THE

DIMWIT'S

DICTIONARY

THE

DIMWIT'S

DICTIONARY

5,000
Overused
Words and Phrases and
Alternatives to Them

Robert Hartwell Fiske

Marion Street Press, Inc.

Library of Congress Cataloging-in-Publication Data

Fiske, Robert Hartwell.
  The dimwit's dictionary : 5,000 overused words and phrases and
alternatives to them / by Robert Hartwell Fiske.
    p. cm.
  ISBN 0-9665176-7-9
1. English language--Synonyms and antonyms--Dictionaries.
2. English language--Usage--Dictionaries. 3. English language--
Terms and phrases.
4. Clichés--Dictionaries. I. Title.
  PE1591 .F566 2002
  423'.1--dc21
                                            2002008424

Cover design by Michelle Crisanti

ISBN 0-9665176-7-9
Printed in U.S.A.
Printing 10 9 8 7 6 5 4 3 2

Marion Street Press, Inc.
PO Box 2249
Oak Park, IL 60304
708-445-8330
Toll-Free 866-443-7987
www.marionstreetpress.com

The Vocabula Review

Robert Hartwell Fiske is the editor and publisher of *The Vocabula Review* (www.vocabula.com), an online journal about the English language.

Along with the evolution of language—the thousands of neologisms that new technologies and new thinking have brought about, for instance—there has been a concurrent, if perhaps less recognizable, devolution of language. The English language has become more precise for some users of it while becoming more plodding for others. Not a small part of this new cumbrousness is due to the loss of distinctions between words, the misuse of words, and other abuses of language.

That a U.S. presidential candidate can cry *Is our children learning*, an admired basketball star can use the word *conversate*, a well-known college professor can say *vociferous* when he means *voracious*, and another can scold a student for using the word *juggernaut* because she believes it means *jigaboo* is disturbing. *The Vocabula Review* strives to combat the degradation of our language.

Equally important, we celebrate its opulence and its elegance. The English language is wonderfully expressive and infinitely flexible. There are many thousands of words and many hundreds of ways in which to use them. *The Vocabula Review* seeks to promote the richness of our language.

In sum, *TVR* battles nonstandard, careless English and embraces clear, expressive English. We hope we can encourage our readers to do as much.

Why not take a look?

The Vocabula Review:
www.vocabula.com

To Betty—unambivalently

CONTENTS

The great enemy of clear language is insincerity. When there is a gap between one's real and one's declared aims, one turns as it were instinctively to long words and exhausted idioms, like a cuttlefish squirting out ink.

GEORGE ORWELL, *Politics and the English Language*

Thoughts, that breathe, and words, that burn.

Thomas Gray, *The Progress of Poesy*

Good as is discourse, silence is better and shames it.

RALPH WALDO EMERSON, *Circles*

For I have neither wit, nor words, nor worth,
Action, nor utterance, nor the power of speech,
To stir men's blood

WILLIAM SHAKESPEARE, *Julius Caesar*, act 3, scene 2

Watch your thoughts; they become words.
Watch your words; they become actions.
Watch your actions; they become habits.
Watch your habits; they become character.
Watch your character; it becomes destiny.

ANONYMOUS

Never do I ever want to hear another word. There isn't one I haven't heard.

ALAN JAY LERNER and FREDERICK LOEWE, *My Fair Lady*

Apologia

The Dimwit's Dictionary will annoy some people and amuse others. People who feel as though I am referring to them in some of the commentary in this book may be annoyed by what I write; those who feel as though I am referring to others may be amused by it. This is an annoying, amusing book.

If the tone of my commentary is sometimes acerbic, it's because tempered persuasion is effete, and considered argument tiresome. Few of us are able to learn well by pedantic or rote methods. But if I disturb or annoy a person, is he not more likely to remember what bothered him; is he not more likely to retain what was said; is he not more likely to learn? This pedagogy may strike some as unworkable, and perhaps its efficacy is suspect, but we surely know that other methods of tutelage are largely unsuccessful.

ROBERT HARTWELL FISKE
info@vocabula.com

The Vocabula Review
www.vocabula.com

Foreword

W hen Robert Hartwell Fiske confronts Saint Peter, I hope he remembers to tell the man that he is the founding editor of *The Vocabula Review*, the online magazine devoted to contemporary language, its delights and its disasters. Saint Peter will immediately understand that Mr. Fiske has been on the side of the angels and therefore been doing the Lord's work. My worry is that, in reply, Saint Peter will commit one or another of the solecisms, illogicalities, or barbarisms that Mr. Fiske spends his days excoriating and that he will feel the need to correct him, causing him to lose his place on the other side of the gates.

Meanwhile, on this side of the gates, to hew to this theological metaphor a bit longer, Robert Hartwell Fiske has been doing a hell of a job.

Mr. Fiske has signed on, evidently for life, for that best of all losing causes, the battle to keep language clear, fresh, free from the pollution of empty jargon, idiotic euphemism, self-serving imprecision, comic redundancy, nonsense generally. He has many famous comrades from among the dead in this battle: Jonathan Swift, H. L. Mencken, George Orwell, H. W. Fowler, Sir Ernest Gowers, and others. And, as I am sure he has discovered, many unknown, still living allies in unexpected places who get quite properly worked up over politicians, advertisers, social scientists, so-called educators, and others attempting to swindle the rest of us through nicely calculated verbal fog.

You are what you eat, the old food faddists used to say. As I read him, Robert Hartwell Fiske is saying that we are, or soon become, what we say and write. Use language slovenly, dully, dopily and we soon ourselves become sloppy, dull, dopey. In *The Dimwit's Dictionary*, he explains his reigning idea in the first paragraph of his first chapter, when he announces that "Dimwitticisms are worn-out words and phrases; they are expressions that dull our reason and dim our insight, formulas that we rely on when we are too lazy to express what we think or even to discover how we feel. The more we use them, the more we conform — in thought and feeling — to everyone else who uses them." We know soon enough what makes them "dim"; the witticism comes into play because most people who adopt such overworked words as "scenario" or such cumbersome academic locutions as "in terms of" think they are being clever, if not highly sophisticated.

Language mavens come in various intensities of aggression. Some come as recent graduates of the Gestapo school of language correction; one has only to read them to feel the leather glove sting across one's cheeks, the word *schweinhund* ringing in one's ears. Some come on as school masters, simply unable to understand why anyone would wish to split an infinitive or end a sentence with a preposition. Some come on as pussycats passing along to us their amazement at the wild and wayward curiosities of language, but always attempting to avoid seeming either formidable or forbidding.

My own favorite among the great language mavens is H. W. Fowler, whose tone I should describe as superior commonsensical. Here, for example, is the great man on those damnable split infinitives: "The English-speaking world may be divided into (1) those who neither know nor care what a split infinitive is; (2) those who do not know but care very much; (3) those who know and condemn; (4) those who know and approve; and (5) those who know and distinguish." Such is Fowler's elevated superiority. Here is his commonsense: "We maintain, however, that a real split infinitive, though not desirable in itself, is preferable to either of two things, to real ambiguity and to patent artificiality." In other words, the Fowler line is, split away before writing anything stupid. But then he adds: "We will split infinitives sooner than be ambiguous or artificial; more than that, we will freely admit that sufficient recasting will get rid of any split infinitives without involving either of those faults, and yet reserve to ourselves the right of deciding in each case whether recasting is worthwhile." Superior, as I say, with a saving commonsense.

Robert Hartwell Fiske's desire — it informs his tone — is to bring us to our senses, to make us understand that "our knowledge of the world expands as our familiarity with words increases" and contracts when we fall back on the categories of ineptitude he has designated the Moribund Metaphor, the Overworked Word, the Plebeian Sentiment, all of which may be said — he, in fact, does say — "blunt our understanding and quash our creativity. They actually shield us from our thoughts and feelings, from any profound sense of ourselves." He is, *au fond*, a reformer who wants us to be the fully developed men and women we "were meant to be."

But Mr. Fiske's reforming impulse doesn't get in the way of his scorning clichés and trite sentiments. His lists of Overworked Words and of Torpid Terms — "off-putting," "operative," "prioritize," "pursuant to," qualify for the latter category — are there because they "keep us dumb and dispassionate. They elicit the least from us." He also suggests words that he thinks worthy of being revitalized — lovely words such as "bedizen," "bootless," "quondam" — while what he calls Withered Words ought, in the phrase of Paul Valery, the great French critic, to be turned over to the "numismaticians of language" to be put "away in their Cabinets, with many another verbal coin that has passed from circulation."

Robert Hartwell Fiske is a verbal trainer, the linguistic equivalent of the personal trainer one sees in gyms and health clubs. He wants us to trim the fat off our mental life; to knock off those Ineffectual Phrases, Inescapable Pairs, Infantile Phrases, and Wretched Redundancies. He has the relentlessness but none of the dogmatism of the drill sergeant.

Reformer, verbal trainer, drill sergeant, in the end Robert Hartwell Fiske is a fisher of souls, a catcher in the wry, a man who, through looking carefully at language, understands its potency and loathes its power, when misused, for making life more dreary than it ought to be. After noting the spread of flat and predictable language in the contemporary world, he exclaims: "No wonder so many of us feel barren or inconsolable: There are few words that inspire us, few words that move us, few words that thrill or overwhelm us. Persuasion has lost much of its sway, conviction, much of its claim."

Mr. Fiske is, in short, a fanatic, an extremist who apparently believes that clear language is our only hope for clear thought, that dull language deadens the mind and dampens the imagination, that a felicitous phrase is good news, that a strong prose style is a gift to be cultivated and cherished, that nothing, no, nothing in the world exceeds language in its significance to the human enterprise. As it happens, I believe in all this, too, which makes it an honor to salute a fellow fanatic and wish him and his book the great good fortune both deserve.

JOSEPH EPSTEIN

Joseph Epstein, former editor of *The American Scholar*, teaches writing and literature at Northwestern University and is the author of many books, including *Narcissus Leaves the Pool* and *Snobbery: The American Version*.

PART 1

On
Dimwitticisms

Chapter 1

Expressions That Dull Our Reason and Dim Our Insight

Whereas a witticism is a clever remark or phrase — indeed, the height of expression — a "dimwitticism" is the converse; it is a commonplace remark or phrase. Dimwitticisms are worn-out words and phrases; they are expressions that dull our reason and dim our insight, formulas that we rely on when we are too lazy to express what we think or even to discover how we feel. The more we use them, the more we conform — in thought and feeling — to everyone else who uses them.

The Dimwit's Dictionary is a compilation of thousands of dimwitticisms (clichés, colloquialisms, idioms, and the like) that people speak and write excessively.*

The Dimwit's Dictionary categorizes dimwitticisms by the following types:†

    Foreign phrases
    Grammatical gimmicks
    Ineffectual phrases
    Inescapable pairs
    Infantile phrases
    Moribund metaphors

---

* Many of the entries in this book are followed by synonyms that may be used in place of the worn-out word or phrase; others are followed by commentary; and still others by both. But even the mere inclusion of an entry — one unaccompanied by synonyms or commentary — damns it as a dimwitticism.

† Many of the entries in this book, quite obviously, could be categorized by more than one of these fourteen types. Many wretched redundancies are also torpid terms, many moribund metaphors also infantile phrases, but I have sought to identify them by their principal type.

Overworked words
Plebeian sentiments
Popular prescriptions
Quack equations
Suspect superlatives
Torpid terms
Withered words
Wretched redundancies

Foreign phrases

Expressions such as *ad infinitum, ad nauseam, c'est la vie, crème de la crème, fait accompli, in loco parentis, je ne sais quoi, joie de vivre, mea culpa, mirabile dictu, modus vivendi, ne plus ultra, non compos mentis, par excellence, persona non grata, quid pro quo, raison d'être, sine qua non, très, verboten,* and *vive la différence,* though perfectly good foreign words and phrases, are, when used by English-speaking people, simply wearisome.

Grammatical gimmicks

Quite simply, *and everything* is a babbler's way of describing what he was unable to. This phrase and so many others like it — *and everything like that; and stuff (things); and (or) stuff (things) like that; and this and that; anyway; I mean; (and that) kind of stuff (thing); or something or other; or whatever; this, that, and the other (thing); you had to be there* — are grammatical gimmicks that we use to make up for the misfashioned words that precede them.

These are devices that we resort to whenever we are unable to adequately explain our thoughts or feelings. Grammatical gimmicks attest to just how dull and dimwitted we have become.

Ineffectual phrases

Ineffectual phrases are the expressions people use to delay or obstruct, to bewilder or make weary. The intent of those who use ineffectual phrases is to make it appear as though their sentences are more substantial than they actually are, but not one sentence is made more meaningful by their inclusion: *(please) be advised that; I'll tell you (something); it has come to (my) attention; it is important to realize (that); it is interesting to note (that); make no mistake (about it); (to) take this opportunity (to); the fact of the matter is; the fact remains; the thing about it is; what happened (is).*

How a person speaks often reveals how he thinks. And how he thinks determines how he behaves. A person who speaks ineffectually may think ineffectually, and a person who thinks ineffectually may behave ineffectually — perhaps badly.

Ineffectual phrases add only to our being ineffectual people.

Inescapable pairs

In an inescapable pair, the first word means much the same as the second or so often accompanies the second that any distinction between them is, in effect, forfeited.

Only occasionally, that is, do we see the word *allied* without the word *closely; asset* without *valuable; baby* without *beautiful; balance* without *delicate; distinction* without *dubious; error* without *egregious; tied* without *inextricably; missed* without *sorely; poverty* without *abject; principle* without *basic.*

And only occasionally do we see the word *aid* without the word *abet; alive* without *well; effective* without *efficient; hope* without *pray; hue* without *cry; pure* without *simple.*

When two words are treated as though they were one — the plight of every inescapable pair — our keenness is compromised, our discernment endangered.

No longer does every word tell; the words themselves have become witless.

Infantile phrases

Any thought or feeling in which these expressions are found is likely to be made instantly laughable: *absolutely, positively; all of the above; because (that's why); because why?; (as) compared to what?; going on (19); I'll bet you any amount of money; in no way, shape, or form; intestinal fortitude; it takes one to know one; me, myself, and I; mission accomplished; mutual admiration society; never (not) in a million years; real, live; really and truly; (you) started it; (I) take it back; the feeling's mutual; the (L)-word; (my) whole, entire life; with a capital (A); without further ado; (62) years young; (a) zillion(s) (of).*

Also included among these phrases that strike all but the dimwitted as derisory are notorious advertising slogans (*inquiring minds want to know; where's the beef*), song and film titles (*a funny thing happened to me on the way to; I can't get no satisfaction*), and alliterative or rhymed phrases (*a bevy of beauties; chrome dome*).

Other infantile phrases are more disturbing, for they reveal an adolescent, unformed reasoning. Explanations like *in the wrong place at the wrong time, it just happened, it's a free country,* and *everything's (it's all) relative* are as farcical as they are possibly fallacious.

Moribund metaphors*

Metaphors, like similes, should have the briefest of lives. Their vitality depends on their evanescence.

Yet must we ever endure the dimwitted *(it's) a jungle (out there), an emotional roller coaster, a stroll (walk) in the park, (like) being run over (getting hit) by a (Mack) truck, (as) cool as a cucumber, everything but the kitchen sink, (as) hungry as a horse, leak like a sieve, light at the end of the tunnel, out to lunch, over the hill, pass like ships in the night, (as) phony as a three-dollar bill, (a) piece of cake, rule the roost, window of opportunity, (every parent's) worst nightmare,* and countless other metaphors that characterize people as dull, everyday speakers and writers, indeed, as platitudinarians? Nothing new do they tell us. Nothing more do they show us.

Moreover, if it weren't for our plethora of metaphors, especially, sports images — *above par, a new ballgame, batting a thousand, do (make) an end run around, down for the count, hit a home run, off base, pull no punches, stand on the sidelines, step up to the plate, took the ball and ran with it* — and war images — *a call to arms, an uphill battle, battle lines are drawn, draw fire, earn his stripes, first line of defense, in the trenches, on the firing line, take by storm* — men and, even, women would be far less able to articulate their thoughts. We would speak and write more haltingly than we already do; our thoughts and feelings more misshapen than they already are.

Moribund metaphors interfere with our understanding not only when we use them singly but also, and especially, when we use them simultaneously, that is, when we use them together, metaphor on metaphor. Frequently incongruous, these metaphors disfigure any sentence in which they are found.

■ And by last Christmas, for any defense contractor, the dwindling Soviet threat had evolved from *meal ticket* into *writing on the wall.*

■ Our restaurant *cost* me and my wife *an arm and a leg,* but we didn't build it without planning and we certainly wouldn't let it *go down the drain.*

■ Right now, USAir's problem is trying to determine whether this is *a soft landing* for the economy or a recession, and *the jury is still out.*

■ For 20 years she was *a rising star* in the business, but by last year her success had *gone to the dogs.*

■ In the face of mounting pressure to gut or eliminate the IRS, it contin-

---

*Rather than have a separate section on "insipid similes," I include them here. Since a metaphor can be thought of as a condensed simile (which often uses the word *as* or *like*) and a simile usually can be converted into a metaphor, this does not strike me as taking too much license.

ues to *shoot itself in the foot* by *biting the hands that feed them*.

■ Looking at those things, *it didn't take a rocket scientist* to see there was *something rotten in Denmark*.

■ Thanks to Clinton, Lewinsky, & Co., I'm *off the hook* and it's *on the table*.

■ Things were already bad, but when we saw those things *coming down the pike*, that was *the last nail in the coffin*.

We rely on metaphors not because we feel they make our speech and writing more vivid and inviting but because we fail to learn how to express ourselves otherwise; we know not the words.

In truth, the more of these metaphors that we use, the less effective is our speech and writing. Neither interesting nor persuasive, their expression fatigues us where we thought it would inform us, annoys us where we believed it would amuse us, and benumbs us where we hoped it would inspire us.

Overworked words

The broader your knowledge of words, the greater your ability to express yourself precisely and persuasively. So many speakers and writers, however, rely on certain words — overworked words like *action, actively, amazing, appreciate, approach, attitude, awesome, basically, crisis, definitely, devastate, effect, excellence, great, impact, implement, incredible, interesting, lasting, major, meaningful, mindset, natural, nice, ongoing, parameter, pretty, really, scenario, significant, situation, strange, thing, unbelievable, very, weird*.

Words, when overworked, diminish the meaning of all that they are used to describe. Our declarations, assertions, and questions are all enfeebled by these tired terms. Nothing that we express with these overworked words has the force or effectiveness of less habitually spoken, less repeatedly written words.

Moreover, since a person understands little more than what the words he is knowledgeable of convey — a word means *only* so much — to rely on so few words reveals just how limited a person's understanding of himself, and those about him, is.

Our knowledge of the world increases as our familiarity with words does.

Plebeian sentiments

Plebeian sentiments reflect the views and values of the least thoughtful among us: *be nice; (I) gave (him) the best years of (my) life; (it) gives (me) something to do; (these things) happen to other people, not to (me); I (just) don't think about it; I just work here; I'm bored (he's boring); (it) keeps (me) busy; (it's) something to look forward to; there are no words to describe (express); you think too much; what can you do; why me?*

What's more, these expressions, base as they are, blunt our understanding and quash our creativity. They actually shield us from our thoughts and feelings, from any profound sense of ourselves.

People who use these expressions have not become who they were meant to be.

Popular prescriptions

Powerless to repeat an author's epigram, unfit to recite a poet's verse, more than many of us are utterly able to echo a society's slogans and clichés: *absence makes the heart grow fonder; actions speak louder than words; a picture is worth a thousand words; beauty is in the eye of the beholder; better late than never; do as I say, not as I do; forgive and forget; hope for the best but expect the worst; it takes two; keep (your) nose to the grindstone; live and learn; misery loves company; money isn't everything; neither a borrower nor a lender be; take it one day (step) at a time; the best things in life are free; the meek shall inherit the earth; the sooner the better; time flies when you're having fun; two wrongs don't make a right; what goes around, comes around; you can't be all things to all people; you can't have everything.*

Popular prescriptions are the platitudes and proverbs by which people live their lives. It is these dicta that determine who we are and how we act; they define our intellectual and moral makeup.

Dull-witted speakers and writers depend on prescriptions like these to guide them through life. For this poor populace, life is, we may surmise, laid out. From the popular or proper course, there is scant deviation; a stray thought is, for them, a gray thought.

Popular prescriptions endure not for their sincerity but for their simplicity. We embrace them because they make all they profess to explain and all they profess to prescribe seem plain and uncomplicated.

Inexorably, we become as simple as they — we people, we platitudes.

Quack equations

This is the sort of simplicity much favored by mountebanks and pretenders, by businesspeople and politicians: *a deal is a deal; a politician is a politician; a promise is a promise; a rule is a rule; bald is beautiful; bigger is better; enough is enough; ethics is ethics; fair is fair; God is love; it is what it is; less is more; more is better; perception is reality; (what's) right is right; seeing is believing; talk is cheap; the law is the law is the law; what happened happened; what's done is done.* Quack equations too readily explain behavior that the undiscerning may otherwise find inexplicable and justify attitudes otherwise unjustifiable. No remedies for shoddy reasoning, no restoratives for suspect thinking, these palliatives soothe only our simple-mindedness.

Equally distressing is that there is no end to these quack equations: *alcohol is alcohol; he is who he is; math is math; money is money is money; people are people; plastic is plastic; prejudice is prejudice; their reasoning is their reasoning; the past is the past; wrong is wrong.* Forever being fabricated and continually being merchandized, shoddy thinking is far more easily dispensed than sound thinking.

Suspect superlatives

In dimwitted usage, superlatives are suspect. That which seems most laudable is often least, that which seems topmost, bottommost, that which seems best, worst: *an amazing person; (I'm) a perfectionist; area of expertise; celebrity; class; gentleman; great; personal friend; pursuit of excellence; the best and (the) brightest; the rich and famous.*

Torpid terms

Torpid terms are vapid words and phrases that we use in place of vital ones: *a majority of; a moving experience; a number of; a step (forward) in the right direction; cautiously optimistic; (take) corrective action; degree; effectuate; extent; (a) factor; incumbent upon; indicate; input; leaves a little (a lot; much; something) to be desired; move forward; negative feelings; off-putting; operative; prioritize; proactive; pursuant to; remedy the situation; represent(s); send a message; shocked (surprised) and saddened (dismayed); significant other; subsequent to; utilize; weight in proportion (proportionate) to height.*

Formulas as flat as these keep us dumb and dispassionate. They elicit the least from us.

With these unsound formulas, little can be communicated and still less can be accomplished. Torpid terms interfere with our understanding and with our taking action; they thwart our thinking and frustrate our feeling.

Withered words

There are many rare and wonderful words that we would do well to become familiar with — words that would revitalize us for our revitalizing them — words like *bedizen; bootless; caliginous; compleat; cotquean; hebdomadal; helpmeet; logorrhea; quondam; wont.*

Withered words, however — words like *albeit; amidst; amongst; behoove; betwixt; ergo; forsooth; perchance; said; sans; save; thence; unbe-*

knownst; verily; whence; wherein; whereon; wherewith; whilst — are archaic and deserve only to be forgotten. People who use them say little that is memorable.

Wretched redundancies*

Reckless writers and slipshod speakers use many words where few would do: *advance planning; at this time; consensus of opinion; dead body; due to the fact that; first and foremost; free gift; just recently; in advance of; in and of itself; in spite of the fact that; in terms of; make a determination; on a ... basis; on the part of; past experience; period of time; (the) reason (why) is because; refer back; the single best (most); until such time as.* Yet for all the words, their expression is but impoverished; more words do not necessarily signify more meaning.

Life is measured by its meaning, and a good deal of that meaning is inherent in the words we use. If so many of our words are superfluous — and thus do not signify — so much of our life is, ineluctably, meaningless.

In the end, we are no more superfluous than are the words we use.

In themselves, dimwitticisms are as innocuous as any other single word or phrase might be, but within sentences, among thoughts struggling to be expressed and ideas seeking to be understood, dimwitticisms ravage the writer's efforts as much as they do the reader's, the speaker's as much as the listener's.

Dimwitticisms give rise to ineloquence, and it is precisely this that marks so much of our speech and writing. Whatever the occasion, whether celebratory or funereal, quotidian or uncommon, people speak and write the same dimwitted words and phrases. No wonder so many of us feel barren or inconsolable: there are few words that inspire us, few words that move us, few words that thrill or overwhelm us. Persuasion has lost much of its sway, conviction, much of its claim.

Consider these further examples of dimwitted usage.

1. From a dialogue between a television correspondent and a school superintendent:

So you feel like you were *left holding the bag*?
Yes, it's fair to say we were *left out in the cold*.

Left holding the bag and *left out in the cold* are both moribund metaphors.

---

*For a more complete listing of redundancies, see my *Dictionary of Concise Writing* (also published by Marion Street Press).

2. From the spoken words of a high school "genius":

> It was *like her worst nightmare or something.*

Like is an infantile phrase, *her worst nightmare* is a moribund metaphor, and *or something* is a grammatical gimmick.

3. From the words of a computer scientist:

> The encryption technology used today is the same as that used twenty years ago by military establishments *and that type of stuff.*

And that type of stuff is a grammatical gimmick.

4. From a business consultant's economic forecast:

> *Basically,* it's a *pretty nice* forecast.

Basically, pretty, and *nice* are all overworked words.

5. From a political lobbyist's analysis:

> If we could *level the playing field,* it would be better than having them *stick out like a sore thumb.*

Level the playing field and *stick out like a sore thumb* are both moribund metaphors.

6. From the author of a college textbook:

> In the beginning, and certainly before democratic forms of government *arrived on the scene,* tribal chieftains used their armies to maintain order.

Arrive on the scene is an infantile phrase.

7. From a news program's report on the death of a woman:

> The company released a statement saying she was an outstanding employee and her colleagues are *shocked and saddened* by her death.

Shocked and saddened is a torpid term.

8. From an article by a health-care professional:

It is interesting to note the impressive array of distinguished mental health professionals who have assumed a derogatory stance on prevention.

It is interesting to note is an ineffectual phrase.

9. From a meteorologist's weather forecast:

Averagewise, around November 10, we see the first snowflakes of the season fall.

Averagewise is a grammatical gimmick.

10. From a police report on the death of a vagrant:

This could have happened to anyone; he happened to be *in the wrong place at the wrong time.*

In the wrong place at the wrong time is an infantile phrase.

11. From a man speaking before a congressional committee:

There are no words to describe how *devastating* this experience has been.

There are no words to describe is a plebeian sentiment, and *devastating* is an overworked word.

12. From a questionnaire soliciting opinions about a business service:

Thank you in advance for your time and assistance; your answers can *make a difference.*

Thank you in advance is a plebeian sentiment, and *make a difference* is a suspect superlative.

13. From the CEO of a multimillion-dollar company:

A mensch is a man *with a capital M.*

With a capital M is an infantile phrase.

14. From an elementary school principal's letter to parents:

Please be advised that Mr. Kline will no longer be your child's fifth-grade teacher as of Monday, November 22.

Please be advised that is an ineffectual phrase.

15. From an interview with a local government official:

> *The fact of the matter is* these are tolls that should have been removed long ago.

The fact of the matter is is an ineffectual phrase.

16. From a television news correspondent:

> Being different can be *a breath of fresh air*.

A breath of fresh air is a moribund metaphor.

17. From a U.S. government official:

> We will *take corrective action to the extent that* we can; we're not going to be *caught asleep at the switch*.

Both *take corrective action* and *to the extent that* are torpid terms, and *caught asleep at the switch* is a moribund metaphor.

18. From a newspaper article:

> But few couples even bother to discuss *the "F" word* — finances — before they *tie the knot*.

The "F" word is an infantile phrase, and *tie the knot* is a moribund metaphor.

19. From a high school counselor's letter of recommendation:

> If he continues to get support in college, with his *incredible* effort to overcome his difficulties, he can *definitely* succeed.

Both *incredible* and *definitely* are overworked words.

20. From a letter written by a town's postmaster:

> The Andover Post Office will soon *be in the process of* computerizing all post office box information *in the near future*.

Both *be in the process of -ing* and *in the near future* are wretched redundancies.

People who rely on dimwitticisms like these appear to express themselves more fluently and articulately than those few who do not. But this is a sham articulateness, for without the use of phrases like *left holding the bag, left out in the cold, her worst nightmare, and that type of stuff, basically, level the playing field, stick out like a sore thumb, arrive on the scene, shocked and saddened, it is interesting to note, in the wrong place at the wrong time, with a capital M, a breath of fresh air, incredible,* and *definitely,* most people would stammer helplessly.

As unsettling and dissatisfying as it can be to read a sentence in which a single dimwitticism occurs, more than one in a sentence heightens our perturbation. Moreover, to *mix* dimwitticisms, as in some of the preceding examples, compounds our distress. To mix metaphors, as in example 5 (and even example 1), has long been frowned upon by grammarians and careful users of the language. But equally disheartening is it to mix one of these categories with another. Joining a plebeian sentiment with an overworked word, as in example 11, or with a suspect superlative, as in example 12, makes a sentence, let us say, less convincing. Joining an infantile phrase with a moribund metaphor, as in example 18, surely makes a sentence less clever. What's more, to join not two but three or more categories, as in example 2, makes a sentence altogether comical and inconsiderable. No less than mixed metaphors are these combinations worthy of our derision.

Dimwitticisms are ubiquitous, and we cannot easily escape them. Few of us can express a thought without them. We learn them unknowingly; insidiously do they become part of our wording unless we recognize what they are and withstand their onslaught. Genuine articulateness is writing and speech that scarcely makes use of dimwitticisms, and it is achieved only with much effort.

Certainly, it is the least effective speakers and writers who use the most dimwitticisms. A person's ability to express himself well is inversely proportional to the number of dimwitticisms he uses.

A person who expresses himself with genuineness instead of in jargon, with feeling instead of in formulas is capable as few have been, as few are, and as few will be; this is a person to heed.

CHAPTER 2

Writing That Demands to Be Read Aloud, Speech That Calls to Be Captured in Print

The *Dimwit's Dictionary* would be incomplete without a brief discussion of what it means to express oneself well and *wittily*.

Though some dictionaries divide usage into standard English and nonstandard English — and others into standard, nonstandard, and substandard — today, our understanding of the English language would be best served if we were to recognize more exacting labels.

Let us then consider the adoption of four categories of usage.

Egregious English
Uneducated English
Everyday English
Elegant English

This scheme is largely an attempt to give recognition to speech and writing that is beyond standard, or everyday, English — to elegant English. Without such a listing, people may not understand that they *can* speak and write elegantly. Certainly, as the superfluity of dimwitticisms makes plain, elegant English is English rarely heard, English seldom seen.

Here, first, are some examples of egregious English, uneducated English, and everyday English.

Egregious English

About egregious English there is little to say — other than it is a lifeless, indeed, death-inducing, dialect that ought not to be said. Here, though, are a few examples.

■ He knew they *was* out there for 10 to 15 minutes before he *done* anything.

■ I *seen* things out there in the world that I never thought I would see.

■ My mom is the one that *brung* me up.

■ Don't you have family members that you could *of went* to?

■ Men have treated me *terrible*.

■ I took everything *literate*.

■ She wasn't being abused about *nothing*.

■ We don't go to parties *no* more; we don't go *no* where.

■ That *don't* matter, I'm still there with you, *ain't* I?

■ I shot *me* a burglar.

■ Let's start over here with the two of *yous*.

■ I *gots* a lot of thinking to do.

Uneducated English

Abuses of language abound, especially among those who speak and write uneducated English.

Whereas people who aspire to write and speak the language well still maintain standards of speech and observe distinctions between words, the uneducated, like some juggernaut, massacre and obliterate. They slay nearly all that they say.

afeard (*ascared*). ■ He says he's *afeard* of being alone in the dark. Use *afraid* or *scared*.

alls. ■ *Alls* I can say is he was a good cop. Use *All.* ■ *Alls* you hear them talk about is their baby. Use *All.* ■ *Alls* I wanted to say is that I forgive him. Use *All.*

anyways. ■ *Anyways,* I have to go now. Use *Anyway* or Delete. ■ You shouldn't be sleeping around when you're married *anyways.* Use *anyway* or Delete.

anywheres. ■ He hasn't got *anywheres* to go. Use *anywhere.*

a (long) ways. ■ I think magazines can go *a long ways* to effecting that. Use *a long way.* ■ Is it *a long ways*? Use *a long way.*

being as. ■ *Being as* he's such a great dad, I thought he wouldn't mind. Use *Because, Considering (that), In that,* or *Since.*

being as how. ■ That's not so bad, *being as how* we didn't even know we would be on the ballot. Use *because, considering (that), in that,* or *since.*

being that. ■ *Being that* we seem to be getting along so well, I thought we might go to dinner. Use *Because, Considering (that), In that,* or *Since.*

better had. ■ You *better had* do as your father says. Use *had better, ought to,* or *should.*

complected. ■ I'm 5'2", 110 lbs., and very *light-complected.* Use *light-complexioned.*

could of. ■ I *could of* if I wanted to. Use *could have.*

don't let's (let's don't). ■ *Don't let's* get upset about it. Use *Let's not.*

drownded. ■ Two men *drownded* when their boat capsized. Use *drowned.*

drug. ■ He *drug* up the past and complained about the argument we had that time. Use *dragged.* ■ What I've done is *drug* all the chapters into one folder. Use *drag.*

good. ■ He did *good* last night. Use *well.* ■ He helps me to do *good* in school. Use *well.*

had(n't) ought. ■ I *had ought* to go. Use *ought* or *should.* ■ You *hadn't ought* tell him what she said. Use *ought not to* or *should not.*

heighth. ■ She's over 6 feet in *heighth.* USE *height.* ■ I am the same size as you in *heighth.* USE *height.*

hisself. ■ I heard it from Walter *hisself.* USE *himself.* ■ I was afraid he was going to hurt *hisself.* USE *himself.*

in regards to. ■ The system has failed me *in regards to* disciplining my kids. USE *in regard to.* ■ *In regards to* your question, the most important thing is that we don't have a father figure in our lives. USE *Concerning.*

irregardless (of). ■ Remember to treat all patients with respect and compassion *irregardless of* their health status. USE *despite, irrespective of, no matter what, regardless of,* or *whatever.*

irregardless of the fact that. ■ *Irregardless of the fact that* she was raised by someone else, she is still our daughter. USE *Although, Even though,* or *Though.*

leastways. ■ There's no sense of accomplishment, *leastways* not for me. USE *at least.*

leave us. ■ *Leave us* go now before it starts to pour. USE *Let us.*

like. ■ It's *like* déjà vu all over again. DELETE *like.* ■ And she's *like,* "*Like,* he wasn't *like* anyone I've, *like,* ever met." DELETE *like.* ■ And I'm *like* I just couldn't believe it. DELETE *like.*

may of. ■ I *may of* met him once before. USE *may have.*

might of. ■ It *might of* been me; I *might of* been sitting in the back seat. USE *might have; might have.*

more -(i)er. ■ You're probably *more busier* than I am. USE *busier* or *more busy.* ■ I've gotten a lot *more braver.* USE *braver* or *more brave.* ■ At Christmas time, people are a little *more friendlier.* USE *friendlier* or *more friendly.*

most -(i)est. ■ We want to take this opportunity to humbly express to you our *most sincerest* appreciation for the many expressions of sympathy you have shown us. USE *most sincere* or *sincerest.* ■ The panel consisted of some of the town's *most lustiest* women. USE *most lusty* or *lustiest.*

muchly. ■ Thank you *muchly.* Use *very much.*

not hardly. ■ Is she plump? *Not hardly.* Use *Hardly.* ■ I *couldn't hardly* breathe because he had broken my ribs. Use *could hardly.*

not scarcely. ■ I *can't scarcely* hear you. Use *can scarcely.*

nowheres. ■ He was *nowheres* near their house. Use *nowhere.*

seeing as. ■ *Seeing as* you're a woman, does the audience respond to you differently? Use *Because, Considering (that), In that,* or *Since.*

seeing as how. ■ Quite possibly it is my fault *seeing as how* I did not respond the way I thought I would. Use *because, considering (that), in that,* or *since.*

seeing that. ■ *Seeing that* this isn't a programming book, you should have little trouble. Use *Because, Considering (that), In that,* or *Since.*

(my)self. ■ How about *yourself?* Use *you.* ■ She told my sister and *myself* that she was pregnant by him. Use *me.* ■ Richard and *myself* are going to lunch. Use *I.* ■ Very large people like *yourselves* can eat tiny amounts of food and not lose an ounce. Use *you.* ■ Let's hope someone comes along, like *myself,* to take his place. Use *me.* ■ We feel Mr. Roedler's comments do an injustice to collectors like *ourselves* who currently pay $1,500 to $2,000 for radios of this type. Use *us.*

should of. ■ I *should of* known. Use *should have.*

somewheres. ■ I left it *somewheres.* Use *somewhere.*

that there (those there). ■ *That there* man was the one who hit her. Delete *there.* ■ *That* way *there,* I can get my degree a few months sooner. Delete *there.*

theirself (theirselves). ■ Irish people I know don't think of *theirselves* as Irish. Use *themselves.*

this here (these here). ■ *This* is my little brother *here.* Delete *here.* ■ *These* shirts *here* are lighter than those. Delete *here.*

thusly. ■ *Thusly,* I feel he was irresponsible and I feel I should tell him. Use *Thus.* ■ Because this was described as school shootings and *thusly* presented as gender neutral, the gendered nature of the killing and shooting was ignored. USE *thus*.

went and. ■ We *went and* called 911. DELETE *went and*. ■ He *went and* left me. DELETE *went and*.

what all. ■ She can't seem to find anyone who understands *what all* she has been through. DELETE *all*. ■ I don't know *what all* the deal was with her, but she rejected me. DELETE *all*.

where at. ■ Nobody knows *where* the $100 is *at*. DELETE *at*. ■ I know *where* she is *at*. DELETE *at*. ■ I know *where* he works *at*. DELETE *at*.

with regards to. ■ Customers are looking for standard-based applications *with regards to* networking. USE *with regard to*. ■ *With regards to* the paper you gave out recently, I don't want to read about what you have against your opponent but what you are going to do for the city. USE *With regard to*.

would have. ■ What I am sure of is if we *would have* never confronted them, these white kids would have never given in to us. USE *had*. ■ If I *would have* been Paula, I would not have started a sexual harassment lawsuit. USE *had*. ■ I wish none of this *would have* ever happened. USE *had*.

would of. ■ I asked myself what I *would of, could of,* and *should of* done. USE *would have, could have,* and *should have*.

Indeed, much uneducated English is everyday English. The language pullulates with people who hover between the uneducated and the everyday.

Everyday English

Though there are many gauges of it, everyday English is certainly marked, as well as marred, by an ignorance of the meanings of words and the distinctions between words.

accidently. Solecistic for *accidentally*. ■ Lee admits he may have *accidently* passed secrets to other countries. USE *accidentally*. ■ Immediately smitten, Guido, who gets a job as a waiter, arranges to *accidently* bump into Dora over the next several days, but eventually realizes that she's engaged — albeit unhappily — to a Fascist official. USE *accidentally*. ■ If a thrown ball *accidently* touches a base coach, or a pitched or thrown ball touches an umpire, the ball is alive and in play. USE *accidentally*.

At least one well-known dictionary does recognize the spelling *accidently*. But let this be a further reminder that dictionaries merely record how people use the language, not necessarily how it ought to be used. Some dictionaries, we can reasonably infer, actually promote illiteracy.

affect. Misused for *effect*. ■ As for the world-wide *affects* of volcanic eruptions this only happens when there are large explosive eruptions that throw material into the stratosphere. USE *effects*. ■ Eventually, these gases escaped and produce a runaway greenhouse *affect*. USE *effect*. ■ The primary *affect* on property values will come from the aerosols associated with the spray. USE *effect*. ■ Now breathe deeply for the full *affect*. USE *effect*. ■ However, producing truth has the opposite *affect*. USE *effect*.

And *effect* is misused for *affect*. ■ The vice president had become self-conscious about the condition of his teeth and aides believed it was directly *effecting* his campaign performance. USE *affecting*. ■ Leslie says she teaches because it gives her a natural high to know she has the power to positively *effect* all who enter her classroom. USE *affect*. ■ Global warming will *effect* many aspects of daily life in the future. USE *affect*. ■ How does HIV *effect* me? USE *affect*.

Though both *affect* and *effect* may be either a noun or a verb, it is usually the verb *affect* that is confused with the noun *effect*. *Affect* as a verb means to influence or have an effect on; as a noun, *affect* means an emotion or emotional response. *Effect* as a verb means to bring about or accomplish; as a noun, *effect* means a result or an influence. The word *affect* is much less often used as a noun than it is as a verb. All the same, it is often misused for, or perhaps misspelled, *effect*.

aggravate. Solecistic for *annoy* (or similar words). ■ What is most needed from us, instead, may be the simple quality of steadfastness — the persistent, open-hearted willingness to simply hang in there with the clients who most confuse, *aggravate*, or discourage us. USE *annoy*. ■ Most of the time, swapping human contacts for electronic ones looks as though it's saving us time, money, and *aggravation*. USE *irritation*. ■ The first set of people I *aggravated* Tuesday were those of you who get angry when I don't stick to financial topics. USE *irritated*. ■ Of course, it's a fear that his kid sister, the irrepressibly *aggravating* D.W., is only too happy to bolster. USE *exasperating*. ■ Skunks stink up campus and *aggravate* students. USE *upset*. ■ Other things have been pre-set at the factory in odd ways that puzzle, frustrate, and *aggravate* the owner. USE *annoy*. ■ Every women knows that satisfying a man is easy, but *aggravating* him takes a special talent! USE *exasperating*.

Aside from the added amusement of "Every *women* knows," the online advertisement for *How to Aggravate a Man Every Time*, a book, offers another example; it's too dear: ■ Learn the best *aggravating* tricks, such as: take over the remote control, make the most of PMS, make friends with his ex-girlfriends....

The modern (as well as, apparently, historical) view is that *aggravate* may mean, along with to make worse or exacerbate, to irritate or annoy. If people who use *aggravate* to mean annoy also had knowledge of its sense of to make worse and could occasionally use it in that sense, perhaps careful writers and speakers of the English language would be less inclined to carp — while, of course, never agreeing to capitulate.

We have words aplenty that mean to annoy; the only other words that mean to aggravate are *worsen* and *exacerbate*, itself often ridiculously confused with *exasperate*.

alright. Solecistic for *all right.* ■ It looks *alright* from this view, but Pooh's Bridge, near Hatfield, England, was recently condemned and rebuilt. Use *all right.* ■ With five games remaining, things are anything but *alright* along the banks of the Mississippi. Use *all right.* ■ "*Alright*, close No. 2 and 3," says the manager of the Mt. Hermon ski resort, Israel's only winter wonderland, as the sight of cable cars with legs and skis dangling from them disappears into sky soup. Use *All right.* ■ The next morning, I knew that everything would be *alright.* Use *all right.*

All it takes for a solecism to become standard English is people misusing or misspelling the word. If enough people do so, lexicographers will enter the originally misused or misspelled word into their dictionaries, and descriptive linguists will embrace it as a further example of the evolution of English. *Alright* is today indefensible, and it ought always to be indefensible. Likewise, *a lot* is correct, and *alot* is not.

amount. Misused for *number.* ■ Prices are set at $10.00/month for a single board or $25/month for an unlimited *amount* of boards. Use *number.* ■ Buy a qualifying *amount* of books and save 10% on all your subsequent purchases of non-discounted books. Use *number.* ■ All these methods will get you a minuscule *amount* of terrorists and a maximum *amount* of drug dealers instead. Use *number.* ■ The trends include aging of the population, a decrease in the *amount* of people who are available to work, an increase in the number of people who are willing to move to get a better paying position, and a change in the way that work is being done. Use *number.*

The word *number* is used with that which can be counted (or count nouns); the word *amount* with that which cannot easily be (or mass nouns).

conversate. Solecistic for *converse* (or similar words). ■ Receive bulletins about news articles and *conversate* with our readers. Use *converse*. ■ Despite this busy workload, he still manages to make time to *conversate* with others. Use *talk*. ■ San Diego Mommies is a place for local mommies and mommies-to-be to congregate and *conversate* about anything and everything under the sun. Use *chat*.

Over the last few years, this ridiculous word has cleaved to young adults, sports figures, and, now, others ill advised. Any dictionary that eventually adds this word born of imbecility to its pages is a dictionary to be disdained. As it is, we ought to consider whether we can gainfully consult a dictionary that includes the comedic, the infantile *humongous.*

discrete. Misused for *discreet*. ■ Our goal is to provide you with a simple, secure and *discrete* method of obtaining Viagra from the privacy of your own home. Use *discreet*. ■ Condom King has twelve different name brands in an assortment of styles; you pick the desired quantity, pay once and have them mailed to your home *discretely* on a monthly basis. Use *discreetly*. ■ The individual briefing must be provided as inconspicuously and *discretely* as possible. Use *discreetly*.

The homonyms *discrete* and *discreet* are often confused. Whereas *discrete* means distinct or separate, *discreet* means circumspect or prudent.

disinterest. Misused for *indifference* (or similar words). ■ We would have named it Apathy.com, but we like the concept: take the typical American voter's *disinterest in* politics, and make more money on it. Use *indifference to*. ■ For Washingtonians, pop culture is a threat, a Pied Piper leading Americans down the road to *disinterest*. Use *apathy*. ■ The lack of fights is not a result of *disinterest* from nationally based promoters, according to Don Hazelton, executive director of the Miccosukee Boxing Commission. Use *uninterest*. ■ Finally, there was lots of talk at Cannes this year about the lack of a Hollywood presence, whether due to the festival's inattention or industry *disinterest*. Use *indifference*.

Disinterest means without bias or impartial; it does not mean uninterest or indifference. To use *disinterest* in the sense of uninterest is to forsake the word itself and, in effect, is a diminution of the foremost way in which we maintain our humanity.

eminent. Misused for *imminent*. ■ Anyone reading one of her romances is in *eminent* danger of addiction. Use *imminent*. ■ Lester Brown, president of the Worldwatch Institute based in Washington, D.C., said the solution to *eminent* water shortages can be found in a water-pricing policy that reflects the real value of water and in research into energy-efficient irrigation technologies. Use *imminent*.

And *imminent* is misused for *eminent*. ■ One *imminent* scholar of its recent history, Charles Cruickshank (1979), says that deception is the art of misleading an enemy into doing something or not doing something so that his strategic or tactical position will be weakened. Use *eminent*. ■ City Manager Ted Staton said the city is trying to find a solution to appease fraternity members but it ultimately could use its power of *imminent* domain to obtain the house. Use *eminent*.

Eminent means lofty; renowned or distinguished. *Eminent domain* is the right of a government to take private property. *Imminent* means impending or about to occur.

flaunt. Misused for *flout*. ■ Why is Ted Kennedy a "pseudo-Catholic" — he claims to be a Catholic but *flaunts* the rules of the church he belongs to. Use *flouts*. ■ Companies regularly *flaunt* the laws, collecting and disseminating personal information. Use *flout*. ■ North Korea continues to *flaunt* international law by speeding ahead with their nuclear program with no consequences whatsoever. Use *flout*. ■ The regime has shown little political will to stop the narcotics exports from Burma and prevent illicit drug money from enriching those who would *flaunt* international rules and profit by destroying the lives of millions. Use *flout*. ■ Leave it up to the Rocky Mountain volleyball team to *flaunt* convention. Use *flout*.

To *flaunt* is to show off or exhibit ostentatiously; to *flout* is to disobey or show contempt for.

graduated. Solecistic for *graduated from*. ■ The study showed 83 percent of Latinos and 80 percent of blacks failed the 10th-grade math exam, which will be a requirement to *graduate* high school in 2003. Use *graduate from*. ■ I *graduated* high school by taking the GED exam. Use *graduated from*. ■ Older cohorts of the population were much less likely to have *graduated* high school than younger cohorts. Of those born in the years 1938 to 1943, only about 76 percent *graduated* high school; of those born between 1973 and 1978, 88 percent had *graduated* high school. Use *graduated from*.

The use of *graduated*, instead of *graduated from* (or, perhaps, *was graduated from*), displays a remarkable lack of learning. More than many solecisms, *graduated* taints the talker and, with each new reader, ridicules the writer.

hecticity. Idiotic for *frenzy* (or similar words). ■ By now I am accustomed to all the *hecticity* of these events. Use *stir*. ■ Since the concept of alienation is too wide and varied, I refined my goal by concentrating on the *hecticity* of contemporary urban life, and the artist's role in creating cultural change in the form of public works that can find a larger audience. Use *franticness*. ■ But even if I was miserable and discouraged — in the *hecticity* of departure I'd left my warm jacket at home, so I had to bundle up as best I could with every shirt I'd brought and a paper-thin rain shell — many others weren't. Use *disorder.* ■ Amid the *hecticity* of existence, we perceive the celestial bodies as phenomena that calm and reassure. Use *chaos.*

This is an abominable word — one that a silly celebrity or a descriptive linguist might love. As you see, many words readily mean what *hecticity* struggles to. That this word is used by a few impressionable people is hardly reason for more discriminating ones to embrace it. Not all words are worthy.

imply. Misused for *infer.* ■ What does it mean that Zaccheus was a chief tax-collector? What can we *imply* about him from that? Use *infer.* ■ Can we *imply* a term into the contract to the effect that you should have the right to terminate on notice, or that the words *termination notice: 1 month* also apply to you? Use *infer.*

To *imply* is to suggest; to *infer* is to conclude. Speakers *imply;* hearers *infer.* Some dictionaries, continuing their disservice to us all, consider these two words synonymous, defining one with the other.

irrelevant. Misused for *irreverent.* ■ It was full of *irrelevant* fun almost to the point of Marx Brothers-style of antics, with a small dose of the horrors of war thrown in. Use *irreverent.* ■ "Vancouver: Secrets of the City": An *irrelevant* look at the lesser-known side of British Columbia's largest city. Use *irreverent.* ■ Andy Armstrong takes an *irrelevant* look at motoring and motorsport. Use *irreverent.* ■ His *irrelevant* style of humour is both witty and makes us think of how we see ourselves. Use *irreverent.*

Irrelevant means not relating to the subject; not pertinent. *Irreverent* means lacking reverence, disrespectful; critical of what is generally accepted; satirical.

it's. Misused for *its.* ■ By now, even the most out of touch among you must realize that the Government of the United States is at war against *it's* own people. Use *its.* ■ You'll get a chance to read my world famous Speed Seduction Newsletters, hear Real Audio Clips from seminars and products, hear testimonials, in their own voices from satisfied customers just like you, join the Speed Seduction private email discussion group, sign up for the Seduction tip of the week, learn all about the Speed Seduction Home Study Course that is turning the world of dating and seduction on *it's* ear, and much, much more. Use *its.* ■ Freemasonry requires that *it's* members confess a belief in a supreme being. Use *its.* ■ Our customers have been absolutely spellbound by *it's* results. Use *its.*

Most often, this confusion is simply a matter of carelessness, but in the end, all good writing is careful writing. *It's* is a contraction for it is or it has; *its* is a possessive pronoun meaning pertaining to or belonging to.

less. Misused for *fewer.* ■ In a survey of 132 jumpers, *less* than half had complaints — all minor. USE *fewer.* ■ *Trust* has a smoother, more rock sound than *Get Happy,* but finds Costello with *less* ideas than ever before. USE *fewer.* ■ The solution to this problem is to download more fonts, thus there are *less* reasons for X to use scaled fonts. USE *fewer.* ■ A posting and handling charge of $3.50 applies once to orders of *less* than 10 books; pre-payment is required for orders of three or *less* books. USE *fewer.*

   Less refers to amounts, to that which cannot be easily counted; *fewer* refers to numbers, to that which can be. *Less* is also used with plural nouns such as periods of time and sums of money.

   Even the confusion between these two words is being sanctioned by lexicographers, for many dictionaries now offer one word as the synonym of the other. In the end, lexicographers who suppress distinctions between words interfere with our ability to see clearly and reason convincingly.

meretricious. Misused for *meritorious.* ■ I informed her that that was a *meretricious* plan except for the fact that it involves lying. USE *meritorious.* ■ They serve the public interest by reminding readers not to believe a message simply because it is widely distributed, and carries the *meretricious* authority of the published word. USE *meritorious.* ■ If the other side is wrong, their arguments, however *meretricious,* will not in the end survive exposure to ours. USE *meritorious.*

   Meretricious means of or relating to a prostitute; falsely or vulgarly attractive; pretentious. It does not mean *meritorious,* having merit, deserving of honor.

mitigate. Misused for *militate.* ■ But this is only one side of the story; inner cities are also rich in culture, institutions, and other resources that can *mitigate* against adversity and promote healthy development and learning. USE *militate.* ■ NUTRI-RICE has been known to increase energy, improve general health, *mitigate* against numerous degenerative diseases and slow the aging process. USE *militate.* ■ Other factors also *mitigate* in favor of appellant. USE *militate.* ■ Personality traits of activists *mitigate* in favor of and against archivists' adoption of marketing as a strategy for advancing the archival service to society, but the reference archivist must use character strengths to overcome the weaknesses. USE *militate.*

   The phrases *against* or *in favor of* invariably follow *militate,* not *mitigate.* To *militate* is to work or fight against (or sometimes for), whereas to *mitigate* is to lessen or alleviate, to improve.

moresome. Idiotic for *more* (or similar words). ■ The Couples Group is for couples and individuals who are part of a couple, triad, foursome or *moresome.* Use *more.* ■ With one devilishly simple activity she manages to get them to delve way back into their pasts, open up and get totally immersed in the activity, as well as potentially use every conceivable English tense and *moresome.* Use *more.* ■ Now Cockshutt, now Moline, now John Deere and Fordson! Then Oliver, Allis, Massey, and *moresome!* Use *others.* ■ Spanish style Hacienda home appr. 6,000 sq. ft. built with high quality construction large lot approximately 450′ x 450′ excellent landscaping, gazebo in rear and much much *moresome* furniture included. Use *more.*

Although meant to describe more than a two-, three-, or foursome — and often used by the sexually ever unsatisfied — *moresome* is finding its way into popular usage. Like the equally odious *moreso*, *moresome* is an abomination (unless perhaps used by James Joyce: "It is most ernst terooly a moresome intartenment").

And then there are instances where the intended meaning of *moresome* is, if not *awesome*, or perhaps *fearsome*, completely elusory: ■ Its extremely fruity bouquet, with that delicate touch of woodiness, makes it extraordinarily *moresome.* ■ In the case of *Satanic Verses* we had a book and an author. But the *moresome* Muslims hit that author the stronger that author became.

opinionation. Idiotic for *opinion.* ■ We started that trip as the usual collection of walking American egos and *opinionations,* and came back uniformly anti-Soviet, the liberals most of all. Use *opinions.* ■ For vinyl geeks and John Cusack groupies *High Fidelity* is an instant collector's object; but even if all the "top five list" gimmickry and pop-insider *opinionations* and Cusack's affected direct addresses to the camera begin to grate on you, the movie still holds up as a great ensemble comedy. Use *opinions.* ■ The essay itself seems to establish pretty firmly, though rather against Hull's will, that the two writers are connected by very little more than Clarke's general knowledge of the world-field occupied by the *opinionations* of Shaw. Use *opinions.* ■ I thank all the readers who have borne with my Novial *opinionations,* especially those who have from time to time written letters of encouragement, and more especially those who have written to the editor. Use *opinions.*

Perhaps people who use the regal-sounding, polysyllabic *opinionation* feel as though it gives more weight to their views than does the plainer *opinion.* If "laxicographers" should ever add *opinionation* to their dictionaries, there will be no reason to consult them further.

permanentized. Idiotic for *make permanent* (or similar words). ■ Once the cognitive elements are manipulated in the desired direction, the programmed conditioning and behavior becomes *permanentized*. USE *permanent*. ■ Instead, I find myself repeatedly disappointed to meet women who insist they want the traditional vagaries, supposedly *permanentized* with a superstitious ceremony. USE *made permanent*. ■ That is why the half million people would come here; to rub some of the (muddy) fame off on themselves, participating as first hand witnesses, *permanentized* in a moment of history. USE *immortalized*.

We know a concoction like *permanentize* is objectionable when it's scarcely pronounceable. *Make permanent* or, perhaps, *immortalize* does nicely; the ungainly, needless *permanentize* does not.

principle. Misused for *principal*. ■ We are delighted to have the generous support and assistance of our *principle* sponsors. USE *principal*. ■ Today, the Russians are our *principle* partner in space exploration, a fact inconceivable in 1957. USE *principal*. ■ Students also must complete the highest level of math offered at their high school before taking a college math class unless an exception is made by the high school *principle*. USE *principal*.

A *principle* (always only a noun) is a truth, law, standard, or rule. *Principal*, as an adjective, means chief or highest in importance; as a noun, it means a person who holds a high position or has a main role.

proscribe. Misused for *prescribe*. ■ We are on record to abide by the 1949 Geneva Conventions and their relevant sections that *proscribe* the rules of war. USE *prescribe*. ■ They often *proscribe* rules of behavior which we must follow to attain rewards or avoid punishment in this or the after world. USE *prescribe*. ■ Apropos to point 6 we as adults must encourage — but not *proscribe* — thinking among young people about a strategy for some kind of healing and reconciliation of the tremendous harm that has been caused by the gender wars (which we adults have caused). USE *prescribe*.

To *proscribe* is to prohibit, forbid, or disallow; to *prescribe* is to set down, order, or recommend.

reoccur. Misused for *recur*. ■ Reading your Aug. 27 front-page article, "Tending to teens' need to sleep," irritated a *reoccurring* wound. USE *recurring*. ■ Jason Kauppi, Swift's spokesman, said yesterday that the initial treatment has been successful and that doctors wanted to keep the girls an extra day to make sure the problem did not *reoccur*. USE *recur*. ■ If you want the appointment or meeting to *reoccur* on a daily basis then tap on the Daily tab. USE *recur*. ■ If a problem did *reoccur*, however, I was puzzled as to why, for the basis of his work is that the problem should be fixed and not recur unless there is new trauma. USE *recur*.

And then there are those who use *reoccurrence* instead of *recurrence*: ■

Basically, what this study is doing is looking at state-of-the-art treatments for depression and looking at how well they work in the short term, but also how well they prevent *reoccurrence*. USE *recurrence*. ■ Gross margins for the three months ended October 31, 1999 increased to 35% from (5%) in the prior year, primarily due to the *non-reoccurrence* of inventory related charges that resulted in the negative margin for the second quarter of last year. USE *non-recurrence*.

Reoccur and *reoccurrence* are errors for *recur* and *recurrence*. Some critics and dictionary makers maintain that *recur* means to happen repeatedly, and *reoccur* to happen, merely, again, but this is a specious explanation for what was at first, and will be to the last, nothing but a blunder.

Neither *reoccur* nor *reoccurrence* exists in any reputable English-language lexicon.

respectively. Misused for *respectfully.* ■ Choose complimentary close according to formality required: Use Sincerely for most business letters. Use *Respectively* yours when writing to the President of the U.S. USE *Respectfully.* ■ Graduates of St. Clare School will act *respectively* towards self and others. USE *respectfully.* ■ Behave *respectively* to adults and each other. USE *respectfully.* ■ I urge you to consider them carefully and I think you will agree that they meet the objectives of the Commission without the negative implications of the proposed wording. *Respectively* yours, Jeffrey W. Pruett CPA. USE *Respectfully.* ■ We assure that all calls are handled in a professional manner aimed at helping the consumer to use products effectively. *Respectively* yours, Frances White, President. USE *Respectfully.*

Respectively means in the order designated or mentioned; *respectfully* means characterized by or showing respect or deference. Even though, in Shakespeare's day, *respectively* apparently meant *respectfully,* the word in that sense has long been obsolete.

Surprisingly, despite the rather widespread misuse, no present-day dictionary has yet suggested that *respectively,* once again, also means *respectfully.*

reticent. Misused for *reluctant.* ■ Despite the seemingly endless challenges, Gallup appears *reticent* to give up either of his jobs. USE *reluctant.* ■ Without this information, leaders are unclear about where to invest resources and thus are *reticent* to do so. USE *reluctant.* ■ Open Port may still be *reticent* about going public, but the company has moved intrepidly into the Dark Continent. USE *reluctant.* ■ In the modern church we have educated pastors who will not take a stand on any biblical issue while they are not *reticent* to take a stand on a political issue. USE *reluctant.*

Reticent means disinclined to speak; taciturn; quiet. *Reluctant* means disinclined to do something; unwilling; loath. Because some people mistakenly use *reticent* to mean *reluctant,* dictionaries now maintain *reticent* means *reluctant.* If we were to rely exclusively on dictionary pronouncements, we'd be altogether undone.

tortuous. Misused for *torturous.* ■ Only water can correct this acid imbalance and relieve the *tortuous* pain it causes. USE *torturous.* ■ His middle childhood years, to be sure, were filled with *tortuous* pain and agony beyond imagination for most of us. USE *torturous.* ■ Dying of starvation and experiencing *tortuous* suffering, he writes how he knows that within a couple of hours the fires raging about him will end his life. USE *torturous.* ■ It was one of the most horrific, slow, *tortuous* deaths ever invented. USE *torturous.*

Tortuous means marked by repeated twists and turns, winding; complex; circuitous; devious. *Torturous* means pertaining to or causing torture; strained.

If enough people, in their everyday dull-wittedness, confuse one of these words with the other, lexicographers and linguists will pronounce the words synonymic, and berate anyone who tries to keep the distinctions alive.

transpire. Solecistic for *occur* (or similar words). ■ After years of research of the Pierce County elections, these skills were necessary to capture an incident that took only a few minutes to *transpire.* USE *happen.* ■ Publishing is in an intense state of flux — which means no one has a clear handle on how to best publish books, what distribution will be like in two years, or what unexpected corporate shifts and mergers will *transpire.* USE *occur.* ■ The communications activities *transpire* within the Communication and Signal Processing Laboratory. USE *take place.*

Transpire means to pass through a surface; to leak out; to come to light; to become known. Unfortunately, its better-known meaning — to come about, happen, or occur — is also its worse one, for no other word means quite what the word's less common usage does. The fewer words we know, the fewer thoughts we have.

trepidacious. Solecistic for *fearful* (or similar words). ■ Together, they decide to write a biography of France and arrive in Galen on a slow, summer day; expectant, delighted, and a little *trepidacious* of what they might find. USE *fearful.* ■ Meanwhile, the Elgar estate, which controlled the copyright to the sketches, became *trepidacious* about anyone continuing work on them, and thus violating their great uncle's deathbed wish. USE *uneasy.* ■ As we introduced ourselves, the common strand which emerged was of a group of people all wanting to improve what they were doing, either unhappy with what had been done or *trepidacious* of their tasks ahead. USE *apprehensive.* ■ In these *trepidacious* times for investors, we at Vanguard believe that discipline and patience are more relevant now than ever. USE *anxious.*

Trepidacious is not a word. Even though people use it (horrible to hear, ridiculous to read though it is), no major dictionary, remarkably, has yet included it in its listing.

vociferous. Misused for *voracious.* ■ No, he wasn't a *vociferous* reader or running a recycling business. USE *voracious.* ■ A *vociferous* reader, he had a fondness for all books, but particularly those slanted towards international history. USE *voracious.* ■ At the age of 18 she opened her own studio and began to teach; a *vociferous* reader, she read everything she could about dance and took master classes from all the recognized leaders. USE *voracious.*

Vociferous means characterized by vehement outcry; clamorous. *Voracious,* greedy in eating; gluttonous; insatiable.

People who confuse *vociferous* with *voracious* may also confuse *vicious* with *viscous,* or *prostrate* with *prostate,* or *rein* with *reign,* or *imply* with *infer,* or *juggernaut* with *jigaboo.* Once we confuse the meanings of words, little is left for us to depend on.

Soon, it is clear, we will be a society unable to distinguish one word from another, sense from nonsense, truth from falsehood, good from evil. We will soon utter only mono- and disyllabic words, be entertained only by what pleases our peers, and adore whatever is easy or effortless. Unfamiliar wording and original phrasing will soon sound incoherent or cacophonic to us, while well-known inanities like *have a nice day, what goes around comes around,* and *hope for the best but expect the worst* will serve as our mantra, our maxim, our motto.

Elegant English

We all know far too well how to write everyday English, but few of us apparently know how to write elegant English — English that is expressed with music as well as meaning, style as well as substance. The point of this category is to show that the language can, indeed, be spoken or written with grace and polish — qualities that much contemporary English is bereft of and could benefit from.

So prevalent is everyday English that the person who speaks correctly and uses words deliberately is often thought less well of than the person who speaks solecistically and uses slang unreservedly. Today, fluency is in disfavor. Neither everyday nor even uneducated English seems to offend people quite as much as does elegant English. People neither fume nor flinch when they hear sentences like those illustrated earlier; but let them listen to someone who speaks, or read someone who writes, elegantly, and they may be instantly repelled. Doubtless, well-turned phrases and orotund tones suggest to them a soul unslain.

Even so, it is not classism but clarity, not snobbery but sensibility that users of elegant English prize and wish to promote. Nothing so patently accessible as usage could ever be justly called invidious. As long as we recognize the categories of usage available to us, we can decide whether to speak and write the language well or badly. And we might more readily decide that elegant English is indeed vital were it more widely spoken by our public figures and more often written in our better books. Countless occasions where elegant English might have been used — indeed, ought to have been used — by a president or politician, a luminary or other notable, have passed with uninspired, if not bumbling, speech or writing.

Further, elegant English needs to be reliably compiled in a new type of dictionary — one that does indeed pay more attention to the phrases and rhetorical figures we use or might use, one that can accommodate the category of elegant English. Such a dictionary would be as new as it is old, for it would also need to note and, more than that, endorse the distinctions between words. It would even prescribe distinctions between words where, perhaps, there have been none.

Here are some examples of elegant English.

The grammatically correct *It is I* is elegant, and the grammatically incorrect *It is me* is not. ■ *It was her* who spoke to me that way. USE *It was she.* ■ He knew it was *her*, but she didn't know it was *him*. USE *she; he.*

The ubiquitous *like* is everyday, whereas *as, as if,* and *as though* are elegant. ■ He felt *like* he had been cheated by the system. USE *as though.* ■ *Like* I was saying, he didn't know what the circumstances were. USE *As.*

Elegant is *graduated from* or *was graduated from*; everyday is *graduated*. ■ Even before *graduating* college, Hughes had published two books of poetry. USE *graduating from* or *he was graduated from.* ■ I *graduated* one of the finest medical schools in the country. USE *graduated from* or *was graduated from.*

How come is everyday English, and *how has it come about that* or *how is it that* is elegant. ■ *How come* everyone else is wrong and you are right? USE *How is it that.*

Me neither, that makes two of us, and *you're not the only one* are everyday; *neither do I, no more do I,* and *nor do I* elegant. ■ I no longer trust her. *You're not the only one.* Use *Neither do I, Nor do I,* or *No more do I.* ■ I myself know nothing about the subject. *Me neither.* Use *Neither do I, Nor do I,* or *No more do I.*

Likewise or *likewise, I'm sure* in the following examples is everyday, even uneducated; the alternatives are not. ■ I'm so happy to have met you. *Likewise, I'm sure.* Use *And I, to have met you,* or *And I, you.* ■ I enjoy meeting intelligent people. *Likewise.* Use *As I do.*

A lot, very, and *very much* are hopelessly everyday expressions; *enormously, hugely, immensely, mightily, monstrously,* and *prodigiously* are not. ■ We are *very* proud of her. Use *enormously.*

All right, O.K., and *whatever* are everyday, but *(just) as you like, (just) as you please,* and *very well* are elegant. ■ I think I'll stay here for the night. *O.K.* Use *Just as you please.* ■ I'm supposed to say that, not you. *Whatever.* Use *Very well.*

Phrases like *aren't I? aren't you?* and *wasn't I?* are everyday, but *am I not? are you not?* and *was I not?* are elegant. ■ *Aren't I* going with you next week? Use *Am I not.* ■ He was right, *wasn't he?* Use *was he not.*

Everyday are words like *awful, bad, horrible,* and *terrible.* Elegant are words like *abominable, dreadful, frightful, ghastly, hideous, insufferable, intolerable, monstrous, unspeakable,* and *unutterable.* ■ What a *terrible* place this city of yours is. Use *monstrous.* ■ This peach pie looks *horrible.* Use *frightful.*

The fact that is everyday, and the largely forgotten *that* elegant. ■ *The fact that* they declared bankruptcy means little to me if not to you. Use *That.* ■ Yes, *the fact that* she behaved like an imbecile did influence any interest we might have had in befriending her. Use *that.*

Similarly, *in order that* and *so that* are everyday; *that* is elegant. ■ We spoke to her sternly *in order that* she might learn from her mistakes. Use *that.* ■ *In order that* we might profit from our experience, he had us write an essay on what we learned from it. Use *That.*

Words like *absolutely, definitely,* and *totally* are everyday; *itself* is elegant. ■ She is *definitely lovely.* Use *loveliness itself.* ■ Throughout the whole affair, he was *absolutely kind.* Use *kindness itself.*

Extremely, so, terribly, and *very* are everyday; *in the extreme* and *too* are not. ■ It's *very* lovely. Use *too.* ■ I found his book *extremely confusing.* Use *confusing in the extreme.*

I don't believe so, I don't think so, and *no (I don't)* are everyday; *I think not* is elegant. ■ Would you like to walk along with us? Thanks, but *I don't think so.* Use *I think not.* ■ Do you have any other questions for our guest? *No.* Use *I think not.*

Phrases such as *am I to* are elegant, but *shall I* or *will I* is everyday. ■ What *will I* do with her? Use *am I to.*

Everyday are *(that's) correct, (most) definitely, I agree, (you're) right, sure;* elegant are *exactly so, just so, precisely so, quite right, quite so,* and *yes.* ■ August is hardly the time to visit Paris. *That's right.* Use *Quite right.* ■ She is the wisest person I know. *Most definitely.* Use *Exactly so.*

Expressions like *that's correct, you're right,* and *yes, she has* are everyday. Expressions like *I am* and *she has* are elegant. ■ Is it really your birthday today? *That's right.* Use *It is.* ■ Are we there already? *Yes.* Use *We are.*

A phrase such as *do you have* is everyday next to the elegant *have you.* ■ *Do I have* time to take a shower? Use *Have I.* ■ *Do you have* anything to drink? Use *Have you.*

An understood *you* is decidedly everyday; the plainly stated *do* is not. ■ We had a little adventure last night. Oh, *tell* me all about it. Use *do tell.* ■ *Leave* me alone. Use *Do leave.*

Although the first three categories of usage, egregious, uneducated, and everyday English, comprise rudimentary structures — a single word, sometimes two or three words — elegant English, a more developed style, generally requires at least a few, and often many, words, as these further examples illustrate.

1. Those who profess to favor freedom, and yet deprecate agitation, are men who want crops without plowing up the ground. They want rain without thunder and lightning. They want the ocean without the awful roar of its waters.

Frederick Douglass, Speech

2. I confess I love littleness almost in all things. A little convenient estate, a little cheerful house, a little company, and a very little feast; and, if I

were to fall in love again (which is a great passion, and therefore, I hope, I have done with it), it would be, I think, with prettiness, rather than with majestical beauty.

ABRAHAM COWLEY, *Of Greatness*

3. Take away but the pomps of death, the disguises and solemn bugbears, the tinsel, and the actings by candle-light, and proper and fantastic ceremonies, the ministrels and the noise-makers, the women and the weepers, the swoonings and the shriekings, the nurses and the physicians, the dark room and the ministers, the kindred and the watchers; and then to die is easy, ready, and quitted from its troublesome circumstances.

JEREMY TAYLOR, *The Rule and Exercises of Holy Dying*

4. Let me wither and wear out mine age in a discomfortable, in an unwholesome, in a penurious prison, and so pay my debts with my bones, and recompense the wastefulness of my youth, with the beggary of mine age; Let me wither in a spittle under sharp, and foul, and infamous diseases, and so recompense the wantonness of my youth, with that loathsomeness in mine age.

JOHN DONNE, *Let Me Wither*

5. A poor relation — is the most irrelevant thing in nature, — a piece of impertinent correspondency, — an odious approximation, — a haunting conscience, — a preposterous shadow, lengthening in the noontide of your prosperity, — an unwelcome remembrancer, — a perpetually recurring mortification, — a drain on your purse, — a more intolerable dun upon your pride, — a drawback upon success, — a rebuke to your rising, — a stain in your blood, — a blot on your scutcheon, — a rent in your garment, — a death's head at your banquet, — Agathocles' pot, — a Mordecai in your gate, — a Lazarus at your door, — a lion in your path, — a frog in your chamber, — a fly in your ointment, — a mote in your eye, — a triumph to your enemy, an apology to your friends, — the one thing not needful, — the hail in harvest, — the ounce of sour in a pound of sweet.

CHARLES LAMB, *Poor Relations*

6. Somewhere, I knew not where — somehow, I knew not how — by some beings, I knew not whom — a battle, a strife, an agony, was conducting, — was evolving like a great drama, or piece of music; with which my sympathy was the more insupportable from my confusion as to its place, its cause, its nature, and its possible issue. I, as is usual in dreams (where, of necessity, we make ourselves central to every movement), had the power, and yet had not the power, to decide it. I had the power, if I could raise myself, to will it; and yet again had not the power,

for the weight of twenty Atlantics was upon me, or the oppression of inexpiable guilt. "Deeper than ever plummet sounded," I lay inactive. Then, like a chorus, the passion deepened. Some greater interest was at stake; some mightier cause than ever yet the sword had pleaded, or trumpet had proclaimed. Then came sudden alarms; hurryings to and fro; trepidations of innumerable fugitives. I knew not whether from the good cause or the bad; darkness and lights; tempest and human faces; and at last, with the sense that all was lost, female forms, and the features that were worth all the world to me, and but a moment allowed — and clasped hands, and heart-breaking partings, and then — everlasting farewells! and, with a sigh, such as the caves of hell sighed when the incestuous mother uttered the abhorred name of death, the sound was reverberated — everlasting farewells! and again, and yet again reverberated — everlasting farewells!

THOMAS DE QUINCEY, *Confessions of an Opium Eater*

7. Great is all townsmen's dread of the Beduw, as if they were the demons of this wild waste earth, ever ready to assail the Haj passengers; and there is no Beduwy durst chop logic in the dark with these often ferocious shooters, that might answer him with lead and who are heard, from time to time, firing backward into the desert all night.

CHARLES M. DOUGHTY, *Travels in Arabia Deserta*

8. Listen! for if you are not totally callous, if your consciences are not seared, I will speak daggers to your souls, and awake you to all the horrors of guilty recollection. I will follow you with whips and stings through every maze of your unexampled turpitude, and plant thorns under the rose of ministerial approbation.

EDMUND BURKE, Speech

9. As to my old opinions, I am heartily sick of them. I have reason, for they have deceived me sadly. I was taught to think, and I was willing to believe, that genius was not a bawd, that virtue was not a mask, that liberty was not a name, that love had its seat in the human heart. Now I would care little if these words were struck out of the dictionary, or if I had never heard them. They are become to my ears a mockery and a dream. Instead of patriots and friends of freedom, I see nothing but the tyrant and the slave, the people linked with kings to rivet on the chains of despotism and superstition. I see folly join with knavery, and together make up public spirit and public opinions. I see the insolent Tory, the blind Reformer, the coward Whig! If mankind had wished for what is right, they might have had it long ago.

WILLIAM HAZLITT, *On the Pleasure of Hating*

10. Poor Cromwell, — great Cromwell! The inarticulate Prophet; Prophet who could not speak. Rude, confused, struggling to utter himself, with his savage depth, with his wild sincerity; and he looked so strange, among the elegant Euphemisms, dainty little Falklands, didactic Chillingworths, diplomatic Clarendons! Consider him. An outer hull of chaotic confusion, visions of the Devil, nervous dreams, almost semi-madness; and yet such a clear determinate man's-energy working in the heart of that. A kind of chaotic man. The ray as of pure starlight and fire, working in such an element of boundless hypochondria, unformed black of darkness! And yet withal this hypochondria, what was it but the very greatness of the man? The depth and tenderness of his wild affections: the quantity of sympathy he had with things, — the quantity of insight he would yet get into the heart of things, the mastery he would yet get over things: this was his hypochondria. The man's misery, as man's misery always does, came of his greatness. Samuel Johnson too is that kind of man. Sorrow-stricken, half-distracted; the wide element of mournful black enveloping him, — wide as the world. It is the character of a prophetic man; a man with his whole soul seeing, and struggling to see.

THOMAS CARLYLE, *Heroes and Hero Worship*

11. The character of the Italian statesman seems, at first sight, a collection of contradictions, a phantom as monstrous as the portress of hell in Milton, half divinity, half snake, majestic and beautiful above, grovelling and poisonous below. We see a man whose thoughts and words have no connection with each other, who never hesitates at an oath when he wishes to seduce, who never wants a pretext when he is inclined to betray. His cruelties spring, not from the heat of blood, or the insanity of uncontrolled power, but from deep and cool meditation. His passions, like well-trained troops, are impetuous by rule, and in their most headstrong fury never forget the discipline to which they have been accustomed. His whole soul is occupied with vast and complicated schemes of ambition, yet his aspect and language exhibit nothing but philosophical moderation. Hatred and revenge eat into his heart; yet every look is a cordial smile, every gesture a familiar caress. He never excites the suspicion of his adversaries by petty provocations. His purpose is disclosed, only when it is accomplished. His face is unruffled, his speech is courteous, till vigilance is laid asleep, till a vital point is exposed, till a sure aim is taken; and then he strikes for the first and last time. Military courage, the boast of the sottish German, of the frivolous and prating Frenchman, of the romantic and arrogant Spaniard, he neither possesses nor values. He shuns danger, not because he is insensible to shame, but because, in the society in which he lives, timidity has ceased to be shameful. To do an injury openly is, in his estimation, as wicked as to do it secretly, and far less profitable. With him the most honorable means are those which are

the surest, the speediest, and the darkest. He cannot comprehend how a man should scruple to deceive those whom he does not scruple to destroy. He would think it madness to declare open hostilities against rivals whom he might stab in a friendly embrace, or poison in a consecrated wafer.

THOMAS BABINGTON MACAULAY, *Machiavelli*

12. Animated by this important object, I shall disdain to cull my phrases or polish my style; — I aim at being useful, and sincerity will render me unaffected; for, wishing rather to persuade by the force of my arguments, than dazzle by the elegance of my language, I shall not waste my time in rounding periods, nor in fabricating the turgid bombast of artificial feelings, which, coming from the head, never reach the heart. — I shall be employed about things, not words! — and, anxious to render my sex more respectable members of society, I shall try to avoid that flowery diction which has slided from essays into novels, and from novels into familiar letters and conversation.

These pretty nothings — these caricatures of the real beauty of sensibility, dropping glibly from the tongue, vitiate the taste, and create a kind of sickly delicacy that turns away from simple unadorned truth; and a deluge of false sentiments and overstretched feelings, stifling the natural emotions of the heart, render the domestic pleasures insipid, that ought to sweeten the exercise of those severe duties, which educate a rational and immortal being for a nobler field of action.

MARY WOLLSTONECRAFT, *A Vindication of the Rights of Woman*

Elegant English, as these examples show, is exhilarating; it stirs our thoughts and feelings as ably as dimwitted English blurs them.

The Dimwit's Dictionary will aid us in our quest for elegant, for *wittier*, speech and writing. The goal is to promote understanding and rouse people to action. The goal is to express ourselves as never before — in writing that demands to be read aloud, in speech that calls to be captured in print.

PART 2

The Dimwit's Dictionary

A

abandon all hope, ye who enter here An infantile phrase (SEE PAGE 18).

(the) ABCs of A moribund metaphor (SEE PAGE 19). *basics; basis; elements; essentials; foundation; fundamentals; principles; rudiments.* ■ The program will discuss *the ABCs of* eating right. REPLACE WITH *fundamentals.*

abject poverty An inescapable pair (SEE PAGE 18).

abortive attempt (effort) An inescapable pair (SEE PAGE 18). *breakdown; failure; malfunction.*

above and beyond the call of duty A moribund metaphor (SEE PAGE 19).

above par A moribund metaphor (SEE PAGE 19). *excellent; exceptional; first-class; first-rate; outstanding; remarkable; superior; superlative.*

absence makes the heart grow fonder A popular prescription (SEE PAGE 21).

absence of A torpid term (SEE PAGE 22). SEE ALSO *lack of; less than (enthusiastic).*

absolutely An overworked word (SEE PAGE 20). *altogether; categorically; completely; entirely; fully; perfectly; positively; quite; roundly; thoroughly; totally; unconditionally; unreservedly; utterly; wholly.* SEE ALSO *definitely; most assuredly; most (very) definitely.*

absolutely, positively An infantile phrase (SEE PAGE 18). ■ A programmer must *absolutely, positively* keep a finger on the format's pulse. DELETE *absolutely, positively.* ■ On a wide range of topics, he is the go-to guy — when you *absolutely, positively* have to know what happened. DELETE *absolutely, positively.*

Here's a variation that the writer may have prided himself on: ■ But what you *positively, absolutely* do not want is to get hurt in a stupid exhibition game. DELETE *positively, absolutely.*

absurd An overworked word (SEE PAGE 20). *comical; extravagant; farcical; foolhardy; foolish; idiotic; illogical; imbecilic; impractical; inane; incongruous; irrational; laughable; ludicrous; moronic; nonsensical; preposterous; ridiculous; senseless; silly; unreasonable.*

accentuate the positive An infantile phrase (SEE PAGE 18). *be confident; be encouraged; be heartened; be hopeful; be optimistic; be positive; be rosy; be sanguine.*

accidents will happen A popular prescription (SEE PAGE 21).

(an) accident waiting to happen A moribund metaphor (SEE PAGE 19). ■ Any network that does not have a standardized backup procedure in place is *an accident waiting to happen*

according to Hoyle An infantile phrase (SEE PAGE 18). *accurately; by the rules; conventionally; correctly; customarily; properly; regularly; rightly; traditionally.*

ace in the hole A moribund metaphor (SEE PAGE 19).

Achilles' heel (tendon) A moribund metaphor (SEE PAGE 19). *defect; deficiency; disadvantage; failing; fault; flaw; foible; fragility; frailness; frailty; handicap; imperfection; liability; limitation; shortcoming; susceptibility; susceptibleness; vulnerability; vulnerableness; weakness.* ■ If the Bruins had an *Achilles' heel* last season, it was that they were a tad oversized. REPLACE WITH *weakness.*

acid test A moribund metaphor (SEE PAGE 19). *assay; crucible; ordeal; proof; test; trial.*

across the board A moribund metaphor (SEE PAGE 19). *(for) all; all over; (for) everyone; everyplace;* everywhere; throughout (the land); universally. ■ There is increased consumer confidence — not just here but *across the board.* REPLACE WITH *everywhere.*

action plan A torpid term (SEE PAGE 22). *action; course; direction; intention; method; move; plan; policy; procedure; route; scheme; strategy.* ■ The UN is expected to produce a global *action plan* aimed at reducing demand and improving treatment, rehabilitation, and interdiction. REPLACE WITH *strategy.*

actions speak louder than words A popular prescription (SEE PAGE 21).

active An overworked word (SEE PAGE 20). Only thoughtless speakers and writers, apes and jackanapes, use the adjective *active* to modify a noun. In doing so, they emasculate the meaning of these words. So common is the adjectival *active*, we might easily wonder if anything is possible or achievable, serious or sincere that does not have this word preceding it. ■ Please believe me when I tell you that the only thing that stands between you and a better, more responsive government is your *active participation* in the process. DELETE *active.* ■ Nor did the president demonstrate *active interest* in the issue. DELETE *active.* ■ Some practitioners think that *active movement* might be the key to a cure. DELETE *active.* ■ An *active search* is on for the shooter. DELETE *active.* SEE ALSO *actively.*

actively An overworked word (SEE PAGE 20). The popular use of *actively* suggests that any verb not affixed to it is feckless.

We cannot simply *consider* an idea lest we be accused of not thinking; we cannot simply *engage* in a pursuit lest we be accused of not trying; we cannot simply *participate* in a conversation lest we be accused of not speaking. ■ Another possibility is *actively being considered* by the administration: the use of force. DELETE *actively*. ■ The core group of ASC founders worried that the membership was restricted too narrowly to policing, so they *actively encouraged* others to participate. DELETE *actively*. ■ I have no intention of mailing a second letter to anyone who does not *actively show* an interest in becoming part of my collectors club. DELETE *actively*. ■ Police are *actively searching* for the killer, *actively looking* in all areas, and *actively examining* all the evidence. DELETE *actively*. ■ Not only do many people not enjoy speaking in public, they *actively* dislike and even fear it. DELETE *actively*. ■ Seek them out *actively*. DELETE *actively*.

Here is an example of just how absurd our fixation on *actively* has become: ■ Among the new features of WSF2 R3.3 that he is *actively looking forward to* is the statistical information that can be provided through SMF records. DELETE *actively*. SEE ALSO *active*.

acutely aware An inescapable pair (SEE PAGE 18). ■ Fans have become *acutely aware* that player strikes and lockouts are battles over who gets the biggest piece of what the fan provides.

adamantly oppose An inescapable pair (SEE PAGE 18).

add fuel to the fire A moribund metaphor (SEE PAGE 19). *activate; aggravate; agitate; animate; arouse; awaken; encourage; enkindle; enliven; exacerbate; excite; feed; foment; heighten; ignite; impassion; incite; increase; inflame; intensify; invigorate; make worse; nourish; prod; provoke; rejuvenate; revitalize; revive; rouse; shake up; stimulate; stir up; vitalize; worsen.*

add insult to injury A moribund metaphor (SEE PAGE 19). *aggravate; arouse; enkindle; enliven; exacerbate; excite; feed; foment; heighten; ignite; impassion; incite; increase; inflame; intensify; invigorate; make worse; nourish; prod; provoke; rouse; shake up; stimulate; stir up; what's worse; worsen.*

ad infinitum A foreign phrase (SEE PAGE 17). *ceaselessly; endlessly; evermore; forever; forevermore; to infinity; without limit.*

ad nauseam A foreign phrase (SEE PAGE 17).

advance planning A wretched redundancy (SEE PAGE 23). *planning.* ■ This project will require a lot of *advance planning*. DELETE *advance*.

advance warning A wretched redundancy (SEE PAGE 23). *warning*. ■ Although the bank's 17,000 employees have known for more than a month that the ax was about to fall, the *advance warning* did little to blunt the effect. DELETE *advance*. SEE ALSO *forewarn; warn in advance.*

advice is cheap A quack equation (SEE PAGE 21).

afraid (frightened; scared) of (his) own shadow A moribund metaphor (SEE PAGE 19). *afraid; alarmed; apprehensive; cowardly; craven; diffident; faint-hearted; fearful; frightened; pavid; pusillanimous; recreant; scared; terror-striken; timid; timorous; tremulous.*

after all is said and done A wretched redundancy (SEE PAGE 23). *all in all; all told; altogether; eventually; finally; in all; in the end; on the whole; overall; ultimately.* ■ *After all is said and done*, it truly was an exceptional decade. REPLACE WITH *On the whole*. SEE ALSO *when all is said and done.*

after the fact A torpid term (SEE PAGE 22). *afterward; later.* ■ We don't have a choice, *after the fact*. REPLACE WITH *afterward*.

age before beauty A popular prescription (SEE PAGE 21).

(the) agony and the ecstasy A moribund metaphor (SEE PAGE 19).

agree to disagree An infantile phrase (SEE PAGE 18).

ahead of the game A moribund metaphor (SEE PAGE 19). *advantageous; auspicious; blessed; charmed; enchanted; favored; felicitous; flourishing; fortuitous; fortunate; golden; happy; in luck; lucky; propitious; prosperous; successful; thriving.*

aid and abet An inescapable pair (SEE PAGE 18). *abet; aid; assist; help; support.* ■ One of the best-known detectives comes from literature in the person of Sherlock Holmes, a private investigator *aided and abetted* by his friend Dr. Watson. REPLACE WITH *assisted*.

airtight alibi An inescapable pair (SEE PAGE 18).

à la A foreign phrase (SEE PAGE 17). *according to; in the manner of; like.* ■ I don't want to put myself in a bad position and get beat *à la* this man. REPLACE WITH *like*. ■ The media may be engaged in a witch hunt *à la* the late U.S. Senator Joe McCarthy and perhaps should cut back on their coverage. REPLACE WITH *in the manner of*.

alas A withered word (SEE PAGE 22). *regrettably; sadly; sorrowfully; unfortunately; unhappily.* ■ *Alas*, the program checks only the first two directory entries. REPLACE WITH *Unfortunately*.

alas and alack An infantile phrase (SEE PAGE 18). *regrettably; sadly; sorrowfully; unfortunately; unhappily.*

albatross around (my) neck A moribund metaphor (SEE PAGE 19). *affliction; burden; charge; cross; difficulty; encumbrance; hardship; hindrance; impediment; load; obstacle; obstruction; onus; oppression; ordeal; problem; trial; trouble; weight.* ■ Then came that unspeakable song, "Begin the Beguine," which is still *an albatross around my neck.* REPLACE WITH *a burden.*

albeit A withered word (SEE PAGE 22). *although; even if; even though; though.* Like other withered words, *albeit* strikes some people as more exquisite sounding — and therefore, apparently, more intellectual sounding — than any of its synonyms. But this is perceived by only the dimwitted. ■ *Albeit* somewhat dated, a study performed eight years ago is attracting attention once again. REPLACE WITH *Although.*

alive and kicking A moribund metaphor (SEE PAGE 19). *alive; blooming; doing well; energetic; existent; existing; extant; fit; flourishing; growing; hale; hardy; healthful; healthy; hearty; live; lively; living; prospering; robust; sound; still exists; strong; surviving; thriving; vigorous; vital; well; well-off.* One of the consequences of endlessly saying and hearing and writing and reading formulaic phrases is that, eventually, people *do* become weary of them.

But instead of expressing themselves differently — more eloquently or more inventively, perhaps — people will simply substitute one word in these selfsame formulas for another.

Thus, along with *alive and kicking,* there is, for instance, *alive and well* (SEE) and even *alive and thriving;* along with *a thing of the past,* there is *a phenomenon of the past;* along with *business as usual,* there is *politics as usual* (SEE) and *life as usual;* along with *mover and shaker,* there is *mover and shaper;* along with *neck of the woods,* there is the noisome *portion of the earth;* along with *needs and wants,* there is *needs and desires;* along with *in no way,* there is *in no way, shape, or form* and the preposterous *in no way, shape, form, or fashion;* along with *remedy the situation,* there is *rectify the situation;* along with *out the window,* there is *out the door;* and along with *nothing could be further from the truth,* there is, incomprehensibly, *nothing could be further from the actual facts.*

Would that it ended here, but there are also far too many people who begin with a hackneyed phrase and then transmogrify it into an ever-so-silly, garish one.

Thus, *between a rock and a hard place* (SEE) becomes: ■ In the past decade, newspaper publishers have felt squeezed *between the Net and a hard place.* ■ The Al Queda fighters are *between an anvil and a hammer.*

From bad to worse (SEE) becomes: ■ Moscow now has about 90 days to try to keep a *bad situation from collapsing into something infinitely worse.*

Doesn't have a snowball's chance in hell (SEE) becomes: ■ There is nobody on Russia's political horizon who embraces Mr. Yeltsin's westernized brand of economic policy and *has a Siberian snowball's chance of winning a presidential election.*

An accident waiting to happen (SEE) becomes: ■ The holidays are *a cornucopia of awkward moments waiting to happen.*

Not with a bang but with a whimper (SEE) becomes: ■ This week *started out with a bang and ended with a whimper* for bank stocks. ■ Hurricane Bonnie hit New England *with a whimper, not a bang.* ■ After *beginning my career there with a bang, I cannot end with a whimper.* ■ It could *end with a whimper or a wallop.*

Walk softly and carry a big stick (SEE) becomes: ■ The guiding principle in foreign policy of this administration seems to be *speak loudly and carry a twig.*

Snatch victory from the jaws of defeat (SEE) becomes: ■ In the end, Republicans will simply *snatch defeat from the jaws of victory* if they successfully oust a president they loathe but lose their majorities in both houses of Congress as a result.

Light at the end of the tunnel (SEE) becomes: ■ Is it possible that we're actually seeing a *light at the end of* Star Trek's *TV continuum?*

Not worth the paper it's written (printed) on (SEE) becomes: ■ Consumers can put their trust in a few of these Web site seals, but in many cases they *aren't worth the pixels that they're painted with.*

Going to hell in a hand basket

(SEE) becomes: ■ The good news, culturally speaking, is that if we're *going to Hell in a Saks shopping bag,* at least we are going there slowly.

People propagate these monstrosities. Equally distressing is that, in doing so, they think they *are* being clever and inventive. Among pedestrian people, this is what it means to be thoughtful, this is what it means to be creative.

Is it any wonder that speech is so often soporific, writing so often wearisome?

alive and well An infantile phrase (SEE PAGE 18). *alive; blooming; doing well; energetic; existent; existing; extant; fit; flourishing; growing; hale; hardy; healthful; healthy; hearty; live; lively; living; prospering; robust; sound; still exists; strong; surviving; thriving; vigorous; vital; well; well-off.* ■ Scholarship and readership are *alive and well* and will outlast the publishing binge of the commercial houses. REPLACE WITH *flourishing.* ■ The work ethic of American workers is unquestionably *alive and well.* REPLACE WITH *sound.*

all and sundry A wretched redundancy (SEE PAGE 23). *all; everybody; everyone; everything.* SEE ALSO *various and sundry.*

all dressed up and no place to go An infantile phrase (SEE PAGE 18).

all ears A moribund metaphor (SEE PAGE 19). *attentive; heedful; listening; paying attention; paying heed.*

(as) all get-out A moribund metaphor (SEE PAGE 19). *acutely; awfully; consumedly; exceedingly; extraordinarily; extremely; greatly; hugely; immensely; intensely; mightily; prodigiously; severely; terribly; very.* ■ He was *funny as all get-out.* REPLACE WITH *extremely funny.*

all hell broke loose A moribund metaphor (SEE PAGE 19).

all of the above An infantile phrase (SEE PAGE 18). ■ Are you just looking for a companion or are you looking for a sexual partner? *All of the above.* SEE ALSO *none of the above.*

all over the lot (map) A moribund metaphor (SEE PAGE 19). *diffuse; dispersed; disseminated; scattered; strewn; unfocused.*

all roads lead to Rome A moribund metaphor (SEE PAGE 19).

all rolled into one A moribund metaphor (SEE PAGE 19). *admixture; amalgam; blend; combination; mix; mixture.*

all's fair in love and war A popular prescription (SEE PAGE 21).

all's well that end's well A popular prescription (SEE PAGE 21).

all systems (are) go A moribund metaphor (SEE PAGE 19).

all that glitters isn't gold A popular prescription (SEE PAGE 21).

(and) all that jazz A grammatical gimmick (SEE PAGE 17). ■ He tells me what to do *and all that jazz.* DELETE *and all that jazz.*

all the world's a stage A moribund metaphor (SEE PAGE 19).

all things considered A wretched redundancy (SEE PAGE 23). *all in all; all told; altogether; in all; on the whole; overall.*

all (good) things must end A popular prescription (SEE PAGE 21).

all thumbs A moribund metaphor (SEE PAGE 19). *awkward; blundering; bumbling; bungling; clumsy; gawky; gauche; ham-handed; heavy-handed; inapt; inept; lubberly; lumbering; maladroit; uncoordinated; uncouth; ungainly; ungraceful; unhandy; unskillful; unwieldy.*

all-time record A wretched redundancy (SEE PAGE 23). *record.* ■ If anyone spent time skiing here this past winter, they'd be happy to find the boycott has resulted in an *all-time record* number of skiers. DELETE *all-time.* SEE ALSO *record-breaking; record-high.*

all to the good A moribund metaphor (SEE PAGE 19). *adequate; advantageous; beneficial; satisfactory; sufficient.*

(from) all walks of life A moribund metaphor (SEE PAGE 19).

all wet A moribund metaphor (SEE PAGE 19). *amiss; astray;*

deceived; deluded; erring; erroneous; fallacious; false; faulty; inaccurate; incorrect; in error; misguided; misinformed; mislead; mistaken; not correct; not right; wrong. ■ Whoever told you that alcohol is less of a problem than drugs is *all wet.* REPLACE WITH *mistaken.*

all wool and a yard wide A moribund metaphor (SEE PAGE 19). *actual; authentic; earnest; genuine; heartfelt; honest; legitimate; pure; real; sincere; sterling; true; unadulterated; unalloyed; veritable.*

all work and no play makes Jack a dull boy A popular prescription (SEE PAGE 21).

along the lines of A wretched redundancy (SEE PAGE 23). *akin to; close to; like; resembling; similar to; such as.* ■ It's generally safe to ask people in the field if they've ever heard of anything *along the lines of* your idea. REPLACE WITH *similar to.*

(the) almighty dollar A moribund metaphor (SEE PAGE 19).

(the) alpha and omega of A moribund metaphor (SEE PAGE 19).

amazing An overworked word (SEE PAGE 20). *astonishing; astounding; extraordinary; marvelous; outstanding; remarkable; spectacular; startling; stunning; wonderful; wondrous.*

(an) amazing person A suspect superlative (SEE PAGE 22). *An amazing person* is so only in the eyes of another who, we can be confident, is not.

(as) American as apple pie An insipid simile (SEE PAGE 19). *all-American; decent; good; honorable; moral; proper; pure; right; straight; upright; virtuous; wholesome.*

(the) American dream A suspect superlative (SEE PAGE 22). ■ *The American dream* has become a nightmare.

America's sweetheart A moribund metaphor (SEE PAGE 19).

amidst A withered word (SEE PAGE 22). *amid; among* . ■ *Amidst* all of life's distractions, what is it that keeps us going? REPLACE WITH *Amid.*

(9:00) a.m. ... (in the) morning A wretched redundancy (SEE PAGE 23). *(9:00) a.m.; (in the) morning.* ■ Monday's events can be defined to occur from *8 a.m.* Monday *morning* to *8 a.m.* Tuesday *morning.* DELETE *morning.* ■ This *morning* at 9:35 *a.m.* a violent clash took place between prisoners. DELETE *a.m..*

amongst A withered word (SEE PAGE 22). *among. Amongst,* among the potentially bright, is preferable to *among,* but only because their potential has yet to be realized. ■ If there is a lack of confidence *amongst* those concerned, the strictly political element will be more obvious. REPLACE WITH *among.* ■ Multiplicity is also common *amongst* elasmobranchs. REPLACE WITH *among*. ■ I'm sorry to say that after passing this *amongst* some colleagues, we've agreed that it is not thorough enough to be a reference book. REPLACE WITH *among*.

analyze to death A moribund metaphor (SEE PAGE 19). *analyze; anatomize; dissect; examine; inspect; investigate; scrutinize; study.* SEE ALSO *to death.*

(that's) ancient history A moribund metaphor (SEE PAGE 19). *aged; ancient; antediluvian; antique; archaic; elderly; history; hoary; old; past; prehistoric; seasoned; superannuated.*

and all A grammatical gimmick (SEE PAGE 17). ■ We're going to look at all these nice buildings *and all.* DELETE *and all.* SEE ALSO *and all like that; and everything (else); and everything like that; and stuff (things); and (or) stuff (things) like that.*

and all like that A grammatical gimmick (SEE PAGE 17). ■ We went to different agencies for help *and all like that.* DELETE *and all like that.* ■ He caught me off guard by asking for my name and address *and all like that.* DELETE *and all like that.* SEE ALSO *and all; and everything (else); and everything like that; and stuff (things); and (or) stuff (things) like that.*

and etc. (et cetera) A wretched redundancy (SEE PAGE 23). *and so forth; and so on; and the like; etc.* ■ We bought the generic-brand products *and et cetera.* REPLACE WITH *and the like.*

and everything (else) A grammatical gimmick (SEE PAGE 17). ■ We're responsible for this baby *and everything else.* DELETE *and everything else.* ■ You guys fight *and everything,* but she really does love you. DELETE *and everything.* SEE ALSO *and all; and all like that; and everything like that; and stuff (things); and (or) stuff (things) like that.*

and everything like that A grammatical gimmick (SEE PAGE 17). ■ They adopted that way of speaking *and everything like that.* DELETE *and everything like that.* ■ Don't you feel cheap and used *and everything like that?* DELETE *and everything like that.* SEE ALSO *and all; and all like that; and everything (else); and stuff (things); and (or) stuff (things) like that.*

and/or A wretched redundancy (SEE PAGE 23). *and; or.* ■ Implant dentistry can be an effective alternative to dentures *and/or* missing teeth. REPLACE WITH *or.* ■ But computers may make both more attractive than the alternatives adopted by those who have abandoned wives *and/or* children by failing to meet their financial obligations. REPLACE WITH *and.*

and so on, and so forth A grammatical gimmick (SEE PAGE 17). *and* *so forth; and so on; and the like; etc.* ■ I'm more interested in films about human relationships *and so on, and so forth.* DELETE *and so on, and so forth.* SEE ALSO *blah, blah, blah; et cetera, et cetera.*

and stuff (things) A grammatical gimmick (SEE PAGE 17). ■ His legs had black bruises on them *and stuff.* DELETE *and stuff.* ■ The customers are really nice people; they're friends *and stuff.* DELETE *and stuff.* ■ They wanted him to go for a bike ride *and things.* DELETE *and things.* ■ We got invited to a lot of Hollywood parties *and things.* DELETE *and things.* SEE ALSO *and all; and all like that; and everything (else); and everything like that; and (or) stuff (things) like that.*

and (or) stuff (things) like that A grammatical gimmick (SEE PAGE 17). ■ I love women — the way they look *and stuff like that.* DELETE *and stuff like that.* ■ People shouldn't shoot others over money or things *or things like that.* DELETE *or things like that.* SEE ALSO *and all; and all like that; and everything (else); and everything like that; and stuff (things).*

and that kind of stuff (thing) A grammatical gimmick (SEE PAGE 17). ■ He's a changed man; he's learned to read and write *and that kind of thing.* DELETE *and that kind of thing.* ■ I was working on getting the house settled *and that kind of stuff.* DELETE *and that kind of stuff.* SEE ALSO *(and that) sort of stuff (thing); (and that) type of stuff (thing).*

and that sort of stuff (thing) A grammatical gimmick (SEE PAGE 17). ■ I enjoy walking in the park *and that sort of thing.* DELETE *and that sort of thing.* SEE ALSO *(and that) kind of stuff (thing); (and that) type of stuff (thing).*

and that type of stuff (thing) A grammatical gimmick (SEE PAGE 17). ■ I like interesting conversation and interacting *and that type of thing.* DELETE *and that type of thing.* SEE ALSO *(and that) kind of stuff (thing); (and that) sort of stuff (thing).*

and (or) stuff (things) like that A grammatical gimmick (SEE PAGE 17). ■ I was upset because my mother went through two divorces *and stuff like that.* DELETE *and stuff like that.* ■ As a big man, they look at you as big and healthy *and things like that.* DELETE *and things like that.* SEE ALSO *and all; and all like that; and everything (else); and everything like that; and stuff (things); and (or) stuff (things) like that.*

and this and that A grammatical gimmick (SEE PAGE 17). ■ He told me how much he cared for me *and this and that.* DELETE *and this and that.* SEE ALSO *and this, that, and the other (thing).*

and this, that, and the other (thing) A grammatical gimmick (SEE PAGE 17). ■ She would say to me, you've got the best of both worlds, you're special, you're loved, *and this, that, and the other thing.* DELETE *and this, that, and the* *other thing.* SEE ALSO *and this and that.*

anent A withered word (SEE PAGE 22). *about; concerning.*

angel of mercy A suspect superlative (SEE PAGE 22). *liberator; redeemer; rescuer; savior.*

anon A withered word (SEE PAGE 22).
1. *at another time; later.*
2. *shortly; soon.*
3. *at once; immediately.*

another day, another dollar A popular prescription (SEE PAGE 21).

an ounce of prevention is worth a pound of cure A popular prescription (SEE PAGE 21).

ants in (his) pants A moribund metaphor (SEE PAGE 19). *aflame; agitated; animated; anxious; eager; ebullient; effervescent; enthusiastic; excitable; excited; fervid; fervid; fidgety; frantic; frenzied; impassioned; impatient; jittery; jumpy; lively; nervous; restive; restless; skittish; spirited.*

any and all A wretched redundancy (SEE PAGE 23). *all; any.* ■ *Any and all* accidental needle sticks must be reported to the physician at once. REPLACE WITH *All.* ■ We welcome *any and all* comments and suggestions regarding this project. REPLACE WITH *any.*

anyhow A grammatical gimmick (SEE PAGE 17). ■ *Anyhow,* we got the divorce in 1992. DELETE *Anyhow.* SEE ALSO *anyway.*

any port in a storm A moribund metaphor (SEE PAGE 19).

anything and everything A wretched redundancy (SEE PAGE 23). *anything; everything.* ■ A deadbeat is generally defined as a person dedicated to getting *anything and everything* possible for nothing. REPLACE WITH *anything* or *everything.*

anything (everything) is possible A popular prescription (SEE PAGE 21).

anyway A grammatical gimmick (SEE PAGE 17). ■ But *anyway,* I'll talk to you later in the week. DELETE *anyway.* ■ So *anyway,* I just wanted to verify that with you. DELETE *anyway.* SEE ALSO *anyhow.*

appearances can be deceiving A popular prescription (SEE PAGE 21).

(first) appear (arrive; come) on the horizon (scene) An infantile phrase (SEE PAGE 18). *appear; arise; become available; begin; be introduced; come forth; develop; emerge; occur; originate; present itself; rise; spring; start; surface; turn up.* ■ TTAPS first *appeared on the scene* in 1983 with a paper in *Science* on the global atmospheric consequences of nuclear war. REPLACE WITH *emerged.* ■ It is at the time of William the Conqueror and the Norman conquest of England that the office of shire reeve first *appears on the scene.* REPLACE WITH *appears.* ■ Clearly, oil used in the internal combustion engine presented such a change when it *came on the scene* in the early part of the twentieth century. REPLACE WITH *became available.* ■ The Component Object Model (COM) has caused more confusion since its inception than any other programming technology that has ever *appeared on the horizon.* REPLACE WITH *been introduced.*

(an) apple a day keeps the doctor away A popular prescription (SEE PAGE 21).

(the) apple doesn't fall far from the tree A popular prescription (SEE PAGE 21).

(the) apple of (my) eye A moribund metaphor (SEE PAGE 19). *hero; idol; star.*

apple polisher A moribund metaphor (SEE PAGE 19). *apparatchik; bootlicker; fawner; flatterer; flunky; follower; lackey; minion; stooge; sycophant; toady; yes-man.*

(like comparing) apples and oranges A moribund metaphor (SEE PAGE 19). *different; discordant; discrepant; dissimilar; dissonant; divergent; incommensurable; incommensurate; incomparable; incompatible; incongruent; incongruous; inconsistent; inconsonant; inharmonious; unlike.*

(I) appreciate (it) An overworked word (SEE PAGE 20).
1. *grateful for; thankful for; thank you.*
2. *admire; cherish; esteem; prize; rel-*ish; treasure; value; welcome.* ■ We *appreciate* your help. REPLACE WITH *are grateful for.* ■ We *appreciate you* being here. REPLACE WITH *thank you for.* ■ I *appreciate* every letter that I have received. REPLACE WITH *treasure.* SEE ALSO *common courtesy.*

(an) approach An overworked word (SEE PAGE 20). For example: *band-aid approach; carrot-and-stick approach; common-sense approach; hands-on approach; holistic approach; shotgun approach; sure-fire approach; team approach; upbeat approach.*

(take) appropriate (corrective) action A torpid term (SEE PAGE 22). This ponderous phrase will stem one person's drive while it saps another's desire. From such a phrase, only dull-minded deeds and uninspired acts may result, which is quite likely all that the user of it, bureaucrat he routinely is, either wishes for or can imagine. ■ If there's enough public pressure, they may rethink their defensiveness and begin to *take corrective action.* REPLACE WITH *behave differently.* ■ The bus driver was not exercising caution in this instance, and *corrective action has been taken.* REPLACE WITH *he was fired.* ■ By the time someone decides to *take corrective action,* the customer may be in too deep. REPLACE WITH *act.* ■ The district will *take appropriate action* to ensure such occurrences do not continue. REPLACE WITH *do what it must.*

April showers bring May flowers A popular prescription (SEE PAGE 21).

area of expertise A suspect superlative (SEE PAGE 22). *area; business; calling; craft; field; forte; job; line; métier; occupation; profession; specialty; strength; trade; vocation.*

(we) aren't going to take it anymore A popular prescription (SEE PAGE 21).

(cost) (an) arm and a leg A moribund metaphor (SEE PAGE 19). 1. *a big (brobdingnagian; colossal; enormous; gargantuan; giant; gigantic; grand; great; huge; immense; large; massive; monstrous; prodigious; tremendous; vast) amount; a great deal; a lot.* 2. *costly; dear; expensive; high-priced; precious; priceless; valuable.*

armed and dangerous An inescapable pair (SEE PAGE 18).

armed (themselves) to the teeth A moribund metaphor (SEE PAGE 19).

(an) army of A moribund metaphor (SEE PAGE 19). SEE ALSO *a barrage of.*

around about A wretched redundancy (SEE PAGE 23). *about; around.* ■ Let's meet *around about* noon. REPLACE WITH *about* or *around*.

(work) around the clock A moribund metaphor (SEE PAGE 19). *always; ceaselessly; constantly; continually; continuously; endlessly; eternally; everlastingly; evermore; forever; forevermore; frequently; interminably; nonstop; permanently; perpetually; persistently; recurrently; regularly; repeatedly; unceasingly; unremittingly.*

(just; right) around the corner A moribund metaphor (SEE PAGE 19). *approaching; at hand; close; close by; coming; forthcoming; imminent; impending; near; nearby; nearing; pending; vicinal.* ■ Deregulation of the utility industry was *just around the corner,* and several other companies were prepared to enter the market. REPLACE WITH *at hand.*

(an) arrow in the heart A moribund metaphor (SEE PAGE 19). *injury; wound.*

art is long, and life is short A popular prescription (SEE PAGE 21).

as a man sows so shall he reap A popular prescription (SEE PAGE 21).

as a matter of fact A wretched redundancy (SEE PAGE 23). *actually; indeed; in fact; in faith; in reality; in truth; truly.* ■ *As a matter of fact,* children get disappointed when they grow up to find the adult's prescription didn't match the real world. REPLACE WITH *In truth.*

as a result of A wretched redundancy (SEE PAGE 23). *after; because of; by; due to; following; for; from; in; out of; owing to; through; with.* ■ *As a result of* this letter, ten of us did not attend the wedding. REPLACE WITH *Because of.*

as defined in (the dictionary) An infantile phrase (SEE PAGE 18). This is a device that only abecedarian writers would ever use; even so, it should always be *x'*d. ■ *As defined in the dictionary,* "Health is the absence of disease." ■ Creationism, *as defined in Webster's New Universal Dictionary,* is the doctrine that matter and all things were created, substantially as they now exist, by an omnipotent creator, and not gradually evolved or developed. SEE ALSO *(the) dictionary defines.*

as far as ... (goes; is concerned) A wretched redundancy (SEE PAGE 23). *about; as for; as to; concerning; for; in; of; on; over; regarding; respecting; to; toward; with.* ■ *As far as* improvements *go,* you'd have a battle. REPLACE WITH *As for.* ■ *As far as* those bargains *are concerned,* attempts to place measures on the table would be regressive and an illegal act. REPLACE WITH *Concerning.* SEE ALSO *where ... is concerned.*

ashes to ashes (dust to dust) A moribund metaphor (SEE PAGE 19).

(like) asking for the moon An insipid simile (SEE PAGE 19).

ask me no questions and I'll tell you no lies A popular prescription (SEE PAGE 21).

asleep at the switch (wheel) A moribund metaphor (SEE PAGE 19). 1. *forgetful; careless; heedless; inattentive; lethean; neglectful; negligent; oblivious; remiss; slack; thoughtless; unmindful; unthinking.* 2. *asleep; daydreaming.*

(as) (wholesome) as mom and apple pie An insipid simile (SEE PAGE 19). *decent; ethical; exemplary; good; honest; honorable; just; moral; pure; righteous; straight; upright; virtuous; wholesome.*

as (you) sow, so shall (you) reap A popular prescription (SEE PAGE 21).

as the crow flies A moribund metaphor (SEE PAGE 19). *by air; directly; lineally; linearly; straight.*

(as) (vain) as the day is long An insipid simile (SEE PAGE 19). *acutely; awfully; consumedly; enormously; exceedingly; extraordinarily; extremely; greatly; hugely; immensely; intensely; mightily; prodigiously; severely; terribly; very.* ■ She's *as neurotic as the day is long.* REPLACE WITH *prodigiously neurotic.* ■ Celeste is *as bright as the day is long.* REPLACE WITH *enormously bright.*

as to A torpid term (SEE PAGE 22). *about; for; from; in; of, on; to; with.* Except when used to begin a sentence, *as to* is if not solecistic then certainly sloppy for a more precise *about* or *of, for* or *with, from* or *to, on* or *in.* This phrase, midsentence, identifies a philistine, a person who, though he writes, doesn't much care to. ■ One hint *as to* his possibly altered standing comes from the latest version of the *Encyclopaedia Britannica,* which, although Roget was an editor of the seventh edition and a contributor of more than 300,000 words to it, gives him somewhat short shrift today, with an entry of a mere twenty lines. REPLACE WITH *of*. ■ Suddenly expectations and pre-conceptions *as to* how things should be done and what steps could be taken disappear, often leaving the displaced family members feeling confused, resentful and, perhaps most importantly, alone. REPLACE WITH *of*. ■ For example, testing of a graphics library will require a very different approach *as to* that of a calendar manager. REPLACE WITH *from*. ■ Depending on the night, the meal and the energy of the evening, I also made distinctions *as to* the drink best suited to the occasion. REPLACE WITH *in*. ■ If your browser is not secure, or there is any question *as to whether* or not it is, please download Netscape Navigator, Microsoft Internet Explorer, or an equivalent browser. DELETE *as to*. ■ Yet there has been some question *as to* whether their hearts can take it. DELETE *as to*.

(even) as we speak An infantile phrase (SEE PAGE 18). *at present; currently; (just; right) now; presently.* ■ The team is having a pep rally on campus *as we speak*. REPLACE WITH *now*. ■ Are your forces, *even as we speak*, looking for him in a military way? REPLACE WITH *currently*.

as you make your bed, so you must lie on it A popular prescription (SEE PAGE 21).

at a crossroad A moribund metaphor (SEE PAGE 19).

at a fast (good) clip A moribund metaphor (SEE PAGE 19). *apace; briskly; expeditiously; fast; hastily; hurriedly; posthaste; quickly; rapidly; speedily; swiftly; wingedly.*

at a loss A moribund metaphor (SEE PAGE 19). *baffled; befuddled; bewildered; confounded; confused; disconcerted; flummoxed; mixed up; muddled; nonplused; perplexed; puzzled.*

at a low ebb A moribund metaphor (SEE PAGE 19).

(hold) at arm's distance (length) A moribund metaphor (SEE PAGE 19).

at a snail's pace A moribund metaphor (SEE PAGE 19). *deliberately; gradually; laggardly; languidly; lazily; leisurely; slothfully; slowly; sluggishly; snail-paced; unhurriedly.* ■ We have been working day after day with him, but he is improving *at a snail's pace*. REPLACE WITH *unhurriedly*.

at (my) beck and call A moribund metaphor (SEE PAGE 19). *accepting; accommodating; acquiescent; complacent; complaisant; compliant; cowed; deferential; docile; dutiful; obedient; passive; prostrate; resigned; submissive; subservient; tolerant; tractable; yielding.*

at death's door A moribund metaphor (SEE PAGE 19). *decaying;*

declining; deteriorating; disintegrating; dying; ebbing; expiring; fading; failing; near death; sinking; waning.

at each other's throats A moribund metaphor (SEE PAGE 19). *arguing; battling; bickering; brawling; clashing; disagreeing; fighting; quarreling; squabbling; wrangling.*

at (my) fingertips A moribund metaphor (SEE PAGE 19).
1. *recall; recollect; remember; think of.*
2. *accessible; at hand; close; close by; handy; near; nearby; neighboring; vicinal.*

at loggerheads A moribund metaphor (SEE PAGE 19). *arguing; battling; bickering; brawling; clashing; disagreeing; disputing; fighting; quarreling; squabbling; wrangling.*

at loose ends A moribund metaphor (SEE PAGE 19).
1. *confused; disorganized; drifting; faltering; in between; irresolute; loose; shaky; swaying; tottering; uncertain; undecided; unfixed; unresolved; unsettled; unsteady; unsure; vacillating; wavering; wobbly.*
2. *bored; idle; inactive; unemployed; unoccupied.*

at one fell swoop A moribund metaphor (SEE PAGE 19).

(all) at sea A moribund metaphor (SEE PAGE 19). *baffled; befuddled; bewildered; confounded; confused; disconcerted; flummoxed; lost; mixed up; muddled; nonplused; perplexed; puzzled.*

at sixes and sevens A moribund metaphor (SEE PAGE 19).
1. *baffled; bewildered; confused; flummoxed; muddled; perplexed; uncertain.*
2. *disarranged; disorganized; entangled; jumbled; in disarray; in disorder; tangled.*

at that time A wretched redundancy (SEE PAGE 23). This phrase and several others like it, including *at that juncture in life, at that moment in our national life, at that point in time, at that stage in the history of my life, at that time in our history,* mean no more than *then.* ■ I wasn't happy with what I was doing *at that juncture in life.* REPLACE WITH *then.* ■ DFSMS did not include any cost input parameters *at that point in time.* REPLACE WITH *then.* SEE ALSO *at this time.*

at the breaking point A moribund metaphor (SEE PAGE 19).

at the crack of dawn A moribund metaphor (SEE PAGE 19). *very early.*

(stand) at the crossroads of history A moribund metaphor (SEE PAGE 19).

at the drop of a hat A moribund metaphor (SEE PAGE 19). *at once; directly; fast; forthwith; hurriedly; immediately; instantly; momentarily; promptly; quickly; rapidly; right away; speedily; straightaway; summarily; swiftly; without delay.* ■ You can get additional information to reporters *at the drop of a hat* if you make up a press kit in advance. REPLACE WITH *speedily.*

at the eleventh hour A moribund metaphor (SEE PAGE 19). *late.*

at the end of (my) rope (tether) A moribund metaphor (SEE PAGE 19). *dejected; despairing; desperate; despondent; disconsolate; distressed; forlorn; frantic; frenetic; frenzied; hopeless; in despair; woebegone; woeful; wretched.*

at the end of the day A moribund metaphor (SEE PAGE 19). *all in all; all told; altogether; eventually; finally; in all; in the end; on the whole; overall; ultimately.*

at the helm A moribund metaphor (SEE PAGE 19). *in charge; in control.*

at the top of (his) game A moribund metaphor (SEE PAGE 19).

at the top of (my) lungs A moribund metaphor (SEE PAGE 19). *blaringly; boisterously; boomingly; deafeningly; earsplittingly; loudly; noisily; obstreperously; resoundingly; roaringly; stentorianly; thunderingly; thunderously; tumultuously; vociferously.*

at (behind) the wheel A moribund metaphor (SEE PAGE 19). *in charge; in control.*

at this time A wretched redundancy (SEE PAGE 23). This phrase and several others like it, including *at the present time, at this juncture in life, at this moment in our national life, at this point in time, at this stage in the history of my life, at*

this time in our history, mean no more than *at present, now, today,* or *yet.* ■ We don't see any significant breakthroughs *at this juncture.* REPLACE WITH *now.* ■ What can she do to help you *at this stage of the game?* REPLACE WITH *now.* ■ *At this point in time,* the conditions for an agreement have not been met. REPLACE WITH *The conditions for an agreement have not yet been met.* SEE ALSO *at that time.*

attitude An overworked word (SEE PAGE 20). For example: *attitude problem; holier-than-thou attitude; patronizing attitude; superior attitude; wait-and-see attitude.*

attributable to the fact that A wretched redundancy (SEE PAGE 23). *because; considering; for; in that; since.* ■ This is *attributable to the fact that* people at Pan Am have done such a good job. REPLACE WITH *because.* SEE ALSO *due to the fact that; owing to the fact that.*

at (his) wit's end A moribund metaphor (SEE PAGE 19). *baffled; befuddled; bewildered; confounded; confused; disconcerted; flummoxed; mixed up; muddled; nonplused; perplexed; puzzled.*

audible (inaudible) to the ear A wretched redundancy (SEE PAGE 23). *audible (inaudible).* SEE ALSO *visible (invisible) to the eye.*

au naturel A foreign phrase (SEE PAGE 17). *bare; disrobed; naked; nude; stripped; unclothed; uncovered; undressed.*

(an) avalanche of A moribund metaphor (SEE PAGE 19). ■ His antics on the court spawned *an avalanche of* imitators. SEE ALSO *a barrage of*.

(your) average Joe A moribund metaphor (SEE PAGE 19). *average; common; commonplace; conventional; customary; everyday; familiar; mediocre; middling; normal; ordinary; quotidian; regular; standard; typical; unexceptional; unremarkable; usual.*

avid reader A suspect superlative (SEE PAGE 22). An *avid reader* suggests someone who reads little more than mysteries, gothic novels, and self-help books. These are people whose avidity is more for how many books they read than it is for any meaning in books — people, that is, who prefer counting to reading. ■ I am an *avid reader* and my advanced education includes writing courses and an intensive two-year writing course.

avoid (it) like the plague An insipid simile (SEE PAGE 19).
1. *abhor; abominate; detest; hate; loathe.* ■ Your clients will probably either love Los Angeles or *avoid it like the plague.* REPLACE WITH *loathe it.*
2. *avoid; dodge; elude; eschew; evade; recoil from; shirk; shrink from; shun; spurn.*

awesome An overworked word (SEE PAGE 20). Like *awful* and *terrific*, the word *awesome* has been made ridiculous by those who are bent on using it solely in its most popular sense. *Awesome* means *awe-inspiring, majestic,* or *terrifying,* but of late, it most often merely means *fantastic* or *terrific* or *great,* worn words all. SEE ALSO *awful; terrific.*

awful An overworked word (SEE PAGE 20). *Awful* means *awe-inspiring* or *terrifying,* but of late, it means no more than *very bad* or *unpleasant.* SEE ALSO *awesome; terrific.*

(the) ax fell A moribund metaphor (SEE PAGE 19).

ax (axe) to grind A moribund metaphor (SEE PAGE 19). *animosity; bitterness; enmity; grievance; grudge; hostility; indignation; ill will; offense; rancor; resentment; spite; umbrage.*

B

babe in the woods A moribund metaphor (SEE PAGE 19). *amateur; apprentice; beginner; greenhorn; neophyte; newcomer; novice; novitiate; tyro.* ■ He's a *babe in the woods* compared to Clinton and the Democrats. REPLACE WITH *neophyte*.

back (up) against the wall A moribund metaphor (SEE PAGE 19). 1. *catch; corner; enmesh; ensnare; entangle; entrap; net; snare; trap.* 2. *at risk; endangered; imperiled; in danger; in jeopardy; threatened.* ■ People will do amazing things when *their backs are against the wall*. REPLACE WITH *they're endangered*.

(meanwhile) back at the ranch A moribund metaphor (SEE PAGE 19).

back in the saddle (again) A moribund metaphor (SEE PAGE 19).

back into a corner A moribund metaphor (SEE PAGE 19). *catch; corner; enmesh; ensnare; entangle; entrap; net; snare; trap.*

(get) back on (his) feet A moribund metaphor (SEE PAGE 19). *ameliorate; amend; come round; convalesce; gain strength; get better; heal; improve; look up; meliorate; mend; rally; recover; recuperate; refresh; regain strength; renew; revive; strengthen.* ■ Even the construction industry is starting to *get back on its feet*. REPLACE WITH *recover*.

back on track A moribund metaphor (SEE PAGE 19).

back to basics A torpid term (SEE PAGE 22). ■ Banks and savings and loans are getting *back to basics* and concentrating on home mortgages.

back to square one A moribund metaphor (SEE PAGE 19).

(go) back to the drawing board A moribund metaphor (SEE PAGE 19). ■ Beware of protracted and angry discussions; they are usually a sign that there is not enough support for the idea, and you should go *back to the drawing board*.

back to the salt mines A moribund metaphor (SEE PAGE 19).

back to the wall A moribund metaphor (SEE PAGE 19). 1. *at risk; endangered; hard-pressed; imperiled; in a bind; in a fix; in a jam; in a predicament; in a quandary; in danger; in difficulty; in jeopardy; in*

peril; in trouble; jeopardized.
2. *at bay; caught; cornered; enmeshed; ensnared; entangled; entrapped; netted; snared; trapped.*

bad apple A moribund metaphor (SEE PAGE 19). *brute; degenerate; fiend; knave; lout; rake; rascal; rogue; ruffian; scamp; scoundrel; villain.*

bad blood (between them) A moribund metaphor (SEE PAGE 19). *abhorrence; anger; animosity; antipathy; aversion; detestation; enmity; hate; hatred; hostility; ill will; loathing; malice; malignity; rancor; repugnance; revulsion; venom; virulence.*

bad egg A moribund metaphor (SEE PAGE 19). *brute; degenerate; fiend; knave; lout; rake; rascal; rogue; ruffian; scamp; scoundrel; villain.*

badge of courage (honor) A moribund metaphor (SEE PAGE 19).

(a) bad penny A moribund metaphor (SEE PAGE 19). *bastard; blackguard; cad; charlatan; cheat; cheater; fake; fraud; impostor; knave; mountebank; phony; pretender; quack; rascal; rogue; scoundrel; swindler; undesirable; villain; wretch.*

(a) bad penny always turns up A popular prescription (SEE PAGE 21).

bag and baggage An inescapable pair (SEE PAGE 18).
1. *accouterments; baggage; bags; belongings; cases; effects; encumbrances; equipment; gear; impedimenta; luggage; portmanteaus; possessions; property; sacks; satchels; stuff; suitcases; supplies; things.*
2. *altogether; completely; entirely; fully; roundly; thoroughly; totally; utterly; wholly.*

bag of bones A moribund metaphor (SEE PAGE 19). *asthenic; attenuated; bony; cachectic; emaciated; gaunt; lank; lanky; lean; narrow; rail-thin; scraggy; scrawny; skeletal; skinny; slender; slight; slim; spare; spindly; svelte; sylphid; thin; trim; wispy.*

bag (bagful) of tricks A moribund metaphor (SEE PAGE 19). *accouterment; equipage; equipment; gear; paraphernalia; resources; supplies; things; tools.*

baker's dozen A moribund metaphor (SEE PAGE 19). *thirteen.*

(as) bald as a baby's backside An insipid simile (SEE PAGE 19). *alopecic; bald; baldheaded; baldpated; glabrous; hairless; depilated; pilgarlic; smooth; tonsured.*

(as) bald as a billiard ball An insipid simile (SEE PAGE 19). *alopecic; bald; baldheaded; baldpated; glabrous; hairless; depilated; pilgarlic; smooth; tonsured.*

bald is beautiful A quack equation (SEE PAGE 21).

ball of fire A moribund metaphor (SEE PAGE 19). *active; animated; ardent; dynamic; emotional; energetic; impassioned; intense; lively; passionate; spirited; sprightly; vigorous; vital; vivacious.*

ballpark figure   A moribund metaphor (SEE PAGE 19). *appraisal; assessment; estimate; estimation; guess; idea; impression; opinion; sense.* ■ Can you give me a *ballpark figure* of how much you made last year? REPLACE WITH *idea.*

(the) ball's in (your) court A moribund metaphor (SEE PAGE 19). ■ I think, nationally, *the ball is* definitely *in our court* now.

bang for (your) buck An infantile phrase (SEE PAGE 18). *quality; value; worth.*

banging (my) head against the wall A moribund metaphor (SEE PAGE 19).

baptism of fire   A moribund metaphor (SEE PAGE 19).

bare-bones (budget) A moribund metaphor (SEE PAGE 19).

bare essentials (necessities)   An inescapable pair (SEE PAGE 18).

barefaced (bold-faced) lie   An inescapable pair (SEE PAGE 18).

bargaining chip   A moribund metaphor (SEE PAGE 19).

(a) barking dog never bites   A popular prescription (SEE PAGE 21).

(her) bark is worse than (her) bite A moribund metaphor (SEE PAGE 19).

bark up the wrong tree A moribund metaphor (SEE PAGE 19). *amiss; astray; deceived; deluded; erring; erroneous; fallacious; false; faulty; inaccurate; incorrect; in error; misguided; misinformed; mislead; mistaken; not correct; not right; wrong.*

(a) barrage of   A moribund metaphor (SEE PAGE 19). If our language seems languid, it's partly because our metaphors are moribund.

This, *a barrage of,* is one of a certain kind of moribund metaphor that is especially irksome to come upon; *a bastion of, a chorus of, a cloud of, a deluge of, a firestorm of, a flood of, a flurry of, a hailstorm of, a mountain of, an army of, an avalanche of, an explosion of, an ocean of, an orgy of, a rising tide of, a sea of, a small army of, a spate of, a storm of, a torrent of, a world of* are all shabby, unimaginative expressions.

These are the least evocative, the least metaphorical, of metaphors. ■ He says *the barrage of marketing* has made teens tougher to teach.

barrel of laughs   A moribund metaphor (SEE PAGE 19). *hilarious; hysterical; side-splitting; uproarious.*

basically   An overworked word (SEE PAGE 20). People often use *basically* thinking it lends an intellectual air to the meaning of their words. *Basically,* in truth, only steals the sense from whatever words accompany it, for it proclaims their uncertainty and inexactitude as loudly as it does the speaker's or writer's pomposity.

Of course, there are also people, with few pretensions, who use *basically* either because they do not know what they say or because they do not know what to say. ■ *Basically*, the program is designed to operate with the same skills used when doing the exercise with a pencil and paper. ■ If the man wants custody, he must prove the woman to be *basically* unfit. ■ The rest of the day will be *basically* partly cloudy. ■ What *basically* began as an experiment to determine whether a family-type YMCA would survive quickly evolved into a challenge to serve a very enthusiastic community. ■ *Basically*, the next step is adding the molasses.

basic (and) fundamental A wretched redundancy (SEE PAGE 23). *basal; basic; elementary; essential; fundamental; primary; rudimentary.*

basic principle An inescapable pair (SEE PAGE 18). Seldom do we find *principle* without the word *basic* preceding it. A principle, however, is a basic truth or assumption. ■ Whether or not you are aware of it, there are *basic principles* of human interaction. DELETE *basic*. ■ The *basic principle* of laser protection is the same as for any direct fire weapon. DELETE *basic*.

basis in fact (reality) A wretched redundancy (SEE PAGE 23). *basis;*

fact; reality; truth; veracity. ■ The June 2 editorial that describes the final, wheezy stages of the movement to eliminate cigarettes has no *basis in fact*. REPLACE WITH *basis*. ■ To see whether such beliefs have any *basis in fact*, five different brands of fruit cocktail were chosen. REPLACE WITH *veracity*.

(a) bastion of A moribund metaphor (SEE PAGE 19). SEE ALSO *a barrage of.*

bathed in tears A moribund metaphor (SEE PAGE 19).

(like a) bat out of hell An insipid simile (SEE PAGE 19). *abruptly; apace; at once; briskly; directly; expeditiously; fast; forthwith; hastily; hurriedly; immediately; instantaneously; instantly; posthaste; promptly; quickly; rapidly; rashly; right away; speedily; straightaway; suddenly; swiftly; wingedly.*

(has) bats in (his) belfry A moribund metaphor (SEE PAGE 19). *batty; cracked; crazy; daft; demented; deranged; fey; foolish; goofy; insane; lunatic; mad; maniacal; neurotic; nuts; nutty; psychotic; raving; silly; squirrelly; touched; unbalanced; unhinged; unsound; wacky; zany.*

batten down the hatches A moribund metaphor (SEE PAGE 19).

batting a thousand A moribund metaphor (SEE PAGE 19).

(good) batting average A moribund metaphor (SEE PAGE 19).

battle lines are drawn A moribund metaphor (SEE PAGE 19).

(a) beacon (ray) of hope A moribund metaphor (SEE PAGE 19). *anticipation; expectancy; expectation; hope; hopefulness; optimism; possibility; promise; prospect; sanguinity.*

(please) be advised that An ineffectual phrase (SEE PAGE 17). This phrase is designed to make the reader pay attention to whatever follows it. The effect it has on anyone with sensibility, however, is quite the opposite: *(Please) be advised that* stupefies the attentive reader thereby ensuring that whatever follows it is hardly attended to. ■ *Please be advised that* some of the ads in this category may require a fee for services or processing. DELETE *Please be advised that.* ■ *Please be advised that* the valuation below is proposed and not final. DELETE *Please be advised that.* ■ *Please be advised that* this office has been retained by North American Mortgage Company to conduct real estate closing for the above-referenced property. DELETE *Please be advised that.* ■ *Please be advised that* it takes seven to ten days to process any request for medical records information. DELETE *Please be advised that.* ■ *Please be advised that* the Norfolk County Mosquito Control Project is now accepting applications for the position of Assistant Superintendent. DELETE *Please be advised that.* ■ *Please be advised that* I will be on vacation from June 26 to July

10. DELETE *Please be advised that.* SEE ALSO *(please) be informed that; this is to inform you that.*

be-all and end-all A moribund metaphor (SEE PAGE 19). *acme; ideal; perfection; quintessence; ultimate.*

beat about (around) the bush A moribund metaphor (SEE PAGE 19). *avoid; be equivocal; be evasive; dissemble; dodge; doubletalk; equivocate; evade; fence; hedge; palter; prevaricate; quibble; shuffle; sidestep; stall; tergiversate; waffle.*

beat a path to (your door) A moribund metaphor (SEE PAGE 19). *dash; hasten; hurry; hustle; make haste; race; run; rush; scamper; scurry; sprint.*

beat a (hasty) retreat A moribund metaphor (SEE PAGE 19). *abscond; clear out; decamp; depart; desert; disappear; escape; exit; flee; fly; go; go away; leave; move on; part; pull out; quit; retire; retreat; run away; take flight; take off; vacate; vanish; withdraw.*

beat (his) brains out A moribund metaphor (SEE PAGE 19).
1. *assail; assault; attack; batter; beat; cudgel; flagellate; flog; hit; lambaste; lash; lick; mangle; pound; pummel; strike; thrash; trounce.*
2. *annihilate; assassinate; butcher; destroy; exterminate; kill; massacre; murder; slaughter; slay.*
3. *beat; conquer; crush; defeat; outdo; overcome; overpower; overwhelm; prevail; quell; rout; succeed; triumph;*

trounce; vanquish; win.
4. *attempt; drudge; endeavor; essay; exert; grind; grub; labor; moil; slave; strain; strive; struggle; sweat; toil; travail; try; work.*

beat (them) hands down A moribund metaphor (SEE PAGE 19). *beat; conquer; crush; defeat; outdo; overcome; overpower; overwhelm; prevail; quell; rout; succeed; triumph; trounce; vanquish; win.*

(like) beating (flogging) a dead horse An insipid simile (SEE PAGE 19). *barren; bootless; effete; feckless; feeble; fruitless; futile; impotent; inadequate; inconsequential; inconsiderable; ineffective; ineffectual; infertile; insignificant; inutile; meaningless; meritless; nugatory; null; of no value; pointless; powerless; profitless; purposeless; redundant; sterile; superfluous; trifling; trivial; unavailing; unimportant; unnecessary; unproductive; unprofitable; unserviceable; unworthy; useless; vain; valueless; weak; worthless.*

beat (it) into the ground A moribund metaphor (SEE PAGE 19). *debilitate; deplete; drain; empty; enervate; exhaust; fatigue; overdo; overwork; sap; tire; wear out; weary.*

beat the bushes A moribund metaphor (SEE PAGE 19). *hunt; look for; quest; ransack; rummage; scour; search; seek.*

beat the (living) daylights out of A moribund metaphor (SEE PAGE 19).
1. *assail; assault; attack; batter; beat;*

cudgel; flagellate; flog; hit; lambaste; lash; lick; mangle; pound; pummel; strike; thrash; trounce.
2. *beat; conquer; crush; defeat; outdo; overcome; overpower; overwhelm; prevail; quell; rout; succeed; triumph; trounce; vanquish; win.*
3. *castigate; chastise; discipline; penalize; punish.*

beat the drum A moribund metaphor (SEE PAGE 19). *advertise; announce; broadcast; cry out; declaim; disseminate; exclaim; proclaim; promulgate; publicize; publish; shout; trumpet; yell.*

beat the stuffing out of A moribund metaphor (SEE PAGE 19).
1. *assail; assault; attack; batter; beat; cudgel; flagellate; flog; hit; lambaste; lash; lick; mangle; pound; pummel; strike; thrash; trounce.*
2. *beat; conquer; crush; defeat; outdo; overcome; overpower; overwhelm; prevail; quell; rout; succeed; triumph; trounce; vanquish; win.*

beat to a pulp A moribund metaphor (SEE PAGE 19).
1. *assail; assault; attack; batter; beat; cudgel; flagellate; flog; hit; lambaste; lash; lick; mangle; pound; pummel; strike; thrash; trounce.*
2. *beat; conquer; crush; defeat; outdo; overcome; overpower; overwhelm; prevail; quell; rout; succeed; triumph; trounce; vanquish; win.*

beat to death A moribund metaphor (SEE PAGE 19).
1. *annihilate; assassinate; butcher; destroy; exterminate; kill; massacre; murder; slaughter; slay.*

2. *debilitate; deplete; drain; empty; enervate; exhaust; fatigue; overdo; overwork; sap; tire; wear out; weary.* SEE ALSO *to death.*

beat (him) to the punch A moribund metaphor (SEE PAGE 19).

beat up on (each other) A moribund metaphor (SEE PAGE 19). *assail; assault; attack; batter; beat; cudgel; flagellate; flog; hit; lambaste; lash; lick; mangle; pound; pummel; strike; thrash; trounce.*

beauteous A withered word (SEE PAGE 22). *beautiful.* ■ Saturday should be a *beauteous* day. REPLACE WITH *beautiful.*

beautiful baby An inescapable pair (SEE PAGE 18).

beauty and the beast A moribund metaphor (SEE PAGE 19).

beauty is in the eye of the beholder A popular prescription (SEE PAGE 21).

because (that's why) An infantile phrase (SEE PAGE 18). ■ Why did you hit him? *Because.* SEE ALSO *it just happened.*

because of the fact that A wretched redundancy (SEE PAGE 23). *because; considering; for; in that; since.* ■ I married him only *because of the fact that* his family has money. REPLACE WITH *because.* ■ Many people told me I had to break off my relationship with her *because of the fact that* I was being

unfair to her. REPLACE WITH *because.* SEE ALSO *by virtue of the fact that; considering the fact that; given the fact that; in consideration of the fact that; in view of the fact that.*

because why? An infantile phrase (SEE PAGE 18). ■ They were afraid of him, too. *Because why?* DELETE *Because.*

(no) bed of roses A moribund metaphor (SEE PAGE 19). *agreeable; ambrosial; beguiling; celestial; charming; delectable; delicious; delightful; divine; enchanting; engaging; enjoyable; fun; heavenly; glorious; gratifying; inviting; joyful; joyous; luscious; pleasant; pleasing; pleasurable.*

(a) beehive of activity A moribund metaphor (SEE PAGE 19). *active; astir; bustling; busy; buzzing; energetic; humming; hopping; hustling; lively; vigorous.*

(a) bee in (her) bonnet A moribund metaphor (SEE PAGE 19). *caprice; crotchet; fixation; fancy; humor; impulse; maggot; notion; obsession; urge; vagary; whim.*

(she's) been around the block (and back) A moribund metaphor (SEE PAGE 19).
1. *adult; aged; aging; elderly; full-grown; hoary; hoary-headed; mature; old; worn.*
2. *able; adept; apt; capable; competent; deft; dexterous; experienced; expert; practiced; proficient; seasoned; skilled; skillful; veteran.*

before (you) can say (Jack Robinson) A moribund metaphor (SEE PAGE 19). *abruptly; apace; at once; briskly; directly; expeditiously; fast; forthwith; hastily; hurriedly; immediately; instantaneously; instantly; posthaste; promptly; quickly; rapidly; rashly; right away; speedily; straightaway; suddenly; swiftly; unexpectedly; wingedly.*

beg, borrow, or steal A moribund metaphor (SEE PAGE 19).

beggers can't be choosers A popular prescription (SEE PAGE 21).

begin (start) a new chapter (in my life) A moribund metaphor (SEE PAGE 19).

behind closed doors A moribund metaphor (SEE PAGE 19). *clandestinely; confidentially; covertly; furtively; mysteriously; in private; in secret; privately; quietly; secludedly; secretly; slyly; stealthily; surreptitiously; undercover.*

behind every successful man stands a woman A popular prescription (SEE PAGE 21).

behind the eight ball A moribund metaphor (SEE PAGE 19). *at risk; endangered; hard-pressed; imperiled; in a bind; in a fix; in a jam; in a predicament; in a quandary; in danger; in difficulty; in jeopardy; in peril; in trouble; jeopardized.*

(work) behind the scenes A moribund metaphor (SEE PAGE 19). *clandestinely; confidentially; covertly; furtively; mysteriously; in private; in secret; privately; quietly; secludedly; secretly; slyly; stealthily; surreptitiously; undercover.*

behind the times A moribund metaphor (SEE PAGE 19). *antediluvian; antiquated; archaic; dead; obsolescent; obsolete; old; old-fashioned; outdated; outmoded; out of date; out of fashion; passé; superannuated.*

(I'll) be honest with you A plebeian sentiment (SEE PAGE 20).

behoove A withered word (SEE PAGE 22).
1. *be advantageous for; benefit; be worthwhile to.*
2. *be necessary for; be proper for.*

(please) be informed that An ineffectual phrase (SEE PAGE 17). ■ *Please be informed that* your wife has retained my office in the matter of her petition for a divorce. DELETE *Please be informed that.* ■ If you are running a version of Almanac earlier than 3.0, *please be informed that* the format of the desktop data files has been changed. DELETE *please be informed that.* SEE ALSO *(please) be advised that; this is to inform you that.*

(like) being run over (getting hit) by a (Mack) truck An insipid simile (SEE PAGE 19). *atomized; crushed; dashed; demolished; depleted; depressed; destroyed; devastated; distraught; distressed; exhausted; obliterated; overcome; overpowered; overwhelmed; prostrate; ravaged; ruined; shattered; undone; upset.* ■ I feel *like I've been run over by a Mac truck.*

bells and whistles A moribund metaphor (SEE PAGE 19). *adornments; attributes; characteristics; decorations; embellishments; features; flourishes; frills; highlights; innovations; novelties; ornaments; properties; qualities; specialties; traits.* ■ They sport few of the *bells and whistles* found in programs like Netscape and Mosaic. REPLACE WITH *features.*

below par A moribund metaphor (SEE PAGE 19). *inferior; poor; second-class; second-rate; shoddy; subordinate; substandard.*

(hit) below the belt A moribund metaphor (SEE PAGE 19). *dishonorable; foul; inequitable; unconscientious; underhanded; unethical; unfair; unjust; unprincipled; unscrupulous; unsportsmanlike.*

belt-tightening (measures) A moribund metaphor (SEE PAGE 19).

bend (my) ear A moribund metaphor (SEE PAGE 19).

bend over backward(s) A moribund metaphor (SEE PAGE 19). *aim; attempt; endeavor; essay; exert; labor; moil; strain; strive; struggle; toil; try hard; undertake; work at.* ■ If anything, he will have to *bend over backward* to not appear to be showing favoritism. REPLACE WITH *struggle.*

be nice A plebeian sentiment (SEE PAGE 20). *"Be nice,"* we often are admonished. There can be no complaint with being agreeable when agreeability is warranted, but to soporiferously accept niceness as a virtue, untarnished and true, is utterly benighted.

To be capable of expressing anger and indignation is thwarted by our society's placing a premium on politeness.

Let us not, of course, be rude gratuitously, nor seek to be singular for its own sake, nor foolish or fantastic for the quick cachet. Do, however, let us become more concerned with giving fuller expression to ourselves.

We do possibly irreparable harm to ourselves when we, to avoid unpleasantness, fail to show another how we truly feel. Unknown to ourselves and unknowable to others we homunculi are, for anonymity is won when anger is lost. SEE ALSO *if you can't say something nice, don't say anything; I'm sorry.*

bent out of shape A moribund metaphor (SEE PAGE 19).
1. *agitated; anxious; aroused; bothered; displeased; disquieted; disturbed; excited; flustered; perturbed; troubled; upset; worried.*
2. *acerbated; angered; annoyed; bothered; disturbed; exasperated; galled; irked; irritated; miffed; nettled; provoked; rankled; riled; roiled; upset; vexed.*

(the) best and (the) brightest A suspect superlative (SEE PAGE 22). *best; brightest; choice; choicest; elite; excellent; finest; first-class; first-rate; foremost; greatest; highest; matchless; optimal; optimum; outstanding; para-*

mount; peerless; preeminent; premium; prominent; select; superior; superlative; top; unequaled; unexcelled; unmatched; unrivaled; unsurpassed. ■ He decried the "cult of efficiency" into which have fallen so many of *the best and brightest* of the conservative young. REPLACE WITH *the brightest.* ■ Bandied about were the names of several of *the best and brightest* of the next generation. REPLACE WITH *the elite.*

(the) best defense is a good offense A popular prescription (SEE PAGE 21).

(the) best (that) money can buy A suspect superlative (SEE PAGE 22).

(in) (the) best of all (possible) worlds A suspect superlative (SEE PAGE 22). *best; choice; elite; excellent; finest; first-class; first-rate; foremost; greatest; highest; ideal; matchless; optimal; optimum; outstanding; paramount; peerless; preeminent; premium; prominent; select; superior; superlative; supreme; top; unequaled; unexcelled; unmatched; unrivaled; unsurpassed.* ■ *In the best of all possible worlds,* test procedures for which neither type of error is possible could be developed. REPLACE WITH *ideally.*

best of the bunch (lot) A suspect superlative (SEE PAGE 22). *best; brightest; choice; choicest; elite; excellent; finest; first-class; first-rate; foremost; greatest; highest; matchless; optimal; optimum; outstanding; paramount; peerless; preeminent; premium; prominent; select; superior;* superlative; top; unequaled; unexcelled; unmatched; unrivaled; unsurpassed.

best-selling author A suspect superlative (SEE PAGE 22). *Best-selling authors,* of course, are often responsible for the worst-written books. SEE ALSO *a good read; a (must) read.*

(the) best (greatest) thing since sliced bread A moribund metaphor (SEE PAGE 19).

(the) best things in life are free A popular prescription (SEE PAGE 21).

(she's) (the) best thing that ever happened to (me) A plebeian sentiment (SEE PAGE 20).

bet (your) bottom dollar (life) A moribund metaphor (SEE PAGE 19). ■ I would have *bet my bottom dollar* that this would not have happened.

(my) better half An infantile phrase (SEE PAGE 18). *consort; helpmate; helpmeet; husband; mate; spouse; wife.*

better late than never A popular prescription (SEE PAGE 21).

better safe than sorry A popular prescription (SEE PAGE 21).

(it's) better than nothing A popular prescription (SEE PAGE 21).

bet the farm (ranch) (on) A moribund metaphor (SEE PAGE 19).

between a rock and a hard place
A moribund metaphor (SEE PAGE
19). *at risk; endangered; hard-pressed;
imperiled; in a bind; in a dilemma; in
a fix; in a jam; in a predicament; in a
quandary; in danger; in difficulty; in
jeopardy; in peril; in trouble; jeopardized.* ■ When you need to regener-
ate a degraded stripe set with par-
ity, you will be faced with a *rock
and a hard place* dilemma. DELETE
rock and a hard place.

between Scylla and Charybdis A
moribund metaphor (SEE PAGE 19).
*at risk; endangered; hard-pressed;
imperiled; in a bind; in a dilemma; in
a fix; in a jam; in a predicament; in a
quandary; in danger; in difficulty; in
jeopardy; in peril; in trouble; jeopardized.*

**between the devil and the deep
blue sea** A moribund metaphor
(SEE PAGE 19). *at risk; endangered;
hard-pressed; imperiled; in a bind; in a
dilemma; in a fix; in a jam; in a
predicament; in a quandary; in danger; in difficulty; in jeopardy; in peril;
in trouble; jeopardized.*

**between you and me (and the
four walls)** A moribund metaphor
(SEE PAGE 19). *classified; confidential;
personal; private; privy; restricted;
secret.*

betwixt A withered word (SEE
PAGE 22). *between.*

betwixt and between An
inescapable pair (SEE PAGE 18).
*divided; drifting; faltering; in
between; irresolute; loose; shaky;
swaying; torn; tottering; uncertain;
undecided; unfixed; unresolved;
unsettled; unsteady; unsure; vacillating; wavering; wobbly.*

beware of Greeks bearing gifts A
popular prescription (SEE PAGE 21).

**beyond (without) a shadow of a
doubt** A moribund metaphor (SEE
PAGE 19). *absolutely; conclusively;
decidedly; definitely; incontrovertibly;
indisputably; indubitably; irrefrag-
ably; irrefutably; positively; unconditionally; uncontestably; undeniably;
undoubtedly; unequivocally; unmis-
takably; unquestionably.*

beyond the pale A moribund
metaphor (SEE PAGE 19). *improper;
inappropriate; unacceptable; unreasonable; unseemly; unsuitable;
unthinkable.*

beyond (my) wildest dreams A
moribund metaphor (SEE PAGE 19).
*astonishing; astounding; beyond
belief; beyond comprehension; breathtaking; extraordinary; fabulous; fantastic; implausible; imponderable;
inconceivable; incredible; marvelous;
miraculous; outlandish; overwhelming; prodigious; sensational; spectacular; unbelievable; unimaginable;
unthinkable; wonderful.*

(a) bevy of beauties An infantile
phrase (SEE PAGE 18).

(as) big as a house An insipid
simile (SEE PAGE 19). *big; brobdingnagian; colossal; enormous; gargantuan; giant; gigantic; grand; great;
huge; immense; large; massive; monstrous; prodigious; tremendous; vast.*

(as) big as life An insipid simile (SEE PAGE 19).

big cheese A moribund metaphor (SEE PAGE 19).
1. *administrator; boss; brass; chief; commander; director; executive; foreman; head; headman; leader; manager; master; (high) muckamuck; officer; official; overseer; president; principal; superintendent; supervisor.*
2. *aristocrat; dignitary; eminence; lord; luminary; magnate; mogul; notable; patrician; personage; ruler; sovereign; worthy.*

big deal An infantile phrase (SEE PAGE 18). *appreciable; central; climacteric; consequential; considerable; critical; crucial; essential; grave; major; material; important; meaningful; momentous; pivotal; pregnant; principal; serious; significant; substantial; vital; weighty.*

big fish in a small pond A moribund metaphor (SEE PAGE 19).

bigger is better A quack equation (SEE PAGE 21).

bigger isn't necessarily better A popular prescription (SEE PAGE 21).

(the) bigger they are, the harder they fall A popular prescription (SEE PAGE 21).

big gun A moribund metaphor (SEE PAGE 19).
1. *administrator; boss; brass; chief; commander; director; executive; foreman; head; headman; leader; manager;*
master; (high) muckamuck; officer; official; overseer; president; principal; superintendent; supervisor.
2. *aristocrat; dignitary; eminence; lord; luminary; magnate; mogul; notable; patrician; personage; ruler; sovereign; worthy.*

(the) big picture A moribund metaphor (SEE PAGE 19). ■ Let's not make decisions without looking at *the big picture.*

big shot A moribund metaphor (SEE PAGE 19).
1. *administrator; boss; brass; chief; commander; director; executive; foreman; head; headman; leader; manager; master; (high) muckamuck; officer; official; overseer; president; principal; superintendent; supervisor.*
2. *aristocrat; dignitary; eminence; lord; luminary; magnate; mogul; notable; patrician; personage; ruler; sovereign; worthy.*

big-ticket (item) A moribund metaphor (SEE PAGE 19). *costly; expensive; high-priced.* ■ We can market these *big-ticket* items, which have a large profit margin. REPLACE WITH *expensive.*

(like a) big weight has been lifted from (my) shoulders An insipid simile (SEE PAGE 19).
1. *allay; alleviate; assuage; lighten; mitigate; relieve; soothe.*
2. *deliver; disburden; disencumber; disentangle; emancipate; extricate; free; liberate; manumit; release; relieve; save; set free; unburden; unchain; unencumber; unfetter; unshackle.*

big wheel A moribund metaphor (SEE PAGE 19).
1. *administrator; boss; brass; chief; commander; director; executive; foreman; head; headman; leader; manager; master; (high) muckamuck; officer; official; overseer; president; principal; superintendent; supervisor.*
2. *aristocrat; dignitary; eminence; lord; luminary; magnate; mogul; notable; patrician; personage; ruler; sovereign; worthy.*

(a) bird in the hand (is worth two in the bush) A popular prescription (SEE PAGE 21).

bird's-eye view A moribund metaphor (SEE PAGE 19). *outline; overview; profile; review; sketch; summary; survey.*

birds of a feather (flock together) A moribund metaphor (SEE PAGE 19). *akin; alike; commensurate; comparable; consonant; duplicate; equal; equivalent; identical; indistinguishable; interchangeable; like; same; similar; undifferentiated.* ■ Politically, they are *birds of a feather.* REPLACE WITH *indistinguishable.*

bite (my) head off A moribund metaphor (SEE PAGE 19). *admonish; animadvert; berate; castigate; censure; chasten; chastise; chide; condemn; criticize; denounce; denunciate; discipline; excoriate; fulminate against; imprecate; impugn; inveigh against; objurgate; punish; rebuke; remonstrate; reprehend; reprimand; reproach; reprobate; reprove; revile; scold; swear at; upbraid; vituperate; warn.*

bite off more than (he) can chew A moribund metaphor (SEE PAGE 19). ■ Even in private circles, there is concern that the government has *bitten off more than it can chew.*

bite the bullet A moribund metaphor (SEE PAGE 19). *bear; endure; put up with; stand; suffer; tolerate.*

bite the dust A moribund metaphor (SEE PAGE 19).
1. *decease; depart; die; expire; extinguish; pass away; pass on; perish; terminate.*
2. *be beaten; be conquered; be crushed; be defeated; be outdone; be overcome; be overpowered; be overwhelmed; be quelled; be routed; be trounced; be vanquished.*
3. *cease; close; complete; conclude; derail; desist; discontinue; end; finish; halt; quit; settle; stop; terminate.*
4. *be unsuccessful; bomb; break down; collapse; fail; fall short; falter; fizzle; flop; fold; founder; mess up; miscarry; not succeed; stumble; topple.*

(they) bite the hand that feeds (them) A moribund metaphor (SEE PAGE 19). *unappreciative; ungrateful; unthankful.*

bite your tongue A moribund metaphor (SEE PAGE 19).

bits and pieces An inescapable pair (SEE PAGE 18). *bits; chunks; components; crumbs; elements; factors; fragments; ingredients; modicums; morsels; nuggets; parts; particles; pieces; scraps; segments; shreds; snips; snippets; specks.* ■ All the bits *and pieces* that make up the whole must be carefully and objectively examined. REPLACE WITH *elements.*

bitter acrimony   An inescapable pair (SEE PAGE 18).

(a) bitter (tough) pill to swallow   A moribund metaphor (SEE PAGE 19).

(as) black as coal   An insipid simile (SEE PAGE 19). *black; blackish; caliginous; dark; ebony; ecchymotic; fuliginous; inky; jet; nigrescent; nigritudinous; raven; sable; swarthy; tenebrific; tenebrous.*

(as) black as pitch   An insipid simile (SEE PAGE 19). *black; blackish; caliginous; dark; ebony; ecchymotic; fuliginous; inky; jet; nigrescent; nigritudinous; raven; sable; swarthy; tenebrific; tenebrous.*

(as) black as the ace of spades   An insipid simile (SEE PAGE 19). *black; blackish; caliginous; dark; ebony; ecchymotic; fuliginous; inky; jet; nigrescent; nigritudinous; raven; sable; swarthy; tenebrific; tenebrous.*

black sheep (of the family)   A moribund metaphor (SEE PAGE 19). *curiosity; deviant; eccentric; extremist; iconoclast; individual; individualist; maverick; misfit; nonconformist; oddball; oddity; renegade; undesirable.*

blah, blah, blah   A grammatical gimmick (SEE PAGE 17). ■ He told me, I want you to come out here; I miss you; *blah, blah, blah.* DELETE *blah, blah, blah.* SEE ALSO *and so on, and so forth; et cetera, et cetera.*

blast from the past   An infantile phrase (SEE PAGE 18).

blatant lie   An inescapable pair (SEE PAGE 18).

blessed event   An infantile phrase (SEE PAGE 18).
1. *baby; infant; newborn.*
2. *birth; childbearing; childbirth; parturition.*

blessed with (has) the gift of gab   An infantile phrase (SEE PAGE 18). *babbling; blathering; chatty; facile; fluent; garrulous; glib; jabbering; logorrheic; long-winded; loquacious; prolix; talkative; verbose; voluble; windy.*

(a) blessing in disguise   A moribund metaphor (SEE PAGE 19).

(as) blind as a bat   An insipid simile (SEE PAGE 19).
1. *blind; eyeless; purblind; sightless; unseeing; unsighted; visionless.*
2. *addleheaded; bovine; cretinous; decerebrate; dense; dull; dull-witted; fatuous; fat-witted; half-witted; harebrained; hebetudinous; idiotic; ignorant; imbecilic; incogitant; insensate; mindless; moronic; muddled; nescient; obtuse; phlegmatic; slow; slow-witted; sluggish; thick; torpid; undiscerning; unintelligent; vacuous; witless.*

blind faith   An inescapable pair (SEE PAGE 18).

(the) blind leading the blind   A moribund metaphor (SEE PAGE 19).

(a) blip on the (radar) screen   A moribund metaphor (SEE PAGE 19).

frivolous; inappreciable; immaterial; inconsequential; inconsiderable; insignificant; meager; meaningless; minor; negligible; next to nothing; nugatory; paltry; petty; scant; scanty; scarcely anything; slight; trifling; trivial; unimportant; unsubstantial; worthless. As laughable as it is moribund, *a blip on the (radar) screen* belies the writing ability of whoever uses it. ■ War and peace abroad was *barely a blip on the screen* compared with gun control at home. REPLACE WITH *inconsiderable.*

blondes have more fun An infantile phrase (SEE PAGE 18).

bloodcurdling scream (yell) An inescapable pair (SEE PAGE 18).

blood is thicker than water A popular prescription (SEE PAGE 21).

blood, sweat, and tears A moribund metaphor (SEE PAGE 19). *assiduity; diligence; discipline; drudgery; effort; endeavor; exertion; grind; hard work; industry; labor; moil; persistence; slavery; strain; struggle; sweat; toil; travail; work.* ■ However unautobiographical or fictional a book is, it still comes out by *blood, sweat, and tears.* REPLACE WITH *toil.*

(the) bloom is off the rose A moribund metaphor (SEE PAGE 19).

blow a fuse A moribund metaphor (SEE PAGE 19). *bellow; bluster; clamor; explode; fulminate; fume; holler; howl; rage; rant; rave; roar; scream; shout; storm; thunder; vociferate; yell.*

blow a gasket A moribund metaphor (SEE PAGE 19). *bellow; bluster; clamor; explode; fulminate; fume; holler; howl; rage; rant; rave; roar; scream; shout; storm; thunder; vociferate; yell.*

blow away A moribund metaphor (SEE PAGE 19).
1. *annihilate; assassinate; butcher; destroy; exterminate; kill; massacre; murder; slaughter; slay.*
2. *amaze; astonish; astound; awe; dazzle; dumbfound; flabbergast; overpower; overwhelm; shock; startle; stun; stupefy; surprise.*

blow by blow A moribund metaphor (SEE PAGE 19).

blow (run) hot and cold A moribund metaphor (SEE PAGE 19).
1. *ambivalent; divided; indecisive; irresolute; torn; uncertain; uncommitted; undecided; unsure.*
2. *capricious; changeable; erratic; fickle; fitful; flighty; fluctuating; haphazard; inconsistent; inconstant; intermittent; irregular; mercurial; occasional; random; sometime; spasmodic; sporadic; unpredictable; unsettled; unstable; unsteady; vacillating; volatile; wavering; wayward.*

blow (my) mind A moribund metaphor (SEE PAGE 19). *amaze; astonish; astound; awe; dazzle; dumbfound; flabbergast; overpower; overwhelm; shock; startle; stun; stupefy; surprise.*

blow off steam A moribund metaphor (SEE PAGE 19).
1. *bellow; bluster; clamor; complain; explode; fulminate; fume; holler; howl;*

object; protest; rage; rant; rave; roar; scream; shout; storm; thunder; vociferate; yell.
2. *be merry; carouse; carry on; celebrate; debauch; disport; frolic; party; play; revel; riot; roister; rollick; romp; skylark.*

blow on the cue ball A moribund metaphor (SEE PAGE 19).

blow (things) out of proportion A moribund metaphor (SEE PAGE 19). *elaborate; embellish; embroider; enhance; enlarge; exaggerate; hyperbolize; inflate; magnify; overdo; overreact; overstress; overstate; strain; stretch.* ■ It was not the sort of event that has now been exaggerated and *blown out of proportion.* DELETE *and blown out of proportion.*

blow (them) out of the water A moribund metaphor (SEE PAGE 19).
1. *annihilate; assassinate; butcher; destroy; exterminate; kill; massacre; murder; slaughter; slay.*
2. *beat; conquer; crush; defeat; outdo; overcome; overpower; overwhelm; prevail; quell; rout; succeed; triumph; trounce; vanquish; win.*
3. *amaze; astonish; astound; awe; dazzle; dumbfound; flabbergast; overpower; overwhelm; shock; startle; stun; stupefy; surprise.*

blow (your) own horn A moribund metaphor (SEE PAGE 19). *acclaim; applaud; bluster; boast; brag; celebrate; cheer; commend; compliment; congratulate; crow; extol; flatter; gloat; hail; honor; laud; praise; puff; salute; self-congratulate; strut; swagger.*

blow smoke A moribund metaphor (SEE PAGE 19). *adumbrate; becloud; befog; camouflage; cloak; cloud; conceal; cover; disguise; dissemble; enshroud; harbor; hide; keep secret; mask; obfuscate; obscure; overshadow; screen; shroud; suppress; veil; withhold.*

blow (his) stack A moribund metaphor (SEE PAGE 19). *bellow; bluster; clamor; explode; fulminate; fume; holler; howl; rage; rant; rave; roar; scream; shout; storm; thunder; vociferate; yell.*

blow the whistle (on) A moribund metaphor (SEE PAGE 19).
1. *bare; betray; disclose; divulge; expose; give away; reveal; show; tell; uncover; unveil.* ■ He *blew the whistle on* company corruption. REPLACE WITH *exposed.*
2. *betray; deliver up; inform on; report; turn in.* ■ Fear of reprisals arises when people consider whether or not to *blow the whistle on* someone who violates ethical standards. REPLACE WITH *report.*

blow to bits A moribund metaphor (SEE PAGE 19). *annihilate; assassinate; butcher; demolish; destroy; devastate; eradicate; exterminate; kill; massacre; murder; obliterate; pulverize; rack; ravage; raze; ruin; shatter; slaughter; slay; smash; undo; wrack; wreck.*

blow (my) top A moribund metaphor (SEE PAGE 19). *bellow; bluster; clamor; explode; fulminate; fume; holler; howl; rage; rant; rave; roar; scream; shout; storm; thunder; vociferate; yell.*

blow to smithereens A moribund metaphor (SEE PAGE 19). *annihilate; assassinate; butcher; demolish; destroy; devastate; eradicate; exterminate; kill; massacre; murder; obliterate; pulverize; rack; ravage; raze; ruin; shatter; slaughter; slay; smash; undo; wrack; wreck.*

(until) (I'm) blue in the face A moribund metaphor (SEE PAGE 19). 1. *angry; annoyed; enraged; exasperated; furious; incensed; infuriated; irate; irked; irritated; mad; raging; wrathful.* 2. *beat; bushed; debilitated; depleted; exhausted; fatigued; fed up; spent; tired; wearied; weary; worn out.*

blue-ribbon commission (committee; panel) A suspect superlative (SEE PAGE 22).

(as) bold as brass An insipid simile (SEE PAGE 19). *audacious; bold; brash; brass; brassy; brazen; cheeky; forward; impertinent; impudent; insolent; outrageous; saucy; shameless; unabashed.*

(a) bolt from (out of) the blue A moribund metaphor (SEE PAGE 19). *bombshell; shock; surprise; thunderbolt; thunderclap.*

bone of contention A moribund metaphor (SEE PAGE 19).

bone to pick A moribund metaphor (SEE PAGE 19). *animosity; bitterness; enmity; grievance; grudge; hostility; indignation; ill will; offense; rancor; resentment; spite; umbrage.*

(cite) book, chapter, and verse A moribund metaphor (SEE PAGE 19). *explain; expound; lecture.* ■ She will give me chapter and verse about the merits of XYZ Chemical and why it should be a glorious investment. REPLACE WITH *lecture me.*

book of woes A moribund metaphor (SEE PAGE 19).

bore the pants off (me) A moribund metaphor (SEE PAGE 19). *annoy; bore; discourage; disgust; exasperate; exhaust; fatigue; irk; irritate; sicken; tire; wear out; weary.*

bore to death (extinction) A moribund metaphor (SEE PAGE 19). *annoy; bore; discourage; disgust; exasperate; exhaust; fatigue; irk; irritate; sicken; tire; wear out; weary.* SEE ALSO *to death.*

bore to tears A moribund metaphor (SEE PAGE 19). *annoy; bore; discourage; disgust; exasperate; exhaust; fatigue; irk; irritate; sicken; tire; wear out; weary.*

born to the purple A moribund metaphor (SEE PAGE 19).

born under a lucky star A moribund metaphor (SEE PAGE 19). *advantageous; auspicious; blessed; charmed; enchanted; favored; felicitous; flourishing; fortuitous; fortunate; golden; happy; in luck; lucky; propitious; prosperous; successful; thriving.*

born with a silver spoon in (his) mouth A moribund metaphor

(SEE PAGE 19). *advantageous; auspicious; blessed; charmed; enchanted; favored; felicitous; flourishing; fortuitous; fortunate; golden; happy; in luck; lucky; propitious; prosperous; successful; thriving.*

(the) bottom fell out A moribund metaphor (SEE PAGE 19). *break down; break up; collapse; crash; crumple; disintegrate; end; fail; fall apart; fold; stop.* ■ He elected to stop financing condominium projects nearly two years before *the bottom fell out* of that business.

bottomless pit A moribund metaphor (SEE PAGE 19). *abyss; hades; hell; inferno; netherworld; perdition.*

(the) bottom line A moribund metaphor (SEE PAGE 19). This is a bottomlessly ordinary term. People bewitched by words that have a trace of technicality to them are inclined to use it. In striving to sound technical, they manage to sound only typical.
1. *conclusion; consequence; culmination; decision; denouement; effect; end; outcome; result; upshot.* ■ The *bottom line* is that America can compete if the politicians are kept out of the picture. REPLACE WITH *upshot.* ■ The *bottom line* is that both kinds of water are generally safe. REPLACE WITH *conclusion.*
2. *crux; essence; key; keynote; main point; salient point.* ■ The *bottom line* is you get what you pay for. REPLACE WITH *main point.* ■ The *bottom line* for parents: choose gifts carefully. REPLACE WITH *keynote.*

SEE ALSO *feedback; input; interface; output; parameters.*

bottom of the barrel A moribund metaphor (SEE PAGE 19).
1. *alluvium; debris; deposit; detritus; dregs; grounds; lees; precipitate; remains; residue; residuum; sediment; settlings; silt; wash.*
2. *close; completion; conclusion; end; ending; finale; finish; termination.*
3. *bums; deadbeats; derelicts; duds; failures; flobs; hobos; losers; pariahs; rabble; renegades; riffraff; scum; tramps; vagabonds; vagrants; washouts.*

bound and determined An inescapable pair (SEE PAGE 18). *bent on; determined; resolute; resolved.*

bow and scrape A moribund metaphor (SEE PAGE 19). *bootlick; bow; crawl; cringe; crouch; fawn; grovel; kowtow; slaver; stoop; toady; truckle.*

(like a) bowl of cherries An insipid simile (SEE PAGE 19). *agreeable; ambrosial; beguiling; celestial; charming; delectable; delicious; delightful; divine; enchanting; engaging; enjoyable; fun; heavenly; glorious; gratifying; inviting; joyful; joyous; luscious; pleasant; pleasing; pleasurable.*

brain drain An infantile phrase (SEE PAGE 18).

brand new An inescapable pair (SEE PAGE 18). ■ Did you forget he got himself a *brand new* car to drive around in? DELETE *brand.*

(the) bread always falls on the buttered side A moribund metaphor (SEE PAGE 19).

bread and butter A moribund metaphor (SEE PAGE 19).
1. *food; keep; livelihood; living; subsistence; support; sustenance.*
2. *basis; center; core; essence; foundation; heart; hub; mainstay; nucleus; root; soul; spirit.* ■ Interfaces are the *bread and butter* of component technology. REPLACE WITH *core.*

breadth and depth An inescapable pair (SEE PAGE 18). *ambit; area; breadth; compass; degree; extent; field; magnitude; range; reach; scope; sphere; sweep.*

break (his) back A moribund metaphor (SEE PAGE 19). *attempt; drudge; endeavor; essay; exert; grind; grub; labor; moil; slave; strain; strive; struggle; sweat; toil; travail; try; work.*

break down (the) barriers A moribund metaphor (SEE PAGE 19).

break (my) neck A moribund metaphor (SEE PAGE 19). *attempt; drudge; endeavor; essay; exert; grind; grub; labor; moil; slave; strain; strive; struggle; sweat; toil; travail; try; work.*

break out of the mold A moribund metaphor (SEE PAGE 19).

(it) breaks (my) heart A moribund metaphor (SEE PAGE 19). *desolate; disappoint; discourage; dishearten; dispirit; distress; sadden.*

break the bank A moribund metaphor (SEE PAGE 19). *bankrupt; deplete; drain; exhaust; impoverish; pauperize; ruin.*

break the ice A moribund metaphor (SEE PAGE 19).

breathe (new) life into A moribund metaphor (SEE PAGE 19). *animate; arouse; enliven; exhilarate; inspire; inspirit; invigorate; revivify; spur; stimulate; vitalize; vivify.* ■ The Citizens for Limited Taxation petition would block school reform at the very time it is needed most to *breathe life into* our public schools. REPLACE WITH *invigorate.*

breathless anticipation An inescapable pair (SEE PAGE 18).

(a welcome) breath of fresh air A moribund metaphor (SEE PAGE 19). *animating; arousing; bracing; enlivening; exciting; exhilarating; inspiring; inspiriting; invigorating; provoking; refreshing; rousing; stimulating; vivifying.*
Of what it purports to describe, *a (welcome) breath of fresh air* offers the opposite. If intelligent or heartfelt sentences are invigorating, this dimwitticism should make us gasp as though we've been throttled by foul-smelling thoughtlessness. ■ A toy industry analyst called the news *a breath of fresh air.* REPLACE WITH *refreshing*

(a) breed apart (unto itself) A moribund metaphor (SEE PAGE 19). *aberrant; abnormal; anomalistic;*

anomalous; atypical; bizarre; curious; deviant; different; distinct; distinctive; eccentric; exceptional; extraordinary; fantastic; foreign; grotesque; idiosyncratic; independent; individual; individualistic; irregular; novel; odd; offbeat; original; peculiar; puzzling; quaint; queer; rare; remarkable; separate; singular; uncommon; unconventional; unexampled; unique; unnatural; unorthodox; unparalleled; unprecedented; unusual; weird.

(it's) (a) breeze A moribund metaphor (SEE PAGE 19). *apparent; basic; clear; clear-cut; conspicuous; distinct; easily done; easy; effortless; elementary; evident; explicit; facile; limpid; lucid; manifest; obvious; patent; pellucid; plain; simple; simplicity itself; straightforward; translucent; transparent; unambiguous; uncomplex; uncomplicated; understandable; unequivocal; unmistakable.*

bright and early An inescapable pair (SEE PAGE 18).

(as) bright as a (new) button An insipid simile (SEE PAGE 19).
1. *beaming; bright; brilliant; burnished; dazzling; effulgent; gleaming; glistening; glittering; glossy; incandescent; luminous; lustrous; radiant; resplendent; shiny; sparkling.*
2. *able; adroit; alert; apt; astute; bright; brilliant; capable; clever; competent; discerning; enlightened; insightful; intelligent; judicious; keen; knowledgeable; learned; logical; luminous; perceptive; perspicacious; quick; quick-witted; rational; reasonable; sagacious; sage; sapient; sensible; sharp; shrewd; smart; sound; understanding; wise.*

(as) bright as a new penny An insipid simile (SEE PAGE 19).
1. *beaming; bright; brilliant; burnished; dazzling; effulgent; gleaming; glistening; glittering; glossy; incandescent; luminous; lustrous; radiant; resplendent; shiny; sparkling.*
2. *able; adroit; alert; apt; astute; bright; brilliant; capable; clever; competent; discerning; enlightened; insightful; intelligent; judicious; keen; knowledgeable; learned; logical; luminous; perceptive; perspicacious; quick; quick-witted; rational; reasonable; sagacious; sage; sapient; sensible; sharp; shrewd; smart; sound; understanding; wise.*

(as) bright as a new pin An insipid simile (SEE PAGE 19).
1. *beaming; bright; brilliant; burnished; dazzling; effulgent; gleaming; glistening; glittering; glossy; incandescent; luminous; lustrous; radiant; resplendent; shiny; sparkling.*
2. *able; adroit; alert; apt; astute; bright; brilliant; capable; clever; competent; discerning; enlightened; insightful; intelligent; judicious; keen; knowledgeable; learned; logical; luminous; perceptive; perspicacious; quick; quick-witted; rational; reasonable; sagacious; sage; sapient; sensible; sharp; shrewd; smart; sound; understanding; wise.*

(she) brightens up a room A moribund metaphor (SEE PAGE 19). *is beaming; is brilliant; is dazzling; is gleaming; is glowing; is incandescent; is luminescent; is luminous; is radiant; is resplendent; is shimmering; is sunny.*

bright-eyed and bushy tailed A moribund metaphor (SEE PAGE 19). *active; adroit; alert; alive; animated; dynamic; energetic; frisky; hearty; lively; nimble; peppy; perky; quick; ready; spirited; sprightly; spry; vibrant; vigorous; vivacious.*

bring (take) (her) down a notch (peg) A moribund metaphor (SEE PAGE 19). *abase; chasten; debase; decrease; deflate; degrade; demean; depreciate; depress; diminish; disgrace; dishonor; embarrass; humble; humiliate; lower; mortify; puncture; shame.*

bring (her) down from (her) high horse A moribund metaphor (SEE PAGE 19). *abase; chasten; debase; decrease; deflate; degrade; demean; depreciate; depress; diminish; disgrace; dishonor; embarrass; humble; humiliate; lower; mortify; puncture; shame.*

bring down the house A moribund metaphor (SEE PAGE 19). *acclaim; applaud; bellow; cheer; clamor; holler; howl; roar; scream; shout; vociferate; yell.*

bring home the bacon A moribund metaphor (SEE PAGE 19). *earn a living; earn money; prosper; succeed* .

bring to a close (a halt; an end; a stop) A wretched redundancy (SEE PAGE 23). *cease; close; complete; conclude; derail; discontinue; end; finish; halt; settle; stop; terminate.* ■ We are pleased to be able to *bring* this longstanding litigation *to a close.* REPLACE WITH *conclude.* ■ You

might be contributing to *bringing* the nation's longest peacetime economic expansion *to a grinding halt.* REPLACE WITH *halting.* SEE ALSO *come to a close (a halt; an end; a stop); grind to a halt.*

bring to a head A moribund metaphor (SEE PAGE 19). *cap; climax; conclude; consummate; crest; crown; culminate; peak.*

bring (come) to closure A torpid term (SEE PAGE 22).
1. *cease; close; complete; conclude; discontinue; end; finish; halt; stop.*
2. *conclude; decide; determine; establish; resolve; settle.*

bring (them) to (their) knees A moribund metaphor (SEE PAGE 19). *beat; conquer; cow; cripple; crush; defeat; disable; dispirit; enervate; enfeeble; humble; incapacitate; lame; make helpless; neutralize; oppress; overcome; overpower; overrun; overthrow; overwhelm; repress; subdue; subjugate; suppress; vanquish.* ■ A network of computers was *brought to its knees* by something out of our control that seemed to live in and even infect the system. REPLACE WITH *vanquished.*

bring to the table A moribund metaphor (SEE PAGE 19). *advance; bring up; broach; contribute; give; introduce; offer; present; proffer; propose; provide; raise; submit; suggest; tender.* ■ As a company that knows education, we thought we had something to *bring to the table.* REPLACE WITH *offer.*

brought it home to (me) A moribund metaphor (SEE PAGE 19).

(as) brown as a berry An insipid simile (SEE PAGE 19). *beige; bronze; bronzed; brown; burnished; chestnut; copper; coppery; ecru; fawn; mahogany; ocherous; russet; sienna; sun-tanned; tan; tanned; tawny.*

(win) brownie points A moribund metaphor (SEE PAGE 19).

brutally honest An inescapable pair (SEE PAGE 18).

brute force An inescapable pair (SEE PAGE 18).

bucket of bolts A moribund metaphor (SEE PAGE 19).

build a better mousetrap (and the world will beat a path to your door) A popular prescription (SEE PAGE 21).

build bridges A moribund metaphor (SEE PAGE 19).

build bridges where there are walls A moribund metaphor (SEE PAGE 19).

build castles in Spain (the air) A moribund metaphor (SEE PAGE 19). *brood; daydream; dream; fantasize; imagine; meditate; muse; reflect.*

building blocks of A moribund metaphor (SEE PAGE 19).

(like) (a) bull in a china closet (shop) An insipid simile (SEE PAGE 19). *awkward; blundering; bumbling; bungling; clumsy; gawky; gauche; ham-handed; heavy-handed; inapt; inept; lubberly; lumbering; maladroit; uncoordinated; uncouth; ungainly; ungraceful; unhandy; unskillful; unwieldy.*

bump in the road A moribund metaphor (SEE PAGE 19). *bar; barrier; block; blockage; check; deterrent; difficulty; encumbrance; handicap; hindrance; hurdle; impediment; interference; obstacle; obstruction.*

(like) (a) bump on a log An insipid simile (SEE PAGE 19). *dead; dormant; dull; immobile; immovable; inactive; inanimate; indolent; inert; inoperative; languid; latent; lethargic; lifeless; listless; motionless; phlegmatic; quiescent; quiet; sluggish; stagnant; static; stationary; still; stockstill; torpid; unresponsive.*

bumpy road (ahead) A moribund metaphor (SEE PAGE 19). *complication; difficulty; dilemma; mess; muddle; ordeal; pickle; plight; predicament; problem; quandary; trial; trouble.*

bunch of baloney A moribund metaphor (SEE PAGE 19). *balderdash; baloney; nonsense; rubbish.*

bundle of joy A moribund metaphor (SEE PAGE 19). *babe; baby; child; infant; neonate; newborn; nursling; suckling; toddler; tot; weanling.*

bundle of nerves A moribund metaphor (SEE PAGE 19). *agitated; anxious; eager; edgy; excitable; excit-*

ed; fidgety; frantic; jittery; jumpy; nervous; ill at ease; on edge; restive; restless; skittish; uncomfortable; uneasy.

burn a hole in (my) pocket A moribund metaphor (SEE PAGE 19).

burn (your) bridges (behind) (you) A moribund metaphor (SEE PAGE 19).

burning desire An inescapable pair (SEE PAGE 18). *ardor; eagerness; fervor; passion; vehemence; zeal.* ■ Suppose you sell group insurance to employers, and your prospect has ten employees and a *burning desire* to expand the business. REPLACE WITH *zeal.*

(it) burns (me) up A moribund metaphor (SEE PAGE 19). *acerbate; anger; annoy; bother; bristle; chafe; enrage; incense; inflame; infuriate; irk; irritate; madden; miff; provoke; rile; roil; vex.*

burn the candle at both ends A moribund metaphor (SEE PAGE 19).
1. *drudge; grind; grub; labor; moil; slave; strain; strive; struggle; sweat; toil; travail; work hard.*
2. *debilitate; deplete; drain; empty; enervate; exhaust; fatigue; overdo; overwork; sap; tire; wear out; weary.*
3. *be merry; carouse; carry on; celebrate; debauch; disport; frolic; party; play; revel; riot; roister; rollick; romp; skylark.*

burn the midnight oil A moribund metaphor (SEE PAGE 19). *drudge; grind; grub; labor; moil;*

slave; strain; strive; struggle; sweat; toil; travail; work hard; work long hours. ■ We are indebted to our wives and families for their patience while we *burned the midnight oil.* REPLACE WITH *worked long hours.*

bursting at the seams A moribund metaphor (SEE PAGE 19).
1. *aflame; agitated; animated; anxious; eager; ebullient; effervescent; enthusiastic; excitable; excited; fervent; fervid; frantic; frenzied; impassioned; impatient; lively; restless; spirited.*
2. *abounding; brimful; brimming; bursting; chock-full; congested; crammed; crowded; dense; filled; full; gorged; jammed; jam-packed; overcrowded; overfilled; overflowing; packed; replete; saturated; stuffed; swarming; teeming.*

burst on (onto) the scene A moribund metaphor (SEE PAGE 19). *appear; arise; come forth; emerge; occur; originate; present itself; rise; surface; turn up.*

bur under (his) saddle A moribund metaphor (SEE PAGE 19). *affliction; annoyance; bane; bother; burden; curse; difficulty; inconvenience; irritant; irritation; load; nuisance; ordeal; pain; pest; plague; problem; torment; tribulation; trouble; vexation; weight; worry.*

bury (her) head in the sand A moribund metaphor (SEE PAGE 19). *cower; cringe; grovel; quail; recoil; shrink.* ■ When confronted with negative press, school officials ought not to *bury their heads in the sand*. REPLACE WITH *cower*.

bury the hatchet A moribund metaphor (SEE PAGE 19). *make peace*.

business as usual A torpid term (SEE PAGE 22). ■ All too many male-dominated workplaces still are doing *business as usual* and denying women equal pay and benefits. ■ In simple terms, it means *business as usual*; specifically, all business will be conducted today as it was yesterday. SEE ALSO *politics as usual*.

business is business A quack equation (SEE PAGE 21).

bust (my) ass A moribund metaphor (SEE PAGE 19). *attempt; drudge; endeavor; essay; exert; grind; grub; labor; moil; slave; strain; strive; struggle; sweat; toil; travail; try; work*.

(as) busy as a beaver An insipid simile (SEE PAGE 19). *assiduous; busy; diligent; grinding; hardworking; indefatigable; industrious; inexhaustible; sedulous; slaving; tireless; toiling; unflagging; unrelenting; untiring*.

(as) busy as a bee An insipid simile (SEE PAGE 19). *assiduous; busy; diligent; grinding; hardworking; indefatigable; industrious; inexhaustible; sedulous; slaving; tireless; toiling; unflagging; unrelenting; untiring*.

butterflies in (her) stomach A moribund metaphor (SEE PAGE 19).

1. *agitated; anxious; eager; edgy; excitable; excited; fidgety; frantic; jittery; jumpy; nervous; ill at ease; on edge; restive; restless; skittish; uncomfortable; uneasy.*
2. *nauseated; nauseous; queasy; sick; squeamish.*

butter (them) up A moribund metaphor (SEE PAGE 19). *acclaim; applaud; celebrate; commend; compliment; extol; flatter; laud; praise.*

butter wouldn't melt in (her) mouth A moribund metaphor (SEE PAGE 19). *affected; artful; artificial; coy; crafty; cunning; deceitful; dishonest; demure; dissembling; dissimulating; duplicitous; fake; false; false-hearted; feigned; foxy; guileful; insincere; lying; mannered; mendacious; phony; plastic; sly; sneaky; tricky; two-faced; uncandid; underhanded; unfrank; unnatural; untrue; untruthful; wily.*

button (zip) your lip A moribund metaphor (SEE PAGE 19).
1. *be silent; be still; hush; keep quiet; quiet; silence.*
2. *be closed-mouthed; be quiet; be reticent; be silent; be speechless; be taciturn; be uncommunicative.*

buy a pig in a poke A moribund metaphor (SEE PAGE 19).

buy into A moribund metaphor (SEE PAGE 19). *accept; adopt; advocate; affirm; agree to; assent to; back; believe in; endorse; espouse; favor; further; hold; sanction; side with; support.* ■ When others witness your confidence in an activity, they are more likely to *buy into* your plans of action. REPLACE WITH *back*.

buy the farm A moribund metaphor (SEE PAGE 19). *cease to exist; depart; die; expire; pass away; pass on; perish.*

buy time A moribund metaphor (SEE PAGE 19). *defer; delay; hold off; hold up; postpone; put aside; put off; set aside; shelve; suspend; table; waive.*

by a hair's breadth A moribund metaphor (SEE PAGE 19). *barely; by a little; hardly; just; merely; narrowly; only just; scarcely.*

(won) by a landslide A moribund metaphor (SEE PAGE 19).

by a whisker A moribund metaphor (SEE PAGE 19). *barely; by a little; hardly; just; merely; narrowly; only just; scarcely.*

by fits and starts A moribund metaphor (SEE PAGE 19). *convulsively; erratically; fitfully; intermittently; irregularly; paroxysmally; randomly; spasmodically; sporadically; unevenly.*

by hook or (by) crook A moribund metaphor (SEE PAGE 19). *somehow; someway.*

(growing) by leaps and bounds A moribund metaphor (SEE PAGE 19). *abruptly; apace; briskly; fast; hastily; hurriedly; posthaste; promptly; quickly; rapidly; rashly; speedily; straightaway; swiftly; wingedly.*

(go; pass) by the board A moribund metaphor (SEE PAGE 19). *abandoned; completed; concluded; disappeared; discarded; done; ended; finished; forfeited; gone (by); lost; over; passed; vanished.* ■ There was a little rain, sleet, and snow, but all that has *gone by the board*. REPLACE WITH *passed*.

(go) by the book A moribund metaphor (SEE PAGE 19).
1. *correctly; properly; rightly.* ■ She's done everything *by the book*. REPLACE WITH *correctly*.
2. *according to the rules.*

by the same token A wretched redundancy (SEE PAGE 23). *also; and; as well; besides; beyond that (this); even; further; furthermore; in addition; likewise; moreover; more than that (this); similarly; still more; too; what is more.*

by the seat of (his) pants A moribund metaphor (SEE PAGE 19). *automatically; by impulse; by instinct; by intuition; by reflex; impulsively; instinctively; intuitively; reflexively; spontaneously; unthinkingly; viscerally.*

by the skin of (his) teeth A moribund metaphor (SEE PAGE 19). *barely; by a little; hardly; just; merely; narrowly; only just; scarcely.*

by the sweat of (his) brow A moribund metaphor (SEE PAGE 19). *arduously; backbreakingly; burdensomely; exhaustingly; fatiguingly; gruelingly; laboriously; onerously; strenuously; toilfully; toilsomely; toughly; wearisomely; with difficulty.*

by virtue of the fact that A wretched redundancy (SEE PAGE 23). *because; considering; for; in that; since.* ■ There are a lot of people who expect too little *by virtue of the fact that* that's all they've known. REPLACE WITH *because.* SEE ALSO *because of the fact that; considering the fact that; given the fact that; in consideration of the fact that; in view of the fact that.*

C

call a halt (an end; a stop) to A wretched redundancy (SEE PAGE 23). *cease; close; complete; conclude; derail; discontinue; end; finish; halt; settle; stop.* ■ Let's *call a halt to* this insanity. REPLACE WITH *end.* SEE ALSO *put a halt (an end; a stop) to.*

call a spade a spade A moribund metaphor (SEE PAGE 19).
1. *be aboveboard; be artless; be candid; be forthright; be frank; be genuine; be guileless; be honest; be ingenuous; be naive; be sincere; be straightforward; be truthful; be veracious; be veridical.*
2. *be blunt; clear; be direct; be explicit; be plain; be specific.*

call into question A wretched redundancy (SEE PAGE 23). *challenge; contradict; dispute; doubt; question.*

call off the dogs A moribund metaphor (SEE PAGE 19).

call (out) on the carpet A moribund metaphor (SEE PAGE 19). *admonish; animadvert; berate; castigate; censure; chasten; chastise; chide; condemn; criticize; denounce; denunciate; discipline; excoriate; fulminate against; imprecate; impugn; inveigh against; objurgate; punish; rebuke;* *remonstrate; reprehend; reprimand; reproach; reprobate; reprove; revile; scold; swear at; upbraid; vituperate; warn.* ■ Popular sentiment indicates that *calling the president on the carpet* is not a labor the people wish to bear. REPLACE WITH *rebuking the president.* ■ She *called Starr on the carpet* as well, notably for alleged leaks to the press. REPLACE WITH *upbraided Starr.*

callow youth An inescapable pair (SEE PAGE 18). *adolescent; artless; callow; green; guileless; immature; inexperienced; inexpert; ingenuous; innocent; juvenile; naive; raw; simple; undeveloped; unfledged; unskilled; unskillful; unsophisticated; untaught; untrained; unworldly; young; youthful.*

call the plays A moribund metaphor (SEE PAGE 19). *administer; boss; choose; command; control; decide; determine; dictate; direct; dominate; govern; in charge; in command; in control; manage; manipulate; master; order; overpower; oversee; predominate; prevail; reign over; rule; superintend.*

call the shots A moribund metaphor (SEE PAGE 19). *administer; boss; choose; command; control;*

decide; determine; dictate; direct; dominate; govern; in charge; in command; in control; manage; manipulate; master; order; overpower; oversee; predominate; prevail; reign over; rule; superintend.

(the) calm before the storm A moribund metaphor (SEE PAGE 19).

calm, cool, and collected An infantile phrase (SEE PAGE 18). *at ease; calm; collected; composed; controlled; cool; imperturbable; insouciant; nonchalant; placid; poised; relaxed; sedate; self-possessed; serene; tranquil; unemotional; unperturbed; unruffled.* ■ She seemed so *calm, cool, and collected* in the interview. REPLACE WITH *calm*.

(we) came, (we) saw, (we) conquered An infantile phrase (SEE PAGE 18).

can chew gum and think (walk) at the same time A moribund metaphor (SEE PAGE 19). *be able; be adept; be adroit; be ambidextrous; be capable; be competent; be deft; be dexterous; be nimble; be proficient; be skilled; be skillful.*

candor and frankness An inescapable pair (SEE PAGE 18). *candor; frankness; honesty; openness; sincerity; truth; truthfulness; veracity.*

can I ask (tell) you something? A plebeian sentiment (SEE PAGE 20). This is a question asked by the ignorant, by the ill-bred, not the well mannered. ■ *Can I tell you something?* I don't really like to go out. DELETE *Can I tell you something?* ■ *Can I ask you something?* Do you want me to give you a check so you can take care of that? DELETE *Can I ask you something?* SEE ALSO *let me ask you something.*

(open up) (a) can of worms A moribund metaphor (SEE PAGE 19). *complication; difficulty; dilemma; mess; muddle; ordeal; pickle; plight; predicament; problem; quandary; trial; trouble.*

(I) can take it or leave it An infantile phrase (SEE PAGE 18). *apathetic; cool; halfhearted; indifferent; insouciant; languid; laodicean; lukewarm; nonchalant; tepid; unenthusiastic.*

(I) can't complain An infantile phrase (SEE PAGE 18). *all right; average; fair; fine; good; mediocre; not bad; passable; pretty good; tolerable; well.*

(you) can't have your cake and eat it too A popular prescription (SEE PAGE 21).

(we) can't help you if you don't want to be helped A popular prescription (SEE PAGE 21).

(he) can't see beyond (the end of) (his) nose A moribund metaphor (SEE PAGE 19).
1. *blind; eyeless; purblind; shortsighted; sightless; unseeing; unsighted; visionless.*
2. *addleheaded; bovine; cretinous; decerebrate; dense; dull; dull-witted; fatuous; fat-witted; half-witted; harebrained; hebetudinous; idiotic; ignorant; imbecilic; incogitant; insensate;*

mindless; moronic; muddled; nescient; obtuse; phlegmatic; slow; slow-witted; sluggish; thick; torpid; undiscerning; unintelligent; vacuous; witless.

can't see the forest (woods) for the trees A moribund metaphor (SEE PAGE 19). *nearsighted; myopic; purblind; shortsighted.*

(with) cap (hat) in hand A moribund metaphor (SEE PAGE 19). *deferentially; diffidently; humbly; modestly; respectfully; sheepishly; unassumingly; unpretentiously.*

captain of industry A moribund metaphor (SEE PAGE 19). *administrator; boss; brass; chief; commander; director; executive; foreman; head; headman; leader; manager; master; (high) muckamuck; officer; official; overseer; owner; president; principal; proprietor; superintendent; supervisor.*

capture the attention of A torpid term (SEE PAGE 22). *absorb; attract; beguile; bewitch; captivate; charm; enamor; engage; engross; enrapture; enthrall; entice; entrance; fascinate; mesmerize; occupy.* ■ The civil rights struggle *captured the attention of* the entire nation. REPLACE WITH *captivated.*

(the) cards (deck) are stacked against (him) A moribund metaphor (SEE PAGE 19).

card up (his) sleeve A moribund metaphor (SEE PAGE 19).

(like) carrying coals to Newcastle An insipid simile (SEE PAGE 19).

barren; bootless; effete; feckless; feeble; fruitless; futile; impotent; inadequate; inconsequential; inconsiderable; ineffective; ineffectual; infertile; insignificant; inutile; meaningless; meritless; nugatory; null; of no value; pointless; powerless; profitless; purposeless; redundant; sterile; superfluous; trifling; trivial; unavailing; unimportant; unnecessary; unproductive; unprofitable; unserviceable; unworthy; useless; vain; valueless; weak; worthless.

carry (his) own weight A moribund metaphor (SEE PAGE 19).

carry the ball A moribund metaphor (SEE PAGE 19).

carry the weight of the world on (my) shoulders A moribund metaphor (SEE PAGE 19).

carte blanche A foreign phrase (SEE PAGE 17).

carved (cast; fixed) in stone A moribund metaphor (SEE PAGE 19). 1. *decided; determined; established; firm; fixed; resolved; set; settled.* 2. *changeless; constant; eternal; everlasting; firm; fixed; immutable; invariable; irreversible; irrevocable; permanent; rigid; stable; unalterable; unchangeable; unchanging; unending.* ■ The state's census count is not yet *fixed in stone.* REPLACE WITH *immutable.* ■ Your choice of per-server or per-seat licensing is not *cast in stone.* REPLACE WITH *unalterable.*

cash in (their) chips A moribund

metaphor (SEE PAGE 19). *cease to exist; decease; depart; die; expire; pass away; pass on; perish.*

cash on the barrel A moribund metaphor (SEE PAGE 19).

cast in (our) lot with A moribund metaphor (SEE PAGE 19). *ally; collaborate; comply; concur; conspire; cooperate; join; unite; work together.*

cast into the pot A moribund metaphor (SEE PAGE 19).

castles in Spain (the air) A moribund metaphor (SEE PAGE 19). *apparition; caprice; chimera; delusion; dream; fanciful idea; fancy; fantasty; fluff; frivolity; hallucination; illusion; imagination; maggot; mirage; phantasm; vagary; vision; whim; whimsy.*

cast (his) net A moribund metaphor (SEE PAGE 19).

cast (your) pearls before swine A moribund metaphor (SEE PAGE 19).

cast the first stone A moribund metaphor (SEE PAGE 19).

catalyst for change A moribund metaphor (SEE PAGE 19). ■ These are the young people who will be the *catalysts for change* in their own communities in the coming decades.

(it's) (a) catch-22 A moribund metaphor (SEE PAGE 19).
1. *contradiction; dilemma; impasse; incongruity; paradox; plight; predicament; quandary; situation.*
2. *conundrum; enigma; puzzle; riddle.*

catch a bear by the tail A moribund metaphor (SEE PAGE 19).

catch as catch can A moribund metaphor (SEE PAGE 19).
1. *aimless; free; irregular; uncontrolled; unplanned.*
2. *by any means; however possible.*

catch forty winks A moribund metaphor (SEE PAGE 19). *doze; go to bed; nap; rest; retire; sleep; slumber.*

catch in the act A moribund metaphor (SEE PAGE 19). *catch; decoy; ensnare; entrap; net; trap.*

catch the wave A moribund metaphor (SEE PAGE 19).

catch (him) with (his) pants down A moribund metaphor (SEE PAGE 19). *catch unawares; surprise.* ■ He isn't the first president to be *caught with his pants down,* nor will he be the last.

(like) (a) cat on a hot tin roof An insipid simile (SEE PAGE 19). *agitated; anxious; eager; edgy; excitable; excited; fidgety; frantic; jittery; jumpy; nervous; ill at ease; on edge; restive; restless; skittish; uncomfortable; uneasy.*

cat's got (your) tongue A moribund metaphor (SEE PAGE 19). *be closed-mouthed; be quiet; be reticent; be silent; be speechless; be taciturn; be uncommunicative.*

(the) cat's out of the bag A moribund metaphor (SEE PAGE 19).

(look) (like) (the) cat that (ate) swallowed the canary An insipid simile (SEE PAGE 19). *complacent; gleeful; pleased; self-satisfied; smug; thrilled.* ■ On the day after an election in which President Clinton was supposed to have been chastened, many of the faces at the White House looked *like the cat that swallowed the canary.* REPLACE WITH *complacent.*

caught in the crossfire A moribund metaphor (SEE PAGE 19).

caught red-handed A moribund metaphor (SEE PAGE 19).

caught with (her) hand in the cookie jar A moribund metaphor (SEE PAGE 19).

cautiously optimistic A torpid term (SEE PAGE 22). *confident; encouraged; heartened; hopeful; optimistic; rosy; sanguine. Optimistic* is a perfectly vigorous word, but modified by *cautiously* or *guardedly,* as it so often is, it becomes valueless. *Cautiously optimistic* is a phrase favored by poltroons and politicians. ■ The retailer was *cautiously optimistic* about its latest report. DELETE *cautiously.* ■ When I realized that CBS was interested, I became *cautiously optimistic.* REPLACE WITH *hopeful.* ■ On the Rhode Island waterfront, the fishermen are *cautious but optimistic.* DELETE *but optimistic.* SEE ALSO *guardedly optimistic.*

cease and desist An inescapable pair (SEE PAGE 18). *cease; desist; end; halt; stop.*

celebrity A suspect superlative (SEE PAGE 22). As the most popular books are sometimes the least worthy of being read, so the most public people are sometimes the least worthy of being known.

If we must acknowledge these creatures — these *celebrities* — let us better understand them for who they are. All dictionary definitions of *celebrity* should include:
1. a mediocrity; a vulgarian; a coxcomb.
2. a scantly talented person who through shameless self-aggrandizement and utter inanity becomes widely known.
SEE ALSO *the rich and famous.*

center around A wretched redundancy (SEE PAGE 23). *center on.* ■ Concern will *center around* military governments. REPLACE WITH *center on.*

center of attention A suspect superlative (SEE PAGE 22). *cynosure.* People who seek to be the *center of attention* are forever peripheral to themselves.

(take) center stage A moribund metaphor (SEE PAGE 19).

c'est la vie A foreign phrase (SEE PAGE 17). To this popular French expression of resignation, there are more than a few English-language equivalents. SEE ALSO *such is life; that's how (the way) it goes; that's how (the way) the ball bounces; that's how (the way) the cookie crumbles; that's life; that's life in the big city; that's show biz; what are you going to do; what can you do.*

chalk it up to experience A popular prescription (SEE PAGE 21).

champing (chomping) at the bit A moribund metaphor (SEE PAGE 19). *anxious; ardent; avid; craving; desiring; desirous; eager; enthusiastic; fervent; fervid; frantic; frenzied; impassioned; impatient; intent; itching; keen; longing; pining; ready; vehement; yearning; zealous.* ■ State corrections officials were *chomping at the bit* to show not only that the program was tightly managed but also that it was benefiting offenders and citizens alike. REPLACE WITH *eager.* ■ It leaves me *chomping at the bit* to be able to do something with these tapes. REPLACE WITH *longing.*

change on a dime A moribund metaphor (SEE PAGE 19). *be adaptable; be flexible; be malleable; be versatile.* ■ He sees AmEx's program as an example of what the smartest marketers will be doing: creating rewards programs that can *change on a dime* based on what consumers tell them. REPLACE WITH *be flexible.*

changing of the guard A moribund metaphor (SEE PAGE 19).

charity begins at home A popular prescription (SEE PAGE 21).

chart a new course A moribund metaphor (SEE PAGE 19).

cheap shot A moribund metaphor (SEE PAGE 19).

cheek by jowl A moribund metaphor (SEE PAGE 19). *attached; close; inseparable; intimate; side by side.*

chew (her) out A moribund metaphor (SEE PAGE 19). *admonish; animadvert; belittle; berate; castigate; censure; chasten; chastise; chide; condemn; criticize; denounce; denunciate; discipline; excoriate; fulminate against; imprecate; impugn; inveigh against; objurgate; punish; rebuke; remonstrate; reprehend; reprimand; reproach; reprobate; reprove; revile; scold; swear at; upbraid; vituperate; warn.*

chew the cud A moribund metaphor (SEE PAGE 19). *brood; cerebrate; cogitate; consider; contemplate; deliberate; excogitate; meditate; ponder; reflect; ruminate; think.*

chew the fat (rag) A moribund metaphor (SEE PAGE 19). *babble; blab; cackle; chaffer; chat; chitchat; chatter; confabulate; converse; gossip; jabber; palaver; prate; prattle; rattle; talk.*

(that's) chicken feed A moribund metaphor (SEE PAGE 19). *frivolous; immaterial; inconsequential; inconsiderable; inferior; insignificant; minor; negligible; niggling; nugatory; petty; secondary; trifling; trivial; unimportant; worthless.*

chicken-or-egg (question) A moribund metaphor (SEE PAGE 19).

(like) (a) chicken with its head cut off An insipid simile (SEE PAGE

19). *agitated; crazed; crazy; demented; deranged; distraught; frantic; frenetic; frenzied; insane; mad; raging; wild.*

children should be seen and not heard A popular prescription (SEE PAGE 21).

(the) child is father of the man A popular prescription (SEE PAGE 21).

(that's) child's play A moribund metaphor (SEE PAGE 19). *apparent; basic; clear; clear-cut; conspicuous; distinct; easily done; easy; effortless; elementary; evident; explicit; facile; limpid; lucid; manifest; obvious; patent; pellucid; plain; simple; simplicity itself; straightforward; translucent; transparent; unambiguous; uncomplex; uncomplicated; understandable; unequivocal; unmistakable.*

chilled to the bone (marrow) A moribund metaphor (SEE PAGE 19). *algid; arctic; brumal; chilly; cold; cool; freezing; frigid; frosty; frozen; gelid; glacial; hibernal; hyperborean; ice-cold; icy; nippy; polar; rimy; wintry.*

chink in (his) armor A moribund metaphor (SEE PAGE 19). *defect; deficiency; disadvantage; failing; fault; flaw; foible; fragility; frailness; frailty; handicap; limitation; shortcoming; susceptibility; susceptibleness; vulnerability; vulnerableness; weakness.*

(a) chip off the old block A moribund metaphor (SEE PAGE 19). *carbon copy; clone; double; duplicate; mirror image; replica; twin.*

chip on (her) shoulder A moribund metaphor (SEE PAGE 19). *ani-*

mosity; bitterness; enmity; grievance; grudge; hostility; indignation; ill will; offense; rancor; resentment; spite; umbrage.

chock full (of) A torpid term (SEE PAGE 22). *abounding; brimful; brimming; bursting; congested; crammed; crowded; dense; filled; full; gorged; jammed; jam-packed; overcrowded; overfilled; overflowing; packed; replete; saturated; stuffed; swarming; teeming.*

a chorus of A moribund metaphor (SEE PAGE 19). SEE ALSO *a barrage of.*

chrome dome An infantile phrase (SEE PAGE 18). *alopecic; bald; bald-headed; baldpated; glabrous; hairless; depilated; pilgarlic; smooth; tonsured.*

Cinderella story A moribund metaphor (SEE PAGE 19).

class A suspect superlative (SEE PAGE 22). The antithesis of culture, *class* is a quality possessed by those who have neither elegance nor grace nor poise nor polish. ■ This always hurts me because I know who he is: a very intelligent, sensitive, *classy* human being. REPLACE WITH *admirable.*

Here's a description of a woman that no discerning man would ever wish to meet: ■ I am a shapely and petite, 31-year-old, exquisitely feminine, *classy* lady. REPLACE WITH *elegant.* SEE ALSO *gentleman; lady.*

(as) clean as a hound's tooth An insipid simile (SEE PAGE 19). *antiseptic; clean; cleansed; disinfected;*

germ-free; hygienic; immaculate; sanitary; sanitized; scoured; scrubbed; spotless; stainless; sterile; unblemished; unsoiled; unspotted; unsullied; untarnished; washed.

(as) clean as a whistle An insipid simile (SEE PAGE 19). *antiseptic; clean; cleansed; disinfected; germ-free; hygienic; immaculate; sanitary; sanitized; scoured; scrubbed; spotless; stainless; sterile; unblemished; unsoiled; unspotted; unsullied; untarnished; washed.*

clean bill of health A moribund metaphor (SEE PAGE 19). *blooming; doing well; energetic; fit; flourishing; good; hale; hardy; healthful; healthy; hearty; robust; sound; strong; vigorous; well; well-off.*

cleanliness is next to godliness A popular prescription (SEE PAGE 21).

clear a (major) hurdle A moribund metaphor (SEE PAGE 19). ■ The proposed sale and redevelopment of Lafayette Place *cleared a final hurdle* yesterday.

(a) clear and present danger An infantile phrase (SEE PAGE 18). *danger; hazard; menace; peril; threat; troublemaker.* ■ He is *a clear and present danger.* REPLACE WITH *a menace.*

(as) clear as a bell An insipid simile (SEE PAGE 19). *audible; clarion; clear; distinct; plain; pure; sharp.*

(as) clear as crystal An insipid simile (SEE PAGE 19). *apparent; basic; clear; clear-cut; conspicuous; crystalline; distinct; easily done; easy; effortless; elementary; evident; explicit; facile; limpid; lucid; manifest; obvious; patent; pellucid; plain; simple; simplicity itself; straightforward; translucent; transparent; unambiguous; uncomplex; uncomplicated; understandable; unequivocal; unmistakable.*

(as) clear as day An insipid simile (SEE PAGE 19). *apparent; basic; clear; clear-cut; conspicuous; crystalline; distinct; easily done; easy; effortless; elementary; evident; explicit; facile; limpid; lucid; manifest; obvious; patent; pellucid; plain; simple; simplicity itself; straightforward; translucent; transparent; unambiguous; uncomplex; uncomplicated; understandable; unequivocal; unmistakable.*

(as) clear as mud An insipid simile (SEE PAGE 19). *ambiguous; blurred; blurry; cloudy; dim; fuzzy; hazy; indistinct; muddy; murky; nebulous; obfuscatory; obscure; opaque; unclear; vague.*

clear sailing A moribund metaphor (SEE PAGE 19). *apparent; basic; clear; clear-cut; conspicuous; distinct; easily done; easy; effortless; elementary; evident; explicit; facile; limpid; lucid; manifest; obvious; patent; pellucid; plain; simple; simplicity itself; straightforward; translucent; transparent; unambiguous; uncomplex; uncomplicated; understandable; unequivocal; unmistakable.*

clear the air A moribund metaphor (SEE PAGE 19).

clear the decks A moribund metaphor (SEE PAGE 19).

climbing the walls A moribund metaphor (SEE PAGE 19). *agitated; anxious; eager; edgy; excitable; excited; fidgety; frantic; jittery; jumpy; nervous; ill at ease; on edge; restive; restless; skittish; uncomfortable; uneasy.*

climb (move up) the ladder (of success) A moribund metaphor (SEE PAGE 19). *advance; flourish; progress; prosper; rise; succeed.*

clinging vine A moribund metaphor (SEE PAGE 19). (SEE) *clinging; dependent; subject; subordinate; subservient.*

cling like a limpet An insipid simile (SEE PAGE 19). *adhere; affix; attach; bind; cleave; cling; cohere; connect; fasten; fuse; hitch; hold; join; stick.*

clip (her) wings A moribund metaphor (SEE PAGE 19). *abase; chasten; debase; decrease; deflate; degrade; demean; depreciate; depress; diminish; disgrace; dishonor; embarrass; humble; humiliate; lower; mortify; puncture; shame.*

(the) clock is ticking A moribund metaphor (SEE PAGE 19).

close (near) at hand A moribund metaphor (SEE PAGE 19). *accessible; at hand; close; close by; handy; near; nearby; neighboring; vicinal.*

close but no cigar An infantile phrase (SEE PAGE 18). *almost; just about; nearly.*

closely allied An inescapable pair (SEE PAGE 18).

close scrutiny An inescapable pair (SEE PAGE 18).

close (shut) the door on (to) A moribund metaphor (SEE PAGE 19). *ban; banish; bar; block; disallow; dismiss; eliminate; exclude; hinder; ignore; impede; obstruct; preclude; prevent; prohibit; proscribe; reject; rule out.*

(hold cards) close to the chest (vest) A moribund metaphor (SEE PAGE 19). *clandestine; cloaked; closed; concealed; confidential; covert; furtive; hidden; masked; mysterious; private; secretive; secret; shrouded; sly; stealthy; surreptitious; veiled.* ■ If police have any leads, they are keeping them *close to the vest.* REPLACE WITH *secret.*

clothes make the man A popular prescription (SEE PAGE 21).

a cloud of A moribund metaphor (SEE PAGE 19). ■ But he did so under *a cloud of* uncertainty over whether what he said could be used against him later by law enforcement officials.

clutch (grasp) at straws A moribund metaphor (SEE PAGE 19).

(the) coast is clear A moribund metaphor (SEE PAGE 19).

cock of the walk A moribund metaphor (SEE PAGE 19). *administrator; boss; brass; chief; commander; director; executive; foreman; head; headman; leader; magnate; manager; master; mogul; (high) muckamuck; notable; officer; official; overseer; patrician; personage; president; principal; ruler; superintendent; supervisor.*

cog in the wheel A moribund metaphor (SEE PAGE 19). *aide; apparatchik; assistant; cog; dependent; drudge; flunky; helper; hireling; inferior; junior; minion; secondary; servant; slave; subaltern; subordinate; underling; vassal.*

cold and calculating An inescapable pair (SEE PAGE 18).

(as) cold as a witch's tit An insipid simile (SEE PAGE 19). *algid; arctic; brumal; chilly; cold; cool; freezing; frigid; frosty; frozen; gelid; glacial; hibernal; hyperborean; ice-cold; icy; nippy; polar; rimy; wintry.*

(as) cold as ice An insipid simile (SEE PAGE 19). *algid; arctic; brumal; chilly; cold; cool; freezing; frigid; frosty; frozen; gelid; glacial; hibernal; hyperborean; ice-cold; icy; nippy; polar; rimy; wintry.*

(as) cold as marble An insipid simile (SEE PAGE 19). *algid; arctic; brumal; chilly; cold; cool; freezing; frigid; frosty; frozen; gelid; glacial; hibernal; hyperborean; ice-cold; icy; nippy; polar; rimy; wintry.*

cold enough to freeze the balls off a brass monkey A moribund metaphor (SEE PAGE 19). *algid; arctic; brumal; chilly; cold; cool; freezing; frigid; frosty; frozen; gelid; glacial; hibernal; hyperborean; ice-cold; icy; nippy; polar; rimy; wintry.*

(get) cold feet A moribund metaphor (SEE PAGE 19). *afraid; alarmed; apprehensive; cowardly; craven; diffident; fearful; frightened; pavid; pusillanimous; recreant; scared; timid; timorous; tremulous.*
■ When the woman heard that the story opened with the theft of the godparents' guns, she *got cold feet*. REPLACE WITH *became apprehensive.*

cold fish A moribund metaphor (SEE PAGE 19). *apathetic; callous; chilly; cold; cool; detached; dispassionate; distant; emotionless; frigid; glacial; hard; hardhearted; harsh; heartless; hostile; icy; impassive; indifferent; passionless; pitiless; reserved; unconcerned; unemotional; unfeeling; unfriendly; unresponsive.*

cold turkey A moribund metaphor (SEE PAGE 19).

collaborate together A wretched redundancy (SEE PAGE 23). *collaborate.* ■ Staff from the American and European sides *collaborate together* to make the journey and the home stay a rewarding experience. DELETE *together.*

collect (gather) dust A moribund metaphor (SEE PAGE 19).

combine together A wretched redundancy (SEE PAGE 23). *combine.* ■ Look at each reviewer's comments separately or *combine* them *together* for a consolidated view. DELETE *together*.

come around   A moribund metaphor (SEE PAGE 19). *agree; consent; feel as (we) do; support (us); think as (I) think.* ■ We believe that in the end the public is going to *come around*. REPLACE WITH *support us*.

come clean A moribund metaphor (SEE PAGE 19). *acknowledge; admit; affirm; allow; avow; be forthright; be frank; be honest; be sincere; be straightforward; be truthful; be veracious; concede; confess; disclose; divulge; expose; grant; own; reveal; tell; uncover; unveil.* ■ It is time for the president to *come clean*. REPLACE WITH *be forthright*.

come forward (with) A moribund metaphor (SEE PAGE 19). *advance; broach; introduce; offer; present; propose; propound; submit; suggest; tender.* ■ Nobody has *come forward with* a good argument for any way to create more jobs and raise the incomes of working people without expanding trade. REPLACE WITH *proposed*. SEE ALSO *put forward*.

come full circle   A moribund metaphor (SEE PAGE 19).

come hell or high water A moribund metaphor (SEE PAGE 19). *no matter what; regardless.*

(chickens) come home to roost A moribund metaphor (SEE PAGE 19).

come in from the cold A moribund metaphor (SEE PAGE 19). ■ Alternative medicine is *coming in from the cold*. REPLACE WITH *gaining respectability.*

come in through the back door A moribund metaphor (SEE PAGE 19).

come knocking (on my door) A moribund metaphor (SEE PAGE 19).

come on like gangbusters   An insipid simile (SEE PAGE 19).
1. *assertive; commanding; dynamic; emphatic; energetic; forceful; intense; mighty; potent; powerful; strong; vehement; vigorous; virile.*
2. *authoritarian; authoritative; autocratic; bossy; despotic; dictatorial; dogmatic; domineering; imperious; iron-handed; lordly; overbearing; peremptory; tyrannical.*

come on strong   A moribund metaphor (SEE PAGE 19).
1. *assertive; commanding; dynamic; emphatic; energetic; forceful; intense; mighty; potent; powerful; strong; vehement; vigorous; virile.*
2. *authoritarian; authoritative; autocratic; bossy; despotic; dictatorial; dogmatic; domineering; imperious; iron-handed; lordly; overbearing; peremptory; tyrannical.*

come out in the wash A moribund metaphor (SEE PAGE 19).

come out of left field A moribund metaphor (SEE PAGE 19).

come out of the closet A moribund metaphor (SEE PAGE 19).

come (crawl) out of the woodwork A moribund metaphor (SEE PAGE 19).

come out (up) smelling like a rose An insipid simile (SEE PAGE 19).

come out swinging A moribund metaphor (SEE PAGE 19). *aggressive; antagonistic; battling; bellicose; belligerent; combative; fighting; militant; pugnacious; truculent; warlike.*

comes (goes) with the territory (turf) A moribund metaphor (SEE PAGE 19). ■ He's got to understand that these questions *go with the territory.*

come to a boil A moribund metaphor (SEE PAGE 19). *cap; climax; conclude; consummate; crest; crown; culminate; peak.*

come to a close (a halt; an end; a stop) A wretched redundancy (SEE PAGE 23). *cease; close; complete; conclude; derail; discontinue; end; finish; halt; settle; stop; terminate.* ■ The days of easy credit, strong liquidity, and speculation are *coming to a close.* REPLACE WITH *ending.* SEE ALSO *bring to a close (a halt; an end; a stop); grind to a halt.*

come to (find) a happy medium A moribund metaphor (SEE PAGE 19). *compromise.*

come to a head A moribund metaphor (SEE PAGE 19). *cap; climax; conclude; consummate; crest; crown; culminate; peak.*

come to blows A moribund metaphor (SEE PAGE 19). *battle; brawl; clash; fight; grapple; jostle; make war; scuffle; skirmish; tussle; war; wrestle; wrangle.*

come to find out An infantile phrase (SEE PAGE 18). *ascertain; determine; discern; discover; find out; learn; realize.*

come to grips with A moribund metaphor (SEE PAGE 19). *accept; comprehend; cope with; deal with; face; handle; struggle with; understand.*

come to pass A moribund metaphor (SEE PAGE 19). *befall; come about; happen; occur; result; take place.*

come to terms with A torpid term (SEE PAGE 22). *accept; comprehend; cope with; deal with; face; handle; struggle with; understand.*

come to the end of the line (road) A moribund metaphor (SEE PAGE 19).

come up empty (handed) A moribund metaphor (SEE PAGE 19). *find nothing.*

come up roses A moribund metaphor (SEE PAGE 19).

(as) comfortable as an old shoe An insipid simile (SEE PAGE 19). *comfortable; cosy; habitable; homey; inhabitable; livable; safe; snug.*

coming apart at the seams A moribund metaphor (SEE PAGE 19).

breaking down; collapsing; crumbling; decaying; decomposing; degenerating; deteriorating; disintegrating; dissipating; dissolving; dying; ending; fading; failing; unraveling. ■ How do you hold it together at work when your life is *coming apart at the seams*? REPLACE WITH *disintegrating.* ■ For the last year and a half it seems the world economy has been *coming apart at the seams.* REPLACE WITH *unraveling.*

(as) common as dirt An insipid simile (SEE PAGE 19). *average; basic; common; commonplace; customary; everyday; normal; omnipresent; ordinary; prevalent; quotidian; regular; standard; typical; ubiquitous; unexceptional; universal; unremarkable; usual; widespread; workaday.*

common courtesy A suspect superlative (SEE PAGE 22). If this expression is not heard as often as it once was, it's because courtesy is today not so common.

Genuine expressions of courtesy such as *please* and *thank you* (SEE) and *you're welcome* have been usurped by glib ones such as *have a nice day* and *I appreciate it* and *no problem.*

What's more, a vapid phrase like *how goes it* (SEE), or a vulgar one like *hey* (SEE), is more popular than an authentic *hello.*

The worsening of our speech accompanies the withering of our selves. SEE ALSO *(I) appreciate (it); have a good (nice) day (evening).*

compare and contrast A wretched redundancy (SEE PAGE 23). *compare; contrast.* ■ Competition is essential to enable consumers to *compare and contrast* alternatives. REPLACE WITH *compare* or *contrast.*

(as) compared to what? An infantile phrase (SEE PAGE 18). SEE ALSO *everything's (it's all) relative; (as) opposed to what?.*

complete and utter A wretched redundancy (SEE PAGE 23). *absolute; compleat; complete; consummate; deadly; outright; perfect; thorough; thoroughgoing; total; unmitigated; unqualified; utter.* ■ She may be my boss, but she is also a *complete and utter* fool. REPLACE WITH *complete.*

component part A wretched redundancy (SEE PAGE 23). *component; part.* ■ Denial is a *component part* of dying. REPLACE WITH *component* or *part.*

comrades in arms A moribund metaphor (SEE PAGE 19).

concerted effort An inescapable pair (SEE PAGE 18).

conflicted A torpid term (SEE PAGE 22). *Conflicted* is a perfectly silly choice of words. It's as if to say having conflicting feelings about something — as common as that is — is more than that, more complicated or less explicable, and only a psychological-sounding term might adequately convey this.

People indefatigably mimic one another; *conflicted,* like so many other ridiculously popular terms, would have less appeal if people were more confident and inclined to think for themselves. ■ Many such parents *feel conflicted* about segregating their children in special classes but think they have no alternative. REPLACE WITH *have conflicting feelings.* ■ The single most important element to a successful production of *Julius Caesar* is to see Brutus as a truly honorable, yet *conflicted* soul whose actions belie his intentions. REPLACE WITH *torn.* ■ My guess is that you have underlying and perhaps, *conflicted* feelings about the way this change occurred. REPLACE WITH *conflicting.*

And some people use *conflicted* to mean war-torn or embattled. ■ RONCO involvement in humanitarian demining in *conflicted* countries evolves from 20 years experience with worldwide development and humanitarian assistance contracts. REPLACE WITH *embattled.* ■ The war on drugs cannot alone explain why the U.S. is sending 60 Black Hawk and Huey helicopters to this *conflicted* nation. REPLACE WITH *war-torn.*

connect together A wretched redundancy (SEE PAGE 23). *connect.* ■ The next step was to *connect* these systems *together* into a system called APRS. DELETE *together.*

consensus of opinion A wretched redundancy (SEE PAGE 23). *consensus.* ■ The *consensus of opinion* is that newspaper endorsements are momentum builders. REPLACE WITH *consensus.*

considering the fact that A wretched redundancy (SEE PAGE 23). *because; considering; for; in that; since; when.* ■ I don't see how you can say you're not a prostitute *considering the fact that* you are paid for your time. REPLACE WITH *when.* SEE ALSO *because of the fact that; by virtue of the fact that; given the fact that; in consideration of the fact that; in view of the fact that.*

conspicuous by (his) absence A torpid term (SEE PAGE 22). ■ If I didn't sing about what I was going through, it would have been *conspicuous by its absence.*

contact An overworked word (SEE PAGE 20). *ask; call; inform; phone; query; question; reach; speak to; talk to; tell; write to.*

continue on A wretched redundancy (SEE PAGE 23). *continue.* ■ We're going to *continue on* with more of this. DELETE *on.*

continuing refrain An inescapable pair (SEE PAGE 18).

contrary to popular belief (opinion) A torpid term (SEE PAGE 22). ■ *Contrary to popular opinion,* a strong dollar does not attract foreign investment to U.S. stocks but to U.S. bonds.

conventional wisdom A suspect superlative (SEE PAGE 22). ■ Washington is in thrall at the moment to two competing *conventional wisdoms.*

conversation piece A plebeian sentiment (SEE PAGE 20). This is an annoying little term. That people might need an object whose purpose is mainly to stimulate conversation reveals just how infertile, just how fallow, our minds are.

convicted felon A wretched redundancy (SEE PAGE 23). *felon.* ■ You were a deputy sheriff and now you're a *convicted felon*? DELETE *convicted.*

cook (his) goose A moribund metaphor.

(the) cook's tour A moribund metaphor (SEE PAGE 19).

cook the books A moribund metaphor (SEE PAGE 19).

(as) cool as a cucumber An insipid simile (SEE PAGE 19). *at ease; calm; collected; composed; controlled; cool; imperturbable; insouciant; nonchalant; placid; poised; relaxed; sedate; self-possessed; serene; tranquil; unemotional; unperturbed; unruffled.*

cool customer A moribund metaphor (SEE PAGE 19). *at ease; calm; collected; composed; controlled; cool; imperturbable; insouciant; nonchalant; placid; poised; relaxed; sedate; self-possessed; serene; tranquil; unemotional; unperturbed; unruffled.*

cool (your) heels A moribund metaphor (SEE PAGE 19). *be patient; hold on; relax; wait.*

cooperate together A wretched redundancy (SEE PAGE 23). *cooperate.* ■ It's important that we *cooperate together* in order to resolve our problems. DELETE *together.*

cost a pretty penny A moribund metaphor (SEE PAGE 19). *costly; dear; expensive; high-priced; precious; priceless; valuable.*

(I) could (should) write a book A plebeian sentiment (SEE PAGE 20). If all those who proclaim *I could write a book* — or all those who are advised *You should write a book* — were to do so, we would be immersed (more than we already are) in the vengeful, petty, or everyday lamentations of hollow-headed homemakers, shameless celebrities, and failed or forgotten businesspeople. ■ *I could write a book* about the way parents pay high prices in raising a disabled child.

course of action A wretched redundancy (SEE PAGE 23). *action; course; direction; intention; method; move; plan; policy; procedure; route; scheme; strategy.*

cover all the bases A moribund metaphor (SEE PAGE 19).

cover a lot of ground A moribund metaphor (SEE PAGE 19).

cover (his) tracks A moribund metaphor (SEE PAGE 19).

crack the whip A moribund metaphor (SEE PAGE 19). 1. *bully; coerce; intimidate; menace; terrorize; threaten.*

2. *castigate; chastise; discipline; penalize; punish.*

crap shoot A moribund metaphor (SEE PAGE 19).

(as) crazy as a coot An insipid simile (SEE PAGE 19). *batty; cracked; crazy; daft; demented; deranged; fey; foolish; goofy; insane; lunatic; mad; maniacal; neurotic; nuts; nutty; psychotic; raving; silly; squirrelly; touched; unbalanced; unhinged; unsound; wacky; zany.*

(as) crazy as a loon An insipid simile (SEE PAGE 19). *batty; cracked; crazy; daft; demented; deranged; fey; foolish; goofy; insane; lunatic; mad; maniacal; neurotic; nuts; nutty; psychotic; raving; silly; squirrelly; touched; unbalanced; unhinged; unsound; wacky; zany.*

crazy like a fox An insipid simile (SEE PAGE 19). *artful; cagey; clever; conniving; crafty; cunning; foxy; guileful; shifty; shrewd; sly; smart; subtle; tricky; wily.*

(the) cream of the crop A moribund metaphor (SEE PAGE 19). *best; brightest; choice; choicest; elite; excellent; finest; first-class; first-rate; foremost; greatest; highest; matchless; optimal; optimum; outstanding; paramount; peerless; preeminent; premium; prominent; select; superior; superlative; top; unequaled; unexcelled; unmatched; unrivaled; unsurpassed.*

crème de la crème A foreign phrase (SEE PAGE 17). *best; brightest;* *choice; choicest; elite; excellent; finest; first-class; first-rate; foremost; greatest; highest; matchless; optimal; optimum; outstanding; paramount; peerless; preeminent; premium; prominent; select; superior; superlative; top; unequaled; unexcelled; unmatched; unrivaled; unsurpassed.* ■ But I have the *crème de la crème* of celebrity users. REPLACE WITH *foremost.* ■ The following list contains the *crème de la crème* of online record retailers. REPLACE WITH *best.*

crisis An overworked word (SEE PAGE 20). We have a "crisis" for all occurrences. For example: *career crisis; crisis in the making; crisis in values; crisis of confidence; crisis proportions; crisis situation; crisis stage; current crisis; economic crisis; educational crisis; energy crisis; extinction crisis; family crisis; financial crisis; fiscal crisis; identity crisis; mid-life crisis; moral crisis; mounting crisis; national crisis; political crisis;* and even, incomprehensibly, *severe crisis.*

Surely, some of these crises are less than that. The terms we use to characterize events and emotions largely decide how we react to them. SEE ALSO *devastate.*

(shed) crocodile tears A moribund metaphor (SEE PAGE 19).

(as) crooked as a dog's hind legs An insipid simile (SEE PAGE 19).

(as) cross as a bear An insipid simile (SEE PAGE 19). *angry; bad-tempered; bilious; cantankerous; chol-*

eric; churlish; crabby; cranky; cross; curmudgeonly; disagreeable; dyspeptic; grouchy; gruff; grumpy; ill-humored; ill-tempered; irascible; irritable; mad; peevish; petulant; quarrelsome; short-tempered; splenetic; surly; testy; vexed.

cross (my) fingers A moribund metaphor (SEE PAGE 19). *hope for; pray for; think positively; wish.*

cross (my) heart and hope to die A moribund metaphor (SEE PAGE 19). *affirm; asseverate; assert; attest; aver; avow; declare; pledge; promise; swear; testify; vow; warrant.*

cross swords A moribund metaphor (SEE PAGE 19).
1. *altercate; argue; disagree; dispute; feud; fight; quarrel; spat; squabble; wrangle.*
2. *battle; brawl; clash; fight; grapple; jostle; make war; scuffle; skirmish; tussle; war; wrestle.*

(we'll) cross that bridge when (we) come to it A moribund metaphor (SEE PAGE 19).

cross the line A moribund metaphor (SEE PAGE 19).

cross the Rubicon A moribund metaphor (SEE PAGE 19).

cross to bear A moribund metaphor (SEE PAGE 19). *affliction; burden; charge; cross; difficulty; encumbrance; hardship; hindrance; impediment; load; obstacle; obstruction; onus; oppression; ordeal; problem; trial; trouble; weight.*

crush like a bug An insipid simile (SEE PAGE 19).
1. *annihilate; assassinate; butcher; destroy; exterminate; kill; massacre; murder; slaughter; slay.*
2. *beat; conquer; crush; defeat; outdo; overcome; overpower; overwhelm; prevail; quell; rout; succeed; triumph; trounce; vanquish; win.*

cry like a baby An insipid simile (SEE PAGE 19). *cry; howl; shriek; sob; ululate; wail; weep; whimper; whine.*

cry over spilt milk A moribund metaphor (SEE PAGE 19). *lament; mourn; sulk.*

crystal clear A moribund metaphor (SEE PAGE 19). *apparent; basic; clear; clear-cut; conspicuous; crystalline; distinct; easily done; easy; effortless; elementary; evident; explicit; facile; limpid; lucid; manifest; obvious; patent; pellucid; plain; simple; simplicity itself; straightforward; translucent; transparent; unambiguous; uncomplex; uncomplicated; understandable; unequivocal; unmistakable.* ■ What seems *crystal clear* to you, and perhaps to others, is not all that obvious to me. REPLACE WITH *obvious.*

cry (say) uncle A moribund metaphor (SEE PAGE 19). *abdicate; accede; acquiesce; bow; capitulate; cede; concede; give in; give up; quit; relinquish; retreat; submit; succumb; surrender; yield.*

cry wolf A moribund metaphor (SEE PAGE 19).

(see) (the) cup (glass) half empty A moribund metaphor (SEE PAGE 19). *despairing; hopeless; pessimistic.*

(see) (the) cup (glass) half full A moribund metaphor (SEE PAGE 19). *cheerful; hopeful; optimistic; pollyanna; pollyannaish; positive; roseate; sanguine; upbeat.*

(not) (everyone's) cup of tea A moribund metaphor (SEE PAGE 19). *bent; choice; leaning; pick; inclination; predilection; preference; propensity; tendency.* ■ Choosing a logo and letterhead design from a catalog may not be everyone's *cup of tea.* REPLACE WITH *preference.*

curiosity killed the cat A popular prescription (SEE PAGE 21). (SEE)

curse a blue streak A moribund metaphor (SEE PAGE 19). *anathematize; blaspheme; condemn; curse; cuss; damn; defile; desecrate; excoriate; execrate; fulminate; imprecate; swear at.*

cushion the blow A moribund metaphor (SEE PAGE 19). ■ We think that will help *cushion the blow* for some people.

(a) cut above (the rest) A moribund metaphor (SEE PAGE 19). *abler; better; exceptional; greater; higher; more able (accomplished; adept; capable; competent; qualified; skilled; talented); outstanding; standout; superior; superlative.*

cut and dried (dry) A moribund metaphor (SEE PAGE 19).
1. *common; commonplace; customary; everyday; normal; ordinary; quotidian; regular; routine; standard; typical; usual.*
2. *anodyne; banal; bland; boring; deadly; dry; dull; everyday; flat; humdrum; insipid; jejune; lifeless; lusterless; mediocre; monotonous; prosaic; stale; tedious; tiresome; unexciting; uninteresting; vapid; watered-down.*

cut a rug A moribund metaphor (SEE PAGE 19). *dance.*

(as) cute as a button An insipid simile (SEE PAGE 19). *appealing; attractive; beautiful; becoming; captivating; comely; cute; dazzling; exquisite; fair; fetching; good-looking; gorgeous; handsome; lovely; nice-looking; pleasing; pretty; pulchritudinous; radiant; ravishing; seemly; stunning.*

cut (them) off at the pass A moribund metaphor (SEE PAGE 19).

cut off (my) nose to spite (my) face A moribund metaphor (SEE PAGE 19).

cut (its) own throat A moribund metaphor (SEE PAGE 19).

cut (her) teeth (on) A moribund metaphor (SEE PAGE 19). ■ Case majored in political science at Williams College and *cut his teeth* as a marketing executive at PepsiCo Inc. and Procter & Gamble.

cut the legs out from under A moribund metaphor (SEE PAGE 19).

cut the mustard A moribund metaphor (SEE PAGE 19). *fare well;*

flourish; prevail; progress; prosper; succeed; thrive; triumph; win.

cutthroat competition An inescapable pair (SEE PAGE 18).

cut through red tape A moribund metaphor (SEE PAGE 19).

(the) cutting edge A moribund metaphor (SEE PAGE 19). *advanced; ground-breaking; innovative; inventive; new; original; pioneering; progressive; radical; revolutionary; unconventional.*

cut to pieces A moribund metaphor (SEE PAGE 19).
1. *annihilate; assassinate; butcher;* *destroy; exterminate; kill; massacre; murder; slaughter; slay.*
2. *beat; conquer; crush; defeat; outdo; overcome; overpower; overwhelm; prevail; quell; rout; succeed; triumph; trounce; vanquish; win.*

cut (costs) to the bone A moribund metaphor (SEE PAGE 19).

cut (stung) to the quick A moribund metaphor (SEE PAGE 19). *affront; crush; dash; devastate; hurt; injure; insult; offend; outrage; shatter; slap; slight; upset; wound.*

cut (it) with a knife A moribund metaphor (SEE PAGE 19).

D

damaged goods A moribund metaphor (SEE PAGE 19).

dancing in the aisles (streets) A moribund metaphor (SEE PAGE 19). *be merry; carouse; carry on; celebrate; debauch; disport; frolic; party; play; revel; riot; roister; rollick; romp; skylark.*

(a) dark day A moribund metaphor (SEE PAGE 19).

(a) day at the beach A moribund metaphor (SEE PAGE 19). 1. *easily done; easy; effortless; elementary; facile; simple; simplicity itself; straightforward; uncomplex; uncomplicated.* 2. *agreeable; beguiling; charming; delightful; enchanting; engaging; enjoyable; fun; glorious; gratifying; inviting; joyful; joyous; pleasant; pleasing; pleasurable.*

(her) day in court A moribund metaphor (SEE PAGE 19).

day in (and) day out A moribund metaphor (SEE PAGE 19). *always; ceaselessly; constantly; continually; continuously; daily; diurnally; endlessly; eternally; everlastingly; evermore; every day; forever; forevermore; frequently; interminably; nonstop; permanently; perpetually; persistently; recurrently; regularly; repeatedly; unceasingly; unremittingly.*

day in the sun A moribund metaphor (SEE PAGE 19).

days of wine and roses An infantile phrase (SEE PAGE 18).

dead and buried A moribund metaphor (SEE PAGE 19). *ceased; completed; concluded; dead; deceased; defunct; departed; done; ended; exanimate; expired; extinct; extinguished; finished; gone; inanimate; lifeless; no more; over; perished; stopped; terminated.*

dead and gone A moribund metaphor (SEE PAGE 19). *ceased; completed; concluded; dead; deceased; defunct; departed; done; ended; exanimate; expired; extinct; extinguished; finished; gone; inanimate; lifeless; no more; over; perished; stopped; terminated.*

(as) dead as a dodo An insipid simile (SEE PAGE 19). 1. *ceased; completed; concluded; dead; deceased; defunct; departed; done; ended; exanimate; expired; extinct;*

118

extinguished; finished; gone; inanimate; lifeless; no more; over; perished; stopped; terminated.
2. antediluvian; antiquated; archaic; dead; obsolescent; obsolete; old; old-fashioned; outdated; outmoded; out of date; out of fashion; passé; superannuated.
3. beat; bushed; debilitated; depleted; drained; drowsy; enervated; exhausted; fatigued; groggy; sapped; sleepy; sluggish; slumberous; somnolent; soporific; spent; tired; weary; worn out.

(as) dead as a doornail An insipid simile (SEE PAGE 19).
1. ceased; completed; concluded; dead; deceased; defunct; departed; done; ended; exanimate; expired; extinct; extinguished; finished; gone; inanimate; lifeless; no more; over; perished; stopped; terminated.
2. antediluvian; antiquated; archaic; dead; obsolescent; obsolete; old; old-fashioned; outdated; outmoded; out of date; out of fashion; passé; superannuated.
3. beat; bushed; debilitated; depleted; drained; drowsy; enervated; exhausted; fatigued; groggy; sapped; sleepy; sluggish; slumberous; somnolent; soporific; spent; tired; weary; worn out.

dead body A wretched redundancy (SEE PAGE 23). body. ■ Their car was abandoned on a bridge, and dead bodies were nowhere to be found. DELETE dead.

dead duck A moribund metaphor (SEE PAGE 19).

deader than a doornail A moribund metaphor (SEE PAGE 19).

1. ceased; completed; concluded; dead; deceased; defunct; departed; done; ended; exanimate; expired; extinct; extinguished; finished; gone; inanimate; lifeless; no more; over; perished; stopped; terminated.
2. antediluvian; antiquated; archaic; dead; obsolescent; obsolete; old; old-fashioned; outdated; outmoded; out of date; out of fashion; passé; superannuated.
3. beat; bushed; debilitated; depleted; drained; drowsy; enervated; exhausted; fatigued; groggy; sapped; sleepy; sluggish; slumberous; somnolent; soporific; spent; tired; weary; worn out.

dead in the water A moribund metaphor (SEE PAGE 19). dead; dormant; dull; inactive; inanimate; indolent; inert; inoperative; languid; latent; lethargic; lifeless; listless; motionless; phlegmatic; quiescent; quiet; sluggish; stagnant; static; stationary; still; stock-still; torpid.
■ The civil rights impulse from the 1960s is dead in the water. REPLACE WITH listless.

dead on arrival A moribund metaphor (SEE PAGE 19).

dead on (her) feet A moribund metaphor (SEE PAGE 19). beat; bushed; debilitated; depleted; drained; drowsy; enervated; exhausted; fatigued; groggy; sapped; sleepy; sluggish; slumberous; somnolent; soporific; spent; tired; weary; worn out.

dead ringer A moribund metaphor (SEE PAGE 19).

dead serious An inescapable pair (SEE PAGE 18).

dead to the world A moribund metaphor (SEE PAGE 19).
1. *asleep; dozing; napping; sleeping.*
2. *anesthetized; benumbed; comatose; insensate; insensible; insentient; oblivious; senseless; soporiferous; soporific; stuporous; unconscious.*

(as) deaf as a post An insipid simile (SEE PAGE 19).
1. *deaf; unhearing.*
2. *heedless; inattentive; oblivious; unmindful.*

deaf, dumb, and blind A moribund metaphor (SEE PAGE 19). *anesthesized; cataleptic; comatose; insensate; insensible; insentient; numb; sensationless; unconscious; unfeeling.*

deal a (crushing; devastating; major; serious) blow to A moribund metaphor (SEE PAGE 19).
1. *annihilate; assassinate; butcher; demolish; destroy; devastate; eradicate; exterminate; kill; massacre; murder; obliterate; pulverize; rack; ravage; raze; ruin; shatter; slaughter; slay; smash; undo; wrack; wreck.*
2. *beat; conquer; crush; defeat; outdo; overcome; overpower; overwhelm; prevail; quell; rout; succeed; triumph; trounce; vanquish; win.*

Still another phrase favored by journalists, *deal a (crushing; devastating; major; serious) blow to*, though it tries mightily to move us, leaves us unimpressed. Drained of any force it might once have had, this dimwitticism exhausts us precisely as much as it is exhausted. ■ Falling real estate values, the stock market crash, and changes in the rules under which S&Ls operate *dealt crushing blows to* the bank's success. ■ Most recently, it was Bennett who *dealt the most devastating blow* yet to Clinton's leadership.

(a) deal is a deal A quack equation (SEE PAGE 21).

(like) death warmed over An insipid simile (SEE PAGE 19). *anemic; ashen; blanched; bloodless; cadaverous; colorless; deathlike; doughy; haggard; lusterless; pale; pallid; pasty; peaked; sallow; sickly; wan; whitish.*

declare war (on) A moribund metaphor (SEE PAGE 19).

deepen the wound A moribund metaphor (SEE PAGE 19).

deeper in (into) the hole A moribund metaphor (SEE PAGE 19).

(has) deep pockets A moribund metaphor (SEE PAGE 19). *affluent; moneyed; opulent; prosperous; rich; wealthy; well-off; well-to-do.*

deep six *(v)* A moribund metaphor (SEE PAGE 19). *discard; eliminate; get rid of; jettison; reject; throw away; toss out.*

definitely An overworked word (SEE PAGE 20). So popular is this word that we might well marvel at the assuredness of those who use it. But, of course, the overuse of *definitely* bespeaks carelessness more than it does confidence. SEE

ALSO *absolutely; most assuredly; most (very) definitely.*

degree A torpid term (SEE PAGE 22). *Degree* — and the superfluity of phrases in which it is found — should be excised from almost all of our speech and writing. No sentence is made more compelling by the use of this word and its diffuse phrases. ■ I believe he has *a very high degree* of integrity and takes extreme pride in his workmanship. REPLACE WITH *a good deal.* ■ Increased employee morale would require *a lesser degree of* accuracy. REPLACE WITH *less.* ■ Their hopes are based, *to a large degree,* on signs that business activity is pulling out of its recent slowdown. REPLACE WITH *largely.* ■ *To a larger degree* than was expected, these economically stunted nations can count on help from the 12-nation organization. REPLACE WITH *More.* ■ Another realm in which schools of choice can and do differ is *the degree to which* the staff and parents are involved in the day-to-day operations of the school. REPLACE WITH *how much.* SEE ALSO *extent.*

déjà vu A foreign phrase (SEE PAGE 17).

déjà vu all over again An infantile phrase (SEE PAGE 18). ■ The police served him with a restraining order; it was *déjà vu all over again.*

delicate balance An inescapable pair (SEE PAGE 18).

a deluge of A moribund metaphor (SEE PAGE 19). SEE ALSO *a barrage of.*

den of iniquity A moribund metaphor (SEE PAGE 19).

den of thieves A moribund metaphor (SEE PAGE 19).

desperately seeking An infantile phrase (SEE PAGE 18).

despite (in spite of) or (maybe; perhaps) because of (the fact that) An ineffectual phrase (SEE PAGE 17). These phrases sound as though they have the ring of respectability to them — that is, they sound intelligent — but since the phrases are formulaic (a staple among journalists and those who write like them) and the contribution they make to a sentence uncertain (*despite* virtually nullifies *because of*), they are actually disreputable — that is, they are dimwitted. ■ *Despite* his old-fashioned style, *or perhaps because of* it, Mansfield remains an extremely popular lecturer. ■ *In spite of or, perhaps, because of the fact that* we humans are normally vision experts at a very young age, we have little intuition about how vision develops or how we accomplish seeing. ■ Excessive weight gain occurred during periods of this pregnancy *despite, or because of,* the mother's emotional problems. ■ Lately, she finds herself having a hard time falling asleep, *despite — or perhaps because of —* her exhaustion. ■ But this is what the harvest is all about, and *despite* the hard work, *or actually,* precisely *because* *of* it, a harvest wants to be celebrated. ■ They sustain a high level of motivation and achieve performance peak after performance peak *in spite of* (*or perhaps because of*) the lack of traditional supervision and rewards.

despite the fact that A wretched redundancy (SEE PAGE 23). *although; but; even if; even though; still; though; yet.* ■ Long a critic of exorbitant executive salaries, he agreed to a 4.7 percent raise, *despite the fact that* his company's profits doubled. REPLACE WITH *even though.* ■ *Despite the fact that* no serious adverse effects have been found, there are still risks. REPLACE WITH *Although.* SEE ALSO *in spite of the fact that; regardless of the fact that.*

devastate An overworked word (SEE PAGE 20). We can hardly wonder why so many of us are so easily *devastated.* This word is pervasive. Rarely are we *disconsolate,* rarely are we *flustered.* If only we would use more measured terms, we might feel less weak and woundable.

   Consider these terms, all more moderate: *agitated; bothered; crestfallen; despondent; disappointed; discomposed; disconsolate; distressed; disturbed; downcast; downhearted; flustered; heartbroken; heartsick; perturbed; ruffled; unsettled; upset.* ■ When Glen was transferred to a city 100 miles away, I was *devastated.* REPLACE WITH *heartbroken.*

   But if devastation it is, here are other terms that might relieve us

of our reliance on this one: *atomized; crushed; demolished; desolate; destroyed; distraught; obliterated; overcome; overpowered; overwhelmed; prostrate; ravaged; ruined; shattered; undone.* ■ Dean and Jenna were *devastated* when she lost their baby. REPLACE WITH *shattered.* SEE ALSO *crisis.*

devil's disciple A moribund metaphor (SEE PAGE 19).

(the) devil finds work for idle hands to do A popular prescription (SEE PAGE 21).

(the) devil take the hindmost A moribund metaphor (SEE PAGE 19).

devil to pay A moribund metaphor (SEE PAGE 19).

develop steam A moribund metaphor (SEE PAGE 19).

diametrically opposed An inescapable pair (SEE PAGE 18).

(a) diamond in the rough A moribund metaphor (SEE PAGE 19).
1. *bad-mannered; coarse; common; crass; crude; ill-bred; ill-mannered; impolite; rough; rude; uncivilized; uncouth; uncultured; unrefined; unsophisticated; vulgar.*
2. *unfulfilled; promising.*

(the) dictionary defines An infantile phrase (SEE PAGE 18). ■ *Webster's New World Dictionary defines* investigate as "to search into; examine in detail; inquire into systematically." ■ *The diction-*

ary defines gratitude as "a feeling of thankful appreciation for favors or benefits received." SEE ALSO *as defined in (the dictionary).*

didn't miss a beat A moribund metaphor (SEE PAGE 19).

die laughing A moribund metaphor (SEE PAGE 19).

die (wither) on the vine A moribund metaphor (SEE PAGE 19). *atrophy; be unsuccessful; bomb; break down; collapse; decay; fail; fall short; falter; fizzle; flop; flounder; fold; founder; languish; mess up; miscarry; miss; not succeed; shrivel; stumble; topple; wilt; wither.* ■ We believe Medicare is going to *wither on the vine* because we think people are going to voluntarily leave it. REPLACE WITH *founder.* ■ The history of computing is littered with great products that *withered on the vine.* REPLACE WITH *failed.*

(the) die is cast A moribund metaphor (SEE PAGE 19).

different strokes for different folks A popular prescription (SEE PAGE 21).

difficult task An inescapable pair (SEE PAGE 18).

digging (your) own grave A moribund metaphor (SEE PAGE 19).

dig in (his) heels A moribund metaphor (SEE PAGE 19). *be adamant; be balky; be bullheaded; be cantankerous; be contrary; be contu-macious; be determined; be dogged; be firm; be headstrong; be inflexible; be intractable; be mulish; be obdurate; be obstinate; be ornery; be perverse; be refractory; be resistant; be resolute; be resolved; be rigid; be stubborn; be unyielding; be willful.* ■ By then, the auto industry was *digging in its heels,* and almost as soon as the law was approved, its provisions were called too stringent. REPLACE WITH *becoming resolute.*

(a) dime a dozen A moribund metaphor (SEE PAGE 19). *average; basic; common; commonplace; customary; everyday; normal; omnipresent; ordinary; prevalent; quotidian; regular; standard; typical; ubiquitous; unexceptional; universal; unremarkable; usual; widespread.* ■ Sikhs in Kenya are *a dime a dozen.* REPLACE WITH *ubiquitous.*

dirt cheap A moribund metaphor (SEE PAGE 19). *cheap; economical; inexpensive; low-cost; low-priced; not costly.*

dirty pool A moribund metaphor (SEE PAGE 19).

a dirty word A moribund metaphor (SEE PAGE 19). *abhorrent; abominable; a curse; an abomination; anathema; antipathetic; detestable; execrable; hateful; loathsome; monstrous; offensive; repugnant.* ■ Some in the academic community may disagree, but to working families corporate takeovers are still *a dirty word.* REPLACE WITH *anathema.*

dis An infantile phrase (SEE PAGE

18). *Dis* is a prefix aspiring to be a word. Are we to allow *un* and *anti, non* and *pre* to follow? People are increasingly mono- and disyllabic as it is; let's rail against this foolishness, this affront, this dimwitted *dis*. ■ And not only does the little *dissing* contest draw the battle lines in today's best-selling music world, but it serves as a reminder of the way *Rolling Stone* manages to embody two sides without appearing totally ridiculous. REPLACE WITH *disparaging*. ■ This issue addresses five other means of *dissing* employees: buck passing, procrastination, inattentiveness, impatience and public reprimands. REPLACE WITH *disrespecting*. ■ More bad news for Leonardo DiCaprio: ABC News is *dissing* him big-time. REPLACE WITH *dismissing*. ■ Gov. Bill Owens made a media splash Monday, playing TV critic and *dissing* first lady of TV news Barbara Walters on national television. REPLACE WITH *disparaging*. ■ Watch Letterman stir up trouble with a Top 10 list or by *dissing* the soft drink Dr. Pepper as "liquid manure." REPLACE WITH *denigrating* ■ Franzen, despised and envied by all writers for his talent, his luck, his good looks, and his marketing acumen, essentially *dissed* the Oprah award for being ... lowbrow. REPLACE WITH *dismissed*.

disappear (vanish) into thin air A moribund metaphor (SEE PAGE 19). *disappear; disperse; dissolve; evaporate; fade; vanish; vaporize; volatilize.*

disappear (vanish) without a trace A moribund metaphor (SEE PAGE 19). *disappear; disperse; dissolve; evaporate; fade; vanish; vaporize; volatilize.*

disconnect A torpid term (SEE PAGE 22). In this brash but silly sense of a gap or a disparity, *disconnect* is to be reviled. Even if we must concede to its usage as a noun in the sense of a computer modem or electrical line disconnection, let that be the end of it. All further development of this word produces only grotesqueries. ■ In other words, there's a *disconnect* between Dubya's policies and his governance. REPLACE WITH *disparity*. ■ We identified a $1.1B projected shortfall and continued to track the *disconnect* between projected and actual sales for subsequent months. REPLACE WITH *variance*. ■ There is an apparent *disconnect* between OO community and systematic reuse community. REPLACE WITH *misunderstanding*. ■ Throughout this decade there has developed a widening *disconnect* between what we expect our national defense forces to do, and the resources supplied to accomplish those missions. REPLACE WITH *gap*. ■ A communications *disconnect* or gap exists between our operations commanders and our logisticians. DELETE *disconnect or*.

discretion is the better part of valor A popular prescription (SEE PAGE 21).

dismal failure An inescapable

pair (SEE PAGE 18). ■ The mayor's attempt at improving the quality of life on Boston Common at night was a *dismal failure*.

divine intervention An inescapable pair (SEE PAGE 18).

do a disappearing act A moribund metaphor (SEE PAGE 19). *abscond; clear out; decamp; depart; desert; disappear; escape; exit; flee; fly; go; go away; leave; move on; part; pull out; quit; retire; retreat; run away; take flight; take off; vacate; vanish; withdraw.*

do a hatchet job on A moribund metaphor (SEE PAGE 19). *asperse; badmouth; belittle; besmirch; bespatter; blacken; calumniate; defame; defile; denigrate; denounce; depreciate; deride; disparage; impugn; insult; libel; malign; profane; revile; scandalize; slander; slap; slur; smear; sully; taint; traduce; vilify; vitiate.*

do a job on A moribund metaphor (SEE PAGE 19).
1. *blight; cripple; damage; deface; disable; disfigure; harm; hurt; impair; incapacitate; injure; lame; maim; mar; mess up; rack; ruin; sabotage; spoil; subvert; undermine; vitiate; wrack; wreck.*
2. *agitate; bother; disquiet; distress; disturb; fluster; jar; jolt; pain; perturb; ruffle; shake; trouble; unsettle; upset; wound.* SEE ALSO *do a number on.*

do all (everything) in (my) power A torpid term (SEE PAGE 22). ■ I believe that Cashbuild has *done everything in its power* to cope with the changing South American environment.

do an about-face A moribund metaphor (SEE PAGE 19). *apostatize; backtrack; flip-flop; recidivate; renege; reverse; tergiversate.* SEE ALSO *do a 180.*

do (make) an end run around A moribund metaphor (SEE PAGE 19). *avoid; bypass; circumvent; dodge; duck; elude; evade; go around; parry; sidestep; skirt.* ■ Trying to *do an end run around* the person responsible for making purchasing decisions isn't advisable. REPLACE WITH *sidestep.*

do a number on A moribund metaphor (SEE PAGE 19).
1. *blight; cripple; damage; deface; disable; disfigure; harm; hurt; impair; incapacitate; injure; lame; maim; mar; mess up; rack; ruin; sabotage; spoil; subvert; undermine; vitiate; wrack; wreck.*
2. *agitate; bother; disquiet; distress; disturb; fluster; jar; jolt; pain; perturb; ruffle; shake; trouble; unsettle; upset; wound.* SEE ALSO *do a job on.*

do a 180 A moribund metaphor (SEE PAGE 19). *apostatize; backtrack; flip-flop; recidivate; renege; reverse; tergiversate.* SEE ALSO *do an about face.*

do as I say, not as I do A popular prescription (SEE PAGE 21).

doctor, lawyer, Indian chief A moribund metaphor (SEE PAGE 19).

dodge the bullet A moribund metaphor (SEE PAGE 19).

(it) doesn't amount to a hill of beans A moribund metaphor (SEE PAGE 19). *barren; bootless; effete; feckless; feeble; fruitless; futile; impotent; inadequate; inconsequential; inconsiderable; ineffective; ineffectual; infertile; insignificant; inutile; meaningless; meritless; nugatory; null; of no value; pointless; powerless; profitless; purposeless; sterile; trifling; trivial; unavailing; unimportant; unproductive; unprofitable; unserviceable; unworthy; useless; vain; valueless; weak; worthless.*

doesn't have a clue A moribund metaphor (SEE PAGE 19). *addlebrained; addleheaded; addlepated; Boeotian; bovine; brainless; clueless; cretinous; decerebrate; dense; dimwitted; doltish; dull; dumb; dunderheaded; empty-headed; fatuous; fatwitted; harebrained; hebetudinous; ignorant; imbecilic; incogitant; insensate; ludicrous; mindless; moronic; muddled; nescient; obtuse; oxlike; phlegmatic; slow-witted; sluggish; stupid; torpid; unaware; unintelligent; unknowing; vacuous; witless.*

doesn't have a snowball's chance in hell A moribund metaphor (SEE PAGE 19). *impossible; unachievable; unattainable; unfeasible.*

doesn't have both oars in the water A moribund metaphor (SEE PAGE 19). *batty; cracked; crazy; daft; demented; deranged; fey; foolish; goofy; insane; lunatic; mad; maniacal; neurotic; nuts; nutty; psychotic; raving; silly; squirrelly; strange; touched; unbalanced; unhinged; unsound; wacky; zany.*

doesn't have two nickels to rub together A moribund metaphor (SEE PAGE 19). *bankrupt; broke; destitute; distressed; impecunious; impoverished; indigent; insolvent; needy; penniless; poor; poverty-stricken; underprivileged.*

doesn't hold water A moribund metaphor (SEE PAGE 19). *baseless; captious; casuistic; casuistical; erroneous; fallacious; false; faulty; flawed; groundless; illogical; inaccurate; incorrect; invalid; irrational; jesuitical; mistaken; nonsensical; non sequitur; paralogistic; senseless; sophistic; sophistical; specious; spurious; unfounded; unreasonable; unsound; untenable; untrue; unveracious; wrong.*

doesn't know (her) ass from a hole in the wall A moribund metaphor (SEE PAGE 19).
1. *addlebrained; addleheaded; addlepated; Boeotian; bovine; brainless; clueless; cretinous; decerebrate; dense; dim-witted; doltish; dull; dumb; dunderheaded; empty-headed; fatuous; fat-witted; harebrained; hebetudinous; ignorant; imbecilic; incogitant; insensate; ludicrous; mindless; moronic; muddled; nescient; obtuse; oxlike; phlegmatic; slow-witted; sluggish; stupid; torpid; unaware; unintelligent; unknowing; vacuous; witless.*
2. *deficient; inadequate; inapt; incapable; incompetent; ineffective; inefficacious; inept; lacking; not able; unable; unfit; unqualified; unsatisfactory; unskilled; wanting.*

doesn't know (his) ass from (his) elbow A moribund metaphor (SEE PAGE 19).
1. *addlebrained; addleheaded; addlepated; Boeotian; bovine; brainless; clueless; cretinous; decerebrate; dense; dim-witted; doltish; dull; dumb; dunderheaded; empty-headed; fatuous; fat-witted; harebrained; hebetudinous; ignorant; imbecilic; incogitant; insensate; ludicrous; mindless; moronic; muddled; nescient; obtuse; oxlike; phlegmatic; slow-witted; sluggish; stupid; torpid; unaware; unintelligent; unknowing; vacuous; witless.*
2. *deficient; inadequate; inapt; incapable; incompetent; ineffective; inefficacious; inept; lacking; not able; unable; unfit; unqualified; unsatisfactory; unskilled; wanting.*

doesn't know enough to come in out of the rain A moribund metaphor (SEE PAGE 19).
1. *addlebrained; addleheaded; addlepated; Boeotian; bovine; brainless; clueless; cretinous; decerebrate; dense; dim-witted; doltish; dull; dumb; dunderheaded; empty-headed; fatuous; fat-witted; harebrained; hebetudinous; ignorant; imbecilic; incogitant; insensate; ludicrous; mindless; moronic; muddled; nescient; obtuse; oxlike; phlegmatic; slow-witted; sluggish; stupid; torpid; unaware; unintelligent; unknowing; vacuous; witless.*
2. *adolescent; artless; callow; green; guileless; immature; inexperienced; inexpert; ingenuous; innocent; juvenile; naive; raw; simple; undeveloped; unfledged; unskilled; unskillful; unsophisticated; untaught; untrained; unworldly; young; youthful.*

dog and pony show A moribund metaphor (SEE PAGE 19).

(the) dog days of summer A moribund metaphor (SEE PAGE 19). *boiling; hot; humid; scorching; sizzling; sweltering.*

dog-eat-dog A moribund metaphor (SEE PAGE 19). *barbarous; bloodthirsty; brutal; cold-blooded; compassionless; cruel; cutthroat; feral; ferocious; fierce; hard; hard-hearted; harsh; heartless; implacable; inexorable; inhuman; merciless; murderous; rancorous; relentless; ruthless; savage; uncompassionate; unmerciful; unrelenting; vicious; virulent; wild.*

(a) dog-eat-dog world A moribund metaphor (SEE PAGE 19). *brutal; cruel; ferocious; fierce; vicious.*

(a) dog's age A moribund metaphor (SEE PAGE 19). *ages; a long time; a long while; an age; an eternity; decades; eons; forever; months; years.*

(lead) (a) dog's life A moribund metaphor (SEE PAGE 19). *misery; unhappiness; wretchedness.*

dollars and sense An infantile phrase (SEE PAGE 18).

(like comparing) dollars to doughnuts A moribund metaphor (SEE PAGE 19). *different; discordant; discrepant; dissimilar; dissonant; divergent; incommensurable; incommensurate; incomparable; incompatible; incongruent; incongruous; inconsistent; inconsonant; inharmonious; unlike.*

(a) done deal A infantile phrase. (SEE PAGE 18). *absolute; completed; concluded; conclusive; consummated; definitive; final; finished.* ■ There seems to be a misconception that this is *a done deal*. REPLACE WITH *consummated*.

don't count your chickens before they're hatched A popular prescription (SEE PAGE 21).

don't cry over spilled milk A popular prescription (SEE PAGE 21).

don't do anything I wouldn't do An infantile phrase (SEE PAGE 18).

don't get mad, get even A popular prescription (SEE PAGE 21). ■ Hillary, *don't get mad, get even* — write a book.

don't get me wrong An infantile phrase (SEE PAGE 18). ■ I'm not trying to condone what I've done. *Don't get me wrong.* REPLACE WITH *Don't misunderstand me.* SEE ALSO *I hear you.*

don't give up the ship A popular prescription (SEE PAGE 21). *carry on; continue; ensue; go on; keep up; persevere; persist; press on; proceed.*

don't hold (your) breath A moribund metaphor (SEE PAGE 19).

don't knock it until you try it A popular prescription (SEE PAGE 21).

don't rock the boat A moribund metaphor (SEE PAGE 19).

don't see eye to eye A moribund metaphor (SEE PAGE 19). *clash; conflict; differ; disagree; think differently.*

don't start anything you can't finish A popular prescription (SEE PAGE 21).

doom and gloom An inescapable pair (SEE PAGE 18).

doomed to failure A torpid term (SEE PAGE 22). *damned; doomed; hopeless; ill-fated.*

do or die A popular prescription (SEE PAGE 21).

do's and don'ts *canon; codes; conventions; conventionality; customs; decorum; directives; etiquette; formula; formulary; guidelines; law; manners; policy; precepts; protocol; proprieties; regulations; rules; standards.*

dot the i's and cross the t's A moribund metaphor (SEE PAGE 19). *careful; conscientious; exact; exacting; fastidious; finical; finicky; fussy; meticulous; nice; painstaking; particular; picky; precise; punctilious; scrupulous; thorough.*

double-edge sword A moribund metaphor (SEE PAGE 19).

doubting Thomas A moribund metaphor (SEE PAGE 19). *cynic; disbeliever; doubter; skeptic.*

down and out A moribund metaphor (SEE PAGE 19). *bankrupt; broke; destitute; distressed; impecunious; impoverished; indigent; insol-*

vent; needy; penniless; poor; poverty-stricken; underprivileged.

down at the heels A moribund metaphor (SEE PAGE 19).
1. dowdy; frowzy; ragged; run-down; seedy; shabby; slipshod; sloppy; slovenly; tattered; threadbare; unkempt; untidy; worn.
2. bankrupt; broke; destitute; distressed; impecunious; impoverished; indigent; insolvent; needy; penniless; poor; poverty-stricken; underprivileged.

down (out) for the count A moribund metaphor (SEE PAGE 19).
1. asleep; napping; sleeping; slumbering; snoozing.
2. cataleptic; comatose; dormant; inactive; insensible; lifeless; passed out; unconscious; unresponsive.

down in the dumps A moribund metaphor (SEE PAGE 19). aggrieved; blue; cheerless; dejected; demoralized; depressed; despondent; disconsolate; discouraged; disheartened; dismal; dispirited; doleful; downcast; downhearted; dreary; forlorn; funereal; gloomy; glum; grieved; low; melancholy; miserable; morose; mournful; plaintive; sad; sorrowful; unhappy; woebegone; woeful.

down in the mouth A moribund metaphor (SEE PAGE 19). aggrieved; blue; cheerless; dejected; demoralized; depressed; despondent; disconsolate; discouraged; disheartened; dismal; dispirited; doleful; downcast; downhearted; dreary; forlorn; funereal; gloomy; glum; grieved; low; melancholy; miserable; morose; mournful; plaintive; sad; sorrowful; unhappy; woebegone; woeful.

(go) down the drain A moribund metaphor (SEE PAGE 19).
1. be misused; be squandered; be thrown way; be wasted.
2. break down; collapse; deteriorate; die; disappear; disintegrate; disperse; dissipate; dissolve; evaporate; fade; fail; finish; forfeit; go; lose; pass; scatter; vanish; vaporize; volatilize; waste. ■ Without new revenue, our schools will go down the drain. REPLACE WITH collapse.
3. annihilated; crushed; demolished; destroyed; obliterated; overturned; ravaged; ruined; scuttled; shattered; smashed; undone; wrecked. ■ One major mistake and your career is down the drain. REPLACE WITH ruined.

down the hatch A moribund metaphor (SEE PAGE 19). drink; gulp; guzzle; imbibe; quaff; swallow.

(later on) down the line (path; pike; road) A wretched redundancy (SEE PAGE 23). at length; before long; eventually; from now; in time; later; ultimately. ■ Even though this knowledge might not seem essential right now, it just might prove invaluable down the line. REPLACE WITH later. ■ Two players will be added to the team later, some months down the road. REPLACE WITH some months later. ■ Later on down the line, we did in fact marry. REPLACE WITH At length.

(go) down the tubes A moribund metaphor (SEE PAGE 19).
1. be despoiled; be destroyed; be devas-

tated; be dissipated; be pillaged; be plundered; be ravaged; be ruined; break down; collapse; disintegrate; fail; fall short; flop; founder; miscarry; topple. ■ Her article points out a major reason why our country is *going down the tubes*. REPLACE WITH *foundering*.

2. *be misused; be squandered; be thrown way; be wasted.* ■ All the money my parents spent on my braces *went down the tubes*. REPLACE WITH *was wasted*.

down to earth A moribund metaphor (SEE PAGE 19). *artless; common; earthly; everyday; genuine; guileless; mortal; mundane; natural; normal; plain; secular; staid; temporal; unaffected; unassuming; unpretentious; worldly.*

(come) down to the wire A moribund metaphor (SEE PAGE 19).

drag (their) feet A moribund metaphor (SEE PAGE 19). *arrest; balk; block; bridle; check; dawdle; defer; delay; detain; encumber; hamper; hesitate; hinder; hold up; impede; inhibit; obstruct; pause; postpone; put off; retard; stall; stay; stonewall; suspend.* ■ The regional Bells have *dragged their feet* in rolling out DSL services. REPLACE WITH *dawdled*.

drag kicking and screaming A moribund metaphor (SEE PAGE 19).

drag through the mud A moribund metaphor (SEE PAGE 19). *asperse; badmouth; belittle; besmirch; bespatter; blacken; calumniate; defame; defile; denigrate; denounce;* depreciate; deride; disparage; impugn; insult; libel; malign; profane; revile; scandalize; slander; slap; slur; smear; sully; taint; traduce; vilify; vitiate.
■ His name was *dragged through the mud* last week thanks to a Harvard Law School professor. REPLACE WITH *defamed*.

draw a bead on A moribund metaphor (SEE PAGE 19).
1. *aim at; focus on; sight; train on.*
2. *admonish; animadvert; berate; castigate; censure; chasten; chastise; chide; condemn; criticize; denounce; denunciate; discipline; impugn; objurgate; punish; rebuke; remonstrate; reprehend; reprimand; reproach; reprobate; reprove; revile; scold; upbraid; vituperate; warn.*

draw a blank A moribund metaphor (SEE PAGE 19).
1. *be addleheaded; be bovine; be cretinous; be decerebrated; be dense; be dull; be dull-witted; be fatuous; be fat-witted; be half-witted; be harebrained; be hebetudinous; be idiotic; be ignorant; be imbecilic; be incogitant; be insensate; be mindless; be moronic; be muddled; be nescient; be obtuse; be phlegmatic; be slow; be slow-witted; be sluggish; be thick; be torpid; be undiscerning; be unintelligent; be vacuous; be witless.* ■ A successful attorney, Caroline *draws a blank* when it comes to men. REPLACE WITH *is witless*.
2. *be absent-minded; be forgetful; be lethean; be oblivious.*

draw a veil over A moribund metaphor (SEE PAGE 19). *adumbrate; becloud; befog; camouflage; cloak;*

cloud; conceal; cover; disguise; dissemble; enshroud; harbor; hide; keep secret; mask; obfuscate; obscure; overshadow; screen; shroud; suppress; veil; withhold.

draw fire (from) A moribund metaphor (SEE PAGE 19).

draw in (his) horns A moribund metaphor (SEE PAGE 19). back away; back down; back off; disengage; evacuate; fall back; recede; regress; retire; retreat; withdraw.

draw in the reins A moribund metaphor (SEE PAGE 19). bridle; check; curb; curtail; halt; restrain; stall; stay; stop.

draw the line (at) A moribund metaphor (SEE PAGE 19).

draw the long bow A moribund metaphor (SEE PAGE 19). elaborate; embellish; embroider; enhance; enlarge; exaggerate; hyperbolize; inflate; magnify; overdo; overreact; overstress; overstate; strain; stretch.

(a) dream (fairy tale) come true A plebeian sentiment (SEE PAGE 20).

dredge up dirt A moribund metaphor (SEE PAGE 19).

dressed (fit) to kill A moribund metaphor (SEE PAGE 19).

dribs and drabs An inescapable pair (SEE PAGE 18). bits; chunks; crumbs; fragments; modicums; morsels; nuggets; particles; pieces; scraps; segments; shreds; snips; snippets; specks.

drink like a fish An insipid simile (SEE PAGE 19). alcoholic; bibulous.

drive a stake through the heart (of) A moribund metaphor (SEE PAGE 19).
1. execute; kill; massacre; murder; slaughter; slay. ■ The IRB's decision drives a stake through the heart of the myth peddled by Carey sympathizers inside and outside the Teamsters. REPLACE WITH slays.
2. annihilate; demolish; destroy; eliminate; eradicate; exterminate; liquidate; obliterate; ravage; ruin; sack; wreck.

drive a wedge between A moribund metaphor (SEE PAGE 19).

drive (me) bananas (crazy; nuts) A moribund metaphor (SEE PAGE 19). annoy; badger; bedevil; bother; chafe; distress; disturb; exasperate; gall; grate; harass; harry; hassle; heckle; hector; hound; irk; irritate; nag; nettle; persecute; pester; plague; provoke; rankle; rile; roil; tease; torment; vex.

drive (me) to drink A moribund metaphor (SEE PAGE 19). annoy; badger; bedevil; bother; chafe; distress; disturb; exasperate; gall; grate; harass; harry; hassle; heckle; hector; hound; irk; irritate; nag; nettle; persecute; pester; plague; provoke; rankle; rile; roil; tease; torment; vex.

drive (me) up the wall A moribund metaphor (SEE PAGE 19). annoy; badger; bedevil; bother; chafe; distress; disturb; exasperate; gall; grate; harass; harry; hassle; heckle;

hector; hound; irk; irritate; nag; nettle; persecute; pester; plague; provoke; rankle; rile; roil; tease; torment; vex.

driving force A wretched redundancy (SEE PAGE 23). *drive; energy; force; impetus; motivation; power.*

drop-dead gorgeous A moribund metaphor (SEE PAGE 19). *attractive; beautiful; comely; exquisite; fair; fetching; good looking; gorgeous; handsome; lovely; pretty; pulchritudinous; ravishing.*

(a) drop in the bucket (ocean) A moribund metaphor (SEE PAGE 19). *frivolous; inappreciable; immaterial; inconsequential; inconsiderable; insignificant; meager; meaningless; negligible; next to nothing; nugatory; paltry; petty; scant; scanty; scarcely anything; slight; trifling; trivial; unimportant; unsubstantial; worthless.* ■ Relative to need, it's *a drop in the bucket.* REPLACE WITH *next to nothing.* ■ When art is part of a larger construction budget, the money is usually *a drop in the bucket* compared with overall costs. REPLACE WITH *inconsiderable.*

drop like a hot potato An insipid simile (SEE PAGE 19). *abandon; abdicate; desert; discard; ditch; drop; forgo; forsake; get rid of; give up; jettison; leave; quit; reject; relinquish; renounce; surrender; throw away; toss out; yield.*

drop like flies An insipid simile (SEE PAGE 19). *annihilate; decimate; demolish; slaughter.*

drop off the face of the earth A moribund metaphor (SEE PAGE 19). *disappear; vanish.*

drop the ball A moribund metaphor (SEE PAGE 19). *be unsuccessful; bomb; break down; collapse; fail; fall short; falter; fizzle; flop; fold; founder; mess up; miscarry; not succeed; stumble; topple.*

(a) drowning man will clutch at a straw A popular prescription (SEE PAGE 21).

(as) drunk as a skunk An insipid simile (SEE PAGE 19). *besotted; crapulous; drunk; inebriated; intoxicated; sodden; stupefied; tipsy.*

(as) dry as a bone An insipid simile (SEE PAGE 19). *arid; dehydrated; desiccated; droughty; dry; exsiccated; parched; sear; shriveled; thirsty; wilted; withered.*

(as) dry as dust An insipid simile (SEE PAGE 19). *anodyne; banal; barren; bland; boring; deadly; dreary; dry; dull; everyday; flat; humdrum; inanimate; insipid; jejune; lifeless; lusterless; mediocre; monotonous; prosaic; routine; spiritless; stale; tedious; tiresome; unexciting; uninteresting; vapid; wearisome.*

dubious distinction An inescapable pair (SEE PAGE 18). ■ Now the Cowboys are coming off a 34-0 shutout in Philadelphia while the Giants have the *dubious distinction* of being the first team to lose to Washington this season.

duck soup A moribund metaphor (SEE PAGE 19). *easily done; easy; effortless; elementary; facile; simple; simplicity itself; straightforward; uncomplex; uncomplicated.*

due to circumstances beyond (our) control An ineffectual phrase (SEE PAGE 17). Of those who use this phrase, we may remark that their speech is no more grammatical than their actions are genuine.

Due to, as often as not, should be *because of* or *owing to,* and only the similarly disingenuous would believe that *circumstances beyond our control* is an explanation rather than an evasion.

In the end, those who express themselves badly are less credible than those who express themselves well. ■ *Due to circumstances beyond our control,* no motel rooms are available in the area on June 25th, 26th, and 27th. ■ *Due to circumstances beyond our control,* the following items may not be available as advertised. SEE ALSO *due to popular demand.*

due to popular demand An ineffectual phrase (SEE PAGE 17). There is with this phrase, as with *due to circumstances beyond (our) control* (See), the same solecism and a similar suspicion. ■ *Due to popular demand,* The Magic Show will be held over another two weeks.

due to the fact that A wretched redundancy (SEE PAGE 23). *because; considering; for; in that; since.* ■ Requirements continue to de-crease slowly *due to the fact that* activity generally decreases with age. REPLACE WITH *since.* ■ Could this be *due to the fact that* it is undecidable? REPLACE WITH *because.* SEE ALSO *attributable to the fact that; owing to the fact that.*

(as) dull as dishwater An insipid simile (SEE PAGE 19).
1. *addleheaded; bovine; cretinous; decerebrate; dense; dull; dull-witted; fatuous; fat-witted; half-witted; hare-brained; hebetudinous; idiotic; ignorant; imbecilic; incogitant; insensate; mindless; moronic; muddled; nescient; obtuse; phlegmatic; slow; slow-witted; sluggish; thick; torpid; undiscerning; unintelligent; vacuous; witless.*
2. *anodyne; banal; barren; bland; boring; deadly; dreary; dry; dull; everyday; flat; humdrum; inanimate; insipid; jejune; lifeless; lusterless; mediocre; monotonous; prosaic; routine; spiritless; stale; tedious; tiresome; unexciting; uninteresting; vapid; wearisome.*

(as) dumb as dirt An insipid simile (SEE PAGE 19). *addlebrained; addleheaded; addlepated; Boeotian; bovine; brainless; clueless; cretinous; decerebrate; dense; dim-witted; doltish; dull; dumb; dunderheaded; empty-headed; fatuous; fat-witted; harebrained; hebetudinous; ignorant; imbecilic; incogitant; insensate; ludicrous; mindless; moronic; muddled; nescient; obtuse; oxlike; phlegmatic; slow-witted; sluggish; stupid; torpid; unaware; unintelligent; unknowing; vacuous; witless.* ■ Frankly, I think these allegations are simply *dumb as dirt.* REPLACE WITH *Boeotian.*

during (in; over) the course of A wretched redundancy (SEE PAGE 23). *during; in; over; throughout.* ■ *In the course of* a 30-minute conversation, she spoke about her married life and her plans for the future. REPLACE WITH *During.* ■ *Over the course of* a woman's life, she may experience a kaleidoscope of health concerns. REPLACE WITH *Throughout.*

during the period (time) that A wretched redundancy (SEE PAGE 23). *while.* ■ *During the time that* we were with him, he called her several uncomplimentary names. REPLACE WITH *While.*

(when) (the) dust settles A moribund metaphor (SEE PAGE 19).

(like) (a) Dutch uncle An insipid simile (SEE PAGE 19).

dyed-in-the-wool A moribund metaphor (SEE PAGE 19). *ardent; constant; devoted; faithful; inflexible; intractable; loyal; refractory; resolute; rigid; staunch; steadfast; unbending; unwavering; unyielding.*

(a) dying breed A moribund metaphor (SEE PAGE 19). *declining; dying; moribund; waning.*

dynamic duo An infantile phrase (SEE PAGE 18).

E

each and every (one) A wretched redundancy (SEE PAGE 23). *all; each; everybody; everyone.* ■ Software developers have changed the way *each and every one* of us does business. REPLACE WITH *each.*

each one A wretched redundancy (SEE PAGE 23). *each.* ■ The fact that these companies do have to compete for business gives *each one* an incentive to work harder and to lower prices. DELETE *one.* SEE ALSO *either one; neither one.*

each to his own A popular prescription (SEE PAGE 21).

eagle eyed A moribund metaphor (SEE PAGE 19). *alert; attentive; observant; vigilant; watchful.*

(the) early bird catches the worm A popular prescription (SEE PAGE 21).

earn (his) stripes A moribund metaphor (SEE PAGE 19).

(as) easy as A B C An insipid simile (SEE PAGE 19). *apparent; basic; clear; clear-cut; conspicuous; distinct; easily done; easy; effortless; elementary; evident; explicit; facile; limpid; lucid; manifest; obvious; patent; pellucid; plain; simple; simplicity itself; straightforward; translucent; transparent; unambiguous; uncomplex; uncomplicated; understandable; unequivocal; unmistakable.*

(as) easy as 1 2 3 An insipid simile (SEE PAGE 19). *apparent; basic; clear; clear-cut; conspicuous; distinct; easily done; easy; effortless; elementary; evident; explicit; facile; limpid; lucid; manifest; obvious; patent; pellucid; plain; simple; simplicity itself; straightforward; translucent; transparent; unambiguous; uncomplex; uncomplicated; understandable; unequivocal; unmistakable.*

(as) easy as pie An insipid simile (SEE PAGE 19). *apparent; basic; clear; clear-cut; conspicuous; distinct; easily done; easy; effortless; elementary; evident; explicit; facile; limpid; lucid; manifest; obvious; patent; pellucid; plain; simple; simplicity itself; straightforward; translucent; transparent; unambiguous; uncomplex; uncomplicated; understandable; unequivocal; unmistakable.* ■ It's *easy as pie* to strike up a conversation with the person sitting next to you. REPLACE WITH *easy.*

easy on the eyes A moribund metaphor (SEE PAGE 19). *attractive; beautiful; comely; exquisite; fair; fetching; good looking; gorgeous; handsome; lovely; pretty; pulchritudinous; ravishing.*

easy on the pocket(book) A moribund metaphor (SEE PAGE 19). *affordable; cheap; economical; inexpensive; low-cost; low-priced; reasonable.*

(an) easy (simple) task A torpid term (SEE PAGE 22). *apparent; basic; clear; clear-cut; conspicuous; distinct; easily done; easy; effortless; elementary; evident; explicit; facile; limpid; lucid; manifest; obvious; patent; pellucid; plain; simple; simplicity itself; straightforward; translucent; transparent; unambiguous; uncomplex; uncomplicated; understandable; unequivocal; unmistakable.* ■ Identifying opinion leaders is not *a simple task* since they tend to be product specific and differ over time. REPLACE WITH *easy*.

eat crow A moribund metaphor (SEE PAGE 19). *be abased; be chastened; be debased; be degraded; be demeaned; be disgraced; be dishonored; be embarrassed; be humbled; be humiliated; be lowered; be mortified; be shamed.*

eat dirt A moribund metaphor (SEE PAGE 19). *be abased; be chastened; be debased; be degraded; be demeaned; be disgraced; be dishonored; be embarrassed; be humbled; be humiliated; be lowered; be mortified; be shamed.*

eat, drink, and be merry A popular prescription (SEE PAGE 21). *be merry; carouse; carry on; celebrate; debauch; disport; frolic; party; play; revel; riot; roister; rollick; romp; skylark.*

eat, drink, and be merry, for tomorrow we die A popular prescription (SEE PAGE 21).

eat (your) heart out A moribund metaphor (SEE PAGE 19). *ache; agonize; grieve; hurt; lament; mourn; pine; sorrow; suffer; worry.*

eat (live) high off (on) the hog A moribund metaphor (SEE PAGE 19). *epicureanly; extravagantly; lavishly; lushly; luxuriantly; opulently; prodigally; profusely; sumptuously; very well.*

eat humble pie A moribund metaphor (SEE PAGE 19). *be abased; be chastened; be debased; be degraded; be demeaned; be disgraced; be dishonored; be embarrassed; be humbled; be humiliated; be lowered; be mortified; be shamed.*

eat like a bird An insipid simile (SEE PAGE 19). *be abstemious.; be ascetic.*

eat like a horse An insipid simile (SEE PAGE 19).
1. *be esurient; be famished; be gluttonous; be greedy; be hungry; be insatiable; be omnivorous; be rapacious; be ravenous; be starved; be starving; be voracious.*
2. *glut; gorge; overdo; overeat; overfeed; overindulge; sate; satiate; stuff; surfeit.*

eat like a pig An insipid simile (SEE PAGE 19).
1. *be esurient; be famished; be gluttonous; be greedy; be hungry; be insatiable; be omnivorous; be rapacious; be ravenous; be starved; be starving; be voracious.*
2. *glut; gorge; overdo; overeat; overfeed; overindulge; sate; satiate; stuff; surfeit.*

eat out of (the palm of) (her) hand A moribund metaphor (SEE PAGE 19). *abide by; acquiesce; comply with; conform; follow; obey; yield.*

eat (me) out of house and home A moribund metaphor (SEE PAGE 19).
1. *be esurient; be famished; be gluttonous; be greedy; be hungry; be insatiable; be omnivorous; be rapacious; be ravenous; be starved; be starving; be voracious.*
2. *glut; gorge; overdo; overeat; overfeed; overindulge; sate; satiate; stuff; surfeit.*

eat (her) words A moribund metaphor (SEE PAGE 19). *disavow; recant; repudiate; retract; take back; withdraw.*

ebb and flow A moribund metaphor (SEE PAGE 19). ■ Optimists try to attribute a linear progression to the *ebb and flow* of history.

effect An overworked word (SEE PAGE 20). For example: *chilling effect; cumulative effect; domino effect; dramatic effect; negative effect; snowball effect; sobering effect; trickle-down effect.* ■ LeBlanc's lawyers

say that would *have a chilling effect on* fraud lawsuits brought by government employees. REPLACE WITH *discourage.* ■ You can learn how to free yourself from the *destructive effects* of negative people in your workplace. REPLACE WITH *detriment.* SEE ALSO *has an effect on.*

effective and efficient An inescapable pair (SEE PAGE 18). Businesspeople, in particular, seem unable to use the word *effective* without also using *efficient.* ■ For these methods, more *effective and efficient* methods are available. REPLACE WITH *effective* or *efficient.* ■ More than an audit, the study should evaluate the *efficiency and effectiveness* of social services and public works. REPLACE WITH *efficiency* or *effectiveness.* ■ The work place should be a safe environment where one can *effectively and efficiently* perform required duties. REPLACE WITH *effectively* or *efficiently.*

effectuate A torpid term (SEE PAGE 22). *bring about; carry out; cause; do; effect; execute; occasion.* SEE ALSO *eventuate.*

(with) egg on (my) face A moribund metaphor (SEE PAGE 19). *abashed; ashamed; chagrined; confused; discomfited; discomposed; disconcerted; embarrassed; flustered; humbled; humiliated; mortified; nonplused; perplexed; red-faced; shamed; shamefaced; sheepish; upset.* ■ Everybody likes to see Harvard *with egg on its face.* REPLACE WITH *embarrassed.*

egregious error An inescapable pair (SEE PAGE 18).

either one A wretched redundancy (SEE PAGE 23). *either.* ■ He doesn't care about *either one* of you. DELETE *one*. SEE ALSO *each one; neither one*.

(an) element A torpid term (SEE PAGE 22). ■ Proper validation is *an* essential *element*. DELETE *an element*. ■ Black turnout was especially low, and that was *a* key *element* to her victory. DELETE *a element*. SEE ALSO *(a) factor*.

elevate to an art form A moribund metaphor (SEE PAGE 19). ■ He would add to the gridlock, then compound the people's frustrations by *elevating* the blame game *to an art form*.

(an) embarrassment of riches A moribund metaphor (SEE PAGE 19). ■ It's a city with *an embarrassment of riches*.

empty void A wretched redundancy (SEE PAGE 23). *emptiness; void.* ■ I know that without me around my mother got lonely and just needed someone to fill the *empty void*. REPLACE WITH *emptiness* or *void*.

enclosed herein (herewith) A wretched redundancy (SEE PAGE 23). *enclosed; here.* ■ *Enclosed herein* is the complete manuscript. REPLACE WITH *Here* or *Enclosed*.

enclosed please find A wretched redundancy (SEE PAGE 23). *enclosed is; here is.* ■ *Enclosed please find* materials that you might find useful prior to your arrival. REPLACE WITH *Enclosed are*. ■ *Enclosed please find* a listing of single family properties that are available for purchase by eligible buyers. REPLACE WITH *Here is*.

endangered species A moribund metaphor (SEE PAGE 19). ■ We all recognize that the nuclear family is an *endangered species*.

(the) end justifies the means A popular prescription (SEE PAGE 21).

end of the line A moribund metaphor (SEE PAGE 19). *close; completion; conclusion; culmination; consummation; end; ending; finale; finish; fulfillment; termination.*

end on a high note A moribund metaphor (SEE PAGE 19).

end result A wretched redundancy (SEE PAGE 23). *result.* ■ The *end result* should be that all mothers and fathers would pay what they can afford. DELETE *end*.

enjoy it while (you) can A popular prescription (SEE PAGE 21).

enough is enough A quack equation (SEE PAGE 21). Though often used to conclude an argument, *enough is enough* is the least compelling of summations. No one can argue *enough is enough* and expect to be persuasive. Indeed, anyone who uses the expression surely loses the argument.

equally as A wretched redundancy (SEE PAGE 23). *as; equally.* ■ *Equally as* important, this program provides comprehensive preventive coverage. REPLACE WITH *As* or *Equally*.

ere A withered word (SEE PAGE 22). *before.* ■ So I avoided the hole and assumed it might likely be June *ere* it was patched. REPLACE WITH *before*.

ergo A withered word (SEE PAGE 22). *consequently; hence; therefore.*

establishment A torpid term (SEE PAGE 22). *business; club; company; firm; outlet; shop; store.* ■ You should park close to the entrance of the *establishment* you are shopping at. REPLACE WITH *store*.

et cetera (etc., etc.; et cetera, et cetera) A grammatical gimmick (SEE PAGE 17). ■ I'm very outgoing and adaptable, *et cetera, et cetera.* DELETE *et cetera, et cetera.* ■ She told me he was everything she was looking for, *et cetera, et cetera.* DELETE *et cetera, et cetera.* ■ Dr. Holmes was a man of brilliant conversational gifts — one of the most notable of that noted circle which composed the "Saturday Club" in Boston — Longfellow, Emerson, Lowell, Whittier, Thoreau, Bayard Taylor, *etc., etc.* DELETE *etc., etc.*
    When thoughts stumble and then stop, words, or at least intelligible words, do as well. As often as

not, *et cetera* is a means of expressing, without having to admit to its meaning, all those words only dimly thought. SEE ALSO *blah, blah, blah; and so on, and so forth.*

et tu, Brute A foreign phrase (SEE PAGE 17).

even Steven An infantile phrase (SEE PAGE 18).

even the score A moribund metaphor (SEE PAGE 19).

eventuate A torpid term (SEE PAGE 22). *befall; come about; end; happen; occur; result; take place.* SEE ALSO *effectuate.*

ever and anon A withered word (SEE PAGE 22). *now and then; occasionally.*

everybody and (his) brother (mother) An infantile phrase (SEE PAGE 18). *all; everybody; everyone.* ■ *Everybody and their mother* is on line today. REPLACE WITH *Everybody.* ■ It's like *everybody and their brother* is having a hearing on Enron. DELETE *and their brother.*

everybody talks about the weather, but nobody does anything about it An infantile phrase (SEE PAGE 18).

every cloud has a silver lining A popular prescription (SEE PAGE 21).

every effort is being made A suspect superlative (SEE PAGE 22). This phrase, disembodied though it is, serves to disarm people as it dismisses them. ■ *Every effort is being made* to find the perpetrators of this heinous crime. ■ *Every effort has been made* to make this verification as simple and painless as possible. ■ During this time, please be patient as *every effort is being made* to process your order in a timely manner. ■ First, we want to be sure that *every effort is being made* to spot, recover, preserve, identify and deliver any human remains to the families of the victims. SEE ALSO *that's interesting; that's nice.*

every nook and cranny A moribund metaphor (SEE PAGE 19). *all around; all over; all through; everyplace; everywhere; throughout.*

everyone under the sun A moribund metaphor (SEE PAGE 19). *all; everybody; everyone.*

every single (solitary) A wretched redundancy (SEE PAGE 23). *every.* ■ *Every single solitary* night we see people dying. REPLACE WITH *Every.*

every step of the way A moribund metaphor (SEE PAGE 19).
1. *always; ceaselessly; constantly; continually; continuously; endlessly; eternally; everlastingly; evermore; forever; forevermore; frequently; interminably; nonstop; permanently; perpetually; persistently; recurrently; regularly; repeatedly; unceasingly; unremittingly.*
2. *all during; all over; all through; everywhere; throughout.*

everything but the kitchen sink A moribund metaphor (SEE PAGE 19). *aggregate; all; all things; entirety; everything; gross; lot; sum; total; totality; whole.*

everything happens for a reason A popular prescription (SEE PAGE 21).

everything's coming up roses An infantile phrase (SEE PAGE 18). *be auspicious; be encouraging; be good; be hopeful; be optimistic; be promising; be propitious; be rosy.*

everything's (it's all) relative An infantile phrase (SEE PAGE 18). SEE ALSO *(as) compared to what? (as) opposed to what?*

everything under the sun A moribund metaphor (SEE PAGE 19). *all; all things; everything.* ■ I tried *everything under the sun* to get her to shape up. REPLACE WITH *everything.*

everything (it) will turn out for the best A popular prescription (SEE PAGE 21).

everything you always wanted to know about ... but were afraid to ask An infantile phrase (SEE PAGE 18).

every time (you) turn around A moribund metaphor (SEE PAGE 19). *always; ceaselessly; constantly; continually; continuously; endlessly; eternally; everlastingly; evermore; forever; forevermore; frequently; interminably; often; permanently; perpetu-*

ally; persistently; recurrently; regularly; repeatedly; unceasingly; unremittingly.

every Tom, Dick, and Harry A moribund metaphor (SEE PAGE 19). *all; citizenry; commonage; commonalty; common people; crowd; everybody; everyone; herd; hoi polloi; masses; mob; multitude; plebeians; populace; proletariat; public; rabble.* ■ I am not advocating that you tip *every Tom, Dick, and Harry.* REPLACE WITH *everyone.*

every trick in the book A moribund metaphor (SEE PAGE 19). ■ They're pulling *every trick in the book* to keep this amendment off the 1992 ballot.

excellence An overworked word (SEE PAGE 20). The word is overworked, and the concept undervalued. Too much, today, passes for *excellence.* Too much of our work is shoddy, too much of our wisdom, suspect, too much of our worth, unsure. ■ With your help, we will continue that tradition of *excellence.* SEE ALSO *pursue (strive for) excellence.*

(the) exception, not (rather than) the rule A torpid term (SEE PAGE 22). *aberrant; abnormal; anomalistic; anomalous; atypical; bizarre; curious; deviant; different; distinct; distinctive; eccentric; exceptional; extraordinary; fantastic; foreign; grotesque; idiosyncratic; independent; individual; individualistic; irregular; notable; noteworthy; novel; odd; offbeat; original; peculiar; puzzling; quaint; queer;* *rare; remarkable; separate; singular; strange; uncommon; unconventional; unexampled; unique; unnatural; unorthodox; unparalleled; unprecedented; unusual; weird.*

Most people find it easier to mimic a repeatedly used phrase like this — however wordy and inexact, however obtuse and tedious — than to remember a rarely used word like *aberrant* or *anomalous.* ■ Today, in region after region, single-town school districts are *the exception, not the rule.* REPLACE WITH *exceptional.* ■ Arrest or issuing a citation is *the exception, not the rule.* REPLACE WITH *atypical.*

(the) exception that proves the rule An infantile phrase (SEE PAGE 18).

(the) exception to the rule A torpid term (SEE PAGE 22). *aberrant; abnormal; anomalistic; anomalous; atypical; bizarre; curious; deviant; different; distinct; distinctive; eccentric; exceptional; extraordinary; fantastic; foreign; grotesque; idiosyncratic; independent; individual; individualistic; irregular; notable; noteworthy; novel; odd; offbeat; original; peculiar; puzzling; quaint; queer; rare; remarkable; separate; singular; strange; uncommon; unconventional; unexampled; unique; unnatural; unorthodox; unparalleled; unprecedented; unusual; weird.*

excess verbiage A wretched redundancy (SEE PAGE 23). *verbiage.*

excruciating pain An inescapable pair (SEE PAGE 18). ■ This medication was initially prescribed to soothe the *excruciating pain* that I was suffering.

excuse me? An infantile phrase (SEE PAGE 18). No longer exclusively a polite way of signifying that you did not hear what a person has said, *excuse me* is also — especially among the young and stupidly egoistic — an impolite way of signifying that you did not like what a person has said. With an autocratic intonation, the person expresses hostility to what he hears. This phrase is particularly loathsome, for those who use it dare not be openly angry or upset; they try to disguise their anger and arrogance behind a mantle of mannerliness. SEE ALSO *I'm sorry; thank you; whatever.*

expert opinion A suspect superlative (SEE PAGE 22).

expletive deleted An infantile phrase (SEE PAGE 18).

explore every avenue A moribund metaphor (SEE PAGE 19).

(an) explosion of A moribund metaphor (SEE PAGE 19). SEE ALSO *a barrage of.*

express (concern) A torpid term (SEE PAGE 22). Phrases like *express concern, express doubt, express opposition, express thanks* make any sentence instantly sodden. ■ Officials *express concern* about the slow pace of economic growth. REPLACE WITH *worry.* ■ House Democrats continue to *express anger* about the state's ethics and campaign finance laws. REPLACE WITH *fume.* ■ I want to *express my appreciation to* all of you who have lent us a hand in this endeavor. REPLACE WITH *thank.*

extend (hold out) the olive branch A moribund metaphor (SEE PAGE 19). *be accommodating; be agreeable; be conciliatory; be obliging; be peaceable; be propitiatory.*

extent A torpid term (SEE PAGE 22). Like *degree,* the word *extent,* along with the phrases in which it is found, is best avoided.

These are lifeless expressions, and it is listless people who use them.

■ In some cases, they've been transformed *to such an extent* that you can no longer recognize them. REPLACE WITH *so much.* ■ The study said that women, *to a greater extent* than men, manage by personal interactions with their subordinates. REPLACE WITH *more.* ■ Re-sources are always used *to the optimum extent.* REPLACE WITH *optimally.* ■ Sooner or later, we will see *to what extent* the central banks are prepared to back up words with actions. REPLACE WITH *how far.* ■ The *extent to which* these practices are seen as flowing in one direction, down from headquarters to subsidiaries, may influence *the extent to which* these practices are adopted and *to what extent* the behavior, beliefs, and values of the corporate culture are incorporated or even complied with.

REPLACE WITH *How much, how much,* and *how much.* SEE ALSO *degree.*

extenuating circumstances An inescapable pair (SEE PAGE 18).

(his) eyes are bigger than (his) stomach A moribund metaphor (SEE PAGE 19).

eyes are the windows of the soul A moribund metaphor (SEE PAGE 19).

(an) eye for an eye (and a tooth for a tooth) A popular prescription (SEE PAGE 21).

(has) eyes in the back of (his) head A moribund metaphor (SEE PAGE 19). *alert; attentive; aware; eagle-eyed; heedful; keen; observant; perceptive; vigilant; wakeful; watchful.*

eyes (are) wide open A moribund metaphor (SEE PAGE 19). *alert; attentive; aware; cognizant; conscious; eagle-eyed; heedful; keen; observant; perceptive; vigilant; wakeful; watchful.*

F

fabulous An overworked word (SEE PAGE 20). As still another synonym for *very good* or *extremely pleasing, fabulous* is indeed overused. In its sense of *hard to believe* or *astounding*, it is now and again used, and in its sense of *like a fable* or *legendary*, it is woefully unused.

(the) face that launched a thousand ships A moribund metaphor (SEE PAGE 19).

face the music A moribund metaphor (SEE PAGE 19). *pay; suffer.*

(the) (plain; simple) fact is (that) An ineffectual phrase (SEE PAGE 17). ■ *The fact is* at least the govenor is trying. DELETE *The fact is.* ■ *The simple fact is* we are now spending nearly $1 trillion on health care. DELETE *The simple fact is.* ■ *The plain fact is* American women are buying guns like they've never bought them before. DELETE *The plain fact is.*

(the) (simple) fact of the matter is An ineffectual phrase (SEE PAGE 17). ■ *The fact of the matter is* the police took the children from you. DELETE *The fact of the matter is.*

■ Despite her behavior, *the simple fact of the matter is* I still love her. DELETE *the simple fact of the matter is.* SEE ALSO *the truth of the matter is.*

(a) factor A torpid term (SEE PAGE 22). ■ I think the TV show *was a contributing factor* to this tragedy. REPLACE WITH *contributed.* ■ They thought the biggest problem we were dealing with was *a jealousy factor.* REPLACE WITH *jealousy.* ■ The *key factor in* the decline appears to be the Irish-American voter's willingness to vote for candidates from other ethnic groups. REPLACE WITH *key to.* ■ The presence of a long umbilical cord *is a contributory factor* to the occurrence of nuchal cord. REPLACE WITH *contributes.* SEE ALSO *(an) element.*

(the) fact remains (that) An ineffectual phrase (SEE PAGE 17). ■ We call this campaign a "snoozer," but *the fact remains* both candidates did behave responsibly. DELETE *the fact remains.* ■ Whether one prefers the proverb's optimism or Euripides' pessimism, *the fact remains that* the way in which investigations are conducted can have a significant impact on the outcome of any case. DELETE *the fact remains that.*

facts and figures An inescapable pair (SEE PAGE 18).

facts and information A wretched redundancy (SEE PAGE 23). *data; facts; information.*

(the) fact that An ineffectual phrase (SEE PAGE 17). ■ *The fact that* many more computers are in communication with one another increases concern that users' privacy will be violated. REPLACE WITH *That.* ■ *The fact that* she was rather attractive did not escape their notice. REPLACE WITH *That.*

fade into the sunset A moribund metaphor (SEE PAGE 19). *disappear; disperse; dissolve; evaporate; fade; vanish; vaporize; volatilize.*

fade into the woodwork A moribund metaphor (SEE PAGE 19). *depart; disappear; disperse; dissolve; evaporate; fade; vacate; vanish; vaporize; volatilize; withdraw.* ■ It is easy to *fade into the woodwork* and never have to deal with those problems. REPLACE WITH *disappear.*

fading fast A moribund metaphor (SEE PAGE 19). *beat; bushed; debilitated; depleted; drained; drowsy; enervated; exhausted; fatigued; groggy; sapped; sleepy; sluggish; slumberous; somnolent; soporific; spent; tired; weary; worn out.*

fair and equitable An inescapable pair (SEE PAGE 18). *equitable; fair; just.* ■ The key to maintaining that system is ensuring that you are treated *fairly and equitably.* REPLACE WITH *equitably* or *fairly.*

fair and square An inescapable pair (SEE PAGE 18). *aboveboard; creditable; equitable; fair; honest; honorable; just; lawful; legitimate; open; proper; reputable; respectable; right; square; straightforward; upright; veracious; veridical.*

fair game A moribund metaphor (SEE PAGE 19).

fair is fair A quack equation (SEE PAGE 21).

fair share A torpid term (SEE PAGE 22). *allocation; allotment; allowance; amount; apportionment; dole; lot; measure; part; piece; portion; quota; ration; share.* ■ We are setting out to get our *fair share* of the residential real estate mortgage business.

fair to middling A wretched redundancy (SEE PAGE 23). *average; common; fair; mediocre; middling; moderate; ordinary; passable; tolerable.*

fait accompli A foreign phrase (SEE PAGE 17).

fall between (through) the cracks A moribund metaphor (SEE PAGE 19). *be discounted; be disregarded; be elided; be forgotten; be ignored; be left out; be missed; be neglected; be omitted; be overlooked; be skipped; be slighted; be snubbed.* ■ Such a caring environment is particularly important for students who have few other sources of support and who might well *fall through the cracks* in a less personalized school setting. REPLACE WITH *be forgotten.*

fall by the wayside A moribund metaphor (SEE PAGE 19). *abate; cease to be; diminish; disappear; dissolve; dwindle; fade; go away; recede; vanish.* ■ Social class distinctions have mostly *fallen by the wayside,* and scientists are now more likely to admit the collective nature of research. REPLACE WITH *disappeared.*

fall flat on (its) face A moribund metaphor (SEE PAGE 19). *be unsuccessful; blunder; bomb; break down; bungle; collapse; fail; fall short; falter; fizzle; flop; fold; founder; mess up; miscarry; not succeed; stumble; topple.* ■ Some professional investors are betting the company will *fall flat on its face.* REPLACE WITH *fail.*

fall from grace A moribund metaphor (SEE PAGE 19). *collapse; decline; downfall; failure; fall; misadventure; misfortune; offense; peccadillo; ruin; sin; transgression; wrongdoing.*

fall in (into) line (place) A moribund metaphor (SEE PAGE 19). *abide by; accede; accommodate; accord; acquiesce; adapt; adhere to; agree; behave; comply; concur; conform; correspond; follow; harmonize; heed; mind; obey; observe; submit; yield.*

fall into (my) lap A moribund metaphor (SEE PAGE 19). ■ It just kind of *fell into my lap.*

fall on deaf ears A moribund metaphor (SEE PAGE 19). *disregard; ignore.*

fall through the floor A moribund metaphor (SEE PAGE 19). *collapse; crash; decline; decrease; descend; dip; drop; ebb; fall; plummet; plunge; recede; sink; slide; slip; subside; topple; tumble.* ■ But Cellucci said the bond rating *fell through the floor* in the late 1980s during the fiscal crisis. REPLACE WITH *collapsed.*

fame and fortune A suspect superlative (SEE PAGE 22). SEE ALSO *the rich and famous.*

(the) family that prays together stays together A popular prescription (SEE PAGE 21).

fan (fuel) the fire (flames) A moribund metaphor (SEE PAGE 19). *activate; agitate; animate; arouse; awaken; encourage; enkindle; enliven; exacerbate; excite; feed; foment; ignite; impassion; incite; inflame; intensify; invigorate; make worse; nourish; prod; provoke; rejuvenate; revitalize; revive; rouse; shake up; stimulate; stir up; vitalize; worsen.*

far and away A wretched redundancy (SEE PAGE 23). *by far; much.*

far and wide An inescapable pair (SEE PAGE 18). *all around; all over; all through; broadly; everyplace; everywhere; extensively; throughout; ubiquitously; universally; widely.* SEE ALSO *high and wide; left and right.*

far-reaching consequences (implications) An inescapable pair (SEE PAGE 18).

fashion statement A plebeian sentiment (SEE PAGE 20). Making a *fashion statement* is the concern of adolescents and addle-brained adults who have yet to fashion for themselves a sense of identity. Their habiliments interest them more than does their humanity.

People so intent on being fashionable make only misstatements. They but blither.

fast and furious An inescapable pair (SEE PAGE 18).

(as) fast as (her) legs can carry (her) An insipid simile (SEE PAGE 19). *abruptly; apace; at once; briskly; directly; expeditiously; fast; forthwith; hastily; hurriedly; immediately; instantaneously; instantly; posthaste; promptly; quickly; rapidly; rashly; right away; speedily; straightaway; swiftly; wingedly.*

fasten your seat belts A moribund metaphor (SEE PAGE 19).

faster than a speeding bullet, (more powerful than a locomotive, able to leap small buildings at a single bound) An infantile phrase (SEE PAGE 18).

fast track A moribund metaphor (SEE PAGE 19).

fast trigger finger A moribund metaphor (SEE PAGE 19).

(as) fat as a cow An insipid simile (SEE PAGE 19). *ample; big; bulky; chubby; chunky; colossal; corpulent; dumpy; enormous; fat; flabby; fleshy;*

gigantic; heavy; hefty; huge; immense; large; mammoth; massive; obese; plump; portly; pudgy; rotund; round; squat; stocky; stout.

(as) fat as a pig An insipid simile (SEE PAGE 19). *ample; big; bulky; chubby; chunky; colossal; corpulent; dumpy; enormous; fat; flabby; fleshy; gigantic; heavy; hefty; huge; immense; large; mammoth; massive; obese; plump; portly; pudgy; rotund; round; squat; stocky; stout.*

fat cat A moribund metaphor (SEE PAGE 19). *billionaire; capitalist; financier; magnate; materialist; millionaire; mogul; multimillionaire; nabob; plutocrat; tycoon.*

(the) fat's in the fire A moribund metaphor (SEE PAGE 19).

fear and trembling An inescapable pair (SEE PAGE 18). *alarm; anxiety; apprehension; consternation; dismay; dread; fear; foreboding; fright; horror; panic; terror; trembling; trepidation.*

feast or famine An inescapable pair (SEE PAGE 18).

(a) feather in (his) cap A moribund metaphor (SEE PAGE 19). *acclaim; acclamation; accolade; approbation; approval; commendation; compliment; endorsement; honor; praise; sanction; tribute.*

feather (their) nest A moribund metaphor (SEE PAGE 19). ■ He repeatedly denied allegations that he used his three years at the

Denver-based thrift to *feather his own nest.*

feed (you) a line   A moribund metaphor (SEE PAGE 19). *deceive; dissemble; distort; equivocate; falsify; fib; lie; misconstrue; mislead; misrepresent; pervert; prevaricate.*

feedback   A torpid term (SEE PAGE 22). *answers; data; feelings; ideas; information; recommendations; replies; responses; suggestions; thoughts; views.* ■ Your *feedback* helps us continually improve. REPLACE WITH *suggestions.* ■ And as *feedback* is obtained, it is the duty of the firm's leaders to convey it to all members of the firm. REPLACE WITH *ideas.* SEE ALSO *(the) bottom line; input; interface; output; parameters.*

feeling no pain   A moribund metaphor (SEE PAGE 19). *besotted; crapulous; drunk; inebriated; intoxicated; sodden; stupefied; tipsy.*

feeling (his) oats   A moribund metaphor (SEE PAGE 19). *active; alive; animated; dynamic; energetic; exuberant; frisky; indefatigable; inexhaustible; invigorated; lively; peppy; spirited; sprightly; spry; tireless; unflagging; vibrant; vigorous; vivacious; zestful; zesty.*

(the) feeling's mutual   An infantile phrase (SEE PAGE 18).

feel the pinch   A moribund metaphor (SEE PAGE 19).

feel the heat   A moribund metaphor (SEE PAGE 19).

fertile ground   A moribund metaphor (SEE PAGE 19).

few and far between   A wretched redundancy (SEE PAGE 23). *exiguous; limited; inadequate; infrequent; meager; rare; scant; scanty; scarce; sparse; uncommon; unusual.* ■ Role models are *few and far between* in those groups. REPLACE WITH *scarce.*

(has a) few screws loose   A moribund metaphor (SEE PAGE 19). *batty; cracked; crazy; daft; demented; deranged; fey; foolish; goofy; insane; lunatic; mad; maniacal; neurotic; nuts; nutty; psychotic; raving; silly; squirrelly; strange; touched; unbalanced; unhinged; unsound; wacky; zany.*

fiddle while Rome burns   A moribund metaphor (SEE PAGE 19).

(a) fifth wheel   A moribund metaphor (SEE PAGE 19). *excessive; extra; extraneous; immaterial; incidental; inconsequential; insignificant; irrelevant; needless; nonessential; superabundant; superfluous; unimportant; unnecessary.* ■ With his mother doing the cooking and other household chores, I would feel *like a fifth wheel.* REPLACE WITH *superfluous.*

fight a losing battle   A moribund metaphor (SEE PAGE 19).

fight fire with fire   A moribund metaphor (SEE PAGE 19).

fight like cats and dogs   An insipid simile (SEE PAGE 19). 1. *altercate; argue; disagree; dispute;*

feud; fight; quarrel; spat; squabble; wrangle.
2. *battle; brawl; clash; fight; grapple; jostle; make war; scuffle; skirmish; tussle; war; wrestle.*

filled to bursting (overflowing) A moribund metaphor (SEE PAGE 19). *abounding; brimful; brimming; bursting; chock-full; congested; crammed; crowded; dense; filled; full; gorged; jammed; jam-packed; overcrowded; overfilled; overflowing; packed; replete; saturated; stuffed; swarming; teeming.*

filled to the brim A moribund metaphor (SEE PAGE 19). *abounding; brimful; brimming; bursting; chock-full; congested; crammed; crowded; dense; filled; full; gorged; jammed; jam-packed; overcrowded; overfilled; overflowing; packed; replete; saturated; stuffed; swarming; teeming.*

fill in the blanks An infantile phrase (SEE PAGE 18).

fill (his) shoes A moribund metaphor (SEE PAGE 19).

fill the bill A moribund metaphor (SEE PAGE 19).
1. *be appropriate; be apt; be befitting; be felicitous; be fit; be fitting; be happy; be meet; be proper; be right; be seemly; be suitable; be suited.*
2. *be acceptable; be adequate; be qualified; be satisfactory; be sufficient.*

fill to capacity A wretched redundancy (SEE PAGE 23). *fill.* ■ Our free public facilities are *filled to capacity,* and there are long waiting

lists for some programs. REPLACE WITH *filled.*

filthy lucre A moribund metaphor (SEE PAGE 19). *money; riches; wealth.*

final and irrevocable An inescapable pair (SEE PAGE 18). *final; firm; irrevocable; unalterable.*

final chapter A moribund metaphor (SEE PAGE 19). *close; completion; conclusion; consummation; culmination; denouement; end; ending; finale; finish; termination.*

final conclusion A wretched redundancy (SEE PAGE 23). ■ We have made no *final conclusions* on responsibility for the attacks in Kenya and Tanzania. DELETE *final.*

final culmination A wretched redundancy (SEE PAGE 23). *culmination.* ■ Owning a farm was the *final culmination* of all our efforts. DELETE *final.*

final decision A wretched redundancy (SEE PAGE 23). *decision.* ■ That's one of the things we have under consideration, but no *final decision* has been made. DELETE *final.*

(the) final (last) frontier A moribund metaphor (SEE PAGE 19).

finalize A torpid term (SEE PAGE 22). *complete; conclude; consummate; end; execute; finish; fulfill; made final; terminate.* ■ Delays in *finalizing* the state budget and its allocations to cities and towns make a special town meeting necessary. REPLACE WITH *completing*. SEE ALSO *utilize*.

(that's) (the) final (last) straw A moribund metaphor (SEE PAGE 19).

finders keepers, losers weepers An infantile phrase (SEE PAGE 18).

(like) finding (looking for) a needle in a haystack An insipid simile (SEE PAGE 19).

find (some) middle ground A moribund metaphor (SEE PAGE 19). *compromise.*

fine and dandy An inescapable pair (SEE PAGE 18). *all right; excellent; fine; good; O.K.; well.* SEE ALSO *well and good.*

(a) fine (pretty) kettle of fish A moribund metaphor (SEE PAGE 19). *complication; difficulty; dilemma; mess; muddle; ordeal; pickle; plight; predicament; problem; quandary; trial; trouble.*

fine line A moribund metaphor (SEE PAGE 19). ■ There is a very *fine line* between vision and delusion.

fingers on the pulse of A moribund metaphor (SEE PAGE 19).

fire (launch) a salvo A moribund metaphor (SEE PAGE 19).

(all) fired (hopped, psyched) up A moribund metaphor (SEE PAGE 19). *afire; aflame; anxious; ardent; burning; eager; enthusiastic; excited; fanatic; fanatical; fervent; fervid; fiery;* *impassioned; inflamed; intense; perfervid; keen; passionate; vehement; zealous.*

(a) firestorm of A moribund metaphor (SEE PAGE 19). ■ That decision unleashed *a firestorm of* protest in the Capitol. SEE ALSO *a barrage of.*

firmly establish An inescapable pair (SEE PAGE 18). Adverbs often modify other words needlessly. Here, *firmly* is superfluous, for *establish* means "to make firm." ■ The play *firmly established* him as a dramatist. DELETE *firmly.*

first and foremost A wretched redundancy (SEE PAGE 23). *chief; chiefly; first; foremost; initial; initially; main; mainly; most important; mostly; primarily; primary; principal; principally.* ■ *First and foremost* these people must have a commitment to public service. REPLACE WITH *Most important*. SEE ALSO *first and most important.*

first and most important A wretched redundancy (SEE PAGE 23). *chief; chiefly; first; foremost; initial; initially; main; mainly; most important; mostly; primarily; primary; principal; principally.* SEE ALSO *first and foremost.*

first begin (start) A wretched redundancy (SEE PAGE 23). *begin; start.* ■ When we *first started* exploring the idea, we didn't even know if it was possible to do. DELETE *first.*

first line of defense A moribund metaphor (SEE PAGE 19).

first of all A wretched redundancy (SEE PAGE 23). *first.* ■ *First of all,* I am delighted about our progress in that area. REPLACE WITH *First.* SEE ALSO *second of all.*

first (highest; number-one; top) priority A torpid term (SEE PAGE 22). Nothing soulful can be said using these expressions, so when a U.S. cardinal drearily sermonizes, "The protection of children must be our *number-one priority,*" we are hardly convinced that this is his or the church's principal concern. When we read, in some corporate promotional piece, "Your satisfaction is our *number-one priority,*" we are likewise, and for good reason, suspicious.

Mechanical expressions like *first (highest; number-one; top) priority* defy tenderness, resist compassion, and counter concern. SEE ALSO *reach epidemic proportions.*

(the) first step is always the hardest A popular prescription (SEE PAGE 21).

fish or cut bait A moribund metaphor (SEE PAGE 19).

(like) (a) fish out of water An insipid simile (SEE PAGE 19). *awkward; blundering; bumbling; bungling; clumsy; gawky; gauche; ham-handed; heavy-handed; inapt; inept; lubberly; lumbering; maladroit; uncoordinated; uncouth; ungainly; ungraceful; unhandy; unskillful; unwieldy.*

(other) fish to fry A moribund metaphor (SEE PAGE 19).

(as) fit as a fiddle An insipid simile (SEE PAGE 19). *athletic; beefy; brawny; energetic; fit; good; hale; hardy; healthful; healthy; hearty; husky; lanky; lean; manly; muscular; powerful; robust; shapely; sinewy; slender; solid; sound; stalwart; stout; strong; sturdy; thin; trim; vigorous; virile; well; well-built.*

fit for a king A moribund metaphor (SEE PAGE 19). *august; awe-inspiring; distinguished; elegant; eminent; exalted; exquisite; extraordinary; extravagant; glorious; grand; great; impressive; kingly; luxurious; magnificent; majestic; monarchical; nobel; opulent; princely; regal; royal; sovereign; splendid; stately; sumptuous.*

fitting and proper An inescapable pair (SEE PAGE 18). *appropriate; apt; befitting; felicitous; fit; fitting; happy; meet; proper; right; seemly; suitable; suited.* ■ And it is generally regarded as *fitting and proper* for women to do this. REPLACE WITH *fitting.*

fit to be tied A moribund metaphor (SEE PAGE 19). *angry; cross; enraged; fuming; furious; incensed; indignant; infuriated; irate; mad; outraged; raging; wrathful.*

fix (her) wagon A moribund metaphor (SEE PAGE 19).
1. *castigate; censure; chasten; chastise; chide; criticize; discipline; penalize; punish; rebuke; reprove; scold.*
2. *spank.*

flaming inferno An infantile phrase (SEE PAGE 18). *blaze; conflagration; fire; inferno.*

flash in the pan A moribund metaphor (SEE PAGE 19). *brief; ephemeral; evanescent; fleeting; momentary; short; short-lived; short-term; temporary; transient; transitory.*

(as) flat as a board An insipid simile (SEE PAGE 19). *even; flat; flush; horizontal; level; plane; smooth.*

(as) flat as a pancake An insipid simile (SEE PAGE 19). *even; flat; flush; horizontal; level; plane; smooth.*

flat on (his) back A moribund metaphor (SEE PAGE 19). *afflicted; ailing; crippled; debilitated; defenseless; disabled; diseased; feeble; fragile; helpless; ill; incapacitated; indisposed; infirm; not (feeling) well; sick; sickly; unhealthy; unwell; valetudinarian; weak.*

(my) (own) flesh and blood A moribund metaphor (SEE PAGE 19). 1. *brother; child; daughter; father; kin; mother; parent; relative; sibling; sister; son.* 2. *depth; reality; substance.*

flight of fancy A moribund metaphor (SEE PAGE 19). *caprice; chimera; crotchet; daydream; delusion; dream; fancy; fantasy; hallucination; humor; illusion; imagination; notion; phantasm; vagary; whim; whimsy.*

flip (her) lid A moribund metaphor (SEE PAGE 19). *bellow; bluster; clamor; explode; fulminate; fume; holler; howl; rage; rant; rave; roar; scream; shout; storm; thunder; vociferate; yell.*

(on the) flip side (of the coin) A moribund metaphor (SEE PAGE 19). 1. *antithesis; contrary; converse; opposite; reverse.* 2. *but; in contrast; conversely; however; inversely; whereas; yet.*

(whatever) floats your boat A moribund metaphor (SEE PAGE 19).

(a) flood of A moribund metaphor (SEE PAGE 19). ■ The evidence indicates NAFTA will lead to *a flood of* auto exports from the United States to Mexico. ■ Should the doctors win, labor leaders predict *a flood of* physicians signing up with unions. SEE ALSO *a barrage of.*

flotsam and jetsam An inescapable pair (SEE PAGE 18). 1. *debris; litter; rack; refuse; rubbish; rubble; wrack; wreckage.* 2. *bits; fragments; modicums; odds and ends; particles; pieces; remnants; scraps; shreds; snippets; trifles.* 3. *itinerants; rovers; tramps; vagabonds; vagrants; wanderers.*

flowing with milk and honey A moribund metaphor (SEE PAGE 19).

(a) flurry of A moribund metaphor (SEE PAGE 19). ■ The U.S. stock market's strong recovery in the last months of 1998 prompted *a flurry of* charitable giving in December. SEE ALSO *a barrage of.*

fly-by-night A moribund metaphor (SEE PAGE 19). *irresponsible; undependable; unreliable; untrustworthy.*

fly by the seat of (his) pants A moribund metaphor (SEE PAGE 19). *be extemporaneous; be instinctive; be spontaneous; impromptu; improvise.* ■ Administrators who *fly by the seat of their pants* typically rely on trial and error because there are no overarching objectives and guidelines. REPLACE WITH *are instinctive.*

flying high A moribund metaphor (SEE PAGE 19).
1. *advantageous; auspicious; blessed; charmed; enchanted; favored; felicitous; flourishing; fortuitous; fortunate; golden; happy; in luck; lucky; propitious; prosperous; successful; thriving.*
2. *blissful; blithe; buoyant; cheerful; delighted; ecstatic; elated; enraptured; euphoric; exalted; excited; exhilarated; exultant; gay; glad; gleeful; good-humored; happy; intoxicated; jolly; jovial; joyful; joyous; jubilant; merry; mirthful; overjoyed; pleased; rapturous; thrilled.*

fly in the face of A moribund metaphor (SEE PAGE 19). *challenge; contradict; defy; disobey; dispute; disregard; flout; go against; ignore; neglect; overlook; resist.* ■ This is nonsensical and *flies in the face of* history and basic economic principles. REPLACE WITH *contradicts.*

fly in the ointment A moribund metaphor (SEE PAGE 19). *bar; barrier; block; blockage; catch; check; deter-* *rent; difficulty; encumbrance; handicap; hindrance; hitch; hurdle; impediment; interference; obstacle; obstruction; rub; snag.*

fly off the handle A moribund metaphor (SEE PAGE 19). *bellow; blow up; bluster; clamor; explode; fulminate; fume; holler; howl; rage; rant; rave; roar; scream; shout; storm; thunder; vociferate; yell.* ■ To tell the truth, investors are *flying off the handle* everywhere you look. REPLACE WITH *howling.* ■ Meditation makes me a much calmer person; I don't *fly off the handle* so much. REPLACE WITH *rant.*

(a) fly on the wall A moribund metaphor (SEE PAGE 19).

fly the coop A moribund metaphor (SEE PAGE 19). *abscond; clear out; decamp; depart; desert; disappear; escape; exit; flee; fly; go; go away; leave; move on; part; pull out; quit; retire; retreat; run away; take flight; take off; vacate; vanish; withdraw.*

fly (too) close to the sun A moribund metaphor (SEE PAGE 19). *chance; dare; endanger; gamble; hazard; imperil; jeopardize; make bold; peril; risk; venture.*

foaming (frothing) at the mouth A moribund metaphor (SEE PAGE 19). *angry; berserk; convulsive; crazed; delirious; demented; demoniac; deranged; enraged; feral; ferocious; fierce; frantic; frenzied; fuming; furious; hysterical; infuriated; in hysterics; insane; incensed; irate; mad; mad-*

dened; maniacal; murderous; possessed; rabid; raging; ranting; raving; savage; seething; wild; wrathful.

focus attention (concentration) on A wretched redundancy (SEE PAGE 23). *concentrate on; focus on.* ■ Microsoft has always *focused its attention on* software products and software standards. REPLACE WITH *focused on.* ■ It is hardly magic to *focus concentration on* success instead of failure. REPLACE WITH *concentrate on.* SEE ALSO *focus effort (energy) on.*

focus effort (energy) on A wretched redundancy (SEE PAGE 23). *concentrate on; focus on.* ■ This downsizing will cut our expenses and allow us to *focus our efforts on* serving our customers. REPLACE WITH *focus on.* ■ Owners can *focus their energy on* expanding the business to a point where it can function outside of a "nurtured" environment. REPLACE WITH *focus on.* SEE ALSO *focus attention (concentration) on.*

focus in on A wretched redundancy (SEE PAGE 23). *focus on.* ■ I have to *focus in on* what I want to accomplish. DELETE *in.*

fold (their) tent A moribund metaphor (SEE PAGE 19). *abscond; clear out; decamp; depart; desert; disappear; escape; exit; flee; fly; go; go away; leave; move on; part; pull out; quit; retire; retreat; run away; take flight; take off; vacate; vanish; withdraw.*

follow in (her) footsteps A moribund metaphor (SEE PAGE 19).

follow suit A moribund metaphor (SEE PAGE 19). *copy; do as much; follow; imitate; mimic.* ■ NYNEX is expected to *follow suit* in the near future. REPLACE WITH *do as much.* ■ When American Airlines slashed fares, TWA *followed suit.* REPLACE WITH *did as much.*

follow the crowd A moribund metaphor (SEE PAGE 19). *abide by; accede; accommodate; accord; acquiesce; adapt; adhere to; agree; behave; comply; concur; conform; correspond; follow; harmonize; heed; mind; obey; observe; submit; yield.*

follow your instincts A popular prescription (SEE PAGE 21).

(bid) (a) fond farewell An infantile phrase (SEE PAGE 18).

food for thought A moribund metaphor (SEE PAGE 19). SEE ALSO *(it's) something to think about.*

food for worms A moribund metaphor (SEE PAGE 19). *dead; deceased; defunct; departed; exanimate; expired; extinct; extinguished; finished; gone; inanimate; lifeless; no more; perished; terminated.*

(a) fool and his money are soon parted A popular prescription (SEE PAGE 21).

fools rush in where angels fear to tread A popular prescription (SEE PAGE 21).

footloose and fancy free A moribund metaphor (SEE PAGE 19). *at liberty; autonomous; free; independent; self-reliant; unattached; unbound; unconfined; unconstrained; unencumbered; unentangled; unfettered; uninhibited; unrestrained; unrestricted; unshackled; untied.*

footprints in the sands of time A moribund metaphor (SEE PAGE 19).

for all intents and purposes A wretched redundancy (SEE PAGE 23). *effectively; essentially; in effect; in essence; practically; virtually.* ■ *For all intents and purposes,* the civil rights acts of 1964 and 1965 signified the demise of official segregation in the United States. REPLACE WITH *In effect.* SEE ALSO *for all practical purposes; to all intents and purposes; to all practical purposes.*

for all practical purposes A wretched redundancy (SEE PAGE 23). *effectively; essentially; in effect; in essence; practically; virtually.* ■ Services are, *for all practical purposes,* sold as products to end users, so the distinction between services and goods is artificial at best. REPLACE WITH *essentially.* SEE ALSO *for all intents and purposes; to all intents and purposes; to all practical purposes.*

(a) force to be reckoned with An infantile phrase (SEE PAGE 18). *adversary; antagonist; challenger; competitor; contender; contestant; force; opponent; rival.* ■ The combination of Walsh, the broadcast of Celtics games this season, and hot Fox network programming will make WFXT *a force to be reckoned with.* REPLACE WITH *a contender.*

forever and a day A moribund metaphor (SEE PAGE 19). *always; ceaselessly; constantly; continually; continuously; endlessly; eternally; everlastingly; evermore; forever; forevermore; immortally; indefinitely; interminably; permanently; perpetually; persistently; unceasingly; unremittingly.*

for every action there's an equal and opposite reaction A popular prescription (SEE PAGE 21).

for every negative there is a positive A popular prescription (SEE PAGE 21).

for everything there is a season A popular prescription (SEE PAGE 21).

forewarn A wretched redundancy (SEE PAGE 23). *warn.* ■ *Forewarn* your clients that they might be stared at by locals. REPLACE WITH *Warn.* SEE ALSO *advance warning; warn in advance.*

forewarned is forearmed A quack equation (SEE PAGE 21).

for free A wretched redundancy (SEE PAGE 23). *free.*

forgive and forget A popular prescription (SEE PAGE 21).

fork in the road A moribund metaphor (SEE PAGE 19).

formative years   A torpid term (SEE PAGE 22). *adolescence; childhood; immaturity; juvenility.*

forsooth   A withered word (SEE PAGE 22). *actually; indeed; in fact; in faith; in reality; in truth; truly.*

(it's) for the birds   A moribund metaphor (SEE PAGE 19).
1. *absurd; asinine; childish; comical; farcical; fatuous; flighty; foolhardy; foolish; frivolous; giddy; idiotic; immature; inane; laughable; ludicrous; nonsensical; preposterous; ridiculous; senseless; silly.*
2. *barren; bootless; effete; feckless; feeble; fruitless; futile; impotent; inadequate; inconsequential; inconsiderable; ineffective; ineffectual; infertile; insignificant; inutile; meaningless; meritless; nugatory; null; of no value; pointless; powerless; profitless; purposeless; sterile; trifling; trivial; unavailing; unimportant; unproductive; unprofitable; unserviceable; unworthy; useless; vain; valueless; weak; worthless.*

for the (simple) fact that   A wretched redundancy (SEE PAGE 23). *because; considering; for; in that; since.* ■ Women received some assistance in the colonial period *for the simple fact that* American Protestants strongly favored "peaceable" and intact families. REPLACE WITH *because.* SEE ALSO *for the (simple) reason that.*

for the most part   A wretched redundancy (SEE PAGE 23). *almost all; chiefly; commonly; generally; greatly; in general; largely; mainly;* *most; mostly; most often; much; nearly all; overall; normally; typically; usually.* ■ The search for solutions to these crises has focused *for the most part* on the legal system. REPLACE WITH *largely.*

for (with) the purpose of -ing   A wretched redundancy (SEE PAGE 23). *for (-ing); so as to; to.* ■ These analyses have been used *for the purpose of criticizing* the shortcomings of Western management. REPLACE WITH *for criticizing* or *to criticize.* ■ The other was the development in 1923 of a comparison microscope that could be used *for the purpose of determining* whether or not a bullet found at the scene of a crime was fired by a particular gun. REPLACE WITH *for determining* or *to determine.*

for the (simple) reason that   A wretched redundancy (SEE PAGE 23). *because; considering; for; in that; since.* ■ Polls dominate political discourse *for the simple reason that* "Everyone else has an opinion; the pollster has a fact." REPLACE WITH *because.* SEE ALSO *for the (simple) fact that.*

for your information   An ineffectual phrase (SEE PAGE 17). ■ *For your information,* he loves me, and I love him. DELETE *For your information.*

foul up (gum up; screw up) the works   A moribund metaphor (SEE PAGE 19).
1. *agitate; confuse; disorder; disorganize; disquiet; disrupt; disturb; fluster;*

jar; jinx; jolt; jumble; mix up; muddle; perturb; rattle; ruffle; shake up; stir up; unnerve; unsettle; upset.
2. *blight; cripple; damage; disable; harm; hurt; impair; incapacitate; lame; mar; mess up; rack; ruin; sabotage; spoil; subvert; undermine; vitiate; wrack; wreck.*

(the) four corners of the earth (world) *all over; everyplace; everywhere; throughout (the land); universally.* A moribund metaphor (SEE PAGE 19). ■ These changes will affect our American patients as well as those who come to the clinic from *the four corners of the world.*

free and easy An inescapable pair (SEE PAGE 18). *casual; carefree; easygoing; informal; insouciant; lighthearted; nonchalant; relaxed; untroubled.*

free and gratis An infantile phrase (SEE PAGE 18). *free.*

(as) free as a bird An insipid simile (SEE PAGE 19). *autonomous; free; independent; self-reliant; unattached; unbound; unconfined; unconstrained; unencumbered; unentangled; unfettered; uninhibited; unrestrained; unrestricted; unshackled; untied.*

(as) free as the wind An insipid simile (SEE PAGE 19). *autonomous; free; independent; self-reliant; unattached; unbound; unconfined; unconstrained; unencumbered; unentangled; unfettered; uninhibited; unrestrained; unrestricted; unshackled; untied.*

free gift A wretched redundancy (SEE PAGE 23). *gift.* ■ With every renewal, you will receive a *free gift.* DELETE *free.*

(no) free lunch A moribund metaphor (SEE PAGE 19).

free ride A moribund metaphor (SEE PAGE 19).

freezing cold An inescapable pair (SEE PAGE 18). *algid; arctic; brumal; chilly; cold; cool; freezing; frigid; frosty; frozen; gelid; glacial; hibernal; hyperborean; ice-cold; icy; nippy; polar; rimy; wintry.*

(as) fresh as a daisy An insipid simile (SEE PAGE 19). *active; alive; animated; blooming; dynamic; energetic; fresh; healthy; hearty; lively; peppy; refreshed; rested; rosy; ruddy; spirited; sprightly; spry; vibrant; vigorous; vivacious.*

fret and fume An inescapable pair (SEE PAGE 18).

(a) friend in need (is a friend indeed) A popular prescription (SEE PAGE 21).

frighten (scare) out of (her) wits A moribund metaphor (SEE PAGE 19). *alarm; appall; benumb; daunt; frighten; horrify; intimidate; panic; paralyze; petrify; scare; shock; startle; terrify; terrorize.*

(go) from a simmer to a hard boil A moribund metaphor (SEE PAGE 19).

from A to Z A moribund metaphor (SEE PAGE 19).
1. *all during; all over; all through; throughout.*
2. *altogether; completely; entirely; fully; perfectly; quite; roundly; thoroughly; totally; unreservedly; utterly; wholly.*

from beginning to end A moribund metaphor (SEE PAGE 19).
1. *always; ceaselessly; constantly; continually; continuously; endlessly; eternally; everlastingly; evermore; forever; forevermore; frequently; interminably; nonstop; permanently; perpetually; persistently; recurrently; regularly; repeatedly; unceasingly; unremittingly.*
2. *all during; all over; all through; throughout.*
3. *altogether; completely; entirely; fully; perfectly; quite; roundly; thoroughly; totally; unreservedly; utterly; wholly.*

from (the) cradle to (the) grave A moribund metaphor (SEE PAGE 19).
1. *always; ceaselessly; constantly; continually; continuously; endlessly; eternally; everlastingly; evermore; forever; forevermore; frequently; interminably; nonstop; permanently; perpetually; persistently; recurrently; regularly; repeatedly; unceasingly; unremittingly.*
2. *all during; all over; all through; throughout.*

from dawn to (until) dusk A moribund metaphor (SEE PAGE 19). *all day; all the time; always; ceaselessly; constantly; continually; continuously; endlessly; eternally; everlastingly;*

evermore; forever; forevermore; frequently; interminably; nonstop; permanently; perpetually; persistently; recurrently; regularly; repeatedly; unceasingly; unremittingly. ■ She has to put up with this kind of stuff *from dawn to dusk.* REPLACE WITH *endlessly.*

(the) (date) from hell A moribund metaphor (SEE PAGE 19).

from hence A wretched redundancy (SEE PAGE 23). *hence.*

from pillar to post A moribund metaphor (SEE PAGE 19). ■ You can't let your convictions be shaken, or you'll jump *from pillar to post* the moment times become difficult.

from rags to riches A moribund metaphor (SEE PAGE 19).

from soup to nuts A moribund metaphor (SEE PAGE 19). *all; all things; everything.*

from start to finish A moribund metaphor (SEE PAGE 19).
1. *always; ceaselessly; constantly; continually; continuously; endlessly; eternally; everlastingly; evermore; forever; forevermore; frequently; interminably; nonstop; permanently; perpetually; persistently; recurrently; regularly; repeatedly; unceasingly; unremittingly.*
2. *all during; all over; all through; throughout.*

from stem to stern A moribund metaphor (SEE PAGE 19).
1. *all during; all over; all through;*

throughout.
2. *altogether; completely; entirely; fully; perfectly; quite; roundly; thoroughly; totally; unreservedly; utterly; wholly.*

from the bottom (depths) of (my) heart A moribund metaphor (SEE PAGE 19). *earnestly; fervently; genuinely; heartily; honestly; sincerely; unreservedly; wholeheartedly.*

from the frying pan into the fire A moribund metaphor (SEE PAGE 19).

(straight) from the horse's mouth A moribund metaphor (SEE PAGE 19).

from top to bottom A moribund metaphor (SEE PAGE 19).
1. *all during; all over; all through; throughout.*
2. *altogether; completely; entirely; fully; perfectly; quite; roundly; thoroughly; totally; unreservedly; utterly; wholly.*

from whence A wretched redundancy (SEE PAGE 23). *whence.* ■ The dolphins were judged sufficiently healthy to be taken back to the sea *from whence* they came. DELETE *from.* ■ And it all boiled over on talk radio — *from whence* it moved into the nation's high schools and junior highs and into late-night television. DELETE *from.*

(on the) front burner A moribund metaphor (SEE PAGE 19). *cardinal; chief; foremost; head; important; leading; main; paramount; predominant; primary; principal; prominent; topmost; uppermost.* ■ Preserving

Yellowstone is probably a priority for most Americans, but at the moment it's not *on anyone's front burner.* REPLACE WITH *paramount.*
■ Procter & Gamble was faced with a *front-burner* actor suffering from a mysterious ailment. REPLACE WITH *leading.*

fuel the fire of A moribund metaphor (SEE PAGE 19).
1. *fire; ignite; inflame; kindle.*
2. *galvanize; goad; incite; induce; needle; poke; prod; prompt; provoke; spur; stimulate; urge.*
3. *activate; animate; arouse; electrify; energize; enliven; excite; inspirit; invigorate; motivate; quicken; stimulate; stir; vitalize; vivify.*

full capacity A wretched redundancy (SEE PAGE 23). *capacity.*
■ Buses are running closer to *full capacity* than at any time since the strike began. DELETE *full.*

full frontal assault A moribund metaphor (SEE PAGE 19).

full of (herself) A moribund metaphor (SEE PAGE 19). *egocentric; egoistic; egotistic; egotistical; narcissistic; self-absorbed; selfish; solipsistic.*

full of beans A moribund metaphor (SEE PAGE 19).
1. *active; alive; animated; dynamic; energetic; exuberant; frisky; indefatigable; inexhaustible; invigorated; lively; peppy; spirited; sprightly; spry; tireless; unflagging; vibrant; vigorous; vivacious; zestful; zesty.*
2. *amiss; astray; deceived; deluded; erring; erroneous; fallacious; false;*

faulty; inaccurate; incorrect; in error; misguided; misinformed; mislead; mistaken; not correct; not right; wrong.

full of holes A moribund metaphor (SEE PAGE 19).
1. defective; faulty; flawed; impaired; imperfect; marred; tainted.
2. baseless; captious; casuistic; casuistical; erroneous; fallacious; false; faulty; flawed; groundless; illogical; inaccurate; incorrect; invalid; irrational; jesuitic; jesuitical; mistaken; nonsensical; non sequitur; paralogistic; senseless; sophistic; sophistical; specious; spurious; unfounded; unreasonable; unsound; untenable; untrue; unveracious; wrong.

full of hot air A moribund metaphor (SEE PAGE 19).
1. aggrandizing; blustering; boasting; bragging; coloring; crowing; elaborating; embellishing; embroidering; exaggerating; fanfaronading; gloating; hyperbolizing; magnifying; overstating; swaggering.
2. amiss; astray; deceived; deluded; erring; erroneous; fallacious; false; faulty; inaccurate; incorrect; in error; misguided; misinformed; mislead; mistaken; not correct; not right; wrong.

full of piss and vinegar A moribund metaphor (SEE PAGE 19). active; alive; animated; dynamic; energetic; hearty; indefatigable; inexhaustible; lively; peppy; spirited; sprightly; spry; tireless; unflagging; vibrant; vigorous; vivacious.

full of vim and vigor A moribund

metaphor (SEE PAGE 19). active; alive; animated; dynamic; energetic; hearty; indefatigable; inexhaustible; lively; peppy; spirited; sprightly; spry; tireless; unflagging; vibrant; vigorous; vivacious.

full plate A moribund metaphor (SEE PAGE 19). booked; busy; employed; engaged; involved; obligated; occupied.

full potential A wretched redundancy (SEE PAGE 23). potential.
■ Youngsters with talents that range from mathematical to musical are not challenged to work to their full potential. DELETE full.

(at) full speed (ahead) A moribund metaphor (SEE PAGE 19). abruptly; apace; at once; briskly; directly; expeditiously; fast; forthwith; hastily; hurriedly; immediately; instantaneously; instantly; posthaste; promptly; quickly; rapidly; rashly; right away; speedily; straightaway; swiftly; wingedly.

(at) full steam (ahead) A moribund metaphor (SEE PAGE 19). abruptly; apace; at once; briskly; directly; expeditiously; fast; forthwith; hastily; hurriedly; immediately; instantaneously; instantly; posthaste; promptly; quickly; rapidly; rashly; right away; speedily; straightaway; swiftly; wingedly.

(a) funny thing happened to me on the way to An infantile phrase (SEE PAGE 18). ■ But a funny thing happened on the way to the Memorial Plaza.

G

gain a foothold A moribund metaphor (SEE PAGE 19).

gain an advantage over A torpid term (SEE PAGE 22). *beat; conquer; crush; defeat; outdo; overcome; overpower; overwhelm; prevail; quell; rout; succeed; triumph; trounce; vanquish; win.*

gain steam A moribund metaphor (SEE PAGE 19).

game plan A moribund metaphor (SEE PAGE 19). *action; course; direction; intention; method; move; plan; policy; procedure; route; scheme; strategy.*

game, set, and match A moribund metaphor (SEE PAGE 19).

garden variety A moribund metaphor (SEE PAGE 19). *average; common; commonplace; customary; everyday; fair; mediocre; middling; normal; ordinary; passable; plain; quotidian; regular; routine; simple; standard; tolerable; typical; uneventful; unexceptional; unremarkable; usual; workaday.*

gather together A wretched redundancy (SEE PAGE 23). *gather.*
■ This summer's training provided all 1,500 youth an opportunity to *gather together* from around the country and to develop their skills and knowledge. DELETE *together.*

(I) gave (him) the best years of (my) life A plebeian sentiment (SEE PAGE 20).

gaze into a crystal ball A moribund metaphor (SEE PAGE 19). *anticipate; augur; divine; envision; forebode; forecast; foreknow; foresee; foretell; predict; prognosticate; prophesy; vaticinate.*

general consensus A wretched redundancy (SEE PAGE 23). *consensus.* ■ The *general consensus* is that house prices have hit bottom. DELETE *general.*

(the) genie is out of the bottle A moribund metaphor (SEE PAGE 19).

(as) gentle as a lamb An insipid simile (SEE PAGE 19). *affable; agreeable; amiable; amicable; compassionate; friendly; gentle; good-hearted; good-natured; humane; kind; kindhearted; kindly; personable; pleasant; tender; tolerant.*

161

gentleman A suspect superlative (SEE PAGE 22). Slipshod usage has reduced *gentleman* to a vulgarism. Common or crude people say *gentleman* when *man* would serve; though *gentleman* may sound dignified, it is actually dimwitted. Moreover, any man who doesn't, in revulsion, quiver at being called a *gentleman* is likely in jeopardy of becoming as vulgar as the word. ■ I am seeking a professional *gentleman* with diversified interests. REPLACE WITH *man*. ■ One *gentleman* told me it is a fantasy world and not to believe everything I hear. REPLACE WITH *man*. SEE ALSO *lady*.

get (our) act together An infantile phrase (SEE PAGE 18). ■ They don't have the luxury of five years to *get their act together*.

get (has) a fix on A moribund metaphor (SEE PAGE 19). *ascertain; assess; comprehend; determine; evaluate; learn; understand.*

get (has) a handle on A moribund metaphor (SEE PAGE 19).
1. *cope with; deal with.*
2. *ascertain; assess; comprehend; determine; evaluate; learn; understand.*

get a life An infantile phrase (SEE PAGE 18).

get away with murder A moribund metaphor (SEE PAGE 19).

get (my) back up A moribund metaphor (SEE PAGE 19). *acerbate; anger; annoy; bother; bristle; chafe; enrage; exasperate; gall; incense; inflame; infuriate; irk; irritate; madden; miff; pique; provoke; rile; roil; vex.*

get (his) dander up A moribund metaphor (SEE PAGE 19). *acerbate; anger; annoy; bother; bristle; chafe; enrage; exasperate; gall; incense; inflame; infuriate; irk; irritate; madden; miff; pique; provoke; rile; roil; vex.*

get down to brass tacks A moribund metaphor (SEE PAGE 19).

get (their) feet wet A moribund metaphor (SEE PAGE 19).

get (your) foot in the door A moribund metaphor (SEE PAGE 19).

get (my) goat A moribund metaphor (SEE PAGE 19). *acerbate; anger; annoy; bother; bristle; chafe; enrage; incense; inflame; infuriate; irk; irritate; madden; miff; provoke; rile; roil; vex.* ■ "In denial" is one of those politically correct terms that *gets my goat*. REPLACE WITH *infuriates me*.

get (her) hackles up A moribund metaphor (SEE PAGE 19). *acerbate; anger; annoy; bother; bristle; chafe; enrage; incense; inflame; infuriate; insult; irk; irritate; madden; miff; offend; provoke; rile; roil; vex.*

get (your) house in order A moribund metaphor (SEE PAGE 19).

get in (my) hair A moribund metaphor (SEE PAGE 19). *annoy;*

badger; bedevil; bother; chafe; distress; disturb; gall; grate; harass; harry; hassle; heckle; hector; hound; irk; irritate; nag; nettle; persecute; pester; plague; provoke; rankle; rile; roil; tease; torment; vex.

get into the act A moribund metaphor (SEE PAGE 19).

get in touch with (your) feelings A popular prescription (SEE PAGE 21). *be aware; be cognizant; be conscious; be insightful; be mindful; be perceptive; be sensitive.*

get off (my) back A moribund metaphor (SEE PAGE 19).

get (it) off (your) chest A moribund metaphor (SEE PAGE 19). *acknowledge; admit; affirm; allow; avow; concede; confess; disclose; divulge; expose; grant; own; reveal; tell; uncover; unveil.*

get off on the wrong foot A moribund metaphor (SEE PAGE 19).

get off the ground A moribund metaphor (SEE PAGE 19). *begin; commence; embark on; inaugurate; initiate; introduce; launch; originate; start.* ■ Like all true entrepreneurs, they were eager to *get* another project *off the ground*. REPLACE WITH *launch.*

get on (my) nerves A moribund metaphor (SEE PAGE 19). *annoy; badger; bedevil; bother; chafe; distress; disturb; gall; grate; harass; harry; hassle; heckle; hector; hound; irk; irritate; nag; nettle; persecute; pester; plague; provoke; rankle; rile; roil; tease; torment; vex.*

get on the stick A moribund metaphor (SEE PAGE 19). *be active; be lively; move; stir.*

get (go) on with (my) life A popular prescription (SEE PAGE 21). SEE ALSO *put (it) behind (us).*

get out of Dodge A moribund metaphor (SEE PAGE 19). *abscond; clear out; decamp; depart; desert; disappear; escape; exit; flee; fly; go; go away; leave; move on; part; pull out; quit; retire; retreat; run away; take flight; take off; vacate; vanish; withdraw.*

get (it) out of (your) system A moribund metaphor (SEE PAGE 19). *acknowledge; admit; affirm; allow; avow; concede; confess; disclose; divulge; expose; grant; own; reveal; tell; uncover; unveil.*

get the ax A moribund metaphor (SEE PAGE 19). *canned; discharged; dismissed; fired; let go; ousted; released; sacked; terminated.*

get (start) the ball rolling A moribund metaphor (SEE PAGE 19). *begin; commence; embark on; inaugurate; initiate; introduce; launch; originate; start.*

get (give) the bum's rush A moribund metaphor (SEE PAGE 19). *chuck; eject; expel; fling; throw out.*

(I) get the picture A moribund metaphor (SEE PAGE 19). *appreciate; apprehend; comprehend; discern; fathom; grasp; know; perceive; realize; recognize; see; understand.*

get the word out   A moribund metaphor (SEE PAGE 19). *advertise; announce; broadcast; disseminate; proclaim; promote; promulgate; publicize; publish; trumpet.*

(let's) get this show on the road   A moribund metaphor (SEE PAGE 19). *begin; commence; embark; inaugurate; initiate; launch; originate; start.*

get to the bottom of (this)   A moribund metaphor (SEE PAGE 19). *appreciate; apprehend; comprehend; discern; fathom; grasp; know; perceive; realize; recognize; see; understand.*

get under (my) skin   A moribund metaphor (SEE PAGE 19). *acerbate; anger; annoy; bother; bristle; chafe; disturb; exasperate; gall; grate; irk; irritate; miff; nettle; provoke; rankle; rile; roil; upset; vex.*

get-up-and-go   A moribund metaphor (SEE PAGE 19). *ambition; bounce; dash; drive; dynamism; élan; energy; enthusiasm; initiative; liveliness; motivation; spirit; verve; vigor; vim; vitalit; vivacity; zeal.*

(full of) get up and go   A moribund metaphor (SEE PAGE 19).
1. *active; alive; animated; dynamic; energetic; exuberant; frisky; indefatigable; inexhaustible; invigorated; lively; peppy; spirited; sprightly; spry; tireless; unflagging; vibrant; vigorous; vivacious; zestful; zesty.*
2. *ambitious; assiduous; busy; determined; diligent; hard-working; industrious; motivated; perseverant; persevering; persistent; sedulous.*

get up on the wrong side of the bed   A moribund metaphor (SEE PAGE 19). *bad-tempered; cantankerous; crabby; cranky; cross; disagreeable; grouchy; ill-humored; ill-natured; ill-tempered; irascible; irritable; quarrelsome; peevish; petulant; splenetic; sullen; surly; testy.*

get (her) walking papers   A moribund metaphor (SEE PAGE 19). *canned; discharged; dismissed; fired; let go; ousted; released; sacked; terminated.*

get wind of   A moribund metaphor (SEE PAGE 19). *ascertain; become aware of; discover; find out; hear about; learn.*

get (our) wires crossed   A moribund metaphor (SEE PAGE 19). *baffle; befuddle; bewilder; confound; confuse; disconcert; flummox; mix up; muddle; nonplus; perplex; puzzle.*

(it'll) get worse before it gets better   A plebeian sentiment (SEE PAGE 20). ■ Things will *get worse* at the bank *before they get better.*

gild (paint) the lily   A moribund metaphor (SEE PAGE 19). *overdo; overstate.*

give (her) a bum steer   A moribund metaphor (SEE PAGE 19). *bamboozle; befool; beguile; betray; bilk; bluff; cheat; con; deceive; defraud; delude; dupe; feint; fool; gyp; hoodwink; lead astray; misdirect; misguide; misinform; mislead; spoof; swindle; trick.*

give (her) a dose (taste) of (her) own medicine A moribund metaphor (SEE PAGE 19).

give and take An inescapable pair (SEE PAGE 18). *collaboration; cooperation; exchange; reciprocity.*

give (them) an inch and (they'll) take a mile A moribund metaphor (SEE PAGE 19).

give (them) a piece of (his) mind A moribund metaphor (SEE PAGE 19). *admonish; animadvert; berate; castigate; censure; chasten; chastise; chide; condemn; criticize; denounce; denunciate; discipline; impugn; objurgate; punish; rebuke; remonstrate; reprehend; reprimand; reproach; reprobate; reprove; revile; scold; upbraid; vituperate; warn.*

give (him) a run for (his) money A moribund metaphor (SEE PAGE 19).

give away the store A moribund metaphor (SEE PAGE 19).

give (her) a wide berth (to) A moribund metaphor (SEE PAGE 19). *avoid; bypass; circumvent; dodge; elude; evade; shun; sidestep; skirt.*

give birth (to) A moribund metaphor (SEE PAGE 19). *bring about; cause; effect; generate; give rise to; inaugurate; initiate; introduce; occasion; produce; provoke; result in.*

give credit where credit is due A popular prescription (SEE PAGE 21).

give (my) eyeteeth (right arm) for A moribund metaphor (SEE PAGE 19).

give it a rest A moribund metaphor (SEE PAGE 19).
1. *be silent; be still; hush; keep quiet; quiet; silence.*
2. *cease; close; complete; conclude; derail; desist; discontinue; end; finish; halt; quit; settle; stop; terminate.*

give it a shot (whirl) A moribund metaphor (SEE PAGE 19). *aim; attempt; endeavor; essay; exert; labor; moil; strain; strive; struggle; toil; try hard; undertake; work at.*

give it (take) (your) best shot A moribund metaphor (SEE PAGE 19). *aim; attempt; endeavor; essay; exert; labor; moil; strain; strive; struggle; toil; try hard; undertake; work at.*

given the fact that A wretched redundancy (SEE PAGE 23). *because; considering; for; in that; since; when.* ■ *Given the fact that* all kibbutz youth were inducted into the army and commingled with tens of thousands of potential mates from outside their kibbutz before they got married, the rate of 200 marriages from within the same kibbutz is far more than could be expected by chance. REPLACE WITH *Since.* ■ I'd be interested in being a guest, but I gather you can't even consider it *given the fact that* I live in Cancun. REPLACE WITH *since.* See also *because of the fact that; by virtue of the fact that; considering the fact that; in consideration of the fact that; in view of the fact that.*

(it) gives (me) something to do A plebeian sentiment (SEE PAGE 20). SEE ALSO *(it) keeps (me) busy; (it) keeps (me) out of trouble; (it's) something to do.*

give (him) the back of (my) hand A moribund metaphor (SEE PAGE 19). *abuse; affront; disdain; insult; offend; outrage; scorn; slap.*

give (her) the brush (brush-off) A moribund metaphor (SEE PAGE 19). *abuse; affront; avoid; disdain; disregard; ignore; insult; neglect; offend; outrage; overlook; rebuff; reject; scorn; shun; sidestep; slap; slight; slur; skirt; sneer; snub; spurn.*

give (him) the business A moribund metaphor (SEE PAGE 19). *admonish; animadvert; berate; castigate; censure; chasten; chastise; chide; condemn; criticize; denounce; denunciate; discipline; impugn; objurgate; punish; rebuke; remonstrate; reprehend; reprimand; reproach; reprobate; reprove; revile; scold; upbraid; vituperate; warn.*

give (him) the cold shoulder A moribund metaphor (SEE PAGE 19). *abuse; affront; avoid; disdain; disregard; ignore; insult; neglect; offend; outrage; overlook; rebuff; reject; scorn; shun; sidestep; slap; slight; slur; skirt; sneer; snub; spurn.*

give the devil his due A moribund metaphor (SEE PAGE 19).

give (him) the runaround A moribund metaphor (SEE PAGE 19). *avoid; dodge; doubletalk; equivocate;* *evade; fence; hedge; palter; prevaricate; quibble; shuffle; sidestep; tergiversate; waffle.*

give (him) the third degree A moribund metaphor (SEE PAGE 19). *catechize; cross-examine; examine; grill; inquire; interrogate; pump; question; quiz; test.*

give the thumbs down (sign) A moribund metaphor (SEE PAGE 19). *decline; deny; disallow; disapprove; forbid; nix; prohibit; proscribe; refuse; reject; rule out; say no; turn down; veto.*

give the thumbs up (sign) A moribund metaphor (SEE PAGE 19). *accredit; affirm; allow; approve; authorize; back; bless; certify; countenance; endorse; favor; permit; ratify; sanction; support.*

give up the ghost A moribund metaphor (SEE PAGE 19). *cease to exist; decease; depart; die; expire; pass away; pass on; perish.*

(a) glimmer of hope A moribund metaphor (SEE PAGE 19). *anticipation; expectancy; expectation; hope; hopefulness; optimism; possibility; promise; prospect; sanguinity.*

gloom and doom An inescapable pair (SEE PAGE 18).

go against the grain (of) A moribund metaphor (SEE PAGE 19). *challenge; contradict; defy; disobey; dispute; disregard; flout; go against; ignore; neglect; overlook; resist.*
■ Does the message *go against the*

grain of corporate philosophy? REPLACE WITH *flout*.

go ahead, make my day An infantile phrase (SEE PAGE 18).

go belly up A moribund metaphor (SEE PAGE 19). *break down; collapse; disintegrate; fail; fall short; flop; founder; miscarry; topple.* ■ All the biotech start-ups in the Bioventures portfolio would likely *go belly up* if the veterinary school is shut down. REPLACE WITH *fail*.

God is love A quack equation (SEE PAGE 21).

go downhill A moribund metaphor (SEE PAGE 19). *decay; decline; degenerate; destroy; deteriorate; disintegrate; ebb; erode; fade; fall off; languish; lessen; plummet; ruin; wane; weaken; wither; worsen.* ■ The bad news is that during the second night, everybody's performance *went downhill*. REPLACE WITH *deteriorated*.

(he) goes An infantile phrase (SEE PAGE 18). Only the adolescent or the addlebrained prefer this gruesome *goes* to *acknowledge; admit; announce; assert; asseverate; aver; avow; comment; confess; cry; declare; disclose; divulge; exclaim; mention; note; observe; proclaim; pronounce; remark; reveal; say; state; utter.* ■ They say they don't know anything, and then they *go*, "if we hear anything, we'll call you." REPLACE WITH *say*. ■ He walked into the room, and she *goes*, "Guess what?" REPLACE WITH *exclaims*. ■ I asked

what do you like about her, and he *went*, "I don't know." REPLACE WITH *confessed*. ■ And then he *goes*, "I don't want to see you any more." REPLACE WITH *announces*.

go for the gold An infantile phrase (SEE PAGE 18).

go for the gusto An infantile phrase (SEE PAGE 18).

go forward A torpid term (SEE PAGE 22). *advance; continue; develop; go on; grow; happen; improve; increase; make headway; make progress; move on; occur; proceed; progress; take place.* ■ The way in which this is drafted will allow those takeovers to *go forward*, which would allow for a greater efficiency and productivity. REPLACE WITH *proceed*. ■ This highlights perhaps the greatest risk to the economy *going forward*. REPLACE WITH *advancing*. ■ It is still our expectation that the summit will *go forward* and be productive. REPLACE WITH *occur*. SEE ALSO *a step forward; a step (forward) in the right direction; move forward; move (forward) in the right direction; proceed forward*.

going, going, gone An infantile phrase (SEE PAGE 18).

going great guns A moribund metaphor (SEE PAGE 19).

going on (19) An infantile phrase (SEE PAGE 18). ■ I'm 69 *going on 70*. ■ I've been there 5 years, *going on 6 years*.

going to hell in a handbasket A moribund metaphor (SEE PAGE 19). *corrode; crumble; decay; decline; degenerate; destroy; deteriorate; disintegrate; ebb; erode; fade; fail; fall off; fester; flag; languish; lessen; plummet; putrefy; regress; rot; ruin; stagnate; ulcerate; wane; weaken; wither; worsen.* ■ The typical reaction people seem to have is that public education is *going to hell in a handbasket.* REPLACE WITH *deteriorating.* ■ For centuries, people have been insisting that the younger generation is *going to hell in a handbasket.* REPLACE WITH *languishing.*

going (have) to live with that for the rest of my life A plebeian sentiment (SEE PAGE 20).

go into a tailspin A moribund metaphor (SEE PAGE 19).
1. *be unsuccessful; bomb; break down; collapse; fail; fall short; falter; fizzle; flop; fold; founder; mess up; miscarry; not succeed; stumble; topple.*
2. *be ailing; be unhealthy; be ill; be sick; be sickly; be unwell.*

go kicking and screaming A moribund metaphor (SEE PAGE 19). *antagonistically; defiantly; disagreeably; grudgingly; recalcitrantly; reluctantly; renitently; resistantly; resistingly; unconsentingly; unwillingly.*

golden opportunity An inescapable pair (SEE PAGE 18). ■ We have a *golden opportunity* to prevent this cycle from continuing.

(a) goldmine of (information) A moribund metaphor (SEE PAGE 19).

SEE ALSO *a barrage of.* ■ His diary is nonetheless *a goldmine of information* about earlier American gay social life.

go (run) like the wind An insipid simile (SEE PAGE 19). *abruptly; apace; at once; briskly; directly; expeditiously; fast; forthwith; hastily; hurriedly; immediately; instantaneously; instantly; posthaste; promptly; quickly; rapidly; rashly; right away; speedily; straightaway; swiftly; wingedly.*

(has) gone with the wind A moribund metaphor (SEE PAGE 19).
1. *be forgotten; dead; disappeared; dissolved; evaporated; past; vanished.* ■ I would retain some of what I read, and then it would very likely *be gone with the wind.* REPLACE WITH *vanish.*
2. *ephemeral; evanescent; fleeting; flitting; fugacious; fugitive; short-lived; transient; transitory; volatile.*

good and sufficient An inescapable pair (SEE PAGE 18). *adequate; good; satisfactory; sufficient.*

(as) good as gold An insipid simile (SEE PAGE 19). *best; excellent; exceptional; fine; finest; first-class; first-rate; good; great; optimal; optimum; superior; superlative.*

good, bad, and (or) indifferent A torpid term (SEE PAGE 22). ■ We really don't know what the effect will be; it could be *good, bad, or indifferent.*

(the) good doctor An infantile phrase (SEE PAGE 18). ■ I think everything *the good doctor* has said is hogwash.

good egg A moribund metaphor (SEE PAGE 19). *agreeable; decent; ethical; forthright; honest; just; moral; righteous; straight; trustworthy; upright; virtuous.*

(a) good man is hard to find A popular prescription (SEE PAGE 21).

(the) good news is (that) An infantile phrase (SEE PAGE 18). ■ *The good news is that* most students report that speaking gets easier as the term progresses.

(the) good old days A suspect superlative (SEE PAGE 22). *antiquity; history; the past; yesterday.* ■ We're going back to *the good old days* on gas prices.

(a) good read An infantile phrase (SEE PAGE 18). This is a hideous expression that only the very badly read — those, that is, who read merely to be entertained — could possibly verbalize. The people who use this phrase are the people who read *best-selling authors* (SEE). ■ This bookstore caters to those looking for *a good read in paperback*. REPLACE WITH *a readable paperback*. ■ While Foley's piece on football stadiums was *a good read*, it is entirely off the mark in terms of the proposed megaplex. REPLACE WITH *entertaining*. ■ It is hard to make air-conditioning repair *a good read*. REPLACE WITH *captivating*. SEE ALSO *a (must) read*.

good riddance to bad rubbish An infantile phrase (SEE PAGE 18).

good things come in small packages A popular prescription (SEE PAGE 21).

(and) (a) good time was had by all An infantile phrase (SEE PAGE 18).

go off half-cocked A moribund metaphor (SEE PAGE 19). *careless; emotional; foolhardy; hasty; headlong; heedless; impulsive; incautious; indiscreet; precipitate; rash; reckless; thoughtless; unmindful; unthinking.*

go off the deep end A moribund metaphor (SEE PAGE 19). *careless; emotional; foolhardy; hasty; headlong; heedless; impulsive; incautious; indiscreet; precipitate; rash; reckless; thoughtless; unmindful; unthinking.*

go (her) one better A moribund metaphor (SEE PAGE 19). *beat; best; better; defeat; eclipse; exceed; excel; outclass; outdo; outflank; outmaneuver; outpace; outperform; outplay; outrank; outrival; outsmart; outstrip; outthink; outwit; overcome; overpower; overshadow; prevail; rout; surpass; top; triumph; trounce; vanquish; whip; win.*

goose egg A moribund metaphor (SEE PAGE 19). *cipher; naught; zero.*

(his) goose is cooked A moribund metaphor (SEE PAGE 19).

(kill) (the) goose that lays the golden egg A moribund metaphor (SEE PAGE 19).

go overboard A moribund metaphor (SEE PAGE 19). *exaggerate; hyperbolize; overdo; overreact; overstress; overstate.*

go (head) south A moribund metaphor (SEE PAGE 19). *collapse; crash; decline; decrease; descend; dip; drop; ebb; fall; plummet; plunge; recede; regress; retire; sink; slide; slip; subside; topple; tumble.* ■ And it is possible that the market may *go south* before the shares can be offered. REPLACE WITH *fall.* ■ Obviously, any of these could cause your spirits to *go south* temporarily. REPLACE WITH *ebb.*

go the extra mile A moribund metaphor (SEE PAGE 19). ■ Average citizens who regularly *go the extra mile* to make this a better world are everywhere.

go the way of all flesh A moribund metaphor (SEE PAGE 19). *cease to exist; decease; depart; die; expire; pass away; pass on; perish.*

go the way of the dinosaur A moribund metaphor (SEE PAGE 19). *become extinct; cease to exist; disappear; vanish.*

go through the ceiling (roof) A moribund metaphor (SEE PAGE 19). *bellow; bluster; clamor; explode; fulminate; fume; holler; howl; rage; rant; rave; roar; scream; shout; storm; thunder; vociferate; yell.*

go through the mill A moribund metaphor (SEE PAGE 19).

go (shoot) through the roof A moribund metaphor (SEE PAGE 19). *ascend; balloon; billow; bulge; climb; escalate; expand; go up; grow; improve; increase; inflate; mount; multiply; rise; skyrocket; soar; surge; swell.* ■ Some people thought it was an extravagance at a time when billings aren't exactly *going through the roof.* REPLACE WITH *soaring.* ■ My quality of life has *gone through the roof* since he quit his job. REPLACE WITH *improved immeasurably.*

go to bat for A moribund metaphor (SEE PAGE 19). *abet; advance; advocate; aid; assist; back; bolster; champion; defend; espouse; fight for; further; help; support; uphold.* ■ All I want to say is that it is easier to *go to bat for* people when they recognize they're wrong. REPLACE WITH *defend.*

go toe to toe with A moribund metaphor (SEE PAGE 19). *battle; compete; contend; fight; struggle; vie.*

(we) got off on the wrong foot A moribund metaphor (SEE PAGE 19).

go to pieces A moribund metaphor (SEE PAGE 19). *decay; decline; degenerate; destroy; deteriorate; disintegrate; ebb; erode; fade; fall off; languish; lessen; ruin; wane; weaken; wither; worsen.*

go to pot A moribund metaphor (SEE PAGE 19). *decay; decline; degenerate; destroy; deteriorate; disintegrate; ebb; erode; fade; fall off; languish; lessen; ruin; wane; weaken; wither; worsen.*

go to (her) reward A moribund metaphor (SEE PAGE 19). *cease to exist; decease; depart; die; expire; pass away; pass on; perish.*

go (run) to seed A moribund metaphor (SEE PAGE 19). *decay; decline; degenerate; deteriorate; devitalize; disintegrate; ebb; erode; fade; fall off; languish; lessen; ruin; wane; weaken; wither; worsen.*

go to the dogs A moribund metaphor (SEE PAGE 19). *decay; decline; degenerate; destroy; deteriorate; disintegrate; ebb; erode; fade; fall off; languish; lessen; ruin; wane; weaken; wither; worsen.*

go up in flames A moribund metaphor (SEE PAGE 19). *annihilate; break down; crumble; demolish; destroy; deteriorate; die; disintegrate; dissolve; end; eradicate; exterminate; obliterate; pulverize; rack; ravage; raze; ruin; shatter; smash; undo; wrack; wreck.*

go up (the chimney) in smoke A moribund metaphor (SEE PAGE 19). *annihilate; break down; crumble; demolish; destroy; deteriorate; die; disappear; disintegrate; dissipate; dissolve; end; eradicate; evaporate; exterminate; fade; obliterate; pulverize; rack; ravage; raze; ruin; shatter; smash; undo; vanish; vaporize; volatilize; wrack; wreck.* ■ Everything I worked for over the last ten years is *going up in smoke*. REPLACE WITH *evaporating.*

go with the flow A moribund metaphor (SEE PAGE 19). *abide by; accede to; accept; accommodate; acquiesce; adapt to; adhere to; adjust to; agree to; assent; be agreeable; be complacent; bend; be resigned; bow; comply with; concede to; concur; conform; consent to; fit; follow; reconcile; submit; succumb; yield.* ■ We have to *go with the flow*. REPLACE WITH *acquiesce.*

(as) graceful as a swan An insipid simile (SEE PAGE 19). *agile; graceful; limber; lissome; lithe; lithesome; nimble; supple.*

grace (us) with (his) presence A torpid term. ■ Most of these essays first appeared in *The New Yorker,* which Liebling *graced with his presence* between 1935 and 1963.

(the) grass is (always) greener (on the other side of) A popular prescription (SEE PAGE 21).

(pure) gravy A moribund metaphor (SEE PAGE 19). *benefit; earnings; gain; money; proceeds; profit.*

gravy train A moribund metaphor (SEE PAGE 19).

grease (her) palm with silver A moribund metaphor (SEE PAGE 19). 1. *bribe; induce; pay; suborn.* 2. *compensate; pay; recompense; tip.*

grease the skids A moribund metaphor (SEE PAGE 19). *arrange; get ready; organize; prepare; set up.*

great A suspect superlative (SEE PAGE 22). That which is called *great* is seldom more than *good,* and that which is *good* is scarcely mentionable.

Great is also, of course, a hugely overworked word. Consider this laughable sentence: ■ When I think of their golf course, the first word that comes to mind is *great*.

Alternatives to the quotidian *great* include: *consequential; considerable; consummate; distinguished; eminent; excellent; exceptional; exemplary; exquisite; extraordinary; fine; flawless; grand; ideal; illustrious; impeccable; imposing; impressive; magnificent; marvelous; matchless; momentous; notable; noteworthy; perfect; preeminent; remarkable; select; splendid; superb; superior; superlative; supreme; transcendent; weighty; wonderful.*

(the) great American novel A suspect superlative (SEE PAGE 22).

(the) great beyond A moribund metaphor (SEE PAGE 19). *afterlife; eternity; everlastingness.*

great expectations A suspect superlative (SEE PAGE 22). Great expectations, of course, often turn out to be slight realizations.

(go) great guns A moribund metaphor (SEE PAGE 19). *abruptly; briskly; expeditiously; fast; hastily; hurriedly; posthaste; promptly; quickly; rapidly; speedily; straightaway; swiftly; wingedly.*

green around the gills A moribund metaphor (SEE PAGE 19).
1. *afflicted; ailing; diseased; ill; indisposed; infirm; not (feeling) well; sick; sickly; suffering; unhealthy; unsound; unwell; valetudinarian.*
2. *nauseated; nauseous; queasy; sick; squeamish; vomiting.*

(as) green as grass An insipid simile (SEE PAGE 19).
1. *aquamarine; emerald; green; greenish; teal; verdant; virescent.*
2. *adolescent; artless; awkward; callow; green; guileless; immature; inexperienced; inexpert; ingenuous; innocent; juvenile; naive; raw; simple; undeveloped; unfledged; unseasoned; unskilled; unskillful; unsophisticated; untaught; untrained; unworldly; young; youthful.*

green-eyed monster A moribund metaphor (SEE PAGE 19). *envy; jealousy.*

green light A moribund metaphor (SEE PAGE 19). *allowance; approval; assent; authority; authorization; blessing; consent; freedom; leave; liberty; license; permission; permit; power; sanction; warrant.* ■ The Baby Bells — which already have *the green light* to go into just about any other venture — have railed against the remaining restrictions since they were imposed. REPLACE WITH *permission.* ■ The FBI was given *the green light* by the Justice Department to continue its investigation. REPLACE WITH *authorization.* ■ Why would we be surprised when others take that message as a *green light* to lie, cheat, steal, and do whatever will benefit them? REPLACE WITH *license.* SEE ALSO *red light.*

green with envy A moribund metaphor (SEE PAGE 19). *covetous; desirous; envious; grudging; jealous; resentful.*

grim reaper A moribund metaphor (SEE PAGE 19). *death.*

grin and bear it A popular prescription (SEE PAGE 21).

grind to a halt A moribund metaphor (SEE PAGE 19). *cease; close; complete; conclude; end; finish; halt; settle; stop; terminate.* ■ Once it becomes apparent that no payment is forthcoming, construction activity can quickly *grind to a halt*. REPLACE WITH *halt*.

grist for the mill A moribund metaphor (SEE PAGE 19).

gross exaggeration An inescapable pair (SEE PAGE 18). *embellishment; exaggeration; hyperbole; overstatement.*

(get in on the) ground floor A moribund metaphor (SEE PAGE 19).

ground zero A moribund metaphor (SEE PAGE 19).

grow (spread) like a cancer An insipid simile (SEE PAGE 19). *augment; breed; duplicate; grow; increase; metastasize; multiply; mushroom; procreate; proliferate; propagate; reproduce; snowball; spread; swell.*

(doesn't) grow on trees A moribund metaphor (SEE PAGE 19). *exiguous; limited; inadequate; infrequent; meager; rare; scant; scanty; scarce; sparse; uncommon; unusual.*

gruesome twosome An infantile phrase (SEE PAGE 18).

guardedly optimistic A torpid term (SEE PAGE 22). *confident; encouraged; heartened; hopeful; optimistic; rosy; sanguine.* ■ Firefighters are *guardedly optimistic* that they have the blaze under control. DELETE *guardedly*. ■ We're *guardedly optimistic* that this synthetic compound may work. DELETE *guardedly*. SEE ALSO *cautiously optimistic*.

guardian angel A suspect superlative (SEE PAGE 22). *liberator; redeemer; rescuer; savior.*

guesstimate An infantile phrase (SEE PAGE 18). *appraisal; assessment; estimate; estimation; guess; impression; opinion.* ■ If you would like a *guesstimate* of time required for your site, we would be happy to give you one. REPLACE WITH *estimate*. ■ Yet with just a few moments of thought you can make a surprisingly good *guesstimate*. REPLACE WITH *guess*. ■ They were asked to guess what the contents were and *guesstimate* how many objects were in the envelope. REPLACE WITH *guess*.

Guesstimate is a perfectly ridiculous merger that people who are uncomfortable with using *guess* will turn to. Most of us prefer knowing to not knowing, or at least we prefer letting others believe we are knowledgeable.

Guesstimate, people reason, adds intelligence and respectability to their wild *guess,* their unsubstantiated *estimate.*

(as) guilty as sin An insipid simile (SEE PAGE 19). *at fault; blamable; blameful; blameworthy; censurable; condemnable; culpable; guilty; in error; reprehensible.*

(a) guilty conscience needs no accuser A popular prescription (SEE PAGE 21).

H

(a) hailstorm of A moribund metaphor (SEE PAGE 19). ■ Thus, President Gerald R. Ford's 1974 pardon of former President Richard M. Nixon provoked *a hailstorm of* criticism and may have contributed to Mr. Ford's defeat two years later by Jimmy Carter. SEE ALSO *a barrage of.*

hale and hearty An inescapable pair (SEE PAGE 18). *energetic; fine; fit; good; hale; healthful; healthy; hearty; robust; sound; strong; vigorous; well.*

(anyone with) half a brain A moribund metaphor (SEE PAGE 19).

half a loaf is better than none A moribund metaphor (SEE PAGE 19).

half-baked (idea) A moribund metaphor (SEE PAGE 19). *bad; blemished; defective; deficient; faulty; flawed; ill-conceived; imperfect; inadequate; incomplete; inferior; malformed; poor; unsound.*

(go at it) hammer and tongs A moribund metaphor (SEE PAGE 19). *actively; aggressively; dynamically; emphatically; energetically; fast; ferociously; fervently; fiercely; forcefully;* *frantically; frenziedly; furiously; hard; intensely; intently; mightily; passionately; powerfully; robustly; savagely; spiritedly; strenuously; strongly; vehemently; viciously; vigorously; violently; wildly; with vigor.*

handed to (her) on a silver platter A moribund metaphor (SEE PAGE 19).

hand and (in) glove A moribund metaphor (SEE PAGE 19). *amiable; amicable; attached; brotherly; chummy; close; confidential; devoted; familiar; friendly; inseparable; intimate; loving; thick.*

(goes) hand in hand A moribund metaphor (SEE PAGE 19). *closely; jointly; together.*

hand over fist A moribund metaphor (SEE PAGE 19). *apace; briskly; expeditiously; fast; hastily; hurriedly; posthaste; quickly; rapidly; speedily; swiftly; wingedly.*

(my) hands are tied A moribund metaphor (SEE PAGE 19).

(the) hand that rocks the cradle (rules the world) A popular prescription (SEE PAGE 21).

handwriting (is) on the wall A moribund metaphor (SEE PAGE 19). *divination; foreboding; forewarning; indication; omen; portent; prediction; premonition; presage; presentiment; sign; signal; warning.*

hang (hold) (on) by a thread A moribund metaphor (SEE PAGE 19). ■ The small towns in Western Massachusetts are *holding on by a thread.*

hang fire A moribund metaphor (SEE PAGE 19).
1. *be delayed; be slow.*
2. *be undecided; be unsettled.*

hang (your) hat on A moribund metaphor (SEE PAGE 19).

hang in there A moribund metaphor (SEE PAGE 19). *carry on; get along; manage; succeed.* ■ Even though profits remain down, most firms are still *hanging in there.* REPLACE WITH *succeeding.* ■ I'm *hanging in there.* REPLACE WITH *managing.*

hang on every word A moribund metaphor (SEE PAGE 19). *attend to; hark; hear; hearken; heed; listen; pay attention; pay heed.*

hang over (our) heads A moribund metaphor (SEE PAGE 19). *hang over; impend; loom; menace; overhang; overshadow; threaten; tower over.*

(these things) happen to other people, not to (me) A plebeian sentiment (SEE PAGE 20).

(as) happy as a clam (at high tide) An insipid simile (SEE PAGE 19). *blissful; blithe; buoyant; cheerful; delighted; ecstatic; elated; enraptured; euphoric; exalted; excited; exhilarated; exultant; gay; glad; gleeful; good-humored; happy; intoxicated; jolly; jovial; joyful; joyous; jubilant; merry; mirthful; overjoyed; pleased; rapturous; thrilled.*

(as) happy as a lark An insipid simile (SEE PAGE 19). *blissful; blithe; buoyant; cheerful; delighted; ecstatic; elated; enraptured; euphoric; exalted; excited; exhilarated; exultant; gay; glad; gleeful; good-humored; happy; intoxicated; jolly; jovial; joyful; joyous; jubilant; merry; mirthful; overjoyed; pleased; rapturous; thrilled.*

happy camper An infantile phrase (SEE PAGE 18). *blissful; blithe; buoyant; cheerful; delighted; ecstatic; elated; enraptured; euphoric; exalted; excited; exhilarated; exultant; gay; glad; gleeful; good-humored; happy; intoxicated; jolly; jovial; joyful; joyous; jubilant; merry; mirthful; overjoyed; pleased; rapturous; thrilled.* ■ The six families who bought in to the project, all at full price, are not *happy campers* these days. REPLACE WITH *pleased.*

(a) hard (tough) act to follow A moribund metaphor (SEE PAGE 19).

hard and fast (rule) A moribund metaphor (SEE PAGE 19). *absolute; binding; certain; defined; dogmatic; entrenched; established; exact; exacting; fast; firm; fixed; hard; immutable; inflexible; invariable; permanent; res-*

olute; rigid; set; severe; solid; steadfast; strict; stringent; unalterable; unbending; uncompromising; unyielding. ■ Events are happening too quickly in Eastern Europe to make *hard and fast* plans at this point. REPLACE WITH *firm.*

(as) hard as a rock An insipid simile (SEE PAGE 19).
1. *adamantine; firm; granitelike; hard; petrified; rock-hard; rocklike; rocky; solid; steellike; steely; stonelike; stony.*
2. *athletic; beefy; brawny; burly; firm; fit; hale; hardy; hearty; husky; manly; mighty; muscular; powerful; puissant; robust; rugged; sinewy; solid; stalwart; stout; strapping; strong; sturdy; tough; vigorous; virile; well-built.*
3. *constant; dependable; determined; faithful; fast; firm; fixed; inexorable; inflexible; loyal; obdurate; resolute; resolved; rigid; solid; stable; staunch; steadfast; steady; stern; tenacious; unflinching; unwavering; unyielding.*

(as) hard as nails An insipid simile (SEE PAGE 19).
1. *athletic; beefy; brawny; burly; firm; fit; hale; hardy; hearty; husky; manly; mighty; muscular; powerful; puissant; robust; rugged; sinewy; solid; stalwart; stout; strapping; strong; sturdy; tough; vigorous; virile; well-built.*
2. *constant; dependable; determined; faithful; fast; firm; fixed; inexorable; inflexible; loyal; obdurate; resolute; resolved; rigid; solid; stable; staunch; steadfast; steady; stern; tenacious; unflinching; unwavering; unyielding.*

(a) hard (tough) nut to crack A

moribund metaphor (SEE PAGE 19).
1. *arduous; backbreaking; burdensome; difficult; exhausting; fatiguing; hard; herculean; laborious; not easy; onerous; severe; strenuous; toilful; toilsome; tough; troublesome; trying; wearisome.*
2. *impenetrable; incomprehensible; inexplicable; inscrutable; mysterious; obscure; unexplainable; unfathomable; ungraspable; unintelligible; unknowable.*
3. *conundrum; difficulty; dilemma; enigma; mystery; nut; plight; poser; predicament; problem; puzzle; quandary; question; riddle.*

hard (rough) on the eyes A moribund metaphor (SEE PAGE 19). *coarse; homely; ill-favored; plain; ugly; unattractive; unbeautiful; uncomely; unsightly.*

hard (tough) row to hoe A moribund metaphor (SEE PAGE 19). *arduous; backbreaking; burdensome; difficult; exhausting; fatiguing; hard; herculean; laborious; not easy; onerous; severe; strenuous; toilful; toilsome; tough; troublesome; trying; wearisome.*

hard to believe A torpid term (SEE PAGE 22). *beyond belief; beyond comprehension; doubtful; dubious; farfetched; implausible; improbable; incomprehensible; inconceivable; incredible; inexplicable; questionable; remote; unbelievable; unimaginable; unlikely; unrealistic.*

hard to swallow A moribund metaphor (SEE PAGE 19). *beyond belief; beyond comprehension; doubt-*

ful; dubious; farfetched; implausible; improbable; incomprehensible; inconceivable; incredible; inexplicable; questionable; remote; unbelievable; unimaginable; unlikely; unrealistic. ■ Some innovations are just a little *hard to swallow.* REPLACE WITH *implausible.*

has a finger in every pie A moribund metaphor (SEE PAGE 19).

has (a) good head on (his) shoulders A moribund metaphor (SEE PAGE 19). *able; adroit; apt; astute; bright; brilliant; capable; clever; competent; discerning; effective; effectual; efficient; enlightened; insightful; intelligent; judicious; keen; knowledgeable; learned; logical; luminous; perceptive; perspicacious; quick; rational; reasonable; sagacious; sage; sapient; sensible; sharp; shrewd; smart; sound; understanding; wise.*

has a heart as big as all outdoors An insipid simile (SEE PAGE 19). *beneficent; benevolent; compassionate; big-hearted; generous; good-hearted; humane; kind; kind-hearted; kindly; sensitive; sympathetic; understanding.*

has a heart of gold A moribund metaphor (SEE PAGE 19). *beneficent; benevolent; compassionate; big-hearted; generous; good-hearted; good-natured; humane; kind; kind-hearted; kindly; sensitive; sympathetic; understanding.*

has a heart of stone A moribund metaphor (SEE PAGE 19). *apathetic; callous; chilly; cold; cool; detached; dispassionate; distant; emotionless; frigid; glacial; hard; hardhearted; harsh; heartless; hostile; icy; impassive; indifferent; passionless; pitiless; reserved; unconcerned; unemotional; unfeeling; unfriendly; unresponsive.*

has an effect on A wretched redundancy (SEE PAGE 23). *acts on; affects; bears on; influences; sways; works on.* ■ That's one of the problems that *has an effect on* everyone's quality of life. REPLACE WITH *affects.* SEE ALSO *effect.*

has an impact on A wretched redundancy (SEE PAGE 23). *acts on; affects; bears on; influences; sways; works on.* ■ That too *had an impact on* the jury. REPLACE WITH *swayed.* SEE ALSO *impact.*

has a swelled head A moribund metaphor (SEE PAGE 19). *arrogant; cavalier; conceited; disdainful; egocentric; egotistic; egotistical; haughty; lofty; pompous; pretentious; proud; narcissistic; self-centered; self-important; self-satisfied; supercilious; superior; vain.*

has both feet on the ground A moribund metaphor (SEE PAGE 19). *businesslike; careful; cautious; circumspect; expedient; judicious; politic; practical; pragmatic; prudent; realistic; reasonable; sensible; utilitarian.*

has (his) hands full A moribund metaphor (SEE PAGE 19). *booked; busy; employed; engaged; involved; obligated; occupied.*

has (him) in the palm of (my) hand A moribund metaphor (SEE PAGE 19). *be in charge; be in command; be in control.*

has the patience of Job A moribund metaphor (SEE PAGE 19). *accepting; accommodating; acquiescent; complacent; complaisant; compliant; cowed; deferential; docile; dutiful; easy; forbearing; gentle; humble; long-suffering; meek; mild; obedient; passive; patient; prostrate; quiet; reserved; resigned; stoical; submissive; subservient; timid; tolerant; tractable; unassuming; uncomplaining; yielding.*

has to do with A wretched redundancy (SEE PAGE 23). *concerns; deals with; is about; pertains to; regards; relates to.* ■ The most recent academy committee mission *has to do with* climate-monitoring satellites. REPLACE WITH *concerns.*

has too many irons in the fire A moribund metaphor (SEE PAGE 19). *booked; busy; employed; engaged; involved; obligated; occupied.*

has two left feet A moribund metaphor (SEE PAGE 19). *awkward; blundering; bumbling; bungling; clumsy; gawky; gauche; ham-handed; heavy-handed; inapt; inept; lubberly; lumbering; maladroit; uncoordinated; uncouth; ungainly; ungraceful; unhandy; unskillful; unwieldy.*

has (him) under (her) thumb A moribund metaphor (SEE PAGE 19). *administer; boss; command; control; dictate; direct; dominate; domineer; govern; in charge; in command; in control; manage; manipulate; master; misuse; order; overpower; oversee; predominate; prevail; reign over; rule; superintend; tyrannize; use.*

haul (rake) over the coals A moribund metaphor (SEE PAGE 19). *admonish; animadvert; berate; castigate; censure; chasten; chastise; chide; condemn; criticize; denounce; denunciate; discipline; excoriate; fulminate against; imprecate; impugn; inveigh against; objurgate; punish; rebuke; remonstrate; reprehend; reprimand; reproach; reprobate; reprove; revile; scold; swear at; upbraid; vituperate; warn.*

have a conniption (fit) A moribund metaphor (SEE PAGE 19). *bellow; bluster; clamor; explode; fulminate; fume; holler; howl; rage; rant; rave; roar; scream; shout; storm; thunder; vociferate; yell.*

have a good (nice) day (evening) A plebeian sentiment (SEE PAGE 20). We are bovine creatures who find that formulas rather than feelings suit us well enough; indeed, they suit us mightily. How pleasant it is not to have to think of a valid sentiment when a vapid one does so nicely; how effortless to rely on triteness rather than on truth.

Dimwitticisms veil our true feelings and avert our real thoughts. SEE ALSO *common courtesy.*

have a hemorrhage A moribund metaphor. *bellow; bluster; clamor;*

explode; fulminate; fume; holler; howl; rage; rant; rave; roar; scream; shout; storm; thunder; vociferate; yell.

(the) have-nots A moribund metaphor (SEE PAGE 19). *bankrupt; broke; destitute; distressed; impecunious; impoverished; indigent; insolvent; needy; penniless; poor; poverty-stricken; underprivileged.* ■ You, me, and many others can afford to pay a little more for health insurance if it gives some to the *have-nots*. REPLACE WITH *indigent*.

(the) haves A moribund metaphor (SEE PAGE 19). *affluent; comfortable; moneyed; opulent; privileged; prosperous; rich; wealthy; well-off; well-to-do.*

(you) have to learn to walk before (you) can run A popular prescription (SEE PAGE 21).

(you) have to love (yourself) before (you) can love another A popular prescription (SEE PAGE 21).

(you) have (your) whole life ahead of (you) A popular prescription (SEE PAGE 21).

(stand) head and shoulders above (the rest) A moribund metaphor (SEE PAGE 19). *abler; better; exceptional; greater; higher; more able (accomplished; adept; capable; competent; qualified; skilled; talented); outstanding; standout; superior; superlative.* ■ By now, a few names should clearly be *heads and shoulders above* all others. REPLACE WITH *better than*.

head for the hills A moribund metaphor (SEE PAGE 19). *abscond; clear out; decamp; depart; desert; disappear; escape; exit; flee; fly; go; go away; leave; move on; part; pull out; quit; retire; retreat; run away; take flight; take off; vacate; vanish; withdraw.*

head in the clouds and feet on the ground A moribund metaphor (SEE PAGE 19).

head into the home stretch A moribund metaphor (SEE PAGE 19).

head on the block A moribund metaphor (SEE PAGE 19).

head over heels A moribund metaphor (SEE PAGE 19). *altogether; ardently; completely; deeply; earnestly; entirely; fervently; fully; intensely; passionately; perfectly; quite; roundly; thoroughly; totally; unreservedly; utterly; wholly; zealously.*

head over heels in love A moribund metaphor (SEE PAGE 19). *besotted; crazed; haunted; infatuated; lovesick; mad; obsessed; possessed; smitten.*

(as) healthy as a horse An insipid simile (SEE PAGE 19). *athletic; beefy; brawny; energetic; fine; fit; good; hale; hardy; hearty; healthful; healthy; husky; lanky; lean; manly; muscular; powerful; robust; shapely; sinewy; slender; solid; sound; stalwart; strong; sturdy; thin; trim; vigorous; virile; well; well-built.*

heap dirt (scorn) on A moribund

metaphor (SEE PAGE 19). *asperse; badmouth; belittle; besmirch; bespatter; blacken; calumniate; defame; defile; denigrate; denounce; depreciate; deride; disparage; impugn; insult; libel; malign; profane; revile; scandalize; slander; slap; slur; smear; sully; taint; traduce; vilify; vitiate.*

hear by (via) the grapevine A moribund metaphor (SEE PAGE 19).

heart and soul A moribund metaphor (SEE PAGE 19).
1. *altogether; completely; entirely; fully; perfectly; quite; roundly; thoroughly; totally; unreservedly; utterly; wholly.*
2. *earnestly; fervently; genuinely; heartily; honestly; sincerely; unreservedly; wholeheartedly.*

(a) heartbeat away A moribund metaphor (SEE PAGE 19).

(his) heart is in the right place A moribund metaphor (SEE PAGE 19). *be well-intentioned.*

(you) hear what I'm saying? An ineffectual phrase (SEE PAGE 17). ■ She's the one who did it, not me. *You hear what I'm saying?* DELETE *You hear what I'm saying?* SEE ALSO *(you) know what I mean? (you) know what I'm saying; (you) know what I'm telling you? (do) you know?.*

(I) hear you An infantile phrase (SEE PAGE 18). *appreciate; apprehend; comprehend; grasp; see; understand.*

(the) heat is on A moribund metaphor (SEE PAGE 19). *be coerced; be compelled; be forced; be pressured.*

heaven on earth A moribund metaphor (SEE PAGE 19). *ambrosial; angelic; beatific; blissful; delightful; divine; enchanting; glorious; godlike; godly; heavenly; joyful; magnificent; resplendent; splendid; sublime.*

(through) hell and high water A moribund metaphor (SEE PAGE 19). *adversity; affliction; calamity; catastrophe; difficulty; distress; hardship; misadventure; misfortune; ordeal; trial; tribulation; trouble; woe.*

hell (hellbent) for leather A moribund metaphor (SEE PAGE 19). *breakneck; fast; madcap; rash; reckless; wild.* ■ Connors clearly thought that he had more to gain by pursuing his *hell-for-leather* expansion in the region.

hell has no fury like (a woman scorned) An insipid simile (SEE PAGE 19).

hell on earth A moribund metaphor (SEE PAGE 19). *chthonian; chthonic; hellish; impossible; infernal; insufferable; insupportable; intolerable; painful; plutonic; sulfurous; unbearable; uncomfortable; unendurable; unpleasant; stygian; tartarean.* ■ Being a stepmother is *hell on earth.* REPLACE WITH *hellish.* SEE ALSO *a living hell.*

hell on wheels A moribund metaphor (SEE PAGE 19).
1. *boisterous; disorderly; feral; obstreperous; rambunctious; riotous; roistering; rowdy; uncontrolled; undisciplined; unrestrained; unruly; untamed; wild.*
2. *angry; bad-tempered; bilious; can-*

tankerous; *choleric; churlish; crabby;
cranky; cross; curmudgeonly; disagreeable; dyspeptic; grouchy; gruff;
grumpy; ill-humored; ill-tempered;
irascible; irritable; mad; peevish; petulant; quarrelsome; short-tempered;
splenetic; surly; testy; vexed.*

hem and haw An inescapable pair
(SEE PAGE 18). *dally; dawdle; hesitate;
vacillate; waver.*

hemorrhage red ink A moribund
metaphor (SEE PAGE 19).

(like) (a) herd of elephants An
insipid simile (SEE PAGE 19).

(right) here and now An
inescapable pair (SEE PAGE 18). *currently; now; nowadays; presently; the
present; today.*

here's the thing An ineffectual
phrase (SEE PAGE 17). ■ *Here's the
thing,* whoever is mayor must be
able to work with the community.
DELETE *Here's the thing.* ■ *Here's the
thing,* men don't even know that
we're different. DELETE *Here's the
thing.* SEE ALSO *that's the thing; the
thing about (of) it is; the thing is.*

here, there, and everywhere A
wretched redundancy (SEE PAGE
23). *all over; everywhere; omnipresent; ubiquitous.*

here today, gone tomorrow An
infantile phrase (SEE PAGE 18). *brief;
ephemeral; evanescent; fleeting; flitting; fugacious; fugitive; impermanent; momentary; passing; short;
short-lived; temporary; transient;*

transitory; volatile.* ■ I still love it
even though nothing is as *here
today, gone tomorrow* as a job in TV.
REPLACE WITH *fleeting.* ■ In politics, issues *that are here today are
gone tomorrow.* REPLACE WITH *are
ephemeral.*

here to stay An infantile phrase
(SEE PAGE 18). *constant; deep-rooted;
enduring; entrenched; established;
everlasting; fixed; lasting; long-lived;
permanent; secure; stable; unending.*
■ They questioned whether ability
grouping is *here to stay.* REPLACE
WITH *permanent.*

hey An infantile phrase (SEE PAGE
18). ■ *Hey,* I'm hardly against men
pitching in around the house and
helping with kids, or listening to
their wives concerns (in fact as a
mother of three with another little
one on the way, I'm all for it).

Certain words do not belong
to the realm of writing, or at least
nonfiction writing: *hey* is clearly
one of them. *Hey* is exclamatory,
but only less than able writers —
however friendly they wish to
appear — would use it, in effect,
as an inverted exclamation mark
with which to capture our flagging
attention.

And as a substitute for *hello* or
hi, hey is a cheerless one. Perhaps
the best way to discourage people
from using *hey* is to respond with a
hearty *diddle, diddle?*

hide (their) heads in the sand A
moribund metaphor (SEE PAGE 19).
*brush aside; avoid; discount; disre-
gard; dodge; duck; ignore; neglect;*

omit; pass over; recoil from; shrink from; shun; shy away from; turn away from; withdraw from. ■ Even when informed of the problem, some denominations are continuing to *hide their heads in the sand.*

(neither) hide nor (or) hair A moribund metaphor (SEE PAGE 19). *nothing; sign; soupçon; trace; vestige.*

(left) high and dry An inescapable pair (SEE PAGE 18). *abandoned; alone; deserted; forgotten; helpless; left; powerless; stranded.*

high and low An inescapable pair (SEE PAGE 18). *all around; all over; all through; broadly; everyplace; everywhere; extensively; throughout; ubiquitously; universally; widely.* SEE ALSO *far and wide; left and right.*

high and mighty An inescapable pair (SEE PAGE 18). *arrogant; cavalier; conceited; condescending; contemptuous; despotic; dictatorial; disdainful; dogmatic; domineering; haughty; imperious; insolent; lofty; overbearing; overweening; patronizing; pompous; pretentious; scornful; self-important; supercilious; superior; vainglorious.*

(as) high as a kite An insipid simile (SEE PAGE 19).
1. *agitated; aroused; ebullient; effusive; enthused; elated; excitable; excited; exhilarated; expansive; impassioned; inflamed; overwrought; stimulated.*
2. *besotted; crapulous; drunk; inebriated; intoxicated; sodden; stupefied; tipsy.*

high (top) man on the totem pole A moribund metaphor (SEE PAGE 19). *administrator; boss; brass; chief; commander; director; executive; foreman; head; headman; leader; manager; master; (high) muckamuck; officer; official; overseer; president; principal; superintendent; supervisor.*

(give) high marks A moribund metaphor (SEE PAGE 19).

high on the hog A moribund metaphor (SEE PAGE 19). *extravagantly; lavishly; luxuriantly.* ■ It's the state officials who are living *high on the hog.* REPLACE WITH *extravagantly.*

high-water mark A moribund metaphor (SEE PAGE 19).

highway robbery A moribund metaphor (SEE PAGE 19).

hindsight is 20/20 A quack equation (SEE PAGE 21).

hired gun A moribund metaphor (SEE PAGE 19).
1. *assassin; killer; mercenary; murderer.*
2. *adviser; authority; consultant; counselor; expert; guru; specialist.*

hit a home run A moribund metaphor (SEE PAGE 19). *advance; fare well; flourish; prevail; progress; prosper; succeed; thrive; triumph; win.*

hit (strike; touch) a nerve A moribund metaphor (SEE PAGE 19).

hit (me) between the eyes A moribund metaphor (SEE PAGE 19). *amaze; astonish; astound; awe; dazzle; dumbfound; flabbergast; overpower; overwhelm; shock; startle; stun; stupefy; surprise.*

hit (rock) bottom A moribund metaphor (SEE PAGE 19). *bankrupt; broke; destitute; distressed; impecunious; impoverished; indigent; insolvent; penniless; poor; poverty-stricken.*

hitch (your) wagon to a star A moribund metaphor (SEE PAGE 19). *be ambitious; be determined; be motivated; be striving.*

hit (close to) home A moribund metaphor (SEE PAGE 19).

hit (me) like a ton of bricks An insipid simile (SEE PAGE 19). *amaze; astonish; astound; awe; confound; daze; dazzle; dumbfound; flabbergast; overpower; overwhelm; shock; stagger; startle; stun; stupefy; surprise.* ■ The report *hit Congress like a ton of bricks.* REPLACE WITH *overwhelmed Congress.*

hit or miss A moribund metaphor (SEE PAGE 19). *aimless; arbitrary; capricious; casual; erratic; haphazard; incidental; inconsistent; infrequent; irregular; lax; loose; occasional; odd; offhand; random; sporadic; uncontrolled; unplanned.*

hit over the head A moribund metaphor (SEE PAGE 19).

hit pay dirt A moribund metaphor (SEE PAGE 19). *flourish; get rich; prevail; prosper; succeed; thrive; triumph; win.*

hit the ceiling A moribund metaphor (SEE PAGE 19). *bellow; bluster; clamor; explode; fulminate; fume; holler; howl; rage; rant; rave; roar; scream; shout; storm; thunder; vociferate; yell.*

hit the ground running A moribund metaphor (SEE PAGE 19). ■ I get up in the morning and *hit the ground running.*

hit the hay A moribund metaphor (SEE PAGE 19). *doze; go to bed; nap; rest; retire; sleep; slumber.*

hit the jackpot A moribund metaphor (SEE PAGE 19). *flourish; get rich; prevail; prosper; succeed; thrive; triumph; win.*

hit the nail (squarely) on the head A moribund metaphor (SEE PAGE 19). *be correct; be right.*

hit the road A moribund metaphor (SEE PAGE 19). *abscond; clear out; decamp; depart; desert; disappear; escape; exit; flee; fly; go; go away; leave; move on; part; pull out; quit; retire; retreat; run away; take flight; take off; vacate; vanish; withdraw.*

hit the roof A moribund metaphor (SEE PAGE 19).
1. *be angry; be annoyed; be enraged; be exasperated; be furious; be incensed; be infuriated; be irate; be irked; be irritated; be mad; be raging; be wrathful.* ■ He *hit the roof.* REPLACE WITH *became enraged.*
2. *bellow; bluster; clamor; explode; fulminate; fume; holler; howl; rage; rant; rave; roar; scream; shout; storm; thunder; vociferate; yell.*

hit the sack A moribund metaphor (SEE PAGE 19). *doze; go to bed; nap; rest; retire; sleep; slumber.*

hit the skids A moribund metaphor (SEE PAGE 19). *decay; decline; degenerate; destroy; deteriorate; disintegrate; ebb; erode; fade; fall off; languish; lessen; ruin; wane; weaken; wither; worsen.*

hit (him) while (he's) down A moribund metaphor (SEE PAGE 19).

(as) hoarse as a crow An insipid simile (SEE PAGE 19). *grating; gravelly; gruff; guttural; harsh; hoarse; rasping; raspy; throaty.*

hoist with (his) own petard A moribund metaphor (SEE PAGE 19).

(can't) hold a candle (to) A moribund metaphor (SEE PAGE 19).
1. *compare; equal; equate; liken; match; measure up; meet; rival.* ■ Various third-party utilities are available to improve this situation, but only one of them *holds a candle to* the NetWare SALVAGE utility. REPLACE WITH *rivals.* ■ When it comes to hosting wackos, the oft-maligned Web can't *hold a candle to* AM radio. REPLACE WITH *compare to.*
2. *be inferior.*

hold a gun to A moribund metaphor (SEE PAGE 19). *coerce; command; compel; constrain; demand; dictate; force; insist; make; order; pressure; require.*

hold all the cards A moribund metaphor (SEE PAGE 19). *administer;*

boss; command; control; dictate; direct; dominate; govern; in charge; in command; in control; manage; manipulate; master; order; overpower; oversee; predominate; prevail; reign over; rule; superintend.

hold (their) feet to the fire A moribund metaphor (SEE PAGE 19). *coerce; command; compel; constrain; demand; enforce; force; goad; impel; importune; incite; induce; insist; instigate; make; oblige; press; pressure; prod; push; require; spur; urge.*
■ The task now for those senators who truly support reform is to *hold their colleagues' feet to the fire* and bring this bill up again and again. REPLACE WITH *pressure their colleagues.* ■ He campaigns by movement-building: helping candidates, running ads to promote tax cuts, and *holding congressional Republicans' feet to the fire.* REPLACE WITH *prodding congressional Republicans.*

hold (your) fire A moribund metaphor (SEE PAGE 19).
1. *be silent; be still; hush; keep quiet; quiet; silence.*
2. *be closed-mouthed; be quiet; be reticent; be silent; be speechless; be taciturn; be uncommunicative.*

hold (their) ground A moribund metaphor (SEE PAGE 19).
1. *hold fast; stand firm.*
2. *assert; command; decree; dictate; insist; order; require.*

hold (my) hand A moribund metaphor (SEE PAGE 19). *accompany; escort; guide.* ■ The intent of this text is to *hold your hand through the learning process.* REPLACE WITH *guide you.*

hold (her) head up (high) A moribund metaphor (SEE PAGE 19). *be proud; show self-respect.*

hold onto your hat A moribund metaphor (SEE PAGE 19).

hold the fort A moribund metaphor (SEE PAGE 19).
1. *defend; guard; protect.*
2. *look after.*

hold the phone A moribund metaphor (SEE PAGE 19). *be patient; hold on; pause; slow down; wait.*

hold the purse strings A moribund metaphor (SEE PAGE 19). *administer; boss; command; control; dictate; direct; dominate; govern; in charge; in command; in control; manage; manipulate; master; order; overpower; oversee; predominate; prevail; reign over; rule; superintend.*

hold (your) tongue A moribund metaphor (SEE PAGE 19).
1. *be silent; be still; hush; keep quiet; quiet; silence.*
2. *be closed-mouthed; be quiet; be reticent; be silent; be speechless; be taciturn; be uncommunicative.*

hold true A wretched redundancy (SEE PAGE 23). *hold.* ■ What *holds true* for them may not *hold true* for others. DELETE *true.*

hold water A moribund metaphor (SEE PAGE 19). *hold; is true; is valid.*

■ We have to ask if the ancient ideas of the roles of bonds still *hold water.* REPLACE WITH *hold.*

hold your horses A moribund metaphor (SEE PAGE 19). *be patient; calm down; hold on; pause; slow down; wait.*

home free A moribund metaphor (SEE PAGE 19). *guarded; protected; safe; secure; sheltered; shielded; undamaged; unharmed; unhurt; unscathed.*

home is where the heart is A popular prescription (SEE PAGE 21).

homely as a mud fence An insipid simile (SEE PAGE 19). *coarse; homely; ill-favored; plain; ugly; unattractive; unbeautiful; uncomely; unsightly.*

(down) (the) home stretch A moribund metaphor (SEE PAGE 19).

(as) honest as the day is long An insipid simile (SEE PAGE 19). *aboveboard; blunt; candid; direct; earnest; faithful; forthright; frank; genuine; honest; reliable; sincere; straightforward; trustworthy; truthful; upright; veracious; veridical.*

honest truth A wretched redundancy (SEE PAGE 23). *honesty; truth.*
■ If you want the *honest truth,* I am in love with him. REPLACE WITH *truth.*

honestly and truly An inescapable pair (SEE PAGE 18). ■ I *honestly and truly* believed he was the best I could hope for. REPLACE WITH *honestly* or *truly*.

honesty is the best policy A popular prescription (SEE PAGE 21).

(the) honeymoon is over A moribund metaphor (SEE PAGE 19).

hook, line, and sinker A moribund metaphor (SEE PAGE 19). *altogether; completely; entirely; fully; perfectly; roundly; quite; thoroughly; totally; unreservedly; utterly; wholly.*

hoot and holler An inescapable pair (SEE PAGE 18). *bay; bawl; bellow; blare; caterwaul; clamor; cry; holler; hoot; howl; roar; screak; scream; screech; shout; shriek; shrill; squawk; squeal; vociferate; wail; whoop; yell; yelp; yowl.*

hope and expect (expectation) A wretched redundancy (SEE PAGE 23). *hope; expect (expectation); trust.* ■ I *hope and expect* you'll be seeing a lot more of this. REPLACE WITH *expect* or *hope.*

hope and pray An inescapable pair (SEE PAGE 18). ■ I *hope and pray* that in future features of this sort, the *Globe* puts the emphasis where it belongs.

hope for the best A popular prescription (SEE PAGE 21). *be confident; be encouraged; be heartened; be hopeful; be optimistic; be positive; be rosy; be sanguine.*

hope for the best but expect the worst A popular prescription (SEE PAGE 21). ■ Since governments can

never know how stable the oil-exporting countries are, governments of importing countries should *hope for the best but prepare for the worst.*

(just) hope (it'll) go away A popular prescription (SEE PAGE 21).

hopeless romantic An inescapable pair (SEE PAGE 18).

hopes and dreams An inescapable pair (SEE PAGE 18).

hope springs eternal A popular prescription (SEE PAGE 21). *confident; encouraged; heartened; hopeful; optimistic; rosy; sanguine.*

hopping mad An inescapable pair (SEE PAGE 18). *agitated; alarmed; angry; annoyed; aroused; choleric; enraged; fierce; fuming; furious; incensed; inflamed; infuriated; irate; irritable; mad; maddened; raging; splenetic.*

(a) hop, skip, and a jump A moribund metaphor (SEE PAGE 19).

hornet's nest A moribund metaphor (SEE PAGE 19). *complexity; complication; difficulty; dilemma; entanglement; imbroglio; labyrinth; maze; muddle; perplexity; plight; predicament; problem; puzzle; quagmire; tangle.* ■ Senator Dodd called the jurisdictional issue a *hornet's nest* but said he was ready to tackle it. REPLACE WITH *imbroglio.*

horse of a different (another) color A moribund metaphor (SEE

PAGE 19). *aberrant; abnormal; anomalistic; anomalous; atypical; bizarre; curious; deviant; different; distinct; distinctive; eccentric; exceptional; extraordinary; fantastic; foreign; grotesque; idiosyncratic; independent; individual; individualistic; irregular; novel; odd; offbeat; original; peculiar; puzzling; quaint; queer; rare; remarkable; separate; singular; uncommon; unconventional; unexampled; unique; unnatural; unorthodox; unparalleled; unprecedented; unusual; weird.*

(the) hostess with the mostess An infantile phrase (SEE PAGE 18).

hot air A moribund metaphor (SEE PAGE 19). *aggrandizement; bluster; boasting; braggadocio; bragging; bravado; crowing; elaboration; embellishment; embroidery; exaggeration; fanfaronade; gasconade; gloating; hyperbole; overstatement; rodomontade; swaggering.*

hot and bothered An inescapable pair (SEE PAGE 18). *agitated; anxious; aroused; bothered; displeased; disquieted; disturbed; excited; flustered; perturbed; troubled; upset; worried.*

hot and heavy An inescapable pair (SEE PAGE 18). *aggressive; dynamic; emphatic; energetic; ferocious; fervent; fierce; forceful; frantic; frenzied; furious; intense; mighty; passionate; powerful; robust; savage; spirited; strenuous; strong; vehement; vicious; vigorous; violent.*

(as) hot as fire An insipid simile (SEE PAGE 19). *aflame; blazing; blistering; boiling; burning; fiery; flaming; heated; hot; ovenlike; roasting; scalding; scorching; searing; simmering; sizzling; steaming; sweltering; torrid; tropical; warm.*

(as) hot as hades (hell) An insipid simile (SEE PAGE 19). *aflame; blazing; blistering; boiling; burning; fiery; flaming; heated; hot; ovenlike; roasting; scalding; scorching; searing; simmering; sizzling; steaming; sweltering; torrid; tropical; warm.*

hot little hands A moribund metaphor (SEE PAGE 19).

hotly contested An inescapable pair (SEE PAGE 18).

hot potato A moribund metaphor (SEE PAGE 19). *card; character; eccentric; exception; original.*

hot ticket A moribund metaphor (SEE PAGE 19). *card; character; eccentric; exception; original.*

hot to trot A moribund metaphor (SEE PAGE 19).
1. *concupiscent; horny; lascivious; lecherous; lewd; libidinous; licentious; lustful; prurient.*
2. *anxious; eager; impatient; ready; willing.*

hot under the collar A moribund metaphor (SEE PAGE 19). *agitated; alarmed; angry; annoyed; aroused; choleric; enraged; fierce; fuming; furious; incensed; inflamed; infuriated; irate; irritable; mad; maddened; raging; splenetic.*

(a) house divided against itself cannot stand A popular prescription (SEE PAGE 21).

(like) (a) house of cards An insipid simile (SEE PAGE 19). *breakable; broken-down; crumbly; decrepit; dilapidated; flimsy; fragile; frangible; friable; precarious; ramshackle; rickety; shabby; shaky; tottering; unsound; unstable; unsteady; unsure; wobbly.* ■ He argued that the government's case against them is *a house of cards.* REPLACE WITH *rickety.*

how could this have happened? A plebeian sentiment (SEE PAGE 20).

how did (I) get into this? A plebeian sentiment (SEE PAGE 20).

how goes it? (how's it going? how you doing?) An ineffectual phrase (SEE PAGE 17). These phrases are uttered by the unalert and inert. *How goes it? how's it going?* and *how you doing?* are gratuitous substitutes for a gracious *hello.*

how much (do) you want to bet? An infantile phrase (SEE PAGE 18).

hue and cry An inescapable pair (SEE PAGE 18). *clamor; commotion; din; hubbub; noise; outcry; protest; racket; shout; tumult; uproar.*

huff and puff An inescapable pair (SEE PAGE 18).
1. *blow; huff; puff.*
2. *bluster; boast; brag; crow; gloat; swagger.*

huge throng A wretched redundancy (SEE PAGE 23). *throng.* ■ A *huge throng* of young people attended the concert. DELETE *huge.*

hugs and kisses An inescapable pair (SEE PAGE 18).

human nature being what it is An ineffectual phrase (SEE PAGE 17) ■ *Human nature being what it is,* most of us would rather speak our own mind than listen to what someone else says. DELETE *Human nature being what it is.* ■ *Human nature being what it is,* when people place demands on others, their initial reaction is to rebel. DELETE *Human nature being what it is.*

(my) humble abode An infantile phrase (SEE PAGE 18). ■ I recently had the opportunity to visit CMD's headquarters in Boulder, Colorado, not far from my *humble abode.* REPLACE WITH *home.*

humongous An infantile phrase (SEE PAGE 18). *big; brobdingnagian; colossal; elephantine; enormous; gargantuan; giant; gigantic; grand; great; huge; immense; large; mammoth; massive; monstrous; prodigious; stupendous; titanic; tremendous; vast.*

Not quite a misusage, *humongous* is altogether a monstrosity. And though it's not fair to say that people who use the word are monstrous as well, at some point we come to be — or at the least are known by — what we say, what we write. ■ My appetite was *humongous.* REPLACE WITH *enormous.* ■ We were up against a *humongous* insurance company. REPLACE WITH *colossal.* ■ My feeling is that there is a *humongous* gap between justice for the rich and the poor and working class. REPLACE WITH *huge.* ■ The players should recognize the exception for what it is: a *humongous* bargaining chip. REPLACE WITH *titanic.*

(as) hungry as a bear An insipid simile (SEE PAGE 19). *esurient; famished; gluttonous; greedy; hungry; insatiable; omnivorous; rapacious; ravenous; starved; starving; voracious.*

(as) hungry as a horse An insipid simile (SEE PAGE 19). *esurient; famished; gluttonous; greedy; hungry; insatiable; omnivorous; rapacious; ravenous; starved; starving; voracious.*

hunt with the hounds and run with the hares A moribund metaphor (SEE PAGE 19).

hurdle to clear A moribund metaphor (SEE PAGE 19). *bar; barrier; block; blockage; check; deterrent; difficulty; encumbrance; handicap; hindrance; hurdle; impediment; interference; obstacle; obstruction.*

hurl insults A moribund metaphor (SEE PAGE 19).

hustle and bustle An inescapable pair (SEE PAGE 18). *bustle; commotion; hustle; stir.* ■ Macau presents a restful alternative to the *hustle and bustle* of Hong Kong. REPLACE WITH *bustle* or *hustle.*

I

I am what (who) I am A quack equation (SEE PAGE 21).

I can't believe I'm telling you this A plebeian sentiment (SEE PAGE 20). SEE ALSO *I don't know why I'm telling you this.*

I can't get no satisfaction An infantile phrase (SEE PAGE 18).

icing on the cake A moribund metaphor (SEE PAGE 19). *a benefit; a bonus; a dividend; a gift; a gratuity; a lagniappe; an extra; a perk; a perquisite; a pourboire; a premium; a tip.* ■ Accreditation is still only *icing on the cake* and does not guarantee a department any rewards beyond the recognition of peers. REPLACE WITH *a perquisite.*

(an) idea whose time has come An infantile phrase (SEE PAGE 18). ■ The good-news section is *an idea whose time has come.*

idle rich An inescapable pair (SEE PAGE 18).

I don't know A plebeian sentiment (SEE PAGE 20). ■ New passion is sweet, but after you know someone for a while, it fades. *I don't know.* ■ I know who I am — I have a good sense of that — but I will never know you, or anyone else, as well. *I don't know.*

For a person to conclude his expressed thoughts and views with *I don't know* would nullify all he seemed to know if it weren't that *I don't know* is less an admission of not knowing than it is an apology for presuming to.

I don't know if (whether) I'm coming or going A moribund metaphor (SEE PAGE 19). *baffled; befuddled; bewildered; confounded; confused; disconcerted; flummoxed; mixed up; muddled; perplexed; puzzled.*

I don't know, what do you want to do? An infantile phrase (SEE PAGE 18).

I don't know why I'm telling you this A plebeian sentiment (SEE PAGE 20). SEE ALSO *I can't believe I'm telling you this.*

I (just) don't think about it A plebeian sentiment (SEE PAGE 20). SEE ALSO *you think too much.*

if and when A wretched redundancy (See page 23). *if; when.* ■ *If and when a conflict should arise, it should be taken care of as soon as possible to protect the harmonious environment.* Replace with *If* or *when.* See also *if, as, and when; when and if; when and whether; when, as, and if; whether and when.*

if, as, and when A wretched redundancy (See page 23). *if; when.* See also *if and when; when and if; when, as, and if; when and whether; whether and when.*

if at first you don't succeed (try, try again) A popular prescription (See page 21).

if it ain't broke, don't fix it A popular prescription (See page 21).

if it feels good, it can't be bad A popular prescription (See page 21).

if it isn't one thing, it's another A plebeian sentiment (See page 20). See also *it's one thing after another.*

if it's (not) meant to be, it's (not) meant to be A popular prescription (See page 21).

if it sounds too good to be true, it (probably) is A popular prescription (See page 21).

if the shoe fits (wear it) A moribund metaphor (See page 19).

if the truth be (were) known (told) An ineffectual phrase (See page 17).

if you can't beat them, join them A popular prescription (See page 21).

if you can't say something nice, don't say anything A plebeian sentiment (See page 20). See also *be nice.*

if you can't stand the heat, stay out of the kitchen A popular prescription (See page 21).

if you don't know, I'm not going to tell you An infantile phrase (See page 18).

ignorance is bliss A plebeian sentiment (See page 20).

I got to (have to) tell you (something) An ineffectual phrase (See page 17). ■ *I got to tell you,* he was the only person I could discuss my frustrations with. Delete *I got to tell you.* ■ *I've got to tell you something,* I'm so proud of you. Delete *I've got to tell you something.* ■ *I have to tell you,* the emerging country rates are up 21 percent. Delete *I have to tell you.* See also *I'll tell you (something); I'll tell you what; I'm telling you; let me tell you (something).*

I just work here A plebeian sentiment (See page 20).

I'll bet you any amount of money An infantile phrase (See page 18).

ill-gotten gains An inescapable pair (See page 18).

I'll tell you (something) An ineffectual phrase (See page 17). ■ You got off easy, *I'll tell you.* Delete *I'll tell you.* ■ *I'll tell you something,* they look like the greatest team ever. Delete *I'll tell you something.* See also *I got to (have to) tell you (something); I'll tell you what; I'm telling you; let me tell you (something).*

I'll tell you what An ineffectual phrase (See page 17). ■ *I'll tell you what,* let's pause for a commercial and then you can tell us your story. Delete *I'll tell you what.* ■ *I'll tell you what,* I'm not bitter against women, but I sure judge them quicker now. Delete *I'll tell you what.* See also *I got to (have to) tell you (something); I'll tell you (something); I'm telling you; let me tell you (something).*

I love (him) but I'm not in love with (him) A popular prescription (See page 21). The need to distinguish between loving someone and being *in* love with someone is fundamentally false. That there are different kinds of love is nothing that any discerning person has to be reminded of.

Some who make such a distinction may do so to ease their conscience, to absolve themselves for not loving someone who likely loves them and whom they surely feel gratitude or obligation to. In these instances, saying *I love (him) but I'm not in love with (him)* is simply a way of feeling good about having made someone feel bad. *Love,* like few other words, ought not to be trifled with. ■ *I love him*

but I'm not in love with him. Replace with *I love him.* See also *be nice; excuse me?.*

I'm bored (he's boring) A plebeian sentiment (See page 20). Being boring is preferable to being bored. The boring are often thoughtful and imaginative; the bored, thoughtless and unimaginative.

We would do well to shun those who whine about how bored they are or how boring another is. It's they, these bored ones, who in their eternal quest for entertainment and self-oblivion are most suited to causing trouble, courting turmoil, and coercing talk. See also *(it) keeps (me) busy.*

I mean A grammatical gimmick (See page 17). Elliptical for "what I mean to say," *I mean* is said by those who do not altogether know what they mean to say. ■ Nobody deserves to die like that. *I mean,* he didn't stand a chance. Delete *I mean.* ■ *I mean,* being in the entertainment field is not easy; *I mean,* I work hard at my job and still have performances to give. Delete *I mean.* ■ I enjoy the outdoors; *I mean,* how can you live here and not enjoy it? Delete *I mean.* ■ *I mean,* if you were in the movies or on TV, *I mean,* many more people would be interested. Delete *I mean.*

imitation is the sincerest form of flattery A popular prescription (See page 21).

I'm not perfect (you know) A plebeian sentiment (SEE PAGE 20). Even though *(I'm) a perfectionist* (SEE) is a suspect superlative (SEE PAGE 22) — meaning that people who proclaim this do not easily disabuse themselves of the notion of being perfect — *I'm not perfect (you know)* is a plebeian sentiment (SEE PAGE 20) — meaning that people who proclaim this all too easily excuse themselves for being imperfect. ■ I have some deep-seated anger. Hey, *I'm not perfect, you know.* SEE ALSO *(I'm) a perfectionist; nobody's perfect.*

I'm not stupid (you know) A plebeian sentiment (SEE PAGE 20). ■ *I'm not stupid, you know;* I'm 24 years old, and I've been around.

impact (on) (*v*) An overworked word (SEE PAGE 20). *act on; affect; bear on; influence; sway; work on.* ■ Let's look at two important trends that may *impact* the future of those languages. REPLACE WITH *influence.* ■ Everybody's district is *impacted* in a different way. REPLACE WITH *affected.* SEE ALSO *has an impact on.*

implement An overworked word (SEE PAGE 20). *accomplish; achieve; carry out; complete; execute; fulfill; realize.*

I'm sorry A plebeian sentiment (SEE PAGE 20). No simple apology, the plebeian *I'm sorry* pretends to soothe while it actually scolds. Even though it may seem like an apology — often for something that requires nothing of the sort — *I'm sorry* is said, unapologetically, in a tone of resentment.

Traditionally a woman's emotion — for women have been, more than men, reluctant to express anger, bare and unbounded — resentment more and more of late finds favor with men and women alike. ■ Nine years old is too young to be left alone, *I'm sorry.* ■ I have to disagree. *I'm sorry.* ■ I know you guys are going to blow up after I'm done talking, but *I'm sorry.* SEE ALSO *excuse me?; nice; thank you.*

I'm telling you An ineffectual phrase (SEE PAGE 17). ■ It has more twists and turns than Route 66, *I'm telling you.* DELETE *I'm telling you.* ■ *I'm telling you,* there are people who take this seriously. DELETE *I'm telling you.* SEE ALSO *I got to (have to) tell you (something); I'll tell you (something); I'll tell you what; let me tell you (something).*

in a bad mood A torpid term (SEE PAGE 22). *angry; annoyed; cheerless; cross; dejected; depressed; despondent; discouraged; dispirited; displeased; downcast; enraged; furious; gloomy; glum; grouchy; irate; irritated; mad; morose; peevish; riled; roiled; sad; testy; troubled; uneasy; unhappy; upset; vexed; worried.* SEE ALSO *negative feelings.*

in a big (major) way A torpid term (SEE PAGE 22). *acutely; a great deal; badly; consumedly; enormously;*

exceedingly; extremely; greatly; hugely; immensely; intensely; largely; mightily; prodigiously; seriously; strongly; very much. ■ He wants to meet me *in a big way*. REPLACE WITH *very much*. ■ It hurt me *in a big way*. REPLACE WITH *badly*. SEE ALSO *in the worst way*.

in a bind A moribund metaphor (SEE PAGE 19). *at risk; endangered; hard-pressed; imperiled; in a bind; in a dilemma; in a fix; in a jam; in a predicament; in a quandary; in danger; in difficulty; in jeopardy; in peril; in trouble; jeopardized.*

in (the) absence of A wretched redundancy (SEE PAGE 23). *absent; having no; lacking; minus; missing; not having; with no; without.* ■ *In the absence of* these articulated linkages, changes introduced will be difficult to monitor. REPLACE WITH *Absent*.

in a class by (itself) A moribund metaphor (SEE PAGE 19). *different; exceptional; extraordinary; incomparable; inimitable; matchless; notable; noteworthy; novel; odd; original; peculiar; peerless; remarkable; singular; special; strange; uncommon; unequaled; unexampled; unique; unmatched; unparalleled; unrivaled; unusual; without equal.*

in a delicate condition A moribund metaphor (SEE PAGE 19). *anticipating; enceinte; expectant; expecting; gravid; parturient; pregnant; with child.*

in a dog's age A moribund metaphor (SEE PAGE 19).

in advance of A wretched redundancy (SEE PAGE 23). *ahead of; before.* ■ *In advance of* introducing our guest, let me tell you why he's here. REPLACE WITH *Before*. SEE ALSO *in advance of; previous to; subsequent to*.

in a (the) family way A moribund metaphor (SEE PAGE 19). *anticipating; enceinte; expectant; expecting; gravid; parturient; pregnant; with child.*

in a (blue) funk A moribund metaphor (SEE PAGE 19). *aggrieved; blue; cheerless; dejected; demoralized; depressed; despondent; disconsolate; discouraged; disheartened; dismal; dispirited; doleful; downcast; downhearted; dreary; forlorn; funereal; gloomy; glum; grieved; low; melancholy; miserable; morose; mournful; plaintive; sad; sorrowful; unhappy; woebegone; woeful.*

in a good mood A torpid term (SEE PAGE 22). *blissful; blithe; buoyant; cheerful; cheery; content; contented; delighted; elated; excited; gay; glad; gleeful; happy; jolly; joyful; joyous; merry; pleased; sanguine; satisfied.* SEE ALSO *positive feelings*.

in a heartbeat A moribund metaphor (SEE PAGE 19). *abruptly; apace; at once; briskly; directly; expeditiously; fast; forthwith; hastily; hurriedly; immediately; instantaneously; instantly; posthaste; promptly; quickly; rapidly; rashly; right away; speedily; straightaway; swiftly; wingedly.*

in a jam A moribund metaphor (SEE PAGE 19). *at risk; endangered;*

hard-pressed; imperiled; in a bind; in a dilemma; in a fix; in a jam; in a predicament; in a quandary; in danger; in difficulty; in jeopardy; in peril; in trouble; jeopardized.

in a lather A moribund metaphor (SEE PAGE 19). *agitated; distraught; disturbed; excited; nervous; shaken; uneasy; upset.*

in a manner of speaking A wretched redundancy (SEE PAGE 23). *as it were; in a sense; in a way; so to speak.* ■ Your contractor is correct *in a manner of speaking.* REPLACE WITH *in a sense.*

in and of itself (themselves) A wretched redundancy (SEE PAGE 23). *as such; in itself (in themselves).* ■ This trend is interesting *in and of itself* but is also quite instructive. REPLACE WITH *in itself.* ■ All the benefits are worthwhile *in and of themselves,* but they have the additional benefit of translating into improved cost efficiency. REPLACE WITH *in themselves.*

in a nutshell A moribund metaphor (SEE PAGE 19). *briefly; concisely; in brief; in short; in sum; succinctly; tersely.*

in any way, shape, form, or fashion An infantile phrase (SEE PAGE 18). *at all; in any way; in some way; in the least; somehow; someway.* That anyone uses this expression, as comical as it is, is wondrous. To discerning listeners and readers, these assemblages are as rickety as they are ridiculous. ■ If students

are asked to leave the University, their return certainly should not be celebrated *in any way, shape, form, or fashion.* DELETE *in any way, shape, form, or fashion.* ■ Do you feel being on television will help you *in any way, shape, or form?* REPLACE WITH *somehow.* ■ That control is no longer there, not *in any way, shape, or form.* REPLACE WITH *at all.* ■ He wants something that doesn't resemble the landmark *in any way, shape, or fashion.* REPLACE WITH *in the least.* SEE ALSO *in every way, shape, and (or) form; in no way, shape, form, or fashion.*

in a pickle A moribund metaphor (SEE PAGE 19). *at risk; endangered; hard-pressed; imperiled; in a bind; in a dilemma; in a fix; in a jam; in a predicament; in a quandary; in danger; in difficulty; in jeopardy; in peril; in trouble; jeopardized.*

in a pig's eye A moribund metaphor (SEE PAGE 19). *at no time; by no means; hardly; in no way; never; no; not at all; not ever; not in any way; not in the least; scarcely; unlikely.*

(stuck) in a rut A moribund metaphor (SEE PAGE 19). *bogged down; caught; cornered; enmeshed; ensnared; entangled; entrapped; netted; mired; snared; stuck; trapped.*

in a (constant) state of flux A torpid term (SEE PAGE 22). *capricious; changeable; erratic; ever-changing; fluid; variable.*

in a timely fashion (manner; way) A wretched redundancy (SEE PAGE

23). *in time; promptly; quickly; rapidly; right away; shortly; soon; speedily; swiftly; timely.* ■ He believes in getting the job done *in a timely fashion* and is very committed to achieving that goal.

(off) in a world of (his) own A moribund metaphor (SEE PAGE 19). *absent; absent-minded; absorbed; abstracted; bemused; captivated; daydreaming; detached; distracted; distrait; dreamy; engrossed; enraptured; faraway; fascinated; immersed; inattentive; lost; mesmerized; oblivious; preoccupied; rapt; spellbound.*

in (her) birthday suit A moribund metaphor (SEE PAGE 19). *bare; disrobed; naked; nude; stripped; unclothed; uncovered; undressed.*

in close (near) proximity to A wretched redundancy (SEE PAGE 23). *close by; close to; in proximity; near; nearby.* ■ Cities were born out of the desire and necessity of human beings to live and work *in close proximity to* each other. REPLACE WITH *close to.* ■ In those cases, the verb will be in agreement with the subject that is *closest in proximity to* the verb. REPLACE WITH *closest to.*

in (the) clover A moribund metaphor (SEE PAGE 19). *affluent; moneyed; opulent; prosperous; rich; successful; wealthy; well-off; well-to-do.*

in cold blood A moribund metaphor (SEE PAGE 19). *deliberately; intentionally; knowingly; mindful-*

ly; *on purpose; premeditatively; willfully.*

in connection with A wretched redundancy (SEE PAGE 23). *about; as for; as to; concerning; for; in; of; on; over; regarding; respecting; to; toward; with.* ■ The police wanted to talk to him *in connection with* a fur store robbery. REPLACE WITH *about.* ■ *In connection with* the hiring incidents, this was the first time he denied any wrongdoing. REPLACE WITH *Concerning.*

in consideration of the fact that A wretched redundancy (SEE PAGE 23). *because; considering; for; in that; since.* ■ *In consideration of the fact that* we have to have something submitted by January 15, we have get to started on this. REPLACE WITH *Since.* SEE ALSO *because of the fact that; considering the fact that; by virtue of the fact that; given the fact that; in view of the fact that.*

in (my) corner A moribund metaphor (SEE PAGE 19).

incredible An overworked word (SEE PAGE 20).
1. *beyond belief; beyond comprehension; doubtful; dubious; implausible; imponderable; improbable; incomprehensible; inconceivable; inexplicable; questionable; unfathomable; unimaginable; unthinkable.*
2. *astonishing; astounding; breathtaking; extraordinary; fabulous; fantastic; marvelous; miraculous; overwhelming; prodigious; sensational; spectacular; wonderful; wondrous.*
Like the platitudinous *unbelievable*

(SEE), this word is very much over-used.

One of the hallmarks of dimwitted language is the unimaginativeness of those who use it. We would do well to try to distinguish ourselves through our speech and writing rather than rely on the words and phrases that so many others are wont to use. Those who speak as others speak, inescapably, think as others think. ■ But that someone would shoot a two-year-old child is *incredible*. REPLACE WITH *unimaginable*. ■ All these people are *incredibly* brave. REPLACE WITH *astonishingly*.

incumbent upon A torpid term (SEE PAGE 22). *binding; compelling; compulsory; essential; imperative; mandatory; necessary; obligatory; required; requisite; urgent.*

in (his) cups A moribund metaphor (SEE PAGE 19). *besotted; crapulous; drunk; inebriated; intoxicated; sodden; stupefied; tipsy.*

indebtedness A torpid term (SEE PAGE 22). *debt.*

indelible impression An inescapable pair (SEE PAGE 18).

in-depth analysis An inescapable pair (SEE PAGE 18).

indicate A torpid term (SEE PAGE 22). *Indicate* has virtually devoured every word that might be used instead of it.

More designative words include *acknowledge; admit; affirm;* *allow; announce; argue; assert; avow; bespeak; betoken; claim; confess; comment; concede; contend; declare; disclose; divulge; expose; feel; hint; hold; imply; insinuate; intimate; maintain; make known; mention; note; point out; profess; remark; reveal; say; show; signal; signify; state; suggest; tell; uncover; unveil.* ■ He *indicated* that he would be fine. REPLACE WITH *said.* ■ People have provided us with documents that *indicate* that veterans were exposed. REPLACE WITH *reveal.* ■ They have *indicated* that they do not understand the managed competition proposals and don't want to. REPLACE WITH *confessed.* ■ Last week's decision of the Federal Reserve Board *indicated* that minority-lending records will be an issue for many years to come. REPLACE WITH *signaled.*

individual(s) (*n*) A torpid term (SEE PAGE 22). *anybody; anyone; everybody; everyone; man; men; people; person; somebody; someone; those; woman; women; you.* ■ This *individual* needs to be stopped. REPLACE WITH *woman.* ■ He seemed like a friendly enough *individual.* Replace with *person.*

in due course (time) A torpid term (SEE PAGE 22). *at length; eventually; in time; ultimately; yet.*

in every way, shape, form, or fashion An infantile phrase (SEE PAGE 18). *altogether; completely; entirely; fully; quite; roundly; thoroughly; in all ways; in every way; perfectly; totally; unreservedly; utterly; wholly.* ■ For centuries, since the first African ancestors were brought here, whites have tried to imitate blacks *in every way, shape, form, or fashion* and I'm tired of it. REPLACE WITH *in all ways.* ■ He supports her *in every way, shape, and form.* REPLACE WITH *thoroughly.* SEE ALSO *in any way, shape, form, or fashion; in no way, shape, form, or fashion.*

in excess of A wretched redundancy (SEE PAGE 23). *above; better than; beyond; faster than; greater than; larger than; more than; over; stronger than.* ■ *In excess of* 10 candidates wanted to make the town of Andover both their profession and their home. REPLACE WITH *More than.* ■ Police said Mr. Howard was driving *in excess of* 90 miles per hour. REPLACE WITH *faster than.*

in extremis A foreign phrase (SEE PAGE 17). *decaying; declining; deteriorating; disintegrating; dying; ebbing; expiring; fading; failing; near death; sinking; waning.*

inextricably tied An inescapable pair (SEE PAGE 18). ■ In good times and in bad, our future and our fortunes are *inextricably tied* together.

in fine fettle A moribund metaphor (SEE PAGE 19). *energetic; fine; fit; good; hale; hardy; healthful; healthy; hearty; robust; sound; strong; vigorous; well.*

in for a rude awakening (shock) A torpid term (SEE PAGE 22). ■ The companies that still think the only ones who are going to make it are Caucasian males are *in for a rude awakening.*

in for a (pleasant) surprise A torpid term (SEE PAGE 22). ■ If she had set out to write a story about a spoiled brat, she was *in for a surprise.*

in full swing A moribund metaphor (SEE PAGE 19).

in harm's way A moribund metaphor (SEE PAGE 19). *exposed; insecure; obnoxious; unguarded; unprotected; unsafe; unsheltered; unshielded; vulnerable.*

in high gear A moribund metaphor (SEE PAGE 19). *abruptly; apace; briskly; directly; expeditiously; fast; hastily; hurriedly; immediately; instantaneously; instantly; posthaste; promptly; quickly; rapidly; rashly; speedily; swiftly; wingedly.*

in hot water A moribund metaphor (SEE PAGE 19). *at risk; endangered; hard-pressed; imperiled; in danger; in difficulty; in jeopardy; in peril; in trouble; jeopardized.*

in its (their) entirety A wretched redundancy (SEE PAGE 23). *all; complete; completely; entire; entirely; every; full; fully; roundly; whole; wholly.* ■ This would leave Wednesday, either partially or *in its entirety,* for coordination. REPLACE WITH *entirely.*

inject (new) life into A moribund metaphor (SEE PAGE 19). *animate;*

energize; enliven; inspirit; invigorate; vitalize.

in less than no time A moribund metaphor (SEE PAGE 19). *abruptly; apace; at once; briskly; directly; expeditiously; fast; forthwith; hastily; hurriedly; immediately; instantaneously; instantly; posthaste; promptly; quickly; rapidly; rashly; right away; speedily; straightaway; suddenly; swiftly; unexpectedly; wingedly.*

(keep) (us) in line A moribund metaphor (SEE PAGE 19). *acquiescent; amenable; behaving; biddable; compliant; docile; dutiful; in conformity; law abiding; obedient; pliant; submissive; tame; tractable; yielding.*

in loco parentis A foreign phrase (SEE PAGE 17).

in (our) midst A wretched redundancy (SEE PAGE 23). *amid; among.* ■ There are growing numbers of crazy people *in our midst*. REPLACE WITH *among us.*

in nature A wretched redundancy (SEE PAGE 23). ■ He said the diaries are personal *in nature*. DELETE *in nature.* ■ Laws governing freedom to protest politically obviously are political *in nature*. DELETE *in nature.*

(as) innocent as a newborn babe (child) An insipid simile (SEE PAGE 19). *artless; guileless; ingenuous; innocent; naïve; simple.*

in nothing (no time) flat A torpid term (SEE PAGE 22). *abruptly; apace;*

at once; briskly; directly; expeditiously; fast; forthwith; hastily; hurriedly; immediately; instantaneously; instantly; posthaste; promptly; quickly; rapidly; rashly; right away; speedily; straightaway; suddenly; swiftly; unexpectedly; wingedly.

in no way, shape, form, or fashion An infantile phrase (SEE PAGE 18). *at no time; by no means; in no way; never; no; not at all; not ever; not in any way; not in the least.* ■ The gas contributed *in no way, shape, or form* to the fire. REPLACE WITH *not at all.* ■ *In no way, shape, or form* did she resemble a 63-year-old woman. REPLACE WITH *In no way.* ■ *In no way, shape, form, or fashion* was there any wrongdoing or misappropriation of funds. REPLACE WITH *Never.* SEE ALSO *in any way, shape, form, or fashion; in every way, shape, and (or) form.*

in one ear and out the other A moribund metaphor (SEE PAGE 19). *forgetful; heedless; inattentive; lethean; neglectful; negligent; oblivious; remiss; thoughtless; unmindful; unthinking.*

(get) in on the ground floor A moribund metaphor (SEE PAGE 19).

in over (my) head A moribund metaphor (SEE PAGE 19).
1. *overburdened; overextended; overloaded; overwhelmed.*
2. *in arrears; in debt.*

(he's) in (his) own world A moribund metahor. *self-absorbed; self-involved; solipsistic.*

in point of fact A wretched redundancy (SEE PAGE 23). *actually; indeed; in fact; in faith; in reality; in truth; truly.* ■ *In point of fact,* we do all the wrong things, and we have for years. REPLACE WITH *In fact.* ■ *In point of fact,* Krakatoa is west of Java, but east apparently sounded better to Hollywood. REPLACE WITH *Actually.* ■ There aren't, *in point of fact,* one or two buildings; there are two exactly. DELETE *in point of fact.*

input A torpid term (SEE PAGE 22). *data; feelings; ideas; information; recommendations; suggestions; thoughts; views.* ■ We would appreciate *input* from anyone who has knowledge in the above areas. REPLACE WITH *information.* ■ Of course, discretion must be used in evaluating their *inputs* since sales reps are biased toward lowering prices and pushing volume. REPLACE WITH *suggestions.* SEE ALSO *(the) bottom line; feedback; interface; output; parameters.*

inquiring minds (want to know) An infantile phrase (SEE PAGE 18).

in (with) reference to A wretched redundancy (SEE PAGE 23). *about; as for; as to; concerning; for; in; of; on; over; regarding; respecting; to; toward; with.* ■ *With reference to* the latest attempt to forge statehood for the District of Columbia, I favor our ancestors' concept that the District ought to be an entity unto itself. REPLACE WITH *As for.*

in (with) regard to A wretched redundancy (SEE PAGE 23). *about; as for; as to; concerning; for; in; of; on; over; regarding; respecting; to; toward; with.* ■ *With regard to* the StataQuest, I am expecting the first six chapters sometime this week. REPLACE WITH *Regarding.*

in (with) respect to A wretched redundancy (SEE PAGE 23). *about; as for; as to; concerning; for; in; of; on; over; regarding; respecting; to; toward; with.* ■ Some history *with respect to* the origins and evolution of the AS/400 will then be discussed. REPLACE WITH *on.*

in seventh heaven A moribund metaphor (SEE PAGE 19). *blissful; blithe; buoyant; cheerful; delighted; ecstatic; elated; enraptured; euphoric; exalted; excited; exhilarated; exultant; gay; glad; gleeful; good-humored; happy; intoxicated; jolly; jovial; joyful; joyous; jubilant; merry; mirthful; overjoyed; pleased; rapturous; thrilled.*

in short order A torpid term (SEE PAGE 22). *abruptly; apace; at once; briskly; directly; expeditiously; fast; forthwith; hastily; hurriedly; immediately; instantaneously; instantly; posthaste; promptly; quickly; rapidly; rashly; right away; speedily; straightaway; swiftly; wingedly.*

in short supply A torpid term (SEE PAGE 22). *exiguous; inadequate; meager; rare; scant; scanty; scarce; sparse; uncommon; unusual.*

inside (and) out A moribund metaphor (SEE PAGE 19). *altogether;*

completely; entirely; fully; perfectly; quite; roundly; thoroughly; totally; unreservedly; utterly; wholly.

(an) inspiration to us all A suspect superlative (SEE PAGE 22). How inspirational could anyone be who is described with such an uninspired expression? ■ He's been *an inspiration to us all*.

in spite of the fact that A wretched redundancy (SEE PAGE 23). *although; but; even if; even though; still; though; yet.* ■ This is true *in spite of the fact that* a separate symbol has been designated for input and output operations. REPLACE WITH *even though*. SEE ALSO *despite the fact that; regardless of the fact that*.

in (within) striking distance A moribund metaphor (SEE PAGE 19).

integral part An inescapable pair (SEE PAGE 18). This is another example of one word modifying another to little or no purpose.

integrate together A wretched redundancy (SEE PAGE 23). *integrate.* ■ The cost of the transmitters can be significantly reduced if all the lasers can be *integrated together* on a single substrate. DELETE *together*.

interesting An overworked word (SEE PAGE 20). *absorbing; alluring; amusing; arresting; bewitching; captivating; charming; curious; diverting; enchanting; engaging; engrossing; entertaining; enthralling; enticing;* exciting; fascinating; gripping; intriguing; invigorating; inviting; pleasing; provocative; refreshing; riveting; spellbinding; stimulating; taking; tantalizing. Not only an overworked word (SEE PAGE 20), *interesting* is also a worsened one, for it connotes uninteresting as often as it denotes interesting. SEE ALSO *that's interesting*.

interface A torpid term (SEE PAGE 22). SEE ALSO *(the) bottom line; feedback; input; output; parameters*.

in terms of A wretched redundancy (SEE PAGE 23). This phrase is most often a plodding replacement for words like *about; as for; as to; concerning; for; in; of; on; regarding; respecting; through; with*. And with some slight thought, *in terms of* frequently can be pared from a sentence. ■ *In terms of* what women need to know about men, I have learned a lot. REPLACE WITH *Regarding*. ■ A key element *in terms of* quality health care is going to be having the best *in terms of the* education and continuing educational abilities to train the best in this country. REPLACE WITH *of*; DELETE *in terms of the*. ■ For further information, you would want to read outside sources that analyze *your competitors in terms of their products*. REPLACE WITH *your competitors' products*.

intestinal fortitude An infantile phrase (SEE PAGE 18). *boldness; bravery; courage; daring; determination; endurance; fearlessness; firmness; fortitude; grit; guts; hardihood;*

hardiness; intrepidity; mettle; nerve; perseverance; resolution; resolve; spirit; spunk; stamina; steadfastness; tenacity. ■ It takes a little luck and a lot of *intestinal fortitude* to break into a game. REPLACE WITH *daring.* ■ Voters will need *intestinal fortitude* to make it to election day. REPLACE WITH *fortitude.*

in the affirmative A wretched redundancy (SEE PAGE 23). *affirmatively; favorably; positively; yes.* ■ The answer is *in the affirmative.* REPLACE WITH *yes.*

in the altogether A moribund metaphor (SEE PAGE 19). *bare; disrobed; naked; nude; stripped; unclothed; uncovered; undressed.*

in the arms of Morpheus A moribund metaphor (SEE PAGE 19). *asleep; dozing; dreaming; napping; sleeping; slumbering; unconscious.*

in the back of (my) mind A moribund metaphor (SEE PAGE 19). *subconsciously; subliminally.* ■ I always knew, *in the back of my mind,* that something was bothering him. REPLACE WITH *subconsciously.*

(it's) in the bag A moribund metaphor (SEE PAGE 19). *assured; certain; definite; guaranteed; incontestable; incontrovertible; indisputable; indubitable; positive; secure; sure; unquestionable.*

in the ballpark of A moribund metaphor (SEE PAGE 19). *about; around; close to; more or less; near;*

nearly; or so; roughly; some. ■ Estimates put the cost of each TAO work time gained or lost *in the ballpark of* $3 million per year. REPLACE WITH *around.* SEE ALSO *in the neighborhood of; in the vicinity of.*

in the black A moribund metaphor (SEE PAGE 19). *debt-free; debtless.*

in the blink of an eye A moribund metaphor (SEE PAGE 19). *abruptly; apace; at once; briskly; directly; expeditiously; fast; forthwith; hastily; hurriedly; immediately; instantaneously; instantly; posthaste; promptly; quickly; rapidly; rashly; right away; speedily; straightaway; suddenly; swiftly; unexpectedly; wingedly.*

in the buff A moribund metaphor (SEE PAGE 19). *bare; disrobed; naked; nude; stripped; unclothed; uncovered; undressed.*

in (on) the cards A moribund metaphor (SEE PAGE 19). *certain; destined; expected; fated; foreordained; foreseeable; imminent; impending; liable; likely; possible; probable; ordained; prearranged; predestined; predetermined; predictable; sure.* ■ I think that kind of complexity is not *in the cards.* REPLACE WITH *likely.*

in the chips A moribund metaphor (SEE PAGE 19). *affluent; moneyed; opulent; prosperous; rich; wealthy; well-off; well-to-do.*

in the clear A moribund metaphor (SEE PAGE 19).
1. *absolved; acquitted; blameless; clear; excused; exonerated; faultless;*

guiltless; inculpable; innocent; irreproachable; unblamable; unblameworthy; vindicated.
2. guarded; protected; safe; secure; sheltered; shielded.
3. debt-free; debtless.

in the closet A moribund metaphor (SEE PAGE 19). clandestine; concealed; confidential; covert; hidden; private; secret; secluded; shrouded; surreptitious; undercover; unspoken; veiled.

(head) in the clouds A moribund metaphor (SEE PAGE 19). absent; absent-minded; absorbed; abstracted; bemused; captivated; daydreaming; detached; distracted; distrait; dreamy; engrossed; enraptured; faraway; fascinated; immersed; inattentive; in thought; lost; mesmerized; oblivious; preoccupied; rapt; spellbound.

in the cold light of reason A moribund metaphor (SEE PAGE 19).

(keep) in the dark A moribund metaphor (SEE PAGE 19). ignorant; incognizant; insensible; mystified; nescient; unacquainted; unadvised; unapprised; unaware; unenlightened; unfamiliar; uninformed; uninitiated; uninstructed; unintelligent; unknowing; unschooled; untaught; unversed. ■ They told me everything; I was never *kept in the dark*. REPLACE WITH *uninformed*.

in the dead of night A moribund metaphor (SEE PAGE 19).

in the depths of depression (despair) A moribund metaphor (SEE PAGE 19). aggrieved; blue; cheerless; dejected; demoralized; depressed; despondent; disconsolate; discouraged; disheartened; dismal; dispirited; doleful; downcast; downhearted; dreary; forlorn; funereal; gloomy; glum; grieved; low; melancholy; miserable; morose; mournful; plaintive; sad; sorrowful; unhappy; woebegone; woeful.

in the distant future A wretched redundancy (SEE PAGE 23). at length; eventually; finally; in the end; in time; later; one day; over the (months); over time; someday; sometime; ultimately; with time. ■ A similar agreement with Mexico could result in a true North American common market *in the distant future*. REPLACE WITH *one day*. SEE ALSO *in the immediate future; in the near future; in the not-too-distant future*.

in the doghouse A moribund metaphor (SEE PAGE 19). in disfavor; in disgrace.

in the doldrums A moribund metaphor (SEE PAGE 19).
1. dead; dormant; dull; immobile; immovable; inactive; inanimate; indolent; inert; inoperative; languid; latent; lethargic; lifeless; listless; motionless; phlegmatic; quiescent; quiet; sluggish; stagnant; static; stationary; still; stock-still; torpid; unresponsive.
2. aggrieved; blue; cheerless; dejected; demoralized; depressed; despondent; disconsolate; discouraged; disheartened; dismal; dispirited; doleful; downcast; downhearted; dreary; forlorn; funereal; gloomy; glum; grieved;

low; melancholy; miserable; morose; mournful; plaintive; sad; sorrowful; unhappy; woebegone; woeful.

in the driver's seat A moribund metaphor (SEE PAGE 19). *administer; boss; command; control; dictate; direct; dominate; govern; in charge; in command; in control; manage; manipulate; master; order; overpower; oversee; predominate; prevail; reign over; rule; superintend.* ■ Buyers are most definitely *in the driver's seat.* REPLACE WITH *in charge.* ■ Unlike traditional pension plans, which your employer controls, 401(k) plans put you *in the driver's seat.* REPLACE WITH *in control.*

(down) in the dumps A moribund metaphor (SEE PAGE 19). *aggrieved; blue; cheerless; dejected; demoralized; depressed; despondent; disconsolate; discouraged; disheartened; dismal; dispirited; doleful; downcast; downhearted; dreary; forlorn; funereal; gloomy; glum; grieved; low; melancholy; miserable; morose; mournful; plaintive; sad; sorrowful; unhappy; woebegone; woeful.*

in the event (that) A wretched redundancy (SEE PAGE 23). *if; should.* ■ *In the event* you think I am overreacting, let me call attention to the realities of the contemporary workplace. REPLACE WITH *If* or *Should.*

in the final (last) analysis A wretched redundancy (SEE PAGE 23). *in the end; ultimately.*

in the first place A wretched

redundancy (SEE PAGE 23). *first.* ■ *In the first place*, I don't want to, and *in the second place*, I can't afford to. REPLACE WITH *First; second.* SEE ALSO *in the second place.*

in the flesh A moribund metaphor (SEE PAGE 19).
1. *alive.*
2. *in person; present.*

in the heat of battle A moribund metaphor (SEE PAGE 19).

in the heat of the moment A moribund metaphor (SEE PAGE 19).

in the immediate future A wretched redundancy (SEE PAGE 23). *at once; at present; before long; currently; directly; immediately; in a (week); next (month); now; presently; quickly; shortly; soon; straightaway; this (month).* ■ I will, *in the immediate future*, contact my fellow mayor in New York and ask him to make a decision. REPLACE WITH *this week.* SEE ALSO *in the distant future; in the near future; in the not-too-distant future.*

in (on) the issue (matter; subject) of A wretched redundancy (SEE PAGE 23). *about; as for; as to; concerning; for; in; of; on; over; regarding; respecting; to; toward; with.* ■ This state used to be a leader *on the issue of* health reform. REPLACE WITH *in.* ■ *On the matter of* quality in teaching, he proposed a more symbiotic relationship between classroom time and research. REPLACE WITH *As for.*

in the know A moribund metaphor (SEE PAGE 19).
1. *able; adept; apt; capable; competent; conversant; deft; dexterous; experienced; expert; familiar; practiced; proficient; seasoned; skilled; skillful; veteran.*
2. *adroit; astute; bright; brilliant; clever; discerning; effective; effectual; efficient; enlightened; insightful; intelligent; judicious; keen; knowledgeable; learned; logical; luminous; perceptive; perspicacious; quick; rational; reasonable; sagacious; sage; sapient; sensible; sharp; shrewd; smart; sound; understanding; wise.*

(live) in the lap of luxury A moribund metaphor (SEE PAGE 19). *affluent; moneyed; opulent; prosperous; rich; wealthy; well-off; well-to-do.*

in (over) the long run (term) A wretched redundancy (SEE PAGE 23). *at length; eventually; finally; in the end; in time; later; long-term; one day; over the (months); over time; someday; sometime; ultimately; with time.* ■ *In the long run,* that may be the most important thing. REPLACE WITH *Over time.* SEE ALSO *in (over) the short run (term).*

in the market for A moribund metaphor (SEE PAGE 19). *able to afford; desire; looking for; need; ready to buy; require; seeking; want; wish for.*

in the midst of A wretched redundancy (SEE PAGE 23). *amid; among; between; encircled by; encompassed by; in; inside; in the middle of; surrounded by.* ■ The United States, *in the midst of* increasing tension over Korea, is softening its tone on China. REPLACE WITH *amid.* ■ My profound conviction is that anytime we are together, Christ is *in the midst of* us. REPLACE WITH *among.*

in the money A moribund metaphor (SEE PAGE 19). *affluent; moneyed; opulent; prosperous; rich; wealthy; well-off; well-to-do.*

in the near future A wretched redundancy (SEE PAGE 23). *before long; directly; eventually; in time; later; one day; presently; quickly; shortly; sometime; soon.* ■ I'm looking forward to the possibility that you might review my work *in the near future.* REPLACE WITH *soon.* SEE ALSO *in the distant future; in the immediate future; in the not-too-distant future.*

in the neighborhood of A wretched redundancy (SEE PAGE 23). *about; around; close to; more or less; near; nearly; or so; roughly; some.* ■ The rebels may have killed *in the neighborhood of* ten people. REPLACE WITH *close to.* SEE ALSO *in the ballpark of; in the vicinity of.*

in the not-too-distant future A wretched redundancy (SEE PAGE 23). *before long; directly; eventually; in time; later; one day; presently; quickly; shortly; sometime; soon.* ■ *In the not-too-distant future,* Americans will have the telephone equivalent of a superhighway to every home and business. REPLACE WITH *Before long.* SEE

ALSO *in the distant future; in the immediate future; in the near future.*

in the not-too-distant past A wretched redundancy (SEE PAGE 23). *before; earlier; formerly; not long ago; once; recently.* ■ *In the not-too-distant past,* women were expected to be home, be nice, be sexy, and be quiet. REPLACE WITH *Not long ago.* SEE ALSO *in the past; in the recent past.*

in the offing A moribund metaphor (SEE PAGE 19). *approaching; at hand; close; coming; expected; forthcoming; imminent; impending; looming; near; nearby.*

in the past A wretched redundancy (SEE PAGE 23). ■ I'm just saying what we did do *in the past.* DELETE *in the past.* ■ We can remember *in the past* when we sometimes had two or three representatives. DELETE *in the past.* SEE ALSO *in the not-too-distant past; in the recent past.*

in the picture A moribund metaphor (SEE PAGE 19). SEE ALSO *not in the picture.*

in the pink A moribund metaphor (SEE PAGE 19). *energetic; fine; fit; good; hale; hardy; healthful; healthy; hearty; robust; sound; strong; vigorous; well.*

in the pipeline A moribund metaphor (SEE PAGE 19).

in the process of -ing A wretched redundancy (SEE PAGE 23). Even though *in the process of* seems to add significance to what is being said — and to who is saying it — it adds nothing, and may even subtract from both. ■ The hurricane is *in the process of* making a slow turn to the northeast. DELETE *in the process of.* ■ I'm *in the process of* going on a lot of interviews. DELETE *in the process of.* ■ The office is still *in the process of* collecting facts. DELETE *in the process of.*

in (within) the realm of possibility A wretched redundancy (SEE PAGE 23). *believable; conceivable; conjecturable; doable; feasible; imaginable; likely; plausible; possible; practicable; supposable; thinkable; workable.* ■ Appointment of a "civilian" generalist public administrator possessing some public safety background is also *within the realm of possibility.* REPLACE WITH *possible.* ■ I'm afraid it is *within the realm of possibility* that that many warheads may be missing. REPLACE WITH *conceivable.*

in the recent past A wretched redundancy (SEE PAGE 23). *before; earlier; formerly; lately; not long ago; of late; once; recent; recently.* ■ *In the recent past,* such performers were on the fringes of American culture. REPLACE WITH *Recently.* SEE ALSO *in the not-too-distant past; in the past.*

in the red A moribund metaphor (SEE PAGE 19). *in arrears; in debt.*

in the right direction A torpid term (SEE PAGE 22). ■ Furthermore, when onerous regulations are brought to the attention of senior officials, the government has taken steps *in the right direction.* REPLACE WITH *to make them less unwieldy.*

in the right place at the right time An infantile phrase (SEE PAGE 18). SEE ALSO *in the wrong place at the wrong time.*

in the saddle A moribund metaphor (SEE PAGE 19). *administer; boss; command; control; dictate; direct; dominate; govern; in charge; in command; in control; manage; manipulate; master; order; overpower; oversee; predominate; prevail; reign over; rule; superintend.*

in the same boat A moribund metaphor (SEE PAGE 19).

in the second place A wretched redundancy (SEE PAGE 23). *second.* ∎ *In the second place,* I sincerely believe that the merger has given it another chance to become the quality institution these students deserve. REPLACE WITH *Second.* SEE ALSO *in the first place.*

in (over) the short run (term) A wretched redundancy (SEE PAGE 23). *at present; before long; currently; directly; eventually; in time; later; next (month); now; one day; presently; quickly; shortly; short-term; sometime; soon; this (month).* ∎ I hope we're able to do something about this *in the short term.* REPLACE WITH *soon.* SEE ALSO *in (over) the long run (term).*

in the soup A moribund meta-

phor (SEE PAGE 19). *at risk; endangered; hard-pressed; imperiled; in a bind; in a dilemma; in a fix; in a jam; in a predicament; in a quandary; in danger; in difficulty; in jeopardy; in peril; in trouble; jeopardized.*

in the spotlight A moribund metaphor (SEE PAGE 19).

in the swim A moribund metaphor (SEE PAGE 19). *absorbed; active; busy; employed; engaged; engrossed; immersed; involved; occupied; preoccupied; wrapped up in.*

in the swing of things A moribund metaphor (SEE PAGE 19). *in step; in sync; in tune.*

in the thick of (it) A moribund metaphor (SEE PAGE 19).
1. *amid; among; encircled; encompassed; in the middle; surrounded.*
2. *absorbed; active; busy; employed; engaged; engrossed; immersed; involved; occupied; preoccupied; wrapped up in.*

in the trenches A moribund metaphor (SEE PAGE 19).

in the twinkling (wink) of an eye A moribund metaphor (SEE PAGE 19). *abruptly; apace; at once; briskly; directly; expeditiously; fast; forthwith; hastily; hurriedly; immediately; instantaneously; instantly; posthaste; promptly; quickly; rapidly; rashly; right away; speedily; straightaway; suddenly; swiftly; unexpectedly; wingedly.*

in the vicinity of A wretched redundancy (SEE PAGE 23). *about;*

around; close to; more or less; near; nearly; or so; roughly; some. ■ The final phase prohibits smoking anywhere *in the vicinity of* the main building's entrance. REPLACE WITH *near.* ■ The public puts its approval of Clinton's conduct *in the vicinity of* 70 percent. REPLACE WITH *around.* SEE ALSO *in the ballpark of; in the neighborhood of.*

in the wake of A moribund metaphor (SEE PAGE 19). *after; behind; ensuing; following; succeeding.* SEE ALSO *(hot) on the heels of; reach epidemic proportions.*

in the wastebasket A moribund metaphor (SEE PAGE 19). *abandoned; discarded; dismissed; jettisoned; rejected; repudiated; thrown out; tossed out.*

in the way of A wretched redundancy (SEE PAGE 23). ■ They don't think they'll meet much *in the way of* resistance. DELETE *in the way of.* ■ The result is a staggering investment in foreign-oriented training with little *in the way of* return on investment. DELETE *in the way of.* ■ They didn't have much *in the way of* money. DELETE *in the way of.* ■ The result is that this disorganized interview usually provides little *in the way of* valuable information. DELETE *in the way of.*

in the worst (possible) way A torpid term (SEE PAGE 22). *acutely; a great deal; badly; consumedly; exceedingly; extremely; greatly; hugely; immensely; intensely; mightily; prodigiously; seriously; very much.* ■ The Eagles want to win *in the worst way.* REPLACE WITH *very much.* SEE ALSO *in a big way.*

in the wrong place at the wrong time An infantile phrase (SEE PAGE 18). An ascription of meaningfulness for those who unhappily speak it, it is an accedence to meaninglessness for those who sadly hear it. Along with *in the right place at the right time* (SEE), this phrase is evidence of what reason has been reduced to. ■ That little girl was just *in the wrong place at the wrong time.*

in this day and age A moribund metaphor (SEE PAGE 19). *at present; currently; now; presently; these days; today.* ■ *In this day and age,* we need to train medical students to see beyond the front door of the hospital and to see the broader issues. REPLACE WITH *Today.*

in (their) time of need A torpid term (SEE PAGE 22). ■ The ultimate beneficiaries are those who turn to the Clinic *in their time of need.*

in two shakes (of a lamb's tail) A moribund metaphor (SEE PAGE 19). *abruptly; apace; at once; briskly; directly; expeditiously; fast; forthwith; hastily; hurriedly; immediately; instantaneously; instantly; posthaste; promptly; quickly; rapidly; rashly; right away; speedily; straightaway; suddenly; swiftly; unexpectedly; wingedly.*

in view of the fact that A wretched redundancy (SEE PAGE

23). *because; considering; for; in that; since.* ■ *In view of the fact that* you couldn't pay your bills, you became a prostitute? REPLACE WITH *Because.* SEE ALSO *because of the fact that; considering the fact that; by virtue of the fact that; given the fact that; in consideration of the fact that.*

(a lot of) irons in the fire A moribund metaphor (SEE PAGE 19).
1. *assignments; chores; duties; involvements; jobs; projects; responsibilities; tasks.*
2. *possibilities; potentialities; prospects.*

I shall return An infantile phrase (SEE PAGE 18).

(money) isn't everything A popular prescription (SEE PAGE 21). ■ Price is important, but *price isn't everything.*

it doesn't take (you don't have to be) a rocket scientist (an Einstein; a PhD) to (know) An infantile phrase (SEE PAGE 18). We can be reasonably certain that the people who use this expression are not rocket scientists, not Einsteins, not PhDs. We can be less certain that the people who use this phrase are not dull-witted, not obtuse, not brainless. ■ *It doesn't take a rocket scientist to* see that a brutal police attack on a peaceful march is unacceptable and outrageous. ■ *It doesn't take a rocket scientist to* understand that high standards and a quality education should rank over diversity. ■ *It doesn't take an Einstein to* know that when kids

see Mark McGwire they're going to head to the mall and buy the supplements. ■ *It doesn't take a rocket scientist to* figure out what's going on here. ■ *It doesn't take a PhD to* realize that the problem with the lagoon is what it contains — trash and polluted water. SEE ALSO *alive and kicking.*

it felt (seemed) like a lifetime An insipid simile (SEE PAGE 19). SEE ALSO *it felt (seemed) like an eternity.*

it felt (seemed) like an eternity An insipid simile (SEE PAGE 19). ■ Although it took 10 hours to convince the man to come down, *it felt like an eternity.* SEE ALSO *it felt (seemed) like a lifetime.*

it has been brought to (my) attention An ineffectual phrase (SEE PAGE 17). ■ *It has been brought to my attention* that we have no record of your order. REPLACE WITH *I have been told.* SEE ALSO *it has come to (my) attention.*

it has come to (my) attention An ineffectual phrase (SEE PAGE 17). ■ *It has come to our attention* that the number 3 is very popular. REPLACE WITH *We have learned.* ■ *It has come to my attention that* your deposit was received too late to be disbursed to your creditors this month. DELETE *It has come to my attention that.* SEE ALSO *it has been brought to (my) attention.*

it is important to note (that) An ineffectual phrase (SEE PAGE 17). Attachments like *it is important to* *note (that)* and *it is interesting to note (that)* suggest that whatever follows them is probably not so important or interesting. Only people who mistrust the import or interest of their own statements use phrases like these — clear signals that their meaning is likely without merit, their message likely without allure. ■ *It is important to note that* you can change these settings for any document. DELETE *It is important to note that.* SEE ALSO *it is interesting to note (that); it is significant to note (that).*

it is important to realize (that) An ineffectual phrase (SEE PAGE 17). ■ *It is important to realize that* analogical reasoning is used to explain and clarify, whereas causal reasoning is used to prove. DELETE *It is important to realize that.*

it is important to remember (that) An ineffectual phrase (SEE PAGE 17). ■ *It is important to remember that* all three phases are important to your success. DELETE *It is important to remember that.*

it is important to understand (that) An ineffectual phrase (SEE PAGE 17). ■ *It is important to understand that* turning the grid lines on and off changes only the display on the monitor and not the printout. DELETE *It is important to understand that.* SEE ALSO *you have to understand (that).*

it is interesting to note (that) An ineffectual phrase (SEE PAGE 17).

■ *It is interesting to note that* although the sex hormone makes men more subject to baldness than women, it is more acceptable for women to wear wigs. DELETE *It is interesting to note that.* ■ *It is interesting to note that* in America bylines were largely an outcome of false reporting in another war, the Civil War. DELETE *It is interesting to note that.* SEE ALSO *it is important to note (that); it is significant to note (that).*

(so) ... it isn't (even) funny An infantile phrase (SEE PAGE 18). ■ We've got so much overcapacity in the securities business *it isn't funny.* ■ I'm so sick of her *it isn't funny.*

it isn't over till it's over A popular prescription (SEE PAGE 21).

it is significant to note (that) An ineffectual phrase (SEE PAGE 17). ■ *It is significant to note that* the original database has not been altered. DELETE *It is significant to note that.* SEE ALSO *it is important to note (that); it is interesting to note (that).*

it is what it is A quack equation (SEE PAGE 21).

it is worth noting (that) An ineffectual phrase (SEE PAGE 17). ■ *It is worth noting that* he regarded her as "one of the finest writers of fiction." DELETE *It is worth noting that.*

it just happened An infantile phrase (SEE PAGE 18). As an explanation for how circumstances or incidents unfold, none is more puerile. And though we might excuse children such a sentiment, it is rarely they who express it.

It just happened is a phrase used by those too slothful or too fearful to know what has happened. ■ It wasn't something I planned; *it just happened.* ■ What can I say? *It just happened.* SEE ALSO *because (that's why); whatever happens happens.*

it makes you (stop and) think A plebeian sentiment (SEE PAGE 20).

it must (should) be mentioned (that) An ineffectual phrase (SEE PAGE 17). ■ *It should be mentioned that* hiperspace is used by authorized programs only. DELETE *It should be mentioned that.*

it must (should) be noted (that) An ineffectual phrase (SEE PAGE 17). ■ *It should be noted that* not all parents require an extensive interview. DELETE *It should be noted that.* ■ In terms of who conducts investigations, *it should be noted that* patrol personnel also may be used as investigators. DELETE *it should be noted that.*

it must (should) be pointed out (that) An ineffectual phrase (SEE PAGE 17). ■ *It should be pointed out that* when you send this type of letter you must follow through with the filing in the court, or it can be looked on as a threat. DELETE *It should be pointed out that.*

it must (should) be realized (that) An ineffectual phrase (SEE PAGE 17). ■ *It should be realized that* uncoupling is complete when the partners have defined themselves and are defined by others as separate and independent of each other. DELETE *It should be realized that.*

it must (should) be understood (that) An ineffectual phrase (SEE PAGE 17). ■ *It should be understood that* a quitting concern assumption would be clearly disclosed on the financial statement. DELETE *It should be understood that.*

it never ends A plebeian sentiment (SEE PAGE 20).

it never rains, but it pours A moribund metaphor (SEE PAGE 19).

I told you (so) An infantile phrase (SEE PAGE 18).

it's a bird, it's a plane, (it's Superman) An infantile phrase (SEE PAGE 18).

it's a dirty job, but someone's got to do it A popular prescription (SEE PAGE 21).

it's a dream come true A moribund metaphor (SEE PAGE 19). ■ To be mentioned in the same sentence as Bette Davis — *it's a dream come true.*

it's a free country An infantile phrase (SEE PAGE 18). This expression is one that only fettered thinkers could possibly use. One of the difficulties with dimwitticisms is that, because they are so familiar, people will most often use them thoughtlessly. Manacled as people are to these well-worn phrases, original thoughts and fresh words are often unreachable. ■ If owners of eating establishments want to allow smoking, let them do so — *it's a free country*.

it's a jungle (out there) A moribund metaphor (SEE PAGE 19).

it's all Greek to me An infantile phrase (SEE PAGE 18). *abstract; abstruse; ambiguous; arcane; blurred; blurry; cloudy; confusing; cryptic; deep; dim; esoteric; impenetrable; inaccessible; incoherent; incomprehensible; indecipherable; indistinct; muddy; murky; nebulous; obscure; puzzling; recondite; unclear; unfathomable; unintelligible; vague.*

it's a long story A torpid term (SEE PAGE 22). *It's a long story* — cipher for *I don't want to tell you* — is a mannerly expression that we use to thwart the interest of a person in whom we are not much interested. SEE ALSO *that's for me to know and you to find out*.

it's always darkest just before dawn A popular prescription (SEE PAGE 21).

it's always something A plebeian sentiment (SEE PAGE 20).

it's an art A suspect superlative (SEE PAGE 22). ■ Parallel parking is not easy; *it's an art*. ■ Creating a seamless event involves skill and experience; *it's an art*.

it's a nice place to visit but I wouldn't want to live there A popular prescription (SEE PAGE 21).

it's a two-way street A moribund metaphor (SEE PAGE 19).

it's a whole different ballgame A moribund metaphor (SEE PAGE 19).

it's better than nothing A popular prescription (SEE PAGE 21).

it's better to have loved and lost than never to have loved at all A popular prescription (SEE PAGE 21).

it's like a death in the family An insipid simile (SEE PAGE 19).

it's like losing a member of the family An insipid simile (SEE PAGE 19).

it's more fun than a barrel of monkeys A moribund metaphor (SEE PAGE 19). *amusing; comical; entertaining; funny; hilarious; humorous; hysterical; riotous; risible; side-splitting.*

it's not over till (until) it's over A quack equation (SEE PAGE 21).

it's not over till (until) the fat lady sings An infantile phrase (SEE PAGE 18).

it's (been) one of those days A plebeian sentiment (SEE PAGE 20).

it's one thing after another A plebeian sentiment (SEE PAGE 20). SEE ALSO *if it isn't one thing, it's another.*

it stands to reason (that) An ineffectual phrase (SEE PAGE 17).

it's what's inside that counts A popular prescription (SEE PAGE 21).

it takes all kinds A popular prescription (SEE PAGE 21).

it takes one to know one An infantile phrase (SEE PAGE 18).

it takes two A popular prescription (SEE PAGE 21).

it takes two to tango A popular prescription (SEE PAGE 21).

it was a dark and stormy night An infantile phrase (SEE PAGE 18).

it will all come out in the wash A moribund metaphor (SEE PAGE 19).

it works both ways A popular prescription (SEE PAGE 21).

J

(Dr.) Jekyll-(Mr.) Hyde (personality) A moribund metaphor (SEE PAGE 19). *capricious; changeable; erratic; fickle; fitful; flighty; fluctuating; haphazard; inconsistent; inconstant; intermittent; irregular; mercurial; occasional; random; sometime; spasmodic; sporadic; unpredictable; unsettled; unstable; unsteady; vacillating; volatile; wavering; wayward.*

je ne sais quoi A foreign phrase (SEE PAGE 17).

John Hancock A moribund metaphor (SEE PAGE 19). *signature.*

Johnny-come-lately A moribund metaphor (SEE PAGE 19). *climber; latecomer; newcomer; parvenu; upstart.*

joie de vivre A foreign phrase (SEE PAGE 17).

join forces A moribund metaphor (SEE PAGE 19). *ally; collaborate; comply; concur; conspire; cooperate; join; unite; work together.*

join together A wretched redundancy (SEE PAGE 23). *join.* ■ ASA *joins* a powerful job scheduler *together* with select elements of automated operations to create a unique software system. DELETE *together.*

judge not, lest you be judged A popular prescription (SEE PAGE 21).

juggling act A moribund metaphor (SEE PAGE 19).

jump all over A moribund metaphor (SEE PAGE 19). *admonish; anathematize; berate; blame; castigate; censure; chastise; chide; condemn; criticize; curse; decry; denounce; execrate; imprecate; inculpate; indict; rebuke; reprimand; reproach; reprove; scold; upbraid.*

jump down (her) throat A moribund metaphor (SEE PAGE 19). *admonish; animadvert; berate; castigate; censure; chasten; chastise; chide; condemn; criticize; denounce; denunciate; discipline; excoriate; fulminate against; imprecate; impugn; inveigh against; objurgate; punish; rebuke; remonstrate; reprehend; reprimand; reproach; reprobate; reprove; revile; scold; swear at; upbraid; vituperate; warn.*

jump for joy A moribund metaphor (SEE PAGE 19). *be blissful; be* blithe; be buoyant; be cheerful; be delighted; be ecstatic; be elated; be enraptured; be euphoric; be exalted; be excited; be exhilarated; be exultant; be gay; be glad; be gleeful; be good-humored; be happy; be intoxicated; be jolly; be jovial; be joyful; be joyous; be jubilant; be merry; be mirthful; be overjoyed; be pleased; be rapturous; be thrilled.

jump from the frying pan into the fire A moribund metaphor (SEE PAGE 19).

jumping-off point A moribund metaphor (SEE PAGE 19).

jump on the bandwagon A moribund metaphor (SEE PAGE 19). be included; be involved; enlist; enroll; join; sign up; take part. ■ Once everyone in an industry has learned about something that works, there's a tendency to *jump on the bandwagon.*

jump out of (her) skin A moribund metaphor (SEE PAGE 19). be afraid; be alarmed; be apprehensive; be cowardly; be craven; be diffident; be faint-hearted; be fearful; be frightened; be pavid; be pusillanimous; be recreant; be scared; be terror-stricken; be timid; be timorous; be tremulous.

jump ship A moribund metaphor (SEE PAGE 19). abandon; desert; for-sake; leave; quit.

jump the gun A moribund metaphor (SEE PAGE 19).

jump through hoops A moribund metaphor (SEE PAGE 19).

(the) jury is still out A moribund metaphor (SEE PAGE 19). be arguable; be debatable; be disputable; be doubtful; be dubious; be in doubt; be moot; be open; be questionable; be uncertain; be unclear; be undecided; be undetermined; be unknown; be unresolved; be unsettled; be unsolved; be unsure. ■ *The jury is still out* on how the Medicare cuts will actually be carried out.

just exactly A wretched redundancy (SEE PAGE 23). exactly; just. ■ *Just exactly* what do you mean? REPLACE WITH *Just* or *Exactly.*

just recently A wretched redundancy (SEE PAGE 23). just; recently. ■ I *just recently* completed my bachelor's degree. REPLACE WITH *just* or *recently.*

just what the doctor ordered A moribund metaphor (SEE PAGE 19).

just when you thought it was safe to An infantile phrase (SEE PAGE 18).

K

keep a (the) lid on A moribund metaphor (SEE PAGE 19). *bridle; check; constrain; control; curb; govern; harness; hold back; inhibit; muzzle; repress; restrain; stifle; suppress.* ■ Its leaders have said they cannot *keep a lid on* popular anger if the government does not begin to respond to citizens' demands. REPLACE WITH *restrain.*

keep a low profile A moribund metaphor (SEE PAGE 19).

keep an ear to the ground A moribund metaphor (SEE PAGE 19). *be alert; be attentive; be awake; be aware; be eagle-eyed; be heedful; be informed; be keen; be observant; be vigilant; be wakeful; be watchful.*

keep an eye out for A moribund metaphor (SEE PAGE 19). *be alert; be attentive; be awake; be aware; be eagle-eyed; be heedful; be informed; be keen; be observant; be vigilant; be wakeful; be watchful; hunt; look for; search.*

keep a stiff upper lip A moribund metaphor (SEE PAGE 19). *be brave; be courageous; be determined; be resolute.*

keep (them) at arm's length A moribund metaphor (SEE PAGE 19).

■ In some cases, you need to *keep hurtful people at arm's length* so they can't continue hurting you.

keep a watchful eye on A moribund metaphor (SEE PAGE 19). *be alert; be attentive; be awake; be aware; be eagle-eyed; be heedful; be informed; be keen; be observant; be vigilant; be wakeful; be watchful.*

keep body and soul together A moribund metaphor (SEE PAGE 19). *endure; exist; keep alive; live; manage; subsist; survive.*

keep (your) chin up A moribund metaphor (SEE PAGE 19). *be brave; be courageous; be determined; be resolute.*

keep (his) cool A moribund metaphor (SEE PAGE 19). *be calm; be composed; be patient; be self-possessed; be tranquil.*

keep (our) distance A moribund metaphor (SEE PAGE 19). *be aloof; be chilly; be cool; be reserved; be standoffish; be unamiable; be unamicable; be uncompanionable; be uncongenial; be unfriendly; be unsociable; be unsocial.*

keep (his) eye on the ball A moribund metaphor (SEE PAGE 19).
1. *be alert; be attentive; be awake; be*

aware; be eagle-eyed; be heedful; be observant; be vigilant; be wakeful; be watchful.

2. be able; be adroit; be apt; be astute; be bright; be brilliant; be capable; be clever; be competent; be discerning; be effective; be effectual; be efficient; be enlightened; be insightful; be intelligent; be judicious; be keen; be knowledgeable; be learned; be logical; be luminous; be perceptive; be perspicacious; be quick; be rational; be reasonable; be sagacious; be sage; be sapient; be sensible; be sharp; be shrewd; be smart; be sound; be understanding; be wise.

keep (your) eyes (open) peeled A moribund metaphor (SEE PAGE 19). *be alert; be attentive; be awake; be aware; be eagle-eyed; be heedful; be observant; be vigilant; be wakeful; be watchful.*

keep (its) finger on the pulse of A moribund metaphor (SEE PAGE 19). ■ The Chinese government has been able to *keep its finger on the pulse of* technology acquisition activities.

keep (your) fingers crossed A moribund metaphor (SEE PAGE 19). *hope for; pray for; think positively; wish.*

keep (me) glued to (my) seat A moribund metaphor (SEE PAGE 19).

keep (my) head above water A moribund metaphor (SEE PAGE 19). *be solvent; exist; live; subsist; survive.*

keep (your) head on (your) shoulders A moribund metaphor (SEE PAGE 19). *be calm; be composed; be patient; be self-possessed; be tranquil.*

keep (your) nose clean A moribund metaphor (SEE PAGE 19). *behave.*

keep (your) nose to the grindstone A popular prescription (SEE PAGE 21). *drudge; grind; grub; labor; moil; slave; strain; strive; struggle; sweat; toil; travail; work hard.*

keep on a short leash A moribund metaphor (SEE PAGE 19).

keep (your) pants (shirt) on A moribund metaphor (SEE PAGE 19). *be calm; be composed; be patient; be self-possessed; be tranquil; calm down; hold on; wait.*

(it) keeps (me) busy A plebeian sentiment (SEE PAGE 20). SEE ALSO *(he's) boring; (it) gives (me) something to do; (it) keeps (me) out of trouble; (it's) something to do.*

(it) keeps (me) going A plebeian sentiment (SEE PAGE 20).

keep smiling A plebeian sentiment (SEE PAGE 20). *Keep smiling* is insisted on by ghoulish brutes who would rob us of our gravity, indeed, steal us from ourselves.

(it) keeps (me) out of trouble A plebeian sentiment (SEE PAGE 20). (SEE) SEE ALSO *(it) gives (me) something to do; (it) keeps (me) busy; (it's) something to do.*

keep the ball rolling A moribund

metaphor (SEE PAGE 19). *continue; go on; keep on; move on; persevere; persist; proceed.*

keep the faith A popular prescription (SEE PAGE 21). *be confident; be encouraged; be heartened; be hopeful; be optimistic; be positive; be sanguine.*

keep the home fires burning A moribund metaphor (SEE PAGE 19).

keep the wolves at bay A moribund metaphor (SEE PAGE 19).

keep under (his) hat A moribund metaphor (SEE PAGE 19). *camouflage; cloak; conceal; cover; disguise; enshroud; harbor; hide; keep secret; mask; screen; shroud; suppress; veil; withhold.*

keep under lock and key A moribund metaphor (SEE PAGE 19).
1. *confine; detain; hold; imprison; intern; jail; lock up; restrain.*
2. *lock up; protect; secure.*

keep up appearances A plebeian sentiment (SEE PAGE 20).

keep up with the Joneses A plebeian sentiment (SEE PAGE 20).

(a) kick in the pants A moribund metaphor (SEE PAGE 19).
1. *encouragement; fillip; goad; impetus; impulse; incentive; incitation; incitement; inducement; jolt; motivation; motive; prod; provocation; push; shove; spur; stimulation; stimulus; thrust; urge.*
2. *animation; ebullience; elation;*

enthusiasm; excitement; exhilaration; exultation; jubilance; jubilation; liveliness; rapture; stimulation; vivacity.
3. *admonishment; castigation; censure; chastisement; disapprobation; disapproval; rebuke; remonstrance; reprimand; reproof; scolding; upbraiding.*

(a) kick in the teeth A moribund metaphor (SEE PAGE 19). *abuse; affront; contempt; contumely; derision; disappointment; disdain; impertinence; indignity; insult; offense; outrage; rebuff; rebuke; rejection; scorn; slap; slight; slur; sneer; snub.*
■ We have received a judgment that has been *a kick in the teeth.* REPLACE WITH *an insult.*

kick the bucket A moribund metaphor (SEE PAGE 19). *cease to exist; decease; depart; die; expire; pass away; pass on; perish.*

kick up (our) heels A moribund metaphor (SEE PAGE 19). *be merry; carouse; carry on; cavort; celebrate; debauch; disport; frolic; gambol; party; play; revel; riot; roister; rollick; romp; skylark.*

(like) (a) kid in a candy shop (store) An insipid simile (SEE PAGE 19).

kill (them) by inches A moribund metaphor (SEE PAGE 19). *afflict; agonize; crucify; excruciate; harrow; martyr; persecute; rack; torment; torture.*

kill the goose that lays the golden egg A moribund metaphor (SEE PAGE 19).

kill two birds with one stone A moribund metaphor (SEE PAGE 19).

kill (her) with kindness A moribund metaphor (SEE PAGE 19).

kind (and) gentle An inescapable pair (SEE PAGE 18). *affable; agreeable; amiable; amicable; compassionate; friendly; gentle; good-hearted; good-natured; humane; kind; kind-hearted; personable; pleasant; tender; tolerant.*

(a) ... kind (sort; type) of thing A grammatical gimmick (SEE PAGE 17). ■ It was *a* spur-of-the-moment *kind of thing*. DELETE *a ... kind of thing.* ■ It's *a* very upsetting *sort of thing*. DELETE *a ... sort of thing.* ■ It's difficult to find a person to commit to in terms of a long-term relationship *type of thing*. DELETE *type of thing*.

kiss and make up A moribund metaphor (SEE PAGE 19).

kiss and tell A moribund metaphor (SEE PAGE 19).

kiss (him) goodbye A moribund metaphor (SEE PAGE 19). *abandon; abdicate; cede; desert; forfeit; forgo; give up; lose (out on); relinquish; renounce; sacrifice; surrender; waive; yield.* ■ Without a new government-funded convention center, Boston will *kiss major gatherings and tourist events goodbye.* REPLACE WITH *forfeit major gatherings and tourist events.*

kiss of death A moribund metaphor (SEE PAGE 19).

(the) (whole) kit and caboodle A moribund metaphor (SEE PAGE 19). *aggregate; all; all things; entirety; everything; gross; lot; sum; total; totality; whole.*

kith and kin An inescapable pair (SEE PAGE 18). *acquaintances; family; friends; kin; kindred; kinfolk; kinsman; kith; relatives.*

knee-high to a grasshopper A moribund metaphor (SEE PAGE 19). 1. *diminutive; dwarfish; elfin; elfish; lilliputian; little; miniature; minikin; petite; pygmy; short; small; teeny; tiny.* 2. *young; youthful.*

knee-jerk reaction A moribund metaphor (SEE PAGE 19). *automatic; habitual; instinctive; inveterate; mechanical; perfunctory; reflex; spontaneous; unconscious; unthinking.*

knight in shining armor A moribund metaphor (SEE PAGE 19).

knock-down, drag-out fight A moribund metaphor (SEE PAGE 19). 1. *altercation; argument; disagreement; discord; disputation; dispute; feud; fight; misunderstanding; quarrel; rift; row; spat; squabble.* 2. *battle; brawl; clash; fight; grapple; jostle; make war; scuffle; skirmish; tussle; war; wrestle.*

knock (me) down with a feather A moribund metaphor (SEE PAGE 19). *amaze; astonish; astound; awe; dazzle; dumbfound; flabbergast; overpower; overwhelm; shock; startle; stun; stupefy; surprise.*

knock (throw) for a loop A moribund metaphor (SEE PAGE 19). *amaze; astonish; astound; awe; dazzle; dumbfound; flabbergast; overpower; overwhelm; shock; startle; stun; stupefy; surprise.*

knock off (his) feet A moribund metaphor (SEE PAGE 19). *amaze; astonish; astound; awe; dazzle; dumbfound; flabbergast; overpower; overwhelm; shock; startle; stun; stupefy; surprise.*

knock on wood A moribund metaphor (SEE PAGE 19). *hope for; pray for; think positively; wish.*

knock (himself) out A moribund metaphor (SEE PAGE 19). *aim; attempt; endeavor; essay; exert; exhaust; labor; moil; strain; strive; struggle; toil; try hard; undertake; work at.*

knock-out punch A moribund metaphor (SEE PAGE 19).

knock (her) socks off A moribund metaphor (SEE PAGE 19).
1. *amaze; astonish; astound; awe; dazzle; dumbfound; flabbergast; overpower; overwhelm; shock; startle; stun; stupefy; surprise.*
2. *beat; better; conquer; defeat; exceed; excel; outclass; outdo; outflank; outmaneuver; outperform; outplay; overcome; overpower; prevail; rout; succeed; surpass; top; triumph; trounce; vanquish; whip; win.*

knock the bottom out of A moribund metaphor (SEE PAGE 19). *belie; confute; contradict; controvert; count-*er; debunk; deny; disprove; discredit; dispute; expose; invalidate; negate; rebut; refute; repudiate.*

knock the spots off A moribund metaphor (SEE PAGE 19). *beat; better; conquer; defeat; exceed; excel; outclass; outdo; outflank; outmaneuver; outperform; outplay; overcome; overpower; prevail; rout; succeed; surpass; top; triumph; trounce; vanquish; whip; win.*

know for a fact An infantile phrase (SEE PAGE 18). ■ I *know for a fact* that he was there with her. DELETE *for a fact.* ■ I'm sure they do; I *know for a fact* they do. DELETE *for a fact.*

(don't) know ... from Adam A moribund metaphor (SEE PAGE 19). *unacquainted; unconversant; unfamiliar; unknown.*

know ... inside out A moribund metaphor (SEE PAGE 19). *be conversant with; be expert in; know thoroughly; know well.*

knowledge is power A quack equation (SEE PAGE 21).

know all the angles A moribund metaphor (SEE PAGE 19).
1. *able; adept; apt; capable; competent; deft; dexterous; experienced; expert; practiced; proficient; seasoned; skilled; skillful; veteran.*
2. *adroit; astute; bright; brilliant; clever; discerning; effective; effectual; efficient; enlightened; insightful; intelligent; judicious; keen; knowledgeable; learned; logical; luminous;*

perceptive; perspicacious; quick; rational; reasonable; sagacious; sage; sapient; sensible; sharp; shrewd; smart; sound; understanding; wise.

(you) know something? An ineffectual phrase (SEE PAGE 17). ■ *You know something? I'm going to do whatever is in my power to end this relationship.* DELETE *You know something?* ■ *You know something? I never loved you either.* DELETE *You know something?* SEE ALSO *(you) know what?*

know what's what An infantile phrase (SEE PAGE 18).
1. *able; adept; apt; capable; competent; deft; dexterous; experienced; expert; practiced; proficient; seasoned; skilled; skillful; veteran.*
2. *adroit; astute; bright; brilliant; clever; discerning; effective; effectual; efficient; enlightened; insightful; intelligent; judicious; keen; knowledgeable; learned; logical; luminous; perceptive; perspicacious; quick; rational; reasonable; sagacious; sage; sapient; sensible; sharp; shrewd; smart; sound; understanding; wise.*

know which side (her) bread is buttered on A moribund metaphor (SEE PAGE 19).

know thyself A popular prescription (SEE PAGE 21).

(you) know what? An ineffectual phrase (SEE PAGE 17). ■ *You know what? When we return, you'll meet her mother.* DELETE *You know what?* ■ *She broke up with me, and you know what?, I've got a* career now, which is good. DELETE *you know what?* SEE ALSO *(you) know something?*

(you) know what I mean? An ineffectual phrase (SEE PAGE 17). ■ *Some people have to work at it more than others. Know what I mean?* DELETE *Know what I mean?* ■ *How can you not be depressed if you don't remember things. You know what I mean?* DELETE *You know what I mean?* SEE ALSO *(you) hear what I'm saying? (you) know what I'm saying? (you) know what I'm telling you? (do) you know?*

(you) know what I'm saying? An ineffectual phrase (SEE PAGE 17). ■ *It was an association that wasn't based on any fact. You know what I'm saying?* DELETE *You know what I'm saying?* ■ *I want a girl that's real. You know what I'm saying?* DELETE *You know what I'm saying?* SEE ALSO *(you) hear what I'm saying? (you) know what I mean? (you) know what I'm telling you? (do) you know?*

(you) know what I'm telling you? An ineffectual phrase (SEE PAGE 17). ■ *I don't know; I can't think of the words. You know what I'm telling you?* DELETE *You know what I'm telling you?* ■ *I like to be with a woman who has the same mindset as I do. You know what I'm telling you?* DELETE *You know what I'm telling you?* SEE ALSO *(you) hear what I'm saying? (you) know what I mean? (you) know what I'm saying? (do) you know?*

knuckle under A moribund metaphor (SEE PAGE 19). *abdicate; accede; acquiesce; bow; capitulate; cede; concede; give in; give up; quit; relinquish; retreat; submit; succumb; surrender; yield.*

kudos A foreign phrase (SEE PAGE 17).

L

(a) labor of love A moribund metaphor (SEE PAGE 19).

lack of A torpid term (SEE PAGE 22). Whatever happened to our negative words, to the prefixes *dis-*, *il-*, *im-*, *in-*, *ir-*, *mis-*, *non-*, and *un-*? No doubt many people say *absence of* or *lack of* because they know so few negative forms of the words that follow these phrases. These people will say *lack of moderation* instead of *immoderation* and *absence of pleasure* instead of *displeasure*.

Others subscribe to society's oral imperative that all things negative be left unsaid. To these people, *lack of respect* is somehow preferable to, and more positive than, *disrespect*. ■ These reports by the media reflect a *lack of sensitivity* to basic human decency. REPLACE WITH *insensitivity*. ■ It was her *lack of judgment* that lost us the sale. REPLACE WITH *misjudgment*. SEE ALSO *absence of; less than (enthusiastic)*.

lady A suspect superlative (SEE PAGE 22). *Lady* has become a pejorative term. No longer does it suggest a cultured, sophisticated woman; rather, it suggests a woman hopelessly common, forever coarse. ■ If you wanted to

sweep one of these *ladies* off her feet, what would you do? REPLACE WITH *women*. ■ I am a *lady*, and I like to be treated as such. REPLACE WITH *well-bred woman*. ■ I have a question for both of you *ladies*. DELETE *ladies*. SEE ALSO *class; gentleman*.

(the) land of milk and honey A moribund metaphor (SEE PAGE 19).

(the) land of nod A moribund metaphor (SEE PAGE 19). *sleep; slumber*.

land on (her) feet A moribund metaphor (SEE PAGE 19). *come through; continue; endure; hold on; persevere; persist; remain; survive*.

landslide victory A moribund metaphor (SEE PAGE 19).

last but (by) no means least An infantile phrase (SEE PAGE 18).

last but not least An infantile phrase (SEE PAGE 18).

lasting An overworked word (SEE PAGE 20). For example: *lasting consequence; lasting contribution; lasting impact; lasting impression; lasting lesson; lasting peace*.

last nail in (his) coffin A moribund metaphor (SEE PAGE 19).

last of the Mohicans An infantile phrase (SEE PAGE 18).

(for) (a) laugh A plebeian sentiment (SEE PAGE 20). This expression is spoken by people who tally their giggles and count their guffaws, people who value numbers and sums more than they do words and concepts, people who consider laughter a commodity and life a comedy. ■ I need *a laugh.* ■ Sue and I want to do these silly things to you *for a laugh.* ■ I'm always looking *for a laugh.* SEE ALSO *avid reader; on a scale of 1 to 10.*

laughing (my) head off A moribund metaphor (SEE PAGE 19). *cachinnate; cackle; chortle; chuckle; convulse; guffaw; hoot; howl; laugh; roar; shriek.*

laughing on the outside and crying on the inside A moribund metaphor (SEE PAGE 19).

laughter is the best medicine A popular prescription (SEE PAGE 21).

launching pad (for) A moribund metaphor (SEE PAGE 19). *base; beginning; foundation; springboard; start*

laundry list A moribund metaphor (SEE PAGE 19).

lavishly illustrated An inescapable pair (SEE PAGE 18).

(the) law is the law A quack equation (SEE PAGE 21).

law of the jungle A moribund metaphor (SEE PAGE 19).

(don't) lay a finger (hand) on A moribund metaphor (SEE PAGE 19). *caress; feel; finger; fondle; handle; pat; paw; pet; rub; stroke; touch.*

lay an egg A moribund metaphor (SEE PAGE 19). *abort; blunder; bomb; fail; fall short; falter; flop; flounder; go wrong; miscarry; not succeed; slip; stumble; trip.*

lay at (their) door A moribund metaphor (SEE PAGE 19). *accredit to; ascribe to; assign to; associate to; attribute to; blame on; charge to; connect with; correlate to; credit to; equate to; impute to; link to; relate to; trace to.*

lay a trap for A moribund metaphor (SEE PAGE 19). *catch; decoy; ensnare; entrap; net; trap.*

lay at the feet of A moribund metaphor (SEE PAGE 19). *accredit to; ascribe to; assign to; associate to; attribute to; blame on; charge to; connect with; correlate to; credit to; equate to; impute to; link to; relate to; trace to.* ■ It doesn't seem that all this volatility can be *laid at the feet of* foreigners. REPLACE WITH *blamed on.*

lay (put) (your) cards on the table A moribund metaphor (SEE PAGE 19). *be aboveboard; be candid; be forthright; be frank; be honest; be open; be straightforward; be truthful.*

lay down the law A moribund

metaphor (SEE PAGE 19).
1. *assert; command; decree; dictate; insist; order; require.*
2. *admonish; berate; castigate; censure; chastise; chide; condemn; criticize; decry; rebuke; reprimand; reproach; reprove; scold; upbraid.*

lay (spread) it on thick A moribund metaphor (SEE PAGE 19).
1. *elaborate; embellish; embroider; enhance; enlarge; exaggerate; hyperbolize; inflate; magnify; overdo; overreact; overstress; overstate; strain; stretch.*
2. *acclaim; applaud; celebrate; commend; compliment; congratulate; eulogize; extol; flatter; hail; laud; panegyrize; praise; puff; salute.*

lay (it) on the line A moribund metaphor (SEE PAGE 19). *be aboveboard; be candid; be forthright; be frank; be honest; be open; be straightforward; be truthful.*

lay (her) out in lavender A moribund metaphor (SEE PAGE 19). *admonish; animadvert; berate; castigate; censure; chasten; chastise; chide; condemn; criticize; denounce; denunciate; discipline; excoriate; fulminate against; imprecate; impugn; inveigh against; objurgate; punish; rebuke; remonstrate; reprehend; reprimand; reproach; reprobate; reprove; revile; scold; swear at; upbraid; vituperate; warn.*

lay the groundwork (for) A moribund metaphor (SEE PAGE 19). *arrange; groom; make ready; plan; prepare; prime; ready.*

lead (her) by the nose A moribund metaphor (SEE PAGE 19). *administer; boss; command; control; dictate; direct; dominate; domineer; govern; in charge; in command; in control; manage; manipulate; master; misuse; order; overpower; oversee; predominate; prevail; reign over; rule; superintend; tyrannize; use.*

lead down the garden path A moribund metaphor (SEE PAGE 19). *bamboozle; befool; beguile; bilk; bluff; cheat; con; deceive; defraud; delude; dupe; feint; fool; gyp; hoodwink; lead astray; misdirect; misguide; misinform; mislead; spoof; swindle; trick; victimize.*

leader of the pack A moribund metaphor (SEE PAGE 19).
1. *administrator; boss; brass; chief; commander; director; executive; foreman; head; headman; leader; manager; master; (high) muckamuck; officer; official; overseer; president; principal; superintendent; supervisor.*
2. *aristocrat; dignitary; eminence; lord; luminary; magnate; mogul; notable; patrician; personage; ruler; sovereign; worthy.*

leak like a sieve An insipid simile (SEE PAGE 19).
1. *leaky; permeable.*
2. *forgetful; heedless; inattentive; lethean; neglectful; negligent; oblivious; remiss; thoughtless; unmindful; unthinking.*

lean and hungry (look) A moribund metaphor (SEE PAGE 19).

lean and mean An inescapable pair (SEE PAGE 18).

leaps off the page   A moribund metaphor (SEE PAGE 19).

learn the ropes   A moribund metaphor (SEE PAGE 19).

leave a bad taste in (my) mouth A moribund metaphor (SEE PAGE 19).

leave a little (a lot; much; something) to be desired   A torpid term (SEE PAGE 22). *be deficient; be inadequate; be insufficient; be lacking; be substandard; be wanting.* ■ In the area of health, the U.S. position *leaves much to be desired.* REPLACE WITH *is sickly.* ■ The plan was great; it was the execution that *left a little to be desired.* REPLACE WITH *was not.* ■ Sorry about that, my handwriting *leaves something to be desired.* REPLACE WITH *is scarcely legible.*

leave holding the bag   A moribund metaphor (SEE PAGE 19). *abandon; depart from; desert; exclude; forsake; leave; quit; withdraw from.*

leave (out) in the cold   A moribund metaphor (SEE PAGE 19). *abandon; ban; banish; bar; desert; exclude; exile; forsake; ostracize; shut out.*

leave (him) in the dust   A moribund metaphor (SEE PAGE 19). *beat; best; better; defeat; eclipse; exceed; excel; outclass; outdo; outflank; outmaneuver; outpace; outperform; outplay; outrank; outrival; outsmart; outstrip; outthink; outwit; overcome; overpower; overshadow; prevail; rout; surpass; top; triumph; trounce; vanquish; whip; win.* ■ It is here where

Homo sapiens *leaves* other species *in the dust,* and the hands usually make it possible. REPLACE WITH *surpasses.*

leave (hanging) in the lurch   A moribund metaphor (SEE PAGE 19). *abandon; depart from; desert; exclude; forsake; leave; quit; withdraw from.* ■ We don't want to *leave* parents *hanging in the lurch.* REPLACE WITH *abandon.*

leave no stone unturned   A moribund metaphor (SEE PAGE 19). *analyze; canvass; comb; examine; explore; filter; forage; hunt; inspect; investigate; look for; probe; quest; ransack; rummage; scour; scrutinize; search; seek; sieve; sift; winnow.*

leave the door (wide) open (for) A moribund metaphor (SEE PAGE 19). ■ The remainder of the majority *left the door open for* a return to capital punishment.

leave well enough alone   A popular prescription (SEE PAGE 21).

left and right   An inescapable pair (SEE PAGE 18). *all around; all over; all through; broadly; everyplace; everywhere; extensively; throughout; ubiquitously; universally; widely.* SEE ALSO *far and wide; high and low.*

(a) legend in (his) own mind   An infantile phrase (SEE PAGE 18).

leg to stand on   A moribund metaphor (SEE PAGE 19).

(has) (a) leg up on   A moribund

metaphor (SEE PAGE 19).
1. *advantage (over)*
2. *predominance over; superiority to; supremacy over.* ■ This is expected to give auto makers *a natural leg up.* REPLACE WITH *a natural advantage.* ■ Even I have *a leg up on* him in that department. REPLACE WITH *an advantage over.*

lend a (helping) hand (to) A moribund metaphor (SEE PAGE 19). *aid; assist; benefit; favor; help; oblige; succor.* ■ During this holiday season, it is fitting for all of us to be thinking of *lending a helping hand to* those in need. REPLACE WITH *aiding.*

lend an ear A moribund metaphor (SEE PAGE 19). *attend to; heed; listen; note.*

(a) leopard cannot change his spots A popular prescription (SEE PAGE 21).

leopards don't lose their spots A moribund metaphor (SEE PAGE 19).

less is more A quack equation (SEE PAGE 21).

(the) less said, the better A popular prescription (SEE PAGE 21).

less than (enthusiastic) A torpid term (SEE PAGE 22). ■ When Fred told his wife about the unbelievable opportunity, he was shocked at her *less than enthusiastic* response. REPLACE WITH *unenthusiastic.* ■ The response from their neighbors has been *less than hos-*

pitable. REPLACE WITH *inhospitable.* SEE ALSO *absence of; lack of.*

let bygones be bygones A popular prescription (SEE PAGE 21).

let go of the past A popular prescription (SEE PAGE 21).

let grass grow under (your) feet A moribund metaphor (SEE PAGE 19). *be idle; be inactive; be lazy; be unemployed; be unoccupied; dally; dawdle; delay; hesitate; linger; loaf; loiter; loll; lounge; pause; relax; repose; rest; tarry; unwind; wait; waste time.*

let (take) (her) hair down A moribund metaphor (SEE PAGE 19). *be casual; be free; be informal; be loose; be natural; be open; be relaxed; be unbound; be unconfined; be unrestrained; be unrestricted.*

let (him) have it with both barrels A moribund metaphor (SEE PAGE 19). *admonish; animadvert; berate; castigate; censure; chasten; chastise; chide; condemn; criticize; denounce; denunciate; discipline; excoriate; fulminate against; imprecate; impugn; inveigh against; objurgate; punish; rebuke; remonstrate; reprehend; reprimand; reproach; reprobate; reprove; revile; scold; swear at; upbraid; vituperate; warn.*

let it all hang out A moribund metaphor (SEE PAGE 19). *acknowledge; admit; affirm; allow; avow; concede; confess; disclose; divulge; expose; grant; own; reveal; tell; uncover; unveil.*

let it be A popular prescription (SEE PAGE 21).

let me ask you something An ineffectual phrase (SEE PAGE 17). ■ *Let me ask you something,* is there anything about school that you like? DELETE *Let me ask you something.* ■ *Let me ask you something:* What would you think if I met three women tonight? DELETE *Let me ask you something.* SEE ALSO *can I ask (tell) you something?*

let me tell you (something) An ineffectual phrase (SEE PAGE 17). ■ This is really class, *let me tell you.* DELETE *let me tell you.* ■ It's been one of those days, *let me tell you.* DELETE *let me tell you.* SEE ALSO *I got to (have to) tell you (something); I'll tell you (something); I'll tell you what; I'm telling you.*

let nature take its course A popular prescription (SEE PAGE 21).

let sleeping dogs lie A popular prescription (SEE PAGE 21). *avoid; discount; disregard; dodge; duck; ignore; neglect; omit; pass over; shun; shy away from; turn away from; withdraw from.*

let the cat out of the bag A moribund metaphor (SEE PAGE 19). *reveal secrets.*

let the chips fall where they may A moribund metaphor (SEE PAGE 19).

let there be no mistake A torpid term (SEE PAGE 22). SEE ALSO *make no mistake (about it).*

let your fingers do the walking An infantile phrase (SEE PAGE 18).

let your mind run wild A moribund metaphor (SEE PAGE 19).

(a) level playing field A moribund metaphor (SEE PAGE 19). *equality; equitableness; equity; fairness; impartiality; justice; justness.* ■ If you live in a democracy, there has to be *a level playing field.* REPLACE WITH *equality.* ■ Many people of goodwill sincerely, but mistakenly, believe that today we have achieved *a level playing field.* REPLACE WITH *fairness.*

level the playing field A moribund metaphor (SEE PAGE 19). *balance; equalize; even out; level; make equal; make level.* ■ The chief aim of the bill is to *level the playing field* so that challengers and incumbents will have an equal opportunity to get their message across. ■ We're not out to hurt anybody, we're just out to *level the playing field.* SEE ALSO *a level playing field.*

lick (his) chops A moribund metaphor (SEE PAGE 19).

lick into shape A moribund metaphor (SEE PAGE 19). *drill; instruct; perfect; train.*

lick (your) wounds A moribund metaphor (SEE PAGE 19).

lie down on the job A moribund metaphor (SEE PAGE 19). *be idle; be inactive; be lazy; be unemployed; be unoccupied; dally; dawdle; linger;*

loaf; loiter; loll; lounge; malinger; tarry.

lie like a rug An insipid simile (SEE PAGE 19). *deceive; dissemble; distort; equivocate; falsify; fib; lie; misconstrue; mislead; misrepresent; pervert; prevaricate.*

lie through (his) teeth A moribund metaphor (SEE PAGE 19). *deceive; dissemble; distort; equivocate; falsify; fib; lie; misconstrue; mislead; misrepresent; pervert; prevaricate.*

life begins at forty A popular prescription (SEE PAGE 21).

life goes on A popular prescription (SEE PAGE 21).

life in a fishbowl A moribund metaphor (SEE PAGE 19).

life in the fast lane A moribund metaphor (SEE PAGE 19).

life is a cabaret A moribund metaphor (SEE PAGE 19).

life is for the living A popular prescription (SEE PAGE 21).

life isn't (always) fair A popular prescription (SEE PAGE 21).

life is short A quack equation (SEE PAGE 21).

(live a) life of luxury A moribund metaphor (SEE PAGE 19). *affluent; moneyed; opulent; prosperous; rich; wealthy; well-off; well-to-do.*

(live) (the) life of Reilly A moribund metaphor (SEE PAGE 19).
1. *be affluent; be moneyed; be opulent; be prosperous; be rich; be wealthy; be well-off; be well-to-do.*
2. *be extravagant; be lavish; be lush; be luxuriant; be sumptuous; be very well.* ■ It was *the life of Reilly*, but something was missing.

lift a finger A moribund metaphor (SEE PAGE 19). *aid; assist; benefit; favor; help; oblige; succor.*

light a fire under A moribund metaphor (SEE PAGE 19). *arouse; awaken; excite; galvanize; goad; impel; incite; induce; motivate; prompt; provoke; push; rouse; spur; stimulate; stir; urge.* ■ May the bishops' counsel encourage those husbands already living their words and *light a fire under* those dozing. REPLACE WITH *rouse*.

(as) light as a feather An insipid simile (SEE PAGE 19). *airy; buoyant; delicate; ethereal; feathery; gaseous; gauzy; gossamer; light; lightweight; slender; slight; sylphid; thin; vaporous; weightless.*

(as) light as air An insipid simile (SEE PAGE 19). *airy; buoyant; delicate; ethereal; feathery; gaseous; gauzy; gossamer; light; lightweight; slender; slight; sylphid; thin; vaporous; weightless.*

light at the end of the tunnel A moribund metaphor (SEE PAGE 19). *anticipation; expectancy; expectation; hope; hopefulness; optimism; possibility; promise; prospect; sanguinity.*

■ When the opportunity arose that he could work for the government, we saw *light at the end of the tunnel*. REPLACE WITH *possibility*.

(a) **light went off in my head** A moribund metaphor (SEE PAGE 19).

like An infantile phrase (SEE PAGE 18). A cachet of all who are grievously adolescent, *like* mars the meaning of every sentence in which it is used. ■ Our family is *like* very open. DELETE *like*. ■ They lived together for *like* twelve years. DELETE *like*. ■ I should, *like*, get up and do something. DELETE *like*. ■ It's *like* just a habit. DELETE *like*. ■ *Like*, you can't really overuse words. DELETE *Like*. ■ My mom said, "Why not circulate a petition and see what happens," which is what I did, but, *like*, I still can't believe it worked. DELETE *like*.

(know) (her) like a book An insipid simile (SEE PAGE 19). *altogether; completely; entirely; fully; perfectly; quite; roundly; thoroughly; totally; unreservedly; utterly; wholly.*

(works) like a charm An insipid simile (SEE PAGE 19). *accurately; easily; exactly; excellently; faultlessly; flawlessly; flowingly; impeccably; indefectibly; methodically; perfectly; precisely; regularly; smoothly; systematically; well.*

like a deer caught in the headlights An insipid simile (SEE PAGE 19). *afraid; alarmed; anxious; apprehensive; fearful; frightened; panicky;* *scared; terrified; timid; timorous.*
■ Tom looked *like a deer caught in the headlights*. REPLACE WITH *terrified*.

(take to it) like a duck to water An insipid simile (SEE PAGE 19). *easily; effortlessly; fluently; naturally; smoothly; with ease.*

(fits) like a glove An insipid simile (SEE PAGE 19). *accurately; easily; exactly; excellently; faultlessly; flawlessly; flowingly; impeccably; indefectibly; methodically; perfectly; precisely; regularly; smoothly; systematically; well.* ■ By having a single, reliable technology solution that fits all of our companies *like a glove*, we are delivering the best technology at the best price to our associates. REPLACE WITH *faultlessly*.

like a hole in the head An insipid simile (SEE PAGE 19). *by no means; hardly; in no way; not at all; not in any way; not in the least; scarcely.*

(go over) like a lead balloon An insipid simile (SEE PAGE 19). *badly; poorly; unsatisfactorily; unsuccessfully.*

like clockwork An insipid simile (SEE PAGE 19). *accurately; easily; exactly; excellently; faultlessly; flawlessly; flowingly; impeccably; indefectibly; methodically; perfectly; precisely; regularly; smoothly; systematically; well.*

like crazy (mad) An insipid simile (SEE PAGE 19).
1. *actively; aggressively; dynamically;*

emphatically; energetically; ferociously; fervently; fiercely; forcefully; frantically; frenziedly; furiously; hard; intensely; intently; mightily; passionately; powerfully; robustly; savagely; spiritedly; strenuously; strongly; vehemently; viciously; vigorously; violently; wildly; with vigor;
2. *ardently; devotedly; eagerly; enthusiastically; fervently; fervidly; passionately; spiritedly; zealously.* ■ He is also eating *like crazy.* Replace with *zealously.*
3. *hastily; hurriedly; posthaste; promptly; quickly; rapidly; speedily; swiftly; very fast; wingedly.*

like hell An insipid simile (See page 19).
1. *actively; aggressively; dynamically; emphatically; energetically; ferociously; fervently; fiercely; forcefully; frantically; frenziedly; furiously; hard; intensely; intently; mightily; passionately; powerfully; robustly; savagely; spiritedly; strenuously; strongly; vehemently; viciously; vigorously; violently; wildly; with vigor.*
2. *ardently; devotedly; eagerly; enthusiastically; fervently; fervidly; passionately; spiritedly; zealously.*
3. *hastily; hurriedly; posthaste; promptly; quickly; rapidly; speedily; swiftly; very fast; wingedly.*

(selling) like hotcakes An insipid simile (See page 19). *briskly; fast; quickly; rapidly; speedily; swiftly; very well; wingedly.* ■ Their current album is selling *like hotcakes.* Replace with *swiftly.*

like it's going out of style An insipid simile (See page 19).

1. *actively; aggressively; dynamically; emphatically; energetically; ferociously; fervently; fiercely; forcefully; frantically; frenziedly; furiously; hard; intensely; intently; mightily; passionately; powerfully; robustly; savagely; spiritedly; strenuously; strongly; vehemently; viciously; vigorously; violently; wildly; with vigor.*
2. *hastily; hurriedly; posthaste; promptly; quickly; rapidly; speedily; swiftly; very fast; wingedly.* ■ I've been taking aspirin *like it's going out of style.* Replace with *aggressively.* See also *like there's no tomorrow.*

like (a streak of; greased) lightning An insipid simile (See page 19). *abruptly; apace; at once; briskly; directly; expeditiously; fast; forthwith; hastily; hurriedly; immediately; instantaneously; instantly; posthaste; promptly; quickly; rapidly; rashly; right away; speedily; straightaway; swiftly; wingedly.*

(works) like magic An insipid simile (See page 19). *amazingly; astonishingly; astoundingly; extraordinarily; inexplicably; magically; miraculously; mysteriously; phenomenally; remarkably; wondrously.*

like nobody's business An insipid simile (See page 19). *brilliantly; consummately; dazzlingly; excellently; exceptionally; expertly; exquisitely; extraordinarily; fabulously; flawlessly; grandly; magnificently; marvelously; perfectly; remarkably; splendidly; superbly; superlatively; supremely; transcendently; very well; wonderfully; wondrously.* ■ Here was the one and only Kronos Quartet in town again, playing — as always — *like nobody's business*. REPLACE WITH *superbly*.

like seeing (looking) … through rose-colored glasses A moribund metaphor (SEE PAGE 19). *hopeful; optimistic; pollyanna; pollyannaish; positive; roseate; sanguine; upbeat.* ■ Life then becomes *like seeing the world through rose-colored glasses*: beautiful and warm. REPLACE WITH *polyannaish*.

(sounds) like something out of a novel An insipid simile (SEE PAGE 19).

like the back of my hand An insipid simile (SEE PAGE 19). *altogether; completely; entirely; fully; perfectly; quite; roundly; thoroughly; totally; unreservedly; utterly; wholly.*

like there's no tomorrow An insipid simile (SEE PAGE 19).
1. *actively; aggressively; dynamically; emphatically; energetically; ferociously; fervently; fiercely; forcefully; frantically; frenziedly; furiously; hard; intensely; intently; mightily; passionately; powerfully; robustly; savagely; spiritedly; strenuously; strongly; vehemently; viciously; vigorously; violently; wildly; with vigor.*
2. *hastily; hurriedly; posthaste; promptly; quickly; rapidly; speedily; swiftly; very fast; wingedly.* SEE ALSO *like it's going out of style.*

like the shifting sands An insipid simile (SEE PAGE 19). *brief; ephemeral; evanescent; fleeting; flitting; fuga-* *cious; fugitive; impermanent; momentary; passing; short; short-lived; temporary; transient; transitory; volatile.*

like watching the grass grow An insipid simile (SEE PAGE 19).
1. *anodyne; banal; barren; bland; boring; deadly; dreary; dry; dull; everyday; flat; humdrum; inanimate; insipid; jejune; lifeless; lusterless; mediocre; monotonous; prosaic; routine; spiritless; stale; tedious; tiresome; unexciting; uninteresting; vapid; wearisome.*
2. *crawling; dallying; dawdling; deliberate; dilatory; faltering; hesitant; laggardly; lagging; leisurely; methodical; plodding; procrastinating; slothful; slow; slow-paced; sluggardly; sluggish; snaillike; systematic; tardy; tortoiselike; unhurried.*

like water (rolling) off a duck's back An insipid simile (SEE PAGE 19) . *to no avail; with no result; without effect.*

line of fire A moribund metaphor (SEE PAGE 19).

lines are drawn A moribund metaphor (SEE PAGE 19).

lining (his) pockets A moribund metaphor (SEE PAGE 19).

link together A wretched redundancy (SEE PAGE 23). *link.* ■ This business will *link together* the telephone, the television, and the computer. DELETE *together.*

(the) lion's share A moribund metaphor (SEE PAGE 19). *almost all;*

most; much; nearly all. ■ The company was late to develop HMOs, and it let competitors grab *the lion's share* of the market. REPLACE WITH *most*.

(my) lips are sealed A moribund metaphor (SEE PAGE 19).

liquid refreshment An infantile phrase (SEE PAGE 18). *beverage; drink; refreshment.*

litany of complaints A moribund metaphor (SEE PAGE 19).

literary event A suspect superlative (SEE PAGE 22).

(a) little bird told me An infantile phrase (SEE PAGE 18).

(the) little boy's (girl's) room An infantile phrase (SEE PAGE 18). *bathroom; lavatory; restroom; toilet.*

(a) little (honesty) goes a long way A popular prescription (SEE PAGE 21).

(a) little knowledge is a dangerous thing A popular prescription (SEE PAGE 21).

little old lady from Dubuque A moribund metaphor (SEE PAGE 19). *boor; bumpkin; commoner; common man; common person; conventional person; peasant; philistine; pleb; plebeian; vulgarian; yokel.* ■ By the time the contest was over, *little, old ladies in Dubuque* could probably discourse on the subject.

(the) little woman An infantile phrase (SEE PAGE 18). *consort; helpmate; helpmeet; mate; spouse; wife.*

lit to the gills A moribund metaphor (SEE PAGE 19). *besotted; crapulous; drunk; inebriated; intoxicated; sodden; stupefied; tipsy.*

lit up like a Christmas tree An insipid simile (SEE PAGE 19).

live and learn A popular prescription (SEE PAGE 21).

live and let live A popular prescription (SEE PAGE 21).

live as though each day were your last A popular prescription (SEE PAGE 21).

live dangerously A popular prescription (SEE PAGE 21).

live each day to the fullest A popular prescription (SEE PAGE 21).

live for the moment A popular prescription (SEE PAGE 21).

live happily ever after A suspect superlative (SEE PAGE 22).

live high off (on) the hog A moribund metaphor (SEE PAGE 19).

live in a pigsty A moribund metaphor (SEE PAGE 19).

live one day at a time A popular prescription (SEE PAGE 21).

live wire A moribund metaphor

(SEE PAGE 19). *card; character; eccentric; exception; original.*

(learn to) live with it A popular prescription (SEE PAGE 21).

(a) living hell A moribund metaphor (SEE PAGE 19). *chthonian; chthonic; hellish; impossible; infernal; insufferable; insupportable; intolerable; painful; plutonic; sulfurous; unbearable; uncomfortable; unendurable; unpleasant; stygian; tartarean.* The force and colorfulness of this metaphor is no longer evident. An uncommonly used word — such as *chthonic, insupportable, plutonic, sulfurous, stygian,* or *tartarean* — is often more potent and captivating than a commonly used metaphor. SEE ALSO *hell on earth.*

(a) living legend A suspect superlative (SEE PAGE 22).

loaded for bear A moribund metaphor (SEE PAGE 19).
1. *eager; prepared; primed; ready; set.*
2. *angry; bad-tempered; bilious; cantankerous; choleric; churlish; crabby; cranky; cross; curmudgeonly; disagreeable; dyspeptic; grouchy; gruff; grumpy; ill-humored; ill-tempered; irascible; irritable; mad; peevish; petulant; quarrelsome; riled; roiled; short-tempered; splenetic; surly; testy; vexed.*

lo and behold A withered word (SEE PAGE 22).

location, location, location An infantile phrase (SEE PAGE 18).

lock horns with A moribund metaphor (SEE PAGE 19). *battle; brawl; clash; fight; grapple; jostle; make war; scuffle; skirmish; tussle; war; wrestle.*

lock, stock, and barrel A moribund metaphor (SEE PAGE 19). *aggregate; all; all things; entirety; everything; gross; lot; sum; total; totality; whole.*

long and hard A torpid term (SEE PAGE 22). *aggressively; dynamically; emphatically; energetically; ferociously; fervently; fiercely; forcefully; frantically; frenziedly; furiously; hard; intensely; intently; mightily; passionately; powerfully; robustly; savagely; spiritedly; strenuously; strongly; vehemently; viciously; vigorously; violently; wildly; with vigor.* ■ The compromise would be a partial victory for Baybanks, which has fought *long and hard* against the legislation. REPLACE WITH *mightily.*

(the) long and (the) short of (it) A wretched redundancy (SEE PAGE 23). *basis; center; core; crux; essence; gist; heart; kernel; pith; substance.*

long in the tooth A moribund metaphor (SEE PAGE 19). *aged; aging; ancient; antediluvian; antique; archaic; elderly; hoary; hoary-headed; old; patriarchal; prehistoric; seasoned; superannuated.*

long overdue An inescapable pair (SEE PAGE 18). ■ This legislation is *long overdue.*

long road ahead A moribund metaphor (SEE PAGE 19).

(a) long shot A moribund metaphor (SEE PAGE 19). *doubtful; dubious; farfetched; implausible; improbable; remote; unlikely; unrealistic.* ■ Something that might happen is *a longer shot* than something that may happen. REPLACE WITH *less likely.*

long time no see An infantile phrase (SEE PAGE 18).

(don't) look a gift horse in the mouth A popular prescription (SEE PAGE 21).

look before you leap A popular prescription (SEE PAGE 21). *be careful; be cautious; be circumspect; be prudent; be safe; be wary.*

look down (her) nose (at) A moribund metaphor (SEE PAGE 19). *contemn; deride; despise; detest; disdain; jeer at; laugh at; mock; ridicule; scoff at; scorn; shun; slight; sneer; snub; spurn.*

look into a crystal ball A moribund metaphor (SEE PAGE 19). *forecast; foreshadow; foretell; portend; predict; prefigure; presage; prognosticate; prophesy.*

look like a drowned rat An insipid simile (SEE PAGE 19). *bedraggled; drenched; dripping; saturated; soaked; sopping; wet.*

looks aren't everything A popular prescription (SEE PAGE 21).

(she) looks like a million bucks (dollars) An insipid simile (SEE PAGE 19).
1. *appealing; attractive; beautiful; becoming; captivating; comely; cute; dazzling; exquisite; fair; fetching; good-looking; gorgeous; handsome; lovely; nice-looking; pleasing; pretty; pulchritudinous; radiant; ravishing; seemly; stunning.*
2. *energetic; fine; fit; good; hale; hardy; healthful; healthy; hearty; robust; sound; strong; vigorous; well.*
3. *affluent; moneyed; opulent; prosperous; rich; successful; wealthy; well-off; well-to-do.*

(take) (a) look see A infantile phrase. This phrase is one of the new illiteracies. Expressions like *a good read, a must have,* and *a look see* are favored today by the "illiterati" — smart, articulate people who find it fashionable to speak unintelligibly. SEE ALSO *a good read; (a) must have; (a) must see; a (must) read.*

look the other way A moribund metaphor (SEE PAGE 19). *brush aside; avoid; discount; disregard; dodge; duck; ignore; neglect; omit; pass over; recoil from; shrink from; shun; shy away from; turn away from; withdraw from.*

look what the tide brought in A moribund metaphor (SEE PAGE 19).

look who's talking An infantile phrase (SEE PAGE 18).

look what (who) the cat dragged in A moribund metaphor (SEE PAGE 19).

loose cannon A moribund metaphor (SEE PAGE 19). *capricious; changeable; erratic; fickle; fluctuating; inconsistent; inconstant; mercurial; unpredictable; unstable; unsteady; variable; volatile; wavering.*

lose (her) head (over) A moribund metaphor (SEE PAGE 19).
1. *alarm; appall; benumb; daunt; frighten; horrify; intimidate; panic; paralyze; petrify; scare; shock; startle; terrify; terrorize.*
2. *infatuated.*

lose (his) marbles (mind) A moribund metaphor (SEE PAGE 19). *batty; cracked; crazy; daft; demented; deranged; fey; foolish; goofy; insane; lunatic; mad; maniacal; neurotic; nuts; nutty; psychotic; raving; silly; squirrelly; touched; unbalanced; unhinged; unsound; wacky; zany.*

lose steam A moribund metaphor (SEE PAGE 19).

a losing battle A moribund metaphor (SEE PAGE 19). *hopeless; impossible; incurable; irreclaimable; irredeemable; irremediable; irreparable; irretrievable; remediless.*

lost in the shuffle A moribund metaphor (SEE PAGE 19). *be discounted; be disregarded; be forgotten; be ignored; be neglected; be omitted; be passed over; be shunned.* ■ There is so much to teach that is writing related, that sometimes the writing itself can *get lost in the shuffle.* REPLACE WITH *be neglected.*

(a) lot of times A wretched redundancy (SEE PAGE 23). *frequently; often.* ■ *A lot of times* people have a tendency to think that others are controlling their destiny. REPLACE WITH *Often.*

loud and clear An inescapable pair (SEE PAGE 18). *apparent; audible; clear; conspicuous; definite; distinct; emphatic; evident; explicit; graphic; lucid; manifest; obvious; patent; pellucid; plain; sharp; translucent; transparent; unambiguous; uncomplex; uncomplicated; understandable; unequivocal; unmistakable; vivid.*

love and cherish An inescapable pair (SEE PAGE 18).

love conquers all A popular prescription (SEE PAGE 21).

love is blind A quack equation (SEE PAGE 21).

love it or leave it An infantile phrase (SEE PAGE 18).

love moves mountains A moribund metaphor (SEE PAGE 19).

low blow A moribund metaphor (SEE PAGE 19). *dishonorable; foul; inequitable; unconscientious; underhanded; unethical; unfair; unjust; unprincipled; unscrupulous; unsportsmanlike.*

lower the boom A moribund metaphor (SEE PAGE 19).
1. *admonish; animadvert; berate; castigate; censure; chasten; chastise; chide; condemn; criticize; denounce;*

denunciate; discipline; excoriate; ful-minate against; imprecate; impugn; inveigh against; objurgate; punish; rebuke; remonstrate; reprehend; repri-mand; reproach; reprobate; reprove; revile; scold; swear at; upbraid; vitu-perate; warn.

2. *abort; annul; arrest; cancel; cease; check; conclude; derail; discontinue; end; halt; nullify; quash; quell; revoke; squelch; stop; suspend; terminate.*

lowest common denominator A torpid term (SEE PAGE 22). For some, frail marketing people and feeble-minded social scientists perhaps, *lowest common denomina-tor* is a convenient way of avoiding more telling, more weighty words. ■ Instead of disseminating the best in our culture, television too often panders to the *lowest common denominator*. REPLACE WITH *worst.* ■ If you fear making anyone mad, then you ultimately probe for the

lowest common denominator of human achievement. REPLACE WITH *nadir.* ■ In that environment, each show tried to appeal to the *lowest common denominator*. RE-PLACE WITH *masses.* ■ The J.D. InterPrizes' *lowest common denomi-nator* design concept allows for the widest possible viewing audience. REPLACE WITH *readily accessible.* ■ So movies must imitate the famil-iar and be pitched to the *lowest common denominator*, causing most of them to be flat, stale and famil-iar. REPLACE WITH *dull-minded.*

low (man) on the totem pole A moribund metaphor (SEE PAGE 19). *inferior; junior; lesser; low ranking; minor; second rate; secondary; subor-dinate.* ■ If you're a freshman member, regardless of what party you're in, you're *low on the totem pole* to be sure. REPLACE WITH *low ranking.*

M

(as) mad as a hatter An insipid simile (SEE PAGE 19). *batty; cracked; crazy; daft; demented; deranged; fey; foolish; goofy; insane; lunatic; mad; maniacal; neurotic; nuts; nutty; psychotic; raving; silly; squirrelly; touched; unbalanced; unhinged; unsound; wacky; zany.*

(as) mad as a hornet An insipid simile (SEE PAGE 19). *angry; berserk; convulsive; crazed; delirious; demented; demoniac; deranged; enraged; feral; ferocious; fierce; frantic; frenzied; fuming; furious; hysterical; infuriated; in hysterics; insane; incensed; irate; mad; maddened; maniacal; murderous; possessed; rabid; raging; ranting; raving; savage; seething; wild; wrathful.*

(as) mad as a March hare An insipid simile (SEE PAGE 19). *batty; cracked; crazy; daft; demented; deranged; fey; foolish; goofy; insane; lunatic; mad; maniacal; neurotic; nuts; nutty; psychotic; raving; silly; squirrelly; touched; unbalanced; unhinged; unsound; wacky; zany.*

(as) mad as a wet hen An insipid simile (SEE PAGE 19). *angry; berserk; convulsive; crazed; delirious; demented; demoniac; deranged; enraged; feral; ferocious; fierce; frantic; frenzied; fuming; furious; hysterical; infuriated; in hysterics; insane; incensed; irate; mad; maddened; maniacal; murderous; possessed; rabid; raging; ranting; raving; savage; seething; wild; wrathful.*

(he) made (me) an offer (I) couldn't refuse An infantile phrase (SEE PAGE 18). ■ We'd still be here today if Bally's hadn't *made us an offer we couldn't refuse.*

(you) made my day A plebeian sentiment (SEE PAGE 20). Often a response to being complimented, *you made my day* appeals to the mass of people who rely on others for their opinion of themselves.

And if they embrace others' approval, so they bow to their criticism.

made of money A moribund metaphor (SEE PAGE 19). *affluent; moneyed; opulent; prosperous; rich; successful; wealthy; well-off; well-to-do.*

magic bullet A moribund metaphor (SEE PAGE 19). *answer; solution.*

(the) main event A moribund metaphor (SEE PAGE 19).

major An overworked word (SEE PAGE 20). For example: *major blow; major breakthrough; major commitment; major concern; major consideration; major defeat; major disaster; major new writer; major opportunity; major player; major ramifications; major road block; major setback; major thrust.*

(a) (the) ... majority (of) A torpid term (SEE PAGE 22). This phrase and others like it — *a large majority; an overwhelming majority; the vast majority* — are indispensable to those who luxuriate in circumlocutory language. They seldom mean more than an unpretentious *almost all, most,* or *nearly all.* ■ *The vast majority* of those people don't receive death sentences. REPLACE WITH *Most.* ■ Within two years, *the overwhelming majority of* Americans will have health coverage. REPLACE WITH *nearly all.* ■ *A large majority of* the participatory lenders have now joined the major banks in supporting our plan. REPLACE WITH *Almost all.* SEE ALSO *a ... number (of).*

make a clean breast of A moribund metaphor (SEE PAGE 19). *acknowledge; admit; affirm; allow; avow; concede; confess; disclose; divulge; expose; grant; own; reveal; tell; uncover; unveil.*

make a concerted effort A wretched redundancy (SEE PAGE 23). *aim; attempt; endeavor; essay; labor; moil; seek; strive; toil; try; undertake; venture; work.* ■ True change will come only when those in power *make a concerted effort* to promote large numbers of women and blacks to high-status jobs. REPLACE WITH *try.*

make a conscious attempt (effort) A wretched redundancy (SEE PAGE 23). *aim; attempt; endeavor; essay; labor; moil; seek; strive; toil; try; undertake; venture; work.* ■ We *made a conscious effort* not to do what most companies do. REPLACE WITH *strived.* ■ Wash your hands and *make conscious attempts* not to touch your face, nose, and eyes. REPLACE WITH *try.*

make a conscious choice (decision) A wretched redundancy (SEE PAGE 23). *Make a conscious choice* means no more than *choose,* and *make a conscious decision* no more than *decide.* Of course, this phrase suggests that those who use it may not otherwise be conscious of what they choose or decide, or even, it could be, do or say. ■ We *made a conscious decision* that this sort of legal terrorism would not affect the way we operate. REPLACE WITH *decided.* ■ They *made a conscious choice* not to have any bedroom scenes in this movie. REPLACE WITH *chose.* SEE ALSO *make an informed choice (decision).*

make a decision A wretched redundancy (SEE PAGE 23). *conclude; decide; determine; resolve.* ■ It's difficult to *make a decision* at this time. REPLACE WITH *decide.* ■

If he *made a decision* not to use protection, he should *make a decision* to support the child. REPLACE WITH *resolved* and *resolve*.

make a determination A wretched redundancy (SEE PAGE 23). *conclude; decide; determine; resolve.* ■ We want the SJC to look at it and *make a determination* to clearly state what is permissible and impermissible. REPLACE WITH *determine*.

make a difference (about; on) A suspect superlative (SEE PAGE 22). Many of us speak of making a difference, some of us strive to make a difference, and few of us succeed in making a difference.
1. *be climacteric; be consequential; be considerable; be critical; be crucial; be effective; be effectual; be helpful; be important; be significant; be useful; be vital; count; matter.* ■ You need to have a sense of humor and to recognize that there's hope, not only despair, in the world — and you need to know that you can *make a difference.* REPLACE WITH *be helpful.* ■ Your answers are important, and they do *make a difference.* REPLACE WITH *matter.*
2. *act on; affect; bear on; influence; sway; work on.* ■ She is part of a great tradition in U.S. society, in which ordinary individuals voice their concerns in order to *make a difference* about issues that matter to them. REPLACE WITH *influence.*
3. *aid; assist; help.*

make a federal case out of A moribund metaphor (SEE PAGE 19). *elaborate; embellish; embroider; enhance; enlarge; exaggerate; hyperbolize; inflate; magnify; overdo; overreact; overstress; overstate; strain; stretch.*

make a getaway A moribund metaphor (SEE PAGE 19). *abscond; clear out; decamp; depart; desert; disappear; escape; exit; flee; fly; go; go away; leave; move on; part; pull out; quit; retire; retreat; run away; take flight; take off; vacate; vanish; withdraw.*

make a monkey out of A moribund metaphor (SEE PAGE 19). *abase; chasten; debase; degrade; demean; deride; disgrace; dishonor; dupe; embarrass; humble; humiliate; mock; mortify; ridicule; shame.*

make a mountain out of a molehill A moribund metaphor (SEE PAGE 19). *elaborate; embellish; embroider; enhance; enlarge; exaggerate; hyperbolize; inflate; magnify; overdo; overreact; overstress; overstate; strain; stretch.*

make an informed choice (decision) A wretched redundancy (SEE PAGE 23). *choose; decide.* SEE ALSO *make a conscious choice (decision).*

make a pig of (myself) A moribund metaphor (SEE PAGE 19). *cloy; cram; glut; gorge; overdo; overeat; overfeed; overindulge; sate; satiate; stuff; surfeit.*

make a quick exit A moribund metaphor (SEE PAGE 19). *abscond; clear out; decamp; depart; desert; dis-*

appear; escape; exit; flee; fly; go; go away; leave; move on; part; pull out; quit; retire; retreat; run away; take flight; take off; vacate; vanish; withdraw.

make a silk purse out of a sow's ear A moribund metaphor (SEE PAGE 19).

make (my) blood boil A moribund metaphor (SEE PAGE 19). acerbate; anger; annoy; bother; bristle; chafe; enrage; incense; inflame; infuriate; irk; irritate; madden; miff; provoke; rile; roil; vex.

make (both) ends meet A moribund metaphor (SEE PAGE 19). economize; endure; exist; live; manage; subsist; survive. ■ Older people are having a tough enough time trying to *make ends meet*. REPLACE WITH *survive*.

make eyes at A moribund metaphor (SEE PAGE 19). flirt.

make false statements A wretched redundancy (SEE PAGE 23). lie. ■ The indictment alleges that he *made false statements* to the FEC and obstructed proceedings. REPLACE WITH *lied*.

make (my) flesh creep A moribund metaphor (SEE PAGE 19). alarm; appall; disgust; frighten; horrify; nauseate; panic; repel; repulse; revolt; scare; shock; sicken; startle; terrify.

make (my) hair stand on end A moribund metaphor (SEE PAGE 19).

alarm; appall; disgust; frighten; horrify; nauseate; panic; repel; repulse; revolt; scare; shock; sicken; startle; terrify.

make hay while the sun shines A moribund metaphor (SEE PAGE 19). capitalize on; exploit; take advantage.

make heads or tails of A moribund metaphor (SEE PAGE 19). appreciate; apprehend; comprehend; discern; fathom; grasp; know; make sense of; perceive; realize; recognize; see; understand. ■ His failures in punctuation make it almost impossible to *make heads or tails of* his convoluted sentences. REPLACE WITH *understand*.

make it big A moribund metaphor (SEE PAGE 19). prevail; succeed; triumph; win.

make mincemeat out of A moribund metaphor (SEE PAGE 19). crush; demolish; destroy; devastate; hammer; obliterate; overpower; overwhelm; rack; ravage; rout; ruin; shatter; slaughter; smash; thrash; undo; wrack; wreck.

make no bones (about it) A moribund metaphor (SEE PAGE 19).

make no mistake (about it) An ineffectual phrase (SEE PAGE 17). ■ *Make no mistake about it*, if we were to leave, other nations would leave, too, and chaos would resume. ■ *Make no mistake*, Jacksonville is not a bad team. ■ *Make no mistake about it*, this impeachment issue has become a battle for who controls the Republican party. SEE ALSO *let there be no mistake.*

make (yourself) scarce An infantile phrase (SEE PAGE 18). *abscond; clear out; decamp; depart; desert; disappear; escape; exit; flee; fly; go; go away; leave; move on; part; pull out; quit; retire; retreat; run away; take flight; take off; vacate; vanish; withdraw.*

make (me) see red A moribund metaphor (SEE PAGE 19). *acerbate; anger; annoy; bother; bristle; chafe; enrage; incense; inflame; infuriate; irk; irritate; madden; miff; provoke; rile; roil; vex.*

(try to) make the best (most) of it A popular prescription (SEE PAGE 21).

make the feathers (fur) fly A moribund metaphor (SEE PAGE 19). *drudge; grind; grub; labor; moil; slave; strain; strive; struggle; sweat; toil; travail; work hard.*

make the grade A moribund metaphor (SEE PAGE 19).
1. *accomplish; achieve; make good; succeed.*
2. *be able; be accomplished; be adept; be adequate; be capable; be competent; be deft; be equal to; be equipped; be fitted; be proficient; be qualified; be skilled; be skillful; be suited; measure up.*

make up (his) mind A wretched redundancy (SEE PAGE 23). *choose; conclude; decide; determine; pick; resolve; select; settle.*

make tracks A moribund metaphor (SEE PAGE 19). *abscond; clear out; decamp; depart; desert; disappear; escape; exit; flee; fly; go; go away; leave; move on; part; pull out; quit; retire; retreat; run away; take flight; take off; vacate; vanish; withdraw.*

make waves A moribund metaphor (SEE PAGE 19). *agitate; disrupt; disturb; perturb; rattle; ruffle; shake up; stir up; unsettle.*

(the) man in the street A moribund metaphor (SEE PAGE 19). *citizen; commoner; everyman; pleb; plebeian; vulgarian.*

(a) man is known by the company he keeps A popular prescription (SEE PAGE 21).

(the) manner (means; mechanism; method; procedure; process) by (in) which A wretched redundancy (SEE PAGE 23). These magisterial-sounding phrases should be replaced by one of the least stately of words: *how.* ∎ I'm not going to discuss *the methods by which* we achieved that. REPLACE WITH *how.* ∎ The philosophical methodology specifies *the procedure by which* concepts will be used to construct a theory. REPLACE WITH *how.* ∎ It does less well in explaining *the process by which* a particular firm decides to implement a price change. REPLACE WITH *how.* ∎ Virtually all of them have been critical of *the manner in which* the administration dealt with the situation. REPLACE WITH *how.*

(a) man's home is his castle A popular prescription (See page 21).

(the) man who came to dinner An infantile phrase (See page 18).

many of my closest friends (are) A plebeian sentiment (See page 20). ■ *Many of my closest friends are* Italian.

marching orders A moribund metaphor (See page 19).

(a) marriage made in heaven A suspect superlative (See page 22). *ideal; model; perfect; wonderful.*

mass exodus A wretched redundancy (See page 23). *exodus.*

(it's) (a) matter of life and death A moribund metaphor (See page 19). *critical; crucial; essential; imperative; important; necessary; pressing; urgent; vital.*

maybe, maybe not An infantile phrase (See page 18).

maybe yes, maybe no An infantile phrase (See page 18).

may (might) possibly A wretched redundancy (See page 23). *may (might).* ■ I *might possibly* be there when you are. Delete *possibly.*

mea culpa A foreign phrase (See page 17).

meal ticket A moribund metaphor (See page 19).

meaningful An overworked word (See page 20). So elusive is meaning in our lives that we apparently feel as though we must modify scores of words with *meaningful* — *meaningful action; meaningful answers; meaningful change; meaningful dialogue; meaningful discussion; meaningful experience; meaningful friendship; meaningful impact; meaningful reform; meaningful relationship; meaningful response.* See also *significant.*

(...) means never having to say you're sorry An infantile phrase (See page 18).

meat and potatoes A moribund metaphor (See page 19). *basal; basic; elementary; essential; fundamental; primary; rudimentary.*

(the) medium is the message A quack equation (See page 21).

(as) meek as a lamb An insipid simile (See page 19). *accepting; accommodating; acquiescent; complacent; complaisant; compliant; cowed; deferential; docile; dutiful; easy; forbearing; gentle; humble; long-suffering; meek; mild; obedient; passive; patient; prostrate; quiet; reserved; resigned; stoical; submissive; subservient; timid; tolerant; tractable; unassuming; uncomplaining; yielding.*

(as) meek as Moses An insipid simile (See page 19). *accepting; accommodating; acquiescent; complacent; complaisant; compliant; cowed; deferential; docile; dutiful; easy; for-*

bearing; gentle; humble; long-suffering; meek; mild; obedient; passive; patient; prostrate; quiet; reserved; resigned; stoical; submissive; subservient; timid; tolerant; tractable; unassuming; uncomplaining; yielding.

(the) meek shall inherit the earth A popular prescription (SEE PAGE 21).

meeting of (the) minds A moribund metaphor (SEE PAGE 19). *accord; accordance; agreement; common view; compatibility; concord; concordance; concurrence; consensus; harmony; unanimity; understanding; unison; unity.* ■ We're talking to him to see if we can have *meeting of minds.* REPLACE WITH *agreement.*

meet (his) Waterloo A moribund metaphor (SEE PAGE 19).

me, myself, and I An infantile phrase (SEE PAGE 18).

mend fences A moribund metaphor (SEE PAGE 19). *reconcile.* ■ Please continue to tell your readers it's never too late to try to *mend those fences.* REPLACE WITH *reconcile.*

(the) men in white coats A moribund metaphor (SEE PAGE 19).

meteoric rise An inescapable pair (SEE PAGE 18). ■ His approach has struck a chord with the American people — hence his unprecedented and *meteoric rise* to prominence.

methodology A torpid term (SEE PAGE 22). A favorite among dimwitted academicians, this polysyllabic word means no more than *method.* ■ How did research *methodologies* change over time in the articles of the *American Journal of Psychology* between 1887 and 1930? REPLACE WITH *methods.*

Mickey-Mouse An infantile phrase (SEE PAGE 18). *inferior; poor; second-class; second-rate; shoddy; subordinate; substandard.*

(the) Midas touch A moribund metaphor (SEE PAGE 19).

middle-of-the-road A moribund metaphor (SEE PAGE 19).
1. *average; common; conservative; conventional; everyday; mediocre; middling; normal; ordinary; quotidian; second-rate; standard; traditional; typical; uneventful; unexceptional; unremarkable; usual.*
2. *careful; cautious; circumspect; prudent; safe; wary.*

might makes right A popular prescription (SEE PAGE 21).

(a) mile a minute A moribund metaphor (SEE PAGE 19). *apace; briskly; expeditiously; fast; hastily; hurriedly; posthaste; quickly; rapidly; speedily; swiftly; wingedly.*

(a) mile wide and an inch deep A moribund metaphor (SEE PAGE 19).
1. *blowhard; boaster; braggadocio; braggart; know-it-all; showoff; swaggerer; trumpeter; windbag.*
2. *glib; silver-tongued; slick; smooth-tongued.*

(the) milk of human kindness A moribund metaphor (SEE PAGE 19). *commiseration; compassion; sympathy; understanding.*

milk the last drop out of A moribund metaphor (SEE PAGE 19).

(a) million miles away A moribund metaphor (SEE PAGE 19). *absent; absent-minded; absorbed; abstracted; bemused; captivated; daydreaming; detached; distracted; distrait; dreamy; engrossed; enraptured; faraway; fascinated; immersed; inattentive; lost; mesmerized; oblivious; preoccupied; rapt; spellbound.*

millstone around (my) neck A moribund metaphor (SEE PAGE 19). *burden; duty; encumbrance; hardship; hindrance; impediment; obligation; obstacle; obstruction; onus; responsibility.*

(has) (a) mind like a sieve An insipid simile (SEE PAGE 19). *forgetful; heedless; inattentive; lethean; neglectful; negligent; oblivious; remiss; thoughtless; unmindful; unthinking.*

mind like a steel trap An insipid simile (SEE PAGE 19). *adroit; astute; bright; brilliant; clever; discerning; enlightened; insightful; intelligent; judicious; keen; knowledgeable; learned; logical; luminous; perceptive; perspicacious; quick; rational; reasonable; sagacious; sage; sapient; sensible; sharp; shrewd; smart; sound; understanding; wise.*

mind (your) P's and Q's A moribund metaphor (SEE PAGE 19). *be accurate; be careful; be exact; be meticulous; be particular; be precise.*

mindset An overworked word (SEE PAGE 20). *attitude; bent; bias; cast; disposition; habit; inclination; leaning; outlook; penchant; perspective; point of view; position; predilection; predisposition; prejudice; proclivity; slant; stand; standpoint; temperament; tendency; view; viewpoint; way of thinking.* ■ You don't have these huge organizations built on patronage anymore, but the *mindset* is still there. REPLACE WITH *predisposition.* ■ What we are doing is changing people's *mindset.* REPLACE WITH *views.* ■ The report is critical of the *mindset* of those in charge of the pipeline. REPLACE WITH *attitude.*

mind the store A moribund metaphor (SEE PAGE 19).

mirabile dictu A foreign phrase (SEE PAGE 17).

misery loves company A popular prescription (SEE PAGE 21).

mission accomplished An infantile phrase (SEE PAGE 18).

(a) miss is as good as a mile A popular prescription (SEE PAGE 21).

miss the boat A moribund metaphor (SEE PAGE 19). *be deprived of; forego; forfeit; give up; lose out; miss out; sacrifice; surrender.* ■ If we define success in terms of material things, we *miss the boat.* REPLACE WITH *lose out.*

mix and mingle An inescapable pair (SEE PAGE 18). *associate; consort; hobnob; fraternize; keep company; mingle; mix; socialize.*

mixed bag A moribund metaphor (SEE PAGE 19).

moan and groan An inescapable pair (SEE PAGE 18). *bawl; bemoan; bewail; blubber; cry; groan; moan; snivel; sob; wail; weep; whimper; whine.*

modus operandi A foreign phrase (SEE PAGE 17).

modus vivendi A foreign phrase (SEE PAGE 17).

Monday morning quarterback-(ing) A moribund metaphor (SEE PAGE 19).

money can't buy everything A popular prescription (SEE PAGE 21).

(like) money in the bank An insipid simile (SEE PAGE 19). *absolute; assured; certain; definite; guaranteed; sure; sure-fire.*

money is the root of all evil A popular prescription (SEE PAGE 21).

money (making) machine A moribund metaphor (SEE PAGE 19).

money talks A moribund metaphor (SEE PAGE 19).

money to burn A moribund metaphor (SEE PAGE 19).

monkey on (my) back A moribund metaphor (SEE PAGE 19). 1. *addiction; fixation; habit; obsession.* 2. *complication; difficulty; dilemma; mess; muddle; ordeal; pickle; plight; predicament; problem; quandary; trial; trouble.*

monkey see, monkey do An infantile phrase (SEE PAGE 18).

(a) month of Sundays A moribund metaphor (SEE PAGE 19). *ages; a long time; a long while; an age; an eternity; decades; eons; forever; months; years.*

mop (wipe) the floor with A moribund metaphor (SEE PAGE 19). 1. *assail; assault; attack; batter; beat; cudgel; flagellate; flog; hit; lambaste; lash; lick; mangle; pound; pummel; strike; thrash; trample; trounce.* 2. *beat; conquer; crush; defeat; outdo; overcome; overpower; overwhelm; prevail; quell; rout; subdue; succeed; triumph; trounce; vanquish; win.* ■ Amazon.com has *mopped the floor with* barnesandnoble.com. REPLACE WITH *routed.*

more is better A quack equation (SEE PAGE 21).

more preferable A wretched redundancy (SEE PAGE 23). *preferable.* ■ While the patient is still at risk to hemorrhage during that time, waiting may be *more preferable* to surgery. DELETE *more.*

more ... than you could shake a stick at A moribund metaphor (SEE PAGE 19). *countless; dozens of;*

hundreds of; incalculable; inestimable; innumerable; many; numerous; scores of; thousands of; untold. ■ He had more women in his life than you could shake a stick at. REPLACE WITH untold.

(the) more the merrier A quack equation (SEE PAGE 21).

(the) more things change, the more they stay the same A popular prescription (SEE PAGE 21).

most assuredly An infantile phrase (SEE PAGE 18). assuredly; certainly; decidedly; definitely; positively; surely; undoubtedly; unequivocally; unhesitatingly; unquestionably. ■ The customer will most assuredly notify the maitre d' if he or she is expecting someone else. REPLACE WITH certainly. SEE ALSO absolutely; definitely; most (very) definitely.

most (very) definitely An infantile phrase (SEE PAGE 18). It is irredeemably dimwitted to say most definitely when the more moderate, indeed, the more civilized certainly, I (am), indeed, just so, quite right, surely, that's right, or yes will do. ■ And you feel your daughter was unjustly treated? Most definitely. REPLACE WITH I do. ■ So whoever you meet has to accommodate your needs? Very definitely. REPLACE WITH Yes. ■ So when you're sitting around, you are the only white person there? Most definitely. REPLACE WITH Just so.

As a synonym for words like assuredly; certainly; decidedly; definitely; positively; surely; undoubtedly; unequivocally; unhesitatingly; unquestionably; the phrase most definitely is ridiculously redundant. ■ Getting this magazine out is a labor of love, but it is most definitely labor. REPLACE WITH decidedly. ■ Colder weather is most definitely on the way. REPLACE WITH unquestionably. ■ Would you do it again? Most definitely. REPLACE WITH Unhesitatingly. SEE ALSO absolutely; definitely; most assuredly.

motivating force A wretched redundancy (SEE PAGE 23). drive; energy; force; impetus; motivation; power.

motley crew An inescapable pair (SEE PAGE 18).

(a) mountain of A moribund metaphor (SEE PAGE 19). SEE ALSO a barrage of. ■ Since January, Starr has assembled a mountain of evidence.

move forward A torpid term (SEE PAGE 22). advance; continue; develop; go on; grow; happen; improve; increase; make headway; make progress; move on; occur; proceed; progress; take place. Politicos and spokespeople endlessly spout fuzzy phrases like move forward and go forward and proceed forward and even move forward in the right direction. Pellucid words like advance, further, improve, proceed, and progress seem to completely elude their intellects. ■ I believe that it was contact with the United

States that has *moved* the process of economic reform *forward,* and hopefully some day will *move* the process of political reform *forward.* REPLACE WITH *advanced* and *advance.* ■ What we need is to empower the city in order to *move* it *forward.* REPLACE WITH *improve.* ■ As the company *moves forward,* it's very important that we hold on to those values. REPLACE WITH *grows.* ■ Serious hurdles remain to make this workable and complete, but this agreement today gives us a way to *move forward.* REPLACE WITH *proceed.* ■ Even if Congress decides they want to play politics this year, we can *move forward and* make progress. DELETE *move forward and.* ■ Using these components as our groundwork, we can now move forward and examine how to apply them in your web application. DELETE *move forward and.*

And here is a truly ludicrous example: ■ As the year *moves forward,* we will see more *forward movement* in global and domestic environmental issues. REPLACE WITH *advances* and *progress.* SEE ALSO *a step forward; a step (forward) in the right direction; go forward; move (forward) in the right direction; proceed forward.*

move heaven and earth A moribund metaphor (SEE PAGE 19). *aim; attempt; endeavor; essay; exert; exhaust; labor; moil; strain; strive; struggle; toil; try hard; undertake; work at.*

move (forward) in the direction (of) -ing A torpid term (SEE PAGE 22). *advance; continue; develop; go on; grow; happen; improve; increase; make headway; make progress; move on; occur; proceed; progress; take place.* ■ We've decided to *move in the direction of helping* the claimants make an educated choice. REPLACE WITH *help.*

move (forward) in the right direction A torpid term (SEE PAGE 22). *advance; continue; develop; go on; grow; happen; improve; increase; make headway; make progress; move on; occur; proceed; progress; take place.* ■ I know the company will resolve its problems and *move forward in the right direction.* REPLACE WITH *grow.* ■ All the numbers are looking pretty good and *moving in the right direction.* REPLACE WITH *increasing.* ■ We are *moving in the right direction,* and I want to keep *moving in the right direction.* REPLACE WITH *making progress* and *making progress.*

Often, formulaic phrases like *move in the right direction* are simply bluster, as in this nearly nonsensical sentence: ■ I'm ready, willing, and able to bring people together and get everybody *moving in the right direction forward.* SEE ALSO *a step forward; a step (forward) in the right direction; go forward; move forward; proceed forward.*

move it or lose it An infantile phrase (SEE PAGE 18).

move mountains A moribund metaphor (SEE PAGE 19). *aim;*

249

attempt; endeavor; essay; exert; exhaust; labor; moil; strain; strive; struggle; toil; try hard; undertake; work at.

mover and shaker A moribund metaphor (SEE PAGE 19).
1. *administrator; boss; brass; chief; commander; director; executive; foreman; head; headman; leader; manager; master; (high) muckamuck; officer; official; overseer; president; principal; superintendent; supervisor.*
2. *aristocrat; dignitary; eminence; lord; luminary; magnate; mogul; notable; patrician; personage; ruler; sovereign; worthy.*

moving target A moribund metaphor (SEE PAGE 19).

(make) much ado about nothing An infantile phrase (SEE PAGE 18). *elaborate; embellish; embroider; enhance; enlarge; exaggerate; hyperbolize; inflate; magnify; overdo; overreact; overstress; overstate; strain; stretch.*

muck and mire A moribund metaphor (SEE PAGE 19).

muddy the waters A moribund metaphor (SEE PAGE 19). *becloud; blur; complicate; confuse; muddy; obscure.*

muscle in on A moribund metaphor (SEE PAGE 19). *break in; encroach; infiltrate; intrude; penetrate; pierce.*

music to (my) ears A moribund metaphor (SEE PAGE 19).

(a) must (miss) An infantile phrase (SEE PAGE 18). Like all badly made terms, *(a) must (miss)* is no sooner said than it sounds stale, no sooner read than it sours. In all its variations — *a must have, a must read, a must see,* and so on — this phrase is altogether too *musty*. ■ A good soundtrack, but a dull story, bad acting and weak special effects make this *a must-miss*. ■ Phone interviewing skills are *a must* for most human resource professionals spend a good portion of their day on the phone. ■ Is that business trip *a must*? ■ It is a *must-stop* location for portfolio-toting high school and college students from across the country. ■ Over 200 *must-do* summer events are listed. ■ Aux Delices is *a must stop* for chowhounds. ■ If ever the Lightning faced *a must-win* game, this was it.

(a) (absolute) must An infantile phrase (SEE PAGE 18). *compulsory; critical; essential; imperative; important; indispensable; mandatory; necessary; needed; obligatory; required; requisite; vital.* ■ Prior experience writing user and technical documentation in the computer field is *a must*. REPLACE WITH *necessary*. ■ It is not *an absolute must* to read this part in order to use the second half of the book. REPLACE WITH *essential*. SEE ALSO *(a) must have; (a) must see; a (definite) plus.*

(a) must have An infantile phrase (SEE PAGE 18). *compulsory; critical; essential; imperative; important;*

indispensable; mandatory; necessary; needed; obligatory; required; requisite; vital. ■ His book is a student's friend, a professional's ally, a *must-have* reference. REPLACE WITH *indispensable.* ■ No application has yet emerged to make a miniaturized computer *a must-have.* REPLACE WITH *essential.* ■ Microsoft Services for NetWare is *a must-have* for any administrator who is managing a network that includes both types of users. REPLACE WITH *vital.* ■ This software is *a must have* in any web marketing company's toolbox. REPLACE WITH *mandatory.* SEE ALSO *(take) a look see; a (absolute) must; (a) must (miss); (a) must see; a (definite) plus.*

(a) must see An infantile phrase (SEE PAGE 18).
1. *compulsory; critical; essential; imperative; important; indispensable; mandatory; necessary; needed; obligatory; required; requisite; vital.* ■ It is the *must-see* event of the season. REPLACE WITH *obligatory.*
2. *compelling; powerful.* ■ This is *must-see* TV. REPLACE WITH *compelling.* SEE ALSO *(take) a look see; a (absolute) must; (a) must (miss); (a) must have; a (definite) plus.*

mutual admiration society An infantile phrase (SEE PAGE 18). *affinity with.*

N

nagging doubts An inescapable pair (SEE PAGE 18).

nail (their) colors (flag) to the mast A moribund metaphor (SEE PAGE 19).

(like) nailing jelly to the wall An insipid simile (SEE PAGE 19). *barren; bootless; effete; feckless; feeble; fruitless; futile; impotent; inadequate; inconsequential; inconsiderable; ineffective; ineffectual; infertile; insignificant; inutile; meaningless; meritless; nugatory; null; of no value; pointless; powerless; profitless; sterile; trifling; trivial; unavailing; unimportant; unproductive; unprofitable; unserviceable; unworthy; useless; vain; valueless; weak; worthless.*

nail (him) to the wall A moribund metaphor (SEE PAGE 19).
1. *admonish; anathematize; berate; blame; castigate; censure; chastise; chide; condemn; criticize; curse; decry; denounce; execrate; imprecate; inculpate; indict; rebuke; reprimand; reproach; reprove; scold; upbraid.*
2. *beat; better; conquer; defeat; exceed; excel; outclass; outdo; outflank; outmaneuver; outperform; outplay; overcome; overpower; prevail; rout; succeed; surpass; top; triumph; trounce;*

vanquish; whip; win.

(as) naked as a jaybird An insipid simile (SEE PAGE 19). *bare; disrobed; naked; nude; stripped; unclothed; uncovered; undressed.*

(my) name is mud A moribund metaphor (SEE PAGE 19).

name of the game A moribund metaphor (SEE PAGE 19). *basis; center; core; crux; essence; gist; heart; kernel; pith; substance.*

(as) narrow as an arrow An insipid simile (SEE PAGE 19). *asthenic; attenuated; bony; cachectic; emaciated; gaunt; lank; lanky; lean; narrow; rail-thin; scraggy; scrawny; skeletal; skinny; slender; slight; slim; spare; spindly; svelte; sylphid; thin; trim; wispy.*

national pastime A moribund metaphor (SEE PAGE 19). *baseball.*

neat and tidy An inescapable pair (SEE PAGE 18). *neat; orderly; tidy.*

(as) neat as a pin An insipid simile (SEE PAGE 19). *methodical; neat; ordered; orderly; organized; systematic; tidy; trim; well-organized.*

necessary evil A torpid term (SEE PAGE 22). ■ Their staunch refusal to concede that new taxes are, at the least, a *necessary evil*, could shut them out of the budget process altogether.

(a) necessary prerequisite A wretched redundancy (SEE PAGE 23). *necessary; prerequisite.* ■ An understanding of expressions is *a necessary prerequisite* to learning any command language. DELETE *necessary.* ■ The transfer of information is *a necessary prerequisite* for the effective transfer of technology. DELETE *a prerequisite.*

necessary requirement A wretched redundancy (SEE PAGE 23). *necessary; requirement.* ■ Because of the labor problems that we have been having with the police patrolmen's union, we will be unable to meet the *necessary requirements* by the deadline. DELETE *necessary.*

necessity is the mother of invention A popular prescription (SEE PAGE 21).

neck and neck A moribund metaphor (SEE PAGE 19). *abreast; close; equal; tied.*

(our) neck of the woods A moribund metaphor (SEE PAGE 19). *area; community; country; county; district; domain; environment; environs; locale; locality; milieu; neighborhood; part; region; section; sector; surroundings; territory; vicinity; zone.*

need(s) and want(s) An inescapable pair (SEE PAGE 18).

negative (*n*) A torpid term (SEE PAGE 22). *burden; deterrence; deterrent; disadvantage; drawback; encumbrance; frailty; hardship; hindrance; liability; limitation; obstacle; onus; shortcoming; weakness.* ■ I don't see how it's a *negative* to the United States to be supporting a democratic government. REPLACE WITH *disadvantage.* SEE ALSO *positive.*

negative effect (impact) A torpid term (SEE PAGE 22). SEE ALSO *positive effect (impact).* ■ The committee is concerned with both short-term and long-term *negative effects.* REPLACE WITH *disruptions.* ■ Imaging helps to overcome the *negative effects* produced by generalizations. REPLACE WITH *inaccuracies.*

negative feelings A torpid term (SEE PAGE 22). This expression tells us how little we listen to how we feel. In our quest for speed and efficiency, we have forfeited our feelings. The niceties of emotion — *anger, animosity, anxiety, depression, despair, displeasure, disquiet, distrust, fear, frustration, fury, gloom, grief, guilt, hatred, hopelessness, hostility, ill will, insecurity, jealousy, malice, melancholy, rage, resentment, sadness, shame, sorrow, stress,* and so on — have been sacrificed to a pointless proficiency. ■ It was reported that IAM headquarters failed to renew a $1 million bond that matured in June, due to their *negative feelings* toward El Al's actions. REPLACE WITH *displeasure.* ■ *Neg-*

ative feelings can trigger a cascade of stress hormones that accelerate the heart rate, shut down the immune system, and encourage blood clotting. REPLACE WITH *Resentment or anger.* ■ But *those negative feelings* can work against you if they render you unwilling or unable to act the next time you face a major decision. REPLACE WITH *anger and embarrassment.* ■ Though little is known about the effects of negative emotions on your heart, there are a few theories about why *negative feelings* can do so much damage. REPLACE WITH *stress and depression.* SEE ALSO *in a bad mood; positive feelings.*

neither a borrower nor a lender be A popular prescription (SEE PAGE 21).

neither fish nor fowl A moribund metaphor (SEE PAGE 19). *indefinite; indeterminate; indistinct; undefined; undetermined.*

neither here nor there A moribund metaphor (SEE PAGE 19). *extraneous; immaterial; impertinent; inapplicable; irrelevant.*

neither one A wretched redundancy (SEE PAGE 23). *neither.* ■ *Neither one* of these choices is exclusive of the other. DELETE *one.* SEE ALSO *each one; either one.*

ne plus ultra A foreign phrase (SEE PAGE 17).

nerves of steel A moribund metaphor (SEE PAGE 19). *bold; brave;*

courageous; dauntless; fearless; intrepid; stouthearted; unafraid.

nest egg A moribund metaphor (SEE PAGE 19). *assets; finances; funds; resources; savings.*

never (not) in a million years An infantile phrase (SEE PAGE 18). *at no time; by no means; in no way; never; no; not at all; not ever; not in any way; not in the least.* ■ I would never have imagined — *not in a million years* — feeling compelled to come to the defense of that grande dame of the administration, the president's wife. DELETE *not in a million years.*

never in my wildest dreams An infantile phrase (SEE PAGE 18). *at no time; by no means; in no way; never; no; not at all; not ever; not in any way; not in the least.* ■ *Never in my wildest dreams* did I imagine that Pinochet would be arrested here in London. DELETE *in my wildest dreams.*

never say die A popular prescription (SEE PAGE 21).

never say never A popular prescription (SEE PAGE 21).

new and improved A suspect superlative (SEE PAGE 22).

new and innovative An inescapable pair (SEE PAGE 18). *innovative; new.* ■ We used some *new and innovative* manufacturing techniques. REPLACE WITH *innovative* or *new.*

(a) (whole) new (different) ball-game A moribund metaphor (SEE PAGE 19). ■ Although the procedure is basically the same, recording a macro is slightly different in Word and PowerPoint than in Excel, and creating a macro in Access is *a whole different ballgame.* REPLACE WITH *wholly different.*

new deck (pack) of cards A moribund metaphor (SEE PAGE 19).

(the) new kid on the block A moribund metaphor (SEE PAGE 19). ■ Being *the new kid on the block* does not excuse them from their responsibilities.

(a) new lease on life A moribund metaphor (SEE PAGE 19). *animated; energized; enlivened; inspired; inspirited; invigorated; refreshed; reinvigorated; rejuvenated; revitalized; revived; roused; stimulated; stired; vitalized.*

(like) new wine in old bottles An insipid simile (SEE PAGE 19).

nice An overworked word (SEE PAGE 20). *affable; agreeable; amiable; amicable; companionable; compassionate; congenial; cordial; delightful; friendly; genial; good; good-hearted; good-natured; humane; kind; kind-hearted; likable; neighborly; personable; pleasant; pleasing; sociable; tender; tolerant.*

The word *nice* we might reserve for its less well-known definitions of *fastidious* and *subtle.*

(as) nice as pie An insipid simile (SEE PAGE 19). *affable; agreeable; amiable; amicable; companionable; compassionate; congenial; cordial; delightful; friendly; genial; good; good-hearted; good-natured; humane; kind; kind-hearted; likable; neighborly; personable; pleasant; pleasing; sociable; tender; tolerant.*

nice work if you can get it A plebeian sentiment (SEE PAGE 20).

nickel-and-dime A moribund metaphor (SEE PAGE 19).
1. *cheap; economical; inexpensive; low-cost; low-priced.*
2. *cheap; frugal; miserly; niggardly; parsimonious; stingy; thrifty.*
3. *inconsequential; insignificant; minor; negligible; paltry; petty; small; small-time; trifling; trivial; unimportant.* ■ The banks were shoveling money into every *nickel-and-dime* developer that walked in. REPLACE WITH *small-time.*

nickel-and-dime (him) to death A moribund metaphor (SEE PAGE 19). ■ Many governors have begun to *nickel-and-dime taxpayers to death* with fees, fines, tolls, and excise taxes. SEE ALSO *to death.*

(like) night and day An insipid simile (SEE PAGE 19). *antipodal; antipodean; antithetical; contrary; converse; diametric; diametrical; different; inverse; opposite; reverse.*

(it's) (a) nightmare A moribund metaphor (SEE PAGE 19). How impoverished our imaginations are. Nightmares ought to be terrifying, but this metaphor — so popular has it become — is hopelessly tame. *It was a nightmare* instills in us as little compassion as it does interest; it makes us yawn rather than yell. No longer is there terror to it.

Though an incident might well be *agonizing, alarming, appalling, awful, disgusting, disquieting, distressing, disturbing, dreadful, excruciating, frightening, frightful, ghastly, grisly, gruesome, harrowing, hideous, horrendous, horrible, horrid, horrific, horrifying, monstrous, nauseating, nightmareish, petrifying, repellent, repulsive, revolting, shocking, sickening, terrifying, tormenting, traumatic,* saying *it was a nightmare* makes it sound as though it were no more than an annoyance, no more than a mere inconvenience.

It was a nightmare, the metaphor, has hardly the force of a sweet dream. ■ It was *a nightmare.* REPLACE WITH *ghastly.* ■ If the birth mother shows up, it's *a nightmare* for the adopting mother. REPLACE WITH *disquieting.*

Altogether remarkable about this expression is that people use it to describe something that tormented or terrified them. They describe an extraordinary event with an ordinary phrase. How can we not doubt the sincerity of their words, the terror of their experience? Is this then what it is to be human, to be able to use language — expressing ourselves in platitudes to illustrate what affects us most deeply? SEE ALSO *(every person's) worst nightmare.*

nip and tuck A moribund metaphor (SEE PAGE 19).

nip (it) in the bud A moribund metaphor (SEE PAGE 19). *abort; annul; arrest; balk; block; cancel; check; contain; crush; derail; detain; end; extinguish; foil; frustrate; halt; hinder; impede; neutralize; nullify; obstruct; prevent; quash; quell; repress; restrain; retard; squash; squelch; squish; stall; stay; stifle; stop; subdue; suppress; terminate; thwart.* ■ Another reader in California has found a sure-fire method for *nipping travel stress in the bud.* REPLACE WITH *squelching travel stress.*

nipping at (your) heels A moribund metaphor (SEE PAGE 19).

no big deal An infantile phrase (SEE PAGE 18). *inappreciable; inconsequential; inconsiderable; insignificant; minor; negligible; niggling; nugatory; petty; trifling; trivial; unimportant; unsubstantial.*

nobody but nobody An infantile phrase (SEE PAGE 18). *nobody; nobody at all; none; no one; no one at all.*

nobody's perfect A popular prescription (SEE PAGE 21). SEE ALSO *(I'm) a perfectionist; I'm not perfect (you know).*

no easy task A torpid term (SEE PAGE 22). *arduous; backbreaking; burdensome; difficult; exhausting; fatiguing; hard; herculean; laborious; not easy; onerous; severe; strenuous; toilful; toilsome; tough; troublesome; trying; wearisome.* ■ Getting this place ready has been *no easy task.* REPLACE WITH *backbreaking.*

no great shakes A moribund metaphor (SEE PAGE 19).
1. *average; common; commonplace; customary; everyday; fair; mediocre; middling; normal; ordinary; passable; quotidian; regular; routine; standard; tolerable; typical; uneventful; unexceptional; unremarkable; usual.*
2. *inappreciable; inconsequential; inconsiderable; insignificant; minor; negligible; niggling; nugatory; petty; trifling; trivial; unimportant; unsubstantial.*

no guts, no glory A popular prescription (SEE PAGE 21).

no holds barred A moribund metaphor (SEE PAGE 19). *candidly; explicitly; openly; overtly; without restraint.*

no ifs, ands, ors, or buts An infantile phrase (SEE PAGE 18). SEE ALSO *period.*

no man is an island A popular prescription (SEE PAGE 21).

non compos mentis A foreign phrase (SEE PAGE 17). *batty; cracked; crazy; cretinous; daft; demented; deranged; insane; lunatic; mad; maniacal; neurotic; nuts; nutty; psychotic; raving; squirrelly; touched; unbalanced; unhinged; unsound.*

none of the above An infantile phrase (SEE PAGE 18). ■ Do you want to talk to me or argue with me? *None of the above.* REPLACE WITH *Neither.* SEE ALSO *all of the above.*

no news is good news A quack equation (SEE PAGE 21). ■ There is a new breed of progressive administrators who do not believe that *no news is good news.*

no offense An infantile phrase (SEE PAGE 18).

(every) nook and cranny A moribund metaphor (SEE PAGE 19). *complexities; details; fine points; intricacies; minutiae; niceties; particulars.* ■ There is lots of time in which to explore the *nooks and crannies* of virtually any topic on AM radio. REPLACE WITH *intricacies.*

no pain, no gain A popular prescription (SEE PAGE 21).

no problem An infantile phrase (SEE PAGE 18).
1. *you're welcome.* ■ Thanks very much. *No problem.* REPLACE WITH *You're welcome.*
2. *not at all; not in the least.*
3. *I'd be glad to; I'd be happy to.*
4. *it's O.K.; that's all right.*
5. *easy; easily; effortlessly; readily.* ■ Can you do it? *No problem.* REPLACE WITH *Easily.* SEE ALSO *common courtesy.*

no pun intended An infantile phrase (SEE PAGE 18).

nose out of joint A moribund metaphor (SEE PAGE 19).
1. *acerbated; angry; annoyed; bothered; cross; displeased; enraged; furious; grouchy; incensed; inflamed; infuriated; irate; irked; irritated; mad; miffed; peeved; provoked; riled; roiled;*

testy; upset; vexed.
2. *covetous; desirous; envious; grudging; jealous; resentful.*

(it's) no skin off (my) nose A moribund metaphor (SEE PAGE 19).

no small feat (task) A torpid term (SEE PAGE 22). *arduous; backbreaking; burdensome; difficult; exhausting; fatiguing; hard; herculean; laborious; not easy; onerous; severe; strenuous; toilful; toilsome; tough; troublesome; trying; wearisome.*

(I'm) no spring chicken A moribund metaphor (SEE PAGE 19). *aged; aging; ancient; antediluvian; antique; archaic; elderly; hoary; hoary-headed; old; patriarchal; prehistoric; seasoned; superannuated.*

no strings attached A moribund metaphor (SEE PAGE 19). *unconditionally; unreservedly.*

no sweat A moribund metaphor (SEE PAGE 19). *easily done; easy; effortless; elementary; facile; simple; simplicity itself; straightforward; uncomplex; uncomplicated.*

not a Chinaman's chance A moribund metaphor (SEE PAGE 19).
1. *doubtful; dubious; farfetched; implausible; improbable; remote; unlikely; unrealistic.*
2. *hopeless; impossible; impracticable; impractical; infeasible; unrealizable; unworkable.*

not a ghost of a chance A moribund metaphor (SEE PAGE 19).
1. *doubtful; dubious; farfetched;*

implausible; improbable; remote; unlikely; unrealistic.
2. *hopeless; impossible; impracticable; impractical; infeasible; unrealizable; unworkable.*

not a hope in hell A moribund metaphor (SEE PAGE 19).
1. *doubtful; dubious; farfetched; implausible; improbable; remote; unlikely; unrealistic.*
2. *hopeless; impossible; impracticable; impractical; infeasible; unrealizable; unworkable.*

not all (what) (it's) cracked up to be A torpid term (SEE PAGE 22). *deficient; disappointing; discouraging; dissatisfying; inadequate; inapt; incapable; incompetent; ineffective; inferior; insufficient; lacking; unfit; unqualified; unsatisfactory; wanting.*

not a mean bone in (her) body A moribund metaphor (SEE PAGE 19). *affable; agreeable; amiable; amicable; compassionate; friendly; gentle; good-hearted; good-natured; humane; kind; kind-hearted; personable; pleasant; tender; tolerant.*

not a snowball's chance in hell A moribund metaphor (SEE PAGE 19).
1. *doubtful; dubious; farfetched; implausible; improbable; remote; unlikely; unrealistic.*
2. *hopeless; impossible; impracticable; impractical; infeasible; unrealizable; unworkable.*

not by a long shot A moribund metaphor (SEE PAGE 19). *at no time; by no means; in no way; never; no; not at all; not ever; not in any way; not in the least.*

not by any stretch of the imagination A moribund metaphor (SEE PAGE 19). *at no time; by no means; in no way; never; no; not at all; not ever; not in any way; not in the least.*

notch in (his) belt A moribund metaphor (SEE PAGE 19). *achievement; attainment; success.*

not for all the tea in China A moribund metaphor (SEE PAGE 19). *at no time; by no means; in no way; never; no; not at all; not ever; not in any way; not in the least.*

not for anything in the world A moribund metaphor (SEE PAGE 19). *at no time; by no means; in no way; never; no; not at all; not ever; not in any way; not in the least.*

not for love or money A moribund metaphor (SEE PAGE 19). *at no time; by no means; in no way; never; no; not at all; not ever; not in any way; not in the least.*

not for the world A moribund metaphor (SEE PAGE 19). *at no time; by no means; in no way; never; no; not at all; not ever; not in any way; not in the least.*

nothing could be further from the truth A torpid term (SEE PAGE 22). 1. *by no means; in no way; never; no; not at all; not ever; nothing of the sort; not in any way; not in the least.*
2. *be amiss; be astray; be deceived; be deluded; be erring; be erroneous; be fallacious; be false; be faulty; be inaccurate; be incorrect; be in error; be misguided; be misinformed; be mislead; be mistaken; be not correct; be not right; be untrue; be wrong.*

You would think that anyone who uses this phrase — anyone, that is, whose words or actions were being questioned or whose honor was being impugned — would choose to speak more eloquently. You would think that unfair or inaccurate accusations would elicit profound and persuasive expressions of denial. When they do not, as they certainly do not when a person resorts to *nothing could be further from the truth,* we have to wonder who is telling the truth and who is not. Formulaic responses like this may make us doubt the sincerity of those who use them. ■ The premise put forth by the administration that employment must be sacrificed to protect the environment *could not be further from the truth.* REPLACE WITH *is erroneous.* ■ I know there will be Republicans who will try to say that because I'm not with you today in Chicago that I'm trying to distance myself from you, but *nothing could be further from the truth.* REPLACE WITH *they are mistaken.* ■ W. R. Grace makes use of my "model citizen" sound bite as though it were some sort of blanket absolution. *Nothing could be further from the truth.* REPLACE WITH *It is not.*

nothing lasts forever A popular prescription (SEE PAGE 21).

nothing to sneeze at A moribund metaphor (SEE PAGE 19). *consequential; considerable; meaningful; mo-*

mentous; *significant; substantial; weighty.* ■ Two hundred thousand jobs is *nothing to sneeze at.* REPLACE WITH *considerable.*

nothing to write home about A moribund metaphor (SEE PAGE 19). 1. *average; common; commonplace; customary; everyday; fair; mediocre; middling; normal; ordinary; passable; quotidian; regular; standard; tolerable; typical; uneventful; unexceptional; unexciting; unremarkable; usual; workaday.*
2. *anodyne; banal; barren; bland; boring; deadly; dreary; dry; dull; everyday; flat; humdrum; inanimate; insipid; jejune; lifeless; lusterless; mediocre; monotonous; prosaic; routine; spiritless; stale; tedious; tiresome; unexciting; uninteresting; vapid; wearisome.*

nothing ventured, nothing gained A popular prescription (SEE PAGE 21).

not in (this) lifetime A moribund metaphor (SEE PAGE 19). *at no time; by no means; in no way; never; no; not at all; not ever; not in any way; not in the least.*

not in (out of) the picture A moribund metaphor (SEE PAGE 19). Some metaphors — so bloodless have they become — accommodate many different meanings. *Not in (out of) the picture* is one of them, for this pale expression could easily mean *dead* or *departed*, conceivably mean *forgotten* or *forgettable*, or imaginably mean *unmentionable* or *nameless*. SEE ALSO *in the picture.*

not on your life A moribund metaphor (SEE PAGE 19). *at no time; by no means; in no way; never; no; not at all; not ever; not in any way; not in the least.*

not what (it) used to be A torpid term (SEE PAGE 22). *deficient; disappointing; discouraging; dissatisfying; inadequate; inapt; incapable; incompetent; ineffective; inferior; insufficient; lacking; unfit; unqualified; unsatisfactory; wanting.*

not with a bang but with a whimper An infantile phrase (SEE PAGE 18).

not worth a continental A moribund metaphor (SEE PAGE 19). *barren; bootless; effete; feckless; feeble; fruitless; futile; impotent; inadequate; inconsequential; inconsiderable; ineffective; ineffectual; infertile; insignificant; inutile; meaningless; meritless; nugatory; null; of no value; pointless; powerless; profitless; sterile; trifling; trivial; unavailing; unimportant; unproductive; unprofitable; unserviceable; unworthy; useless; vain; valueless; weak; worthless.*

not worth a (tinker's) damn A moribund metaphor (SEE PAGE 19). *barren; bootless; effete; feckless; feeble; fruitless; futile; impotent; inadequate; inconsequential; inconsiderable; ineffective; ineffectual; infertile; insignificant; inutile; meaningless; meritless; nugatory; null; of no value; pointless; powerless; profitless; sterile; trifling; trivial; unavailing; unimportant; unproductive; unprofitable; unserviceable; unworthy; useless; vain; valueless; weak; worthless.*

not worth a plugged nickel A moribund metaphor (SEE PAGE 19). *barren; bootless; effete; feckless; feeble; fruitless; futile; impotent; inadequate; inconsequential; inconsiderable; ineffective; ineffectual; infertile; insignificant; inutile; meaningless; meritless; nugatory; null; of no value; pointless; powerless; profitless; sterile; trifling; trivial; unavailing; unimportant; unproductive; unprofitable; unserviceable; unworthy; useless; vain; valueless; weak; worthless.*

not worth a straw A moribund metaphor (SEE PAGE 19). *barren; bootless; effete; feckless; feeble; fruitless; futile; impotent; inadequate; inconsequential; inconsiderable; ineffective; ineffectual; infertile; insignificant; inutile; meaningless; meritless; nugatory; null; of no value; pointless; powerless; profitless; sterile; trifling; trivial; unavailing; unimportant; unproductive; unprofitable; unserviceable; unworthy; useless; vain; valueless; weak; worthless.*

not worth the paper it's written (printed) on A moribund metaphor (SEE PAGE 19). *barren; bootless; effete; feckless; feeble; fruitless; futile; impotent; inadequate; inconsequential; inconsiderable; ineffective; ineffectual; infertile; insignificant; inutile; meaningless; meritless; nugatory; null; of no value; pointless; powerless; profitless; sterile; trifling; trivial; unavailing; unimportant; unproductive; unprofitable; unserviceable; unworthy; useless; vain; valueless; weak; worthless.* ■ I say to you that the governor's budget is *not worth the paper it's written on.* REPLACE WITH *useless.* ■ He went on to say that he did not believe in the United States Constitution, and that it was *not worth the paper it's printed on.* REPLACE WITH *nugatory.*

no use crying over spilt milk A popular prescription (SEE PAGE 21).

no way An infantile phrase (SEE PAGE 18). *at no time; by no means; in no way; never; no; not at all; not ever; not in any way; not in the least.*

no way José An infantile phrase (SEE PAGE 18). *at no time; by no means; in no way; never; no; not at all; not ever; not in any way; not in the least.*

now it's my time (turn) A plebeian sentiment (SEE PAGE 20). ■ I've done my family duty and brought up my children, and *now it's my turn.*

now you see it, now you don't An infantile phrase (SEE PAGE 18).

null and void An inescapable pair (SEE PAGE 18). *abolished; annulled; canceled; countermanded; invalid; null; nullified; recalled; repealed; rescinded; revoked; void; withdrawn; worthless.* ■ We aren't sure what the terms of the deal are, or what may be expected of them, or what may make them *null and void.* REPLACE WITH *invalid.*

(her) number is up A moribund metaphor (SEE PAGE 19).

(a) ... number (of) A torpid term

(SEE PAGE 22). ■ You can use the computer to discover students who are making *a large number of* mistakes. REPLACE WITH *many.* ■ *A good number* of troops have arrived in Moscow. REPLACE WITH *Hundreds.* ■ *An overwhelming number of* the participatory lenders have now joined the major banks in supporting our plan. REPLACE WITH *Almost all.* ■ They are dependent upon the teacher's pension, which is fully given at the age of 62 after *a large number of teaching years.* REPLACE WITH *years of teaching.* SEE ALSO *a (the) ... majority (of); a sufficient number (of).*

number-one A moribund metaphor (SEE PAGE 19). *chief; foremost; leading; main; primary; prime; principal.*

number one (two) A wretched redundancy (SEE PAGE 23). *first (second).* ■ *Number one,* I don't feel that qualifies her as black. *Number two,* a person's color shouldn't be worn on their sleeve. REPLACE WITH *First; Second.*

nuts and bolts A moribund metaphor (SEE PAGE 19). *basics; essentials; facts; foundation; fundamentals; principles.* ■ In this text, we explore the *nuts and bolts* of radio production. REPLACE WITH *essentials.*

nuttier than a fruitcake A moribund metaphor (SEE PAGE 19). *batty; cracked; crazy; daft; demented; deranged; fey; foolish; goofy; insane; lunatic; mad; maniacal; neurotic; nuts; nutty; psychotic; raving; silly; squirrelly; touched; unbalanced; unhinged; unsound; wacky; zany.*

(as) nutty as a fruitcake An insipid simile (SEE PAGE 19). *batty; cracked; crazy; daft; demented; deranged; fey; foolish; goofy; insane; lunatic; mad; maniacal; neurotic; nuts; nutty; psychotic; raving; silly; squirrelly; touched; unbalanced; unhinged; unsound; wacky; zany.*

O

object of one's affection An infantile phrase (SEE PAGE 18). *admirer; beau; beloved; boyfriend (girlfriend); companion; darling; dear; flame; infatuate; inamorato (inamorata); lover; paramour; steady; suiter; swain; sweetheart; wooer.* SEE ALSO *significant other.*

obscene An overworked word (SEE PAGE 20). *abhorrent; abominable; accursed; appalling; atrocious; awful; beastly; blasphemous; detestable; disagreeable; disgusting; dreadful; execrable; frightening; frightful; ghastly; grisly; gruesome; hateful; horrendous; horrible; horrid; horrifying; indecent; indelicate; inhuman; insulting; loathesome; monstrous; obnoxious; odious; offensive; repellent; repugnant; repulsive; revolting; tasteless; terrible; terrifying; unspeakable; unutterable; vulgar.* ■ Certain levels of expenditure are *obscene* and do a great injustice to our concept of social justice. REPLACE WITH *offensive.* ■ It's an *obscene* scenario that's being played out. REPLACE WITH *unspeakable.*

obviate the need for A wretched redundancy (SEE PAGE 23). *obviate.*

■ If indicated, create a limited-access, safe unit to *obviate the need for* activity restriction. DELETE *the need for.*

(an) ocean of A moribund metaphor (SEE PAGE 19). SEE ALSO *a barrage of.*

oceans of ink A moribund metaphor (SEE PAGE 19). *bureaucracy; formalities; paperwork; procedures; regulations; rules.*

(disaster) of biblical proportions A moribund metaphor (SEE PAGE 19). *colossal; elephantine; enormous; gargantuan; giant; gigantic; great; huge; immense; mammoth; massive; monstrous; prodigious; stupendous; titanic; tremendous; vast.*

off and running A moribund metaphor (SEE PAGE 19).

off base A moribund metaphor (SEE PAGE 19). *amiss; astray; deceived; deluded; erring; erroneous; fallacious; false; faulty; inaccurate; incorrect; in error; misguided; misinformed; mislead; mistaken; not correct; not right; wrong.* ■ Given all the uncertainty surrounding the nation's economic future, no one is prepared to say the administration is *off base.* REPLACE WITH *incorrect.*

off-putting A torpid term (SEE PAGE 22).
1. *agitating; discomfiting; discomposing; disconcerting; disquieting; disturbing; unsettling.*
2. *abhorrent; abominable; appalling; atrocious; awful; disagreeable; disgusting; distasteful; objectionable; offensive; repellent; repugnant; repulsive; revolting.* ■ This fact will undoubtedly be *off-putting* to some students. REPLACE WITH *repellent.*

off (her) rocker A moribund metaphor (SEE PAGE 19). *batty; cracked; crazy; daft; demented; deranged; fey; foolish; goofy; insane; lunatic; mad; maniacal; neurotic; nuts; nutty; psychotic; raving; silly; squirrelly; touched; unbalanced; unhinged; unsound; wacky; zany.*

off the beaten path (track) A moribund metaphor (SEE PAGE 19).
1. *aberrant; abnormal; anomalistic; anomalous; atypical; bizarre; curious; deviant; different; distinct; distinctive; eccentric; exceptional; extraordinary; fantastic; foreign; grotesque; idiosyncratic; independent; individual; individualistic; irregular; novel; odd; offbeat; original; peculiar; queer; strange; uncommon; unconventional; unexampled; unique; unnatural; unorthodox; unusual; weird.*
2. *inaccessible; isolated; remote; secluded; unreachable.* ■ A lot of smaller towns of 800 to 3000 people are *off the beaten path.* REPLACE WITH *remote.*

off the cuff A moribund metaphor (SEE PAGE 19). *extemporaneous; extempore; impromptu; improvised; spontaneous; unprepared; unprompted; unrehearsed.*

(go) off the deep end A moribund metaphor (SEE PAGE 19). *batty; cracked; crazy; daft; demented; deranged; fey; foolish; goofy; insane; lunatic; mad; maniacal; neurotic; nuts; nutty; psychotic; raving; silly; squirrelly; touched; unbalanced; unhinged; unsound; wacky; zany.*

(let) off the hook A moribund metaphor (SEE PAGE 19). *absolve; acquit; clear; condone; exculpate; excuse; exonerate; forgive; overlook; pardon; remit; vindicate.* ■ Confronting sexual issues is so taboo in most African culture that rapists are frequently *let off the hook* because few families will endure the public shame of acknowledging the abuse. REPLACE WITH *acquitted.* ■ But as news events in the scandal coverage ebb, the media have had to find new ways to *let Clinton off the hook.* REPLACE WITH *absolve Clinton.* ■ Now she's calling for Nicaragua and Honduras to be *let off the hook* for at least two years. REPLACE WITH *excused.*

off the record A moribund metaphor (SEE PAGE 19). *classified; confidential; personal; private; privy; restricted; secret.*

off the top of (my) head A moribund metaphor (SEE PAGE 19). *extemporaneous; extempore; im-*

promptu; improvised; spontaneous; unprepared; unprompted; unrehearsed.

off the wall A moribund metaphor (SEE PAGE 19). *aberrant; abnormal; anomalistic; anomalous; atypical; bizarre; curious; deviant; different; distinct; distinctive; eccentric; exceptional; extraordinary; fantastic; foreign; grotesque; idiosyncratic; independent; individual; individualistic; irregular; novel; odd; offbeat; original; peculiar; puzzling; quaint; queer; rare; remarkable; separate; singular; strange; uncommon; unconventional; unexampled; unique; unorthodox; unparalleled; unprecedented; unusual; weird.*

off to the races A moribund metaphor (SEE PAGE 19).

off track A moribund metaphor (SEE PAGE 19). *amiss; astray; deceived; deluded; erring; erroneous; fallacious; false; faulty; inaccurate; incorrect; in error; misguided; misinformed; mislead; mistaken; not correct; not right; wrong.*

off (her) trolley A moribund metaphor (SEE PAGE 19). *batty; cracked; crazy; daft; demented; deranged; fey; foolish; goofy; insane; lunatic; mad; maniacal; neurotic; nuts; nutty; psychotic; raving; silly; squirrelly; touched; unbalanced; unhinged; unsound; wacky; zany.*

oftentimes A wretched redundancy (SEE PAGE 23). *frequently; often; repeatedly.* ■ *Oftentimes*, this results in overloading the office staff with the added responsibility of planning the company's meetings and events. REPLACE WITH *Often*.

of the first water A moribund metaphor (SEE PAGE 19). *best; brightest; choice; choicest; elite; excellent; finest; first-class; first-rate; foremost; greatest; highest; highest quality; matchless; optimal; optimum; outstanding; paramount; peerless; preeminent; premium; prominent; select; superior; superlative; top; unequaled; unexcelled; unmatched; unrivaled; unsurpassed.*

ofttimes A withered word (SEE PAGE 22). *frequently; often; repeatedly.*

of two minds A moribund metaphor (SEE PAGE 19). *ambivalent; confused; divided; indecisive; in doubt; irresolute; neutral; torn; uncertain; uncommitted; undecided; unsure.*

O.K.? An infantile phrase (SEE PAGE 18). ■ I don't have a lot of respect for people who judge others by their skin tone, *O.K.?* DELETE *O.K.?* ■ I have a master's degree, *O.K.?* but if I dress bad or speak bad, I'm treated bad, *O.K.?* DELETE *O.K.?* ■ Once that sperm hits that egg, *O.K.?* you have no rights after that, *O.K.?* DELETE *O.K.?* ■ What I did was wrong, *O.K.?* I shouldn't have done it, *O.K.?* I did my time for it, *O.K.?* DELETE *O.K.?*

old adage A wretched redundancy (SEE PAGE 23). *adage.* ■ The *old adage* "The first half of our lives is ruined by our parents and the last half by our children" need not be and should not be. DELETE *old*.

old and decrepit An inescapable pair (SEE PAGE 18).

(as) old as Adam An insipid simile (SEE PAGE 19). *aged; aging; ancient; antediluvian; antique; archaic; elderly; hoary; hoary-headed; old; patriarchal; prehistoric; seasoned; superannuated; venerable.*

(as) old as the hills An insipid simile (SEE PAGE 19). *aged; aging; ancient; antediluvian; antique; archaic; elderly; hoary; hoary-headed; old; patriarchal; prehistoric; seasoned; superannuated; venerable.*

(as) old as time An insipid simile (SEE PAGE 19). *aged; aging; ancient; antediluvian; antique; archaic; elderly; hoary; hoary-headed; old; patriarchal; prehistoric; seasoned; superannuated; venerable.*

old-boy network A moribund metaphor (SEE PAGE 19).

old cliché A wretched redundancy (SEE PAGE 23). *cliché.* ■ Working for these guys I feel like the *old cliché* "a cog in the wheel." DELETE *old*.

old enough to know better An infantile phrase (SEE PAGE 18).

old enough to know better but young enough not to care An infantile phrase (SEE PAGE 18).

(an) old hand A moribund metaphor (SEE PAGE 19). *able; adept; apt; capable; competent; deft; dexterous; experienced; expert; practiced; proficient; seasoned; skilled; skillful; veteran.*

old hat A moribund metaphor (SEE PAGE 19).
1. *antediluvian; antiquated; archaic; dead; obsolescent; obsolete; old; old-fashioned; outdated; outmoded; out of date; out of fashion; passé; superannuated.*
2. *anodyne; banal; barren; bland; boring; deadly; dreary; dry; dull; everyday; flat; humdrum; inanimate; insipid; jejune; lifeless; lusterless; mediocre; monotonous; prosaic; routine; spiritless; stale; tedious; tiresome; unexciting; uninteresting; vapid; wearisome.*

old maxim A wretched redundancy (SEE PAGE 23). *maxim.* ■ A number of studies indicate that, in deciding what punishment is appropriate for different crimes, individuals typically rely on an *old maxim*: Let the punishment fit the crime. DELETE *old*.

old saw A wretched redundancy (SEE PAGE 23). *saw.* ■ The claim is similar to the *old saw* from the tobacco industry, now proven false, that there is no direct link between cancer and smoking. DELETE *old*.

old saying A wretched redundancy (SEE PAGE 23). *saying.* ■ The *old saying* "A picture is worth a thousand words" is usually true. DELETE *old*.

old wives' tale A moribund metaphor (SEE PAGE 19).

on a ... basis A wretched redundancy (SEE PAGE 23). ■ Meat production is the major use of goats *on a worldwide basis*. REPLACE WITH *worldwide*. ■ I am tortured *on a daily basis*. REPLACE WITH *daily*. ■ I see him for my treatment *on a regular basis*. REPLACE WITH *regularly*. ■ You meet the students *on a weekly basis*. REPLACE WITH *weekly*. ■ We should look at these issues *on a case by case basis*. REPLACE WITH *case by case*.

on a collision course A moribund metaphor (SEE PAGE 19).

on a different wavelength A moribund metaphor (SEE PAGE 19). *conflict; differ; disagree; disharmonize; feel differently; think unalike.*

(working) on all cylinders A moribund metaphor (SEE PAGE 19). 1. *able; adept; apt; capable; competent; conversant; deft; dexterous; experienced; expert; familiar; practiced; proficient; seasoned; skilled; skillful; veteran.* ■ This rapid growth cycle is a challenge opportunity and needs good *people working on all cylinders* to take advantage of it. REPLACE WITH *capable people*. 2. *adroit; astute; bright; brilliant; clever; discerning; effective; effectual; efficient; enlightened; insightful; intelligent; judicious; keen; knowledgeable; learned; logical; luminous; perceptive; perspicacious; quick; rational; reasonable; sagacious; sage; sapient; sensible; sharp; shrewd; smart; sound; understanding; wise.*

on an even keel A moribund metaphor (SEE PAGE 19). *balanced; even; firm; fixed; stable; steadfast; steady; unfaltering; unwavering.*

on a ... note A wretched redundancy (SEE PAGE 23). ■ *On a personal note*, I would not be all that appalled if my children were to perform well only 99 percent of the time. REPLACE WITH *Personally*.

on a roll A moribund metaphor (SEE PAGE 19). *doing well; flourishing; prospering; succeeding; thriving.*

on a scale of 1 to 10 An infantile phrase (SEE PAGE 18). The popularity of this phrase is further evidence of the delight some people have with numbers and counting and the distaste they have for words and concepts. Of course, their fondness for numbers may not go much beyond the count of 10 — so, too, perhaps the number of words in their vocabulary. ■ *On a scale of 1 to 10*, how much does uncertainty surrounding laws and regulations in [COUNTRY] increase the risk of equities in that country? ■ *On a scale of 1 to 10*, just how good a student are you? ■ *On a scale of 1 to 10* (1 being the lowest, 10 being the highest) please rank the usefulness and intuitiveness of the website's navigational elements. ■ How would you rank your programming skills (in your best language) *on a scale of 1 to 10*, with 1 being lowest and 10 being highest? SEE ALSO *(for) a laugh; avid reader.*

on a shoestring   A moribund metaphor (SEE PAGE 19). *cheaply; economically; inexpensively; reasonably.*

on automatic pilot   A moribund metaphor (SEE PAGE 19). *automatic; habitual; mechanical; routine.*

(come) on board   A moribund metaphor (SEE PAGE 19). ■ Some doctors are starting to *come on board,* but many haven't got a clue what's going on. REPLACE WITH *take alternative medicine seriously.*

on both sides of the fence   A moribund metaphor (SEE PAGE 19). *ambivalent; divided; indecisive; in doubt; irresolute; neutral; torn; uncertain; uncommitted; undecided; unsure.*

once bitten (burned), twice shy   A popular prescription (SEE PAGE 21).

once in a blue moon   A moribund metaphor (SEE PAGE 19). *hardly; infrequently; not often; occasionally; rarely; scarcely; seldom; sporadically; uncommonly.*

once in a lifetime (opportunity)   A moribund metaphor (SEE PAGE 19). *different; exceptional; extraordinary; incomparable; inimitable; matchless; notable; noteworthy; novel; odd; original; peculiar; peerless; rare; remarkable; singular; special; strange; uncommon; unequaled; unexampled; unique; unmatched; unparalleled; unrivaled; unusual; without equal.* ■ This is a *once in a lifetime* opportunity. REPLACE WITH *singular.*

once upon a time   An infantile phrase (SEE PAGE 18).

on cloud nine   A moribund metaphor (SEE PAGE 19). *blissful; blithe; buoyant; cheerful; delighted; ecstatic; elated; enraptured; euphoric; exalted; excited; exhilarated; exultant; gay; glad; gleeful; good-humored; happy; intoxicated; jolly; jovial; joyful; joyous; jubilant; merry; mirthful; overjoyed; pleased; rapturous; thrilled.*

on (our) doorstep   A moribund metaphor (SEE PAGE 19). *approaching; at hand; close; coming; expected; forthcoming; imminent; impending; looming; near; nearby.*

(the) one and only   A wretched redundancy (SEE PAGE 23). *one; only; sole.* ■ In the early days of any business, the *one and only* thing you understand is that the customer is king. REPLACE WITH *one* or *only.*

one and the same   A wretched redundancy (SEE PAGE 23). *identical; one; the same.* ■ Are you saying that submission and competition are *one and the same*? REPLACE WITH *the same.* ■ Some people believe that marketing and advertising are *one and the same.* REPLACE WITH *identical.*

on easy street   A moribund metaphor (SEE PAGE 19). *affluent; moneyed; opulent; prosperous; rich; wealthy; well-off; well-to-do.*

one big, happy family   A suspect superlative (SEE PAGE 22).

one foot in and one foot out A moribund metaphor (SEE PAGE 19). *ambivalent; divided; indecisive; irresolute; torn; uncertain; uncommitted; undecided; unsure.*

(put) one foot in front of the other A moribund metaphor (SEE PAGE 19).

one foot in the grave A moribund metaphor (SEE PAGE 19). *decaying; declining; deteriorating; disintegrating; dying; ebbing; expiring; fading; failing; moribund; near death; sinking; very ill; waning.*

one for the books A moribund metaphor (SEE PAGE 19). *different; exceptional; extraordinary; incomparable; inimitable; matchless; notable; noteworthy; novel; odd; original; peculiar; peerless; remarkable; singular; special; strange; uncommon; unequaled; unexampled; unique; unmatched; unparalleled; unrivaled; unusual; without equal.*

one good turn deserves another A popular prescription (SEE PAGE 21).

one hundred (100) percent An infantile phrase (SEE PAGE 18). *absolutely; altogether; categorically; completely; entirely; fully; perfectly; positively; quite; roundly; thoroughly; totally; unconditionally; unreservedly; utterly; wholly.* ■ I agree with you *one hundred percent*. REPLACE WITH *unreservedly*.

one in a million A moribund metaphor (SEE PAGE 19). *different; exceptional; extraordinary; incompa-rable; inimitable; matchless; notable; noteworthy; novel; odd; original; peculiar; peerless; remarkable; singular; special; strange; uncommon; unequaled; unexampled; unique; unmatched; unparalleled; unrivaled; unusual; without equal.* ■ One teacher commented that Philip is *one in a million*. REPLACE WITH *peerless*.

one man's meat is another man's poison A popular prescription (SEE PAGE 21).

one man's trash is another man's treasure A popular prescription (SEE PAGE 21).

one of a kind A torpid term (SEE PAGE 22). *different; exceptional; extraordinary; incomparable; inimitable; matchless; notable; noteworthy; novel; odd; original; peculiar; peerless; remarkable; singular; special; strange; uncommon; unequaled; unexampled; unique; unmatched; unparalleled; unrivaled; unusual; without equal.*

one size fits all An infantile phrase (SEE PAGE 18). *procrustean.* ■ We do not advocate a *one-size-fits-all* approach in making decisions about how students should be educated. REPLACE WITH *procrustean*.

one step at a time A popular prescription (SEE PAGE 21).

(well) one thing led to another A grammatical gimmick (SEE PAGE 17).

one-two punch A moribund metaphor (SEE PAGE 19).

one-way street A moribund metaphor (SEE PAGE 19).

one-way ticket to A moribund metaphor (SEE PAGE 19).

on firm (solid) ground A moribund metaphor (SEE PAGE 19). *firm; solid; sound; stable; sturdy.*

ongoing An overworked word (SEE PAGE 20). *Ongoing* has superseded practically all of its synonyms. We have *ongoing basis; ongoing care; ongoing commitment; ongoing destruction; ongoing discussions; ongoing education; ongoing effort; ongoing investigation; ongoing plan; ongoing process; ongoing program; ongoing relationship; ongoing service; ongoing support;* and so many more.

Consider these synonyms: *ceaseless; constant; continual; continuing; continuous; endless; enduring; incessant; lifelong; long-lived; nonstop; progressing; unbroken; unceasing; unremitting.* ■ With this new rehabilitation center, patients will no longer have to travel outside the community to receive the *ongoing* care they need. DELETE *ongoing.* ■ Establishing paternity also may force more women into *ongoing* relationships with fathers who are abusive or violent. REPLACE WITH *lifelong.*

(up) on (her) high horse A moribund metaphor (SEE PAGE 19). *arrogant; cavalier; condescending; contemptuous; despotic; dictatorial; disdainful; dogmatic; domineering; haughty; imperious; insolent; lofty;* *overbearing; overweening; patronizing; pompous; pretentious; scornful; self-important; supercilious; superior; vainglorious.*

on (its) last legs A moribund metaphor (SEE PAGE 19).
1. *decaying; declining; deteriorating; disappearing; disintegrating; dying; ebbing; expiring; fading; failing; moribund; near death; sinking; vanishing; waning.*
2. *beat; bushed; debilitated; depleted; drained; drowsy; enervated; exhausted; fatigued; groggy; sapped; sleepy; sluggish; slumberous; somnolent; soporific; spent; tired; weary; worn out.*
■ The battle for a smoke-free environment is hardly *on its last legs.* REPLACE WITH *moribund.*

(the) only good (cat) is a dead (cat) A quack equation (SEE PAGE 21).

only the strong survive A popular prescription (SEE PAGE 21).

on (his) part A wretched redundancy (SEE PAGE 23). *among; by; for; from; of; -s.* ■ I think this is really irresponsible *on your part.* REPLACE WITH *of you.* ■ I guess this is selfish *on my part.* REPLACE WITH *of me.* SEE ALSO *on the part of.*

on pins and needles A moribund metaphor (SEE PAGE 19). *agitated; anxious; apprehensive; disquieted; distressed; disturbed; edgy; fretful; ill at ease; impatient; in suspense; nervous; on edge; restive; restless; troubled; uneasy; unquiet; unsettled; worried.* ■ Democrats — already *on pins and needles* over the release of

Clinton's grand jury testimony — were scrambling yesterday with how to cope over the second tape. REPLACE WITH *uneasy.*

on (her) plate A moribund metaphor (SEE PAGE 19). *awaiting (her); before (her); pending.*

on safe ground A moribund metaphor (SEE PAGE 19). *guarded; protected; safe; secure; sheltered; shielded.*

on shaky ground A moribund metaphor (SEE PAGE 19). *indefensible; shaky; unsound; unsustainable.*

(right) on target A moribund metaphor (SEE PAGE 19). *accurate; correct; exact; irrefutable; precise; right; true.* ■ The Jan. 19 editorial identifying the inconsistent, but vociferous, antitax group as "the haters" is *right on target.* REPLACE WITH *irrefutable.*

on tenterhooks A moribund metaphor (SEE PAGE 19). *agitated; anxious; apprehensive; disquieted; distressed; disturbed; edgy; fretful; ill at ease; impatient; in suspense; nervous; on edge; restive; restless; troubled; uneasy; unquiet; unsettled; worried.*

on the back burner A moribund metaphor (SEE PAGE 19). *in abeyance; on hold; pending; suspended.*

on the ball A moribund metaphor (SEE PAGE 19).
1. *alert; attentive; awake; aware; eagle-eyed; heedful; observant; vigi-*
lant; wakeful; watchful.
2. *able; adroit; apt; astute; bright; brilliant; capable; clever; competent; discerning; effective; effectual; efficient; enlightened; insightful; intelligent; judicious; keen; knowledgeable; learned; logical; luminous; perceptive; perspicacious; quick; rational; reasonable; sagacious; sage; sapient; sensible; sharp; shrewd; smart; sound; understanding; wise.*

on the basis of A wretched redundancy (SEE PAGE 23). *after; based on; because of; by; due to; for; from; in; on; owing to; through; via; with.* ■ NABCO chooses material for this site *on the basis of* its timely and useful content. REPLACE WITH *based on.* ■ Exemption from IRB review and approval is determined *on the basis of* the risks associated with the study. REPLACE WITH *by.* ■ There shall be no discrimination against any individual *on the basis of* ethnic group, race, religion, gender, sexual orientation, age, or record of public offense. REPLACE WITH *because of.*

on the blink A moribund metaphor (SEE PAGE 19). *broken; defective; in disrepair; not working; not functioning; out of order.*

on the brink of A moribund metaphor (SEE PAGE 19). *about to; (very) close (to); (very) near (to).*

(right) on the button A moribund metaphor (SEE PAGE 19). *accurate; correct; exact; irrefutable; precise; right; true.*

on the chopping block A moribund metaphor (SEE PAGE 19). *at risk; endangered; imperiled; in danger; in jeopardy; in peril; in trouble; jeopardized.*

(ride) on the coattails of A moribund metaphor (SEE PAGE 19).

on the cuff A moribund metaphor (SEE PAGE 19). *on credit.*

on the cutting (leading) edge A moribund metaphor (SEE PAGE 19). *first; forefront; foremost; leading; vanguard.*

on the dot A moribund metaphor (SEE PAGE 19). *on time; precisely; promptly; punctually.*

on the drawing board A moribund metaphor (SEE PAGE 19). ■ The university now has seven new schools *on the drawing board.*

on the edge of (their) seats A moribund metaphor (SEE PAGE 19). *absorb; arrest; bewitch; captivate; charm; curious; divert; enchant; engage; engross; entertain; enthrall; entice; excite; fascinate; intrigue; rivet; spellbind; stimulate; tantalize.* ■ People are *on the edge of their seats* about this report. REPLACE WITH *fascinated.*

on the fast track A moribund metaphor (SEE PAGE 19).

(sit) on the fence A moribund metaphor (SEE PAGE 19). *ambivalent; divided; impartial; indecisive; irresolute; neutral; noncommittal; torn; uncertain; uncommitted; undecided; unsettled; unsure.*

on the firing line A moribund metaphor (SEE PAGE 19).

on the fly A moribund metaphor (SEE PAGE 19). *ad-lib; extemporize; improvise.*

on the fritz A moribund metaphor (SEE PAGE 19). *broken; defective; in disrepair; not working; not functioning; out of order.*

on the front lines A moribund metaphor (SEE PAGE 19).

on the go A moribund metaphor (SEE PAGE 19). *absorbed; active; busy; employed; engaged; engrossed; going; immersed; involved; moving; occupied; preoccupied; wrapped up in.*

(hot) on the heels of A moribund metaphor (SEE PAGE 19). *after; behind; ensuing; following; succeeding.* SEE ALSO *in the wake of.*

on the horizon A moribund metaphor (SEE PAGE 19). *approaching; at hand; close; coming; expected; forthcoming; imminent; impending; near; nearby.*

(caught) on the horns of a dilemma A moribund metaphor (SEE PAGE 19). *at risk; endangered; hardpressed; imperiled; in a bind; in a dilemma; in a fix; in a jam; in a predicament; in a quandary; in danger; in difficulty; in jeopardy; in peril; in trouble; jeopardized.*

(take it) on the lam A moribund metaphor (SEE PAGE 19). *abscond; clear out; decamp; depart; desert; disappear; escape; exit; flee; fly; go; go away; leave; move on; part; pull out; quit; retire; retreat; run away; take flight; take off; vacate; vanish; withdraw.*

on the level A torpid term (SEE PAGE 22). *aboveboard; creditable; equitable; fair; genuine; honest; honorable; just; lawful; legitimate; open; proper; reputable; respectable; right; sincere; square; straightforward; truthful; upright; veracious; veridical.*

on the loose A torpid term (SEE PAGE 22). *at large; at liberty; free; loose; unattached; unbound; unconfined; unrestrained; unrestricted.*

on the mend A torpid term (SEE PAGE 22). *ameliorating; amending; coming round; convalescent; convalescing; gaining strength; getting better; healing; improving; looking up; meliorating; mending; rallying; recovering; recuperating; refreshing; renewing; reviving; strengthening.*

(right) on the money A moribund metaphor (SEE PAGE 19). *accurate; correct; exact; fact; irrefutable; precise; right; true.* ■ I think it was *right on the money.* REPLACE WITH *irrefutable.*

on the nose A moribund metaphor (SEE PAGE 19). *accurate; correct; exact; irrefutable; precise; right; true.*

(on the) other side of the coin A moribund metaphor (SEE PAGE 19). 1. *antithesis; contrary; converse; opposite; reverse.* 2. *but; in contrast; conversely; however; inversely; whereas; yet.* ■ *On the other side of the coin,* if you're astute you can occasionally buy them at big discounts. REPLACE WITH *But.*

on the part of A wretched redundancy (SEE PAGE 23). *among; by; for; from; of; -s. On the part of* is a preposition phrase that apparently appeals to bombastic men and women who may not fully consider what they say, for they certainly do not consider how they say it. ■ As a result, and following vigorous lobbying *on the part of* CFS victims, the disease is now called chronic fatigue immunodeficiency syndrome. REPLACE WITH *by.* ■ There is some cultural resistance *on the part of* some U.S. racial and ethnic groups to government-sponsored contraceptive programs. REPLACE WITH *from.* ■ *Misconduct on the part of the police* sometimes also violates the criminal law. REPLACE WITH *Police misconduct.* ■ It has also sometimes been attributed to an attitude *on the part of* health counselors that the poor are charity cases who should be satisfied with whatever they get since they are probably not paying for their own care. REPLACE WITH *among.* ■ If you are to get over the current crisis, *sacrifices on the part of everyone will have to be made.* REPLACE WITH *everyone will have to make sacrifices.* SEE ALSO *on (his) part.*

on the Q.T. A moribund metaphor (SEE PAGE 19). *clandestinely; confidentially; covertly; furtively; mysteri-*

ously; in private; in secret; privately; quietly; secludedly; secretly; slyly; stealthily; surreptitiously; undercover.

on the razor's edge A moribund metaphor (SEE PAGE 19). *at risk; endangered; hard-pressed; imperiled; in danger; in difficulty; in jeopardy; in peril; in trouble; jeopardized.*

(start) on the right foot A moribund metaphor (SEE PAGE 19). *auspiciously; favorably; positively; propitiously; well.*

on the right track A moribund metaphor (SEE PAGE 19). *on target; on track.*

on the road A moribund metaphor (SEE PAGE 19). *traveling.*

on the road to recovery A moribund metaphor (SEE PAGE 19). *ameliorating; amending; coming round; convalescent; convalescing; feeling better; gaining strength; getting better; healing; improving; looking up; meliorating; mending; rallying; recovering; recuperating; refreshing; renewing; reviving; strengthening.* ■ His wife has been ill, but she's *on the road to recovery.* REPLACE WITH *improving.*

on the rocks A moribund metaphor (SEE PAGE 19). *at risk; collapsing; endangered; failing; imperiled; in danger; in difficulty; in jeopardy; in peril; in trouble; jeopardized.* ■ Our marriage is *on the rocks.* REPLACE WITH *imperiled.*

on the ropes A moribund metaphor (SEE PAGE 19).
1. *at risk; endangered; hard-pressed; imperiled; in danger; in difficulty; in jeopardy; in peril; in trouble; jeopardized.*
2. *defenseless; helpless; impotent; powerless.*

on the same wavelength A moribund metaphor (SEE PAGE 19). *agree; concur; feel similarly; harmonize; match; mesh; think alike.*

on the ... side A wretched redundancy (SEE PAGE 23). ■ Tuesday will be *on the chilly side.* REPLACE WITH *chilly.* ■ She is *on the thin side.* REPLACE WITH *thin.* ■ That means the 550,000 estimate is probably *on the low side.* REPLACE WITH *low.*

on the sly A torpid term (SEE PAGE 22). *clandestinely; confidentially; covertly; furtively; mysteriously; in private; in secret; privately; quietly; secludedly; secretly; slyly; stealthily; surreptitiously; undercover.*

on the spot A torpid term (SEE PAGE 22).
1. *at once; directly; forthwith; immediately; instantly; momentarily; promptly; right away; straightaway; summarily; without delay.*
2. *at risk; endangered; hard-pressed; imperiled; in danger; in difficulty; in jeopardy; in peril; in trouble; jeopardized.*

on the spur of the moment A wretched redundancy (SEE PAGE 23). *impetuously; impulsively; spontaneously; suddenly; unexpectedly; without warning.*

on the table A moribund

274

metaphor (SEE PAGE 19). *before us; being considered; under discussion.* ■ A healthy dialog on value systems when there is no pressing issue *on the table* may help clear the air. REPLACE WITH *before us.* ■ There is nothing that is not *on the table.* REPLACE WITH *being considered.*

(out) on the town A moribund metaphor (SEE PAGE 19). *be merry; carouse; carry on; celebrate; debauch; disport; frolic; party; play; revel; riot; roister; rollick; romp; skylark.*

on the up-and-up A torpid term (SEE PAGE 22). *aboveboard; creditable; equitable; fair; honest; honorable; just; lawful; legitimate; open; proper; reputable; respectable; right; sincere; square; straightforward; upright; veracious; veridical.*

on the warpath A moribund metaphor (SEE PAGE 19).
1. *angry; bad-tempered; bilious; cantankerous; choleric; churlish; crabby; cranky; cross; curmudgeonly; disagreeable; dyspeptic; grouchy; gruff; grumpy; ill-humored; ill-tempered; irascible; irritable; mad; peevish; petulant; quarrelsome; riled; roiled; short-tempered; splenetic; surly; testy; vexed.*
2. *aggressive; antagonistic; arguing; argumentative; battling; bellicose; belligerent; bickering; brawling; clashing; combative; contentious; fighting; militant; pugnacious; quarrelsome; querulous; squabbling; truculent; warlike; wrangling.*

on the wings of the wind A moribund metaphor (SEE PAGE 19). *abruptly; apace; at once; briskly;* *directly; expeditiously; fast; forthwith; hastily; hurriedly; immediately; instantaneously; instantly; posthaste; promptly; quickly; rapidly; rashly; right away; speedily; straightaway; swiftly; wingedly.*

(start) on the wrong foot A moribund metaphor (SEE PAGE 19). *adversely; inauspiciously; negatively; unfavorably; unpropitiously.*

on the wrong track A moribund metaphor (SEE PAGE 19). *amiss; astray; deceived; deluded; erring; erroneous; fallacious; false; faulty; inaccurate; incorrect; in error; misguided; misinformed; mislead; mistaken; not correct; not right; wrong.*

(skate) on thin ice A moribund metaphor (SEE PAGE 19). *chance; dare; endanger; gamble; hazard; imperil; jeopardize; make bold; peril; risk; venture.*

(keep) on (his) toes A moribund metaphor (SEE PAGE 19). *(be) alert; (be) attentive; (be) awake; (be) aware; (be) heedful; (be) vigilant; (be) wakeful.*

(sitting) on top of the world A moribund metaphor (SEE PAGE 19).
1. *advantageous; auspicious; blessed; charmed; enchanted; favored; felicitous; flourishing; fortuitous; fortunate; golden; in luck; lucky; propitious; prosperous; successful; thriving.*
2. *blissful; blithe; buoyant; cheerful; delighted; ecstatic; elated; enraptured; euphoric; exalted; excited; exhilarated; exultant; gay; glad; gleeful; good-humored; happy; intoxicated; jolly;*

jovial; joyful; joyous; jubilant; merry; mirthful; overjoyed; pleased; rapturous; thrilled.

onward and upward An inescapable pair (SEE PAGE 18).

open and aboveboard A moribund metaphor (SEE PAGE 19). *aboveboard; creditable; equitable; fair; honest; honorable; just; lawful; legitimate; open; proper; reputable; respectable; right; square; straightforward; upright; veracious; veridical.*

(an) open-and-shut case A moribund metaphor (SEE PAGE 19). *apparent; clear; evident; open; plain; straightforward; unambiguous; uncomplex; uncomplicated.*

open (up) a Pandora's box A moribund metaphor (SEE PAGE 19).

(an) open book A moribund metaphor (SEE PAGE 19).
1. *apparent; clear; clear-cut; crystalline; evident; explicit; limpid; lucid; manifest; obvious; open; patent; pellucid; plain; translucent; transparent; unambiguous; uncomplex; uncomplicated; understandable; unequivocal; unmistakable.*
2. *aboveboard; artless; blunt; candid; direct; forthright; frank; genuine; guileless; honest; ingenuous; naive; sincere; straightforward; truthful; veracious; veridical.*

(the) opening (latest) salvo A moribund metaphor (SEE PAGE 19).

(an) (wide) open question A wretched redundancy (SEE PAGE

23). *a question; debatable; disputable; moot; open; questionable; uncertain; unclear; undecided; undetermined; unknown; unsettled; unsure.* ■ Whether it's still possible for us to complete the project by next season is *an open question* at this point. REPLACE WITH *questionable.*

open the door for (on; to) A moribund metaphor (SEE PAGE 19). *bring about; cause; create; effect; generate; give rise to; inaugurate; initiate; introduce; lead to; occasion; produce; provoke; result in; usher in.* ■ This breakthrough could *open the door to* a wide range of new varieties of important crops. REPLACE WITH *result in.* ■ Human embryo cells have been isolated and grown in the test tube for the first time, a development that could *open the door to* new drug therapies. REPLACE WITH *lead to.*

open the floodgates A moribund metaphor (SEE PAGE 19).

operative A torpid term (SEE PAGE 22). ■ The *operative* philosophy is spelled out early on: Winning is the most important thing in life.

opportunity knocks only once A popular prescription (SEE PAGE 21).

(as) opposed to what? An infantile phrase (SEE PAGE 18). SEE ALSO *(as) compared to what?; everything's (it's all) relative.*

opposites attract A popular prescription (SEE PAGE 21).

or anything A grammatical gimmick (SEE PAGE 17). ■ I didn't go beat her up, *or anything*. DELETE *or anything*. ■ Not to be rude *or anything*, but I don't think we should talk to each other. DELETE *or anything*. SEE ALSO *or anything like that*.

or anything like that A grammatical gimmick (SEE PAGE 17). ■ He wasn't my first boyfriend *or anything like that*. DELETE *or anything like that*. ■ He didn't go out and say, "Who goes there?" *or anything like that*. DELETE *or anything like that*. ■ I really apologize if I was inappropriate or upset you *or anything like that*. DELETE *or anything like that*. SEE ALSO *or anything*.

(an) orgy of A moribund metaphor (SEE PAGE 19). SEE ALSO *a barrage of*.

or (a; the) lack thereof A torpid term (SEE PAGE 22). ■ He was ousted because the majority of voters believe he didn't do a good job as mayor — not because of his skin color, but because of his merit *or lack thereof*.

or something A grammatical gimmick (SEE PAGE 17). ■ This is like something I'd wear in third grade, *or something*. DELETE *or something*. ■ It makes you mad when they make them sound like they're vicious people — that if you walk the street, they're going to grab you *or something*. DELETE *or something*. SEE ALSO *or something like that; or something or other*.

or something like that A grammatical gimmick (SEE PAGE 17). ■ Why couldn't they have shot him in his arm or leg *or something like that*? DELETE *or something like that*. SEE ALSO *or something; or something or other*.

or something or other A grammatical gimmick (SEE PAGE 17). ■ We might go to the movies *or something or other*. DELETE *or something or other*. SEE ALSO *or something; or something like that*.

or what A grammatical gimmick (SEE PAGE 17). ■ Did you see an opportunity for escape, or plan it for a long time, *or what*? DELETE *or what*. ■ Was he being vulgar *or what*? DELETE *or what*. ■ Did you make enough money so you can retire *or what*? REPLACE WITH *or not*.

or whatever A grammatical gimmick (SEE PAGE 17). ■ They say he corrupted my mind *or whatever*. DELETE *or whatever*. ■ Is it a good thing, is it a bad thing, is it useless, *or whatever*? DELETE *or whatever*. ■ She just wants the extra attention, *or whatever*. DELETE *or whatever*. ■ You can call this arrogance or way too much self-assurance *or whatever*. DELETE *or whatever*. ■ The percent remembered is the same whether the audience is a business audience, a college audience, a PTA audience, *or whatever*. DELETE *or whatever*.

or words to that effect A grammatical gimmick (SEE PAGE 17).

out and out A torpid term (SEE PAGE 22). *absolute; compleat; complete; consummate; deadly; outright; perfect; thorough; thoroughgoing; total; unmitigated; unqualified; utter.*

out at the elbows A moribund metaphor (SEE PAGE 19).
1. *dowdy; frowzy; ragged; run-down; seedy; shabby; slipshod; sloppy; slovenly; tattered; threadbare; unkempt; untidy; worn.*
2. *bankrupt; broke; destitute; distressed; impecunious; impoverished; indigent; insolvent; needy; penniless; poor; poverty-stricken; underprivileged.*

out for blood A moribund metaphor (SEE PAGE 19).

out in left field A moribund metaphor (SEE PAGE 19).
1. *amiss; astray; confused; deceived; deluded; erring; erroneous; fallacious; false; faulty; inaccurate; incorrect; in error; misguided; misinformed; mislead; mistaken; not correct; not right; uninformed; wrong.*
2. *ignorant; incognizant; insensible; nescient; unacquainted; unadvised; unapprised; unaware; unenlightened; unfamiliar; unintelligent; unknowing; un-schooled; untaught; unversed.*
■ On this issue, feminists are truly *out in left field.* REPLACE WITH *misguided.*

(they're) out in the cold A moribund metaphor (SEE PAGE 19). *abandoned; alone; assailable; attackable; defenseless; deserted; exposed; forsaken; obnoxious; penetrable; pregnable; stranded; undefended; unguarded; unprotected; unshielded; vulnerable.*

out in the sun too much A moribund metaphor (SEE PAGE 19). *bewildered; confounded; confused; dazed; mixed up; muddled; perplexed.*

out like a light An insipid simile (SEE PAGE 19).
1. *asleep; dozing; napping; sleeping.*
2. *anesthetized; benumbed; comatose; insensate; insensible; insentient; oblivious; senseless; soporiferous; soporific; stuporous; unconscious.*

out of a clear blue sky A moribund metaphor (SEE PAGE 19). *by surprise; suddenly; unexpectedly; without warning.*

out of circulation A moribund metaphor (SEE PAGE 19).
1. *broken; defective; in disrepair; not working; not functioning; out of order.*
2. *afflicted; ailing; diseased; ill; indisposed; infirm; not (feeling) well; sick; sickly; suffering; unhealthy; unsound; unwell; valetudinarian.*

out of commission A moribund metaphor (SEE PAGE 19).
1. *broken; defective; in disrepair; not working; not functioning; out of order.*
2. *afflicted; ailing; diseased; ill; indisposed; infirm; not (feeling) well; sick; sickly; suffering; unhealthy; unsound; unwell; valetudinarian.*

out of gas A moribund metaphor (SEE PAGE 19). *beat; bushed; debilitated; depleted; drained; drowsy; enervated; exhausted; fatigued; groggy; sapped; sleepy; sluggish; slumberous; somnolent; soporific; spent; tired; weary; worn out.*

out of harm's way A moribund metaphor (See page 19). *guarded; protected; safe; secure; sheltered; shielded; undamaged; unharmed; unhurt; unscathed.*

out of it A moribund metaphor (See page 19). *ignorant; incognizant; insensible; nescient; unacquainted; unadvised; unapprised; unaware; unenlightened; unfamiliar; uninformed; unintelligent; unknowing; unschooled; untaught; unversed.*

out of kilter A moribund metaphor (See page 19).
1. *broken; defective; in disrepair; not working; not functioning; out of order.*
2. *lopsided; shaky; unbalanced; unsettled; unsound; unstable; wobbly.*

out of line A moribund metaphor (See page 19).
1. *improper; inappropriate; inapt; indecorous; unbefitting; uncalled for; unfit; unfitting; unsuitable; unsuited.*
2. *boisterous; contrary; contumacious; disobedient; disorderly; fractious; insubordinate; misbehaving; obstreperous; rebellious; recalcitrant; refractory; rowdy; uncontrolled; undisciplined; unruly.*

out of reach A moribund metaphor (See page 19).
1. *inaccessible; remote; unapproachable; unreachable.*
2. *impossible; impracticable; improbable; unfeasible; unlikely; unworkable.*

out of sorts A moribund metaphor (See page 19). *angry; annoyed; cheerless; cross; dejected; depressed; despondent; discouraged; dispirited; displeased; downcast; enraged; furious; gloomy; glum; grouchy; irate; irritated; mad; morose; peevish; riled; roiled; sad; testy; troubled; uneasy; unhappy; upset; vexed; worried.*

out of sync A moribund metaphor (See page 19).
1. *broken; defective; in disrepair; not working; not functioning; out of order.*
2. *lopsided; shaky; unbalanced; unsettled; unsound; unstable; wobbly.*

out of the blue A moribund metaphor (See page 19). *by surprise; suddenly; unexpectedly; without warning.*

out of the frying pan and into the fire A moribund metaphor (See page 19). *aggravate; complicate; exacerbate; heighten; increase; intensify; irritate; make worse; worsen.*

out of the game A moribund metaphor (See page 19).

out of the realm of possibility A wretched redundancy (See page 23). *implausible; imponderable; impossible; impracticable; inconceivable; infeasible; not likely; unbelievable; unconjecturable; unimaginable; unsupposable; unthinkable; unworkable.* ■ It's not *out of the realm of possibility* that he wants to embarrass the president. Replace with *unthinkable*.

out of the running A moribund metaphor (See page 19). *noncontender; not competing; not contending.*

out of the woods A moribund metaphor (SEE PAGE 19). *guarded; protected; safe; secure; sheltered; shielded; undamaged; unharmed; unhurt; unscathed.*

out of thin air A moribund metaphor (SEE PAGE 19).

out of this world A moribund metaphor (SEE PAGE 19). *consummate; distinguished; eminent; excellent; exceptional; exemplary; exquisite; extraordinary; fabulous; fantastic; flawless; grand; great; ideal; illustrious; magnificent; marvelous; matchless; perfect; preeminent; remarkable; splendid; superb; superior; superlative; supreme; terrific; transcendent; tremendous; wonderful; wondrous.*

out of whack A moribund metaphor (SEE PAGE 19).
1. *broken; defective; in disrepair; not working; not functioning; out of order.*
2. *lopsided; shaky; unbalanced; unsettled; unsound; unstable; wobbly.*

out on a limb A moribund metaphor (SEE PAGE 19).
1. *at risk; endangered; hard-pressed; imperiled; in a bind; in a dilemma; in a fix; in a jam; in a predicament; in a quandary; in danger; in difficulty; in jeopardy; in peril; in trouble; jeopardized.*
2. *abandoned; alone; assailable; attackable; defenseless; deserted; exposed; forsaken; obnoxious; penetrable; pregnable; stranded; undefended; unguarded; unprotected; unshielded; vulnerable.*
3. *be adventuresome; be adventurous; be bold; be daring.*

output A torpid term (SEE PAGE 22). SEE ALSO *(the) bottom line; feedback; input; interface; parameters.*

out the window A moribund metaphor (SEE PAGE 19).
1. *abandoned; discarded; dismissed; jettisoned; rejected; repudiated; thrown out; tossed out.* ■ It's 1999 in America, a land where common sense *went out the window* long ago. REPLACE WITH *was jettisoned.*
2. *dead; disappeared; dissolved; dispersed; evaporated; finished; forfeited; gone; inapplicable; inappropriate; inoperative; insignificant; irrelevant; lost; no longer applicable (apply); over; passed; scattered; unimportant; vanished.* ■ It's just that old rules are *out the window*, like most of last year's assumptions about Europe. REPLACE WITH *inapplicable.*

out to lunch A moribund metaphor (SEE PAGE 19).
1. *absent-minded; absorbed; abstracted; bemused; daydreaming; distrait; dreamy; faraway; lost; preoccupied.*
2. *forgetful; heedless; inattentive; lethean; neglectful; oblivious; unmindful.*
3. *ignorant; incognizant; insensible; nescient; unacquainted; unadvised; unapprised; unaware; unenlightened; unfamiliar; unintelligent; unknowing; unschooled; untaught; unversed.*
4. *amiss; astray; confused; deceived; deluded; erring; erroneous; fallacious; false; faulty; inaccurate; incorrect; in error; misguided; misinformed; mislead; mistaken; not correct; not right; uninformed; wrong.*

(put) out to pasture A moribund metaphor (SEE PAGE 19). *discharge;*

dismiss; fire; lay off; let go; release; retire; sack; set aside; shelve. ■ Motors Inc. said Joe will be *put out to pasture* when it introduces next year's lineup of vehicles. REPLACE WITH *retired.*

over a barrel A moribund metaphor (SEE PAGE 19). *defenseless; helpless; impotent; powerless.*

over and done with A wretched redundancy (SEE PAGE 23). *completed; concluded; done; ended; finished; over; passed; through.* ■ But in reality, it is the same old story, one we'd like to think of as *over and done with.* REPLACE WITH *concluded.*

over (my) dead body A moribund metaphor (SEE PAGE 19). *at no time; by no means; in no way; never; no; not at all; not ever; not in any way; not in the least*

overplay (his) hand A moribund metaphor (SEE PAGE 19).

(go) over the edge A moribund metaphor (SEE PAGE 19). *batty;*

cracked; crazy; daft; demented; deranged; fey; foolish; goofy; insane; lunatic; mad; maniacal; neurotic; nuts; nutty; psychotic; raving; silly; squirrelly; touched; unbalanced; unhinged; unsound; wacky; zany.

over the hill A moribund metaphor (SEE PAGE 19). *aged; aging; ancient; antediluvian; antique; archaic; elderly; hoary; hoary-headed; old; patriarchal; prehistoric; seasoned; superannuated; venerable.*

over the transom A moribund metaphor (SEE PAGE 19).

overworked and understaffed An inescapable pair (SEE PAGE 18).

owing to the fact that A wretched redundancy (SEE PAGE 23). *because; considering; for; in that; since.* ■ *Owing to the fact that* many companies are members of more than one EDI system, it is helpful if they all change in recognizable ways. REPLACE WITH *Since.* SEE ALSO *attributable to the fact that; due to the fact that.*

P

pack a punch (wallop) A moribund metaphor (SEE PAGE 19). *cogent; convincing; dynamic; effective; effectual; emotional; energetic; ferocious; fierce; forceful; formidable; gripping; hard-hitting; herculean; impassioned; inspiring; intense; lively; mighty; moving; passionate; persuasive; potent; powerful; strong; vehement; vigorous; vital.* ■ No doubt hurricane Bonnie is still *packing a punch.* REPLACE WITH *mighty.*

packed in like sardines An insipid simile (SEE PAGE 19). *abounding; brimful; brimming; bursting; chock-full; congested; crammed; crowded; dense; filled; full; gorged; jammed; jam-packed; overcrowded; overfilled; overflowing; packed; replete; saturated; stuffed; swarming; teeming.*

pack to the rafters A moribund metaphor (SEE PAGE 19). *abounding; brimful; brimming; bursting; chock-full; congested; crammed; crowded; dense; filled; full; gorged; jammed; jam-packed; overcrowded; overfilled; overflowing; packed; replete; saturated; stuffed; swarming; teeming.*

pack up and leave A moribund metaphor (SEE PAGE 19). *abscond; clear out; decamp; depart; desert; disappear; escape; exit; flee; fly; go; go away; leave; move on; part; pull out; quit; retire; retreat; run away; take flight; take off; vacate; vanish; withdraw.*

paddle (my) own canoe A moribund metaphor (SEE PAGE 19). *autonomous; free; independent; self-reliant.* ■ I like to *paddle my own canoe* in life, but when you have holes in your canoe, it's hard to know what to do.

pain and suffering An inescapable pair (SEE PAGE 18). *agony; anguish; distress; grief; misery; pain; suffering; torment; worry.*

painfully shy An inescapable pair (SEE PAGE 18). *afraid; apprehensive; bashful; coy; demure; diffident; distant; fearful; humble; introverted; meek; modest; pavid; quiet; reserved; reticent; retiring; sheepish; shrinking; shy; timid; timorous; tremulous; unassuming; unobtrusive; unsociable; unsocial; withdrawn.*

(a) pain in the ass (rear) A moribund metaphor (SEE PAGE 19). *affliction; annoyance; bane; bother;*

burden; curse; difficulty; inconvenience; irritant; irritation; load; nuisance; ordeal; pain; pest; plague; problem; torment; tribulation; trouble; vexation; weight; worry.

(a) pain in the neck A moribund metaphor (SEE PAGE 19). affliction; annoyance; bane; bother; burden; curse; difficulty; inconvenience; irritant; irritation; load; nuisance; ordeal; pain; pest; plague; problem; torment; tribulation; trouble; vexation; weight; worry.

paint a (rosy) picture of A moribund metaphor (SEE PAGE 19). delineate; demonstrate; depict; describe; document; draw; evince; illustrate; indicate; paint; picture; portray; present; report; represent; reveal; show. ■ The document will paint a picture of the nation's worsening financial system and warn that many large banks are near insolvency. REPLACE WITH describe. ■ Together, they paint a picture of hard times ahead. REPLACE WITH portray.

paint (himself) into a corner A moribund metaphor (SEE PAGE 19). at bay; catch; corner; enmesh; ensnare; entangle; entrap; net; snare; trap.

paint the town red A moribund metaphor (SEE PAGE 19). be merry; carouse; carry on; celebrate; debauch; disport; frolic; party; play; revel; riot; roister; rollick; romp; skylark.

paint with a broad brush A moribund metaphor (SEE PAGE 19). generalize; universalize.

pair of (two) twins A wretched redundancy (SEE PAGE 23). twins. ■ There were two twins at the mall who came up to him and asked him out. DELETE two.

(as) pale as a ghost An insipid simile (SEE PAGE 19). anemic; ashen; blanched; bloodless; cadaverous; colorless; deathlike; doughy; haggard; lusterless; pale; pallid; pasty; peaked; sallow; sickly; wan; whitish.

parameter An overworked word (SEE PAGE 20).
1. boundary; guideline; guidepost; limit; limitation; perimeter. ■ We would like to send you our most recent catalog to see if any of our books fit within your reviewing parameters. REPLACE WITH guidelines.
2. characteristic; factor. ■ At this time, potential funding parameters may change in a variety of ways. REPLACE WITH characteristics. SEE ALSO (the) bottom line; feedback; input; interface; output.

pardon my French An infantile phrase (SEE PAGE 18).

par excellence A foreign phrase (SEE PAGE 17). incomparable; preeminent.

par for the course A moribund metaphor (SEE PAGE 19). average; common; commonplace; customary; everyday; mediocre; middling; normal; ordinary; quotidian; regular; routine; standard; typical; uneventful; unexceptional; unremarkable; usual. ■ That is par for the course for foreign businesses here, which have descended upon the Soviet Union much as they descended upon China. REPLACE WITH *normal*. ■ It's *par for the course* for this administration to blame all of its troubles on someone else. REPLACE WITH *customary*.

part and parcel An inescapable pair (SEE PAGE 18). *component; element; factor; part; portion.*

parting is such sweet sorrow A popular prescription (SEE PAGE 21).

parting of the ways A moribund metaphor (SEE PAGE 19). *altercation; argument; conflict; disagreement; discord; disputation; dispute; feud; fight; misunderstanding; quarrel; rift; row; spat; squabble.*

partner in crime A moribund metaphor (SEE PAGE 19). *abettor; accessory; accomplice; affiliate; ally; assistant; associate; co-conspirator; cohort; collaborator; colleague; compatriot; compeer; comrade; confederate; consort; co-worker; crony; partner; peer.*

part of the landscape A moribund metaphor (SEE PAGE 19).

pass the buck A moribund metaphor (SEE PAGE 19). *ascribe; assign; attribute; impute.*

pass the time of day A moribund metaphor (SEE PAGE 19). *babble; blab; cackle; chaffer; chat; chitchat; chatter; confabulate; converse; gossip; jabber; palaver; prate; prattle; rattle; talk.*

pass with flying colors A moribund metaphor (SEE PAGE 19). *ace; do well; excel; shine.*

past experience A wretched redundancy (SEE PAGE 23). *experience.* ■ I know from *past experience* that a lot of you are not going to like what I have to say. DELETE *past.*

past history A wretched redundancy (SEE PAGE 23). *history.* ■ We did not anticipate that the town would attempt to live off of its *past history.* DELETE *past.*

past (his) prime A torpid term (SEE PAGE 22). *aged; aging; ancient; antediluvian; antique; archaic; elderly; hoary; hoary-headed; old; patriarchal; prehistoric; seasoned; superannuated; venerable.*

past the point of no return A moribund metaphor (SEE PAGE 19).

patience is a virtue A popular prescription (SEE PAGE 21).

(as) patient as Job An insipid simile (SEE PAGE 19). *accepting; accommodating; acquiescent; complacent; complaisant; compliant; cowed; deferential; docile; dutiful; easy; forbearing; gentle; humble; long-suffering; meek; mild; obedient; passive; patient; prostrate; quiet; reserved; resigned; stoical; submissive; subservient; timid; tolerant; tractable; unassuming; uncomplaining; yielding.*

pat on the back A moribund metaphor (SEE PAGE 19). *acclaim;*

accolade; acknowledgment; applause; appreciation; approval; compliment; congratulation; felicitation; homage; honor; plaudits; praise; recognition; tribute. ■ The selections are a nice *pat on the back* for our talented staff around the world. REPLACE WITH *compliment.* ■ To me, it's *a pat on the back* for hard work well done. REPLACE WITH *an acknowledgment.*

pat (myself) on the back A moribund metaphor (SEE PAGE 19). *acclaim; applaud; celebrate; cheer; commend; compliment; congratulate; extol; flatter; hail; honor; laud; plume; praise; puff; salute; self-congratulate.* ■ After *patting himself on the back,* he incidentally points out that many other people may have had something to do with it. REPLACE WITH *congratulating himself.*

pave the way (for) A moribund metaphor (SEE PAGE 19).
1. *arrange; groom; make ready; plan; prepare; prime; ready.* ■ Chartering all schools *paves the way* for a new way to organize public education. REPLACE WITH *prepares.*
2. *bring about; cause; create; effect; generate; give rise to; inaugurate; initiate; introduce; lead to; occasion; produce; provoke; result in; usher in.*

pay (their) debt to society A moribund metaphor (SEE PAGE 19).

pay (my) dues A moribund metaphor (SEE PAGE 19).

pay the fiddler (piper) A moribund metaphor (SEE PAGE 19). *pay; suffer.*

pay the price A moribund metaphor (SEE PAGE 19).*pay; suffer.*

pay through the nose A moribund metaphor (SEE PAGE 19). *costly; dear; excessive; exorbitant; expensive; high-priced.*

peace and harmony A wretched redundancy (SEE PAGE 23). *harmony; peace.* ■ I want there to be *peace and harmony* between us. REPLACE WITH *harmony* or *peace.*

peace and quiet An inescapable pair (SEE PAGE 18). *calm; calmness; composure; equanimity; peace; peacefulness; poise; quiet; quietude; repose; rest; serenity; silence; stillness; tranquility.*

peaches and cream (complexion) A moribund metaphor (SEE PAGE 19).

pea in (my) shoe A moribund metaphor (SEE PAGE 19). *affliction; annoyance; bane; bother; burden; curse; difficulty; inconvenience; irritant; irritation; load; nuisance; ordeal; pain; pest; plague; problem; torment; tribulation; trouble; vexation; weight; worry.*

peaks and valleys A moribund metaphor (SEE PAGE 19). *alterations; changes; erraticism; fluctuations; fortuitousness; inconstancies; shifts; uncertainties; vacillations; variations; vicissitudes.*

peanut gallery An infantile phrase (SEE PAGE 18). *audience; spectators; viewers.*

pearls of wisdom A moribund metaphor (SEE PAGE 19). *acumen; astuteness; erudition; insight; intelligence; perspicacity; sagacity; wisdom.* ■ In addition to the $50,000 fee, his *pearls of wisdom* will cost three first-class airplane tickets. REPLACE WITH *insights.*

pencil pusher A moribund metaphor (SEE PAGE 19).
1. *assistant; clerk; office worker; recorder; scribe; secretary; typist.*
2. *drudge; menial; scullion; toiler.*

(the) pen is mightier than the sword A moribund metaphor (SEE PAGE 19).

(a) penny saved is a penny earned A popular prescription (SEE PAGE 21).

people are who (what) they are A quack equation (SEE PAGE 21).

people who live in glass houses shouldn't throw stones A popular prescription (SEE PAGE 21).

(as) per (your request) A torpid term (SEE PAGE 22). *according to; as.* Quintessentially dimwitted, *(as) per (your request)* is used by people who cannot manage to sustain an original thought. These are the people who rely on ready-made phrases and formulas; the people who unquestioningly do as they're told; the people who join mass movements because they themselves cannot bear the burden of making decisions; the people who hate on instruction and fear forev-

er. ■ *As per your request,* you have been unsubscribed. REPLACE WITH *As you requested.* ■ Enclosed are chapters 1 through 6, *as per your request.* REPLACE WITH *as you requested.* ■ *As per usual,* he refuses to choose between his chief of staff and his chief of budget. REPLACE WITH *As usual.* ■ *Per our discussion,* please substitute the version developed in the earlier tool for all but the last two sentences of this. REPLACE WITH *As we discussed.* ■ OPEC crude production in the first half of 1989 was supposed to be 18.5 million b/d, *as per* the November 1988 agreement. REPLACE WITH *as stated in.* ■ *As per* the Semiconductor Industry Association, U.S. manufacturers accounted for nearly $137 billion in revenues during the year 1997. REPLACE WITH *According to.*

perception is reality A quack equation (SEE PAGE 21). Perception is too often purblind for there to be much reality to this quack equation. Still, it is a formula, uttered by mountebanks and managers alike, that has done much to disturb the life and livelihood of people.

perchance A withered word (SEE PAGE 22).
1. *conceivably; feasibly; maybe; perhaps; possibly.*
2. *accidentally; by chance.*

perennially popular An inescapable pair (SEE PAGE 18).

(I'm) (a) perfectionist A suspect superlative (SEE PAGE 22). SEE ALSO

I'm not perfect (you know); nobody's perfect.

period An infantile phrase (See page 18). ■ The lesson of the women's movement is clearly that no one makes it on their own. *Period.* Delete *period.* ■ I know some professional, single women who would not date married men. *Period.* Delete *period.* See also *no ifs, ands, or buts.*

period of time A wretched redundancy (See page 23). *period; time.* ■ I've been wanting to watch this movie for a long *period of time.* Replace with *time.* ■ Over a considerable *period of time,* this therapy gradually provides immunization. Replace with *period.*

personal friend A suspect superlative (See page 22). A *personal friend* is but a friend, and a friend, more often than not, but an acquaintance.

persona non grata A foreign phrase (See page 17). *undesirable.*

(as) phony (queer) as a three-dollar bill An insipid simile (See page 19). *artificial; bogus; counterfeit; ersatz; fake; false; feigned; fictitious; forged; fraudulent; imitation; mock; phony; pseudo; sham; simulated; spurious; synthetic.*

phony baloney An infantile phrase (See page 18). *artificial; bogus; counterfeit; ersatz; fake; false; feigned; fictitious; forged; fraudulent; imitation; mock; phony; pseudo; sham; simulated; spurious; synthetic.*

physician, heal thyself A popular prescription (See page 21).

pick and choose An inescapable pair (See page 18). *choose; cull; decide; determine; elect; pick; select.* ■ For years, we could *pick and choose* where our students worked. Replace with *select.*

pick of the litter A moribund metaphor (See page 19). *best; choice; elite; excellent; finest; first-class; first-rate; foremost; greatest; highest; matchless; optimal; optimum; outstanding; paramount; peerless; preeminent; premium; prominent; select; superior; superlative; top; unequaled; unexcelled; unmatched; unrivaled; unsurpassed.*

pick up speed A moribund metaphor (See page 19). *accelerate; advance; bestir; bustle; hasten; hurry; precipitate; quicken; rush; speed up.*

pick up steam A moribund metaphor (See page 19).
1. *accelerate; advance; bestir; bustle; hasten; hurry; precipitate; quicken; rush; speed up.*
2. *advance; awaken; better; expand; flourish; gain; gain strength; grow; heal; improve; increase; pick up; progress; prosper; rally; recover; recuperate; refresh; renew; revive; rouse; strengthen; thrive.*

pick up (take) the ball (and run with it) A moribund metaphor (See page 19). *activate; bring about; cause; create; effect; enter on; generate; give rise to; inaugurate; initiate; instigate; introduce; lead to; occasion; produce; provoke; usher in.*

pick up the pace   A moribund metaphor (SEE PAGE 19). *accelerate; advance; bestir; bustle; hasten; hurry; precipitate; quicken; rush; speed up.*

pick up the pieces   A moribund metaphor (SEE PAGE 19).

(a) picture is worth a thousand words   A popular prescription (SEE PAGE 21).

picture perfect   A moribund metaphor (SEE PAGE 19). *absolute; beautiful; consummate; excellent; exemplary; exquisite; faultless; flawless; ideal; impeccable; lovely; magnificent; matchless; model; peerless; perfect; pretty; pure; sublime; superb; supreme; transcendent; ultimate; unblemished; unequaled; unexcelled; unrivaled; unsurpassed; untarnished.*

pièce de résistance   A foreign phrase (SEE PAGE 17).

(a) piece of cake   A moribund metaphor (SEE PAGE 19). *apparent; basic; clear; clear-cut; conspicuous; distinct; easily done; easy; effortless; elementary; evident; explicit; facile; limpid; lucid; manifest; obvious; patent; pellucid; plain; simple; simplicity itself; straightforward; translucent; transparent; unambiguous; uncomplex; uncomplicated; understandable; unequivocal; unmistakable.* Evoking only the silliest of images, *a piece of cake* ought to tell us that those who use this expression have nothing serious to say, and perhaps little thoughtful to think. ■ Choosing the menu for the wedding reception isn't always *a piece of cake*. REPLACE WITH *easy*. ■ Setting up a Palm device to use GoType! is *a piece of cake*. REPLACE WITH *simplicity itself*. ■ At my high school, preparing for college is not *a piece of cake*. REPLACE WITH *effortless*.

(a) piece of the action   An infantile phrase (SEE PAGE 18). ■ Similar to the U.S. model, it will give companies the capital and technology they need while giving employees a *piece of the action* and establishing a constituency for capitalism.

(a) piece (slice) of the pie   A moribund metaphor (SEE PAGE 19).

(a) piece of the puzzle   A moribund metaphor (SEE PAGE 19). *clue; hint; inkling; pointer; sign.*

(a) piece of work   A moribund metaphor (SEE PAGE 19). *aberrant; abnormal; anomalistic; anomalous; atypical; bizarre; curious; deviant; different; distinct; distinctive; eccentric; exceptional; extraordinary; fantastic; foreign; grotesque; idiosyncratic; independent; individual; individualistic; irregular; novel; odd; offbeat; original; peculiar; puzzling; quaint; queer; rare; remarkable; separate; singular; strange; uncommon; unconventional; unexampled; unique; unnatural; unorthodox; unparalleled; unprecedented; unusual; weird.*

pie in the sky   A moribund metaphor (SEE PAGE 19). *artificial; capricious; chimeric; chimerical; delusive; dreamy; fanciful; fantastical; fictitious; frivolous; hallucinatory; illu-*

sory; imaginary; maggoty; phantasmal; phantasmic; unreal; whimsical. ■ The only alternatives to testing she proposes are scarcely more than *pie in the sky.* REPLACE WITH *illusory.* ■ Other predictions were laughably *pie-in-the-sky.* REPLACE WITH *chimerical.*

pillar of society (the church; the community) A suspect superlative (SEE PAGE 22). It is the pillars of society — whether powerful, knowledgeable, or moneyed — who are often the most wobbly among us.

Few who have power do not misapply it, few who have knowledge do not misuse it, and few who have money do not misspend it.

For these reasons and others, before long and before others, pillars totter and then topple. ■ But beware — you'll be going up against the well-informed dealer who might be viewed as *a pillar of the community.*

pillar (tower) of strength A moribund metaphor (SEE PAGE 19). *constant; dependable; determined; faithful; fast; firm; fixed; inexorable; inflexible; loyal; obdurate; reliable; resolute; resolved; rigid; solid; stable; staunch; steadfast; steady; stern; strong; supportive; tenacious; true; trustworthy; trusty; unflinching; unwavering; unyielding.*

pin (his) ears back A moribund metaphor (SEE PAGE 19).
1. *beat; better; cap; defeat; exceed; excel; outclass; outdo; outflank; out-*maneuver; outperform; outplay; outrank; outsmart; outthink; outwit; overcome; overpower; prevail over; surpass; top; triumph over; trounce; whip; win out.*
2. *admonish; animadvert; berate; castigate; censure; chasten; chastise; chide; condemn; criticize; denounce; denunciate; discipline; impugn; objurgate; punish; rebuke; remonstrate; reprehend; reprimand; reproach; reprobate; reprove; revile; scold; upbraid; vituperate; warn.*

pin the blame on A moribund metaphor (SEE PAGE 19). *accuse; blame; censure; charge; condemn; criticize; implicate; incriminate; inculpate; rebuke; reprimand; reproach; reprove; scold.*

(the) pits A moribund metaphor (SEE PAGE 19).
1. *abhorrent; abominable; appalling; atrocious; awful; beastly; detestable; disagreeable; disgusting; dreadful; frightening; frightful; ghastly; grisly; gruesome; horrendous; horrible; horrid; horrifying; inhuman; loathesome; objectionable; obnoxious; odious; offensive; repellent; repugnant; repulsive; revolting; terrible; terrifying; unspeakable; unutterable.*
2. *calamitous; deplorable; depressing; distressing; disturbing; grievous; lamentable; unfortunate; upsetting; sad; tragic; woeful.*

(a) place for everything and everything in its place A popular prescription (SEE PAGE 21).

place the blame on (her) shoulders A moribund metaphor (SEE PAGE 19). *accuse; blame; censure;*

charge; condemn; criticize; implicate; incriminate; inculpate; rebuke; reprimand; reproach; reprove; scold.

plain and simple An inescapable pair (SEE PAGE 18). *apparent; basic; clear; clear-cut; conspicuous; distinct; easily done; easy; effortless; elementary; evident; explicit; facile; limpid; lucid; manifest; obvious; patent; pellucid; plain; simple; simplicity itself; straightforward; translucent; transparent; unambiguous; uncomplex; uncomplicated; understandable; unequivocal; unmistakable.*

(as) plain as a pikestaff An insipid simile (SEE PAGE 19). *apparent; basic; clear; clear-cut; conspicuous; distinct; easily done; easy; effortless; elementary; evident; explicit; facile; limpid; lucid; manifest; obvious; patent; pellucid; plain; simple; simplicity itself; straightforward; translucent; transparent; unambiguous; uncomplex; uncomplicated; understandable; unequivocal; unmistakable.*

(as) plain as day An insipid simile (SEE PAGE 19). *apparent; basic; clear; clear-cut; conspicuous; distinct; easily done; easy; effortless; elementary; evident; explicit; facile; limpid; lucid; manifest; obvious; patent; pellucid; plain; simple; simplicity itself; straightforward; translucent; transparent; unambiguous; uncomplex; uncomplicated; understandable; unequivocal; unmistakable.*

(as) plain as the nose on (your) face An insipid simile (SEE PAGE 19). *apparent; basic; clear; clear-cut;*

conspicuous; distinct; easily done; easy; effortless; elementary; evident; explicit; facile; limpid; lucid; manifest; obvious; patent; pellucid; plain; simple; simplicity itself; straightforward; translucent; transparent; unambiguous; uncomplex; uncomplicated; understandable; unequivocal; unmistakable.

plain (smooth) sailing A moribund metaphor (SEE PAGE 19). *apparent; basic; clear; clear-cut; conspicuous; distinct; easily done; easy; effortless; elementary; evident; explicit; facile; limpid; lucid; manifest; obvious; patent; pellucid; plain; simple; simplicity itself; smooth; straightforward; translucent; transparent; unambiguous; uncomplex; uncomplicated; understandable; unequivocal; unmistakable.*

plain vanilla A moribund metaphor (SEE PAGE 19). *basic; common; conservative; conventional; customary; general; normal; ordinary; quotidian; regular; routine; standard; traditional; typical; uncreative; undaring; unimaginative; usual.* ■ He was uninterested in staying now that the bank has been limited to *plain vanilla* banking. REPLACE WITH *basic*.

plan ahead A wretched redundancy (SEE PAGE 23). *plan*. ■ It's important that you *plan ahead* for your retirement. DELETE *ahead*.

plan for the worst, but hope for the best A popular prescription (SEE PAGE 21).

plan of action A torpid term (SEE PAGE 22). *action; course; direction; intention; method; move; plan; policy; procedure; route; scheme; strategy.*

plans and specifications A wretched redundancy (SEE PAGE 23). *plans; specifications.* ■ Allowed expenditures include architectural and engineering services and related costs for *plans and specifications* for the renovation. USE *plans* or *specifications.*

play ball A moribund metaphor (SEE PAGE 19). *collaborate; comply; concur; conspire; cooperate; join in; participate; work together.*

play both ends against the middle A moribund metaphor (SEE PAGE 19).

play (your) cards right A moribund metaphor (SEE PAGE 19).

play cat and mouse A moribund metaphor (SEE PAGE 19). *fool; tease.*

play (his cards) close to the chest (vest) A moribund metaphor (SEE PAGE 19). *be clandestine; be confidential; be covert; be furtive; be mysterious; be private; be secretive; be secret; be sly; be stealthy; be surreptitious.*

play cupid A moribund metaphor (SEE PAGE 19).

play fast and loose (with) A moribund metaphor (SEE PAGE 19). *be careless; be dishonest; be disloyal; be false; be undependable; be unpredictable; be unreliable; be untrue; be untrustworthy.*

play games (with) A moribund metaphor (SEE PAGE 19). *confuse; deceive; trick.*

play hardball A moribund metaphor (SEE PAGE 19). *be demanding; be hard-hitting; be harsh; be rough; be severe; be stern; be strict; be tough.*

play hard to get A moribund metaphor (SEE PAGE 19). *be coy; be fickle.*

play (raise) havoc with A moribund metaphor (SEE PAGE 19). *disturb; mess up; devastate; rack; ravage; ruin; shatter; smash; undo; upset; wrack; wreck.*

play hell (the devil) with A moribund metaphor (SEE PAGE 19). *disturb; mess up; devastate; rack; ravage; ruin; shatter; smash; undo; upset; wrack; wreck.*

play hide and seek A moribund metaphor (SEE PAGE 19).

(like) playing Russian roulette An insipid simile (SEE PAGE 19). ■ Licensees who sell on Sundays in violation of state law are *playing Russian roulette* with their licenses.

(will it) play in Peoria A moribund metaphor (SEE PAGE 19).

play it by ear A moribund metaphor (SEE PAGE 19). *ad-lib; extemporize; improvise.*

play musical chairs A moribund metaphor (SEE PAGE 19).

play out A torpid term (SEE PAGE 22).
1. *carry out; execute; perform; play.*
2. *develop; evolve; unfold.* ■ We will report to you how all this *plays out.* REPLACE WITH *unfolds.*

play possum A moribund metaphor (SEE PAGE 19).

play second fiddle A moribund metaphor (SEE PAGE 19).

play the field A moribund metaphor (SEE PAGE 19).

play the fool A moribund metaphor (SEE PAGE 19). *be silly; clown; fool around; mess around.*

play the game A moribund metaphor (SEE PAGE 19). *abide by; accommodate; accord; acquiesce; act fairly; adapt; adhere to; agree; behave; comply; concur; conform; correspond; follow; harmonize; heed; mind; obey; observe; submit; yield.*

play the waiting game A moribund metaphor (SEE PAGE 19). *be patient; wait.*

play to the crowd A moribund metaphor (SEE PAGE 19). *perform; play up; posture; show off.*

play (your) trump card A moribund metaphor (SEE PAGE 19).

play with fire A moribund metaphor (SEE PAGE 19). *chance; dare; endanger; gamble; hazard; imperil; jeopardize; make bold; peril; risk; venture.*

pleasant surprise An inescapable pair (SEE PAGE 18).

(as) pleased as Punch An insipid simile (SEE PAGE 19). *blissful; buoyant; cheerful; delighted; elated; excited; gay; glad; gladdened; gleeful; good-humored; gratified; happy; jolly; jovial; joyful; joyous; jubilant; merry; mirthful; pleased; tickled.*

pleasingly plump An inescapable pair (SEE PAGE 18). *ample; big; bulky; chubby; chunky; colossal; corpulent; dumpy; enormous; fat; flabby; fleshy; gigantic; heavy; hefty; huge; immense; large; mammoth; massive; obese; plump; portly; pudgy; rotund; round; squat; stocky; stout.*

plow new ground A moribund metaphor (SEE PAGE 19).
1. *arrange; groom; make ready; plan; prepare; prime; ready.*
2. *bring about; cause; create; effect; generate; give rise to; inaugurate; initiate; introduce; lead to; occasion; produce; provoke; result in; usher in.*

(5:00) p.m. ... (in the) afternoon (evening) A wretched redundancy (SEE PAGE 23). *(5:00) p.m.; (in the) afternoon (evening).* ■ The city school legislature was called to order at 2 *p.m.* on a Monday *afternoon.* DELETE *afternoon.*

(he's) (a) poet but (he) doesn't know it An infantile phrase (SEE PAGE 18).

poetry in motion A moribund metaphor (SEE PAGE 19). *agile; graceful; limber; lissome; lithe; lithesome; nimble; supple.*

(a) point in time   A wretched redundancy (SEE PAGE 23). *a time.* ■ There comes *a point in time* when we all pass into adulthood. REPLACE WITH *a time.*

(the) point of no return   A moribund metaphor (SEE PAGE 19).

point the finger (of blame) at   A moribund metaphor (SEE PAGE 19). *accuse; blame; censure; charge; condemn; criticize; implicate; incriminate; inculpate; rebuke; reprimand; reproach; reprove; scold.* ■ When the problem is that severe, regulators have to *point the finger at* someone. REPLACE WITH *blame.*

poke (her) nose into   A moribund metaphor (SEE PAGE 19). *encroach; entrench; infringe; interfere; intrude; invade; meddle; pry; tamper; trespass.*

politics as usual   A torpid term (SEE PAGE 22). This is but a euphemism, a politic phrase, for words like *cheating; deceit; deceitfulness; deception; dishonesty; duplicity; falsehood; fraudulence; lying; mendacity; perfidy; self-interest; selfishness; tergiversation; treachery.* ■ In the course of this election, there has been too much *politics as usual.* REPLACE WITH *dishonesty.* SEE ALSO *business as usual.*

pomp and circumstance   An inescapable pair (SEE PAGE 18). *array; ceremony; circumstance; dazzle; display; fanfare; grandeur; magnificence; ostentation; pageantry; panoply; parade; pomp; resplendence; ritual; show; spectacle; splendor.*

(as) poor as a churchmouse   An insipid simile (SEE PAGE 19). *bankrupt; broke; destitute; distressed; impecunious; impoverished; indigent; insolvent; needy; penniless; poor; poverty- stricken; underprivileged.*

poor cousin to   A moribund metaphor (SEE PAGE 19). ■ Independent TV stations were once viewed as *poor cousins to* networked-owned stations and affiliates.

pose no immediate (imminent) danger (threat)   A torpid term (SEE PAGE 22). ■ And though the radioactive fuel may *pose no immediate threat*, the canisters continue to deteriorate.

positive (*n*)   A torpid term (SEE PAGE 22). *advantage; asset; benefit; gain; good; strength.* SEE ALSO *negative.*

positive effect (impact)   A torpid term (SEE PAGE 22). ■ The breakup doesn't undo any of the *positive effects,* and it doesn't mean I revert to the way I was 10 years ago. REPLACE WITH *goodness.* ■ A small but growing number of school programs on problem solving show *positive effects* in preventing depression. REPLACE WITH *success.* ■ It's a defeat for minority children who can't afford to attend private schools through grade 6, thus missing out on the *positive effect* of a private school education. REPLACE WITH *benefit.* SEE ALSO *negative effect (impact).*

positive feelings   A torpid term (SEE PAGE 22). As the following variety of synonyms shows, *positive feelings* is a pulpous expression that arouses only our inattention: *affection; approval; blissfulness; courage; delectation; delight; ecstasy; enjoyment; fondness; friendliness; friendship; generosity; goodwill; happiness; hope; joy; kindness; lightheartedness; like; liking; love; loyalty; merriment; passion; peace; pleasure; rapture; relish; respect; warmth.* ■ I feel she may have *positive feelings* for me, and I'd like to know for sure. REPLACE WITH *affection.* ■ The goal is to capture the *positive feelings* about making special purchases. REPLACE WITH *delectation.* ■ The better in touch you are with your *positive feelings* for each other, the less likely you are to act contemptuous of your spouse when you have a difference of opinion. REPLACE WITH *fondness and admiration.* SEE ALSO *in a good mood; negative feelings.*

(like) (the) pot calling the kettle black An insipid simile (SEE PAGE 19).

pot of gold A moribund metaphor (SEE PAGE 19). *affluence; fortune; money; opulence; prosperity; riches; treasure; wealth.*

(exact) (a) pound of flesh A moribund metaphor (SEE PAGE 19).

pound the pavement A moribund metaphor (SEE PAGE 19). *hunt; look for; quest; ransack; rummage; scour; search; seek.*

pouring (down) rain A wretched redundancy (SEE PAGE 23). *pouring; raining; storming.*

pour oil on troubled waters A moribund metaphor (SEE PAGE 19). *allay; alleviate; appease; assuage; calm; compose; ease; mitigate; mollify; pacify; palliate; quiet; relieve; soothe; still; tranquilize.*

pour (rub) salt on (our) wounds A moribund metaphor (SEE PAGE 19). *aggravate; complicate; exacerbate; heighten; increase; intensify; irritate; make worse; worsen.*

(the) power of the purse A moribund metaphor (SEE PAGE 19).

practice makes perfect A popular prescription (SEE PAGE 21).

practice what (you) preach A popular prescription (SEE PAGE 21).

praise (them) to the skies A moribund metaphor (SEE PAGE 19). *acclaim; applaud; celebrate; commend; compliment; congratulate; eulogize; extol; flatter; hail; laud; panegyrize; praise; puff; salute.*

precarious position An inescapable pair (SEE PAGE 18).

pretty An overworked word (SEE PAGE 20). *adequately; amply; enough; fairly; moderately; quite; rather; reasonably; somewhat; sufficiently; tolerably.* ■ She's a *pretty* bright woman. REPLACE WITH *reasonably.* ■ We're suffering some *pretty* devastating effects right now. DELETE *pretty.*

Pretty, in these senses, proclaims its users have a vocabulary of little more than disyllabic words. For a person who says *pretty* also says *little* and *logy*, *really* and *leery*, *input* and *impact*. And with so few words, only so much can be known, only so much can be conveyed.

(as) pretty as a picture An insipid simile (SEE PAGE 19). *appealing; attractive; beautiful; becoming; captivating; comely; cute; dazzling; exquisite; fair; fetching; good-looking; gorgeous; handsome; lovely; nice-looking; pleasing; pretty; pulchritudinous; radiant; ravishing; seemly; stunning.*

(a) pretty picture A moribund metaphor (SEE PAGE 19).

prevailing winds of A moribund metaphor (SEE PAGE 19).

previous to A torpid term (SEE PAGE 22). *before.* ■ *Previous to* meeting her, I showed no interest in women. REPLACE WITH *Before*. SEE ALSO *in advance of; previous to; subsequent to.*

prick (puncture) (his) balloon A moribund metaphor (SEE PAGE 19). *abase; chasten; debase; decrease; deflate; degrade; demean; depreciate; depress; diminish; disgrace; dishonor; embarrass; humble; humiliate; lower; mortify; puncture; shame.*

prick up (her) ears A moribund metaphor (SEE PAGE 19). *attend to; hark; hear; hearken; heed; listen; pay attention; pay heed.*

pride and joy An inescapable pair (SEE PAGE 18).

prim and proper An inescapable pair (SEE PAGE 18).

primrose path A moribund metaphor (SEE PAGE 19).

(a) prince among men A suspect superlative (SEE PAGE 22).

prince charming An infantile phrase (SEE PAGE 18).

princely price An inescapable pair (SEE PAGE 18). *costly; dear; excessive; exorbitant; expensive; high-priced.*

prioritize A torpid term (SEE PAGE 22). *arrange; classify; list; order; place; put; rank; rate.* ■ He *prioritizes* this relationship above all his "after high school plans," such as going to college. REPLACE WITH *ranks*.

prior to A torpid term (SEE PAGE 22). *before.* ■ Select only the cells to be printed *prior to* selecting the Print command. REPLACE WITH *before.* ■ Certain verbs in English require the use of a pronoun *prior to* and after an infinitive phrase. REPLACE WITH *before.* SEE ALSO *in advance of; previous to; subsequent to.*

prize(d) possession An inescapable pair (SEE PAGE 18). ■ In an era of spiraling costs, a good indirect cost rate is a *prized possession.*

proactive A torpid term (SEE PAGE

22).

1. *anticipatory; involved; participatory.* ■ To educate parents to take this more *proactive* role in the education of their children, the board has authorized the creation of a parent-controlled Family Education Resources Center. REPLACE WITH *participatory.*

2. *aggressive; assertive; enterprising.* ■ It is vital to obtain sell-through information from retailers so that you can take *proactive* steps to get a new order. REPLACE WITH *aggressive.* ■ A school needs a PR person to develop a *proactive* approach that anticipates problems before they develop. REPLACE WITH *enterprising.* ■ Smaller, specialty firms, such as Bath & Body Works, or apparel stores, such as Bloomingdale's, Nordstrom, and Canada's famed Harry Rosen, teach their employees to *proactively* ask customers if they need assistance. DELETE *proactively.*

proceeded to A torpid term (SEE PAGE 22). ■ The team *proceeded to develop* the recently generated ideas into a concrete curriculum. REPLACE WITH *developed.* ■ He then *proceeded to declare* his undying love for me. REPLACE WITH *declared.*

proceed forward A torpid term (SEE PAGE 22). *advance; continue; develop; go on; grow; happen; improve; increase; make headway; make progress; move on; occur; proceed; progress; take place.* ■ Reducing operating losses in this business will give us increased flexibility to *proceed forward* with other endeavors. REPLACE WITH *proceed.* SEE ALSO *a step forward; a step (forward) in the right direction; go forward; move forward; move (forward) in the right direction.*

(the) promised land A moribund metaphor (SEE PAGE 19). *Eden; El Dorado; Elysian Fields; Elysium; heaven; kingdom come; nirvana; paradise; utopia; Valhalla.*

(a) promise is a promise A quack equation (SEE PAGE 21).

(the) proof of the pudding (is in the eating) A popular prescription (SEE PAGE 21).

(as) proud as a peacock An insipid simile (SEE PAGE 19). *arrogant; cavalier; conceited; disdainful; egocentric; egotistic; egotistical; haughty; lofty; pompous; pretentious; prideful; proud; narcissistic; self-centered; self-important; self-satisfied; supercilious; superior; vain.*

proud parent An inescapable pair (SEE PAGE 18).

pull a fast one A moribund metaphor (SEE PAGE 19). *bamboozle; befool; beguile; bilk; bluff; cheat; con; deceive; defraud; delude; dupe; feint; fool; gyp; hoodwink; lead astray; misdirect; misguide; misinform; mislead; spoof; swindle; trick; victimize.*

pull a rabbit out of the hat A moribund metaphor (SEE PAGE 19). *be creative; be ingenious; be inventive; be resourceful.*

pull (my) leg A moribund metaphor (SEE PAGE 19). *bamboozle; befool; beguile; bilk; bluff; cheat; con; deceive; defraud; delude; dupe; feint; fool; gyp; hoodwink; jest; joke; kid; lead astray; misdirect; misguide; misinform; mislead; spoof; swindle; tease; trick; trifle with.*

(like) pulling teeth An insipid simile (SEE PAGE 19). *arduous; backbreaking; burdensome; difficult; exhausting; fatiguing; hard; herculean; laborious; not easy; onerous; severe; strenuous; toilful; toilsome; tough; troublesome; trying; wearisome.* ■ Getting these people to level with reporters is often *like pulling teeth.* REPLACE WITH *arduous.*

pull no punches A moribund metaphor (SEE PAGE 19). *be blunt; be candid; be direct; be forthright; be frank; be open; be outspoken; be straightforward.*

pull (it) off A moribund metaphor (SEE PAGE 19). *accomplish; bring about; do; carry out; perform; succeed.*

pull out all the stops A moribund metaphor (SEE PAGE 19). *aim; attempt; endeavor; essay; exert; exhaust; labor; moil; strain; strive; struggle; toil; try hard; undertake; work at.*

pull strings A moribund metaphor (SEE PAGE 19).

pull the plug (on) A moribund metaphor (SEE PAGE 19). *abandon; abort; annul; arrest; ban; cancel; cease;* *check; conclude; derail; desert; desist; discontinue; end; forsake; halt; invalidate; leave; quit; repeal; rescind; revoke; stop; suspend; terminate; withdraw.* ■ Organizers say they'll *pull the plug* on the parade if a gay and lesbian group is allowed to participate. REPLACE WITH *cancel.* ■ Cellucci *pulled the plug on* the PAC last summer after learning it was being organized by inmates at some of the states' toughest prisons. REPLACE WITH *banned.*

pull the rug out from under A moribund metaphor (SEE PAGE 19). *capsize; founder; invert; overset; overthrow; overturn; reverse; sink; tip; topple; tumble; upend; upset.*

pull the wool over (his) eyes A moribund metaphor (SEE PAGE 19). *bamboozle; befool; beguile; bilk; bluff; cheat; con; deceive; defraud; delude; dupe; fake; feign; feint; fool; gyp; hoodwink; lead astray; lie; misdirect; misguide; misinform; mislead; misrepresent; pretend; spoof; swindle; trick; victimize.*

pull (yourself) up by (your) own bootstraps A moribund metaphor (SEE PAGE 19).

pull up stakes A moribund metaphor (SEE PAGE 19). *abscond; clear out; decamp; depart; desert; disappear; escape; exit; flee; fly; go; go away; leave; move on; part; pull out; quit; retire; retreat; run away; take flight; take off; vacate; vanish; withdraw.*

pure and simple An inescapable pair (SEE PAGE 18). *basic; elementary;*

fundamental; pure; simple; straight-forward; uncomplicated.

(as) pure as the driven snow An insipid simile (SEE PAGE 19).
1. *decent; ethical; exemplary; good; honest; honorable; just; moral; pure; righteous; straight; upright; virtuous; wholesome.*
2. *celibate; chaste; immaculate; maidenly; modest; snowy; spotless; stainless; unblemished; unsoiled; untarnished; virgin; virginal; virtuous.*

pursuant to A torpid term (SEE PAGE 22). *according to; by; following; under.*

pursue (strive for) excellence A suspect superlative (SEE PAGE 22). ■ *Striving for excellence* is not just a goal but a way of life. ■ The recipients had to prepare brief statements on what inspires them to *strive for excellence.* SEE ALSO *excellence.*

push and shove An inescapable pair (SEE PAGE 18). *bulldoze; drive; propel; push; shove; thrust.*

(when) push comes to shove A moribund metaphor (SEE PAGE 19).

push the envelope A moribund metaphor (SEE PAGE 19).
1. *be adventuresome; be adventurous; be bold; be daring.*
2. *beat; exceed; outdo; outstrip; surpass; top.*

push the panic button A moribund metaphor (SEE PAGE 19). *be alarmed; be anxious; be excited; be*

frightened; be jumpy; be nervous; be panicky; be panic-stricken; be scared; be unnerved.

push the right buttons A moribund metaphor (SEE PAGE 19).

pushed (me) to the wall A moribund metaphor (SEE PAGE 19).
1. *coerced; compelled; constrained; dictated; enforced; enjoined; forced; made; ordered; pressed; pressured; required.*
2. *at bay; caught; cornered; enmeshed; ensnared; entangled; entrapped; netted; snared; trapped.*

put a bug in (his) ear A moribund metaphor (SEE PAGE 19). *allude to; clue; connote; cue; hint; imply; indicate; insinuate; intimate; prompt; suggest; tip off.*

put a damper on A moribund metaphor (SEE PAGE 19). *check; dampen; deaden; depress; discourage; hinder; impede; inhibit; obstruct; repress; restrain.*

put a gun to (my) head A moribund metaphor (SEE PAGE 19). *coerce; command; compel; constrain; demand; dictate; enforce; enjoin; force; insist; make; order; pressure; require.* ■ Nobody *put a gun to your head.* REPLACE WITH *forced you.*

put a halt (an end; a stop) to A wretched redundancy (SEE PAGE 23). *cease; close; complete; conclude; derail; discontinue; end; finish; halt; settle; stop.* ■ It's time we *put a stop to* all the violence. REPLACE WITH *stop.* SEE ALSO *call a halt (an end; a stop) to.*

put a lid on (it) A moribund metaphor (SEE PAGE 19).
1. *abandon; abort; annul; arrest; ban; cancel; cease; check; conclude; desert; desist; discontinue; end; forsake; halt; leave; quit; stop; suspend; terminate.*
2. *censor; hush up; muffle; quash; smother; squash; squelch; stifle.*
3. *be closed-mouthed; be quiet; be reticent; be silent; be speechless; be still; be taciturn; be uncommunicative; keep quiet.* ■ *Put a lid on it.* REPLACE WITH *Be quiet.*

(don't) put all (your) eggs in one basket A moribund metaphor (SEE PAGE 19).

put a spin on A moribund metaphor (SEE PAGE 19).

put (it) behind (us) A moribund metaphor (SEE PAGE 19). ■ She is eager to testify before the grand jury and to *put this part of the investigation behind her.* SEE ALSO *get (go) on with (my) life.*

put (his) best foot forward A moribund metaphor (SEE PAGE 19).

put (your) finger on A moribund metaphor (SEE PAGE 19). *detect; discern; discover; distinguish; find; identify; know; locate; make out; note; notice; perceive; pick out; pinpoint; place; point out; recall; recognize; recollect; remember; see; specify; spot; think of.*

put (her) foot down A moribund metaphor (SEE PAGE 19).
1. *hold fast; stand firm.*
2. *assert; command; decree; dictate;*

insist; order; require.
3. *deny; disallow; forbid; prohibit; refuse; reject.* ■ *I put my foot down.* REPLACE WITH *refused.*

put (his) foot in (his) mouth A moribund metaphor (SEE PAGE 19).

put forward A torpid term (SEE PAGE 22). *advance; broach; introduce; offer; present; propose; propound; submit; suggest; tender.* ■ There is speculation that he opposed Moynihan's plan so he could *put forward* his own. REPLACE WITH *propose.* SEE ALSO *come forward (with).*

put (his) head in the lion's mouth A moribund metaphor (SEE PAGE 19). *chance; dare; endanger; gamble; hazard; imperil; jeopardize; make bold; peril; risk; venture.*

put (our) heads together A moribund metaphor (SEE PAGE 19). *collaborate; conspire; cooperate; work together.*

put (your) house (back) in order A moribund metaphor (SEE PAGE 19). *correct; rectify; redress; remedy; restore; right.* ■ Ravaged by losses after it lost direction in a period of rapid growth, Phoenix is attempting to *put its house back in order.* REPLACE WITH *right itself.*

put in a plug for A moribund metaphor (SEE PAGE 19). *acclaim; applaud; celebrate; commend; compliment; congratulate; eulogize; extol; flatter; hail; laud; panegyrize; praise; puff; salute.*

put (him) in bad light A moribund metaphor (SEE PAGE 19).

put in cold storage A moribund metaphor (SEE PAGE 19). *defer; delay; forget; hold off; hold up; ignore; pigeonhole; postpone; procrastinate; put aside; put off; set aside; shelve; suspend; table; waive.*

put in motion A moribund metaphor (SEE PAGE 19). *begin; commence; embark; inaugurate; initiate; launch; originate; start; undertake.*

put (her) in (her) place A moribund metaphor (SEE PAGE 19). *abase; chasten; debase; decrease; deflate; degrade; demean; depreciate; depress; diminish; disgrace; dishonor; embarrass; humble; humiliate; lower; mortify; puncture; shame.*

put (yourself) in (her) place A moribund metaphor (SEE PAGE 19). *be sorry for; commiserate; empathize; feel for; feel sorry for; identify with; pity; sympathize; understand.*

put (myself) in (his) shoes A moribund metaphor (SEE PAGE 19). *be sorry for; commiserate; empathize; feel for; feel sorry for; identify with; pity; sympathize; understand.*

put (your) life on the line A moribund metaphor (SEE PAGE 19). *chance; dare; endanger; gamble; hazard; imperil; jeopardize; make bold; peril; risk; venture.*

put money on A moribund metaphor (SEE PAGE 19). *bet; gamble; wager.*

put (his) neck on the line A moribund metaphor (SEE PAGE 19). *chance; dare; endanger; gamble; hazard; imperil; jeopardize; make bold; peril; risk; venture.*

put new life into A moribund metaphor (SEE PAGE 19). *animate; energize; enliven; inspire; inspirit; invigorate; refresh; reinvigorate; rejuvenate; revitalize; revive; rouse; stimulate; stir; vitalize.*

put on airs A moribund metaphor (SEE PAGE 19). *be affected; be arrogant; be conceited; be condescending; be contumelious; be disdainful; be egotistic; be egotistical; be haughty; be high-handed; be magisterial; be overbearing; be pompous; be pretentious; be proud; be prideful; be self-important; be snobbish; be supercilious; be superior.*

put on an act A moribund metaphor (SEE PAGE 19). *affect; fake; feign; make believe; pretend; simulate.*

put (her) on a pedestal A moribund metaphor (SEE PAGE 19). *adore; cherish; esteem; eulogize; exalt; extol; glorify; honor; idealize; idolize; laud; love; panegyrize; prize; revere; treasure; venerate; worship.*

put one over on (her) A moribund metaphor (SEE PAGE 19). *bamboozle; befool; beguile; bilk; bluff; cheat; con; deceive; defraud; delude; dupe; feint; fool; gyp; hoodwink; lead astray; misdirect; misguide; mislead; spoof; swindle; trick; victimize.*

put on hold A torpid term (SEE

PAGE 22). *defer; delay; forget; hold off; hold up; ignore; pigeonhole; postpone; procrastinate; put aside; put off; set aside; shelve; suspend; table; waive.* ■ The agreement had been scheduled to go into effect on Tuesday, after being *put on hold* for 30 days. REPLACE WITH *delayed.*

put on ice A moribund metaphor (SEE PAGE 19). *defer; delay; forget; hold off; hold up; ignore; pigeonhole; postpone; procrastinate; put aside; put off; set aside; shelve; suspend; table; waive.*

put on the back burner A moribund metaphor (SEE PAGE 19). *defer; delay; forget; hold off; hold up; ignore; pigeonhole; postpone; procrastinate; put aside; put off; set aside; shelve; suspend; table; waive.* ■ She understands the necessity of *putting* her own emotional needs *on the back burner* when these would otherwise interfere with her goal. REPLACE WITH *waiving.*

put on the front burner A moribund metaphor (SEE PAGE 19). *advance.*

put (us) on the map A moribund metaphor (SEE PAGE 19). ■ At the time analysts thought Ames was just the tonic Zayre needed, and the deal *put* the 30-year-old Ames *on the map.*

put (it) on the table A moribund metaphor (SEE PAGE 19). *be aboveboard; be candid; be forthright; be frank; be honest; be open; be straightforward; be truthful.*

put out to pasture A moribund metaphor (SEE PAGE 19).
1. *cast off; discard; dismiss; drop; dump; eliminate; exclude; expel; jettison; lay aside; reject; retire; set aside; shed.*
2. *ax; discharge; dismiss; fire; let go; retire.* ■ Playing a hot-blooded parent helps you feel like you haven't yet been *put out to pasture.* REPLACE WITH *dismissed.*

put (his) pants on one leg at a time A moribund metaphor (SEE PAGE 19). *average; common; commonplace; conservative; conventional; customary; everyday; mediocre; middling; normal; ordinary; quotidian; regular; routine; standard; traditional; typical; uneventful; unexceptional; unremarkable; usual.*

put pen to paper A moribund metaphor (SEE PAGE 19). *author; compose; indite; inscribe; jot down; pen; scrabble; scratch; scrawl; scribble; scribe; write.*

put (your) shoulder to the wheel A moribund metaphor (SEE PAGE 19). *drudge; grind; grub; labor; moil; slave; strain; strive; struggle; sweat; toil; travail; work hard.*

put (your) stamp of approval on A moribund metaphor (SEE PAGE 19). *approve of; authorize; certify; endorse; sanction.* ■ To portray our community as *putting a stamp of approval on* the execution is inaccurate. REPLACE WITH *approving of.*

put that in your pipe and smoke it A moribund metaphor (SEE PAGE 19).

put the brakes on A moribund metaphor (SEE PAGE 19). *abandon; abort; arrest; block; bridle; cancel; cease; check; conclude; control; curb; derail; desert; desist; discontinue; disturb; end; forsake; halt; interrupt; leave; obstruct; quit; repress; restrain; stop; suppress; suspend; terminate.* ■ The parent's problems with its retail divisions effectively *put the brakes on* the project and helped stall other downtown projects as well. REPLACE WITH *stopped.* ■ It *put the brakes on* the decline of political talk radio. REPLACE WITH *checked.*

put the cart before the horse A moribund metaphor (SEE PAGE 19). *backward; counterclockwise; inside-out; inverted; reversed; upside-down.*

put the best face on A moribund metaphor (SEE PAGE 19). ■ In the aftermath, AT&T management tried to *put the best face on* an embarrassing and costly mix-up.

put the fear of God into (them) A torpid term (SEE PAGE 22). *alarm; appall; benumb; daunt; frighten; horrify; intimidate; panic; paralyze; petrify; scare; shock; startle; terrify; terrorize.*

put the finger on A moribund metaphor (SEE PAGE 19). *betray; deliver up; inform on; turn in.*

put the finishing touches on A moribund metaphor (SEE PAGE 19). *complete; conclude; consummate; finish.*

put the genie back in the bottle A moribund metaphor (SEE PAGE 19).

put the kibosh on A moribund metaphor (SEE PAGE 19). *abort; annul; arrest; balk; block; bridle; cancel; check; derail; detain; end; foil; frustrate; halt; harness; neutralize; nullify; restrain; retard; stall; stay; stop; terminate; thwart.*

put the screws to A moribund metaphor (SEE PAGE 19). *bulldoze; bully; coerce; compel; constrain; demand; drive; enforce; enjoin; goad; force; impel; incite; intimidate; make; necessitate; obligate; oblige; order; press; pressure; prod; require; threaten; tyrannize; urge.*

put the skids on A moribund metaphor (SEE PAGE 19). *abandon; abort; arrest; cancel; cease; check; conclude; derail; desert; desist; discontinue; end; forsake; halt; leave; quit; stop; suspend; terminate.*

put through (her) paces A moribund metaphor (SEE PAGE 19). *catechize; cross-examine; examine; grill; inquire; interrogate; pump; question; quiz; test.*

put through the wringer A moribund metaphor (SEE PAGE 19). *catechize; cross-examine; examine; grill; inquire; interrogate; pump; question; quiz; test.*

put together the pieces of the puzzle A moribund metaphor (SEE PAGE 19). *clear up; decipher; disentangle; explain; explicate; figure out; resolve; solve; unravel; untangle; work out.*

put (them) to the test A torpid term (SEE PAGE 22). *catechize; cross-examine; examine; grill; inquire; interrogate; pump; question; quiz; test.*

put two and two together A moribund metaphor (SEE PAGE 19). *comprehend; conclude; decipher; deduce; discern; fathom; figure out; gather; grasp; infer; interpret; perceive; realize; reason; see; understand.*

(like) putty in (my) hands An insipid simile (SEE PAGE 19). *accommodating; acquiescent; adaptable; agreeable; amenable; complacent; complaisant; compliant; deferential; docile; ductile; elastic; flexible; malleable; manageable; moldable; obedient; obliging; persuasible; pliant; responsive; submissive; tractable; trained; yielding.*

put up or shut up An infantile phrase (SEE PAGE 18).

Q

queer fish A moribund metaphor (SEE PAGE 19). *aberrant; abnormal; anomalistic; anomalous; atypical; bizarre; curious; deviant; different; distinct; distinctive; eccentric; exceptional; extraordinary; fantastic; foreign; grotesque; idiosyncratic; independent; individual; individualistic; irregular; novel; odd; offbeat; original; peculiar; puzzling; quaint; queer; rare; remarkable; separate; singular; strange; uncommon; unconventional; unexampled; unique; unnatural; unorthodox; unparalleled; unprecedented; unusual; weird.*

(the) quick and the dead A moribund metaphor (SEE PAGE 19).

(as) quick as a bunny An insipid simile (SEE PAGE 19). *brisk; expeditious; fast; fleet; hasty; hurried; immediate; instant; instantaneous; prompt; quick; rapid; speedy; spry; sudden; swift; winged.*

(as) quick as a flash An insipid simile (SEE PAGE 19). *brisk; expeditious; fast; fleet; hasty; hurried; immediate; instant; instantaneous; prompt; quick; rapid; speedy; spry; sudden; swift; winged.*

(as) quick as a wink An insipid simile (SEE PAGE 19). *brisk; expeditious; fast; fleet; hasty; hurried; immediate; instant; instantaneous; prompt; quick; rapid; speedy; spry; sudden; swift; winged.*

(as) quick as lightning An insipid simile (SEE PAGE 19). *brisk; expeditious; fast; fleet; hasty; hurried; immediate; instant; instantaneous; prompt; quick; rapid; speedy; spry; sudden; swift; winged.*

quick on (his) feet A moribund metaphor (SEE PAGE 19).
1. *brisk; expeditious; fast; fleet; hasty; hurried; immediate; instant; instantaneous; prompt; quick; rapid; speedy; spry; sudden; swift; winged.*
2. *able; adroit; alert; apt; astute; bright; brilliant; capable; clever; competent; discerning; enlightened; insightful; intelligent; judicious; keen; knowledgeable; learned; logical; luminous; perceptive; perspicacious; quick; rational; reasonable; sagacious; sage; sapient; sensible; sharp; shrewd; smart; sound; understanding; wise; witty.*

quick on the draw A moribund metaphor (SEE PAGE 19). *fast; fast-acting; quick; rapid; speedy; swift.*

quid pro quo A foreign phrase (SEE PAGE 17).

(as) quiet as a mouse An insipid simile (SEE PAGE 19). *dumb; hushed; motionless; mum; mute; noiseless; quiet; reticent; silent; speechless; stationary; still; stock-still; subdued; taciturn; unmoving; voiceless; wordless.*

quiet desperation An inescapable pair (SEE PAGE 18).

quit the scene A torpid term (SEE PAGE 22). *abscond; clear out; decamp; depart; desert; disappear; escape; exit; flee; fly; go; go away; leave; move on; part; pull out; quit; retire; retreat; run away; take flight; take off; vacate; vanish; withdraw.*

quit while (you're) ahead A popular prescription (SEE PAGE 21).

quote, unquote An infantile phrase (SEE PAGE 18). *as it were; so-called; so to speak; such as it is.* ■ It's too soon in the *quote, unquote* relationship for that. REPLACE WITH *so-called.* ■ I was referred to them by a friend of mine, *quote, unquote.* REPLACE WITH *as it were.*

R

(a) race to the finish (line) A moribund metaphor (SEE PAGE 19).

(gone to) rack (wrack) and ruin An inescapable pair (SEE PAGE 18). *broken down; crumbly; decayed; deteriorated; dilapidated; run-down; shabby.*

rack (wrack) (my) brains A moribund metaphor (SEE PAGE 19). *endeavor; exert; labor; moil; slave; strain; strive; struggle; toil; try; work.*

radiantly happy An inescapable pair (SEE PAGE 18). *blissful; blithe; buoyant; cheerful; delighted; ecstatic; elated; enraptured; euphoric; exalted; excited; exhilarated; exultant; gay; glad; gleeful; good-humored; happy; intoxicated; jolly; jovial; joyful; joyous; jubilant; merry; mirthful; overjoyed; pleased; rapturous; thrilled.*

raid the cookie jar A moribund metaphor (SEE PAGE 19). *filch; pilfer; pinch; purloin; rob; steal; take; thieve.*

raining cats and dogs A moribund metaphor (SEE PAGE 19). *pouring; raining; storming.*

raining pitchforks A moribund metaphor (SEE PAGE 19). *pouring; raining; storming.*

rain on (your) parade A moribund metaphor (SEE PAGE 19). *blight; cripple; damage; disable; harm; hurt; impair; incapacitate; lame; mar; mess up; rack; ruin; sabotage; spoil; subvert; undermine; vitiate; wrack; wreck.*

(come) rain or shine A moribund metaphor (SEE PAGE 19). *no matter what; regardless.*

raise a (red) flag A moribund metaphor (SEE PAGE 19). *alert; apprise; caution; forewarn; inform; notify; signal; warn.*

raise a stink A moribund metaphor (SEE PAGE 19).

raise Cain A moribund metaphor (SEE PAGE 19).
1. *bellow; bluster; clamor; complain; explode; fulminate; fume; holler; howl; object; protest; rage; rant; rave; roar; scream; shout; storm; thunder; vociferate; yell.*
2. *be merry; carouse; carry on; celebrate; debauch; disport; frolic; party; play; revel; riot; roister; rollick; romp; skylark.*

raise (some) eyebrows (of) A moribund metaphor (SEE PAGE 19).

amaze; astonish; astound; awe; dumbfound; flabbergast; jar; jolt; shock; start; startle; stun; stupefy; surprise.
■ An executive at one financial institution that participated in the bailout said Goldman Sachs's dual role *raised the eyebrows of* some participants. REPLACE WITH *surprised*.

raise hell A moribund metaphor (SEE PAGE 19).
1. *bellow; bluster; clamor; complain; explode; fulminate; fume; holler; howl; object; protest; rage; rant; rave; roar; scream; shout; storm; thunder; vociferate; yell.*
2. *be merry; carouse; carry on; celebrate; debauch; disport; frolic; party; play; revel; riot; roister; rollick; romp; skylark.*

raise the dead A moribund metaphor (SEE PAGE 19). *be merry; carouse; carry on; celebrate; debauch; disport; frolic; party; play; revel; riot; roister; rollick; romp; skylark.*

raise the flag A moribund metaphor (SEE PAGE 19). *be delighted; be elated; be glad; be overjoyed; be pleased; celebrate; cheer; exult; glory; jubilate; rejoice; triumph.*

raise the hackles A moribund metaphor (SEE PAGE 19). *acerbate; anger; annoy; bother; bristle; chafe; enrage; incense; inflame; infuriate; insult; irk; irritate; madden; miff; nettle; offend; provoke; rile; roil; vex.*

raise the roof A moribund metaphor (SEE PAGE 19).
1. *bellow; bluster; clamor; complain; explode; fulminate; fume; holler; howl;*

object; protest; rage; rant; rave; roar; scream; shout; storm; thunder; vociferate; yell.
2. *be merry; carouse; carry on; celebrate; debauch; disport; frolic; party; play; revel; riot; roister; rollick; romp; skylark.*

raison d'être A foreign phrase (SEE PAGE 17).

rally 'round the flag A moribund metaphor (SEE PAGE 19).

rank and file A moribund metaphor (SEE PAGE 19). *all; citizenry; commonage; commonalty; common people; crowd; everybody; everyone; followers; herd; hoi polloi; laborers; masses; mob; multitude; plebeians; populace; proletariat; public; rabble; workers.*

rant and rave An inescapable pair (SEE PAGE 18). *bellow; bluster; clamor; explode; fulminate; fume; holler; howl; rage; rant; rave; roar; scream; shout; storm; thunder; vent; vociferate; yell.*

rap (his) knuckles A moribund metaphor (SEE PAGE 19). *admonish; animadvert; berate; castigate; censure; chasten; chastise; chide; condemn; criticize; denounce; denunciate; discipline; impugn; objurgate; punish; rebuke; remonstrate; reprehend; reprimand; reproach; reprobate; reprove; revile; scold; upbraid; vituperate; warn.*

rara avis A foreign phrase (SEE PAGE 17). *aberrant; abnormal; anomalistic; anomalous; atypical; bizarre;*

curious; deviant; different; distinct; distinctive; eccentric; exceptional; extraordinary; fantastic; foreign; grotesque; idiosyncratic; independent; individual; individualistic; irregular; novel; odd; offbeat; original; peculiar; puzzling; quaint; queer; rare; remarkable; separate; singular; strange; uncommon; unconventional; unexampled; unique; unnatural; unorthodox; unparalleled; unprecedented; unusual; weird.

rarely (seldom) ever A wretched redundancy (SEE PAGE 23). *rarely (seldom).* ■ We are brothers, but we *rarely ever* speak. DELETE *ever.*

rat race A moribund metaphor (SEE PAGE 19).

(like) rats abandoning a ship An insipid simile (SEE PAGE 19).

rave reviews An inescapable pair (SEE PAGE 18). ■ The new LapLink for Windows is already getting *rave reviews* from both industry experts and users like you. ■ But it turned out *Maximumrocknroll* gave it a *rave review.* ■ In 1995, CeCe got *rave reviews* for her solo debut.

raving lunatic An inescapable pair (SEE PAGE 18).

(a) ray of light (sunshine) A moribund metaphor (SEE PAGE 19). *anticipation; expectancy; expectation; hope; hopefulness; optimism; possibility; promise; prospect; sanguinity.* ■ I don't see any *ray of sunshine* when we have all these interplaying forces in conflict. REPLACE WITH *hope.*

reach epidemic proportions A torpid term (SEE PAGE 22). This phrase and journalistic junk of its kind — for example, *(breathe; heave) a collective sigh of relief* (SEE); *an uphill battle (fight)* (SEE); *deal a (crushing; devastating; major; serious) blow to* (SEE); *first (number-one; top) priority* (SEE); *grind to a halt* (SEE); *in the wake of; send a message (signal)* (SEE); *shocked (surprised) and saddened (dismayed)* (SEE); *weather the storm (of)* (SEE) — ensure the writers of them will never be seriously read, and the readers of them never thoroughly engaged. ■ The availability of guns on the street has *reached epidemic proportions.* ■ Dog bites among children are reportedly *reaching epidemic proportions.*

reach for the sky A moribund metaphor (SEE PAGE 19). *exceed; excel; outclass; outdo; outrival; outshine; outstrip; shine; stand; surpass.*

reach out and touch An infantile phrase (SEE PAGE 18).

reach the end of (our) rope (tether) A moribund metaphor (SEE PAGE 19). *exhausted; frazzled; harassed; stressed; stressed out; tense; weary; worn out.*

(a) (must) read An infantile phrase (SEE PAGE 18). Colloquial usage such as this leads only to everyday thoughts and commonplace actions; few insights, fewer epiph-anies, can be had with mediocre language. In essence, *a (must) read* is an expression that secures the banality of what it describes. ■ Tom Wolfe's *Bonfire of the Vanities* is *an enormously entertaining read.* REPLACE WITH *enormously entertaining.* ■ This book is *a tough read* but one of the most important recent accounts of personal identity. REPLACE WITH *tough to understand.* ■ There are a few books on the list that I feel are clearly *easy reads.* REPLACE WITH *easy to read.* ■ There are thousands of great books out there, but how many are *must reads?* REPLACE WITH *compelling.* ■ It's a very challenging *read.* REPLACE WITH *book.* ■ Is it Tolstoy? is it Dostoyevsky? no, but it is a wonderfully satisfying *read.* REPLACE WITH *story.* ■ The manuscript is 312 pages long and *a pretty easy read.* REPLACE WITH *easily readable.* ■ But the problem with the "ho-hum" approach to a life story is that it makes for *a tiresome read.* REPLACE WITH *tiresome reading.* SEE ALSO *a good read; (take) a look see; (a) must (miss); (a) must have; (a) must see.*

read between the lines A moribund metaphor (SEE PAGE 19). *assume; conclude; conjecture; deduce; gather; guess; hypothesize; imagine; infer; presume; speculate; suppose; surmise; theorize; venture.*

read it and weep An infantile phrase (SEE PAGE 18).

read (her) like a (an open) book An insipid simile (SEE PAGE 19). *empathize; identify with; know; sympathize; understand.*

read my lips An infantile phrase (SEE PAGE 18).

read (him) the riot act A moribund metaphor (SEE PAGE 19). *admonish; animadvert; berate; castigate; censure; chasten; chastise; chide; condemn; criticize; denounce; denunciate; discipline; excoriate; fulminate against; imprecate; impugn; inveigh against; objurgate; punish; rebuke; remonstrate; reprehend; reprimand; reproach; reprobate; reprove; revile; scold; swear at; upbraid; vituperate; warn.*

ready, willing, and able An infantile phrase (SEE PAGE 18). ■ She described her client as being *ready, willing, and able* to testify. REPLACE WITH *willing.* ■ We have a lot of social problems that need to be addressed, and I'm *ready, willing, and able* to do that. REPLACE WITH *ready.*

re- again A wretched redundancy (SEE PAGE 23). *re-.* ■ I divorced him, and then I *remarried again.* DELETE *again.* ■ We missed the first ten minutes of his talk, so he *repeated* it *again* for us. DELETE *again.*

real An overworked word (SEE PAGE 20). For example: *real contribution; real difference; real obvious; real possibility; real progress; real tragedy.*

reality check An infantile phrase (SEE PAGE 18).

real, live An infantile phrase (SEE PAGE 18).

really An overworked word (SEE PAGE 20). If such an intensive is needed at all, alternatives to the word *really* include *consumedly; enormously; especially; exceedingly; exceptionally; extraordinarily; extremely; genuinely; particularly; remarkably; specially; truly; uncommonly; very.*

Often, however, such highlighting seems only to moderate the value of our statements. ■ At the *London Review* we take serious pride in our role as one of the *really* significant participants in the international exchange of ideas and information. DELETE *really.* ■ He did a *really* good job of convincing us to buy. DELETE *really.* SEE ALSO *very.* ■ This speechlessness is *really* affecting his moods, his behavior, and his mental state. DELETE *really.*

really? An infantile phrase (SEE PAGE 18). SEE ALSO *you're kidding; you've got to be kidding.*

really (and) truly An infantile phrase (SEE PAGE 18). ■ I *really and truly* love being in love. DELETE *really and truly.* ■ Do you *really truly* believe that your mom thinks you're a whore? DELETE *really.* ■ They *really and truly* thought I would never make it. DELETE *really and.*

(the) real McCoy A moribund metaphor (SEE PAGE 19). *actual; authentic; genuine; legitimate; pure; real; sterling; true; unadulterated; unalloyed; veritable.* ■ When you

are talking about classical scholarship, he is *the real McCoy.*

rear (its) (ugly) head A moribund metaphor (SEE PAGE 19). *appear; emerge; materialize; surface.* ■ That hypocritical axiom, "Do as I say, not as I do" seems to have *reared its ugly head* on the editorial pages of the *Globe* once again. ■ None of us knows for sure whether there is another problem in this volatile environment which could *rear its ugly head* soon.

reasonable facsimile An inescapable pair (SEE PAGE 18).

(the) reason (why) is because A wretched redundancy (SEE PAGE 23). *because; reason is (that).* ■ One of *the reasons why* people keep this to themselves *is because of* the stigma. REPLACE WITH *the reasons ... is.*

(the) reason why A wretched redundancy (SEE PAGE 23). *reason.* ■ There is a *reason why* she is the way she is. DELETE *why.* ■ The researchers are not certain as to the *reason why.* DELETE *why.*

receive back A wretched redundancy (SEE PAGE 23). *receive.* ■ DPL now communicates with Excel, sending the input values and *receiving back* the output value Profit. DELETE *back.*

reckless abandon An inescapable pair (SEE PAGE 18).

record-breaking A wretched

redundancy (SEE PAGE 23). *record.* ■ We'll take a look at some *record-breaking* snowfalls. REPLACE WITH *record.* SEE ALSO *all-time record; record-high.*

record-high A wretched redundancy (SEE PAGE 23). *record.* ■ In Concord, it was a *record-high* 12 degrees. REPLACE WITH *record.* SEE ALSO *all-time record; record-breaking.*

(as) red as a beet An insipid simile (SEE PAGE 19).
1. *beet-red; blood-red; burgundian; burgundy; cardinal; carmine; cerise; cherry; crimson; fire-engine-red; maroon; purple; purplish; red; reddish; rose; rose-colored; rosy; rubefacient; rubescent; rubicund; rubied; rubiginous; ruby; ruddy; rufescent; rufous; russet; sanguine; sanguineous; scarlet; vermilion; wine; wine-colored.*
2. *abashed; ashamed; blushing; chagrined; confused; discomfited; discomposed; disconcerted; embarrassed; flushed; flustered; mortified; nonplused; perplexed; red-faced; shamed; shamefaced; sheepish.*

(as) red as a cherry An insipid simile (SEE PAGE 19).
1. *beet-red; blood-red; burgundian; burgundy; cardinal; carmine; cerise; cherry; crimson; fire-engine-red; maroon; purple; purplish; red; reddish; rose; rose-colored; rosy; rubefacient; rubescent; rubicund; rubied; rubiginous; ruby; ruddy; rufescent; rufous; russet; sanguine; sanguineous; scarlet; vermilion; wine; wine-colored.*
2. *abashed; ashamed; blushing; cha-*

grined; confused; discomfited; discomposed; disconcerted; embarrassed; flushed; flustered; mortified; nonplused; perplexed; red-faced; shamed; shamefaced; sheepish.

(as) red as a rose An insipid simile (SEE PAGE 19).
1. *beet-red; blood-red; burgundian; burgundy; cardinal; carmine; cerise; cherry; crimson; fire-engine-red; maroon; purple; purplish; red; reddish; rose; rose-colored; rosy; rubefacient; rubescent; rubicund; rubied; rubiginous; ruby; ruddy; rufescent; rufous; russet; sanguine; sanguineous; scarlet; vermilion; wine; wine-colored.*
2. *abashed; ashamed; blushing; chagrined; confused; discomfited; discomposed; disconcerted; embarrassed; flushed; flustered; mortified; nonplused; perplexed; red-faced; shamed; shamefaced; sheepish.*

(as) red as a ruby An insipid simile (SEE PAGE 19).
1. *beet-red; blood-red; burgundian; burgundy; cardinal; carmine; cerise; cherry; crimson; fire-engine-red; maroon; purple; purplish; red; reddish; rose; rose-colored; rosy; rubefacient; rubescent; rubicund; rubied; rubiginous; ruby; ruddy; rufescent; rufous; russet; sanguine; sanguineous; scarlet; vermilion; wine; wine-colored.*
2. *abashed; ashamed; blushing; chagrined; confused; discomfited; discomposed; disconcerted; embarrassed; flushed; flustered; mortified; nonplused; perplexed; red-faced; shamed; shamefaced; sheepish.*

red herring A moribund metaphor (SEE PAGE 19). *decoy; distraction; diversion; lure; ploy; trick.*

red in the face A moribund metaphor (SEE PAGE 19). *abashed; ashamed; blushing; chagrined; confused; discomfited; discomposed; disconcerted; embarrassed; flushed; flustered; mortified; nonplused; perplexed; red-faced; shamed; shamefaced; sheepish.*

red-letter day A moribund metaphor (SEE PAGE 19).

red light A moribund metaphor (SEE PAGE 19). *ban; disallowance; enjoinment; exclusion; interdiction; prohibition; proscription; veto.* SEE ALSO *green light.*

red tape A moribund metaphor (SEE PAGE 19). *bureaucracy; formalities; paperwork; procedures; regulations; rules.*

refer back A wretched redundancy (SEE PAGE 23). *refer.* ■ *Refer back* to Chapter 4. DELETE *back.*

reflect back A wretched redundancy (SEE PAGE 23). *reflect.* ■ Part of the energy is *reflected back* into medium 1 as a reflected ray, and the remainder passes into medium 2 as a refracted ray. DELETE *back.*

regardless of the fact that A wretched redundancy (SEE PAGE 23). *although; but; even if; even though; still; though; yet.* ■ *Regardless of the fact that* these products are low in sucrose, they still contain energy from other nutrients. REPLACE WITH *Though.* SEE ALSO *despite the fact that; in spite of the fact that.*

(as) regular as clockwork An insipid simile (SEE PAGE 19). *cyclic; established; fixed; habitual; periodic; recurrent; recurring; regular; repetitive; rhythmic; rhythmical.*

reinvent the wheel A moribund metaphor (SEE PAGE 19).

relate back A wretched redundancy (SEE PAGE 23). *relate.* ■ Like the Chicago School, anomie theory *relates back* to the European sociology of the 1800s. DELETE *back.*

relic of the past A wretched redundancy (SEE PAGE 23). *relic.* ■ The very idea of a single, domestic market has become a *relic of the past.* REPLACE WITH *relic.*

(it) remains to be seen A torpid term (SEE PAGE 22). *I don't know; (it's) not (yet) known; (that's) uncertain; (that's) unclear; (it's) unknown.* This phrase is often euphemistic for *(I) don't know* and similar admissions. ■ So much *remains to be seen.* REPLACE WITH *is unknown.* ■ *It remains to be seen* whether dietary soybeans can protect women against breast cancer. REPLACE WITH *We do not know.* ■ How the French public, fond of both cigarettes and alcohol, will respond *remains to be seen.* REPLACE WITH *is not yet known.* SEE ALSO *your guess is as good as mine; (just have to) wait and see.*

remedy the situation A torpid term (SEE PAGE 22). Like all torpid terms, *remedy the situation* neither moves nor motivates us; its use practically ensures that nothing will be righted, nothing remedied.

An ill we might be moved to correct, a problem we might be inspired to solve, but a situation we might never be roused to remedy. ■ If the decisions actually turn out to hamper civil rights enforcement, obviously I would want to take steps to *remedy the situation*. ■ To *remedy the situation* and make the process fairer, the SEC should require that voting be strictly confidential. ■ One issue has been bothering management for quite a while, but they feel somewhat helpless to *remedy the situation*. SEE ALSO *(a) situation*.

reminisce about the past A wretched redundancy (SEE PAGE 23). *reminisce*. ■ She's now 89 years old and she spends most of her time *reminiscing about the past*. DELETE *about the past*.

remove the cotton from (my) ears A moribund metaphor (SEE PAGE 19).

replace back A wretched redundancy (SEE PAGE 23). *replace*. ■ When a change needs to be made, a developer reserves that file from the library, makes the change, and then *replaces* it *back*. DELETE *back*.

reports of (my) death are greatly exaggerated An infantile phrase (SEE PAGE 18).

represent(s) A torpid term (SEE PAGE 22). Increasingly, *represents* is being used for a sad, simple *is* (and *represent* for *are*). ■ The budgeted capacity level *represents* the level of expected business activity under normal operating conditions. REPLACE WITH *is*. ■ Newstar and BASYS currently *represent* the major newsroom computer systems in the broadcasting field. REPLACE WITH *are*. ■ Radiosurgery *represents* a major step forward in our ability to treat tumors that previously have been untreatable. REPLACE WITH *is*. ■ I think Ginger, Patty, and I *represent* three very hardworking, committed faculty members. REPLACE WITH *are*.

respond back A wretched redundancy (SEE PAGE 23). *respond*. ■ The OPP will review each request and *respond back* within ten business days. DELETE *back*.

rest and relaxation An inescapable pair (SEE PAGE 18). *calm; calmness; leisure; peace; peacefulness; quiet; quietude; relaxation; repose; rest; serenity; stillness; tranquility*.

(and) (the) rest is history An infantile phrase (SEE PAGE 18).

rest on (her) laurels A moribund metaphor (SEE PAGE 19).

restore back A wretched redundancy (SEE PAGE 23). *restore*. ■ The new Undo feature allows you to *restore* the disk *back* to its original state. DELETE *back*.

return back A wretched redundancy (SEE PAGE 23). *return.* ■ When SEU is exited, the user will be *returned back* to the Programmer Menu. DELETE *back.*

revenge is sweet A quack equation (SEE PAGE 21).

revert back A wretched redundancy (SEE PAGE 23). *revert.* ■ Scientists speculate that the rapid spread of the disease may be due to farmland *reverting back* to woodland. DELETE *back.* ■ Not knowing what to do, I would *revert right back* to my old eating habits. DELETE *right back.*

revolving door policy A moribund metaphor (SEE PAGE 19).

(the) rich and famous A suspect superlative (SEE PAGE 22). *The rich and famous* infatuate only foolish people, who are as boring to themselves as they are barren of themselves. ■ It has become a summer hideaway for *the rich and famous.* SEE ALSO *celebrity; fame and fortune.*

(as) rich as Croesus An insipid simile (SEE PAGE 19). *affluent; moneyed; opulent; prosperous; rich; wealthy; well-off; well-to-do.*

richly deserves An inescapable pair (SEE PAGE 18) ■ Instead of vilifying him, we should be giving him the encouragement and support he *richly deserves.*

rich man, poor man, beggerman, thief A moribund metaphor (SEE PAGE 19). ■ It doesn't matter whether you are *rich man, poor man, beggar, or thief,* if you are black, there's an artificial ceiling on your ambition.

ride herd on A moribund metaphor (SEE PAGE 19). *control; direct; guard; manage; mind; watch over.*

ride off into the sunset A moribund metaphor (SEE PAGE 19). *abscond; clear out; decamp; depart; desert; disappear; escape; exit; flee; fly; go; go away; leave; move on; part; pull out; quit; retire; retreat; run away; take flight; take off; vacate; vanish; withdraw.*

ride on (her) coattails A moribund metaphor (SEE PAGE 19).

ride out the storm A moribund metaphor (SEE PAGE 19).

ride roughshod over A moribund metaphor (SEE PAGE 19). *boss; browbeat; brutalize; bully; dictate; domineer; enslave; master; oppress; overpower; overrule; reign over; repress; rule; subjugate; suppress; tyrannize.*

(as) right as rain An insipid simile (SEE PAGE 19).
1. *accurate; correct; exact; irrefutable; precise; right; true.*
2. *fit; good; hale; hardy; healthful; healthy; hearty; robust; sound; strong; well.*

(a case of) (the) right hand not knowing what the left hand is doing A moribund metaphor (SEE PAGE 19).

(what's) right is right A quack equation (SEE PAGE 21).

right off the bat A moribund metaphor (SEE PAGE 19). *abruptly; apace; at once; briskly; directly; expeditiously; fast; forthwith; hastily; hurriedly; immediately; instantaneously; instantly; posthaste; promptly; quickly; rapidly; rashly; right away; speedily; straightaway; swiftly; wingedly.*

(on the) right track A moribund metaphor (SEE PAGE 19).

(doesn't) ring a bell A moribund metaphor (SEE PAGE 19).

ring down the curtain (on) A moribund metaphor (SEE PAGE 19). *cease; close; complete; conclude; discontinue; end; finish; halt; settle; stop.*

ringing endorsement An inescapable pair (SEE PAGE 18).

ringing off the hook A moribund metaphor (SEE PAGE 19). *ceaselessly; constantly; continually; continuously; nonstop; perpetually; steadily.* ■ The phones are *ringing off the hook.* REPLACE WITH *constantly ringing.*

rip (tear) to shreds A moribund metaphor (SEE PAGE 19). *demolish; destroy; devastate; obliterate; rack; ravage; ruin; shatter; smash; undo; wrack; wreck.*

rise from the ashes A moribund metaphor (SEE PAGE 19). *rise anew.*

rise to the bait A moribund metaphor (SEE PAGE 19). *get angry; react; respond.*

(a) rising tide of A moribund metaphor (SEE PAGE 19). ■ The report found in the nation's public schools *a rising tide of* mediocrity. SEE ALSO *a barrage of.*

road less traveled A moribund metaphor (SEE PAGE 19).

(the) road to hell is paved with good intentions A popular prescription (SEE PAGE 21).

road to ruin A moribund metaphor (SEE PAGE 19). ■ To permit lying is a step down the *road to ruin.*

roar (in) like a lion An insipid simile (SEE PAGE 19). *growl; roar.*

rob Peter to pay Paul A moribund metaphor (SEE PAGE 19).

(the) rock of Gibraltar A moribund metaphor (SEE PAGE 19).
1. *beefy; brawny; burly; energetic; firm; fit; hale; hardy; healthful; healthy; hearty; husky; manly; mighty; muscular; powerful; puissant; robust; rugged; sinewy; solid; sound; stalwart; stout; strapping; strong; sturdy; tough; vigorous; virile; well-built.*
2. *constant; dependable; determined; faithful; fast; firm; fixed; inexorable; inflexible; loyal; obdurate; resolute; resolved; rigid; solid; stable; staunch; steadfast; steady; stern; strong; tenacious; unflinching; unwavering; unyielding.*

rock the boat A moribund metaphor (SEE PAGE 19). *agitate;*

confuse; disorder; disorganize; disquiet; disrupt; disturb; fluster; jar; jolt; jumble; mess up; mix up; muddle; perturb; rattle; ruffle; shake up; stir up; trouble; unnerve; unsettle; upset.

(a) rogue's gallery of A moribund metaphor (SEE PAGE 19).

(positive) role model A torpid term (SEE PAGE 22). *archetype; example; exemplar; good example; good man (woman); guide; hero; ideal; inspiration; model; paragon; prototype.*

(like) (a) (an emotional) roller-coaster (ride) A moribund metaphor (SEE PAGE 19). Without relentless amusement, endless diversions, people might manage to speak tolerably well. As it is, the need to be entertained so overcomes us that we can speak in little but laughable images. The expression *(like) a (an emotional) roller-coaster (ride),* one such image, results from and gives rise to only carnival-like conversation, sideshow prose. ■ But the next season, it's the same thing, a game filled with ups and downs; it really is *like a roller coaster ride.* ■ The stock market is *like a roller coaster ride.* ■ If you find that the everyday activities of your daily life are being interrupted by intense emotions or *a roller coaster* of emotions, call EAP Preferred to schedule a session. ■ When I started TTC again, I knew that this pregnancy would be a bit of *an emotional roller coaster,* but I had no idea just how terrified I would be.

rolling in money A moribund metaphor (SEE PAGE 19). *affluent; moneyed; opulent; prosperous; rich; wealthy; well-off; well-to-do.*

(a) rolling stone gathers no moss A popular prescription (SEE PAGE 21).

roll in the aisles A moribund metaphor (SEE PAGE 19). *cachinnate; cackle; chortle; chuckle; convulse; guffaw; hoot; howl; laugh; roar; shriek.*

roll out the red carpet A moribund metaphor (SEE PAGE 19). *esteem; honor; respect; venerate; welcome.*

roll up (her) sleeves A moribund metaphor (SEE PAGE 19). *drudge; grind; grub; labor; moil; slave; strain; strive; struggle; sweat; toil; travail; work hard.*

roll with the punches A moribund metaphor (SEE PAGE 19). *abide by; accede to; accept; accommodate; acquiesce; adapt to; adhere to; adjust to; agree to; assent; be agreeable; be complacent; bend; be resigned; bow; comply with; concede to; concur; conform; consent to; fit; follow; reconcile; submit; succumb; yield.*

romantic interlude A suspect superlative (SEE PAGE 22). *intercourse; love-making; sex.*

Rome wasn't built in a day A popular prescription (SEE PAGE 21).

(the) roof fell in A moribund metaphor (SEE PAGE 19). *break* *down; break up; collapse; crash; crumple; disintegrate; end; fail; fall apart; fold; stop.*

(money is) (the) root of all evil A popular prescription (SEE PAGE 21).

(a) roof over (their) heads A moribund metaphor (SEE PAGE 19). *asylum; cover; harbor; harborage; haven; housing; lodging; protection; refuge; retreat; safety; sanctuary; shelter.*

root cause A wretched redundancy (SEE PAGE 23). *cause; origin; reason; root; source.* ■ It does not truly solve the problem of rising health care costs since it does not address the *root cause* of the problem. REPLACE WITH *root.*

rootin', tootin', shootin' An infantile phrase (SEE PAGE 18).

(a) rose by any other name (would smell as sweet) A popular prescription (SEE PAGE 21).

(a) rose is a rose (is a rose) A quack equation (SEE PAGE 21).

rotten apple A moribund metaphor (SEE PAGE 19). *bastard; blackguard; cad; charlatan; cheat; cheater; fake; fraud; impostor; knave; mountebank; phony; pretender; quack; rascal; rogue; scoundrel; swindler; undesirable; villain.*

rotten to the core A moribund metaphor (SEE PAGE 19). *bad; base; contemptible; corrupt; crooked; deceitful; despicable; dishonest; evil;* *immoral; iniquitous; malevolent; mean; miserable; nefarious; pernicious; praetorian; rotten; sinister; underhanded; unethical; untrustworthy; venal; vicious; vile; wicked.*

rough and ready An inescapable pair (SEE PAGE 18).

rough and tumble A moribund metaphor (SEE PAGE 19). *boisterous; disorderly; raucous; riotous; rough; tempestuous; tumultuous; turbulent; uproarious; violent; wild.*

rough around the edges A moribund metaphor (SEE PAGE 19).
1. *bad-mannered; boorish; coarse; crude; ill-mannered; loutish; oafish; rough; rude; uncouth; uncultured; unrefined; unsophisticated; vulgar.*
2. *imperfect; incomplete; unfinished.*

(a) round peg in a square hole A moribund metaphor (SEE PAGE 19). *curiosity; deviant; eccentric; iconoclast; individual; individualist; maverick; misfit; nonconformist; oddball; oddity; renegade; undesirable.*

rousing success An inescapable pair (SEE PAGE 18).

rub elbows A moribund metaphor (SEE PAGE 19). *associate; consort; hobnob; fraternize; keep company; mingle; mix; socialize.*

rub (me) the wrong way A moribund metaphor (SEE PAGE 19).
1. *acerbate; anger; annoy; chafe; gall; grate; irk; irritate; miff; nettle; provoke; rankle; rile; roil; upset; vex.* ■ I wouldn't want to do anything that

would *rub her the wrong way*. REPLACE WITH *annoy her*.
2. *affront; agitate; bother; disrupt; disturb; fluster; insult; jar; offend; perturb; rattle; ruffle; shake up; stir up; trouble; unnerve; unsettle; upset.*

ruffle (her) feathers A moribund metaphor (SEE PAGE 19). *affront; agitate; bother; disrupt; disturb; fluster; insult; jar; offend; perturb; rattle; ruffle; shake up; stir up; trouble; unnerve; unsettle; upset.*

(a) rule is a rule A quack equation (SEE PAGE 21).

(the) rule rather than the exception A torpid term (SEE PAGE 22). *basic; common; commonplace; conventional; customary; general; normal; ordinary; quotidian; regular; routine; standard; typical; uneventful; unexceptional; unremarkable; usual.*
■ New advertising campaigns costing $5 million or even $10 million are becoming *the rule rather than the exception*. REPLACE WITH *common*.

rules and regulations An inescapable pair (SEE PAGE 18). *regulations; rules.* ■ You may have a player that's disappointed, but we're adhering to our *rules and regulations*. REPLACE WITH *regulations* or *rules*.

rules are made to be broken A popular prescription (SEE PAGE 21).

(the) rules of the game A moribund metaphor (SEE PAGE 19).

(the) rules of the road A moribund metaphor (SEE PAGE 19).

rule the roost A moribund metaphor (SEE PAGE 19). *administer; be in charge; be in command; be in control; boss; command; control; dictate; direct; dominate; govern; manage; manipulate; master; order; overpower; oversee; predominate; preponderate; prevail; reign over; rule; superintend.*
■ High school football no longer *rules the roost*. REPLACE WITH *predominates*.

rule with an iron fist (hand) A moribund metaphor (SEE PAGE 19). *authoritarian; authoritative; autocratic; cruel; despotic; dictatorial; dogmatic; domineering; hard; harsh; imperious; iron-handed; lordly; oppressive; overbearing; peremptory; repressive; rigorous; severe; stern; strict; tough; tyrannical.*

run a tight ship A moribund metaphor (SEE PAGE 19). *controlled; ordered; organized; structured.*

run circles (rings) around A moribund metaphor (SEE PAGE 19). *beat; better; cap; defeat; exceed; excel; outclass; outdo; outflank; outmaneuver; outperform; outplay; outrank; outsmart; outstrip; outthink; outwit; overcome; overpower; prevail over; surpass; top; triumph over; trounce; whip; win out.*

(a) run for (his) money A moribund metaphor (SEE PAGE 19).

run (it) into the ground A moribund metaphor (SEE PAGE 19).

running on empty A moribund metaphor (SEE PAGE 19).

running on fumes A moribund metaphor (SEE PAGE 19).

run off at the mouth A moribund metaphor (SEE PAGE 19). *babbling; blathering; chatty; facile; fluent; garrulous; glib; jabbering; logorrheic; long-winded; loquacious; prolix; talkative; verbose; voluble; windy.*

run of the mill A moribund metaphor (SEE PAGE 19). *average; common; commonplace; customary; everyday; fair; mediocre; middling; normal; ordinary; passable; plain; quotidian; regular; routine; simple; standard; tolerable; typical; uneventful; unexceptional; unremarkable; usual; workaday.*

run out of steam A moribund metaphor (SEE PAGE 19). *be exhausted; be fatigued; conclude; decline; deteriorate; die; droop; dwindle; end; expire; fade; fail; finish; flag; languish; perish; quit; regress; stop; tire; weaken; wear out.* ■ Market rallies within ongoing bear markets tend to *run out of steam* as soon as the market climbs back up to the vicinity

of its 200-day moving average. REPLACE WITH *languish.*

(money) runs through (his) fingers A moribund metaphor (SEE PAGE 19).

run the gauntlet A moribund metaphor (SEE PAGE 19). *bear; endure; experience; face; suffer; undergo.*

run the show A moribund metaphor (SEE PAGE 19). *administer; boss; command; control; dictate; direct; dominate; govern; in charge; in command; in control; manage; manipulate; master; order; overpower; oversee; predominate; prevail; reign over; rule; superintend.*

run with the pack A moribund metaphor (SEE PAGE 19). *abide by; accommodate; accord; acquiesce; adapt; adhere to; agree; behave; comply; concur; conform; correspond; follow; harmonize; heed; mind; obey; observe; submit; yield.*

run with the hare and hunt with the hounds A moribund metaphor (SEE PAGE 19).

S

sacred cow A moribund metaphor (SEE PAGE 19).

sacrificial lamb A moribund metaphor (SEE PAGE 19). *sacrifice; victim.*

safe and sound An inescapable pair (SEE PAGE 18). *all right; unharmed; uninjured; safe.*

safe haven A wretched redundancy (SEE PAGE 23). *asylum; haven; refuge; sanctuary; shelter.* ■ Massachusetts, which likes to think of itself as a liberal mecca, is no *safe haven*. REPLACE WITH *haven.*

safety net A moribund metaphor (SEE PAGE 19).

said A withered word (SEE PAGE 22). ■ Therefore, the relative pronouns used to introduce clauses will retain *said* function. REPLACE WITH *this.*

sail (too) close to the wind A moribund metaphor (SEE PAGE 19). *chance; dare; endanger; gamble; hazard; imperil; jeopardize; make bold; peril; risk; venture.*

sail under false colors A moribund metaphor (SEE PAGE 19). *bamboozle; befool; beguile; belie; bilk; bluff; cheat; color; con; deceive; defraud; delude; disguise; dissemble; dissimulate; dupe; fake; falsify; feign; feint; fool; gyp; hoodwink; lead astray; masquerade; misdirect; misguide; misinform; mislead; misrepresent; pretend; simulate; spoof; swindle; trick.*

(the) salt of the earth A moribund metaphor (SEE PAGE 19).

(the) same but different An infantile phrase (SEE PAGE 18). SEE ALSO *same difference.*

sans A withered word (SEE PAGE 22). *bereft; lacking; without.* ■ He has a reckless streak, as revealed in his tendency to go swimming *sans* suit. REPLACE WITH *without a.* ■ Using this button will allow you to see what the dialog box will look like to the user, *sans* any personal or company information that you'll eventually add to it. REPLACE WITH *without.*

save A withered word (SEE PAGE 22). *but; except.* ■ The room was quiet during his performance, *save* when he would take a deep breath and let out some of it. REPLACE WITH *except*. ■ In 1990, the Emirate of Kuwait — tiny in all respects *save* its role in oil affairs — was invaded by fellow OPEC and Arab League member Iraq. REPLACE WITH *but*.

saved by the bell An infantile phrase (SEE PAGE 18).

save (it) for a rainy day A moribund metaphor (SEE PAGE 19).

save (his) neck (skin) A moribund metaphor (SEE PAGE 19).

save your breath A moribund metaphor (SEE PAGE 19). *be quiet; be silent; be still; hush; keep quiet; keep still.*

(as) scarce (scarcer) as hen's teeth An insipid simile (SEE PAGE 19). *exiguous; inadequate; meager; rare; scant; scanty; scarce; sparse; uncommon; unusual.*

scare the (living) daylights out of (me) A moribund metaphor (SEE PAGE 19). *alarm; appall; benumb; daunt; frighten; horrify; intimidate; panic; paralyze; petrify; scare; shock; startle; terrify; terrorize.*

scare the pants off (me) A moribund metaphor (SEE PAGE 19). *alarm; appall; benumb; daunt; frighten; horrify; intimidate; panic; paralyze; petrify; scare; shock; startle; terrify; terrorize.*

scare to death A moribund metaphor (SEE PAGE 19). *alarm; appall; benumb; daunt; frighten; horrify; intimidate; panic; paralyze; petrify; scare; shock; startle; terrify; terrorize.* SEE ALSO *to death.*

scenario An overworked word (SEE PAGE 20). ■ The worst-case *scenario* would be for Question 3 to pass and for Question 5 to fail. DELETE *scenario.* ■ He believes that putting the question of rent control before the voters will lead to *an absurd scenario.* REPLACE WITH *absurdity.*

school of hard knocks A moribund metaphor (SEE PAGE 19).

(just) scratch the surface A moribund metaphor (SEE PAGE 19).

scream and yell An inescapable pair (SEE PAGE 18). *bay; bawl; bellow; blare; caterwaul; clamor; cry; holler; hoot; howl; roar; screak; scream; screech; shout; shriek; shrill; squawk; squeal; vociferate; wail; whoop; yell; yelp; yowl.* ■ If parents are *screaming and yelling* at each other, that causes fear in children. REPLACE WITH *yelling.* ■ It's very flattering that women *scream and yell* when you walk on stage. REPLACE WITH *scream.* SEE ALSO *yell and scream.*

scream (yell) at the top of (my) lungs A moribund metaphor (SEE PAGE 19). *bay; bawl; bellow; blare; caterwaul; clamor; cry; holler; hoot; howl; roar; screak; scream; screech; shout; shriek; shrill; squawk; squeal; vociferate; wail; whoop; yell; yelp; yowl.*

scream (yell) bloody murder A moribund metaphor (SEE PAGE 19). 1. *bay; bawl; bellow; blare; caterwaul; clamor; cry; holler; hoot; howl; roar; screech; shout; shriek; shrill; squawk; squeal; vociferate; wail; whoop; yell; yelp; yowl.*
2. *clamor; complain; explode; fulminate; fume; fuss; gripe; grumble; holler; howl; object; protest; rage; rant; rave; remonstrate; roar; scream; shout; storm; thunder; vociferate; yell.*
■ The Jones lawyers would have *screamed bloody murder,* and rightly so. REPLACE WITH *protested.*

screech to a halt A moribund metaphor (SEE PAGE 19). *cease; close; complete; conclude; derail; discontinue; end; finish; halt; settle; stop.*
■ Work in 535 congressional offices *screeched to a halt.* REPLACE WITH *ceased.*

(a) sea of A moribund metaphor (SEE PAGE 19). ■ He was surrounded by *a sea of* concerned women. DELETE *a sea of.* SEE ALSO *a barrage of.*

(the) second American Revolution A moribund metaphor (SEE PAGE 19).

second banana A moribund metaphor (SEE PAGE 19). *aide; assistant; associate; inferior; junior; minion; secondary; subordinate; underling.* ■ Murphy's greatest political need is to convince the public that she is a leader, and not just the governor's long-suffering *second banana.*

second of all A wretched redundancy (SEE PAGE 23). *second.*
■ *Second of all,* you're going to get hurt if you continue this behavior. REPLACE WITH *Second.* SEE ALSO *first of all.*

second to none A torpid term (SEE PAGE 22). *best; different; exceptional; extraordinary; finest; first; greatest; highest; incomparable; inimitable; matchless; notable; noteworthy; novel; odd; optimal; optimum; original; outstanding; peculiar; peerless; remarkable; singular; special; strange; superlative; uncommon; unequaled; unexampled; unique; unmatched; unparalleled; unrivaled; unusual; without equal.*

(plant) (the) seeds of A moribund metaphor (SEE PAGE 19).

see eye to eye A moribund metaphor (SEE PAGE 19). *agree; concur; think alike.* ■ We *see eye to eye* on most all matters. REPLACE WITH *agree.*

seeing is believing A quack equation (SEE PAGE 21).

seek and you shall find A popular prescription (SEE PAGE 21).

see red A moribund metaphor (SEE PAGE 19). *acerbate; anger; annoy; bother; bristle; chafe; enrage; incense; inflame; infuriate; irk; irritate; madden; miff; provoke; rile; roil; vex.*

see the glass half empty A moribund metaphor (SEE PAGE 19). *cyn-*

ical; dark; despairing; doubtful; gloomy; hopeless; morbid; pessimistic; sullen.

see the light A moribund metaphor (SEE PAGE 19). *appreciate; apprehend; comprehend; discern; fathom; grasp; know; make sense of; perceive; realize; recognize; see; understand.*

see the light of day A moribund metaphor (SEE PAGE 19).
1. *be actualized; be carried out; be implemented; be initiated; be instituted; be realized; be undertaken.* ■ The proposal will never *see the light of day.* REPLACE WITH *be realized.*
2. *be accomplished; be achieved; be completed; be consummated; be executed; be finished; be fulfilled.*

seething mass of humanity A moribund metaphor (SEE PAGE 19).

self-fulfilling prophecy A torpid term (SEE PAGE 22). ■ If retailers think negatively and pessimistically in terms of Christmas, it's going to be a *self-fulfilling prophecy.*

sell (him) a bill of goods A moribund metaphor (SEE PAGE 19). *cheat; deceive; defraud; dupe; fool; lie to; swindle; trick; victimize.* ■ We realize that we've been *sold a bill of goods.* REPLACE WITH *swindled.*

sell (him) down the river A moribund metaphor (SEE PAGE 19). *betray; deliver up; inform on; turn in.*

send a (loud) message (signal) A torpid term (SEE PAGE 22). This phrase is a favorite among journalists and politicians — scrawlers and stammerers — who are accustomed to expressing themselves with dead and indifferent words. And from such words, only the faintest of feelings and the shallowest of thoughts can be summoned. ■ The patent system that protects new drugs from competition *sends a message* to pharmaceutical companies: if you invest enough money and come up with a hit, you can make a killing. REPLACE WITH *says.* ■ We want to *send a message* that this kind of behavior will not be tolerated. REPLACE WITH *make clear.* ■ The police department *sent out a message* that we would not allow such looting to occur again. REPLACE WITH *made it known.* ■ By agreeing to act now, we are *sending a signal* that we do not want this plan to fail. REPLACE WITH *announcing.* ■ I think the MFA, by hosting this exhibit, is *sending the wrong message to* the public. REPLACE WITH *misguiding.* ■ A triple-spaced term paper *sends the loud message* that the writer probably has very little to say. REPLACE WITH *proclaims.* SEE ALSO *reach epidemic proportions.*

send chills (shivers) down (my) spine A moribund metaphor (SEE PAGE 19).
1. *agitate; disquiet; disrupt; disturb; fluster; jar; jolt; perturb; rattle; ruffle; shake up; stir up; trouble; unnerve; unsettle; upset.*
2. *alarm; appall; benumb; daunt; frighten; horrify; intimidate; panic; paralyze; petrify; scare; shock; startle; terrify; terrorize.*

send into a tailspin A moribund metaphor (SEE PAGE 19).

send (them) packing A moribund metaphor (SEE PAGE 19). *discard; dismiss; discharge.*

send shock waves (through) A moribund metaphor (SEE PAGE 19). *agitate; arouse; astound; bother; confuse; discomfit; disconcert; disquiet; disrupt; disturb; excite; jolt; shock; startle; stimulate; stir; stun; unsettle; upset.* ■ When Swiss pharmaceutical giant Roche Holding Ltd. announced that it would buy 60 percent of Genentech Inc., it *sent shock waves through* the biotechnology community. REPLACE WITH *shocked.*

send up a trial balloon A moribund metaphor (SEE PAGE 19). *assess; check; explore; inspect; investigate; look into; probe; test; try.*

separate and distinct A wretched redundancy (SEE PAGE 23). *distinct; separate.* ■ Nor are the stages *separate and distinct*; they may occur at the same time. REPLACE WITH *distinct.*

separate and independent A wretched redundancy (SEE PAGE 23). *independent; separate.* ■ Since the audio and video in an Interactive Multipoint videoconference travel over *separate and independent* paths, the audio must be delayed to synchronize it with the video. REPLACE WITH *separate.*

separate out A wretched redundancy (SEE PAGE 23). *separate.* ■ I don't think you can *separate out* those two things. DELETE *out.* ■ The entire nation of Israel is not much bigger than the state of New Hampshire, and if you *separate out* the territories Israel captured in 1967, it is even smaller than the New England state. DELETE *out.* ■ Our objective was to *separate out* the NLR from the continuum emission by subtracting the different filter images. DELETE *out.* ■ One of the things that became very clear to us early on was that you simply can't *separate out* issues like curriculum and teachers' professional development and learning and instruction. DELETE *out.*

separate the men from the boys A moribund metaphor (SEE PAGE 19). *choose; cull; differentiate; discriminate; distinguish; divide; filter; isolate; pick; screen; segregate; select; separate; sieve; sift; sort; strain; weed out; winnow.*

separate the sheep from the goats A moribund metaphor (SEE PAGE 19). *choose; cull; differentiate; discriminate; distinguish; divide; filter; isolate; pick; screen; segregate; select; separate; sieve; sift; sort; strain; weed out; winnow.*

separate the wheat from the chaff A moribund metaphor (SEE PAGE 19). *choose; cull; differentiate; discriminate; distinguish; divide; filter; isolate; pick; screen; segregate; select; separate; sieve; sift; sort; strain; weed out; winnow.*

serious reservations An inescapable pair (SEE PAGE 18).

set in concrete A moribund metaphor (SEE PAGE 19). *eternal; everlasting; firm; immutable; invariable; irreversible; irrevocable; permanent; rigid; stable; unalterable; unchangeable; unchanging.*

set (her) teeth on edge A moribund metaphor (SEE PAGE 19). 1. *acerbate; anger; annoy; bristle; chafe; enrage; incense; inflame; infuriate; irk; irritate; madden; miff; nettle; offend; provoke; rile; roil; vex.* 2. *agitate; bother; disconcert; disturb; fluster; perturb; unnerve; upset.*

set the record straight A torpid term (SEE PAGE 22). ■ There are a lot of things I can do in my book in terms of *setting the record straight.* ■ EPA believes it's time to *set the record straight* about an indisputable fact: secondhand smoke is a real and preventable health risk.

set the stage (for) A moribund metaphor (SEE PAGE 19). *arrange; groom; make ready; plan; prepare; prime; ready.*

set the wheels in motion A moribund metaphor (SEE PAGE 19). *begin; commence; embark; inaugurate; initiate; launch; originate; start; undertake.*

set the world on fire A moribund metaphor (SEE PAGE 19). *amaze; animate; awe; captivate; dazzle; electrify; excite; exhilarate; fascinate; impress; intoxicate; thrill; overwhelm.*

settle the score A moribund metaphor (SEE PAGE 19).

seventh heaven A moribund metaphor (SEE PAGE 19). *bliss; delight; ecstasy; joy; rapture.*

(he's) (a) shadow of (his) former self A moribund metaphor (SEE PAGE 19). *apparition; specter; wraith.*

shake to its foundations A moribund metaphor (SEE PAGE 19). *agitate; disquiet; disrupt; disturb; fluster; jar; jerk; jolt; perturb; quake; quiver; rattle; ruffle; shake up; shudder; stir up; unnerve; unsettle; tremble; upset.*

shaking in (his) boots A moribund metaphor (SEE PAGE 19). 1. *afraid; alarmed; apprehensive; cowardly; craven; diffident; faint-hearted; fearful; frightened; pavid; pusillanimous; recreant; scared; terror-striken; timid; timorous; tremulous.* 2. *jittery; jumpy; nervous; quivering; shaking; shivering; shivery; shuddering; skittish; trembling.*

shaking like a leaf An insipid simile (SEE PAGE 19). 1. *jittery; jumpy; nervous; quivering; shaking; shivering; shivery; shuddering; skittish; trembling.* 2. *afraid; alarmed; apprehensive; cowardly; craven; diffident; faint-hearted; fearful; frightened; pavid; pusillanimous; recreant; scared; terror-striken; timid; timorous; tremulous.*

shank's mare A moribund metaphor (SEE PAGE 19). *by foot.*

share and share alike A popular prescription (SEE PAGE 21).

(as) sharp as a razor An insipid simile (SEE PAGE 19). *able; adroit;*

apt; astute; bright; brilliant; capable; clever; competent; discerning; enlightened; insightful; intelligent; judicious; keen; knowledgeable; learned; logical; luminous; perceptive; perspicacious; quick; rational; reasonable; sagacious; sage; sapient; sensible; sharp; shrewd; smart; sound; understanding; wise.

(as) sharp as a tack An insipid simile (SEE PAGE 19).
1. *dapper; neat; smart; trim; well dressed; well groomed.*
2. *able; adroit; apt; astute; bright; brilliant; capable; clever; competent; discerning; enlightened; insightful; intelligent; judicious; keen; knowledgeable; learned; logical; luminous; perceptive; perspicacious; quick; rational; reasonable; sagacious; sage; sapient; sensible; sharp; shrewd; smart; sound; understanding; wise.*

shed (throw) light on A moribund metaphor (SEE PAGE 19). *clarify; clear up; describe; disentangle; elucidate; enlighten; explain; explicate; illume; illuminate; interpret; make clear; make plain; reveal; simplify.*

shift (switch) gears A moribund metaphor (SEE PAGE 19).

shift (swing) into high gear A moribund metaphor (SEE PAGE 19). ■ The lawyer is *shifting into high gear*, summoning all his persuasive powers for a rhetorical flourish that will dazzle the jury and save his client a multimillion-dollar court award.

ship of fools A moribund metaphor (SEE PAGE 19).

(like) (two) ships passing in the night An insipid simile (SEE PAGE 19).

(my) ship to come in A moribund metaphor (SEE PAGE 19).

(cost) (the) shirt off (my) back A moribund metaphor (SEE PAGE 19).

shocked (surprised) and saddened (dismayed) A torpid term (SEE PAGE 22). These are formulas that people — especially spokespeople and journalists it seems — use to express indignation. And, as formulas, the *shock and sadness*, the *shock and dismay*, the *shock and outrage* is scarcely heartfelt. ■ I was *shocked and saddened* by the news of his death. ■ Shoppers and shop owners were also *shocked and saddened* by Mr. Stuart's suicide. ■ Relatives were *shocked and dismayed* by what they saw today. ■ When Kissinger was selected instead of the banking mogul, Rockefeller's staff were *shocked and dismayed*. ■ Sullivan says she is *surprised and saddened* by the recent turn of events. ■ We are *saddened and outraged* by the tragic death of a young man just starting to fulfill his life promise. ■ We are terribly *shocked and dismayed*; Ed was an active and important member of our community who will be missed by his colleagues. ■ Needless to say, my dear husband was, and is, *shocked and saddened*. ■ I am *shocked and saddened* by these allegations. ■ I want to begin by saying that Hillary and I are profoundly *shocked and saddened* by the tragedy today in Littleton. ■ The man who was at the heart of the Cape Verdean neighborhood leaves behind a wife, five children, and a *shocked and saddened* community.

A newspaper editor who has just learned of the mutilation of one of his female reporters in a strife-torn country remarks he is *saddened and distressed* by her death. This is the same soulless formula; anyone who has not surrendered to this dimwitticism would surely have said it differently. SEE ALSO *reach epidemic proportions.*

shoot down A moribund metaphor (SEE PAGE 19). *belie; confute; contradict; controvert; counter; debunk; deny; disprove; discredit; dispute; expose; invalidate; negate; rebut; refute; repudiate.*

(the) shoe is on the other foot A moribund metaphor (SEE PAGE 19).

shoot from the hip A moribund metaphor (SEE PAGE 19).
1. *be aboveboard; be artless; be blunt; be candid; be direct; be forthright; be frank; be genuine; be guileless; be honest; be ingenuous; be naive; be outspoken; be sincere; be straightforward.*
2. *hasty; headlong; heedless; hot-headed; impetuous; impulsive; incautious; precipitate; rash; reckless; thoughtless; unthinking.* ■ Congress is feeling very ambivalent, there are very complicated questions of government here, and these *shoot-from-the-hip* folks already have their

opinion locked in cement. RE-PLACE WITH *incautious.*

shoot full of holes A moribund metaphor (SEE PAGE 19). *belie; confute; contradict; controvert; counter; debunk; deny; disprove; discredit; dispute; expose; invalidate; negate; rebut; refute; repudiate.*

(like) shooting fish in a barrel An insipid simile (SEE PAGE 19). *easily done; easy; effortless; elementary; facile; simple; simplicity itself; straightforward; uncomplex; uncomplicated.*

shoot the breeze (bull) A moribund metaphor (SEE PAGE 19). *babble; blab; cackle; chaffer; chat; chitchat; chatter; confabulate; converse; gossip; jabber; palaver; prate; prattle; rattle; talk.* ■ He would come down every couple of weeks just to *shoot the breeze.* REPLACE WITH *chat.*

shoot the messenger A moribund metaphor (SEE PAGE 19).

shoot the works A moribund metaphor (SEE PAGE 19).

shop till you drop A moribund metaphor (SEE PAGE 19).

short and sweet An inescapable pair (SEE PAGE 18). *brief; compact; concise; condensed; curt; laconic; pithy; short; succinct; terse.*

short end of the stick A moribund metaphor (SEE PAGE 19).

(a) shot across the bow A moribund metaphor (SEE PAGE 19). *warning.*

shot heard around the world A moribund metaphor (See page 19).

shot (himself) in the foot A moribund metaphor (See page 19).

(a) shot in the arm A moribund metaphor (See page 19). *boost; encouragement; fillip; goad; impetus; impulse; incentive; incitation; incitement; inducement; jolt; motivation; motive; prod; provocation; push; shove; spur; stimulus; thrust; urge.* ■ Their success will give *a shot in the arm* to the rest of the economy. Replace with *a thrust*.

(a) shot in the dark A moribund metaphor (See page 19). *appraisal; assessment; assumption; conjecture; estimate; estimation; guess; hypothesis; impression; opinion; presumption; speculation; supposition; surmise.*

shot to hell A moribund metaphor (See page 19).
1. *demolished; destroyed; devastated; obliterated; racked; ruined; shattered; smashed; wracked; wrecked.*
2. *damaged; decayed; decrepit; deteriorated; dilapidated; ragged; shabby; shopworn; tattered; worn.*

(stand) shoulder to shoulder A moribund metaphor (See page 19). *collaborate; comply; concur; conspire; cooperate; work together.*

shout (it) from the housetops (rooftops) A moribund metaphor (See page 19). *advertise; announce; broadcast; cry out; declaim; disseminate; exclaim; proclaim; promulgate; publicize; publish; shout; trumpet; yell.*

shove down (their) throats A moribund metaphor (See page 19). *bulldoze; bully; coerce; compel; constrain; demand; drive; enforce; enjoin; goad; force; impel; incite; intimidate; make; necessitate; obligate; oblige; order; press; pressure; prod; require; threaten; tyrannize; urge.*

show me a ... and I'll show you a ... An infantile phrase (See page 18). ■ *Show me a* person who's lived a normal, conventional life, *and I'll show you a* dullard.

(the) show must go on A popular prescription (See page 21).

(not) (a) shred of (evidence) A moribund metaphor (See page 19). ■ There was not a *shred of evidence* to support his contentions.

shrinking violet A moribund metaphor (See page 19). *diffident; quiet; reserved; retiring; self-effacing; shy; timid.*

shut (his) eyes to A moribund metaphor (See page 19). *brush aside; avoid; discount; disregard; dodge; duck; ignore; neglect; omit; pass over; recoil from; shrink from; shun; shy away from; turn away from; withdraw from.*

sick and tired (of) An inescapable pair (See page 18).
1. *annoyed; bored; discouraged; disgusted; exasperated; exhausted; fatigued; fed up; impatient; irked; irritated; sick; sickened; tired; wearied; weary.* ■ I'm *sick and tired* of seeing the welfare bashing in the newspa-

per. REPLACE WITH *weary*. ■ No matter how desperate and *sick and tired* and lonely I felt, I was also vibrant and alive. REPLACE WITH *discouraged*.
2. *cloyed; glutted; gorged; jaded; sated; satiated; surfeited.*

(as) sick as a dog An insipid simile (SEE PAGE 19).
1. *afflicted; ailing; diseased; ill; indisposed; infirm; not (feeling) well; sick; sickly; suffering; unhealthy; unsound; unwell; valetudinarian.*
2. *nauseated; nauseous; queasy; sick; squeamish; vomiting.*

sick to death A moribund metaphor (SEE PAGE 19). *annoyed; bored; discouraged; disgusted; exasperated; exhausted; fatigued; fed up; impatient; irked; irritated; sick; sickened; tired; wearied; weary.* SEE ALSO *to death*.

(breathe; exhale; heave) (a) (collective) sigh of relief A torpid term (SEE PAGE 22). *be allayed; be alleviated; be assuaged; be calmed; be comforted; be mollified; be palliated; be relieved; be soothed; calm down; quiet down; relax; rest; unwind.* ■ Investors *breathed a sigh of relief* there was nothing more in the report than they expected. REPLACE WITH *were relieved*. ■ Emergency workers were *breathing a collective sigh of relief*. REPLACE WITH *relieved*. ■ Every morning when I come in and see them, I *breathe a sigh of relief*. REPLACE WITH *relax*. ■ After holding its breath for days, the city finally *exhaled a sigh of relief*. REPLACE WITH *relaxed*. SEE ALSO *reach epidemic proportions*.

(a) sight for sore eyes A moribund metaphor (SEE PAGE 19).

signed, sealed, and delivered A moribund metaphor (SEE PAGE 19). *completed; concluded; consummated; ended; executed; finished; fulfilled; made final; terminated.*

significant An overworked word (SEE PAGE 20). For example: *significant development; significant effect; significant impact; significant progress.* SEE ALSO *meaningful*.

significant other A torpid term (SEE PAGE 22). The use of this dispassionate expression will likely result in a bloodless relationship with whomever it is used to describe. Any one of the following words is a far better choice: *admirer; beau; beloved; boyfriend (girlfriend); companion; confidant; darling; dear; dearest; familiar; family member; flame; friend; husband (wife); inamorata (inamorato); infatuate; intimate; love; lover; paramour; partner; spouse; steady; suitor; swain; sweetheart.*

The term *significant other* (SO) gives rise to sentiments like this:
Lover: I love you so.
Loved: I love you so, so.
■ Whether it be with instructors, *significant others*, children, or bosses, you practice the art of gentle persuasion continually. REPLACE WITH *spouses*. ■ My *significant other* is always calling me a spoil sport because I won't compromise on things. REPLACE WITH *lover*. ■ Men trying to use it to cheat on their *significant others*

should know that a pager number will work on a woman for only a short time. REPLACE WITH *girlfriends or wives.* ■ I am being stalked by a former *significant other.* REPLACE WITH *boyfriend.* SEE ALSO *object of one's affection.*

(a) significant part (portion; proportion) A wretched redundancy (SEE PAGE 23). *a good (great) deal; a good (great) many; almost all; many; most; much; nearly all.* ■ Many programmers spend *a significant portion* of their working day maintaining software. REPLACE WITH *a good deal.* SEE ALSO *a substantial part (portion; proportion).*

silence is golden A quack equation (SEE PAGE 21).

(as) silent as the dead An insipid simile (SEE PAGE 19). *dumb; hushed; mum; mute; noiseless; quiet; reticent; silent; speechless; still; stock-still; taciturn; voiceless; wordless.*

(the) silent majority A moribund metaphor (SEE PAGE 19). *all; citizenry; commonage; commonalty; common people; crowd; everybody; everyone; followers; herd; hoi polloi; masses; mob; multitude; plebeians; populace; proletariat; public; rabble.*

(as) silly as a goose An insipid simile (SEE PAGE 19). *absurd; asinine; childish; comical; farcical; fatuous; flighty; foolhardy; foolish; frivolous; giddy; idiotic; immature; inane; laughable; ludicrous; nonsensical; ridiculous; senseless; silly.*

silver lining A moribund metaphor (SEE PAGE 19).

simultaneously at the same time A wretched redundancy (SEE PAGE 23). *at the same time; simultaneously.* ■ This machine does four welds *simultaneously at the same time.* REPLACE WITH *at the same time* or *simultaneously.* SEE ALSO *while at the same time; while simultaneously.*

(a) sine qua non A foreign phrase (SEE PAGE 17). *critical essential; indispensable; necessary; requisite; vital.* ■ A comprehensive neurologic assessment is *a sine qua non* in assessing cases of cerebral palsy. REPLACE WITH *indispensable.*

sing a different tune A moribund metaphor (SEE PAGE 19).

sing for (her) supper A moribund metaphor (SEE PAGE 19).

single best (biggest; greatest; highest; largest; most) A wretched redundancy (SEE PAGE 23). *best (most).* This expression is a good example of how people pay scant attention to what they say or write. Idiom or no, superlatives like *best* and *most* need not be qualified by the word *single.* People attend more to what others say — copying, as they do, one another's words — than to what they themselves say. ■ The *single most* important problem is discrimination among one another. DELETE *single.* ■ Good records are the *single best* way to avoid having deductions disallowed in the event you are audited. DELETE *single*. ■ The *single biggest* issue is the cost of upgrading a substandard system. DELETE *single*. ■ The school committee and the superintendent place student safety as their *single highest* priority. DELETE *single*.

sing like a bird An insipid simile (SEE PAGE 19). *dulcet; harmonious; melodic; melodious; pleasant-sounding; sonorous; sweet.*

sing (his) praises A torpid term (SEE PAGE 22). *acclaim; applaud; celebrate; commend; compliment; congratulate; eulogize; extol; flatter; hail; laud; panegyrize; praise; puff; salute.*

(enough to) sink a ship A moribund metaphor (SEE PAGE 19). *a big (brobdingnagian; colossal; enormous; gargantuan; giant; gigantic; grand; great; huge; immense; large; massive; monstrous; prodigious; tremendous; vast) amount; a great deal; a lot.*

sink or swim A moribund metaphor (SEE PAGE 19).

sink (my) teeth into A moribund metaphor (SEE PAGE 19). *absorb; engage; engross; immerse; involve.*

sit on (her) duff A moribund metaphor (SEE PAGE 19). *be idle; be inactive; be lazy; be unemployed; be unoccupied; dally; dawdle; loaf; loiter; loll; lounge; relax; repose; rest.*

sit on (their) hands A moribund metaphor (SEE PAGE 19). *be idle; be inactive; be lazy; be unemployed; be unoccupied; dally; dawdle; loaf; loiter; loll; lounge; relax; repose; rest.*

sit on the fence A moribund metaphor (SEE PAGE 19). *ambivalent; divided; indecisive; in doubt; irresolute; neutral; torn; uncertain; uncommitted; undecided; unsure.* ■ If you're *sitting on the fence* or your answer is yes, you're in luck. REPLACE WITH *undecided*.

sit tight A moribund metaphor (SEE PAGE 19). *be patient; hold on; wait.*

(a) sitting duck A moribund metaphor (SEE PAGE 19).

sitting on a gold mine A moribund metaphor (SEE PAGE 19).

(a) situation An overworked word (SEE PAGE 20). For example: *crisis situation; difficult situation; life-threatening situation; push-pull situation; no-lose situation; no-win situation; open-ended situation; problematic situation; sad situation; tragic situation; win-win situation.* ■ It's really *a* pathetic *situation*. DELETE *a situation*. ■ If there is an emergency *situation*, then that person can exit as well. DELETE *situation*. ■ It's nice to be *in a situation where you are* recognized for the work you're doing. DELETE *in a situation where you are*. ■ The *air conditioning situation* is currently under repair. DELETE *situation* or REPLACE WITH *air conditioner*. ■ The network approach *is a win-win situation for* all involved. REPLACE

WITH *benefits.* SEE ALSO *remedy the situation.*

(sit) with (his) head in (his) hands A moribund metaphor (SEE PAGE 19). *brood; despair; despond; mope.*

(it's) six of one, half dozen of the other A moribund metaphor (SEE PAGE 19). *either; either way; it doesn't matter; no matter.*

(the) $64,000 question An infantile phrase (SEE PAGE 18). ■ That's *the $64,000 question* for a number of people.

skate on thin ice A moribund metaphor (SEE PAGE 19). *chance; dare; endanger; gamble; hazard; imperil; jeopardize; make bold; peril; risk; venture.*

skeletons in the closet (cupboard) A moribund metaphor (SEE PAGE 19). *secret; surprise.*

(all) skin and bones A moribund metaphor (SEE PAGE 19). *asthenic; attenuated; bony; cachectic; emaciated; gaunt; lank; lanky; lean; narrow; rail-thin; scraggy; scrawny; skeletal; skinny; slender; slight; slim; spare; spindly; svelte; sylphid; thin; trim; wispy.*

(as) skinny as a stick An insipid simile (SEE PAGE 19). *asthenic; attenuated; bony; cachectic; emaciated; gaunt; lank; lanky; lean; narrow; rail-thin; scraggy; scrawny; skeletal; skinny; slender; slight; slim; spare; spindly; svelte; sylphid; thin; trim; wispy.*

(the) sky's the limit A moribund metaphor (SEE PAGE 19).

(a) slap in the face A moribund metaphor (SEE PAGE 19). *abuse; affront; contempt; contumely; derision; disappointment; disdain; dishonor; impertinence; indignity; insult; offense; outrage; rebuff; rebuke; rejection; scorn; slap; slight; slur; sneer; snub.* ■ Megan's mother called the judge's decision *a slap in the face.* REPLACE WITH *an insult.* ■ The document is *a slap in the face* to the democratic principles that Americans expect their leaders to uphold. REPLACE WITH *an affront.*

slap on the wrist A moribund metaphor (SEE PAGE 19). *admonish; animadvert; berate; castigate; censure; chastise; chide; condemn; criticize; denounce; discipline; objurgate; punish; rebuke; remonstrate; reprehend; reprimand; reproach; reprobate; reprove; revile; scold; upbraid; vituperate; warn.* ■ When the story proved false, Oliver and Smith were fired, but Arnett was *slapped on the wrist* and retained by CNN. REPLACE WITH *chided.*

(a) slap on the wrist A moribund metaphor (SEE PAGE 19). *admonishment; admonition; animadversion; berating; castigation; censure; chastisement; chiding; condemnation; criticism; denouncement; denunciation; disapprobation; disapproval; disciplining; objurgation; punishment; rebuke; remonstrance; reprehension; reprimand; reproach; reprobation; reproof; revilement; scolding; upbraiding; vituperation; warning.* ■ Nearly as many seem willing to let him off with *a slap on the wrist* because they believe they see the changes involving mostly private matters. REPLACE WITH *a scolding.*

sleep like a log An insipid simile (SEE PAGE 19). *doze; nap; rest; sleep; slumber.*

sleep like a top An insipid simile (SEE PAGE 19). *doze; nap; rest; sleep; slumber.*

sleep the sleep of the just A moribund metaphor (SEE PAGE 19). *doze; nap; rest; sleep; slumber.*

slice of life A moribund metaphor (SEE PAGE 19).

slim and trim An inescapable pair (SEE PAGE 18). *asthenic; attenuated; bony; cachectic; emaciated; gaunt; lank; lanky; lean; narrow; rail-thin; scraggy; scrawny; skeletal; skinny; slender; slight; slim; spare; spindly; svelte; sylphid; thin; trim; wispy.*

slings and arrows A moribund metaphor (SEE PAGE 19).
1. *assault; attack; blow.*
2. *adversity; bad luck; calamity; catastrophe; hardship; ill fortune; misadventure; mischance; misfortune; mishap; reversal; setback.*

(the) slings and arrows of outrageous fortune A moribund metaphor (SEE PAGE 19).

(as) slippery as an eel An insipid simile (SEE PAGE 19).
1. *elusive; ephemeral; evanescent; eva-sive; fleeting; fugitive; passing; short-lived; slippery; volatile.*
2. *crafty; cunning; deceitful; dishonest; foxy; shifty; slick; tricky; wily.*

slippery character (customer) A moribund metaphor (SEE PAGE 19). *bastard; blackguard; cad; charlatan; cheat; cheater; fake; fraud; impostor; knave; mountebank; phony; pretender; quack; rascal; rogue; scoundrel; swindler; undesirable; villain.*

slippery slope A moribund metaphor (SEE PAGE 19). *declivity.*

slip through (our) fingers A moribund metaphor (SEE PAGE 19). *abscond; clear out; decamp; depart; desert; disappear; escape; exit; flee; fly; go; go away; leave; move on; part; pull out; quit; retire; retreat; run away; take flight; take off; vacate; vanish; withdraw.*

slip through the cracks A moribund metaphor (SEE PAGE 19). *discount; disregard; elide; ignore; leave out; miss; neglect; omit; overlook; slight.*

slow and steady wins the race A popular prescription (SEE PAGE 21).

(as) slow as molasses (in January) An insipid simile (SEE PAGE 19). *crawling; dallying; dawdling; deliberate; dilatory; faltering; hesitant; laggardly; lagging; leisurely; methodical; plodding; procrastinating; slothful; slow; slow-paced; sluggardly; sluggish; snaillike; systematic; tardy; tortoiselike; unhurried.*

(a) slow boat to China (nowhere) A moribund metaphor (SEE PAGE 19).

slow(ly) but sure(ly) An inescapable pair (SEE PAGE 18).

slower than molasses (in January) A moribund metaphor (SEE PAGE 19). *crawling; dallying; dawdling; deliberate; dilatory; faltering; hesitant; laggardly; lagging; leisurely; methodical; plodding; procrastinating; slothful; slow; slow-paced; sluggardly; sluggish; snaillike; systematic; tardy; tortoiselike; unhurried.*

smack dab in the middle of An infantile phrase (SEE PAGE 18). ■ It puts readers *smack dab in the middle of* the action.

(a) small army of A moribund metaphor (SEE PAGE 19). ■ *A small army of* labor leaders came to Washington for a final assault against the agreement. SEE ALSO *a barrage of.*

small potatoes A moribund metaphor (SEE PAGE 19). *immaterial; inappreciable; inconsequential; inconsiderable; insignificant; meaningless; minor; negligible; niggling; nugatory; petty; trifling; trivial; unimportant; unsubstantial.* ■ And 10,000 cases is *no small potatoes.* REPLACE WITH *not insignificant.*

(as) smart as a whip An insipid simile (SEE PAGE 19). *able; adroit; alert; apt; astute; bright; brilliant; capable; clever; competent; discerning; enlightened; intelligent; judicious;* *keen; knowledgeable; learned; logical; luminous; perceptive; perspicacious; quick; quick-witted; rational; reasonable; sagacious; sage; sapient; sensible; sharp; shrewd; smart; sound; understanding; wise.*

smart cookie A moribund metaphor (SEE PAGE 19). *able; adroit; apt; astute; bright; brilliant; capable; clever; competent; discerning; enlightened; intelligent; judicious; keen; knowledgeable; learned; logical; luminous; perceptive; perspicacious; quick; rational; reasonable; sagacious; sage; sapient; sensible; sharp; shrewd; smart; sound; understanding; wise.*

smell a rat A moribund metaphor (SEE PAGE 19).

smell fishy A moribund metaphor (SEE PAGE 19). *doubtful; dubious; questionable; shady; shaky; suspect; suspicious.*

smell (stink) to high heaven A moribund metaphor (SEE PAGE 19). *reek; smell; stink.*

smoke and mirrors A moribund metaphor (SEE PAGE 19). *artfulness; artifice; chicanery; cover-up; cozenage; craftiness; cunning; deceit; deceiving; deception; dissembling; dissimulation; duplicity; feigning; fraud; guile; pretense; shamming; trickery; wile.*

smokes like a chimney An insipid simile (SEE PAGE 19).

smoking gun A moribund metaphor (SEE PAGE 19). *evidence; proof.*

(as) smooth as glass An insipid simile (SEE PAGE 19).
1. *burnished; even; glassy; glossy; greasy; lustrous; oily; polished; satiny; silky; sleek; slick; slippery; smooth; velvety.*
2. *apparent; basic; clear; clear-cut; conspicuous; distinct; easily done; easy; effortless; elementary; evident; explicit; facile; limpid; lucid; manifest; obvious; patent; pellucid; plain; simple; simplicity itself; smooth; straightforward; translucent; transparent; unambiguous; uncomplex; uncomplicated; understandable; unequivocal; unmistakable.*

(as) smooth as silk An insipid simile (SEE PAGE 19).
1. *burnished; even; glassy; glossy; greasy; lustrous; oily; polished; satiny; silky; sleek; slick; slippery; smooth; velvety.*
2. *apparent; basic; clear; clear-cut; conspicuous; distinct; easily done; easy; effortless; elementary; evident; explicit; facile; limpid; lucid; manifest; obvious; patent; pellucid; plain; simple; simplicity itself; smooth; straightforward; translucent; transparent; unambiguous; uncomplex; uncomplicated; understandable; unequivocal; unmistakable.*

smooth (her) feathers A moribund metaphor (SEE PAGE 19). *allay; appease; assuage; calm; comfort; compose; conciliate; console; moderate; modulate; mollify; pacify; placate; propitiate; quiet; soften; soothe; still; temper; tranquilize.*

snake in the grass A moribund metaphor (SEE PAGE 19). *animal; barbarian; beast; brute; degenerate; fiend; knave; lout; monster; rake; rascal; reptile; rogue; ruffian; savage; scamp; scoundrel; villain.*

snatch victory from the jaws of defeat A moribund metaphor (SEE PAGE 19).

snow job A moribund metaphor (SEE PAGE 19). *deception; dishonesty.*

(as) snug as a bug in a rug An insipid simile (SEE PAGE 19). *comfortable; cosy; habitable; homey; inhabitable; livable; safe; snug.*

(like) (a) soap opera An insipid simile (SEE PAGE 19). *exaggerated; excessive; histrionic; hyperbolic; maudlin; mawkish; melodramatic; overblown; overdone; overemotional; sensational; sentimental; soppy.*

(as) sober as a judge An insipid simile (SEE PAGE 19).
1. *dignified; earnest; formal; grave; pensive; reserved; sedate; self-controlled; self-restrained; serious; severe; sober; solemn; somber; staid; stern; strict; subdued; thoughtful.*
2. *abstemious; sober; teetotal; temperate.*

social butterfly A moribund metaphor (SEE PAGE 19). *fin-lover; gadabout; pleasure-seeker.*

(as) soft as velvet An insipid simile (SEE PAGE 19). *delicate; downy; feathery; fine; fluffy; satiny; silken; silky; smooth; soft; velvety.*

soft landing A moribund metaphor (SEE PAGE 19). ■ The airline industry's problem is trying to determine whether this is a *soft landing* for the economy or a recession.

(a) soft touch A moribund metaphor (SEE PAGE 19).

(as) solid as a rock An insipid simile (SEE PAGE 19).
1. *adamantine; firm; granitelike; hard; petrified; rock-hard; rocklike; rocky; solid; steellike; steely; stonelike; stony.*
2. *athletic; beefy; brawny; burly; firm; fit; hale; hardy; hearty; husky; manly; mesomorphic; mighty; muscular; powerful; puissant; robust; rugged; sinewy; solid; stalwart; stout; strapping; strong; sturdy; tough; vigorous; virile; well-built.*
3. *constant; dependable; determined; faithful; fast; firm; fixed; inexorable; inflexible; loyal; obdurate; resolute; resolved; rigid; solid; stable; staunch; steadfast; steady; stern; strong; tenacious; unflinching; unwavering; unyielding.*

some of my best friends are A plebeian sentiment (SEE PAGE 20).

(thirty)-something An infantile phrase (SEE PAGE 18). ■ But they're not the typical self-absorbed, *30-something* crowd. ■ If you give a speech on social security, your purpose will vary for audiences made up of *twenty-something, forty-something,* or *seventy-something* individuals.

(there's) something in the wind A moribund metaphor (SEE PAGE 19).

(there's) something rotten in the state of Denmark A moribund metaphor (SEE PAGE 19).

(like) something out of a (Norman Rockwell painting) An insipid simile (SEE PAGE 19). ■ Li River cruises can take your clients past dreamlike rock formations; they *look like something out of a Salvador Dali painting.*

(it's) something to do A plebeian sentiment (SEE PAGE 20). SEE ALSO *(it) gives (me) something to do; (it) keeps (me) busy; (it) keeps (me) out of trouble.*

(it's) something to look forward to A plebeian sentiment (SEE PAGE 20). Those who use this phrase acknowledge the future appeals to them more than does the present, as they do the apparent pallor of their lives.

(it's) something to think about A plebeian sentiment (SEE PAGE 20). SEE ALSO *food for thought.*

(a) sometime thing A torpid term (SEE PAGE 22). *erratic; fitful; haphazard; inconsistent; intermittent; irregular; occasional; random; sometime; spasmodic; sporadic; unpredictable.*

song and dance A moribund metaphor (SEE PAGE 19).
1. *pattern; routine.*
2. *deception; dissimulation; duplicity; equivocation; evasion; excuse; fabrication; falsehood; fib; invention; lie; mumbo-jumbo; nonsense; prevarication.*

son of a gun A moribund metaphor (SEE PAGE 19). *brute; degenerate; fiend; knave; lout; rake; rascal; rogue; ruffian; scamp; scoundrel; villain.*

(the) sooner the better A quack equation (SEE PAGE 21).

sorely missed An inescapable pair (SEE PAGE 18). Let us not die only to have it said we will be *sorely missed.* We should prefer silence to such insipidity. More disturbing still is that we should be spoken of so blandly, so, indeed, badly. This is hardly wording from a tribute, hardly an encomium. ■ He is going to be *sorely missed* by his teammates. ■ He will be *sorely missed* by those of us who were privileged to call him our friend. ■ He will be *sorely missed* by his family, fiends and neighbors.

(the) sound and the fury A moribund metaphor (SEE PAGE 19).

(as) sound as a bell An insipid simile (SEE PAGE 19).
1. *cogent; convincing; intelligent; judicious; just; logical; prudent; rational; reasonable; sensible; sound; telling; valid; well-founded; well-grounded; wise.*
2. *athletic; beefy; brawny; energetic; fit; good; hale; hardy; healthful; healthy; hearty; lanky; lean; manly; mesomorphic; muscular; powerful; robust; shapely; sinewy; slender; solid; sound; stalwart; strong; sturdy; thin; trim; vigorous; virile; well; well-built.*

(as) sound as a dollar An insipid simile (SEE PAGE 19).
1. *cogent; convincing; intelligent;*

judicious; just; logical; prudent; rational; reasonable; sensible; sound; telling; valid; well-founded; well-grounded; wise.
2. *athletic; beefy; brawny; energetic; fit; good; hale; hardy; healthful; healthy; hearty; lanky; lean; manly; mesomorphic; muscular; powerful; robust; shapely; sinewy; slender; solid; sound; stalwart; strong; sturdy; thin; trim; vigorous; virile; well; well-built.*

(she) sounds like a broken record An insipid simile (SEE PAGE 19).

(as) sour as vinegar An insipid simile (SEE PAGE 19).

sour grapes A moribund metaphor (SEE PAGE 19). *bile; bitterness; resentment; umbrage.*

sour note A moribund metaphor (SEE PAGE 19).

so what else is new? An infantile phrase (SEE PAGE 18).

sow the seeds of A moribund metaphor (SEE PAGE 19). *circulate; disseminate; distribute; propagate; sow; spread.*

sow (his) wild oats A moribund metaphor (SEE PAGE 19). *be dissolute; be licentious; be wild; have sex.*

spare the rod and spoil the child A popular prescription (SEE PAGE 21).

(a) spate of A moribund metaphor (SEE PAGE 19). ■ The legislation was proposed in response to *a* spate of violent incidents. SEE ALSO *a barrage of.*

speaks volumes A moribund metaphor (SEE PAGE 19).

(she's) special A suspect superlative (SEE PAGE 22).

(that) special someone A suspect superlative (SEE PAGE 22). *admirer; amorist; beau; boyfriend; flame; gallant; girlfriend; inamorata; inamorato; lover; paramour; steady; suitor; swain; sweetheart; wooer.* ■ I still haven't met *that special someone,* but I am confident it will happen soon.

(the) specter of A moribund metaphor (SEE PAGE 19). ■ The Troika's standard response to all who raised *the specter of* diminished social services has been insult, invective, and ire.

spick and span An inescapable pair (SEE PAGE 18). *antiseptic; clean; cleansed; disinfected; germ-free; hygienic; immaculate; neat; orderly; sanitary; sanitized; scoured; scrubbed; spotless; spruce; stainless; sterile; tidy; unblemished; unsoiled; unspotted; unsullied; untarnished; washed.*

spilled milk A moribund metaphor (SEE PAGE 19).

spill (his) guts A moribund metaphor (SEE PAGE 19). *acknowledge; admit; affirm; allow; avow; concede; confess; disclose; divulge; expose; grant; own; reveal; tell; uncover; unveil.*

spill the beans A moribund metaphor (SEE PAGE 19). *confess; disclose; divulge; leak; make known; reveal; tell.*

spinning (my) wheels A moribund metaphor (SEE PAGE 19). *mired; stalled; stuck.*

spit and image (spitting image) An inescapable pair (SEE PAGE 18). *clone; copy; counterpart; doppelgänger; double; duplicate; exact likeness; match; twin.*

spit and polish A moribund metaphor (SEE PAGE 19).

spoil rotten A moribund metaphor (SEE PAGE 19). *coddle; gratify; humor; indulge; mollycoddle; overindulge; overprotect; pamper; spoil.*

spread like wildfire An insipid simile (SEE PAGE 19). *breed; multiply; proliferate; propagate; reproduce; spread.*

spread (himself) too thin A moribund metaphor (SEE PAGE 19).

sprout up like mushrooms An insipid simile (SEE PAGE 19). *breed; multiply; proliferate; propagate; reproduce; spread.*

(on the) spur of the moment A moribund metaphor (SEE PAGE 19). *abrupt; extemporaneous; extempore; immediate; impromptu; improvised; impulsive; instant; quick; rash; spontaneous; sudden; unexpected; unprepared; unprompted; unrehearsed.*

square peg in a round hole A moribund metaphor (SEE PAGE 19). *aberrant; abnormal; anomalistic; anomalous; atypical; bizarre; curious; deviant; different; distinct; distinctive; eccentric; exceptional; extraordinary; fantastic; foreign; grotesque; idiosyncratic; independent; individual; individualistic; irregular; novel; odd; offbeat; original; peculiar; puzzling; quaint; queer; rare; remarkable; separate; singular; uncommon; unconventional; unexampled; unique; unnatural; unorthodox; unparalleled; unprecedented; unusual; weird.*

(a) square peg in a round hole A moribund metaphor (SEE PAGE 19). *curiosity; deviant; eccentric; iconoclast; individual; individualist; maverick; misfit; nonconformist; oddball; oddity; renegade; undesirable.*

squeaky clean A moribund metaphor (SEE PAGE 19). *high-minded; moralistic; principled; strait-laced; upright; upstanding.*

(the) squeaky wheel gets the grease A popular prescription (SEE PAGE 21).

stab (her) in the back A moribund metaphor (SEE PAGE 19).
1. *assail; attack; badmouth; complain; criticize; denounce; knock; put down.*
2. *abuse; harm; hurt; injure; maltreat; mistreat; wound.* ■ If I stop trusting people because they may *stab me in the back,* I could miss out on some valuable and enriching friendships. REPLACE WITH *mistreat me.*

stack the cards (deck) A moribund metaphor (SEE PAGE 19). ■

While such efforts must invariably fail, the climate of distrust and fear *stacks the deck* against individuals who must move into a hostile environment.

(the) staff of life A moribund metaphor (SEE PAGE 19). *bread.*

(the) stage has been set A moribund metaphor (SEE PAGE 19). ■ *The stage has been set* for a contract that will have to contain genuine reforms.

(old) stamping (stomping) ground A moribund metaphor (SEE PAGE 19). *hangout; haunt; rendezvous.*

stamp of approval A moribund metaphor (SEE PAGE 19). *approval; authorization; certification; endorsement; sanction.*

stand (their) ground A moribund metaphor (SEE PAGE 19).
1. *hold fast; persevere; persist; stand firm; stick with.*
2. *be adamant; be balky; be bullheaded; be cantankerous; be contrary; be contumacious; be dogged; be headstrong; be inflexible; be intractable; be mulish; be obdurate; be obstinate; be ornery; be perverse; be refractory; be resolute; be rigid; be stubborn; be unyielding; be willful.*

stand on (his) own two feet A moribund metaphor (SEE PAGE 19). *assured; confident; independent; self-assured; self-confident; self-contained; self-governing; self-reliant; self-ruling; self-sufficient; self-supporting; sure.*

stand on the sidelines A moribund metaphor (SEE PAGE 19). ■ Surgeons who have been *standing on the sidelines* are beginning to take up the procedure themselves.

stand out from (in) the crowd (pack) A moribund metaphor (SEE PAGE 19). *aberrant; abnormal; anomalistic; anomalous; atypical; bizarre; curious; deviant; different; distinct; distinctive; eccentric; exceptional; extraordinary; fantastic; foreign; grotesque; idiosyncratic; independent; individual; individualistic; irregular; novel; odd; offbeat; original; peculiar; puzzling; quaint; queer; rare; remarkable; separate; singular; strange; uncommon; unconventional; unexampled; unique; unnatural; unorthodox; unparalleled; unprecedented; unusual; weird.*

stand (stick) out like a sore thumb An insipid simile (SEE PAGE 19). *apparent; arresting; blatant; conspicuous; evident; flagrant; glaring; gross; manifest; noticeable; observable; obtrusive; obvious; outstanding; patent; prominent; salient.*

(his) star is on the rise A moribund metaphor (SEE PAGE 19).

(has) stars in her eyes A moribund metaphor (SEE PAGE 19). *dreamy; happy; idealistic; optimistic; starry-eyed.*

start the ball rolling A moribund metaphor (SEE PAGE 19). *begin; commence; enter on; initiate.*

start with a clean slate A moribund metaphor (SEE PAGE 19). *begin anew; start afresh; start over.*

state of seige A moribund metaphor (SEE PAGE 19).

staying power A moribund metaphor (SEE PAGE 19). *determination; durability; endurance; firmness; fortitude; permanence; permanency; perseverance; resolution; resolve; spunk; stability; stamina; steadfastness; tenacity.*

stay on target A moribund metaphor (SEE PAGE 19).

(as) steady as a rock An insipid simile (SEE PAGE 19). *constant; dependable; determined; faithful; fast; firm; fixed; inexorable; inflexible; loyal; obdurate; reliable; resolute; resolved; rigid; solid; stable; staunch; steadfast; steady; stern; strong; supportive; tenacious; true; trustworthy; trusty; unflinching; unwavering; unyielding.*

steal the show A moribund metaphor (SEE PAGE 19).

steal (her) thunder A moribund metaphor (SEE PAGE 19).

steer clear (of) A moribund metaphor (SEE PAGE 19). *avoid; bypass; circumvent; dodge; elude; evade; shun; sidestep; skirt.* ■ It was a signal to the new mayor to *steer cleer of* divisiveness and cliquishness. REPLACE WITH *shun.*

steer wrong A moribund metaphor (SEE PAGE 19). *beguile; betray;*

deceive; lead astray; misdirect; misguide; mislead. ■ I trust that you won't *steer* them *wrong*. REPLACE WITH *mislead*.

stem the flow A moribund metaphor (SEE PAGE 19). *abort; arrest; block; check; curb; decelerate; delay; end; halt; hamper; hinder; impede; obstruct; plug; quash; quell; retard; slow; squash; stay; stem; stop; suspend; terminate.*

stem the tide A moribund metaphor (SEE PAGE 19). *abort; arrest; block; check; curb; decelerate; delay; end; halt; hamper; hinder; impede; obstruct; plug; quash; quell; retard; slow; squash; stay; stem; stop; suspend; terminate.* ■ But twenty years of effort have failed to *stem the tide of* environmental degradation. REPLACE WITH *retard*.

(a) step backward A torpid term (SEE PAGE 22). *backset; reversal; setback.*

(a) step forward A torpid term (SEE PAGE 22). *advancement; betterment; development; furtherance; growth; headway; improvement; progress.* ■ This is *a step forward* for us all. REPLACE WITH *betterment*. For some writers, *a step forward* isn't positive enough: ■ Although the IFS interface is *a positive step forward* for DOS, it remains in a sort of twilight zone. REPLACE WITH *an advancement*. SEE ALSO *a step (forward) in the right direction; go forward; move forward; move (forward) in the right direction; proceed forward.*

(a) step (forward) in the right direction A torpid term (SEE PAGE 22). *advancement; betterment; development; furtherance; growth; headway; improvement; progress.* Like many dimwitticisms, *a step forward in the right direction* is an ungainly creation. The English language is wonderfully expressive and infinitely flexible, but this maladroit phrase is stiff, wooden. ■ Incentives to attract and retain nurses would be *a step in the right direction*. REPLACE WITH *an improvement*. ■ Mr. Singh describ-ed the arrests of Mr. Saeed and other militants as *a step forward in the right direction* but said more action was necessary. REPLACE WITH *progress*. SEE ALSO *a step forward; go forward; move forward; move (forward) in the right direction; proceed forward.*

step on (his) toes A moribund metaphor (SEE PAGE 19). *abuse; affront; anger; annoy; bother; displease; harm; hurt; insult; irk; irritate; offend; outrage; provoke; rile; roil; slap; slight; smart; trouble; upset; vex; wound.* ■ During his five months as acting mayor, he *stepped on many people's toes*. REPLACE WITH *offended many people*.

step up to the plate A moribund metaphor (SEE PAGE 19). 1. *aim for; attempt; endeavor; engage; participate; pursue; seek; strive for; try.* ■ Industry is *stepping up to the plate on* this. REPLACE WITH *pursuing*. 2. *advance; appear; approach; come forth; come forward; emerge; rise; show; surface.* ■ Because his public

presence has been tainted greatly, she's going to have to *step up to the plate* and do more. REPLACE WITH *come forward.* ■ Rumors of an imminent buyout circulated, but no one *stepped up to the plate.* REPLACE WITH *came forward.*
3. *be accountable; be answerable; be responsible.*

stewed to the gills A moribund metaphor (SEE PAGE 19). *besotted; crapulous; drunk; inebriated; intoxicated; sodden; stupefied; tipsy.*

stew in (her) own juice A moribund metaphor (SEE PAGE 19). *brood; fret; mope; stew; worry.*

stick in (my) craw (throat) A moribund metaphor (SEE PAGE 19). *acerbate; anger; annoy; bother; bristle; chafe; enrage; envenom; exacerbate; gall; incense; inflame; infuriate; insult; irk; irritate; madden; miff; nettle; offend; provoke; rankle; rile; roil; vex.*

stick (your) neck out A moribund metaphor (SEE PAGE 19). *chance; dare; endanger; gamble; hazard; imperil; jeopardize; make bold; peril; risk; venture.* ■ They do not *stick their necks out* to initiate change — they are followers. REPLACE WITH *venture.*

sticks and stones will break my bones, but words will never hurt me An infantile phrase (SEE PAGE 18).

stick to (your) guns A moribund metaphor (SEE PAGE 19).
1. *hold fast; persevere; persist; stand firm; stick with.*
2. *be adamant; be balky; be bullheaded; be cantankerous; be contrary; be contumacious; be dogged; be headstrong; be inflexible; be intractable; be mulish; be obdurate; be obstinate; be ornery; be perverse; be refractory; be resolute; be rigid; be stubborn; be unyielding; be willful.*

stick to (your) ribs A moribund metaphor (SEE PAGE 19). *fill; sate; satiate; satisfy.*

stick to the knitting A moribund metaphor (SEE PAGE 19).

sticky wicket A moribund metaphor (SEE PAGE 19). *affliction; annoyance; bane; bother; burden; curse; difficulty; inconvenience; irritant; irritation; load; nuisance; ordeal; pain; pest; problem; tribulation; trouble; vexation; weight; worry.*

(as) stiff as a board An insipid simile (SEE PAGE 19).
1. *firm; inelastic; inflexible; rigid; stiff; unbending; unmalleable; unpliable; unyielding.*
2. *awkward; ceremonious; constrained; formal; precise; priggish; prim; proper; prudish; punctilious; puritanical; reserved; starched; stiff; stilted; strait-laced; stuffy; unrelaxed; uptight.*

still and all A wretched redundancy (SEE PAGE 23). *even so; still; yet.* ■ *Still and all,* I love her. REPLACE WITH *Even so* or *Still.*

(as) still as death An insipid simile (SEE PAGE 19). *dead; dormant; dull;*

immobile; immovable; inactive; inanimate; indolent; inert; inoperative; languid; latent; lethargic; lifeless; listless; motionless; phlegmatic; quiescent; quiet; sluggish; stagnant; static; stationary; still; stock-still; torpid; unresponsive.

still kicking　A moribund metaphor (SEE PAGE 19). *alive; animate; breathing; live; living.*

still waters run deep　A popular prescription (SEE PAGE 21).

stink like hell　An insipid simile (SEE PAGE 19). *reek; smell; stink.*

stir up a hornet's nest　A moribund metaphor (SEE PAGE 19). SEE ALSO *hornet's nest.*

stitch in time　A moribund metaphor (SEE PAGE 19).

(a) stitch in time saves nine　A popular prescription (SEE PAGE 21).

(a) stone's throw (away)　A moribund metaphor (SEE PAGE 19). *accessible; at hand; close; close by; handy; near; nearby; neighboring; vicinal.*

stop and smell the flowers (roses)　A moribund metaphor (SEE PAGE 19). *be idle; be inactive; be lazy; be unemployed; be unoccupied; dally; dawdle; loaf; loiter; loll; lounge; relax; repose; rest.*

stop the world I want to get off　An infantile phrase (SEE PAGE 18).

storm brewing　A moribund metaphor (SEE PAGE 19).

(a) storm of　A moribund metaphor (SEE PAGE 19). SEE ALSO *a barrage of.*

(the) story of (my) life　A plebeian sentiment (SEE PAGE 20). ■ I've always felt like an outcast; it's *the story of my life.*

straddle the fence　A moribund metaphor (SEE PAGE 19). *ambivalent; divided; indecisive; in doubt; irresolute; neutral; torn; uncertain; uncommitted; undecided; unsure.*

(the) straight and narrow (path)　A moribund metaphor (SEE PAGE 19). *decent; ethical; exemplary; good; honest; honorable; just; moral; pure; righteous; straight; upright; virtuous; wholesome.*

(as) straight as an arrow　An insipid simile (SEE PAGE 19).
1. *direct; lineal; linear; straight.*
2. *decent; ethical; exemplary; good; honest; honorable; just; moral; pure; righteous; straight; upright; virtuous; wholesome.*

straight from the horse's mouth　A moribund metaphor (SEE PAGE 19).

straight from the shoulder　A moribund metaphor (SEE PAGE 19). *bluntly; candidly; directly; forthrightly; frankly; man to man; openly; outspokenly; plainly; straightforwardly; unambiguously; unequivocally.*

straight shooter A moribund metaphor (SEE PAGE 19). *decent; ethical; forthright; honest; just; moral; righteous; straight; trustworthy; upright; virtuous.*

strange An overworked word (SEE PAGE 20). *aberrant; abnormal; anomalistic; anomalous; atypical; bizarre; curious; deviant; different; distinct; distinctive; eccentric; exceptional; extraordinary; fantastic; foreign; grotesque; idiosyncratic; independent; individual; individualistic; irregular; novel; odd; offbeat; original; peculiar; puzzling; quaint; queer; rare; remarkable; separate; singular; uncommon; unconventional; unexampled; unique; unnatural; unorthodox; unparalleled; unprecedented; unusual; weird.* SEE ALSO *weird.*

strange bedfellows A moribund metaphor (SEE PAGE 19).

(the) straw that broke the camel's back A moribund metaphor (SEE PAGE 19).

stretch the point (truth) A moribund metaphor (SEE PAGE 19). *elaborate; embellish; embroider; enhance; enlarge; exaggerate; hyperbolize; inflate; magnify; overdo; overstress; overstate; strain; stretch.*

strike a (sympathetic) chord A moribund metaphor (SEE PAGE 19). ■ These words *struck a familiar chord* with many of the 6,000 conference participants.

strike gold A moribund metaphor (SEE PAGE 19).

strike while the iron is hot A moribund metaphor (SEE PAGE 19). *capitalize on; exploit.*

strings attached A moribund metaphor (SEE PAGE 19). *conditions; limitations; preconditions; prerequisites; provisions; qualifications; requirements; stipulations; terms.*

stroll down memory lane A moribund metaphor (SEE PAGE 19). *be nostalgic; recall; recollect; remember; reminisce; think back.*

(a) stroll (walk) in the park A moribund metaphor (SEE PAGE 19). 1. *casual; easily done; easy; effortless; elementary; facile; simple; simplicity itself; straightforward; uncomplex; uncomplicated.*
2. *agreeable; beguiling; charming; delightful; enchanting; engaging; enjoyable; fun; glorious; gratifying; inviting; joyful; joyous; pleasant; pleasing; pleasurable.* ■ Building high-rise buildings, dams, and bridges isn't exactly *a walk in the park.* REPLACE WITH *simple.* ■ Compared to NetWare 3.x, installing Windows NT Server is *a stroll in the park.* REPLACE WITH *effortless.*

(as) strong as a horse An insipid simile (SEE PAGE 19). *athletic; beefy; brawny; burly; energetic; fit; hale; hardy; healthful; healthy; hearty; husky; manly; mesomorphic; mighty; muscular; powerful; puissant; robust; rugged; sinewy; solid; sound; stalwart; stout; strapping; strong; sturdy; vigorous; virile; well-built.*

(as) strong as a lion An insipid simile (SEE PAGE 19). *athletic; beefy; brawny; burly; energetic; fit; hale; hardy; healthful; healthy; hearty; husky; manly; mesomorphic; mighty; muscular; powerful; puissant; robust; rugged; sinewy; solid; sound; stalwart; stout; strapping; strong; sturdy; vigorous; virile; well-built.*

(as) strong as an ox An insipid simile (SEE PAGE 19). *athletic; beefy; brawny; burly; energetic; fit; hale; hardy; healthful; healthy; hearty; husky; manly; mesomorphic; mighty; muscular; powerful; puissant; robust; rugged; sinewy; solid; sound; stalwart; stout; strapping; strong; sturdy; vigorous; virile; well-built.*

(as) stubborn as a mule An insipid simile (SEE PAGE 19). *adamant; balky; bullheaded; cantankerous; contrary; contumacious; dogged; headstrong; inflexible; intractable; mulish; obdurate; obstinate; ornery; perverse; refractory; resolute; rigid; stubborn; unyielding; willful.*

stuff and nonsense An inescapable pair (SEE PAGE 18). *absurdity; fatuousness; folly; foolishness; ludicrousness; nonsense; preposterousness; ridiculousness; rubbish; silliness.*

(the) stuff dreams (legends) are made of A moribund metaphor (SEE PAGE 19).

stuff to the gills A moribund metaphor (SEE PAGE 19). *abounding; brimful; brimming; bursting; chock-full; congested; crammed; crowded; dense; filled; full; gorged; jammed; jam-packed; overcrowded; overfilled; overflowing; packed; replete; saturated; stuffed; swarming; teeming.*

(major) stumbling block A moribund metaphor (SEE PAGE 19). *barrier; hindrance; hurdle; impediment; obstacle; obstruction.* ■ Modernization of the Chinese HRM system is fraught with significant *stumbling blocks*.

stupid An overworked word (SEE PAGE 20). This epithet, along with others as common, is much overused. Let's do our best to convince *stupid* people that they are by calling them, instead, *addlebrained; addleheaded; addlepated; Boeotian; bovine; cretinous; decerebrate; doltish; dull-witted; dunderheaded; fatuous; fat-witted; harebrained; hebetudinous; imbecilic; incogitant; insensate; ludicrous; moronic; muddled; nescient; obtuse; oxlike; pedestrian; phlegmatic; sluggish; torpid; vacuous; witless.*

(as) sturdy as an oak An insipid simile (SEE PAGE 19). *athletic; beefy; brawny; burly; energetic; fit; hale; hardy; healthful; healthy; hearty; husky; manly; mesomorphic; mighty; muscular; powerful; puissant; robust; rugged; sinewy; solid; sound; stalwart; stout; strapping; strong; sturdy; vigorous; virile; well-built.*

subsequent to A torpid term (SEE PAGE 22). *after; following.* ■ *Subsequent to* the initiation of the Ethics Committee investigation, the senator took back some tapes in my possession which I had not yet transcribed. REPLACE WITH *Following.* SEE ALSO *in advance of; previous to; subsequent to.*

(a) substantial part (portion; proportion) A wretched redundancy (SEE PAGE 23). *a good (great) deal; a good (great) many; almost all; many; most; much; nearly all.* ■ It is unconscionable that *a substantial proportion* of our population does not have adequate access to health care. REPLACE WITH *much.* ■ I assume that Boston will be eligible for *a substantial portion* of the distressed communities fund. Replace with *a good deal.* SEE ALSO *a significant part (portion; proportion).*

such is life A plebeian sentiment (SEE PAGE 20). SEE ALSO *that's how (the way) it goes; that's how (the way) the ball bounces; that's how (the way) the cookie crumbles; that's life; that's life in the big city; that's show biz; what are you going to do; what can you do.*

suck the life out of A moribund metaphor (SEE PAGE 19). *bleed dry; deplete; drain; exhaust; sap; suck dry.*

suddenly and without warning A wretched redundancy (SEE PAGE 23). *impetuously; impulsively; spontaneously; suddenly; unexpectedly; without warning.*

sufficient enough A wretched redundancy (SEE PAGE 23). *enough; sufficient.* ■ Just tell them your new number, and that should be *sufficient enough.* REPLACE WITH *sufficient* or *enough.* SEE ALSO *adequate enough.*

(a) sufficient number (of) A wretched redundancy (SEE PAGE 23). *enough.* ■ Effective groups contain *a sufficient number of* members to ensure good interaction. REPLACE WITH *enough.* SEE ALSO *a ... number (of).*

sugar and spice A moribund metaphor (SEE PAGE 19).

sum and substance An inescapable pair (SEE PAGE 18). *basis; center; core; crux; essence; gist; heart; kernel; pith; substance; sum.*

(the) sun, the moon, and the stars A moribund metaphor (SEE PAGE 19).

(as) sure as death An insipid simile (SEE PAGE 19). *assured; certain; destined; established; fated; fixed; foreordained; ineluctable; inescapable; inevitable; inexorable; irresistible; irreversible; irrevocable; ordained; prearranged; predestined; predetermined; sure; unalterable; unavoidable; unchangeable; unpreventable; unstoppable.*

(as) sure as death and taxes An insipid simile (SEE PAGE 19). *assured; certain; destined; established; fated; fixed; foreordained; ineluctable; inescapable; inevitable; inexorable; irresistible; irreversible; irrevocable; ordained; prearranged; predestined; predetermined; sure; unalterable; unavoidable; unchangeable; unpreventable; unstoppable.*

survival of the fittest A popular prescription (SEE PAGE 21).

swallow (her) pride A moribund metaphor (SEE PAGE 19). *abase; chasten; debase; degrade; demean; disgrace; dishonor; embarrass; humble; humiliate; lower; mortify; shame.*

swan song A moribund metaphor (SEE PAGE 19). *farewell; good-bye.*

swear by all that's holy A moribund metaphor (SEE PAGE 19). *affirm; asseverate; assert; attest; aver; avow; declare; pledge; promise; swear; testify; vow; warrant.*

swear like a sailor (trooper) An insipid simile (SEE PAGE 19). *abusive; blackguardly; coarse; crude; fescennine; foul-mouthed; indecent; lewd; obscene; profane; ribald; scurrilous; thersitical; vulgar.*

swear on a stack of bibles A moribund metaphor (SEE PAGE 19). *affirm; asseverate; assert; attest; aver; avow; declare; pledge; promise; swear; testify; vow; warrant.*

sweat bullets A moribund metaphor (SEE PAGE 19).
1. *excrete; exude; ooze; perspire; sweat; swelter; wilt.*
2. *be afraid; be agitated; be anxious; be apprehensive; be distraught; be distressed; be fearful; be fretful; be impatient; be nervous; be panicky; be tense; be uneasy; be worried.*
3. *drudge; grind; grub; labor; moil; slave; strain; strive; struggle; sweat; toil; travail; work hard.*

sweep off (her) feet A moribund metaphor (SEE PAGE 19). *amaze; astonish; astound; awe; dazzle; dumbfound; flabbergast; overpower; overwhelm; shock; startle; stun; stupefy; surprise.*

sweep (it) under the (carpet) rug A moribund metaphor (SEE PAGE 19).
1. *brush aside; avoid; discount; disregard; dodge; duck; ignore; neglect; omit; pass over; recoil from; shrink from; shun; shy away from; turn away from; withdraw from.* ■ The strategy was to *sweep it under the rug*. REPLACE WITH *ignore it*.
2. *camouflage; cloak; conceal; cover; disguise; enshroud; harbor; hide; keep secret; mask; screen; shroud; suppress; veil; withhold.*

sweep (it) under the table A moribund metaphor (SEE PAGE 19).
1. *brush aside; avoid; discount; disregard; dodge; duck; ignore; neglect; omit; pass over; recoil from; shrink from; shun; shy away from; turn away from; withdraw from.* ■ We see the word *anti-Semitism* every day in our secular newspapers, but the word *anti-Catholic* is *swept under the table*. REPLACE WITH *brushed aside*.
2. *camouflage; cloak; conceal; cover; disguise; enshroud; harbor; hide; keep secret; mask; screen; shroud; suppress; veil; withhold.*

(as) sweet as honey An insipid simile (SEE PAGE 19).
1. *honeyed; luscious; saccharine; sugary; sweet; sweetened; syrupy.*
2. *agreeable; ambrosial; beguiling; celestial; charming; delectable; deli-*

cious; delightful; divine; enchanting; engaging; enjoyable; fun; heavenly; glorious; gratifying; inviting; joyful; joyous; luscious; pleasant; pleasing; pleasurable.

(as) sweet as pie An insipid simile (SEE PAGE 19).
1. honeyed; luscious; saccharine; sugary; sweet; sweetened; syrupy.
2. agreeable; ambrosial; beguiling; celestial; charming; delectable; delicious; delightful; divine; enchanting; engaging; enjoyable; fun; heavenly; glorious; gratifying; inviting; joyful; joyous; luscious; pleasant; pleasing; pleasurable.

sweeten the pot A moribund metaphor (SEE PAGE 19). add to; augment; enhance; improve; increase; supplement.

sweeter than honey A moribund metaphor (SEE PAGE 19).
1. honeyed; luscious; saccharine; sugary; sweet; sweetened; syrupy.
2. agreeable; ambrosial; beguiling; celestial; charming; delectable; delicious; delightful; divine; enchanting;

engaging; enjoyable; fun; heavenly; glorious; gratifying; inviting; joyful; joyous; luscious; pleasant; pleasing; pleasurable.

sweet smell of success A moribund metaphor (SEE PAGE 19).

(as) swift as an arrow An insipid simile (SEE PAGE 19). brisk; expeditious; fast; fleet; hasty; hurried; immediate; instant; instantaneous; prompt; quick; rapid; speedy; spry; sudden; swift; winged.

swim against the current (tide) A moribund metaphor (SEE PAGE 19).
1. drudge; grind; grub; labor; moil; slave; strain; strive; struggle; sweat; toil; travail; work hard.
2. battle; fight; tussle; wrestle.

swim like a fish An insipid simile (SEE PAGE 19).

swim upstream A moribund metaphor (SEE PAGE 19).

swim with the tide A moribund metaphor (SEE PAGE 19).

T

tabula rasa A foreign phrase (SEE PAGE 17).

(a case of) (the) tail wagging the dog A moribund metaphor (SEE PAGE 19). *backward; in reverse.*

take a back seat A moribund metaphor (SEE PAGE 19). *be ancillary; be inferior; be lesser; be lower; be minor; be second; be secondary; be subordinate; be subservient.* ■ Just a few years after this work, machine learning *took a back seat* to expert knowledge systems. REPLACE WITH *became subordinate.* ■ As in most races for most offices, issues have *taken a back seat* to personality, image, footwork, money, and most important, field organization. REPLACE WITH *became ancillary.* ■ Power based on expertise frequently *takes a back seat* to power based on position. REPLACE WITH *is second.*

take a bath A moribund metaphor (SEE PAGE 19). *lose money.*

take a beating A moribund metaphor (SEE PAGE 19).
1. *be beaten; be conquered; be crushed; be defeated; be outdone; be overcome; be overpowered; be overwhelmed; be quelled; be routed; be trounced; be vanquished.*
2. *be assailed; be assaulted; be attacked; be battered; be beaten; be cudgeled; be flagellated; be flogged; be hit; be lambasted; be lashed; be licked; be mangled; be pounded; be pummeled; be struck; be thrashed; be trounced.*

take a breather An infantile phrase (SEE PAGE 18). *be idle; be inactive; be lazy; be unemployed; be unoccupied; dally; dawdle; loaf; loiter; loll; lounge; relax; repose; rest.*

take a dim view of A moribund metaphor (SEE PAGE 19). *deprecate; disapprove; dislike; frown on; object; protest.*

take a fancy (shine) to A moribund metaphor (SEE PAGE 19). *delight in; enjoy; fancy; like; relish.*

take a gander (at) An infantile phrase (SEE PAGE 18). *gaze; glance; glimpse; look; observe; stare; watch.*

take a haircut A moribund metaphor (SEE PAGE 19). *lose money.* ■ He suggested what has been plain for some time — that holders of $1.7 billion in junk bonds would probably *take a haircut*. REPLACE WITH *lose money*.

take a hit A moribund metaphor (SEE PAGE 19). *be assailed; be assaulted; be attacked; be battered; be beaten; be cudgeled; be flagellated; be flogged; be hit; be lambasted; be lashed; be licked; be mangled; be pounded; be pummeled; be struck; be thrashed; be trounced.*

take a leaf (page) out of (their) book A moribund metaphor (SEE PAGE 19). *copy; duplicate; emulate; follow; imitate; mimic.*

take a load off (your) mind A moribund metaphor (SEE PAGE 19). *acknowledge; admit; affirm; allow; avow; concede; confess; disclose; divulge; expose; grant; own; reveal; tell; uncover; unveil.*

take a long, hard look (at) A torpid term (SEE PAGE 22). *analyze; assay; check out; delve into; examine; investigate; probe; scrutinize; study.* ■ We need leaders with the will and the determination to *take a long, hard look at* the structure of our government. REPLACE WITH *examine.*

take a nose dive A moribund metaphor (SEE PAGE 19). *collapse; crash; dive; drop; fall; nose-dive; plummet; plunge.*

take a powder A moribund metaphor (SEE PAGE 19). *abscond; clear out; decamp; depart; desert; disappear; escape; exit; flee; fly; go; go away; leave; move on; part; pull out;* *quit; retire; retreat; run away; take flight; take off; vacate; vanish; withdraw.*

take a turn for the better A moribund metaphor (SEE PAGE 19). *ameliorate; amend; come round; convalesce; gain strength; get better; heal; improve; look up; meliorate; mend; rally; recover; recuperate; refresh; regain strength; renew; revive; strengthen.*

take a turn for the worse A moribund metaphor (SEE PAGE 19). *decay; decline; degenerate; deteriorate; disintegrate; ebb; erode; fade; fall off; languish; lessen; wane; weaken; wither; worsen.*

take (my) ball (toys) and go home An infantile phrase (SEE PAGE 18).

take (your) breath away A moribund metaphor (SEE PAGE 19). *amaze; astonish; astound; awe; dazzle; dumbfound; flabbergast; overpower; overwhelm; shock; startle; stun; stupefy; surprise.*

take by storm A moribund metaphor (SEE PAGE 19). *amaze; animate; awe; captivate; dazzle; electrify; excite; exhilarate; fascinate; impress; intoxicate; thrill; overwhelm.* ■ In the two years since it was introduced as the newest drug for depression, Prozac has *taken* the mental health community *by storm*. REPLACE WITH *captivated.*

take each day as it comes A popular prescription (SEE PAGE 21).

take exception to A wretched redundancy (SEE PAGE 23). *challenge; demur; disagree with; disapprove of; dispute; find fault with; object to; oppose; protest; question; resent.* ■ I *take exception to* your analysis of his difficulties. REPLACE WITH *disagree with*. SEE ALSO *take issue with*.

take (him) for a ride A moribund metaphor (SEE PAGE 19). *bamboozle; befool; beguile; bilk; bluff; cheat; con; deceive; defraud; delude; dupe; feint; fool; gyp; hoodwink; lead astray; misdirect; misguide; misinform; mislead; spoof; swindle; trick; victimize.*

take (my) hat off to A moribund metaphor (SEE PAGE 19). *acclaim; applaud; commend; compliment; congratulate; extol; hail; laud; praise.*

take heart A moribund metaphor (SEE PAGE 19). *be confident; be encouraged; be optimistic.*

take (a lot of) heat A moribund metaphor (SEE PAGE 19).

take into account A wretched redundancy (SEE PAGE 23). *allow for; consider; contemplate; examine; inspect; investigate; look at; ponder; provide for; regard; scrutinize; study; think over; weigh.* ■ The character of the army is also an important factor to be *taken into account*. REPLACE WITH *considered*. SEE ALSO *take into consideration*.

take into consideration A wretched redundancy (SEE PAGE 23). *allow for; consider; contemplate; examine; inspect; investigate; look at; ponder;*

provide for; regard; scrutinize; study; think over; weigh. ■ All this will be *taken into consideration*, and financial analysis will be done. REPLACE WITH *examined*. SEE ALSO *take into account*.

take issue with A wretched redundancy (SEE PAGE 23). *challenge; demur; disagree with; disapprove of; dispute; find fault with; object to; oppose; protest; question; resent.* ■ Some *take issue with* the state requiring people to use seat belts. REPLACE WITH *object to*. SEE ALSO *take exception to*.

take it as it comes A popular prescription (SEE PAGE 21).

(I) take it (that) back An infantile phrase (SEE PAGE 18).
1. *be incorrect; be in error; be misguided; be misinformed; be mislead; be mistaken; be not right; be wrong.* ■ Joanie is in third place; no, I *take it back* — it's another runner. REPLACE WITH *I'm wrong*.
2. *disavow; recant; renounce; repudiate; retract; withdraw* ■ I always wanted to be with someone more respectable; not respectable, I *take that back*, professional. REPLACE WITH *I retract that*.

take it one day (step) at a time A popular prescription (SEE PAGE 21).

take it on the chin A moribund metaphor (SEE PAGE 19).
1. *be beaten; be conquered; be crushed; be defeated; be flattened; be outdone; be overcome; be overpowered; be trampled; be trounced; be vanquished.*
2. *abide; accept; bear; brook; endure; stand; stomach; suffer; take; tolerate; withstand.*

take (her) life in (her) hands A moribund metaphor (SEE PAGE 19). *chance; dare; endanger; gamble; hazard; imperil; jeopardize; make bold; peril; risk; venture.*

take (his) lumps A moribund metaphor (SEE PAGE 19). ■ We fought our way back to profitability after *taking our lumps.*

take (their) medicine A moribund metaphor (SEE PAGE 19).

take the bait A moribund metaphor (SEE PAGE 19).

take the bit between (in) (her) teeth A moribund metaphor (SEE PAGE 19). *defy; disobey; rebel; resist; revolt; take charge; take control.*

take the bitter with the sweet A popular prescription (SEE PAGE 21).

take the bull by the horns A moribund metaphor (SEE PAGE 19). *meet head-on.*

take the cake A moribund metaphor (SEE PAGE 19).
1. *be best; be finest; be first; be first-rate; be outstanding; win.*
2. *be absurd; be disgraceful; be inane; be lowest; be outrageous; be poorest; be preposterous; be ridiculous; be worst.*
■ I am accustomed to being shocked by John Ellis, but "Beyond manifest destiny" *takes the cake.* REPLACE WITH *is outrageous.*

take the heat A moribund metaphor (SEE PAGE 19).

take the high road A moribund metaphor (SEE PAGE 19).
1. *be beneficent; be benevolent; be broad-minded; be charitable; be civil; be courteous; be gracious; be high-minded; be kind; be liberal; be magnanimous; be noble.*
2. *be decent; be ethical; be exemplary; be good; be honest; be honorable; be just; be moral; be pure; be respectful; be righteous; be straight; be upright; be virtuous; be wholesome.*

take the money and run A moribund metaphor (SEE PAGE 19). *abscond; clear out; decamp; depart; desert; disappear; escape; exit; flee; fly; go; go away; leave; make off; move on; part; pull out; quit; retire; retreat; run away; steal away; take flight; take off; vacate; vanish; withdraw.*

take the plunge A moribund metaphor (SEE PAGE 19). *dive in; do it; jump in.*

take the wind out of (his) sails A moribund metaphor (SEE PAGE 19).
1. *abase; chasten; debase; decrease; deflate; degrade; demean; depreciate; depress; diminish; disgrace; dishonor; embarrass; humble; humiliate; lower; mortify; puncture; shame.*
2. *arrest; balk; block; bridle; check; curb; derail; detain; end; foil; frustrate; halt; harness; hold up; impede; inhibit; obstruct; restrain; retard; slow; stall; stay; stop; suppress; terminate; thwart.*

(to) take this opportunity (to) An ineffectual phrase (SEE PAGE 17). On the podium and before others, people speak what they're expected to say. Alone and on their deathbeds, they moan that no one knew who they were. *(To) take this opportunity (to)* is one of the phrases that people learn to mimic before they know to moan. ■ I would like *to take this opportunity* to apologize to my family and friends. DELETE *to take this opportunity*. ■ I'd like *to take this opportunity* to renew our commitment to you — to provide you with superior service. DELETE *to take this opportunity*. ■ Let me *take this opportunity to* thank our most inspirational guest. DELETE *take this opportunity to*.

take to (his) heels A moribund metaphor (SEE PAGE 19). *abscond; clear out; decamp; depart; desert; disappear; escape; exit; flee; fly; go; go away; leave; move on; part; pull out; quit; retire; retreat; run away; take flight; take off; vacate; vanish; withdraw.*

take (him) to task A torpid term (SEE PAGE 22). *admonish; animadvert; berate; blame; castigate; censure; chasten; chastise; chide; condemn; criticize; denounce; denunciate; discipline; impugn; objurgate; punish; rebuke; remonstrate; reprehend; reprimand; reproach; reprobate; reprove; revile; scold; upbraid; vituperate; warn.* ■ In polite, carefully chosen words, the auditors *take* management *to task* for a multitude of sins. REPLACE WITH *censure*.

take (her) to the cleaners A moribund metaphor (SEE PAGE 19).

take (them) to the woodshed A moribund metaphor (SEE PAGE 19). *admonish; animadvert; berate; castigate; censure; chasten; chastise; chide; condemn; criticize; denounce; denunciate; discipline; excoriate; fulminate against; imprecate; impugn; inveigh against; objurgate; punish; rebuke; remonstrate; reprehend; reprimand; reproach; reprobate; reprove; revile; scold; swear at; upbraid; vituperate; warn.*

take umbrage at A wretched redundancy (SEE PAGE 23). *disagree with; dislike; object to; resent.* ■ I *take umbrage at* the comment he made in response to my criticism of the DA's poor performance. REPLACE WITH *resent*.

take with a grain of salt A moribund metaphor (SEE PAGE 19). *disbelieve; distrust; doubt; have doubts; have misgivings; have reservations; mistrust; question; suspect; wonder.* ■ But this pane's data should be *taken with a grain of salt*. REPLACE WITH *doubted*.

(like) taking candy from a baby An insipid simile (SEE PAGE 19). *apparent; basic; clear; clear-cut; conspicuous; distinct; easily done; easy; effortless; elementary; evident; explicit; facile; limpid; lucid; manifest; obvious; patent; pellucid; plain; simple; simplicity itself; straightforward; translucent; transparent; unambiguous; uncomplex; uncomplicated; understandable; unequivocal; unmistakable.*

(like) taking lambs to the slaughter An insipid simile (SEE PAGE 19).

(a) tale never loses in the telling A popular prescription (SEE PAGE 21).

talk a blue streak A moribund metaphor (SEE PAGE 19). *babbling; blathering; chatty; facile; fluent; garrulous; glib; jabbering; logorrheic; long-winded; loquacious; prolix; talkative; verbose; voluble; windy.*

talk (my) ear (head) off A moribund metaphor (SEE PAGE 19). *babbling; blathering; chatty; facile; fluent; garrulous; glib; jabbering; logorrheic; long-winded; loquacious; prolix; talkative; verbose; voluble; windy.*

talk is cheap A quack equation (SEE PAGE 21).

talk (speak) out of both sides of (his) mouth A moribund metaphor (SEE PAGE 19). *be ambivalent; be indecisive; be irresolute; be uncertain; be unsure; be wishy-washy; dodge; doubletalk; equivocate; evade; fence; hedge; palter; prevaricate; quibble; shuffle; sidestep; tergiversate; waffle.*

(he) talks a good game A moribund metaphor (SEE PAGE 19).

talk through (his) hat A moribund metaphor (SEE PAGE 19). *babble; blather; jabber; prate; prattle.*

talk turkey A moribund metaphor (SEE PAGE 19).

tan (warm) (her) hide A moribund metaphor (SEE PAGE 19). *spank.*

tar and feather A moribund metaphor (SEE PAGE 19). *admonish; animadvert; berate; castigate; censure; chasten; chastise; chide; condemn; criticize; denounce; denunciate; discipline; impugn; objurgate; punish; rebuke; remonstrate; reprehend; reprimand; reproach; reprobate; reprove; revile; scold; upbraid; vituperate; warn.*

tar (him) with the same brush A moribund metaphor (SEE PAGE 19).

teach (me) the ropes A moribund metaphor (SEE PAGE 19). *coach; educate; initiate; instruct; teach; train; tutor.*

team player A suspect superlative (SEE PAGE 22). This term is much favored by those in the business world for an employee who thinks just as others do and behaves just as he is expected to. A *team player* is a person who has not the spirit to think for or be himself.

Of course, nothing new, nothing innovative is likely to be realized by insisting, as the business world does, on objectivity and consensus.

A team player is often no more than a *bootlicker;* no more than a *fawner,* a *flatterer,* a *follower;* no more than a *lackey,* a *minion,* a *stooge;* no more than a *sycophant,* a *toady,* a *yes-man.* ■ Mulvey, whose termination is perhaps the most striking — he was one of the bank's stellar performers — was not regarded as a *team player.*

tear (out) (my) hair A moribund

metaphor (SEE PAGE 19).

1. *acerbated; angry; annoyed; bothered; cross; displeased; enraged; furious; grouchy; incensed; inflamed; infuriated; irate; irked; irritated; mad; miffed; peeved; provoked; riled; roiled; testy; upset; vexed.*

2. *agitated; anxious; apprehensive; distraught; distressed; fearful; frustrated; nervous; panicky; stressed; stressful; tense; tormented; troubled; uneasy; worried.*

teeter on the brink (of) A moribund metaphor (SEE PAGE 19).

tell it like it is An infantile phrase (SEE PAGE 18). *be honest; honest; speak the truth; truthful.* ■ He's not whining; he's just *telling it like it is*. REPLACE WITH *being honest*. ■ These videos may be informative and *tell it like it is* but are far too explicit and do not belong in a coed classroom. REPLACE WITH *truthful*.

tell it to the Marines A moribund metaphor (SEE PAGE 19).

tell tales out of school A moribund metaphor (SEE PAGE 19). *reveal secrets.* ■ A lot of people thought they were *telling tales out of school*. REPLACE WITH *revealing secrets*.

tempest in a teapot A moribund metaphor (SEE PAGE 19).

terra firma A foreign phrase (SEE PAGE 17).

terrific An overworked word (SEE PAGE 20). *Terrific* means *causing terror* or *terrifying*, but of late, it means only *very bad* or, annoyingly, *very good*. ■ I have a *terrific* stomachache. REPLACE WITH *very bad*. ■ We had a *terrific* time at the party. REPLACE WITH *very good*. SEE ALSO *awesome; awful*.

(the) temper of our time A moribund metaphor (SEE PAGE 19).

test the waters A moribund metaphor (SEE PAGE 19).

thank goodness it's Friday An infantile phrase (SEE PAGE 18).

thanks but no thanks An infantile phrase (SEE PAGE 18). *thanks; thanks all the same; thanks anyway; thanks just the same.*

thank you A plebeian sentiment (SEE PAGE 20). Even *thank you* — once a sure sign of civility — becomes part of the plebeian patois when it is spoken mechanically.

Only a spectacularly thoughtless person would thank others for having been abused or berated by them, for having been refused or rejected by them. SEE ALSO *excuse me?; I'm sorry*.

thank(ing) you in advance A plebeian sentiment (SEE PAGE 20). These phrases are more than plebeian, they are impudent. Only the lowbred or harebrained would presume to thank another for something while requesting it of him. ■ We *thank you in advance* for your understanding in this situation. ■ *Thank you in advance* for taking the time to help us. ■ *Thanks in advance* for your cooperation. ■ I have contacted the folks at ArtistDirect as well, and wanted to *thank you in advance* for your compliance in this matter.

And now variations of this phrase are being used in other, even more facile and sillier, constructions: ■ If I offend any man, woman, beast, or anything in between, *I apologize in advance.* ■ *He apologizes in advance* to those with a more normal sense of humor.

that makes two of us An infantile phrase (SEE PAGE 18). *as I do; I do too; neither do I; no more do I; nor do I; so do I.*

that's for me to know and you to find out An infantile phrase (SEE PAGE 18). SEE ALSO *it's a long story.*

that's how (the way) it goes A plebeian sentiment (SEE PAGE 20). *That's how (the way) it goes* and other expressions of resignation are often spoken by some people and rarely, if at all, spoken by others.

It is dimwitted people who are too often resigned when they should be complaining, too often resigned when they should be demanding, too often resigned when they should be raging. SEE ALSO *such is life; that's how (the way) the ball bounces; that's how (the way) the cookie crumbles; that's life; that's life in the big city; that's show biz; what are you going to do; what can you do.*

that's how (the way) the ball bounces A plebeian sentiment (SEE PAGE 20). SEE ALSO *such is life; that's how (the way) it goes; that's how (the way) the cookie crumbles; that's life; that's life in the big city; that's show biz; what are you going to do; what can you do.*

that's how (the way) the cookie crumbles A plebeian sentiment (SEE PAGE 20). SEE ALSO *such is life; that's how (the way) it goes; that's how (the way) the ball bounces; that's life; that's life in the big city; that's show biz; what are you going to do; what can you do.*

that's interesting A plebeian sentiment (SEE PAGE 20). *That's interesting*, like *that's nice* (SEE), is most often a witless response to what a person has said. As such, it is no more than an acknowledgment of having been bored, an admission of not having listened, or a confession of having nothing clever to say. SEE ALSO *every effort is being made; interesting.*

that's life A plebeian sentiment (SEE PAGE 20). SEE ALSO *such is life; that's how (the way) it goes; that's how (the way) the ball bounces; that's how (the way) the cookie crumbles; that's life in the big city; that's show biz; what are you going to do; what can you do.*

that's life in the big city A plebeian sentiment (SEE PAGE 20). SEE ALSO *such is life; that's how (the way) it goes; that's how (the way) the ball bounces; that's how (the way) the* cookie crumbles; that's life; that's show biz; what are you going to do; what can you do.

that's nice A plebeian sentiment (SEE PAGE 20). This phrase is used to dismiss what a person has said. *That's nice* is a perfunctory response that, though it suggests interest in a person, actually reveals indifference to the person. SEE ALSO *every effort is being made; that's interesting.*

that's show biz A plebeian sentiment (SEE PAGE 20). SEE ALSO *such is life; that's how (the way) it goes; that's how (the way) the ball bounces; that's how (the way) the cookie crumbles; that's life; that's life in the big city; what are you going to do; what can you do.*

that's the thing An ineffectual phrase (SEE PAGE 17). SEE ALSO *here's the thing; the thing about (of) it is; the thing is.*

that's what it's all about A popular prescription (SEE PAGE 21). ■ It's the little things, not the big things — like playing with my son — *that's what it's all about.*

that's where (you) enter the picture A moribund metaphor (SEE PAGE 19).

thence A withered word (SEE PAGE 22).
1. *from that place; from there.* ■ Saudi Arabia pumps some crude through the IPSA pipeline to the Red Sea and *thence* through the

Suez canal. REPLACE WITH *from there.*
2. *from that time.*
3. *hence; therefore; thus.*

there are no words to describe (express) A plebeian sentiment (SEE PAGE 20). There are many more words than people seem to think, and far more is expressible with them than people seem to imagine.

Those who depend on dimwitticisms to convey thought and feeling are more apt to believe *there are no words to describe ...*, for these people are, necessarily, most frustrated by the limits of language.

Dimwitticisms do permit us to describe our most universal feelings, our most banal thoughts, but they prevent us from describing more individual feelings, more brilliant thoughts. These are reserved for a language largely unknown to everyday speakers and writers. SEE ALSO *words cannot describe (express).*

there are other fish in the sea A moribund metaphor (SEE PAGE 19).

there are two sides to every (question) story A popular prescription (SEE PAGE 21).

there's a first time for everything A popular prescription (SEE PAGE 21).

there's a time and a place for everything A popular prescription (SEE PAGE 21).

there's more than one way to skin a cat A popular prescription (SEE PAGE 21).

there's no accounting for taste A popular prescription (SEE PAGE 21).

there's no fool like an old fool A popular prescription (SEE PAGE 21).

there's no (such thing as a) free lunch A popular prescription (SEE PAGE 21).

there's no going back A popular prescription (SEE PAGE 21).

there's no harm in trying A popular prescription (SEE PAGE 21).

there's no place like home A popular prescription (SEE PAGE 21).

there's no rest for the weary A popular prescription (SEE PAGE 21).

there's nothing new under the sun A popular prescription (SEE PAGE 21).

there's no time like the present A popular prescription (SEE PAGE 21). ■ They say *there's no time like the present* and that's never been truer.

there's nowhere to go but up A popular prescription (SEE PAGE 21).

there's safety (strength) in numbers A popular prescription (SEE PAGE 21).

(as) thick as molasses An insipid simile (SEE PAGE 19). *concentrated; congealed; gelatinous; gluey; glutinous; gooey; gummy; inspissated; jellied; jellified; jellylike; mucilaginous; sticky; thick; viscid; viscous.*

(as) thick as thieves An insipid simile (SEE PAGE 19). *amiable; amicable; attached; brotherly; chummy; close; confidential; devoted; familiar; friendly; inseparable; intimate; loving; thick.*

(as) thin as a reed An insipid simile (SEE PAGE 19). *asthenic; attenuated; bony; cachectic; emaciated; gaunt; lank; lanky; lean; narrow; rail-thin; scraggy; scrawny; skeletal; skinny; slender; slight; slim; spare; spindly; svelte; sylphid; thin; trim; wispy.*

(as) thin as a rail An insipid simile (SEE PAGE 19). *asthenic; attenuated; bony; cachectic; emaciated; gaunt; lank; lanky; lean; narrow; rail-thin; scraggy; scrawny; skeletal; skinny; slender; slight; slim; spare; spindly; svelte; sylphid; thin; trim; wispy.*

(a) thing An overworked word (SEE PAGE 20). ■ The mind is *an* amazing *thing.* DELETE *an thing.* ■ It's *a* very important *thing.* DELETE *a thing.* ■ We have won the battle, but the war is *an* ongoing *thing.* DELETE *an thing.* ■ I think that change is *a* good *thing.* DELETE *a thing.* ■ You do this by comparing something your listeners know a lot about with something they know little or nothing about in order to make the unfamiliar *thing* clear. DELETE *thing.*

(the) thing about (of) it is An ineffectual phrase (SEE PAGE 17). ■ *The thing about it is* it's humiliating and destructive to the psyche to be hit. DELETE *The thing about it is.* ■ *The thing about it is* what they say or do has no influence on what I do. DELETE *The thing about it is.* ■ *The thing about it is* I could never tell her anything. DELETE *The thing about it is.* SEE ALSO *here's the thing; that's the thing; the thing is.*

(the) thing is An ineffectual phrase (SEE PAGE 17). ■ *The thing is* we know sexual orientation is discovered prior to adolescence. DELETE *The thing is.* ■ *The thing is* I work two jobs, and when I get home I want to relax. DELETE *The thing is.* ■ But *the thing is,* there's always someone who knows where they are. DELETE *the thing is.* SEE ALSO *here's the thing; that's the thing; the thing about (of) it is.*

(a) thing of beauty is a joy forever A popular prescription (SEE PAGE 21).

(a) thing of the past A torpid term (SEE PAGE 22).
1. *ceased; completed; concluded; dead; deceased; defunct; departed; done; ended; exanimate; expired; extinct; extinguished; finished; gone; inanimate; lifeless; no more; over; perished; stopped; terminated.*
2. *antediluvian; antiquated; archaic; dead; obsolescent; obsolete; old; old-fashioned; outdated; outmoded; out of date; out of fashion; passé; superannuated.* ■ All agree that the days of students being able to work their way through college are *a thing of the past.* REPLACE WITH *over.* ■ The 8-hour day has become *a thing of the past.* REPLACE WITH *obsolete.*

this and that A grammatical gimmick (SEE PAGE 17).

this can't be happening (to me) A plebeian sentiment (SEE PAGE 20).

this is the first day of the rest of your life A popular prescription (SEE PAGE 21).

this is to inform you that An ineffectual phrase (SEE PAGE 17). ■ *This is to inform you that* your credit application has been approved and your account is now open. DELETE *This is to inform you that.* SEE ALSO *(please) be advised that; (please) be informed that.*

thorn in (my) flesh (side) (of) A moribund metaphor (SEE PAGE 19). *affliction; annoyance; bane; blight; bother; burden; curse; difficulty; inconvenience; irritant; irritation; load; nuisance; ordeal; pain; pest; plague; problem; torment; tribulation; trouble; vexation; weight; worry.* ■ Inventory collateral valuations have been a *thorn in the side of* the agricultural industry for years. REPLACE WITH *bane to.*

those who can, do; those who can't, teach A popular prescription (SEE PAGE 21).

(the) three musketeers An infantile phrase (SEE PAGE 18).

three sheets to the wind A moribund metaphor (SEE PAGE 19). *besotted; crapulous; drunk; inebriated; intoxicated; sodden; stupefied; tipsy.*

three strikes and you're out An infantile phrase (SEE PAGE 18).

thrilled to death A moribund metaphor (SEE PAGE 19). *blissful; blithe; buoyant; cheerful; delighted; ecstatic; elated; enraptured; euphoric; exalted; excited; exhilarated; exultant; gay; glad; gleeful; good-humored; happy; intoxicated; jolly; jovial; joyful; joyous; jubilant; merry; mirthful; overjoyed; pleased; rapturous; thrilled.* SEE ALSO *to death.*

thrills and chills An inescapable pair (SEE PAGE 18).

through thick and thin A moribund metaphor (SEE PAGE 19).

throw (a dog) a bone A moribund metaphor (SEE PAGE 19).

throw (her) a curve A moribund metaphor (SEE PAGE 19). *bamboozle; befool; beguile; bilk; bluff; cheat; con; deceive; defraud; delude; dupe; feint; fool; gyp; hoodwink; lead astray; misdirect; misguide; misinform; mislead; spoof; swindle; trick; victimize.*

throw a monkey wrench into the works A moribund metaphor (SEE PAGE 19).
1. *agitate; confuse; disorder; disorganize; disquiet; disrupt; disturb; fluster; jar; jinx; jolt; jumble; mix up; muddle; perturb; rattle; ruffle; shake up; stir up; trouble; unnerve; unsettle; upset.*
2. *blight; cripple; damage; disable; harm; hurt; impair; incapacitate; lame; mar; mess up; rack; ruin; sabotage; spoil; subvert; undermine; vitiate; wrack; wreck.*

throw a wet blanket on A moribund metaphor (SEE PAGE 19). *bridle; check; constrain; contain; curb; curtail; dampen; discourage; foil; harness; hinder; impede; inhibit; obstruct; quell; repress; restrain; restrict; retard; stifle; subdue; suppress; thwart; weaken.* SEE ALSO *throw cold water on.*

throw caution to the wind A moribund metaphor (SEE PAGE 19).
1. *be adventuresome; be adventurous; be audacious; be bold; be brave; be courageous; be daring; be dauntless; be fearless; be intrepid; be mettlesome; be plucky; be stalwart; be unafraid; be valiant; be valorous; be venturesome.*
2. *be careless; be foolhardy; be hasty; be heedless; be impetuous; be incautious; be precipitate; be rash; be reckless; be thoughtless.*

throw cold water on A moribund metaphor (SEE PAGE 19). *bridle; check; constrain; contain; curb; curtail; dampen; discourage; foil; harness; hinder; impede; inhibit; obstruct; quell; repress; restrain; restrict; retard; stifle; subdue; suppress; thwart; weaken.* SEE ALSO *throw a wet blanket on.*

throw down the gauntlet (glove) A moribund metaphor (SEE PAGE 19). *affront; brave; call; challenge; confront; dare; defy; encounter; face; meet.*

throw dust in (your) eyes A moribund metaphor (SEE PAGE 19). *bamboozle; befool; beguile; bilk; bluff; cheat; con; deceive; defraud; delude; dupe; feint; fool; gyp; hoodwink; lead astray; misdirect; misguide; misinform; mislead; spoof; swindle; trick; victimize.*

throw enough dirt, and some will stick A moribund metaphor (SEE PAGE 19).

throw for a loop A moribund metaphor (SEE PAGE 19). *amaze; astonish; astound; awe; dazzle; dumbfound; flabbergast; overpower; overwhelm; shock; startle; stun; stupefy; surprise.*

throw (toss) (his) hat in the ring A moribund metaphor (SEE PAGE 19).
1. *join; run.*
2. *commence; begin; enter into; start; undertake.*

throw (toss) in the sponge (towel) A moribund metaphor (SEE PAGE 19). *abdicate; accede; acquiesce; bow; capitulate; cede; concede; give in; give up; quit; relinquish; retreat; submit; succumb; surrender; yield.* ■ The bloated bureaucracy remains unscathed, spending continues uncontrolled, and the House leadership has *thrown in the towel* to the governor. REPLACE WITH *acquiesced.* ■ If I get any more overwhelmed, I'm going to *throw in the towel.* REPLACE WITH *quit.*

throw (them) off the scent A moribund metaphor (SEE PAGE 19).

bamboozle; befool; beguile; bilk; bluff; cheat; con; hoodwink; lead astray; deceive; defraud; delude; dupe; feint; fool; gyp; misdirect; misguide; misinform; mislead; spoof; swindle; trick.

throw out the baby with the bath water A moribund metaphor (SEE PAGE 19).

throw (toss) out the window A moribund metaphor (SEE PAGE 19). *abandon; chuck; discard; dismiss; dump; jettison; reject; repudiate; throw out; toss out.* ■ Everything I tried to teach them about getting along and togetherness has been *thrown out the window.* REPLACE WITH *jettisoned.*

throw the book at A moribund metaphor (SEE PAGE 19). *admonish; animadvert; berate; castigate; censure; chasten; chastise; chide; condemn; criticize; denounce; denunciate; discipline; excoriate; fulminate against; imprecate; impugn; inveigh against; objurgate; penalize; punish; rebuke; remonstrate; reprehend; reprimand; reproach; reprobate; reprove; revile; scold; swear at; upbraid; vituperate; warn.*

throw (them) to the wolves A moribund metaphor (SEE PAGE 19).

throw (his) weight around A moribund metaphor (SEE PAGE 19). *awe; browbeat; bully; frighten; intimidate; menace; push around; scare; threaten; torment.*

thumb (his) nose (at) A moribund metaphor (SEE PAGE 19). *contemn;*

deride; despise; detest; disdain; jeer at; laugh at; mock; ridicule; scoff at; scorn; shun; slight; sneer; snub; spurn. ■ We burden our own banks with record keeping and reporting while offshore bankers *thumb their noses at* us. REPLACE WITH *mock.*

(turn) thumbs down A moribund metaphor (SEE PAGE 19). *decline; deny; disallow; disapprove; forbid; nix; prohibit; proscribe; refuse; reject; rule out; say no; turn down; veto.*

thunderous applause An inescapable pair (SEE PAGE 18).

tickled pink A moribund metaphor (SEE PAGE 19). *blissful; buoyant; cheerful; delighted; elated; excited; gay; glad; gladdened; gleeful; good-humored; gratified; happy; jolly; jovial; joyful; joyous; jubilant; merry; mirthful; pleased; tickled.*

tickled to death A moribund metaphor (SEE PAGE 19). *blissful; buoyant; cheerful; delighted; elated; excited; gay; glad; gladdened; gleeful; good-humored; gratified; happy; jolly; jovial; joyful; joyous; jubilant; merry; mirthful; pleased; tickled.* SEE ALSO *to death.*

(the) tide of A moribund metaphor (SEE PAGE 19). SEE ALSO *a barrage of.*

tied to (her) apron strings A moribund metaphor (SEE PAGE 19). *clinging; dependent; subject; subordinate; subservient.*

(a) tidal wave of A moribund metaphor (SEE PAGE 19). ■ There's just *a tidal wave of* vital information that gets delivered by telephone. SEE ALSO *a barrage of.*

tie the knot A moribund metaphor (SEE PAGE 19). *marry; wed.*

tie up loose ends A moribund metaphor (SEE PAGE 19).

(as) tight as a drum An insipid simile (SEE PAGE 19). *firm; snug; strained; stretched; taut; tense; tight.*

tighten (our) belts A moribund metaphor (SEE PAGE 19). *reduce costs; save money.* ■ We are constantly looking for ways to *tighten our belts.* REPLACE WITH *save money.*

tighten the screws A moribund metaphor (SEE PAGE 19). *coerce; command; compel; constrain; demand; dictate; enforce; enjoin; force; insist; make; order; press; pressure; push.*

tight rein on A moribund metaphor (SEE PAGE 19).

(talk) till (I'm) blue in the face A moribund metaphor (SEE PAGE 19). *always; ceaselessly; constantly; continually; continuously; endlessly; eternally; everlastingly; evermore; forever; forevermore; immortally; indefinitely; interminably; permanently; perpetually; persistently; unceasingly; unremittingly.*

till (until) (her) dying days A moribund metaphor (SEE PAGE 19). *always; ceaselessly; constantly; con-*

tinually; continuously; endlessly; eternally; everlastingly; evermore; forever; forevermore; immortally; indefinitely; interminably; permanently; perpetually; persistently; unceasingly; unremittingly.

till (until) hell freezes over A moribund metaphor (SEE PAGE 19). *always; ceaselessly; constantly; continually; continuously; endlessly; eternally; everlastingly; evermore; forever; forevermore; immortally; indefinitely; interminably; permanently; perpetually; persistently; unceasingly; unremittingly.*

till (until) it's coming out (of) (my) ears A moribund metaphor (SEE PAGE 19). *excessively; exorbitantly; extravagantly; immoderately; in excess; inordinately; profligately; unrestrainedly.*

till (until) the cows come home A moribund metaphor (SEE PAGE 19). *always; ceaselessly; constantly; continually; continuously; endlessly; eternally; everlastingly; evermore; forever; forevermore; immortally; indefinitely; interminably; permanently; perpetually; persistently; unceasingly; unremittingly.* ■ You can press Escape *until the cows come home*, and it will do nothing. REPLACE WITH *unceasingly.*

tilt at windmills A moribund metaphor (SEE PAGE 19).

time and effort An inescapable pair (SEE PAGE 18). ■ He still puts a lot of *time and effort* into his commercials.

time and energy An inescapable pair (SEE PAGE 18). ■ Boiling water also is cheaper than buying bottled water, but it takes more *time and energy.*

time and tide wait for no man A popular prescription (SEE PAGE 21).

time flies when you're having fun A popular prescription (SEE PAGE 21).

(the) time has come An infantile phrase (SEE PAGE 18). ■ *The time has come* to recognize that personal diaries must be accorded greater protection than business records.

time heals all wounds A popular prescription (SEE PAGE 21).

time is a great healer A popular prescription (SEE PAGE 21).

time is money A quack equation (SEE PAGE 21).

time period A wretched redundancy (SEE PAGE 23). *period; time.* ■ Would you go along with this for a *time period*? REPLACE WITH *period* or *time.*

time was when A torpid term (SEE PAGE 22). *before; earlier; formerly; long ago; once; previously.*

time will tell A moribund metaphor (SEE PAGE 19). ■ We have made many changes in attitude and practice, and only *time will tell* whether these are for the ultimate good or merely more mischief.

tip (my) hat to A moribund metaphor (SEE PAGE 19).
1. *acknowledge; flag; greet; hail; recognize; salute; wave to; welcome.* ■ I *tip my hat to* Mayor Menino for having the vision to see that Boston does not require a professional football team to remain a world-class city. REPLACE WITH *salute.* ■ I'd also like to *tip my hat to* Jeff Staples for his fast editing and feedback. REPLACE WITH *acknowledge.*
2. *acclaim; applaud; cheer; commend; compliment; congratulate; hail; praise; salute; support; toast.*

(a) tip of the hat A moribund metaphor (SEE PAGE 19).

tip of the iceberg A moribund metaphor (SEE PAGE 19). *beginning; commencement; foundation; inauguration; inception; least of it; onset; start.* The monstrous and omnipresent *tip of the iceberg,* like so many other dimwitted usages, alerts us to an inarticulate speaker, a tentative writer. ■ We have just seen the *tip of the iceberg* of corporations that have loaded up with too much debt and gone broke because of the merger and takeover wars. REPLACE WITH *beginning.* ■ I feel these issues and programs are just the *tip of the iceberg.* REPLACE WITH *start.*

And here are a couple of examples no less than wonderful: ■ It's difficult to tell whether my study is the iceberg and the tip is yet to be found, or whether my study was the *tip of the iceberg.* ■

These attacks are only the *tip of the iceberg;* they are the part of the iceberg that is visible above the water, in clear view — but as everyone knows, the largest part of the iceberg, and possibly the most dangerous, lies beneath the surface of the water and is difficult to detect.

tip the scales A moribund metaphor (SEE PAGE 19).

(as) tired as a dog An insipid simile (SEE PAGE 19). *beat; bushed; debilitated; depleted; drained; drowsy; enervated; exhausted; fatigued; groggy; sapped; sleepy; sluggish; slumberous; somnolent; soporific; spent; tired; weary; worn out.*

to all intents and purposes A wretched redundancy (SEE PAGE 23). *effectively; essentially; in effect; in essence; practically; virtually.* ■ *To all intents and purposes,* you were dating two women at a time. REPLACE WITH *In effect.* SEE ALSO *for all intents and purposes; for all practical purposes; to all practical purposes.*

to all practical purposes A wretched redundancy (SEE PAGE 23). *effectively; essentially; in effect; in essence; practically; virtually.* ■ The ruling Unionist party is, *to all practical purposes,* a Protestant party. REPLACE WITH *in essence.* SEE ALSO *for all intents and purposes; for all practical purposes; to all intents and purposes.*

to a T A moribund metaphor (SEE PAGE 19). *accurately; correctly; exact-*

ly; faultlessly; flawlessly; ideally; just right; perfectly; precisely; rightly; strictly; to perfection; unerringly; very well.

(the) toast of the town A moribund metaphor (SEE PAGE 19).

to beat the band A moribund metaphor (SEE PAGE 19). *actively; aggressively; dynamically; emphatically; energetically; fast; ferociously; fervently; fiercely; forcefully; frantically; frenziedly; furiously; hard; intensely; intently; mightily; passionately; powerfully; robustly; savagely; spiritedly; strenuously; strongly; vehemently; viciously; vigorously; violently; wildly; with vigor.* ■ When you wake up, it should be snowing *to beat the band.* REPLACE WITH *mightily.*

to burn A moribund metaphor (SEE PAGE 19).
1. *enormous; great; huge; immense; large; massive; monstrous; prodigious; tremendous; vast.* ■ And Mrs. Dole has *Southern charm to burn.* REPLACE WITH *immense Southern charm.*
2. *excessive; exorbitant; extreme; immoderate; inordinate; undue.*

today is the first day of the rest of (your) life A popular prescription (SEE PAGE 21).

to death A moribund metaphor (SEE PAGE 19). *consumedly; enormously; exceedingly; excessively; exorbitantly; extraordinarily; extremely; greatly; hugely; immensely; immoderately; inordinately; intem-* *perately; intensely; mightily; prodigiously; unreasonably; unrestrainedly; very much.* ■ I love him *to death.* REPLACE WITH *prodigiously.*

And as if *to death* were not persuasive enough: ■ The DoD and VA appeared content to study Gulf War illnesses *literally to death.* REPLACE WITH *unrestrainedly.*

to each (his) own A popular prescription (SEE PAGE 21).

to err is human A popular prescription (SEE PAGE 21).

to err is human, to forgive divine A popular prescription (SEE PAGE 21).

toe the line (mark) A moribund metaphor (SEE PAGE 19). *abide by; accede; accommodate; accord; acquiesce; adapt; adhere to; agree; behave; comply; concur; conform; correspond; follow; harmonize; heed; mind; obey; observe; submit; yield.*

(leveraged) to (their) eyebrows A moribund metaphor (SEE PAGE 19).

to make a long story short A torpid term (SEE PAGE 22). *briefly; concisely; in brief; in short; in sum; succinctly; tersely.*

(with) tongue in cheek A moribund metaphor (SEE PAGE 19). *facetiously; humorously; in fun; in jest; in play; jocosely; jokingly; kiddingly; playfully; teasingly.*

(set) tongues wagging A moribund metaphor (SEE PAGE 19). *bab-*

ble; blab; cackle; chaffer; chat; chitchat; chatter; confabulate; converse; gossip; jabber; palaver; prate; prattle; rattle; talk.

too big for (his) breeches A moribund metaphor (SEE PAGE 19). *arrogant; cavalier; condescending; contemptuous; despotic; dictatorial; disdainful; dogmatic; domineering; haughty; imperious; insolent; lofty; overbearing; overweening; patronizing; pompous; pretentious; scornful; self-important; supercilious; superior; vainglorious.*

too hot to handle A moribund metaphor (SEE PAGE 19).

(you) took the words (right) out of (my) mouth A moribund metaphor (SEE PAGE 19).

too many chiefs (and not enough Indians) A moribund metaphor (SEE PAGE 19).

too many cooks spoil the broth (brew) A popular prescription (SEE PAGE 21).

too smart for (his) own good A plebeian sentiment (SEE PAGE 20).

(fight) tooth and nail A moribund metaphor (SEE PAGE 19). *actively; aggressively; dynamically; emphatically; energetically; ferociously; fervently; fiercely; forcefully; frantically; frenziedly; furiously; hard; intensely; intently; mightily; passionately; powerfully; robustly; savagely; spiritedly; strenuously; strongly; vehemently; viciously; vigorously; violently; wild-*

ly; with vigor. ■ Bank of Boston, the state's largest bank, lobbied *tooth and nail* against the interstate law. REPLACE WITH *intensely.*

toot (your) own horn A moribund metaphor (SEE PAGE 19). *acclaim; applaud; bluster; boast; brag; celebrate; cheer; commend; compliment; congratulate; crow; extol; flatter; gloat; hail; honor; laud; praise; puff; salute; self-congratulate; strut; swagger.* ■ Engineers are the world's worst at *tooting their own horn.* REPLACE WITH *applauding themselves.* ■ Even so, the group president of Lucent Technologies' Global Service Provider business division isn't the type to *toot her own horn.* REPLACE WITH *boast.*

top brass A moribund metaphor (SEE PAGE 19). *administrator; boss; brass; chief; commander; director; executive; foreman; head; headman; leader; manager; master; (high) muckamuck; officer; official; overseer; president; principal; superintendent; supervisor.*

(a) torrent of A moribund metaphor (SEE PAGE 19). SEE ALSO *a barrage of.*

toss and turn An inescapable pair (SEE PAGE 18).

to tell you the truth An ineffectual phrase (SEE PAGE 17).

(march) to the beat of a different drummer A moribund metaphor (SEE PAGE 19). *aberrant; abnormal; anomalistic; anomalous; atypical;*

bizarre; curious; deviant; different; distinct; distinctive; eccentric; exceptional; extraordinary; fantastic; foreign; grotesque; idiosyncratic; independent; individual; individualistic; irregular; novel; odd; offbeat; original; peculiar; puzzling; quaint; queer; rare; remarkable; separate; singular; strange; uncommon; unconventional; unexampled; unique; unnatural; unorthodox; unparalleled; unprecedented; unusual; weird.

to the ends (far reaches) of the earth A moribund metaphor (SEE PAGE 19).
1. *always; ceaselessly; constantly; continually; continuously; endlessly; eternally; everlastingly; evermore; forever; forevermore; frequently; interminably; nonstop; permanently; perpetually; persistently; recurrently; regularly; repeatedly; unceasingly; unremittingly.*
2. *all during; all over; all through; everyplace; everywhere; throughout.*

(up) to the hilt A moribund metaphor (SEE PAGE 19). *altogether; completely; entirely; fully; perfectly; quite; roundly; thoroughly; totally; unreservedly; utterly; wholly.*

to the letter A moribund metaphor (SEE PAGE 19). *accurately; correctly; exactly; faultlessly; flawlessly; ideally; just right; perfectly; precisely; rightly; strictly; to perfection; unerringly.*

to the nines A moribund metaphor (SEE PAGE 19). *lavishly; profusely; richly.* ■ The house was decorated to the nines. REPLACE WITH *lavishly.*

to the point of (that; where) A wretched redundancy (SEE PAGE 23). *so; so far (that); so much (that); so that; to; to when; to where.* ■ It's gotten *to the point that* I even flirt with operators. REPLACE WITH *so that.* ■ But it has now evolved *to the point where* they do it all the time. REPLACE WITH *to where.*

to the teeth A moribund metaphor (SEE PAGE 19). *altogether; completely; entirely; fully; perfectly; quite; roundly; thoroughly; totally; unreservedly; utterly; wholly.*

to the tune of A wretched redundancy (SEE PAGE 23). ■ It cost him *to the tune of* $4,500 to buy his new computer system. DELETE *to the tune of.*

to the victor belong the spoils A popular prescription (SEE PAGE 21).

to thine own self be true A popular prescription (SEE PAGE 21).

touch and go A moribund metaphor (SEE PAGE 19). *dangerous; precarious; risky; uncertain.*

touch base with A moribund metaphor (SEE PAGE 19).

(as) tough as leather An insipid simile (SEE PAGE 19).
1. *athletic; beefy; brawny; burly; energetic; firm; fit; hale; hardy; hearty; healthful; healthy; husky; leathery; manly; mesomorphic; mighty; muscular; powerful; puissant; robust; rugged; sinewy; solid; sound; stalwart; stout; strapping; strong; sturdy;*

tough; vigorous; virile; well-built.
2. *constant; dependable; determined; faithful; fast; firm; fixed; inexorable; inflexible; loyal; obdurate; resolute; resolved; rigid; solid; stable; staunch; steadfast; steady; stern; strong; tenacious; unflinching; unwavering; unyielding.*

(as) tough as nails An insipid simile (SEE PAGE 19).
1. *athletic; beefy; brawny; burly; energetic; firm; fit; hale; hardy; healthful; healthy; hearty; leathery; manly; mesomorphic; mighty; muscular; powerful; puissant; robust; rugged; sinewy; solid; sound; stalwart; stout; strapping; strong; sturdy; tough; vigorous; virile; well-built.*
2. *constant; dependable; determined; faithful; fast; firm; fixed; inexorable; inflexible; loyal; obdurate; resolute; resolved; rigid; solid; stable; staunch; steadfast; steady; stern; strong; tenacious; unflinching; unwavering; unyielding.*

tough sledding A moribund metaphor (SEE PAGE 19). *arduous; backbreaking; burdensome; difficult; exhausting; fatiguing; hard; herculean; laborious; not easy; onerous; severe; strenuous; toilful; toilsome; tough; troublesome; trying; wearisome.*

tough to swallow A moribund metaphor (SEE PAGE 19).

(it's) tough to teach an old dog new tricks A moribund metaphor (SEE PAGE 19).

towering inferno An infantile phrase (SEE PAGE 18). *blaze; conflagration; fire; holocaust; inferno.*

tow the (party) line (mark) A moribund metaphor (SEE PAGE 19). *abide by; accommodate; accord; acquiesce; adapt; adhere to; agree; behave; comply; concur; conform; correspond; follow; harmonize; heed; mind; obey; observe; submit; yield.*

(proven) track record A moribund metaphor (SEE PAGE 19).

tread water A moribund metaphor (SEE PAGE 19). ■ He is now *treading water,* deciding what to do next.

treat (us) like royalty An insipid simile (SEE PAGE 19).

très A foreign phrase (SEE PAGE 17). *very.* ■ She is *très* happy now that she is working. REPLACE WITH *very.* ■ Two New Yorkers we recently sent out on a discount shopping spree were *très* impressed with the hippness quotient. REPLACE WITH *very.*

trials and tribulations An inescapable pair (SEE PAGE 18). *adversity; affliction; calamity; catastrophe; difficulty; distress; hardship; misadventure; misfortune; ordeal; trial; tribulation; trouble; woe.* ■ It also presents a first-hand account of the *trials and tribulations* of living in a lesbian family. REPLACE WITH *ordeal.*

tried and true An inescapable pair (SEE PAGE 18).
1. *constant; dependable; faithful; firm; loyal; reliable; solid; staunch; steadfast; strong; true; trustworthy; trusty.*

2. *authentic; authenticated; established; reliable; substantiated; sound; verified; well-founded; well-grounded.*

trim (her) sails   A moribund metaphor (SEE PAGE 19).

trip the light fantastic   A moribund metaphor (SEE PAGE 19). *dance.*

triumphant return   An inescapable pair (SEE PAGE 18).

trouble in paradise   A moribund metaphor (SEE PAGE 19).

(a) trouble shared is a trouble halved   A popular prescription (SEE PAGE 21).

true blue   A moribund metaphor (SEE PAGE 19). *constant; dependable; faithful; firm; loyal; reliable; solid; staunch; steadfast; strong; true; trustworthy; trusty.*

true facts   A wretched redundancy (SEE PAGE 23). *facts; truth.* ■ Sometimes I wish the papers would print the *true facts*. REPLACE WITH *facts* or *truth*.

true love   A suspect superlative (SEE PAGE 22).

(the course of) true love never runs smooth   A popular prescription (SEE PAGE 21).

truthfully honest   A wretched redundancy (SEE PAGE 23). *honest; truthful.* ■ To be *truthfully honest*, I do want to be her friend. REPLACE WITH *truthful.*

truth is stranger than fiction   A popular prescription (SEE PAGE 21).

truth, justice, and the American way   An infantile phrase (SEE PAGE 18).

(the) truth of the matter is   An ineffectual phrase (SEE PAGE 17). ■ *The truth of the matter is* half of the people who get married end up divorced. DELETE *The truth of the matter is.* ■ *The truth of the matter is,* I don't understand it, but I'm against it. DELETE *The truth of the matter is.* SEE ALSO *the fact of the matter is.*

(the) truth will set you free   A popular prescription (SEE PAGE 21).

try it, you'll like it   An infantile phrase (SEE PAGE 18).

try, try again   A popular prescription (SEE PAGE 21).

(a) tug of war   A moribund metaphor (SEE PAGE 19). ■ There's *a tug of war* between people who like the economy and people who are afraid.

turn a blind eye to (toward)   A moribund metaphor (SEE PAGE 19). *brush aside; avoid; discount; disregard; dodge; duck; ignore; look away from; neglect; omit; overlook; pass over; shrink from; shun; shy away from; turn away from; withdraw from.* ■ And Chile, at least, is learning the risks of *turning a blind eye to* the past. REPLACE WITH *ignoring.* ■ Yet some of Bolt's advertisers, while lured by the site's demographics, may be *turning a blind eye to* content they normally find questionable in other media. REPLACE WITH *overlooking.* ■ The donors have *turned a blind eye toward* allegations of corruption. REPLACE WITH *disregarded.*

turnabout is fair play A popular prescription (SEE PAGE 21).

turn a deaf ear to A moribund metaphor (SEE PAGE 19). *brush aside; avoid; discount; disregard; dodge; duck; ignore; neglect; omit; pass over; recoil from; shrink from; shun; shy away from; turn away from; withdraw from.* ■ Wilson should *turn a deaf ear to* HMO lobbyists and sign it. REPLACE WITH *disregard.*

turn a negative into a positive A torpid term (SEE PAGE 22). ■ The revolution in traditional family ties has *turned a negative into a positive* for most singles today. SEE ALSO *negative; positive.*

turn (their) back on A moribund metaphor (SEE PAGE 19). *abandon; abdicate; avoid; brush aside; deny; desert; disavow; discount; disinherit; disown; disregard; dodge; drop; duck; forgo; forsake; give up; ignore; leave; neglect; omit; pass over; quit; recoil from; reject; relinquish; renounce; shrink from; shun; shy away from; snub; surrender; turn away from; withdraw from; yield.* ■ It will be unfortunate, indeed, if the countries of Western Europe *turn their backs on* their Eastern neighbors. REPLACE WITH *disregard.*

turn back the clock (of time) A moribund metaphor (SEE PAGE 19).

turn (your) dreams into reality A popular prescription (SEE PAGE 21).

turn inside out A moribund metaphor (SEE PAGE 19). *agitate; confuse; disorder; disorganize; disquiet; disrupt; disturb; fluster; jar; jolt; jumble; mess up; mix up; muddle; perturb; rattle; ruffle; shake up; stir up; trouble; unnerve; unsettle; upset.*

turn into (to) stone A moribund metaphor (SEE PAGE 19). *calcify; fossilize; harden; petrify; solidify.*

turn like the weather An insipid simile (SEE PAGE 19). *capricious; changeable; erratic; fickle; fitful; flighty; fluctuating; haphazard; inconsistent; inconstant; intermittent; irregular; mercurial; occasional; random; sometime; spasmodic; sporadic; unpredictable; unsettled; unstable; unsteady; vacillating; volatile; wavering; wayward.*

(another) turn of the screw A moribund metaphor (SEE PAGE 19).

turn over a new leaf A moribund metaphor (SEE PAGE 19). *alter; begin again; change; convert; improve; metamorphose; modify; reform; remake; remodel; rethink; transform.*

(a) turn on A moribund metaphor (SEE PAGE 19). *animating; arousing; bracing; enlivening; exciting; exhilarating; inspiring; inspiriting; invigorating; provoking; refreshing; rousing; stimulating; vivifying.*

turn over in (his) grave A moribund metaphor (SEE PAGE 19).

turn sour A moribund metaphor (SEE PAGE 19). ■ Banks caught in the euphoria of a construction boom have watched the economy *turn sour.*

turn (my) stomach A moribund metaphor (SEE PAGE 19). *appall; disgust; horrify; nauseate; offend; outrage; repel; repulse; revolt; shock; sicken.*

turn tail A moribund metaphor (SEE PAGE 19). *abscond; clear out; decamp; depart; desert; disappear; escape; exit; flee; fly; go; go away; leave; move on; part; pull out; quit; retire; retreat; run away; take flight; take off; vacate; vanish; withdraw*

turn the corner A moribund metaphor (SEE PAGE 19). *advance; awaken; better; expand; flourish; gain; gain strength; grow; heal; improve; increase; pick up; progress; prosper; rally; recover; recuperate; refresh; renew; revive; rouse; strengthen; thrive.* ■ Our No. 1 goal is to reestablish reliability and customer satisfaction, and we think we have started to *turn the corner.* REPLACE WITH *improve.*

turn the other cheek A moribund metaphor (SEE PAGE 19).

turn the tables (on) A moribund metaphor (SEE PAGE 19).

turn the tide A moribund metaphor (SEE PAGE 19).

turn up (her) nose A moribund metaphor (SEE PAGE 19). *contemn; deride; despise; detest; disdain; jeer at; laugh at; mock; ridicule; scoff at; scorn; shun; slight; sneer; snub; spurn.*

turn up the heat A moribund metaphor (SEE PAGE 19). *coerce; command; compel; constrain; demand; enforce; force; goad; impel; importune; incite; induce; insist; instigate; make; oblige; press; pressure; prod; push; spur; urge.*

(sit and) twiddle (our) thumbs A moribund metaphor (SEE PAGE 19). *be idle; be inactive; be lazy; be unemployed; be unoccupied; dally; dawdle; loaf; loiter; loll; lounge; relax; repose; rest.*

twilight zone A moribund metaphor (SEE PAGE 19).

twist (his) arm A moribund metaphor (SEE PAGE 19). *bulldoze; bully; coerce; compel; constrain; demand; drive; enforce; enjoin; exhort; goad; force; impel; incite; insist; intimidate; make; necessitate; obligate; oblige; order; press; pressure; prod; require; threaten; tyrannize; urge.*

twist (wrap) around (her) little finger A moribund metaphor (SEE PAGE 19). *administer; boss; command; control; dictate; direct; dominate; domineer; govern; in charge; in control; in command; manage; manipulate; master; misuse; order; overpower; oversee; predominate; prevail; reign over; rule; superintend; tyrannize; use.*

twist of fate A moribund metaphor (SEE PAGE 19).

twists and turns (of fate) A moribund metaphor (SEE PAGE 19).

twist slowly in the wind A moribund metaphor (SEE PAGE 19). *afflict; agonize; crucify; excruciate; harrow; martyr; persecute; rack; torment; torture.*

two heads are better than one A popular prescription (SEE PAGE 21).

(like) two peas in a pod An insipid simile (SEE PAGE 19). *akin; alike; correspondent; corresponding; equal; equivalent; identical; indistinguishable; kindred; like; matching; one; same; selfsame; similar; twin.*

two's company, three's a crowd A popular prescription (SEE PAGE 21).

two-way street A moribund metaphor (SEE PAGE 19).

two wrongs don't make a right A popular prescription (SEE PAGE 21).

U

(as) ugly as a toad An insipid simile (SEE PAGE 19). *deformed; disfigured; disgusting; displeasing; distorted; freakish; frightful; ghastly; gorgonian; grisly; grotesque; gruesome; hideous; homely; horrendous; horrible; horrid; monstrous; offensive; plain; repellent; repulsive; revolting; ugly; unsightly.*

(as) ugly as sin An insipid simile (SEE PAGE 19). *deformed; disfigured; disgusting; displeasing; distorted; freakish; frightful; ghastly; gorgonian; grisly; grotesque; gruesome; hideous; homely; horrendous; horrible; horrid; monstrous; offensive; plain; repellent; repulsive; revolting; ugly; unsightly.*

ugly duckling A moribund metaphor (SEE PAGE 19). *deformed; disfigured; disgusting; displeasing; distorted; freakish; frightful; ghastly; gorgonian; grisly; grotesque; gruesome; hideous; homely; horrendous; horrible; horrid; monstrous; offensive; plain; repellent; repulsive; revolting; ugly; unsightly.*

unbeknownst A withered word (SEE PAGE 22). *unbeknown; unknown.* ■ *Unbeknownst* to his girlfriend, he made a videotape of them having sex. REPLACE WITH *Unknown.*

unbelievable An overworked word (SEE PAGE 20).
1. *beyond belief; beyond comprehension; doubtful; dubious; implausible; imponderable; improbable; incomprehensible; inconceivable; inexplicable; questionable; unfathomable; unimaginable; unthinkable.*
2. *astonishing; astounding; breathtaking; extraordinary; fabulous; fantastic; marvelous; miraculous; overwhelming; prodigious; sensational; spectacular; wonderful; wondrous.*

unchartered waters A moribund metaphor (SEE PAGE 19).

under a cloud A moribund metaphor (SEE PAGE 19). *discredited; disfavored; disgraced; dishonored; distrusted; in disfavor; in disgrace; in disrepute; in ignominy; in shame; suspect; under suspicion.* ■ He became the only vice president to leave *under a cloud.* REPLACE WITH *in disgrace.* ■ He left the police department *under a cloud of suspicion.* REPLACE WITH *under suspicion.*

under (my) belt A moribund metaphor (SEE PAGE 19). *background; education; experience; grooming; grounding; instruction; learning;*

knowledge; maturity; practice; preparation; qualifications; schooling; seasoning; skill; teaching; training.

(come) under fire A moribund metaphor (SEE PAGE 19). *be admonished; be assailed; be attacked; be castigated; be censured; be chastised; be chided; be condemned; be criticized; be denounced; be rebuked; be reprimanded; be reproached; be reproved; be scolded; be set on; be upbraided.*

(keep) under lock and key A moribund metaphor (SEE PAGE 19).
1. *confined; imprisoned; in jail; locked up.*
2. *guarded; protected; safe; secure; sheltered; shielded.*

under (his) own steam A moribund metaphor (SEE PAGE 19).

understaffed and overworked An inescapable pair (SEE PAGE 18).

under the gun A moribund metaphor (SEE PAGE 19). *be at risk; be at stake; be endangered; be imperiled; be in danger; be in jeopardy; be jeopardized; be menaced; be threatened.* ■ The American way of life, long taken for granted, was *under the gun*. REPLACE WITH *being threatened*.

under the table A moribund metaphor (SEE PAGE 19). *clandestinely; confidentially; covertly; furtively; mysteriously; in private; in secret; privately; quietly; secludedly; secretly; slyly; stealthily; surreptitiously; undercover.*

under the weather A moribund

metaphor (SEE PAGE 19).
1. *afflicted; ailing; debilitated; diseased; enervated; feeble; frail; ill; indisposed; infirm; not (feeling) well; sick; sickly; suffering; unhealthy; unsound; unwell; valetudinarian.* ■ It doesn't matter if some days I'm feeling a little low or *under the weather*. REPLACE WITH *unwell*.
2. *besotted; crapulous; drunk; inebriated; intoxicated; sodden; stupefied; tipsy.*

under the wire A moribund metaphor (SEE PAGE 19).

under (his) thumb A moribund metaphor (SEE PAGE 19). *dependent; subject; subordinate; subservient; under.*

under (his) wing A moribund metaphor (SEE PAGE 19).

(keep) under wraps A moribund metaphor (SEE PAGE 19). *camouflage; clandestine; cloak; conceal; cover; covert; disguise; enshroud; harbor; hide; out of sight; secret; mask; screen; shroud; suppress; surreptitious; veil; withhold.* ■ Radcliffe tried, and failed, to keep its list *under wraps*. REPLACE WITH *hidden*. ■ Negotiations have been kept largely *under wraps*. REPLACE WITH *secret*.

uneasy calm An inescapable pair (SEE PAGE 18). ■ By midafternoon, an *uneasy calm* returned to much of the capital.

uneasy lies the head that wears a crown A popular prescription (SEE PAGE 21).

374

united we stand (divided we fall) A popular prescription (SEE PAGE 21).

unite in holy wedlock (marriage) A wretched redundancy (SEE PAGE 23). *marry; wed.*

unless and (or) until A wretched redundancy (SEE PAGE 23). *unless; until.* ■ I am opposed to the imposition of any new taxes *unless and until* major cuts in spending have been implemented. REPLACE WITH *unless* or *until.*

unmitigated gall An inescapable pair (SEE PAGE 18).

untenable position An inescapable pair (SEE PAGE 18).

until and (or) unless A wretched redundancy (SEE PAGE 23). *unless; until.* ■ *Until and unless* these two conditions are met, the second rule does not fire. REPLACE WITH *Unless* or *Until.*

until such time as A wretched redundancy (SEE PAGE 23). *until.* ■ Lessee shall not be liable for any rent *until such time as* Lessor can deliver possession. REPLACE WITH *until.* ■ The FBI would cooperate but play a subordinate role *until such time as* it became evident that the explosion was caused by a criminal act. REPLACE WITH *until.*

up a blind alley A moribund metaphor (SEE PAGE 19).
1. *at risk; endangered; hard-pressed; imperiled; in a bind; in a dilemma; in a fix; in a jam; in a predicament; in a*

quandary; in danger; in difficulty; in jeopardy; in peril; in trouble; jeopardized.
2. *caught; cornered; enmeshed; ensnared; entangled; entrapped; netted; snared; trapped.*

up a creek A moribund metaphor (SEE PAGE 19). *at risk; endangered; hard-pressed; imperiled; in a bind; in a dilemma; in a fix; in a jam; in a predicament; in a quandary; in danger; in difficulty; in jeopardy; in peril; in trouble; jeopardized.*

up against the wall A moribund metaphor (SEE PAGE 19).
1. *at risk; desperate; endangered; frantic; hard-pressed; imperiled; in a bind; in a dilemma; in a fix; in a jam; in a predicament; in a quandary; in danger; in difficulty; in jeopardy; in peril; in trouble; jeopardized.*
2. *caught; cornered; enmeshed; ensnared; entangled; entrapped; netted; snared; trapped.*

(right) up (her) alley A moribund metaphor (SEE PAGE 19).

up and running A moribund metaphor (SEE PAGE 19). *at work; functioning; going; in action; in operation; operational; operating; performing; producing; running; working.* ■ We intend to have a smoothly functioning, well-integrated unit *up and running* when we start in February. REPLACE WITH *in operation.*

up a tree A moribund metaphor (SEE PAGE 19).
1. *at risk; endangered; hard-pressed;*

imperiled; in a bind; in a fix; in a jam; in a predicament; in danger; in difficulty; in jeopardy; in peril; in trouble; jeopardized.

2. *caught; cornered; enmeshed; ensnared; entangled; entrapped; netted; snared; trapped.*

up close and personal An infantile phrase (SEE PAGE 18).

(an) uphill battle (fight) A moribund metaphor (SEE PAGE 19).
1. *an endeavor; an undertaking; a struggle; a task; drudgery; hard work; labor; moil; toil; travail; work.* ■ Alleging sexual harassment against a supervisor is *an uphill battle.* REPLACE WITH *a struggle.*
2. *arduous; difficult; hard; laborious; strenuous.* ■ Even though it's been *an uphill battle,* I've learned a lot. REPLACE WITH *difficult.* SEE ALSO *reach epidemic proportions.*

up in arms A moribund metaphor (SEE PAGE 19).
1. *agitated; alarmed; angry; annoyed; aroused; choleric; enraged; fierce; fuming; furious; incensed; indignant; inflamed; infuriated; irate; irked; irritable; mad; maddened; raging; resentful; splenetic; vexatious.* ■ The nurses were *up in arms* because of their work conditions. REPLACE WITH *incensed.*
2. *factious; insubordinate; insurgent; mutinous; rebellious; seditious.*

up in the air A moribund metaphor (SEE PAGE 19). *confused; dubious; indecisive; in doubt; irresolute; open; questionable; tentative; uncertain; unconcluded; undecided;*

undetermined; unresolved; unsettled. ■ The issue is still very much *up in the air* despite a series of rulings in the 1980s. REPLACE WITH *unsettled.*

ups and downs A moribund metaphor (SEE PAGE 19). *alterations; changes; erraticism; fluctuations; fortuitousness; inconstancies; shifts; uncertainties; vacillations; variations; vicissitudes.* ■ A community that can meet many of its needs by using locally available natural, human, and financial resources will be less affected by the *ups and downs* of the national and global economies. REPLACE WITH *vicissitudes.*

upset the apple cart A moribund metaphor (SEE PAGE 19). *confuse; damage; disorder; disrupt; disturb; jumble; mess up; mix up; muddle; ruin; scramble; spoil; upset.*

up the ante A moribund metaphor (SEE PAGE 19).

up the creek (without a paddle) A moribund metaphor (SEE PAGE 19).
1. *at risk; endangered; hard-pressed; imperiled; in a bind; in a dilemma; in a fix; in a jam; in a predicament; in a quandary; in danger; in difficulty; in jeopardy; in peril; in trouble; jeopardized.*
2. *caught; cornered; enmeshed; ensnared; entangled; entrapped; netted; snared; trapped.*

up till (until) A wretched redundancy (SEE PAGE 23). *till (until).* ■ *Up until* the day he left, they hoped that he would play a major role in the new company as a key senior executive. REPLACE WITH *Until.*

up till (until) this point (time) A wretched redundancy (SEE PAGE 23). *until now.* ■ *Up until this point* we have been working in the dark. REPLACE WITH *Until now.*

up to (my) ears A moribund metaphor (SEE PAGE 19).
1. *bury; deluge; flood; glut; immerse; infest; inundate; overburden; overload; overpower; overrun; overwhelm; sate; swamp.*
2. *altogether; completely; entirely; fully; perfectly; quite; roundly; thoroughly; totally; unreservedly; utterly; wholly.*

up to (my) eyeballs (eyebrows; eyes) A moribund metaphor (SEE PAGE 19).
1. *bury; deluge; glut; immerse; infest; inundate; overburden; overload; overpower; overrun; overwhelm; sate; swamp.* ■ The campaigns' organizations are all *up to their eyeballs* with delegate-counting. REPLACE WITH *overrun.*
2. *altogether; completely; entirely; fully; perfectly; quite; roundly; thoroughly; totally; unreservedly; utterly; wholly.* ■ We are in this now, *up to our eyebrows* and for the long haul. REPLACE WITH *fully.*

up to par A moribund metaphor (SEE PAGE 19).
1. *average; common; commonplace; customary; everyday; mediocre; middling; normal; ordinary; quotidian;* *regular; routine; standard; typical; uneventful; unexceptional; unremarkable; usual.*
2. *acceptable; adequate; fine; good; good enough; healthy; passable; satisfactory; sufficient; suitable; tolerable; well.*

up to scratch A moribund metaphor (SEE PAGE 19). *acceptable; adequate; fine; good; good enough; healthy; passable; satisfactory; sufficient; suitable; tolerable; well.*

up to snuff A moribund metaphor (SEE PAGE 19). *acceptable; adequate; fine; good; good enough; healthy; passable; satisfactory; sufficient; suitable; tolerable; well.*

up to speed A moribund metaphor (SEE PAGE 19). *acceptable; adequate; fine; good; good enough; healthy; passable; satisfactory; sufficient; suitable; well.*

use and abuse An inescapable pair (SEE PAGE 18). ■ We all agree that we have been racially *used and abused.* ■ Lil Franklin said her son had been *used and abused* by two fundamentalist ministers.

utilize A torpid term (SEE PAGE 22). *apply; employ; make use of; use.* ■ I *utilize* my bike for nearly everything. REPLACE WITH *use.* ■ These are all expository techniques that you will be *utilizing* once you have mastered the basics of writing. REPLACE WITH *using.* SEE ALSO *finalize.*

V

valuable asset An inescapable pair (SEE PAGE 18). This phrase is, like many inescapable pairs, also redundant, for an *asset* is *valuable*.

variety is the spice of life A popular prescription (SEE PAGE 21).

various and sundry An inescapable pair (SEE PAGE 18). *assorted; diverse; sundry; varied; various; varying.* ■ I tried *various and sundry* ways to get her to see me. REPLACE WITH *various*. SEE ALSO *all and sundry*.

vehemently oppose An inescapable pair (SEE PAGE 18). ■ MCA *vehemently opposed* Sony's Betamax and the VCR invasion.

verboten A foreign phrase (SEE PAGE 17). *banned; disallowed; enjoined; forbidden; prohibited; proscribed.* ■ But once everything was set up, my analog modem worked on a previously *verboten* digital phone. REPLACE WITH *disallowed*.

verily A withered word (SEE PAGE 22). *actually; indeed; in fact; in faith; in reality; in truth; truly.*

very An overworked word (SEE PAGE 20). The word *very* is often a needless intensive, but preceding words like *excellent, major,* and *delightful,* it is ludicrous. ■ I think that's a *very* excellent thought. DELETE *very*. ■ It's a *very* major plus for our state and our region. DELETE *very*. ■ You seem *very* delightful. DELETE *very*. ■ She's a biochemist and *very* brilliant. DELETE *very*. ■ If the test cells were to be shut down, it would be *very* detrimental to the operation. DELETE *very*. ■ More-over, the wind at the peak can be *very* deadly. DELETE *very*. SEE ALSO *really*.

viable alternative An inescapable pair (SEE PAGE 18).

vicious circle An inescapable pair (SEE PAGE 18).

vicious rumor An inescapable pair (SEE PAGE 18).

vim and vigor An inescapable pair (SEE PAGE 18). *animation; ardor; dash; dynamism; élan; energy; fervor; force; intensity; liveliness; passion; potency; power; spirit; stamina; strength; verve; vigor; vitality; vivacity; zeal.*

virtue is its own reward A popular prescription (SEE PAGE 21).

vis-à-vis A foreign phrase (SEE PAGE 17).

viselike grip A moribund metaphor (SEE PAGE 19).

visible (invisible) to the eye A wretched redundancy (SEE PAGE 23). *visible (invisible)*. SEE ALSO *audible (inaudible) to the ear*.

vive la différence A foreign phrase (SEE PAGE 17).

voice (crying) in the wilderness A moribund metaphor (SEE PAGE 19).

vote with (their) feet A moribund metaphor (SEE PAGE 19). ■ People are *voting with their feet*, and politicians know this.

W

wages of sin A moribund metaphor (SEE PAGE 19).

(just have to) wait and see (what happens) A torpid term (SEE PAGE 22). *I don't know; (it's) not (yet) known; (that's) uncertain; (that's) unclear; (it's) unknown.* SEE ALSO *(it) remains to be seen; your guess is as good as mine.*

wait for the ax to fall A moribund metaphor (SEE PAGE 19).

wait for the other shoe to drop A moribund metaphor (SEE PAGE 19).

waiting for Godot An infantile phrase (SEE PAGE 18).

waiting in the wings A moribund metaphor (SEE PAGE 19).

wake the dead A moribund metaphor (SEE PAGE 19). *blaring; boisterous; booming; deafening; ear-splitting; fulminating; loud; noisy; obstreperous; piercing; plangent; resounding; roaring; shrill; stentorian; strident; thundering; thunderous; tumultuous; vociferous.*

wake up and smell the coffee A moribund metaphor (SEE PAGE 19).

wake-up call A moribund metaphor (SEE PAGE 19). ■ The priest sexual scandal is a *wake-up call* for the church.

walk a fine line A moribund metaphor (SEE PAGE 19).

walk a tightrope A moribund metaphor (SEE PAGE 19). *chance; dare; endanger; gamble; hazard; imperil; jeopardize; make bold; peril; risk; venture.*

walk away from A moribund metaphor (SEE PAGE 19). *abandon; abdicate; avoid; brush aside; deny; desert; disavow; discount; disinherit; disown; disregard; dodge; drop; duck; forgo; forsake; give up; ignore; leave; neglect; omit; pass over; quit; recoil from; reject; relinquish; renounce; shrink from; shun; shy away from; snub; spurn; surrender; turn away from; withdraw from; yield.* ■ The state cannot *walk away from* that obligation. REPLACE WITH *disregard.*

(the) walking dead A moribund metaphor (SEE PAGE 19).

(a) walking, talking An infantile phrase (SEE PAGE 18).

walk on air A moribund metaphor (SEE PAGE 19). *blissful; blithe; buoyant; cheerful; delighted; ecstatic; elated; enraptured; euphoric; exalted; excited; exhilarated; exultant; gay; glad; gleeful; good-humored; happy; intoxicated; jolly; jovial; joyful; joyous; jubilant; merry; mirthful; overjoyed; pleased; rapturous; thrilled.*

walk on eggs (eggshells) A moribund metaphor (SEE PAGE 19). ■ For years, Robinson *walked on eggshells* as the first black baseball player in the major leagues.

(all) walks of life A moribund metaphor (SEE PAGE 19).

walk softly and carry a big stick A popular prescription (SEE PAGE 21).

wall of silence A moribund metaphor (SEE PAGE 19).

(the) walls have ears A moribund metaphor (SEE PAGE 19).

want to bet? An infantile phrase (SEE PAGE 18).

war clouds A moribund metaphor (SEE PAGE 19).

war is hell A quack equation (SEE PAGE 21).

(as) warm as toast An insipid simile (SEE PAGE 19). *heated; lukewarm; mild; temperate; tepid; toasty; warm; warmish.*

warm the cockles of (my) heart A moribund metaphor (SEE PAGE 19).

warn in advance A wretched redundancy (SEE PAGE 23). *warn.* ■ Management should be *warned in advance* that fines are no longer the way to satisfy the system for a careless disaster. DELETE *in advance.* SEE ALSO *advance warning; forewarn.*

war of words A moribund metaphor (SEE PAGE 19). *altercation; argument; bickering; conflict; contention; controversy; disagreement; disputation; dispute; feud; polemics; quarrel; row; spat; squabble; strife; wrangle.* ■ Yesterday's *war of words* seemed like a replay of the bitter 1988 campaign. REPLACE WITH *squabble.*

wash (their) dirty linen in public A moribund metaphor (SEE PAGE 19).

(all) washed up A moribund metaphor (SEE PAGE 19). *beaten; condemned; conquered; cowed; cursed; damned; defunct; doomed; fated; finished; gone; lost; ruined; vanquished.*

wash (her) hands of (it) A moribund metaphor (SEE PAGE 19). *abandon; abdicate; avoid; brush aside; deny; desert; disavow; discount; disinherit; disown; disregard; dodge; drop; duck; forgo; forsake; give up; ignore; leave; neglect; omit; pass over; quit; recoil from; reject; relinquish; renounce; shrink from; shun; shy away from; snub; surrender; turn away from; withdraw from; yield.*

waste not, want not A popular prescription (SEE PAGE 21).

(a) watched pot never boils A popular prescription (SEE PAGE 21).

(like) watching grass grow An insipid simile (SEE PAGE 19). *banal; barren; bland; boring; deadly; dreary; dry; dull; everyday; flat; humdrum; inanimate; insipid; jejune; lifeless; lusterless; mediocre; monotonous; prosaic; routine; spiritless; stale; tedious; tiresome; unexciting; uninteresting; vapid; wearisome.*

watch (him) like a hawk An insipid simile (SEE PAGE 19). *be alert; be attentive; be awake; be aware; be eagle-eyed; be heedful; be informed; be keen; be observant; be vigilant; be wakeful; be watchful.*

water over the dam A moribund metaphor (SEE PAGE 19).
1. *completed; concluded; done; ended; finished; over; passed; through.*
2. *history; the past; yesterday.*

water under the bridge A moribund metaphor (SEE PAGE 19).
1. *completed; concluded; done; ended; finished; over; passed; through.*
2. *history; the past; yesterday.*

(the) wave of the future A moribund metaphor (SEE PAGE 19).

(like) waving a red flag (rag) in front of a bull An insipid simile (SEE PAGE 19).

wax and wane An inescapable pair (SEE PAGE 18).

ways and means An inescapable pair (SEE PAGE 18). *approaches; means; mechanisms; methods; techniques; ways.*

(the) way to a man's heart is through his stomach A popular prescription (SEE PAGE 21).

(as) weak as a baby An insipid simile (SEE PAGE 19). *dainty; debilitated; delicate; enervated; feeble; fragile; frail; infirm; nonmuscular; puny; sickly; unhealthy; unwell; valetudinarian; weak; weakly.*

(as) weak as a kitten An insipid simile (SEE PAGE 19). *dainty; debilitated; delicate; enervated; feeble; fragile; frail; infirm; nonmuscular; puny; sickly; unhealthy; unwell; valetudinarian; weak; weakly.*

weak in the knees A moribund metaphor (SEE PAGE 19). *dizzy; faint; giddy; lightheaded; weak.*

(the) weak link (in the chain) A moribund metaphor (SEE PAGE 19).

wears (her) heart on (her) sleeve A moribund metaphor (SEE PAGE 19). *demonstrative; emotional; emotive; sensitive; sentimental.*

wear the pants A moribund metaphor (SEE PAGE 19). *administer; boss; command; control; dictate; direct; dominate; govern; in charge; in command; in control; manage; manipulate; master; order; overpower; oversee; predominate; prevail; reign over; rule; superintend.*

weather the storm (of) A moribund metaphor (SEE PAGE 19). ■ A tremendous thank you goes out to each of you who has helped our family *weather this storm*. SEE ALSO *reach epidemic proportions*.

weight in proportion (proportionate) to height A torpid term (SEE PAGE 22). Men should eschew women (and women, men) whom they've not yet met and who describe their physiques as *weight in proportion (proportionate) to height*.

Let us men prefer an *athletic; brawny; firm; fit; medium-build; mesomorphic; muscular; robust; sinewy; well-built* woman or a *bony; ectomorphic; lanky; lean; petite; rail-thin; scraggy; scrawny; skeletal; skinny; slender; slight; slim; small; spare; spindly; svelte; sylphid; thin; tiny; trim; wispy* woman or a *big-boned, big-breasted, big-bellied, or big-bottomed; bulbous; bulky; busty; buxom; chubby; chunky; corpulent; curvaceous; dumpy; endomorphic; enormous; fat; flabby; fleshy; globular; heavy; hefty; huge; large; obese; plump; portly; pudgy; rotund; round; squat; steatopygic; stocky; stout; voluptuous* woman — if not for her *womanliness* then at least for her *words*.

weird An overworked word (SEE PAGE 20). *aberrant; abnormal; anomalistic; anomalous; atypical; bizarre; curious; deviant; different; distinct; distinctive; eccentric; exceptional; extraordinary; fantastic; foreign; grotesque; idiosyncratic; independent; individual; individualistic; irregular; novel; odd; offbeat; original; peculiar; puzzling; quaint; queer; rare; remark-*

able; separate; singular; strange; uncommon; unconventional; unexampled; unique; unnatural; unorthodox; unparalleled; unprecedented; unusual. SEE ALSO *strange*.

(all) well and good A wretched redundancy (SEE PAGE 23). *adequate; all right; excellent; fine; good; O.K.; satisfactory; well*. ■ That's *all well and good* for the hobbyist running a bulletin board or the IT worker who does side programming jobs in his off-hours at home. REPLACE WITH *good*. ■ Well, this is *all well and good*, but who's going to pay for it — not my insurance company! REPLACE WITH *fine*. ■ This is *all well and good*, but what do experts say? REPLACE WITH *good*. ■ That's *all well and good*, but what about my son? REPLACE WITH *fine*. SEE ALSO *fine and dandy; still and all*.

well-nigh A withered word (SEE PAGE 22). *almost; nearly*.

wet behind the ears A moribund metaphor (SEE PAGE 19). *artless; awkward; callow; green; guileless; immature; inexperienced; inexpert; ingenuous; innocent; naive; raw; simple; undeveloped; unfledged; unskilled; unskillful; unsophisticated; untaught; untrained; unworldly*.

wet (my) whistle A moribund metaphor (SEE PAGE 19). *drink; guzzle; imbibe; quaff*.

we've all got to go sometime A popular prescription (SEE PAGE 21).

we've got to stop meeting like this An infantile phrase (SEE PAGE 18).

what are you going to do A plebeian sentiment (SEE PAGE 20). This is still another expression of resignation. Though phrased as a question, it is rarely spoken interrogatively, so resigned, so hopeless are those who use it. SEE ALSO *such is life; that's how (the way) it goes; that's how (the way) the ball bounces; that's how (the way) the cookie crumbles; that's life; that's life in the big city; that's show biz; what can you do.*

what can I say? An infantile phrase (SEE PAGE 18).

what can I tell you? An infantile phrase (SEE PAGE 18).

what can you do A plebeian sentiment (SEE PAGE 20). SEE ALSO *such is life; that's how (the way) it goes; that's how (the way) the ball bounces; that's how (the way) the cookie crumbles; that's life; that's life in the big city; that's show biz; what are you going to do.*

what (he) doesn't know won't hurt (him) A popular prescription (SEE PAGE 21).

whatever An infantile phrase (SEE PAGE 18). As a one-word response to another's comment or question, *whatever* is as dismissive as it is ill-mannered. SEE ALSO *excuse me.*

whatever happens happens An infantile phrase (SEE PAGE 18). SEE ALSO *it just happened; what(ever) must (will) be, must (will) be.*

what goes around, comes around A popular prescription (SEE PAGE 21). This is the secular equivalent of "as you sow, so shall you reap." As such, it is nonetheless a moralistic prescription — intoned by those who think in circles — that too easily explains the way of the world.

what goes up must come down A popular prescription (SEE PAGE 21).

what happened (is) An ineffectual phrase (SEE PAGE 17). ■ *What happened was* I woke up one morning and just decided to leave. DELETE *What happened was.* ■ *What happened was* we applied for welfare. DELETE *What happened was.* ■ *What happened was* when I said that to him he got upset and left in a huff. DELETE *What happened was.* ■ *What has happened is,* my identity has gotten lost in this ordeal. DELETE *What has happened is.* SEE ALSO *what is.*

what ... is An ineffectual phrase (SEE PAGE 17). ■ *What* you want *is* someone who will stand by his work once it is completed. DELETE *What is.* ■ *What* we are finding *is* that they want to measure up to our standards of integrity. DELETE *What is.* ■ *What* this course is about *is* empowerment. DELETE *What is.* ■ *What* we have *is* a program that asks some important questions. DELETE *What is.* SEE ALSO *what happened (is).*

what is the world coming to? A plebeian sentiment (SEE PAGE 20).

what's done is done A quack equation (SEE PAGE 21). ■ *What's done is done,* but rethinking the choice now will help you make a better choice next time.

what's good for (the goose) is good for (the gander) A popular prescription (SEE PAGE 21).

what will they think of next? A plebeian sentiment (SEE PAGE 20).

what you don't know can't (won't) hurt you A popular prescription (SEE PAGE 21).

what you see is not always what you get A quack equation (SEE PAGE 21).

what you see is what you get A quack equation (SEE PAGE 21).

wheel and deal An inescapable pair (SEE PAGE 18). *bargain; contrive; deal; do business; negotiate; plan; plot; scheme.*

when all is said and done A wretched redundancy (SEE PAGE 23). *all in all; all told; altogether; eventually; finally; in all; in the end; on the whole; overall; ultimately.* ■ *When all is said and done,* we humans are a curious species. REPLACE WITH *All told.* SEE ALSO *after all is said and done.*

when and if A wretched redundancy (SEE PAGE 23). *if; when.*

■ People are asking *when and if* there will be a democratic government. REPLACE WITH *if* or *when.* SEE ALSO *if and when; if, as, and when; when and whether; when, as, and if; whether and when.*

when and whether A wretched redundancy (SEE PAGE 23). *when; whether.* ■ She will decide *when and whether* and under what circumstances she'll become a mother. REPLACE WITH *when* or *whether.* SEE ALSO *if and when; if, as, and when; when and if; when, as, and if; whether and when.*

when, as, and if A wretched redundancy (SEE PAGE 23). *if; when.* SEE ALSO *if and when; if, as, and when; when and if; when and whether; whether and when.*

whence A withered word (SEE PAGE 22).
1. *from where.*
2. *from what source.*
3. *from which.*

when (you) come right down to it A wretched redundancy (SEE PAGE 23). *all in all; all told; altogether; eventually; finally; in all; in the end; on the whole; overall; ultimately.*

when hell freezes over A moribund metaphor (SEE PAGE 19). *never; no; not at all; not ever; not in any way; not in the least.*

when in Rome (do as the Romans do) A popular prescription (SEE PAGE 21). *abide by; accede; accommodate; accord; acquiesce; adapt; adhere* *to; agree; behave; comply; concur; conform; correspond; follow; harmonize; heed; mind; obey; observe; submit; yield.*

when it comes to   A wretched redundancy (SEE PAGE 23). *about; as for; as to; concerning; for; in; of; on; over; regarding; respecting; to; toward; when; with.* ■ I feel I'm more experienced *when it comes to* looking for a job. REPLACE WITH *in.* ■ I'm an expert *when it comes to* marriage. REPLACE WITH *about.* ■ *When it comes to* middle-age dating, there are four stages. REPLACE WITH *As for.* ■ She is not reasonable *when it comes to* me. REPLACE WITH *with.*

when it rains, it pours   A moribund metaphor (SEE PAGE 19).

when push comes to shove   A moribund metaphor (SEE PAGE 19). ■ *When push comes to shove*, liberalism collapses, society polarizes itself, and the gloves are removed.

when the cat's away, the mice will play   A moribund metaphor (SEE PAGE 19).

when the going gets tough, the tough get going   A popular prescription (SEE PAGE 21).

where angels fear to tread   A moribund metaphor (SEE PAGE 19).

whereat   A withered word (SEE PAGE 22). *at which point.*

wherefore   A withered word (SEE PAGE 22).
1. *why.*
2. *for which.*
3. *therefore.*

wherein   A withered word (SEE PAGE 22). *how; in what way.*

where ... is concerned   A wretched redundancy (SEE PAGE 23). *about; as for; as to; concerning; for; in; of; on; over; regarding; respecting; to; toward; with.* ■ Our gangs are just getting off the ground *where* violence *is concerned*. REPLACE WITH *concerning.* ■ Obviously, time doesn't heal all wounds, especially *where* the Red Sox *are concerned*. REPLACE WITH *regarding*. SEE ALSO *as far as ... (goes; is concerned).*

whereon   A withered word (SEE PAGE 22). *on what; on which.*

where's the beef?   An infantile phrase (SEE PAGE 18).

where there's a will, there's a way   A popular prescription (SEE PAGE 21).

where there's smoke there's fire   A popular prescription (SEE PAGE 21).

where the rubber hits the road   A moribund metaphor (SEE PAGE 19). ■ That, for Christians, is *where the rubber hits the road* — where we intersect with people who are poor or marginalized.

wherethrough   A withered word (SEE PAGE 22). *through which.*

whereto A withered word (SEE PAGE 22). *to what; to which.*

whereunto A withered word (SEE PAGE 22). *to what; to which.*

wherewith A withered word (SEE PAGE 22). *with what; with which.*

whet (my) appetite A moribund metaphor (SEE PAGE 19).

whether and when A wretched redundancy (SEE PAGE 23). *when; whether.* ■ Lee will be the one to determine *whether and when* he isn't up to the job. REPLACE WITH *when* or *whether.* SEE ALSO *if and when; if, as, and when; when and if; when and whether; when, as, and if.*

which way the wind blows A moribund metaphor (SEE PAGE 19).

while at the same time A wretched redundancy (SEE PAGE 23). *at the same time; while.* ■ It provides us with an opportunity to honor his memory *while at the same time* assisting future students. REPLACE WITH *at the same time* or *while.* SEE ALSO *simultaneously at the same time; while simultaneously.*

while simultaneously A wretched redundancy (SEE PAGE 23). *simultaneously; while.* ■ So you can work on applications *while simultaneously* watching TV in a resizable window. DELETE *simultaneously.* SEE ALSO *simultaneously at the same time; while at the same time.*

whilst A withered word (SEE PAGE 22). *while.* ■ *Whilst* it delivers the required protection, most users will probably feel strangely unsatisfied after some hard use. REPLACE WITH *While.* ■ Some imply a functional relationship between variables *whilst* others are of a more exploratory nature. REPLACE WITH *while.*

whip into a frenzy A moribund metaphor (SEE PAGE 19). *acerbate; anger; annoy; bother; bristle; chafe; enrage; incense; inflame; infuriate; irk; irritate; madden; miff; provoke; rile; roil; vex.*

whip into shape A moribund metaphor (SEE PAGE 19).

whistle in the dark A moribund metaphor (SEE PAGE 19).

whistling Dixie A moribund metaphor (SEE PAGE 19).

(as) white as a sheet An insipid simile (SEE PAGE 19).
1. *anemic; ashen; blanched; bloodless; cadaverous; colorless; deathlike; doughy; haggard; lusterless; pale; pallid; pasty; peaked; sallow; sickly; wan; whitish.*
2. *achromatic; alabaster-white; albescent; bleached; chalky; colorless; ivory; milk-white; milky; niveous; pearly; pearly-white; snow-white; snowy; uncolored; whitish.*

(as) white as snow An insipid simile (SEE PAGE 19).
1. *achromatic; alabaster-white; albescent; bleached; chalky; colorless; ivory; milk-white; milky; niveous;*

pearly; pearly-white; snow-white; snowy; uncolored; whitish.

2. anemic; ashen; blanched; bloodless; cadaverous; colorless; deathlike; doughy; haggard; lusterless; pale; pallid; pasty; peaked; sallow; sickly; wan; whitish.

(like) white on rice An insipid simile (SEE PAGE 19).

1. congenital; fundamental; genetic; hereditary; inborn; inbred; ingrained; inherent; inherited; innate; intrinsic; native; natural.

2. all over; everywhere; omnipresent; ubiquitous.

whither A withered word (SEE PAGE 22).

1. where.

2. wherever.

(the) whole ball of wax A moribund metaphor (SEE PAGE 19). aggregate; all; all things; entirety; everything; gross; lot; sum; total; totality; whole.

(my) whole, entire (life) An infantile phrase (SEE PAGE 18). ■ People like you laughed at me my whole, entire life. ■ With this on, you will attract more women than you have in your whole, entire lives.

(the) whole is greater than the sum of its parts A popular prescription (SEE PAGE 21).

(the) whole nine yards A moribund metaphor (SEE PAGE 19). aggregate; all; all things; entirety; everything; gross; lot; sum; total; totality; whole. ■ You've won the

Sony TV, the VCR, the stereo system, the camcorder, the whole nine yards. REPLACE WITH everything.

(the) whole shebang A moribund metaphor (SEE PAGE 19). aggregate; all; all things; entirety; everything; gross; lot; sum; total; totality; whole.

(the) whole shooting match A moribund metaphor (SEE PAGE 19). aggregate; all; all things; entirety; everything; gross; lot; sum; total; totality; whole.

who let the cat out of the bag? A moribund metaphor (SEE PAGE 19).

whoop it up A moribund metaphor (SEE PAGE 19).

1. be merry; carouse; carry on; celebrate; debauch; disport; frolic; party; play; revel; riot; roister; rollick; romp; skylark.

2. bay; bawl; bellow; blare; caterwaul; cheer; clamor; cry; holler; hoot; howl; roar; screak; scream; screech; shout; shriek; shrill; squawk; squeal; vociferate; wail; whoop; yell; yelp; yowl.

who's minding the store? A moribund metaphor (SEE PAGE 19).

who would have (ever) thought A plebeian sentiment (SEE PAGE 20).

(the) why and (the) wherefore A wretched redundancy (SEE PAGE 23). aim; cause; design; end; goal; intent; intention; motive; object; objective; purpose; reason.

why didn't (I) think of that? A plebeian sentiment (SEE PAGE 20).

why me? A plebeian sentiment (SEE PAGE 20).

(the) why and (the) wherefore A wretched redundancy (SEE PAGE 23). *aim; cause; goal; motive; purpose; reason.*

wild and crazy An inescapable pair (SEE PAGE 18).

wild and woolly An inescapable pair (SEE PAGE 18).

wild blue yonder A moribund metaphor (SEE PAGE 19). *air; atmosphere; biosphere; empyrean; ether; firmament; heaven; heavens; outer space; sky; space; stratosphere.*

wild goose chase A moribund metaphor (SEE PAGE 19).

wild horses couldn't (keep me away) A moribund metaphor (SEE PAGE 19).

wild horses couldn't drag it from (me) A moribund metaphor (SEE PAGE 19).

window dressing A moribund metaphor (SEE PAGE 19).

window of opportunity A moribund metaphor (SEE PAGE 19). *chance; occasion; opening; opportunity; possibility; prospect; time.* ■ I think we have a terrific *window of opportunity* to make progress this year. REPLACE WITH *chance.* ■ There may be *a window of opportunity* between 12 and 1 for us to talk. REPLACE WITH *time.* ■ One

redesign of an ASIC can cause the system vendor to completely miss the *window of opportunity* for a particular product. REPLACE WITH *opportunity.* SEE ALSO *a barrage of.*

window on the (world) A moribund metaphor (SEE PAGE 19).

winds of change A moribund metaphor (SEE PAGE 19).

wine and dine An inescapable pair (SEE PAGE 18).

win hands down A moribund metaphor (SEE PAGE 19). *beat; conquer; crush; defeat; outclass; outdo; overcome; overpower; overwhelm; prevail; quell; rout; succeed; triumph; trounce; vanquish; win.*

win, lose, or draw A moribund metaphor (SEE PAGE 19). *regardless.*

win (his) spurs A moribund metaphor (SEE PAGE 19).

wipe the slate clean A moribund metaphor (SEE PAGE 19). *begin anew; start afresh; start over.*

-wise A grammatical gimmick (SEE PAGE 17). We fasten the suffix *-wise* to words when we have not sufficiently thought about what we want to say or, even more so, how we want to say it. With *-wise,* though there may be some substance to our thought, there is scant style. ■ I've been very successful *businesswise.* REPLACE WITH *in business.* ■ *Burialwise,* I don't feel they're responsible enough to take care of *my wishes*. REPLACE WITH *my burial wishes*. ■ I do have a photo of a model *who resembles me bodywise*. REPLACE WITH *whose body resembles my own*. ■ And *academicwise*, he's made the honor roll every year. REPLACE WITH *academically*. ■ She is attractive and much smaller *sizewise* than me. DELETE *sizewise*. ■ I'll let you know *what I get from them informationwise*. REPLACE WITH *what information I get from them*.

(the) winter (summer) of (our) discontent A moribund metaphor (SEE PAGE 19).

(as) wise as Solomon An insipid simile (SEE PAGE 19). *astute; bright; brilliant; clever; discerning; enlightened; insightful; intelligent; judicious; keen; knowledgeable; learned; logical; luminous; penetrating; perceptive; perspicacious; rational; reasonable; sagacious; sage; sapient; sensible; sharp; shrewd; smart; sound; understanding; wise*.

wit and wisdom An inescapable pair (SEE PAGE 18).

with a big (capital) (A) An infantile phrase (SEE PAGE 18). ■ It's crisp, *with a capital C*. DELETE *with a capital C*. ■ He loves conversation — *with a big C*. DELETE *with a big C*. ■ These establishments offer dining *with a capital D*. REPLACE WITH *elegant dining*.

(go over) with a fine-toothed comb A moribund metaphor (SEE PAGE 19). *analyze; canvass; comb; examine; explore; filter; forage; hunt; inspect; investigate; look for; probe; quest; ransack; rummage; scour; scrutinize; search; seek; sieve; sift; winnow*.

with a heavy hand A moribund metaphor (SEE PAGE 19). *coercively; draconianly; harshly; oppressively; severely*.

with all (my) heart A moribund metaphor (SEE PAGE 19). *earnestly; fervently; genuinely; heartily; honestly; sincerely; unreservedly; wholeheartedly*.

with an open hand A moribund metaphor (SEE PAGE 19). *altruistically; beneficently; bountifully; charitably; generously; liberally; munificently; unselfishly; unstintingly*.

with a vengeance A moribund metaphor (SEE PAGE 19). *actively; aggressively; dynamically; emphatically; energetically; fast; furiously; fervently; fiercely; forcefully; frantically; frenziedly; furiously; hard; intensely; intently; mightily; passionately; powerfully; robustly; savagely; spiritedly; strenuously; strongly; vehemently; viciously; vigorously; violently; wildly; with vigor*.

with a wink and a nod A moribund metaphor (SEE PAGE 19). *clandestinely; confidentially; covertly; furtively; mysteriously; in private; in secret; privately; quietly; secludedly; secretly; slyly; stealthily; surreptitiously; undercover*. ■ Boston's most infamous criminal partnership began *with a wink and a nod*. REPLACE WITH *furtively*.

with bated breath A moribund metaphor (SEE PAGE 19). *agitatedly; anxiously; apprehensively; excitedly; fearfully; nervously; suspensefully; timidly; timorously; tremulously; worriedly.*

with bells on A moribund metaphor (SEE PAGE 19). *animatedly; eagerly; ebulliently; effervescently; effusively; enthusiastically; excitedly; lively; spiritedly; sprightly; vivaciously.*

with flying colors A moribund metaphor (SEE PAGE 19). *beautifully; brilliantly; dazzlingly; excellently; grandly; impressively; magnificently; marvelously; outstandingly; splendidly; sublimely; successfully; superbly; triumphally; triumphantly; victoriously; wonderfully.*

with (her) heart in (her) mouth A moribund metaphor (SEE PAGE 19). *anxiously; apprehensively; fearfully; pavidly; timidly; timorously; tremblingly; tremulously.*

within a hair's breadth of A moribund metaphor (SEE PAGE 19). *(very) close (to); (very) near (to).* ■ Some visionaries are *within a hair's breadth of* achieving unattended computer center operation. REPLACE WITH *close to*.

(beaten) within an inch of (his) life A moribund metaphor (SEE PAGE 19). *brutally; cruelly; ferociously; fiercely; harshly; ruthlessly; severely; viciously; violently.*

within a whisker of A moribund metaphor (SEE PAGE 19). *(very) close (to); (very) near (to).*

(handle) with kid gloves A moribund metaphor (SEE PAGE 19). *carefully; cautiously; delicately; gently; gingerly; mildly; sensitively; with care.*

with machinelike precision An insipid simile (SEE PAGE 19). *accurately; easily; exactly; excellently; faultlessly; flawlessly; flowingly; impeccably; indefectibly; methodically; perfectly; precisely; regularly; smoothly; systematically; well.*

with might and main A moribund metaphor (SEE PAGE 19). *actively; aggressively; dynamically; emphatically; energetically; ferociously; fervently; fiercely; forcefully; frantically; frenziedly; furiously; hard; intensely; intently; mightily; passionately; powerfully; robustly; savagely; spiritedly; strenuously; strongly; vehemently; viciously; vigorously; violently; wildly; with vigor.*

with (her) nose in the air A moribund metaphor (SEE PAGE 19). *arrogant; cavalier; condescending; contemptuous; despotic; dictatorial; disdainful; dogmatic; domineering; haughty; imperious; insolent; lofty; overbearing; overweening; patronizing; pompous; pretentious; scornful; self-important; supercilious; superior; vainglorious.*

(welcome) with open arms A moribund metaphor (SEE PAGE 19). *affectionately; cheerfully; eagerly;*

gladly; happily; joyously; readily; unreservedly; warmly. ■ We have welcomed them *with open arms.* REPLACE WITH *cheerfully.* ■ I hope I am welcomed back *with open arms.* REPLACE WITH *unreservedly.*

(went off) without a hitch A moribund metaphor (SEE PAGE 19). *accurately; easily; exactly; excellently; faultlessly; flawlessly; flowingly; impeccably; indefectibly; methodically; perfectly; precisely; regularly; smoothly; systematically; well.*

without cost or obligation A wretched redundancy (SEE PAGE 23). *free.*

without further ado An infantile phrase (SEE PAGE 18). *at once; directly; forthwith; immediately; instantly; promptly; right away; straightaway; summarily; unfalteringly; unhesitatingly; without delay.*

Of course, any speaker who drones *without further ado* at the end of his prefatory remarks probably ought never himself to be introduced.

without missing a beat A moribund metaphor (SEE PAGE 19). *accurately; easily; exactly; excellently; faultlessly; flawlessly; flowingly; impeccably; indefectibly; methodically; perfectly; precisely; regularly; smoothly; systematically; well.*

without rhyme or reason A moribund metaphor (SEE PAGE 19). *decerebrate; foolish; idiotic; illogical; incomprehensible; meaningless; nonsensical; senseless; stupid; unintelligent; unintelligible.*

with (my) tail between (my) legs A moribund metaphor (SEE PAGE 19). *abjectly; ashamedly; humbly; ignobly; ignominiously; ingloriously; in humility; in shame; meekly; shamefully; submissively.* ■ But she was not happy at the school and left before graduation *with her tail between her legs.* REPLACE WITH *ingloriously.*

with the exception of A wretched redundancy (SEE PAGE 23). *apart from; aside from; barring; besides; but for; except; except for; excepting; excluding; other than; outside of.* ■ We found that our first 50 patients were wide awake and alert the next day *with the exception of* one patient. REPLACE WITH *except for.*

woefully inadequate An inescapable pair (SEE PAGE 18). Little is *inadequate* that isn't *woefully* so.

(the) wolf at the door A moribund metaphor (SEE PAGE 19).

wolf in sheep's clothing A moribund metaphor (SEE PAGE 19). *apostate; charlatan; deceiver; dissembler; fake; fraud; hypocrite; impostor; knave; mountebank; pharisee; phony; pretender; quack; rascal; recreant; renegade; scoundrel; swindler; tergiversator; traitor.*

(a) woman's place is in the home A popular prescription (SEE PAGE 21).

(a) woman's work is never done A popular prescription (SEE PAGE 21).

(the) wonderful world of A moribund metaphor (SEE PAGE 19).

(he) won't bite A moribund metaphor (SEE PAGE 19).

won't budge (an inch) A moribund metaphor (SEE PAGE 19). *adamant; close-minded; contumacious; firm; immovable; immutable; inflexible; intransigent; invariable; obstinate; resolute; resolved; rigid; steadfast; stubborn; unalterable; unbending; unchangeable; unchanging; unwavering; unyielding.*

won the battle but lost the war A moribund metaphor (SEE PAGE 19).

won't take no for an answer An infantile phrase (SEE PAGE 18). *insist.*

(the) (F)-word An infantile phrase (SEE PAGE 18). ■ Many men have trouble with *the C-word*. REPLACE WITH *commitment*. ■ During the holidays, many people write and ask about *the D-word*, depression. DELETE *the D-word*. ■ Nearly everyone involved with the contract was using *the H-word*, "historic," to describe it. DELETE *the H-word*. ■ Journalists agonized over asking about the *"A" word*. REPLACE WITH *affair*. ■ For most middle-aged women, *the M-word* is not a laughing matter. REPLACE WITH *menopause*. ■ The see-through Clinton has three schemes in his playbook to divert us all from *the "M" word*. REPLACE WITH *Monica*.

words cannot describe (express) A plebeian sentiment (SEE PAGE 20). ■ *Words cannot express* the terrible emptiness we feel or how much we miss her. SEE ALSO *there are no words to describe (express)*.

work (my) butt (tail) off A moribund metaphor (SEE PAGE 19). *drudge; grind; grub; labor; moil; slave; strain; strive; struggle; sweat; toil; travail; work hard.*

work (his) fingers to the bone A moribund metaphor (SEE PAGE 19). *drudge; grind; grub; labor; moil; slave; strain; strive; struggle; sweat; toil; travail; work hard.*

working stiff A moribund metaphor (SEE PAGE 19). *aide; apparatchik; assistant; cog; dependent; drudge; flunky; helper; hireling; inferior; junior; minion; secondary; servant; slave; subaltern; subordinate; underling; vassal.*

work like a dog An insipid simile (SEE PAGE 19). *drudge; grind; grub; labor; moil; slave; strain; strive; struggle; sweat; toil; travail; work hard.*

(the) world is (his) oyster A moribund metaphor (SEE PAGE 19).

(a) (whole new) world of A moribund metaphor (SEE PAGE 19). ■ Mail merge can make your word processor more useful and can open up *a whole new world of power*. SEE ALSO *a barrage of*.

worlds apart A moribund metaphor (SEE PAGE 19).

(and) (the) world will beat a path to (your) door A moribund metaphor (SEE PAGE 19).

worn threadbare A moribund metaphor (SEE PAGE 19).
1. *banal; bromidic; common; commonplace; hackneyed; overused; overworked; pedestrian; platitudinous; prosaic; stale; trite.*
2. *damaged; decayed; decrepit; deteriorated; dilapidated; ragged; shabby; shopworn; tattered; worn.*

worried to death A moribund metaphor (SEE PAGE 19). *agitated; anxious; apprehensive; distraught; distressed; fearful; nervous; panicky; stressed; stressful; tense; tormented; troubled; uneasy; worried.* SEE ALSO *to death.*

(looks) (the) worse for wear A moribund metaphor (SEE PAGE 19).
1. *broken-down; crumbly; damaged; decayed; decrepit; deteriorated; dilapidated; dingy; dirty; filthy; flimsy; foul; frayed; grimy; grubby; grungy; ragged; ramshackle; rickety; seedy; shabby; shaky; soiled; sordid; sullied; squalid; tattered; tottering; unclean; unsound; worn.*
2. *aged; aging; elderly; hoary; old; seasoned.*

(he) worships the ground (I) walk on A moribund metaphor (SEE PAGE 19). *adore; cherish; esteem; eulogize; exalt; extol; glorify; honor; idealize; idolize; laud; love; panegyrize; prize; revere; treasure; venerate; worship.*

(every parent's) worst nightmare A moribund metaphor (SEE PAGE 19). ■ It's *every mother's worst nightmare.* ■ This defendant is *every person's worst nightmare.* ■ Being a stepparent is *my worst nightmare.* ■ Perhaps the cliché is true about its being a woman's greatest fantasy and *a man's worst nightmare.* SEE ALSO *it was a nightmare.*

(the) worst of all (possible) worlds A moribund metaphor (SEE PAGE 19).

worth (her) salt A moribund metaphor (SEE PAGE 19). *advantageous; beneficial; cost-effective; effective; effectual; efficacious; gainful; lucrative; productive; profitable; serviceable; useful; valuable; worthwhile.*

worth (its) weight in gold A moribund metaphor (SEE PAGE 19).
1. *costly; dear; expensive; inestimable; invaluable; precious; priceless; prized; valuable.*
2. *advantageous; beneficial; effective; effectual; efficacious; essential; helpful; indispensable; profitable; serviceable; useful; valuable; vital; worthwhile.*

would appear (hope; imagine; seem; submit; suggest; suspect; think) A wretched redundancy (SEE PAGE 23). *appear (hope; imagine; seem; submit; suggest; suspect; think).* ■ I *would think* so. DELETE *would.* ■ I *would hope* a decision would be reached before the term of office expires. DELETE *would.* ■ It *would appear* that the state wants to jeopardize the project. REPLACE WITH *appears.*

Not only is the *would* in *would appear* (*hope; imagine; seem; submit; suggest; suspect; think*) superfluous, it calls into question the accuracy and knowledge of whoever uses the phrase. Only the intellectually timorous, the dimwitted, need to so qualify their words.

(he) wouldn't hurt a flea (fly) A moribund metaphor (SEE PAGE 19).
1. *affable; agreeable; amiable; amicable; compassionate; friendly; gentle; good-hearted; good-natured; humane; kind; kind-hearted; personable; pleasant; tender; tolerant.*
2. *dovish; irenic; nonviolent; pacific; pacifist; pacifistic; peaceable; peaceful; peace-loving; unbelligerent; uncontentious.*

(I) wouldn't touch it with a ten-foot pole A moribund metaphor (SEE PAGE 19).

wrapped up in (herself) A moribund metaphor (SEE PAGE 19). *egocentric; egoistic; egotistic; egotistical; narcissistic; self-absorbed; selfish; solipsistic.*

wreak havoc An inescapable pair (SEE PAGE 18). *demolish; destroy; devastate; injure; obliterate; rack; ravage; ruin; shatter; smash; undo; wrack; wreck.* ■ A handful of companies is *wreaking havoc on* the rest of the industry. REPLACE WITH *ravaging.*

wreathed in smiles A moribund metaphor (SEE PAGE 19). *beaming; glowing; smiling.*

(it's) written all over (you) A moribund metaphor (SEE PAGE 19).

wrong end of the stick A moribund metaphor (SEE PAGE 19).

(what's) wrong is wrong A quack equation (SEE PAGE 21).

(the) wrong side of the tracks A moribund metaphor (SEE PAGE 19).

(he) wrote the book (on) A moribund metaphor (SEE PAGE 19).

X, Y, Z

x marks the spot A moribund metaphor (SEE PAGE 19).

year in (and) year out A moribund metaphor (SEE PAGE 19). *always; ceaselessly; constantly; continually; continuously; endlessly; eternally; everlastingly; evermore; forever; forevermore; immortally; indefinitely; interminably; permanently; perpetually; persistently; unceasingly; unremittingly.*

(62) years young An infantile phrase (SEE PAGE 18). ■ *I'm 43 years young.* DELETE *years young.*

yell and scream An inescapable pair (SEE PAGE 18). *bay; bawl; bellow; blare; caterwaul; clamor; cry; holler; hoot; howl; roar; screak; scream; screech; shout; shriek; shrill; squawk; squeal; vociferate; wail; whoop; yell; yelp; yowl.* ■ Two months later, he'd lost all his hair, and his wife started *yelling and screaming* about my not making him continue. REPLACE WITH *scream* or *yell.* SEE ALSO *yell and scream.*

yell (her) head off A moribund metaphor (SEE PAGE 19). *bay; bawl; bellow; blare; caterwaul; clamor; cry; holler; hoot; howl; roar; screak; scream; screech; shout; shriek; shrill; squawk; squeal; vociferate; wail; whoop; yell; yelp; yowl.*

yes, Virginia, (there is) An infantile phrase (SEE PAGE 18).

(the) yin and the yang A moribund metaphor (SEE PAGE 19).

you are what you eat A popular prescription (SEE PAGE 21).

you can catch more flies with honey than with vinegar A popular prescription (SEE PAGE 21).

you can fool some of the people some of the time, but you can't fool all of the people all of the time A popular prescription (SEE PAGE 21).

you can lead a horse to water, but you can't make (him) drink A popular prescription (SEE PAGE 21).

you can make a difference A popular prescription (SEE PAGE 21).

you can say that again An infantile phrase (SEE PAGE 18).

you can't be all things to all people A popular prescription (SEE PAGE 21).

you can't buy love A popular prescription (SEE PAGE 21).

you can't change the world in a day A popular prescription (SEE PAGE 21).

you can't fight city hall A popular prescription (SEE PAGE 21).

you can't fit a square peg in a round hole A popular prescription (SEE PAGE 21).

you can't get blood from (out of) a stone A popular prescription (SEE PAGE 21).

you can't get there from here An infantile phrase (SEE PAGE 18).

you can't go home again A popular prescription (SEE PAGE 21).

you can't have everything A popular prescription (SEE PAGE 21).

you can't have it both ways A popular prescription (SEE PAGE 21).

you can't have something for nothing A popular prescription (SEE PAGE 21).

you can't have your cake and eat it too A popular prescription (SEE PAGE 21).

you can't judge a book by its cover A popular prescription (SEE PAGE 21).

you can't live on love alone A popular prescription (SEE PAGE 21).

you can't live with (them) and you can't live without (them) A popular prescription (SEE PAGE 21).

you can't lose what you never had A popular prescription (SEE PAGE 21).

you can't make a silk purse out of a sow's ear A popular prescription (SEE PAGE 21).

you can't please everyone A popular prescription (SEE PAGE 21).

you can't put new wine in old bottles A popular prescription (SEE PAGE 21).

you can't serve God and mammon A popular prescription (SEE PAGE 21).

you can't take it with you A popular prescription (SEE PAGE 21).

you can't teach an old dog new tricks A popular prescription (SEE PAGE 21).

you can't win them all A popular prescription (SEE PAGE 21).

(so quiet) you could hear a pin drop A moribund metaphor (SEE PAGE 19).
1. *dumb; hushed; motionless; mum; mute; noiseless; quiet; reticent; silent; soundless; speechless; stationary; still; stock-still; subdued; taciturn; unmoving; voiceless; wordless.*

2. *becalmed; calm; halcyon; irenic; pacific; peaceable; peaceful; placid; quiescent; reposeful; serene; tranquil.*

you don't miss what you never had A popular prescription (SEE PAGE 21).

you (have to) do what you have to (do) A popular prescription (SEE PAGE 21).

you get what you pay for A popular prescription (SEE PAGE 21).

you had to be there A grammatical gimmick (SEE PAGE 17). This is merely an admission of having badly told a tale.

you have everything to gain and nothing to lose A popular prescription (SEE PAGE 21).

you have nothing to lose A popular prescription (SEE PAGE 21).

you have to give to get A popular prescription (SEE PAGE 21).

you have (got) to start somewhere A popular prescription (SEE PAGE 21).

you have to understand (that) An ineffectual phrase (SEE PAGE 17). ■ First of all, *you have to understand that* many black men are in prison. DELETE *you have to understand that.* SEE ALSO *it is important to understand (that).*

(do) you know? An ineffectual phrase (SEE PAGE 17). ■ I felt like I was enlightened, *you know?* DELETE *you know?* ■ You never know what's going to happen, *you know?* DELETE *you know?* ■ The translation sounded too straightforward, *you know?* DELETE *you know?* ■ To an extent, I think everybody is racist. *You know?* DELETE *You know?* SEE ALSO *(you) hear what I'm saying? (you) know what I mean? (you) know what I'm saying? (you) know what I'm telling you?*

you learn something new every day A plebeian sentiment (SEE PAGE 20). It's the event of having learned something — something taught, not thought — that gives rise to the remark.

you made your bed, now lay in it A popular prescription (SEE PAGE 21).

you name it A grammatical gimmick (SEE PAGE 17). *and others; and so forth; and so on; and the like; etc.* ■ Today, in our state, those who do the public's work — teachers, cops, public-health nurses, social workers, highway builders, prison guards, *you name it* — are held up to ridicule.

you never know A plebeian sentiment (SEE PAGE 20).

you never know till you try A popular prescription (SEE PAGE 21).

young and foolish An inescapable pair (SEE PAGE 18).

you owe it to yourself A popular

prescription (SEE PAGE 21). ■ Believe me, *you owe it to yourself* to take advantage of this exciting opportunity.

you're (only) as old as you feel A popular prescription (SEE PAGE 21).

you're either part of the solution or part of the problem A popular prescription (SEE PAGE 21).

you're either with (me) or against (me) A popular prescription (SEE PAGE 21).

you're kidding An infantile phrase (SEE PAGE 18). This expression is among the most banal we utter. We say it uncontrollably — less in stupefaction than in stupidity — and without a moment's reflection.

The more commonplace the words you use, the more commonplace the person you are. SEE ALSO *really? you've got to be kidding.*

you're not alone A plebeian sentiment (SEE PAGE 20). ■ Feeling depressed, lonely, restless, bored, upset? *You're not alone.*

you're not the only one An infantile phrase (SEE PAGE 18). *as I do; I do too; neither do I; no more do I; nor do I; so do I.*

you're only young once A popular prescription (SEE PAGE 21).

your guess is as good as mine An infantile phrase (SEE PAGE 18). *I don't know; (it's) not (yet) known;*

(that's) uncertain; (that's) unclear; (it's) unknown. SEE ALSO *(it) remains to be seen; (just have to) wait and see.*

yours truly An infantile phrase (SEE PAGE 18). *I; me.* ■ And you can bet that *yours truly* will do something crazy. REPLACE WITH *I.*

you scratch my back, I'll scratch yours A popular prescription (SEE PAGE 21). ■ It's an approach that resonates equally with businessmen steeped in the win-win jargon of negotiations and politicians deep in the pragmatic *you-scratch-my-back-I'll-scratch-yours* conversations that make Washington run.

you think too much A plebeian sentiment (SEE PAGE 20). *You think too much* is, of course, commentary that only those who rarely think could ever offer. These are the people who cower from consciousness. SEE ALSO *I (just) don't think about it.*

you've come a long way (baby) An infantile phrase (SEE PAGE 18).

you've got to be kidding An infantile phrase (SEE PAGE 18). SEE ALSO *really? you're kidding.*

you win a few (some), you lose a few (some) A popular prescription (SEE PAGE 21).

zigs and zags An inescapable pair (SEE PAGE 18).

(a) zillion(s) (of) An infantile phrase (SEE PAGE 18). Doubly infantile are the phrases *ba-zillion* and *ga-zillion*. ■ I'll bet their mothers spent *a zillion* hours trying to get their sons to clean up after themselves. Replace with *countless*. ■ I made *a zillion* mistakes. Replace with *innumerable*. ■ There may be grating aspects to 20- and 30-somethings earning *kazillion*-dollar bonuses, but at least wealth gives them the self-confidence to ask for a date. Replace with *million*.